International Conference on ICT, Society, and Human Beings 2019, International Conference on Connected Smart Cities 2019 and International Conference on Web Based Communities and Social Media 2019

Held at the Multi-Conference on Computer Science and Information Systems (MCCSIS 2019)

Porto, Portugal
16-19 July 2019

Editors:

Piet Kommers
Guo Chao Peng
Luís Rodrigues
Pedro Isaías

ISBN: 978-1-5108-9241-5

Printed from e-media with permission by:

Curran Associates, Inc.
57 Morehouse Lane
Red Hook, NY 12571

Some format issues inherent in the e-media version may also appear in this print version.

Printed by Curran Associates, Inc. (2019)

For permission requests, please contact International Association for Development of the Information Society (IADIS) at the address below.

International Association for Development of the Information Society (IADIS)
Rua Sao Sebastiao Da Pedreira
No. 100, 30, 1050-209
Lisbon, Portugal

Phone: 351 21 3151373
Fax: 351 21 3151244

secretariat@iadis.org

Additional copies of this publication are available from:

Curran Associates, Inc.
57 Morehouse Lane
Red Hook, NY 12571 USA
Phone: 845-758-0400
Fax: 845-758-2633
Email: curran@proceedings.com
Web: www.proceedings.com

MULTI CONFERENCE ON COMPUTER SCIENCE AND INFORMATION SYSTEMS

MCCSIS 2019

16-19 JULY PORTO, PORTUGAL

Proceedings of the International Conferences

ICT, Society and Human Beings 2019
Connected Smart Cities 2019
Web Based Communities and Social Media 2019

Edited by
Piet Kommers
Guo Chao Peng

iadis
international association for development of the information society

Volume Editors:
Piet Kommers and Guo Chao Peng

Computer Science and Information Systems Series Editors:
Piet Kommers and Pedro Isaías

Associate Editor: Luís Rodrigues

INTERNATIONAL CONFERENCES ON

ICT, SOCIETY AND HUMAN BEINGS 2019

CONNECTED SMART CITIES 2019

and

WEB BASED COMMUNITIES AND SOCIAL MEDIA 2019

part of the

MULTI CONFERENCE ON COMPUTER SCIENCE AND

INFORMATION SYSTEMS 2019

PROCEEDINGS OF THE INTERNATIONAL CONFERENCES

ICT, SOCIETY AND HUMAN BEINGS 2019

CONNECTED SMART CITIES 2019

and

WEB BASED COMMUNITIES AND SOCIAL MEDIA 2019

Porto, Portugal
JULY 17 - 19, 2019

Organised by

iadis
international association for development of the information society

Co-Organised by

isep Instituto Superior de Engenharia do Porto

TABLE OF CONTENTS

WEB BASED COMMUNITIES AND SOCIAL MEDIA

SHORT PAPERS

ICT, SOCIETY, AND HUMAN BEINGS

CONNECTED SMART CITIES

WEB BASED COMMUNITIES AND SOCIAL MEDIA

REFLECTION PAPERS

ICT, SOCIETY, AND HUMAN BEINGS

CONNECTED SMART CITIES

POSTER

ICT, SOCIETY, AND HUMAN BEINGS

FOREWORD

These proceedings contain the papers and a poster of the 12th International Conference on ICT, Society and Human Beings (ICT 2019), the 5th International Conference on Connected Smart Cities (CSC 2019) and of the 16th International Conference Web Based Communities and Social Media (WBC 2019), which were organised by the International Association for Development of the Information Society and co-organised by ISEP – Instituto Superior de Engenharia do Porto, from 17 - 19 July, 2019. These conferences are part of the Multi Conference on Computer Science and Information Systems 2019, 16 - 19 July, which had a total of 926 submissions.

The Network period in the evolution of computer technology is very much based on the convergence and integration of three main technologies; computer technology, tele technology and media technology. Telecommunication technology is playing a more and more dominant role in this convergence, especially internet and web technology. Embedded (ubiquitous) computer technology is making the process invisible, and media technologies converge within itself (multimedia and cross media). The convergence process is enforced all the time by smaller, cheaper, and more powerful components.

ICT and its applications are interacting with environments, roles, and processes which can also be modelled by converging circles. The process of social and psychosocial change and ICT from a global perspective is described graphically in the convergence model in figure 1 (Bradley 2006 Routledge) with concepts and their interrelations. Both "convergence" and "interactions" are important features in the model. Read from the left hand side in the model for the titles of some main tracks of the conference:

- Globalisation and ICT: When technology, economy, norms/values and labour market are converging on a global level, what are the hard questions? When the geographical space in the future will be both global and beyond – including virtual reality (VR) what is the state of art in research? (see the list of key words under ´globalisation´)
- Information and Communication Technology (ICT), next cluster of circles to the left in the figure, what applications contribute to desirable goals in the society?
- When Work Environment, Home Environment, and Public Environment are converging and the work and public issues tend to merge into the private sphere of our homes – what main changes in peoples Life Environment occur?.
- If the Professional Role (Work Life), Private Role (Private Life) and Citizen's Role (Public Life) converge forming a Life Role, what are the main social-psychologial changes?
- Four circles representing Virtual Reality (VR) are marked with dotted lines and are surrounding the set of converging circles. These circles reflect our participation in cyberspace on various levels. To the left part in figure we could talk about Virtual Worlds on the global level. Within the concept of ICT, the steps taken by applied Embedded and ubiquitous technology make technology more hidden to the individual and society as a whole.

  Virtual Environments are already a common concept. Finally, we could talk about Virtual Human Roles, which could in more extreme forms be another personality that you play e g avatars. The converging circles are forming a Life Role and new life styles are being shaped.
- Effects on humans become more multi faceted and complex. Research focusing upon the individual is crucial i. e. research on how the use of ICT interacts with and impacts identity, social competence, creativity, integrity, trust, dependency etc.

A compass rose (card) for "Effects on Humans" (to the right) is used as a metaphor reminding us of the importance to keep the direction towards desirable human and societal goals and qualities at the development and use of ICT.

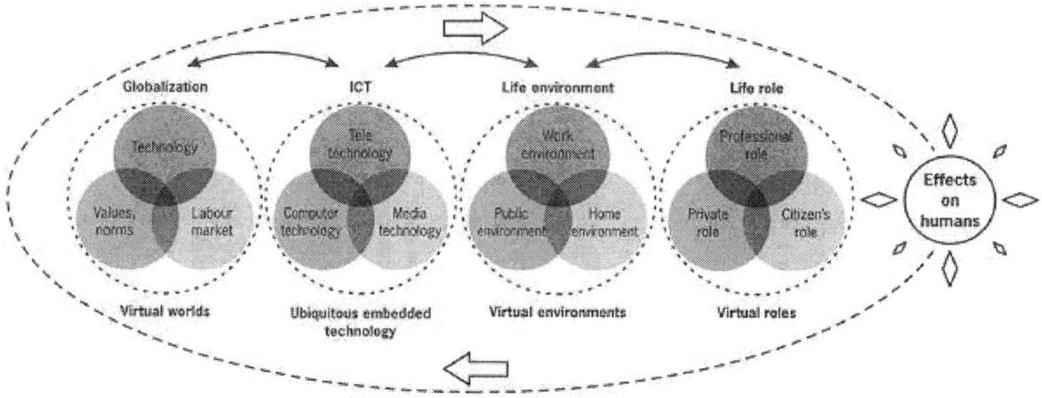

Figure 1. Convergence Model on ICT and Psychosocial Life Environment (Source: Bradley, 2005, 2006)

ICT can provide tools for promoting sustainability (environmental, economic, and social sustainability) but can also be a threat for sustainability. Sustainability as a guiding principle involves system perspective, holism, human aspects, bottom up approach, common good, and equality. A change in focus regarding research and development is taking place. Analysis and design increasingly address both the work process and management connected to the sphere of production life and people's life environment. Analysis and design of ICT and societal systems both at local level and globally become important. What research in the field exists or is needed?

Community research in a broad sense comes to the fore – both physical and virtual communities. There is also a requirement to involve new and additional actors at the deeper and broader integration of ICT in the society (children, elderly, and consumer organisations). Educational programs on Community Informatics and Social Informatics are appearing in many academic institutions. Can a new infrastructure of the society be identified?

The effects of ICT on human beings as well as the interaction between ICT, individuals, and society are all within the focus of this conference. Both analyses of interactions and effects are important. Changes in behaviour, perspectives, values, competencies, human and psychological aspects and feelings are all of interest. Reflections on past, present, and future challenges – especially planning for handling the latter – are encouraged.

Today, computer science and ICT-related disciplines are working more and more together with various behavioural and social sciences including child psychology and developmental psychology. For this reason, the conference pays attention to societal changes, global and more local organisational and institutional changes, changes in values and in lifestyles, as well as individual cognitive effects and changes, motivational and emotional changes. It also appeals to solution-building in terms of desirable goals and actions for reaching a Good Information Society.

In general, all types of research strategies are encouraged, and especially cross-disciplinary and multi-disciplinary studies. Case studies, broader empirical field studies, theoretical analyses, cross-cultural studies, scenarios, ethnographic studies, epistemological analyses may all be presented.

The ICT, Society and Human Beings 2019 conference addresses in detail seven main aspects:
- Globalization and ICT
- Life environment and ICT
- Life role and ICT
- ICT and effects on humans
- Perspectives on ICT
- Desirable goals and ICT
- Actions for reaching the Good Information Society

Significant societal challenges in the form of demographics, urbanisation, climate change, resource crises and global competition are driving profound changes within our cities. In order to cope, governments and businesses are turning to 'smart city' concepts with the aim to enhance the efficiency of key infrastructure, utilities and services to create a sustainable urban environment that improves the quality of life for its citizens and enhances economic development. Smart cities are essentially built by utilising a set of latest information and communication technologies (ICT), including Wi-Fi and mobile networks, wireless sensors, the Internet of things, big data analytic tools, cloud services, mobile devices, and mobile apps. In this context, ICT as an enabling Smart City technology will generate radically new "smart" services and facilities. The UK's Department of Business, Innovation and Skills values the smart city industry at more than $400 billion globally by 2020.

The CSC 2019 conferences aims to provide a premier and exciting forum for the exchange of scientific ideas, research findings, and industrial practices among academics and practitioners, who are from different disciplines (e.g. information systems, computer science, telecommunication engineering, urban studies, and business and economics) but have common interests in smart cities. It welcomes all forms of relevant research, including conceptual, theoretical, quantitative, qualitative, and mixed-method studies. Papers with an interdisciplinary nature are particularly encouraging. In order to offer wide-ranging discussion opportunities, the conference seeks the most recent and relevant research on the following main topics:
- Wireless Connectivity in Smart Cities;
- New Business Concerns in Smart Cities;
- Data and Software Applications in Smart Cities;
- User-Centric Smart Cities;
- Security, Privacy and Identity Issues in Smart Cities;
- Greenness and Sustainability of Smart Cities;
- Smart City as an Integrated Ecosystem.

The World Wide Web has migrated from information space into opportunities for social communication. Social Media are growing rapidly and play an increasingly important role in the development of Online Communities. They are all about identity, reputation, presence and relationships. Web based communities announce themselves both in your professional and private life through several new media such as LinkedIn, Twitter, Plaxo, etc. In order to keep you up to date with the pace of these new technological developments this Conference offers a dedicated overview and informative discussion on today's most relevant issues in new media for social life on the web.

Social Media are growing rapidly and play an increasingly important role in the development of Online Communities. Social Network Sites and Web-based communities announce themselves both in your professional and private life through new media such as Facebook, LinkedIn, Twitter, Plaxo, etc. Social media allow more dynamic roles in participation, virtual presence and online communities. These new ways to communicate via online social media have great societal effects and are motivating the creation of best practices to help individuals, corporations and authorities to make the best of it. It raises the awareness of the growing impact of social media and the influence of web based communities in today's users / consumers behavior; many organizations spend an increasing share of their budget in online social marketing strategies.

The mission of the Web Based Communities and Social Media 2019 conference is to publish and integrate scientific results and act catalytically to the fast developing culture of web communities, while helping to disseminate and understand the latest developments social media and their impact.

Submissions were accepted under the following 6 main topics:
- The History, Architecture and Future of Virtual Communities
- Cyborgs, Teleworking, Telemedicine, Art Games and Learning Communities
- Virtual Communities for People with Special Needs
- Group Processes and Self-Organization
- Expanding Markets through Virtual Communities
- Collaborative Technologies
- Social Media

These conferences received 244 submissions from more than 36 countries. Each submission has been anonymously reviewed by an average of four independent reviewers, to ensure that accepted submissions were of a high standard. Consequently, only 42 full papers were approved which means an acceptance rate of 17%. A few more papers were accepted as short papers, reflection papers and poster. An extended version of the best papers may be published in the IADIS International Journal on Computer Science and Information Systems (ISSN: 1646-3692) and/or in the IADIS International Journal on WWW/Internet (ISSN: 1645-7641), International Journal of Web Based Communities" (IJWBC - ISSN: 1477 – 8394) and also in other selected journals, including journals from Inderscience.

Besides the presentation of full, short and reflection papers and a poster, these conferences also included two keynote presentations by Prof. Jaime Villate, Faculty of Engineering, University of Porto, Portugal and Prof. Frederico Custódio, Director of the Intelligence and Explorative Research Group at CEiiA, Portugal. We would therefore like to express our gratitude to Prof. Jaime Villate and Prof. Frederico Custódio for accepting our invitation to be keynote speakers.

This volume has taken shape as a result of the contributions from a number of individuals. We are grateful to all authors who have submitted their papers to enrich the conference proceedings. We wish to thank all members of the organizing committee, delegates, invitees and guests whose contribution and involvement are crucial for the success of the conference.

Last but not the least, we hope that everybody had a good time in Porto, and we invite all participants for the next years´ edition of these conferences.

Piet Kommers, University of Twente, The Netherlands
ICT 2019 & Web Based Communities and Social Media 2019 Program Chair

Guo Chao (Alex) Peng, School of Information Management, Sun Yat-sen University, Guangzhou, China
CSC 2019 Program Chair

Piet Kommers, University of Twente, The Netherlands
Pedro Isaías, The University of Queensland, Australia
MCCSIS 2019 General Conference Co-Chairs

Bertil Marques, ISEP, Portugal
MCCSIS 2019 Local Organising Chair

Porto, Portugal
July 2019

PROGRAM COMMITTEE

ICT, SOCIETY AND HUMAN BEINGS
&
WEB BASED COMMUNITIES AND SOCIAL MEDIA
PROGRAM CHAIR

Piet Kommers, University of Twente, The Netherlands

CONNECTED SMART CITIES
PROGRAM CHAIR

Guo Chao (Alex) Peng, School of Information Management, Sun Yat-sen University, Guangzhou, China

MCCSIS GENERAL CONFERENCE CO-CHAIRS

Piet Kommers, University of Twente, The Netherlands
Pedro Isaías, The University of Queensland, Australia

MCCSIS LOCAL ORGANISING CHAIR

Bertil Marques, ISEP, Portugal

ICT, SOCIETY AND HUMAN BEINGS

COMMITTEE MEMBERS

Alrence Halibas, Gulf College, Oman
Ana Isabel Paraguay, CIDACS/FIOCRUZ-BA, Brazil
Cecile K. M. Crutzen, Open University of the Netherlands, Netherlands
Christophe Trefois, Université du Luxembourg, Luxembourg
Daniel Pimienta, Funredes , Dominican Republic
Eila Jarvenpaa, Aalto University, Finland
Elspeth Mckay, Rmit University , Australia
Elvis Mazzoni, University of Bologna, Italy
Fabio Cassano, Università Degli Studi di Bari, Italy
Farshad Badie, Aalborg University, Denmark
Francisco Garcia, University of Murcia, Spain
Gordon Huang, University of Regina, Canada
Jan Kubicek, Technical University of Ostrava, Czech Republic
Jan Meyer (Pr.M), Faculty Member, GSB&GL, NWU, South Africa
John Sören Pettersson, Karlstad University, Sweden
Jorge Franco, Universidade Presbiteriana Mackenzie, Brazil
Kai Kimppa, University of Turku, Finland
Krzysztof Hauke, Wroclaw University of Economics, Poland
Lech Zacher, Kozminski Business School, Poland
Manuela Repetto, INDIRE, Italy
Marco Lazzari, University of Bergamo, Italy
Margaret Tan, A*STAR IHPC, Singapore
Monica Banzato, University of Ca' Foscari - Venice, Italy

Nestor Garay-Vitoria, Universidad del País Vasco/Euskal Herriko Uniberts, Spain
Nicola Doering, Ilmenau University of Technology, Germany
Patrick Rau, Tsinghua University, China
Pertti Jarvinen, University of Tampere, Finland
Pertti Saariluoma, University of Jyvaskyla, Finland
Przemyslaw Falkowski-Gilski, Gdansk University of Technology, Poland
Robert Pintér , Corvinus University of Budapest, Hungary
Sarai Lastra, Universidad Ana G. Méndez, Recinto de Gurabo, Puerto Rico
Stina Giesecke, Aalto University, Finland
Vincenzo D Andrea, University of Trento, Italy
Virve Siirak, Tallinn University of Technology, Estonia

CONNECTED SMART CITIES

COMMITTEE MEMBERS

Agusti Solanas, Rovira i Virgili University, Catalonia
Davide Careglio, Universitat Politècnica de Catalunya, Spain
Giovanni Merlino, University of Messina, Italy
Jorge Gómez-sanz Gomez-sanz, Universidad Complutense De Madrid, Spain
José Luis Hernández Ramos, European Commission, Join Research Centre (JRC), Belgium
Juan Antonio Alvarez-garcía, University of Seville, Spain
Lasse Berntzen, University of South-eastern Norway, Norway
Mani Krishna, University of Massachusetts Amherst, USA
Maria Bermudez-edo, University of Granada, Spain
Maria Blanca Caminero Herraez, University of Castilla-la Mancha, Spain
Peter Mechant, Ghent University, Belgium
Pierfrancesco Bellini, University of Florence, Italy
Rabinarayan Mahapatra, Texas A&m University, United States
Ramin Yahyapour, GWDG/University Goettingen, Germany
Raquel Martínez España, Catholic University of Murcia, Spain
Riccardo Bettati, Texas A&M University, USA
Rosaldo Rossetti, University of Porto, Portugal
Sandro Leuchter, Mannheim University of Applied Sciences, Germany
Saurabh Garg, University of Tasmania, Australia
Yeh-ching Chung, National Tsing Hua University, Taiwan
Zeeshan Pervez, University of the West of Scotland, United Kingdom
Zena Wood, University of Greenwich, United Kingdom
Zhu Ye, Cleveland State University, USA

WEB BASED COMMUNITIES AND SOCIAL MEDIA

COMMITTEE MEMBERS

Allan Jeong, Florida State University, USA
Andrei Semeniuta, Belarus Trade Economics University, Belarus
Anirban Kundu, Kuang-Chi Institute of Advanced Technology, Shenzh, China
Apostolos Gkamas, University Ecclesiastical Academy of Vella of Ioan, Greece
Arianna D'ulizia, National Research Council - Irpps, Italy
Atsuo Hazeyama, Tokyo Gakugei University, Japan
Carmen Celina Torres Arcadia, Tecnológico de Monterrey, Mexico
Charalampos Karagiannidis, University of Thessaly, Greece

KEYNOTE LECTURES

HOW TO USE E-LEARNING FOR TESTING AND ASSESSING LARGE CLASSES

Prof. Jaime Villate,
Faculty of Engineering, University of Porto, Portugal

ABSTRACT

On-line quizzes provide many advantages for students and teachers. The student doesn't have to be in the same place as the examiner, results and feedback can be given to the student immediately, and the student might be able to keep a copy of the quiz in digital form. However, exams given simultaneously to a large class are usually conducted in the traditional written form, because an on-line approach would pose many issues hard to solve. Students might have to wait several days before getting the results and feedback. We report on a hybrid method we have been using with over 200 students enrolled in Engineering Physics courses. Traditional written exams are used, but the results and feedback are published in an e-learning site, as if the exam had been taken on-line. The e-learning platform is also used to help students prepare for the exams.

SMART AND SUSTAINABLE LIVING COLAB: A ROADMAP TO ACCELERATE URBAN SUSTAINABILITY

Prof. Frederico Custódio,
Director of the Intelligence and Explorative Research Group at CEiiA,
Portugal

ABSTRACT

Cities represent around 75% of global energy demand and total energy-related carbon emissions. But they also have a tremendous power to act on climate ambitions, through the definition of policies, the implementation of new solutions to foster sustainable mobility, energy-efficiency and renewable energy production. Recently, CEiiA, a technology center from Portugal, launched a new Collaborative Lab – the Smart and Sustainable Living CoLAB – which focuses on the development of new solutions to accelerate the transformation of cities into smart and sustainable ecosystems. The research agenda of the CoLAB goes beyond a technocratic conception of smart cities, to propose new human and living centred concepts, capable to meet sustainable goals. A particular focus is given to the development of new approaches to empower citizens to reduce their carbon footprint, thus accelerating the decarbonization of cities. Namely, the CoLAB recently presented at the New York Smart-Cities Summit the AYR Platform - a trading system for saved carbon emissions, which is based on a disruptive concept of 'valuing what is not emitted'. The AYR platform, developed on blockchain technology, accounts on real time saved CO_2 emissions from sustainable mobility services, rewarding users with digital credits – AYRs. Users can later buy products and services from a network of partners. The project is currently being piloted in the city of Matosinhos, Portugal.

Full Papers

TECHNOLOGY EXPOSURE IN LARGE PORTUGUESE CATHOLIC FAMILIES

Adriana José de Oliveira and Luciana Oliveira
CEOS.PP ISCAP Polytechnic of Porto
Rua Jaime Lopes Amorim, s/n 4465-004 S. Mamede de Infesta, Matosinhos, Portugal

ABSTRACT

Despite the tremendous opportunities provided by current unparalleled advancements in communication and connectivity among individuals, many concerns have been raising, from many fields, regarding the effects of intensive use and exposure to technology in the escalation of social dehumanization. As the main social control mechanism, religion diffuses normative instruments that are not immediately open to progress, as they typically propel a broader resistance to normative, behavioral and social change. In this paper, we focus on the relation between religious practice and the use of technology, and on how religious families curate for the family well-being while conceding to technology exposure within their homes. Large catholic families were selected as the subject of research as they constitute, at least in Portugal, as the most conservative and resistant to change group. A mixed-methods research strategy, with surveys and interviews, was used to identify how these families regulate the use of technology, how and when they use digital devices and internet connection, and which are the norms and strategies used to preserve the values of the Catholic church while engaging with digital devices and networks.

KEYWORDS

Technology Exposure, WWW, Large Catholic Families

1. INTRODUCTION

Technology and the WWW have brought multiple changes into the work and family fields (Livingstone, 2002, Roe, 2000, Toffler, 1984). The impacts and changes brought by the 4th Industrial Revolution (4IR) have been and will remain on the agenda of much of the controversial scientific, technological, economic and social debate. Unlike previous industrial revolutions, which were characterized by advancements in technology, the 4IR biggest impact is to improve quality of life and reduce inequalities among the worlds' population. This marks a new era of metaphorical and literal technology embedding into individuals' bodies and environment. As much of the potential of this era relies on advances on communication and connectivity, a social revolution regarding the way we live, work and relate to one another is unavoidable.

Despite the tremendous opportunities provided by current unparalleled advancements in communication and connectivity among individuals, many concerns have been raising, from many fields, regarding the effects of intensive use and exposure to technology in the escalation of social dehumanization.

This scenario, which affects societies at large, collides directly with the core of the formation of individuals, where fundamental principles and values are learned, by hindering the necessary socialization in the family nucleus. Technology has become the key vehicle to connect family members when they are apart as much as it has become the main barrier to keep them from socializing when they are together.

A notorious stream of warnings and precautions associated with the need of maintenance of off-screen socialization and off-line communication and leisure has been advocated by psychologists, neurologists, pediatricians, and other health and social authorities. Curiously, most of these recommendations tend to recall, recapture and boost what could be understood as the core pre-modern and pre-technological most traditional social and family values, framed into sets of precautionary cross-filed measures aimed at preserving the family well-being. As the main social control mechanism, religion diffuses normative instruments that are not most open to any type of immediate progress, as they typically propel a broader resistance to normative, behavioral and social change.

In this context, families with high prominent religious involvement appear most prone to resist to the technological advancements which are believed to result in the corruption of the families' core values, dehumanization, isolation, neglection and social marginalization of individuals in close circles and in society. This happens because when highly involved in religious practices, there is a regular direct contact with a set of reinforced normative that establish morals and conduct on how to manage, among others, the integration of technology in the family environment without corrupting it. Since religion has always been the most powerful mean for the preservation of self-regulation and self-control, we believe that, within it, it is possible to identify and report on behaviors, strategies, norms and values they may be useful in addressing some of the current concerns of the dehumanization of families and individuals.

However, very little research has been devoted to the relation between religious practice and the use of technology, and on how religious families curate for the family well-being while conceding to technology exposure within their homes. In this work, large catholic families were selected as the subject of research as they constitute, at least in Portugal, as the most conservative and resistant to change group. A mixed-methods research strategy, with surveys and interviews, was used to identify how these families regulate the use of technology, how and when they use digital devices and internet connection, and which are the norms and strategies used to preserve the values of the Catholic church while engaging with digital devices and networks.

2. EXPOSURE TO TECHNOLOGY: TIME AND PLACE

Acknowledging the levels of exposure, role and power of technology, and namely internet access, the need to claim locations for certain purposes has grown (Morgan, 1996). In fact, internet access began by occupying public spaces and later the private ones, resulting not only in different ways to look at the private and public life, but also turning the family environment into a more collectivist or individualistic interaction space (Livingstone, 2002).

In Portugal, in 2017 (INE, 2017), 77% of households had internet access, with a large majority of families who have children. Portugal is one of the countries where children and teenagers are more exposed to technology and internet in their bedrooms (67%), being above the European average (49%). Among these, the ones with higher economic resources use their bedrooms and shared spaces (86%), as opposed to those who have lower income and less access to the Internet in shared spaces (73%) (Ponte et al., 2012).

Private and individualized use of the internet has been growing concerning the internet's possession, contact with outer world, creation of original content in platforms such as Youtube, Facebook or blogs without parental supervision, which has been leading to negotiations or conflicting situations in the family environment (Livingstone, 2002, Morgan, 1996, Monteiro and Policarpo, 2011). Understanding teenager's use of the ICTs continues to be the key to comprehend the internet's omnipresence in people's homes, the conditions of access and involvement, the lifestyles of both teenagers and parents, the differences between amount, quality and consumption and the attitudes and values of the families. Given all this, religion, age group, ethnicity, gender and regional and national cultures' differences and similarities must be considered, regardless of variables such as "privatization, individualization and consumerism" (Livingstone, 2002, Roberts, 2000).

Individuals need to claim their own time, like time to take a shower, eat (Morgan, 1996), or surf the web. Teenager's behavior towards the internet usage leads to time being more dedicated to these platforms rather than the family. This increases individualism and isolation in the family environment (Livingstone, 2002).
Mesch's model (2006), represented in Figure 1, establishes direct and indirect connections between several key variables linked to the use of the internet and the family settings.

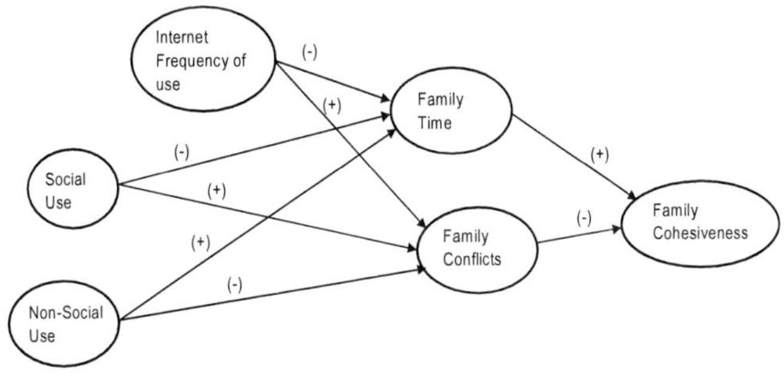

Figure 1. Behavior of uses model (Mesch, 2006)

According to the author, the time dedicated to the internet usage represents time that is taken away from the family. This may lead to low levels of family cohesion and bonding and several family conflicts (Lee, 2009, Nie et al., 2004, Lenhart et al., 2001). Contrarily, when one dedicates more time to the family than to the media, one may see higher levels of family cohesion and fewer family conflicts. This equation may become more relevant if applied to bigger families, since there is more competition among members for the time dedicated to the media (and more competition for personal attention). This may lead to conflicts between parents and their children, because teenagers may find sharing digital resources consists of restrictions on freedom (Mesch, 2006).

In 2018, 79% of Portuguese individuals had internet in their homes (INE, 2018) and according to the study 'Eu kids Online', 87% of teenagers had access to the internet (Ponte and Batista, 2019). The Americans dedicate nearly 8 hours a day to internet usage, with more than half of them using the computer daily, to the detriment of other activities (Roberts, 2000). On average, they devote three daily hours to surfing the web, being that 57% of this time is spent on email, instant messages and chats. Adults use the e-mail more often than teenagers, who use instant messages and chats more frequently (Nie et al., 2004).

Given the values that guide the individual and family life, the theoretical possibility of this study is that the Catholic religion is a relevant factor when choosing the place where internet access is available, and the time devoted to it.

3. LARGE CATHOLIC FAMILIES

A family is a polysemic subjective concept, which definition depends on the social, political and demographic context. It involves many religious, moral, legal, cultural and social conceptions that provide family typologies according to nature and size (Osswald, 2015, Saraceno and Naldini, 2003, Segrin and Flora, 2011, Simionato and Oliveira, 2003).

At the beginning of the 20th century, a family was seen as the relationship between a man (father), a woman (wife) and their child, in which the man assumed the main role (Durkheim, 1975, Parsons, 1971). As the years went by, the ideology of family, marriage and conjugality acquired a new paradigm, where Portugal is included (Aboim, 2005a, Aboim, 2005b, Amaro, 2014, Dias, 2011, Wall, 2005, Wall and Guerreiro, 2005).

Regarding the size of the family, despite the lack of documentation (Hutchins, 2013), it is said that a family with three or more children is considered a large family (Drysdale et al., 1984, Fahey et al., 2012, Knowlton, 1832, Rogers and Nikkel, 1979). According to the European Large Families Confederation (ELFAC) and the Portuguese Association for Large Families (APFN), a family with 3 or more children is considered large.

Even though it's open to change, Catholic Church defines the family as built by the father, mother and children, in several biblical texts. The ideology of family is defined on the basis of the "emotional ties and mutual consent"(Goody et al., 1995). In this conception, the children are seen as "God's blessings" or as gifts given by God to the couple. Therefore, it is not uncommon to find Catholic families in which the children assume the central role which is "intrinsic to the religious ideology" (Goody et al., 1995). In this paper, a large Catholic family is one with three or more children, where the commandments of the Catholic Doctrine are prophesied.

4. METHODOLOGY

Mixed methods research was the strategy adopted, since quantitative and qualitative methods were used to gather data and evidence, which was later triangulated. This approach is frequently used in investigation on social sciences, namely in the studies about communication and the media.

Two samples were formed with two different purposes: a national sample of families (N=333), using simple random sampling, where questionnaires were applied; and a regional snowball sample (N=39) where families were interviewed and observed, with semi-structured interviews, field diaries and non-structured observation.

The accuracy of the sample along with its unanimity construction allowed the overcoming of the "answers' superficiality" (Quivy & Campenhoudt, 2008, pp. 189-190). The semi-structured interview allowed the exploration of certain ideas, testing of answers, investigation of motives and feelings, things a questionnaire would never do (Bell, 1997). The field diaries allowed a thorough comprehension of the role of a computer connected to the internet in the family environment. The observation consisted of the spontaneous collection of data, capture of authentic moments and learning of behaviors and events in the specific moments these happened (Quivy and Campenhoudt, 2008). The interview data and field diaries were analyzed based on the "speech-cognition-society" (Van Dijk, 2000, Van Dijk, 2006), because of the wide understanding of "speech", in other words, as a "communicative event". This includes the face-to-face interaction, writing as well as body, facial language, text formatting, images and any other semiosis (Van Dijk et al., 2013).

4.1 Samples

The used qualification criterion was the same for both samples: large, Catholic, wealthy families. Altogether, both samples totalize 372 individuals, as depicted in Table 1.

Table 1. Depiction of national and regional samples

Participants	National	Regional	Total
Parents	128	14	142
Children	205	25	230
Total	**333**	39	372

Most of the parents are aged of 42-47, with higher education degrees (79%) and work as specialists in intellectual and scientific activities (52%). The children are aged between of 12-13 and the majority of them (97%) attends school. 26% of these are currently on the 9th grade, followed by 6th graders (25%) and fourth graders (24%).

All respondents, parents and children, follow the foundations of the Catholic Church. However, the majority of parents (68%) and children (62%) don't attend any specific religious community. Around 30% of parents and 27% of children are integrated in some kind of religious community. Amongst the communities that have a higher number of followers are the Teams of Our Lady (28%), Schoenstatt Apostolic Movement (16%) and the Neocatechumenal Way (14%). With the same percentage of answers (9%) are the Emmanuel Community, Opus Dei and the Communion and Liberation. Regarding the children, the Neocatechumenal Way (21%) and the Teams of Our Lady (20%) are the most common.

5. RESULTS

In this section we present results concerning the number of computers connected to the internet, the location of those devices inside the families' houses and the time of exposure to the internet.

5.1 Number of Computers Connected to the Internet

The national surveys - see Table 2 - show that 55% of the Portuguese Catholic families have a computer with internet connection at home, for N=333. While the interviews and the field diaries show that there are 17 computers connected to the internet for N=39.

Table 2. Number and location of the computer connected to the internet

Type of device	National			Regional/Local
	% of families with a computer connected to the internet	Location in the house where the computers connected to the internet are		Data from the interviews and field diaries in absolute value
		Shared	Private	
Computer connected to the internet	54.8%	86.2%	13.8%	17

Even though the surveyed families belong to an educated, upper social class with no financial difficulties, the number of computers connected to the internet is low in the family environment. Therefore, it is clear that our data doesn't match the studies that mention Portugal as a country that is at the forefront regarding the number of personal computers (Livingstone et al., 2011, Ponte, 2011a, Ponte et al., 2012), nor there is a direct relation between family income and available amount of devices. The low number of digital devices is due to the fact that parents value sharing. This orients not only the amount, but also the location and time dedicated to the media/IT, as we will verify later. Since sharing is something that's encouraged since childhood, there was no competition nor family conflicts for the use of the media/ICTs. This goes against Mesch's perspective (2006), which states that the bigger the family, the higher the levels of conflict for the use of the media. He adds that teenagers may see shared access to the media platforms as a restriction of autonomy (Mesch, 2006). Therefore, it is common to listen to parents and children saying that the fact that there's only one computer is positive, since it allows sharing. This confirms that large families are formed by people who share feelings and values molding ties of interest, solidarity and reciprocity (Simionato and Oliveira, 2003).

5.2 Location of Computers Connected to the Internet

In terms of location, the computers connected to the internet are usually placed in shared spaces that can be accessed easily and quickly, instead of private spaces (Livingstone, 2002, Hall, 1990). There's no intention of moving them to private rooms (mother C), since they promote, for example, "isolation" or "sharing" (mother G). Parents want a family environment that allows for intrapersonal communication and avoids isolation. These results don't support the idea that Portugal is a country where media platforms are located in private rooms, like the bedroom (Livingstone et al., 2011, Ponte, 2011a, Ponte, 2011b, Ponte et al., 2012). They also don't support the privatization, individualization and consumerism perspective, nor the easiness of mobility and privacy on the internet that the abundance of portable computers and networks allowed. The promotion of the value of sharing allows the practice of other values, like "solidarity" (mother G), "participation" (father A) or "common good" (mother G; father A).

Regarding the amount, location and time of use, the father figure may be more important than the mother one. This exposes not only the gender inequality, noticeable in the Portuguese family environment (Wall, 2005), but also the idea passed on by the Catholic Church that "the lack of a father-figure in many families causes major imbalances in households and uncertainty in gender identification in children" (Synod of Bishops, 2014, p.27) Excerpts of the interviews reveal just that: "My father is usually the one who decides [on the purchase] For example, the computer So, we choose, then my father sees if (laughs) the price is fit or not" (daughter F3); "My father is the one who decides that it should be this way [amount, type and location] and that's it!" (daughter A3).

5.3 Time of Exposure the Internet

Relating to the time spent on the internet, questionnaires show that, on a national level, 11% of parents and 6% of children don't use it. 34% of parents surf the web up until thirty minutes, 28% of children surf the web for between thirty minutes and one hour, 5% of parents and 10% of children surf the web three or more daily hours, as depicted in Table 3. The interviews and the field diaries confirm that people don't spend a lot of time on the internet. The majority dedicates the internet around two daily hours, this mainly during the week. When compared to the majority of Portuguese people, that surf the web for more than two daily hours, sometimes getting to five daily hours, these results are rather low.

Table 3. Daily time spent on the internet (regional/local) N = 39

	0 hours	Up to 30 min	30 min-1 hour	1 hour-2 hours	2 hours-3 hours	3 hours or more
Children	10	2	6	5	0	2
Parents	3	7	1	2	1	0

For these families, time is a "value", it's a "gift of God" and it should be dedicated to the family or educational activities like reading, scouting, or catechesis, instead of using the internet, namely social networks like Facebook, Twitter or Instagram. The concept of time in the families of this research reflects the principles of the Catholic Church, as shown in statements of the participants:

- "it is a Christian standard, so we, as Christians, can't waste time... It is a gift of God" (father D);

-" Time is a great value... it's a little related to faith..." (mother D);

-" We don't waste a lot of time, that's it! ...we have to use it to talk about our lives, problems, to pray" (father F);

-" Thinking if there's a lot of time for praying and I pray, here at home, instead of being on the internet. Hum, I also spend more time with my family than being on the internet..." (daughter F6).

Mostly, a time of use is not established, since the children agree not to spend a lot of it on the internet, spending their time on other activities. It is common that each one has a limited period of time for the use of the internet, as shown in this excerpt of the interview: "It's usually about an hour, an hour and a half for each, and no time in the morning. That's when we help out, read, play and that's it!" (Son C5); "When I'm on vacation, my mom gives me a little more time for the computer. She usually does (son B4)". The qualitative analysis also reveals that the time of exposure to the internet should be controlled. This perspective is found in the statements of both parents and children, as well as the idea that it's up to the parents to ensure that the family uses the internet in a "cautious" and "moderate" way. As the main guardians for education, it is the parent's duty to control their children. In fact, for these families, this role itself is a value (Dias, 2011).

6. CONCLUSION

We attempted to understand the time and location of the use of the internet in large Portuguese Catholic families, mentioning the role of religion.

In conclusion, the number of computers connected to the internet is low and they are found mainly in shared rooms, not private ones. This makes sharing easier and prevents isolation. The time of exposure is also short: parents spend a daily amount of 30 minutes maximum on the internet, while children dedicate between thirty minutes and one hour to it. Time should be dedicated to doing things that please the Lord because time is sacred. This restrains the use of the internet, which doesn't have an active role in these families.

This work is not without limitations, as we believe that bigger samples would increase its robustness and the level of trust in the obtained results.

Despite this limitation, we consider that this study introduced new family environments in which the time and location of the use of the internet do not obey the (apparent) generalized trend of the omnipresence of internet and technology amongst the families.

For future work, we set the studies of mobile devices as well as studies with bigger samples and ones that have different particularities. This will allow the identification of other uses of the internet that don't fit the (apparent) generalized trend in the majority of families.

REFERENCES

Aboim, S. 2005a. As orientações normativas da conjugalidade. *Famílias em Portugal-Percursos, Interacções, Redes Sociais*, 169-230.

Aboim, S. 2005b. Dinâmicas de interacção e tipos de conjugalidade. *Famílias em Portugal. Percursos, Interacções, Relações Sociais, Lisboa, Imprensa de Ciências Sociais*, 231-302.

Amaro, F. 2014. *Sociologia da família,* Lisboa, Pactor.

Bell, J. 1997. Como realizar um projecto de investigação. *Gradiva.*

Dias, M. O. 2011. Um olhar sobre a família na perspetiva sistémica no processo de comunicação no sistema familiar. *Gestão e desenvolvimento,* 19, 139-156.

Drysdale, C. V., Ellis, H., Robinson, W. J. & Grotjahn, A. 1984. Small or large families: Birth control from the moral, racial and eugenic standpoint.

Durkheim, E. 1975. *Textes, fonctions sociales et institutions,* Paris, Minuit.

Fahey, T., Keilthy, P. & Polek, E. 2012. Family relationships and family well-being: A study of the families of nine year-olds in Ireland. *Dublin: University College Dublin and the Family Support Agency*, 1-108.

Goody, J., Barradas, A. & Mariz, J. 1995. *Família e casamento na Europa.*

Hall, E. T. 1990. *The hidden dimension,* United States of America, Anchor.

Hutchins, H. R. 2013. Cheaper by the dozen: communication in large families.

INE. 2017. *Portal do Instituto Nacional de Estatística* [Online]. Available: www.ine.pt [Accessed 10 fevereiro 2018].

INE. 2018. *Portal do Instituto Nacional de Estatística* [Online]. Lisboa Instituto Nacional de Estatística. Available: www.ine.pt [Accessed 12 dezembro 2018].

Knowlton, C. 1832. Fruits of philosophy. San Francisco: The Reader's Library.

Lee, S. J. 2009. Online communication and adolescent social ties: Who benefits more from Internet use? *Journal of Computer-Mediated Communication,* 14, 509-531.

Lenhart, A., Rainie, L. & Lewis, O. 2001. Teenage life online: The rise of the instant-message generation and the Internet's impact on friendships and family relationships. 1-46.

Livingstone, S. 2002. *Young people and new media: Childhood and the changing media environment*, Sage.

Livingstone, S., Haddon, L., Görzig, A. & Ólafsson, K. 2011. EU kids online II: final report 2011.

Mesch, G. S. 2006. Family relations and the Internet: Exploring a family boundaries approach. *The Journal of Family Communication,* 6, 119-138.

Monteiro, T. L. & Policarpo, V. 2011. Media e entretenimento. *In:* MATTOSO, J. (ed.) *História da vida privada em Portugal. Maia: .* Maia: Temas e debates

Morgan, D. 1996. *Family connections: An introduction to family studies*, Polity Press Cambridge.

Nie, N. H., Simpser, A., Stepanikova, I. & Zheng, L. 2004. The ten years after the birth of the Internet, how do Americans use the Internet in their daily lives?, *Stanford Center for the Quantitative Study of Society*, 2-20.

Osswald, H. 2015. Em Torno da história da família. *In:* FERNANDES, O. M. & MAIA, C. (eds.) *A família portuguesa no século XXI.* Lisboa: Parsifal.

Parsons 1971. A estrutura social da família. *In:* ASHEN, R. (ed.) *A família: Sua função e destino* Lisboa: Edições Meridiano.

Ponte, C. 2011a. Acessos e literacias digitais: resultados portugueses do inquérito europeu EU Kids Online. *Literacia, Media e Cidadania*, 23-38.

Ponte, C. 2011b. Uma geração digital? A influência familiar na experiência mediática de adolescentes. *Sociologia, problemas e práticas*, 31-50.

Ponte, C. & Batista, S. 2019. EU Kids Online Portugal. Usos, competências, riscos e mediações da internet reportados por crianças e jovens. EU Kids

Ponte, C., Jorge, A., Simões, J. A. & Cardoso, D. 2012. *Crianças e internet em Portugal,* Coimbra, Minerva.

Quivy, R. & Campenhoudt, L. 2008. *Manual de investigação em ciências sociais.* , Lisboa, Gradiva.

Roberts, D. F. 2000. Media and youth: Access, exposure, and privatization. *Journal of adolescent health,* 27, 8-14.

Roe, K. 2000. Adolescents' media use: a European view. *Journal of adolescent health,* 27, 15-21.

Rogers, E. C. & Nikkel, S. R. 1979. The housing satisfaction of large urban families. *Housing and Society,* 6, 73-87.

Saraceno, C. & Naldini, M. 2003. *Sociologia Da Família,* Lisboa, Estampa.

Segrin, C. & Flora, J. 2011. *Family communication*, Routledge.

Simionato, M. A. W. & Oliveira, R. G. 2003. Funções e transformações da família ao longo da história. *Anais do I Encontro Paranaense de Psicopedagogia*, 57.

Toffler, A. 1984 *A terceira vaga,* Lisboa, Livros do Brasil.

Van Dijk, T. A. 2000. Cognitive discourse analysis: an introduction. *University of Amsterdam. Disponível em: www. discourses. org/MainPage2. html. Acesso em,* 20, 2004.

Van Dijk, T. A. 2006. Discourse, context and cognition. *Discourse studies,* 8, 159-177.

Van Dijk, T. A., Medeiros, B. W. L. & ANDRADE, M. L. C. 2013. Análise crítica do discurso multidisciplinar: um apelo em favor da diversidade. *Linha D'Água,* 26, 351-381.

Wall, K. 2005. *Famílias em Portugal,* Lisboa, Imprensa de Ciências Sociais.

Wall, K. & Guerreiro, M. D. 2005. A divisão familiar do trabalho. *In:* WALL, K. (ed.) *Famílias em Portugal* Lisboa: Imprensa das Ciências Sociais.

FACTORS AFFECTING THE SUSTAINED USE OF CHATBOTS: AN ORGANIZATIONAL PERSPECTIVE

Karine Aoun Barakat and Amal Dabbous
Saint Joseph University of Beirut, Lebanon

ABSTRACT

Artificial intelligence innovations including conversational user interfaces have become widely adopted within the banking sector, as they present numerous advantages such as cost reduction, increased efficiency and quicker servicing of customers. However, these benefits will materialize only if organizations ensure the sustained use of these technologies. Hence, identifying the main factors that drive the sustained use of these services is critical to assess new technology adoption given that a very high number of IT implementations might fail. Researchers have relied on technology acceptance models to analyze the adoption of these new technologies within organizations, however little is known about the factors that ensure their sustained use. Using a qualitative methodology based on in-depth interviews with employees of a leading bank operating in developing economies, the study addresses this shortcoming by investigating the factors that contribute to the sustained use of conversational user interfaces, taking chatbots as a case study. Findings reveal that eight main internal and external factors are essential to promote the sustained use of chatbots, the most prominent of which are: a positive human-technology relationship, a favorable corporate culture, and the technology's high perceived efficiency.

KEYWORDS

Technology Sustained Use, Artificial Intelligence, Chatbots, Organizational Perspective

1. INTRODUCTION

Artificial intelligence (AI) and the use of digital technologies including chatbots are shaping the banking industry and facilitating the transition from traditional to conversational channels. They represent the current market trend and are expected to be used within several segments of large companies (Wilson et al., 2017). According to a survey conducted by Oracle, 80% of the decision makers participating in a global study confirm that they already used or plan to use chatbots by 2020 (Business Insider, 2016).

The use of chatbots presents numerous advantages for banks and financial institutions. These benefits include cost reduction, increased efficiency and quicker servicing of customers. Embracing conversational user interfaces might therefore enrich the performance of an organization as this channel can offer advanced customer care and personalized services while saving time and costs. However, significant cost reduction and increased efficiency due to the adoption of conversational interfaces can only materialize if this technology is continuously used.

The concept of sustained use is different from first time acceptance as instead of investigating the initial use behavior of a new technology, it has a long-term focus and analyzes a person's or organization's use behavior and interaction with this system over a longer period of time (Bhattacherjee, 2001).

Previous studies in the literature have carried research and developed theories that explain the acceptance and adoption of a new technology such as Venkatesh et al. (2003). However, none of these studies investigate the factors that drive the sustained use of a new technology. Although initial acceptance and use of new technologies can depict its success rate at the beginning, an information technology's long-term success rate and viability largely depends on its sustained and continuous use (Ratten, 2016; Wang et al., 2008). Continuous use behavior is therefore the extension of the initial use and is considered a critical factor to assess when adopting a new technology, particularly that some researchers advocate that almost 70% of all IT implementations fail (Balogun, & Hope Hailey, 2004). Hence it is crucial to depict and specify which factors foster the sustained use of a new technology within an organization.

This study aims to determine the significant factors that affect the sustained use of chatbots within an organization. To answer the research question, the study adopts an organizational perspective to conduct a qualitative analysis. Data collected from semi-structured interviews conducted with employees from a leading bank operating in several developing economies is examined using thematic analysis. Findings identify eight internal and external factors that promote the sustained use of conversational user interfaces.

To the best of the authors' knowledge, this study is considered among the first to examine factors that influence the sustained of use of chatbots within the banking environment context and to classify these factors as internal and external drivers for the continuous use of a new technology. Moreover, the findings of this study constitute the building block to develop and test a conceptual model for the sustained use of conversational user interfaces.

The paper is organized as follows, section two presents a summary of the concepts of Artificial Intelligence and chatbots and a review of the literature on technology acceptance, use and sustained use, section three develops the research methodology, section four reports and discusses the findings and section five concludes and portrays contributions and future research directions.

2. THEORETICAL BACKGROUND

2.1 Artificial Intelligence and Chatbots

Numerous financial institutions including banks are beginning to introduce within their activities various types of AI technologies namely those based on voice and text such as chatbots. A conversational interface or natural user interface is defined as an interface that the user can interact with by using natural inputs such as, speech, touch or hand gestures (Wigdor & Wixon, 2011). This study focuses only on chatbots that use textual inputs.

These conversational AIs present the advantage of combining historical interactions with current real time data as well as internal and external data. Hence, this process makes the individualized engagement by a machine or a robot possible through the use of big data. Most importantly, this technology offers the advantages of reducing costs while making organizational processes more efficient which in turn enhances the value to both organizations and customers (Pannu, 2015).

Several factors encourage the adoption of chatbots by banks, the most important factor being the reduced cost of data storage, analytical tools and the advancements in machine learning which permit the automation of repetitive customer support tasks and will eventually allow the processing of more complicated interactions at lower costs. Furthermore, as more firms and consumers use chatbots, the increased demand for this technology will trigger additional development of chatbots, making the implementation process easier for organizations. Moreover, chatbot features are improving, thus making mass personalization possible due to innovations in artificial intelligence and machine learning technologies, big data analysis, improved analytics as well as predictive models. As a result, the number of financial institutions using chatbots and consumers that adopt this channel of communication will increase as the quality of delivered services improves across industries. Even though chatbots can be used in several segments such as marketing and payments, they are most frequently used for servicing customers and providing information to them. Within the global market, almost 45% of end users favor the use of chatbots as the primary channel of communication for customer service queries (Nguyen, 2017).

While the use of chatbots presents various advantages for banks and financial institutions, in order for these organizations to leverage this inexpensive and wide-reaching channel of communication to engage with a larger number of customers, it is important to depict the factors that are essential to ensure the sustained use of this technology within the organization. Identifying these factors is of major importance given that the use of this conversational user interface can face many challenges both internally and externally.

2.2 Technology Acceptance, Implementation and Use

2.2.1 Theoretical Models

Previous studies in the literature discussed the concept of technology acceptance and adoption. These studies primarily focused on the issues of technology acceptance explaining the technical aspects of design and implementation in a particular ICT infrastructure; among others we cite, Kane (2016) and Dahiya, (2017). Theories such as the technology acceptance model, TAM (Venkatesh & Davis, 2000), the unified theory of acceptance and use of technology, UTAUT (Venkatesh et al., 2003) have been widely used to investigate the intention to adopt and use a new technology. These theories are nevertheless primarily concerned with the initial adoption of a technology and not its continuous and sustained use. They have been criticized for focusing on the exploitation stage and trying to forecast and model the behavior of the users that take the decision to adopt the technology or reject it (Aizstrauta et al., 2015).

Studies that proceed to further analyze the factors that ensure the sustained use of a technology are important because interiorized usage cannot be predicted by studies based solely on concepts such as acceptance and adoption or short-term use (Al-Sharafi et al., 2017). Sustained use also called continued use by some authors (Jennex & Olfman, 2006) has a long term focus and analyzes the use behaviour and interaction with a particular system over a long period of time (Bhattacherjee, 2001). A given technology is not considered successful unless its usage is sustained by users who are supposed to benefit from this use (Bhattacherjee & Lin, 2015). However, the literature tackling this issue is very scarce and to the best of the authors' knowledge none of the previous studies explored the factors that affect the sustained use of chatbots within an organization.

To further investigate the sustained use of a new technology within the existing literature, the IASAM2 of Aizstrauta et al. (2015) provides an in-depth view of a new technology sustainability and proposes to calculate an index to measure it. According to IASAM2 model, technology sustainability depends on four flows: Management, Quality of Technology, Acceptance and Domain Development. Management of the technology development and the quality of the technology used are considered to be internal flows as they are controlled by the organization itself, while technology acceptance and domain development are considered as external flows. Each of these flows is characterized by various socio-technical factors. However, the IASAM2 model presents a very large number of factors that affect the sustainability of a technology and is more suitable for a quantitative study. As the scope of the present study is to identify the most important factors that support the sustained use of a technology within an organization, this model is not suitable and an exploratory approach is used with the aim of refining the conceptual understanding of the sustained phenomenon under investigation.

2.2.2 Sustained Use

To explore the sustained use behaviour, this study draws on the technology adoption and use literature to identify possible internal and external factors that might influence the sustained use of a new technology. Particularly, among the internal factors that could affect the adoption of a new technology is its expected ability to fulfill the organization's needs (Kim et al., 2013) and to improve the job performance (Venkatesh et al., 2003). In addition, some advocate that the use of a new technology such as the conversational interface could replace human-based customer service capabilities, hence threatening the job security of the organization's employees. It is known that the use of a new technology within the organization will modify several organizational processes and tasks, hence affecting the nature of jobs (Dewett & Jones, 2001; Taylor, 2004). Findings from the literature reveal that the success of the implementation of a new technology and the use of this technology by employees depends on their perceptions of how this new technology might affect their jobs (Bhattacherjee & Premjumar, 2004; Owen & Demb, 2004). Employees who perceive that the new technology will enhance their ability to accomplish their job tasks are more willing to adopt and use this new technology and might help to strengthen the technology adoption-performance link (Schraeder et al., 2006). Inversely, those who feel threatened by this new technology and are unwilling to embrace change will hinder the implantation and use of the technology.

Moreover, previous studies identify organizational culture as one of the factors that have a large influence on innovation within an organization as it could both stimulate or restrain the development and use of this innovation (Naranjo-Valencia et al., 2016). Organizational culture affects employees' behaviour and can lead the staff to consider innovation as a fundamental value of the organization and to feel more engaged in it (Hartmann, 2006). Stakeholders and leaders have also been considered to play an important role to facilitate the transition phase and transfer people from one state to another (Elrod & Tippett, 2002), which might drive the sustained use of a new technology. Finally, as the degree to which a technology is used is determined by the sum of its use by individual users, another factor that influences the transition to conversational engagement and sustained use of this channel is the consumers' acceptance for this conversational interface. Hence, it is fundamental to continuously adjust, change and modify the processes within the organization when using a new technology to meet the expectations and the needs of the users (Bouwman et al., 2005).

Several external factors could also affect the adoption of a new technology, some of which are directly linked to the industry or market regulations (Bouwman et al., 2005). In fact, the adoption of a new technology would be promoted under the existence of a favorable macro-policy, detailed regulations and rules that do not hinder the development of this technology (Shen et al., 2015). The way a technological product is used is also highly affected by the technical and social contexts. The technical context could restrain what the technology can achieve, while the social aspect establishes what will be acceptable in a given social system (Liebenau & Harindranath, 2002). In addition, the decision to adopt a new technology could be either specific to the individuals or organizations that chose to adopt this technology or associated with environmental factors and characteristics specific to this innovation (Rogers, 2003; Frambach & Schillewaert, 2002).

3. METHODOLOGY

The aim of this research being to understand the factors that lead to the sustained use of technology, a qualitative research approach was chosen. Qualitative studies capture the reality in substantial detail and are particularly useful when focusing on contemporary subjects (Chan and Ngai, 2007).

For this purpose, ten face-to-face semi-structured interviews with managers and employees within a bank that has implemented and is currently using a chatbot were conducted. The bank which is the object of this study operates in several developing economies and is considered to have a high level of experience with the chatbot as it has been continuously used for over a year and currently carries out 3,500 successful conversations every month. Interviewees were selected based on their experience as decision makers, implementers and users of the chatbot within the bank. Five of the employees which were interviewed are involved in the project as managers and strategic decision makers and the other five are implicated at the operation level and have a daily contact with the chatbot.

The guiding conceptual framework used during the interviews revolved around understanding the interaction between the organization itself, employees, the technology and the environment (Linton, 2002). The questions included in the interview guide aimed to determine the socio-technical factors that impacted the way the chatbot technology was developed, implemented and maintained, and the way in which this contributed to the continuous use of this technology.

Data collected through the ten interviews was then thematically analyzed. Thematic analysis can be widely used across a range of epistemologies and research questions. It is a method for identifying, analyzing organizing, describing and reporting themes found within a data set (Braun and Clarke, 2006). Within the context of this paper, a six-step analysis approach was adopted. Firstly, all the collected data was carefully read, and the sections which are of interest to the research were identified and captured. Secondly, initial codes were manually generated from the data by the two authors. Thirdly, the coded data extracts were sorted and collated into potential themes using an inductive approach. During the fourth step, themes were refined; those with not enough data to support them were merged into other themes and others which were too broad were broken down into separate themes. During the fifth step, the authors determined the aspects of the data each theme captured. The final step consisted of analyzing each theme and transcribing the findings (Braun and Clarke, 2006, Nowell et al, 2017).

4. FINDINGS AND DISCUSSION

Following the collection, coding, collation, refinement and analysis of the data derived from the ten face-to-face interviews, the resulting themes along with their corresponding verbatims were reported in Table 1 below. Some themes which were not adequately supported were excluded or integrated into other themes such as: the contribution to employees' job enhancement, top management support, and having realistic expectations about the technology.

Table 1. Thematic analysis results

Themes	Verbatim
Favorable Corporate Culture	"The bank already has a mindset of continuous growth… The technology culture is there and has always been there" "The culture change that now accepts failure has led us to unleash our innovation capabilities" "We are a bank which loves to innovate and try new things…it's a question of having the right mentality geared towards openness and new technologies"
Technological Advancement	"There is a general trend towards using chatbots around the world" "Once the chatbot technology became accessible to end users we thought it was time to start using it" "The chatbot can grow as far as technology allows it"
Perceived Efficiency	"The chatbot enhances both the efficiency and the customer experience at the bank" "Chatbot use has increased customer satisfaction" "The chatbot allows us to save time"
Compliance with Regulations	"The scope of the chatbot is being hindered because of the regulatory framework" "Regulations remain however a hurdle to developing chatbots further especially that they can sometimes be difficult to interpret"
Positive Human-Technology Relationship	"No jobs were lost, no threats…On the contrary new jobs were created" "Our chatbot was given an identity, a name…employees working with the chatbot consider it as their baby" "We are very happy to have the chatbot, we love him a lot" "Customers have easily accepted the idea of chatting with a bot" "More and more customers prefer to interact with the chatbot than contact us through our call center"
Multi-Stakeholder Implication	"All parties are on-board" "People from different departments are constantly solicited to be involved in the project" "Our vendors have to understand how we work, they have to be part of the team"
Continuous Improvement	"We have a roadmap of enhancements…we are continually working on improving the chatbot" "Technology enhancements cannot only be done from the company side, we need to know what customers require" "Continuous development not only from the operational side but at the managerial and strategic level as well is essential"
Strategic Alignment	"In line with the bank's positioning as a leader in the field of technology" "Our customers and competitors admire the Bank's innovations" "Having a chatbot reflects positively on the bank's image as a pioneer and innovator"

After reviewing the resulting eight themes, a distinction appeared between factors that could be controlled by the bank and those that are the product of its environment. Results are summarized in Figure 1 below. For instance, when discussing the technological advancement, it appeared clearly that the bank was dependent on the evolution of the AI technology environment as a whole and that in this case the sustained and continuous use of the chatbot was tied to how fast and far this technology would progress. Likewise, the prolonged use of the chatbot relies to a great extent on the regulatory environment and can be hindered in case stricter laws are passed. In terms of factors that could be controlled by the company which are favorable to the continuous use of chatbots, these were: having a corporate culture that encourages innovation, the technology's perceived efficiency, the multi-stakeholder approach mentality, the will to continuously improve and enhance the technology, as well as the alignment of the technology with the company's strategy. The final key factor which appeared was a positive human-technology relationship where not only employees and technology work side by side, but also customers have readily accepted and are satisfied with using this technology.

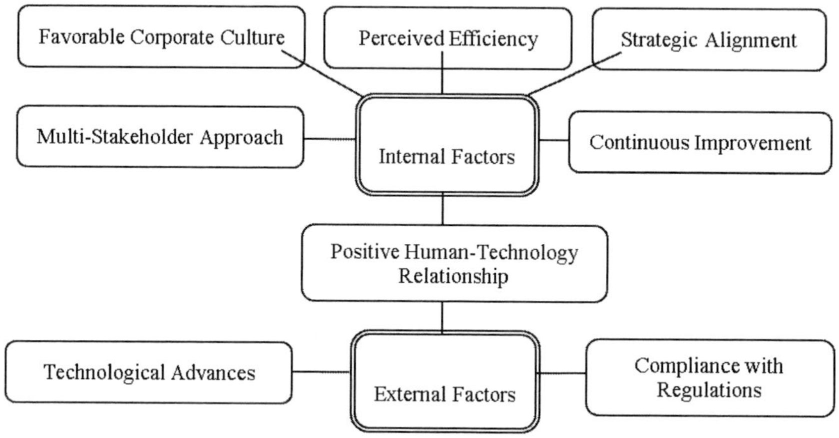

Figure 1. Factors affecting the continuous use of chatbots

Furthermore, among the noteworthy findings of the study was identifying which of the eight factors initially appear during the adoption phase of the technology and continue to play a crucial role in maintaining the continuous use of this technology. The first of these factors is strategic alignment, as mentioned by Lin & Chen (2012), who considered that a key factor affecting cloud computing adoption is the technology's compatibility with the company's business model and customer demands. Another such factor is the perceived efficiency, which proved to be a motivator for travel and tourism companies adopting robots as it translates into a reduction of costs and an increase in productivity (Ivanov & Webster, 2017). Finally, the technology's compliance with regulations is considered as a vital factor which determines its adoption, given that any new technology would be promoted under the existence of a favorable macro-policy, as well as detailed regulations and rules that do not hinder its development (Shen et al., 2015).

5. CONCLUSION

The present study contributes to the literature on the use of technology by including the sustained use behavior and identifying eight main internal and external factors that are considered essential to ensure the sustained use of chatbots within an organization. Semi structured interviews were conducted and a thematic analysis was adopted to select and validate eight main themes which are considered crucial internal and external factors that affect the sustained use of conversational user interfaces like chatbots.

The findings can be used both by academics and practitioners. For academics, it enriches the current models by including a long-term view into the use of technology, particularly chatbots. And as such, it opens new research streams. For practitioners, the paper which is based on a case study highlights the essential factors managers should take into account to ensure sustained use when adopting a new technology. Identifying these factors is crucial as it will help decision makers within an organization to increase proficiency, decide on the suitability of a new technology adoption and whether this technology can be continuously used or not. It stems from the authors' belief that acceptance and adoption are not enough to justify the substantial investments made by companies in the field of technology.

Even though the organization chosen to conduct this study operates in different developing countries, the findings of this research will have the typical limitations and threats to validity of a case study research, particularly with respect to generalization of results to other regions. Other limitations relate to the sector of activity of the studied organization which might also make the generalization of results difficult for organizations which are not in the banking sector.

As a future work, it would be interesting to include a larger number of organizations operating in different geographical regions and in different sectors of activity to increase the validity and generalizability of the results. Moreover, the next step could entail an in-depth quantitative analysis to hypothesize on the relations between the identified factors and their impact on the sustained use of chatbots within organizations. These hypotheses will constitute the basis for a new testable research model.

REFERENCES

Aizstrauta, D., *et al.*, 2015. Applying theory of diffusion of innovations to evaluate technology acceptance and sustainability. *Procedia Computer Science*, 43, pp. 69-77.

Al-Sharafi, M.A., *et al.*, 2017. Factors Influencing the Continuous Use of Cloud Computing Services in Organization Level. In *Proceedings of the International Conference on Advances in Image Processing* (pp. 189-194). ACM.

Balogun, J. and Hope Hailey, V., 2004. Exploring Strategic Change. Prentice Hall, London.

Bhattacherjee, A., 2001. Understanding Information Systems Continuance: An Expectation-Confirmation Model. *MIS Quarterly*, 25 (3), pp. 351-370.

Bhattacherjee, A., and Lin, C. P., 2015. A unified model of IT continuance: three complementary perspectives and crossover effects. *European Journal of Information Systems*, 24(4), pp. 364-373.

Bhattacherjee, A., and Premjumar, G., 2004. Understanding changes in belief and attitude toward information technology usage: A theoretical model and longitudinal test. *MIS Quarterly*, 28(2), pp. 229-254.

Bouwman, H., *et al.*, 2005. *Information and communication technology in organizations: adoption, implementation, use and effects*, Sage.

Braun, V. and Clarke, V., 2006. Using thematic analysis in psychology. *Qualitative research in psychology*, 3(2), pp 77-101.

Chan, S. C. and Ngai, E. W., 2007. A qualitative study of information technology adoption: how ten organizations adopted Web-based training. *Information Systems Journal*, 17(3), pp. 289-315.

Dahiya, M., 2017. A Tool of Conversation: Chatbot. *International Journal of Computer Sciences and Engineering*, 5(5), pp. 158-161.

Dewett, T., and Jones, G. R., 2001. The role of information technology in the organization: A review, model, and assessment. *Journal of Management*, 27, pp. 313-346.

Elrod, P. D., and Tippett, D. D., 2002. The "Death Valley" of change. *Journal of organizational change management*, 15(3), pp. 273-291.

Frambach, R. T., and Schillewaert, N., 2002. Organizational innovation adoption: A multilevel framework of determinants and opportunities for future research. *Journal of Business Research*, 55(2), pp.163-176.

Hartmann, A., 2006. The role of organizational culture in motivating innovative behaviour in construction firms. *Construction Innovation*, *6*(3), pp. 159-172.

Ivanov, S. H., & Webster, C., 2017. Adoption of robots, artificial intelligence and service automation by travel, tourism and hospitality companies–a cost-benefit analysis. *Artificial Intelligence and Service Automation by Travel, Tourism and Hospitality Companies–A Cost-Benefit Analysis.*

Jennex, M.E., and Olfman, L., 2006. A Model of Knowledge Management Success. *International Journal of Knowledge Management*, vol. 2, pp. 51-68.

Kane, D. A., 2016. The Role of Chatbots in Teaching and Learning. *E-Learning and the Academic Library: Essays on Innovative Initiatives*, 131.

Kim, Y. H., *et al.*, 2013. A study of mobile user engagement (MoEN): Engagement motivations, perceived value, satisfaction, and continued engagement intention. *Decision Support Systems*, 56, pp. 361-370.

Liebenau, J. and Harindranath, G., 2002. Organizational reconciliation and its implications for organizational decision support systems: a semiotic approach. *Decision Support Systems*, 33(4): pp. 339-398.

Lin, A., & Chen, N. C., 2012. Cloud computing as an innovation: Percepetion, attitude, and adoption. *International Journal of Information Management*, 32(6), 533-540.

Linton, J.D., 2002. Implementation research: state of the art and future directions, *Technovation*, 22(2), pp. 65– 79.

Naranjo-Valencia, J. C., *et al.*, 2016. Studying the links between organizational culture, innovation, and performance in Spanish companies. *Revista Latinoamericana de Psicología*, *48*(1), pp. 30-41.

Nguyen, M.H., 2017. The latest market research, trends & landscape in the growing AI chatbot industry. *Business Insider*, October issue.

Nowell, L. S., *et al*., 2017. Thematic analysis: Striving to meet the trustworthiness criteria. *International Journal of Qualitative Methods*, 16(1), 1609406917733847.

Owen, P. S. and Demb, A., 2004. Change dynamics and leadership in technology implementation. *Journal of Higher Education*, 75(6), pp. 636-666.

Pannu, A., 2015. Artificial intelligence and its application in different areas. *Artificial Intelligence*, 4(10), pp. 79-84.

Ratten, V., 2016. Continuance use intention of cloud computing: Innovativeness and creativity perspectives, *Journal of Business Research,* 69(5), pp. 1737-1740.

Rogers E.M., 2003. *Diffusion of Innovations*. Free Press, New York.

Schraeder, M., *et al.,* 2006. Employee involvement, attitudes and reactions to technology changes. *Journal of Leadership & Organizational Studies*, 12(3), 85.

Shen, G., *et al*., 2015. Factors influencing the adoption and sustainable use of clean fuels and cookstoves in China-a Chinese literature review. *Renewable and Sustainable Energy Reviews*, *51*, pp.741-750.

Taylor, D. S., 2004. Technology acceptance: Increasing new technology use by applying the right messages. *Performance Improvement*, 43(9), pp. 21-26.

Trott, P., 2001. The Role of Market Research in the Development of Discontinuous New Products. *European Journal of Innovation Management*, 4, pp. 117-125

Venkatesh, V., and Davis, F. D., 2000. A theoretical extension of the technology acceptance model: Four longitudinal field studies. *Management Science*, 46(2), pp. 186-204.

Venkatesh, V., *et al.,* 2003. User acceptance of information technology: Toward a unified view. *MIS Quarterly*, 27(3)

Wang, S.C., *et al.,* 2008. A study on the continuous adoption intention model of information systems—cognitive process, emotional states, and belief bases. In *Service Systems and Service Management International Conference*

Wigdor, D., and Wixon, D., 2011. *Brave NUI world: designing natural user interfaces for touch and gesture*. Elsevier.

Wilson, H. J., *et al.,* 2017. The jobs that artificial intelligence will create. *MIT Sloan Management Review*, 58(4), 14-17

Business Insider, 2016 https://www.businessinsider.com/80-of-businesses-want-chatbots-by-2020-2016-12

FROM NICHE TO MAINSTREAM TRANSITIONS: DIGITAL SECOND-HAND MARKETS FOR MILLENNIALS

Swati Srivastava and Alma Leora Culén
Department of Informatics, University of Oslo
PB 1080, 0316 Blindern, Oslo, Norway

ABSTRACT

This paper addresses the issue of over-consumption among millennials by repositioning reacquisition of consumer goods and digital platforms that support peer-to-peer exchange. We use transition design to frame our thinking and provide the focus on local communities and global technologies. To understand millennials, we have used in-depth interviews as the main method. The analysis of the interview data led to the recognition of five significant barriers for the uptake of second-hand platforms. Synthesis of findings, together with consumer behavior archetypes that we have identified previously, led to nine implication for the design of future services. These are a significant step toward re-conceptualization of peer-to-peer services and building of local communities of interest based on lifestyles and interests, including being greener.

KEYWORDS

Sustainable Services, Transition Design, Socio-Cultural Factors, Second-Hand Markets, Green Choices

1. INTRODUCTION

In this paper, we describe a real-life collaborative project with industrial partners interested in more sustainable consumption and the new business models that support it. We approached the project with the transition design framework (Escobar, 2018; Irwin, 2015, 2018; Manzini, 2015) and aimed to understand how to mitigate over-consumption amongst millennials.

Transition design is an emerging field of design, based on deeper entanglement of design with socio-cultural factors and systemic thinking, technology and future-oriented positioning. In proposing transition design, Irwin states that "transition to sustainable futures will require a sweeping change at every level of our society" (Irwin, 2015). Furthermore, the success of transformational change "will depend upon our ability to change our ideas about change itself – how it manifests and how it can be initiated and directed" (ibid.). Transition design, thus, advocates the re-conception of entire lifestyles, based on a deep understanding of underlying systems dynamics, aiming to make them place and community-based. It forwards four main areas in which design and research activities unfold to scaffold transitions in positive directions: visions of the future, finding and using the appropriate theories of change, understanding internal mindset and values, as well as external attitudes, and finally, discovering and using new ways of designing.

While the thinking behind our methodological approach is novel, our method involving in-depth interviews is well proven. With fifteen millennials we discussed their present consumption habits and the use of digital re-distribution (second-hand markets) platforms. The analysis of interviews played a crucial role in the proposal of design strategies based on thinking ecologically and including social, cultural and sustainability perspectives. In line with transition design, these strategies are to actively engage young people in re-thinking over-consumption and 'throw away' culture that they are a part of. Millennials represent the segment of the population inheriting serious global problems that span every aspect of human life, from environmental to social. They are already living in times of change, and are increasingly engaged in creating alternatives to present day consumer practices, e.g., (Peyer, Balderjahn, Seegebarth, & Klemm, 2017), but these are still far from mainstream ideas. We have specifically focussed on millennials, who often have a strong role as influencers for other age groups (Prensky, 2001; Selwyn, 2013).

The research presented here was done at the beginning of our collaboration with the industrial partners. However, contrary to the habitual linear paths of dissemination of academic results, it was not published first. The design practice outcomes were shared with the community first, where the main outcome was a future oriented service. The assemblage of design outcomes, i.e., the set of artefacts representing the service concept and supporting the service, was exhibited at a conference (Srivastava, 2017). An academic paper discussing the service (Srivastava & Culén, 2018) was also published. Furthermore, we have discussed the value of finding consumer behaviour archetypes and using this knowledge to support transitions to more sustainable consumption in (Srivastava & Culén, 2019).

The findings from the interviews that are presented in this paper, provided the basis to discuss opportunities regarding the re-positioning of the digital second-hand markets from niche to mainstream, and from global to place and community-based ones.

In what follows, we first outline the background work that helps us to position and frame this research towards transitioning to decreased consumption of consumer goods among millenials. We then discuss the findings from the interviews, focusing exclusively on challenges and opportunities to reduce consumption using digital platforms and novel services. We outline implications for design of future services, within the context of digital re-acquisition services featuring everyday things, and scaffolding local connections and community building.

2. BACKGROUND

Starting from transitional thinking (aiming to make a shift from todays to better consumption practices on digital platforms), we present the transition design framework first, then look briefly at sustainable consumption research within interaction design. We also provide a short summary of our research on finding consumers behavioural archetypes based on their current consumption practices and lifestyles. Together, these provide the conceptual background for the work and the way to contextualize our findings.

2.1 Transition design

Irwin defines transition design as *"a proposition for a new area of design practice, study, and research that advocates design-led societal transition toward more sustainable futures"*, (Irwin, 2015). To frame this practice, four areas of design and research activities are foundational for scaffolding transitions in a positive direction. Those are visions of the future, finding and using the appropriate theories of change, understanding internal mindset and values, as well as external attitudes, and finally, discovering and using new ways of designing (Escobar, 2018; Irwin, 2018; Lockton & Candy, 2018; Tonkinwise, 2015), see Figure 1.

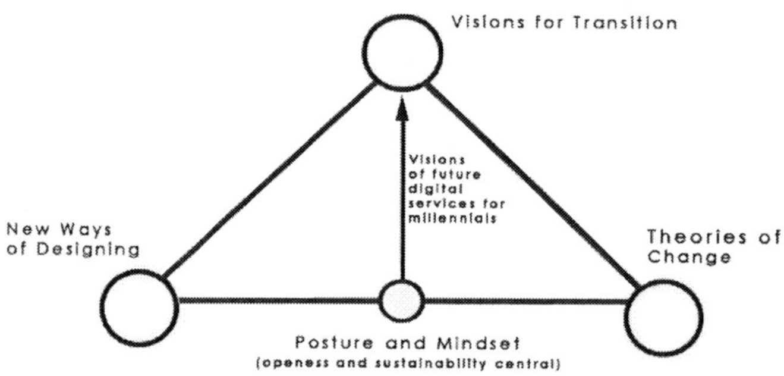

Figure 1. Transition Design Framework to transform consumer practices. Source: modified from (Irwin, 2018)

Furthermore, as any other design activity, transition design oscillates between the concrete, every day actions, and the more abstract theories and concepts and explorations, thus actively combining the research and the design. This is reminiscent of the processes described by Fallman (Fallman, 2008) for research through design, but what sets transition design apart is the intent to effectuate large scale societal changes.

The necessary changes from the perspective of transitions thinking involve changes in lifestyles and socio-cultural norms, and as such are more complex and challenging. The role of transition designers is to act as transformation agents, enabling thinking and action towards change. However, sustainability transitions need to be addressed by cross-disciplinary approaches in which design and designers stands together with different scientific disciplines needed to address the challenges at hand, as well as other types of knowledge that can lead towards finding better ways to frame the solution space in terms of plural opportunities (Escobar, 2018; Leach et al., 2012).

2.2 Sustainable Consumption Practices in Interaction Design

Social practice theories are particularly suitable for supporting sustainability transitions, focusing on horizontal trajectories and interconnectedness of everyday, place based practices (Ingram, Shove, & Watson, 2007; Shove, Pantzar, & Watson, 2012). To understand and engage people in re-thinking situated practices, (understood as routinized and everyday activities in some context), it is helpful to frame them as a unit of design. This way of looking at practices, since introduction in (Kuijer, Jong, & Eijk, 2013), has been gaining traction.

Using social practice theories as a way to understand how to change people's behaviors, has made its way in sustainable interaction design work. For example, Pierce and Paulos discuss consumption and frame it as practices related to acquisition, possession, dispossession and reacquisition, exploring reacquisition (purchasing used, second-hand goods) in particular, as a possible pathway toward more sustainable consumption practices (Pierce & Paulos, 2011). They point to an important distinction between designing *for* or *with* communities of reacquisition, and designing *from* communities of reacquisition. The former has to do with improving reacquisition as practices (better technologies, services, more profound concerns for the environment), while the latter engages in processes and practices of reacquisition as the basis for seeking and shaping of new solutions. The latter relates well to social practice theories, and thus was well in tune with our previous choices of designing for transitions using social practice as a theory of change. Their rich qualitative study of reacquisition informed on the importance of values, social acceptance, and challenges with current practices of reacquisition. Furthermore, it brought attention to the relation between dispossession and reacquisition, and the importance of experientially desirable acquisition. Also, in (Odom, Pierce, Stolterman, & Blevis, 2009), authors discuss dispossession and reacquisition, focusing on what things mean and outlining four areas of importance for relations between things and people: engagement (with things), histories (personal stories, memories), augmentation (creative ways of using, enhancing) and perceived durability.

2.3 Behavioral Archetypes

Behavioral archetypes are understood as behaviors carried forward from deep historical roots that are used to anchor socio-cultural norms. We subscribe to a culturally coded view of the archetype, i.e., archetypes are understood as iconic representations of social meanings and behavioral norms. In (Srivastava & Culén, 2019), we have identified three basic archetypes that millennials' consumption patterns follow. All three highlight the transient character of their living situation as the most important factor that shapes their purchase decisions, such as buying brand new or second-hand goods. We named these three categories *Spirited Nurtured Dwellers* (age 16 – 19, lived at home with their parents), *Busy Frugal Nomads* (age 20 – 23, moved out of their parents' home into the temporary living situations such as collectives or the student housing), and *Steady Independent Movers* (age 24 – 27, employed and building their careers). We point out to their mutual inter-connectedness and interdependences, and underlying transience as the key motivation behind the engagement with re-distribution services within this demographic. Thus, we identified the opportunity to explore ways of scaffolding transience by visioning different transitions and relations between the archetypes, creating pathways for movements of well-functioning consumer goods, but also knowledge, skills and time, within a familiar, similar-minded demographic. This can provide a foundation for new local, community-based social practices, leading to prolonged life of goods and a more sustainable consumption.

3. METHOD

We approached the issue of consumption among youth with a *mindset of openness*: we wished to do a broad, open, reflective and exploratory inquiry into routinised behaviours, focusing archetypal understanding of youth and their consumption practices around second-hand goods, and particularly, second-hand digital markets and platforms.

The method of choice were semi-structured in-depth interviews. We engaged fifteen young people (7 males and 8 females), see Table 1, in conversations lasting between one and two hours. The interviews were recorded, anonymized, then transcribed and coded using emergent, thematic coding. The analysis started with each author coding transcripts of two interviews and then discussing the emerging themes to help guide the remaining work with content analysis.

Table 1. The table provides the participants' pseudonyms, gender and age. The archetypes are color-coded

#	G	Pseudonym	Age	8	F	Nomadine-3	21
1	F	Dwelline-1	17	9	M	Nomad-4	19
2	F	Dwelline-2	16	10	M	Mover- 1	27
3	M	Dweller-3	17	11	F	Moverine-2	26
4	F	Dwelline-4	16	12	F	Moverine-3	24
5	F	Dwelline-5	16	13	M	Mover-4	24
6	M	Nomad-1	22	14	M	Mover-5	24
7	F	Nomadine-2	21	15	M	Mover-6	26

The analysis presented in this paper focuses on the use of digital platforms and design implications for future digital services.

4. FINDINGS

Several categories of findings emerged through he analysis. The largest category constitutes challenges related to trust, positioning of the market as the place to get rid of things, on-line presentation of goods, difficulties with communication, and the effort that it takes to find things.

4.1 Perceptions of the Existing Services and Platforms

The majority of the existing digital reacquisition services are peer-to-peer systems. Consequently, the participants' experiences with such services and platforms focused primarily on peer-to-peer interactions, necessity of engaging in direct communication and exchange of assets, representing contextually situated *social challenges*. In addition, second-hand markets are culturally coded as places where one *gets rid of things*, not as a re-distribution of quality things. These traits of the peer-to-peer economy for re-distribution of second-hand goods pose a very real set of challenges for millennials.

The social challenges had to do with issues of *trust* and *familiarity*. They preferred to avoid transactions when profiles seemed very different from their own age group, citing unfamiliarity, security and a sense of general awkwardness as primary reasons. For instance, Dwelline-2 considers someone who is at the university, and a student, to be trustworthy and close to her own profile: *"I am going to the university next year. I would gladly buy a used book if there are not too many scribblings and notes in it. I am open to that because the person I would buy it from would be a trustworthy student from the same campus."*

When asked why she believes that a person she would meet for such exchange is more trustworthy, she replied: *"I guess the age, it matters a lot."* The issue of trust is sensitive and Dwelline-2 thinks that people close to her own age are in principle more trustworthy because *"I do not trust old men. I do not know why. Something stereotypical, probably. Maybe, when I see pictures of their faces, I am judgmental, I don't know, but maybe I am."*

While Dwelline-2 did not have a direct experience with peer-to-peer transactions, but was open to it under certain conditions, Nomadine-3 has the first-hand experience. However, certain sensibility around trust was present in her experience as well: *"Yeah, I bought a lamp from a guy who lived on my block. I went to his place, because he was not living far away. I could just walk there. I didn't think that this was a* [safety] *problem for me, because he was also talking to another guy who wanted to buy. When the other guy didn't come through, he decided to sell to me".* Elaborating on safety issues, Nomadine-3 added:

"When I'm on FIND [the largest online platform called Finn ('finn' means find, see finn.no) in Norway], *I check the seller. But not like, 'Okay, he looks like a particular kind of a person.' Some pictures do make me more sceptical regarding the seller, but it is not very often I feel that. But for me, he* [the lamp owner] *just seemed like an okay person. He was nice, and also, when I was going to his place, I think he was returning home from work or something. So, I just came up to his flat and waited at the door until he arrived."*

Participants expressed some hesitance when considering exchange within own social circles. For most of the participants this hesitance stemmed from the risk of making their friends uncomfortable by, for example, unintentional spamming with advertisements on social media, which could affect their relations and reputation within the social circle.

"If I was selling something expensive, I would like to tell my friends and family on Facebook, and they could get a lower price. I wouldn't post my clothes or things like that on Facebook, because I think that would be like spamming them. It's personal. Small stuff. If I was selling a boat or something, I would let people know. Or a car", Nomad-1.

When asked further, if he thought that people do not care in general about the stuff he is selling, or they do not care for him doing it on the Facebook, Nomad-1 explained: *"Both actually. If you want something second-hand, you go on FIND. You don't want to get your social media spammed with advertisements. It already has enough ads."*

These few examples illustrate inclinations to trust people of their own age more, but not within own social circles, where they are afraid of being judged negatively. The middle ground was found to be young people who were not friends, but lived in their neighbourhood, or in a place they know. They were situated between the extreme familiarity (friends and family) and non-familiarity. Open profiles on FIND allowed for trust judgments, but this openness added a time and effort consuming task of filtering profiles, potentially leading to an overall less positive experience.

Furthermore, a prevailing perception of second-hand platforms was that of a market for *unwanted things.* This perception is reinforced by services providers themselves by advertising their services as means of *getting rid of things*, and making easy money and space for first-hand purchases. This led to a creation of a vicious circle regarding positioning of the market as a place to get rid of things. This perception was very evident among our young participants. For instance, Mover-1 describes the sale of very expensive shoes very cheaply on FIND by saying: *"I just wanted to get rid of them."* Many other participants used the exact same wording, and admitted to being motivated by the intent to 'get rid of things', which Moverine-3 describes as *"It can be a bit difficult because part of why people put up things on FIND is just so that someone else will get rid of them* [instead of disposing of things themselves]*."*

While most of the participants expressed willingness to buy, use and sell functional goods at reduced prices at online platforms, these remained largely unpopular within this age group. When the re-distribution platforms were used, and thought of in more positive ways, it was related to making fast money, personal gain, niche hobbies or treasure-hunts. Not one participant thought of these digital platforms as platforms representing greener choices.

4.2 Stories, Attachments, Quality of Goods

The participants admitted to being willing to accept minor visible flaws as a trade-off for acquiring things at a lower price, as long as the flaws were clearly communicated by the seller. However, along with the current state of goods, and clarity in conveying it, the participants underlined that if the flaw has an interesting story behind it, the story was important to their decision-making process. They recounted several instances where they themselves worked to discover the story behind the artefact of interest. Examples provided told stories about purchases from a famous person, a brand item at an unbelievable price, or a brand-new artefact at a low price. Even if the presentation of the artefact on the platform had an interesting story, distinct content or style, it was found to increase their interest. Furthermore, if the attachment of the previous owner to the item was visible, it also has a positive effect. As Mover-6 pointed out *"You need to know that it* [a musical instrument in this case] *has been taken care of, its been dealt with properly and not misused because its about to become something personal for me, yeah, so that is an aspect I look at."*

Many other participants also explained that they limited their purchases to objects they had expertise on, or experience with, as it allowed them to judge its condition easily. Most reacquisition services, naturally, do not offer any guarantee on the object itself. Therefore, for many users, an open platform with little familiarity with the community influences their trust not only in people, but also in the durability/quality of the goods.

4.3 Communication and (In)Conveniences

It was clear from the interviews that none of the participants were looking to build social relationships through second-hand platforms, it was not seen as a means to meet new people. They expected (and sometimes wanted) a cordial transaction and were open to the idea of a serendipitous social connections but it was not a reward they anticipated from the engagement. However, most of the participants cited communication as one of the key inconveniences of the process.

"You have to meet up with this person. You have to decide, 'Oh, we can meet on this day, then you can give me the money, I'll give you the clothing.' Just setting that up that meeting, it is... I don't know. I don't want to do it".

When selling, they preferred minimal communications. Rather than answering requests and inquiries from multiple users, they preferred to be able to connect with one or two potential buyers and concluding the transaction fast and with minimum negotiations.

4.4 Lack of Reliability, Commitment, and Information

A common concern raised by most of the participants was a lack of support of any kind on second-hand platforms, besides affordance to connect. Even though expectations, in contrast to the first-hand platforms, were lower, figuring to out every step of the way on their own can quickly became time-consuming. For instance, the decision-making process to sell or buy second-hand requires information gathering on its demand and estimated selling price in the market. This further requires spending time identifying and checking out similar listings. The participants have to decide on a selling price, evaluate the user profiles, the logistics of carrying things, mutually deciding a meetup times, and negotiating modes of monetary transactions. While the second-hand marketplace is often presented as an instant and easily accessible platform to buy or list/sell disused items (mainly because of their presence as smartphone apps), engaging in a transaction in this marketplace carries along many uncertainties. The drop-offs (a point of failure) in the all services available at present, also played a significant role in deterring the participants from investing time in reacquisition. Participants having experience with reacquisition platforms said that making a commitment to make a transaction and setting time aside for it did not mean that the other party would show up as agreed, and sometimes things were sold, but the change in status not updated on the app (a common concern). Moverine-3 expresses these common concerns as follows:

"Sometimes I've tried to buy things, but they have been sold. I just wish I could have had an overview of the transaction. It would have been better because sometimes you ask the person: 'Hey can I buy that thing?' They are like 'Yeah, it's still available.' Then you say 'Cool, when can I pick it up?' You then never hear from that person again. Then you're like, 'Hey, I haven't heard from you.' And then they say 'Oh, I sold it to someone else'. I just feel 'What? Why? We had a deal!'"

Moverine-3 expresses frustration with such communication and the lack of transparency. However, she is almost conflicted when she justifies such a bad user experience as an acceptable trade-off for getting things at a considerably lower price than at the first-hand markets. It points towards an implicit positioning of sellers over buyers, adding to the lack of accountability and transparency in the transaction. Mover-1 points to the following:

"In a way, I was expecting some help, with putting it [the item] *in the car and everything. No such help, it was like okay, put the money there and get rid of that, you're helping me get rid of that. Practically, she paid me for the job of getting rid of it, I wasn't paying her for the table. I was actually paying her for doing a small job for her, but then that's why the price was really, really cheap. It was easier for her to get rid of the table in this way."*

This implied that sellers view transactions as a free labour with a small profit, not as a value of the item. Unlike large peer-to-peer systems such as Uber, or Airbnb, most re-distribution platforms do not rate sellers, freeing them from the pressure of earning ratings or reputation, resulting in a lack of ongoing commitment.

4.5 Invisibility of the Market

Engagement with digital reacquisition marketplaces remains a deliberate act within this age group. Unlike looking at storefronts that can give a sense for the goods available in the first-hand market, discovering the second-hand market remains effort-demanding and requiring an intentional and planned activity involving high screen-time. Mover-1 explains that he is not willing to do this work. Instead, he says: *"That would be my girlfriend* [who is willing to put in the effort]. *I prefer to buy new things just because I don't deal with this. Also, even if you went to find used stuff, you still need to go to particular places. Together, that's more time consuming for me."*

This is quite ironic since desired second-hand goods and the marketplace are often present in the user's physical locality, close to home. Still, even a casual exploration of the second-hand inventory demands careful and undivided user attention. The invisibility of the market, and effort of discovery required, often presented a barrier to engagement with second-hand markets, even when the possibility of saving money, getting access to durable goods and making greener choices are all considered.

5. IMPLICATIONS FOR DESIGN AND DISCUSSION

We now draw on the finding to outline the implications for design, where our vision focussed on designing for wider uptake of reacquisition, within the mainstream communities of teens and young adults.

1. Re-positioning reacquisition within the existing practices and transient lifestyles of millennials

As evident from the interviews, the practices of possession and dispossession of everyday consumer goods pivot around transient living situations. Reacquisition services have the potential to offer larger assistance to sustainably manage the flow of consumer goods, instead of using a generic peer-to peer approach of simply connecting the buyers and the sellers. Rather than designing a prescriptive solution for a seamless point-to-point peer transaction, redistribution services should offer a holistic system addressing the material needs and challenges of the dynamic, aspirational, and busy lifestyles of this young demographic. Going beyond the possibility of making greener choices, monetary benefits, and riddance, a reacquisition service should be built to connect peers with familiar needs rituals/practices around usage of possessions.

2. Design to create pathways for movements of things to a context of value

Pierce et. al. emphasise the *context* as a means of re-coding the value of domestic objects and the potential of digital technologies to facilitate the articulating this intent (Pierce & Paulos, 2011). The pivotal position of both the context as well as the digital medium is evident in our research as well. Building on this, we explore the agency of design in building a robust pathway for the movement of durable goods across meaningful contexts. We argue for designing the path of reacquisition by connecting peers with complimentary lifestyles as well as a familiar routine of use.

3. Simplifying research and evaluation through intelligent information curation

Discovery and time-effort needed to identify desirable items are important barriers for many young users of reacquisition services. However, intelligent data processing systems are becoming increasingly common, opening new opportunities also in relation to reselling platforms. Sophisticated algorithms can reduce the manual evaluation process at the user's end, by capturing details and recognizing patterns and predicting outcomes. This can lead to a highly customized and relevant marketplace for all, reducing the time investment.

4. Design to eliminate the reputation of "easy riddance"

Lack of quality control in second-hand platforms' inventory was one of the common concerns amongst all the participants. It has a cascading negative effect on the service experience. Given the subjective nature of acceptance criteria of goods amongst the users, a clinical quality check alone cannot manage this challenge.

Reselling systems need to be designed and branded to eliminate their reputation of being platforms for "getting rid of unwanted things". The subtle inclination of these services towards selling as opposed to buying, through narratives and systems interactions encourages the use of these platforms as a convenient disposal strategy as well as a source of cheap throwaway goods, countering the intent of reducing consumption. Instead, reselling platforms need to be designed to adopt and promote the narrative of movement/circulation rather than *riddance of unwanted things*, where the community views the goods as a representation of their intents, practices, and aspiration. Additionally, by positioning the service as a clear and defined platform for mainstream utilitarian goods for the younger population with a transient lifestyle, the quality standards can be tailored towards maintenance and monitoring the peers and the service providers.

5. Design to engage durable brands directly with reacquisition

Durable inventory is fundamental to reacquisition services aiming to promote sustainable consumption. However, preventing the inflow of nondurable goods, in these services can be immensely challenging. A possible step in resolving this issue is for reacquisition services would be to be use branding and design to make goods having a longer lifespan an essential part of their identity, moving consciously away from the popular strategy of *riddance of unwanted things*. Durable brands can potentially utilize second-hand marketplace to advertise the high build quality of their offerings. With intelligent algorithms becoming more and more commonplace, this change in the brand identity and strategy can be supported through effective quality control and management of the inventory.

6. Design for positive social friction amongst the users

As reflected in the interview accounts, on the one hand, social interactions required for reselling transactions were deemed uncomfortable and unwanted by an otherwise usually social user group of millennial and digital natives. At the same time, the participants also admitted to these interpersonal conversations being essential to both product and peer evaluation. A sustained and positive *social friction* can assist in building trust and familiarity in a peer-to-peer service, especially in the case of reacquisition services where the engagement of both the buyers and sellers are often infrequent and need-based. Designed for engagements in addition to merely buying and selling can encourage a sense of community and possibly leading to other peripheral social interactions between the users. For instance, reacquisition market platforms can also function as forum for the young millennials to assist each other settling down in a new city, or offering reviews on second hand values and lifespan of various goods.

7. Design for a visible market

Making the availability of second-hand goods in the locality more prominent is important. The issue of time is essential, and a more mainstream positioning of reacquisition services requires a more visible presence of the goods available locally, to reduce the efforts of searching through a large inventory. For instance, customized ads of curated goods for individuals in their university campus can make the available inventory more visible through the use of technology beyond mobile and web platforms. To be sure, we do not necessarily imply that second-hand markets need to emulate the first-hand model of opening physical shops and showrooms. However emerging technology like connected objects and augmented reality can be used to make the inventory 'visible' in inventive ways. This can enable the youth easily and contextually discover second-hand objects and the marketplace in general while going about their lives.

8. Design for closed platforms and curated community

Closed platforms imply the control over who is a member of the peer-to-peer service. It allows for the community to be shaped through connections and familiarity and enables organic building of trust and empathy leading to more reliability and commitment to the community. It implies setting new norms, re-coding the culture of the platform, defining clearly what participants should expect from the other members, people worth similar and complimentary intents and lifestyle participate and interact with other with the intent of helping out each other and also fulfilling their needs of domestic goods.

9. Design to support the environmental/green motivations

The interviews show that millennials are motivated to make greener choices, and second-hand market places can use that as a leverage point. The services should clearly and visibly communicate this intent and focus on this issue in a transparent and factual way. The design itself needs to convey the honest efforts to support sustainable practices.

6. CONCLUSION

Conducting in-depth interviews with 15 young people, we have discovered five significant barriers for the uptake of second-hand services among millennials. These have served as starting points for synthesis that led to the articulation of nine implications for future services. To implement the findings in the real world, cross-disciplinary collaboration is needed to discuss and implement them, as well as chart the best ways to achieve transition visions toward more sustainable consumption by millennials. The results of this paper are a significant step in understanding how to re-conceptualize services and allow them to support communities of interest in ways that are in line with their lifestyles and interests, including the motivation to be greener.

ACKNOWLEDGEMENT

This work was conducted as part of the research and innovation project Conserve and Consume, funded by the Norwegian Research Council (project number 235526/O30).

REFERENCES

Escobar, A. (2018). *Designs for the Pluriverse: Radical Interdependence, Autonomy, and the Making of Worlds*. Durham: Duke University Press Books.

Fallman, D. (2008). The Interaction Design Research Triangle of Design Practice, Design Studies, and Design Exploration. *Design Issues*, *24*(3), 4–18.

Ingram, J., Shove, E., & Watson, M. (2007). Products and Practices: Selected Concepts from Science and Technology Studies and from Social Theories of Consumption and Practice1. *Design Issues*, *23*(2), 3–16.

Irwin, T. (2015). Transition Design: A Proposal for a New Area of Design Practice, Study, and Research. *Design and Culture*, *7*(2), 229–246.

Irwin, T. (2018). The Emerging Transition Design Approach. *DRS 2018: Catalyst*, Volume 3, pp. 968–989.

Kuijer, L., Jong, A. de, & Eijk, D. van. (2013). Practices as a Unit of Design: An Exploration of Theoretical Guidelines in a Study on Bathing. *ACM Trans. Comput.-Hum. Interact.*, *20*(4), 21:1–21:22.

Leach, M., Rockström, J., Raskin, P., Scoones, I., Stirling, A. C., Smith, A., Thompson, J., Millstone, E., Ely, A., Arond, E., Folke, C., & Olsson, P. (2012). Transforming innovation for sustainability. *Ecology and Society*, *17*(2):11.

Lockton, D., & Candy, S. (2018). Vocabulary for Visions in Designing for Transitions. *DRS 2018: Catalyst*, Volume 3, pp. 908–926.

Manzini, E. (2015). *Design, When Everybody Designs: An Introduction to Design for Social Innovation* (R. Coad, Trans.). Cambridge, Massachusetts: The MIT Press.

McDonald, S., & Oates, C. J. (2006). Sustainability: Consumer Perceptions and Marketing Strategies. *Business Strategy and the Environment*, *15*(3), 157–170.

Odom, W., Pierce, J., Stolterman, E., & Blevis, E. (2009). Understanding why we preserve some things and discard others in the context of interaction design. *Proceedings of the SIGCHI Conference on Human Factors in Computing Systems*, 1053–1062.

Peyer, M., Balderjahn, I., Seegebarth, B., & Klemm, A. (2017). The role of sustainability in profiling voluntary simplifiers. *Journal of Business Research*, *70*, 37–43.

Pierce, J., & Paulos, E. (2011). Second-hand Interactions: Investigating Reacquisition and Dispossession Practices Around Domestic Objects. *Proceeding of SIGCHI Conference on Human Factors in Computing Systems*, 2385–2394.

Prensky, M. (2001). Digital Natives, Digital Immigrants Part 1. *On the Horizon*, *9*(5), 1–6.

Selwyn, N. (2013). The digital native – myth and reality. *Aslib Proceedings*. https://doi.org/10.1108/00012530910973776

Shove, E., Pantzar, M., & Watson, M. (2012). *The dynamics of social practice: Everyday life and how it changes*. Sage.

Srivastava, S., 2017. Zygo: Design led reframing of secondhand marketplaces, *Nordes: Design + Power*. Exhibit.

Srivastava, S., Culén, A.L., 2018. Transition-oriented Futuring: Integrated Design for Decreased Consumption amongst Millennials, *DRS 2018: Catalyst*, Volume 3, pp. 927–940.

Srivastava, S., Culén, A.L., 2019. Implications for Transitions to Sustainable Consumption: Finding Millennials' Behavior Archetypes. Forthcoming.

Tonkinwise, C. (2015). Design for Transitions – from and to what? *Design Philosophy Papers*, *13*(1), 85–92.

AVATAR 1, MEDIA AND SOCIO-TECHNOLOGICAL IMAGINARIES: IMPLICATIONS FOR HCI RESEARCH

Jorun Børsting[1], Alma Leora Culén[1] and William Odom[2]
[1]*University of Oslo, Oslo, Norway*
[2]*Simon Fraser University, Surrey, Canada*

ABSTRACT

In this paper, we discuss the media coverage of a research product made for social innovation and its implications on our research and commercialization of the product that followed. We were interested in how media coverage shaped socio-technological imaginaries, cultural and social views of people around this new technology. The research product that was in the eye of the media interest was a networked artifact in the shape of a small robot called AV1, developed to reduce isolation among long-term ill children and adolescents. Discourse analysis was used to examine 170 news articles to explore diverse perspectives on AV1. Our work uncovers potential opportunities and challenges for researchers working with responsible social innovation and research products before commercialization. Further, it highlights the opportunities for research products to surface deeper entanglements between socio-cultural factors and technology innovation.

KEYWORDS

Research through Design, Research Products, Social Entrepreneurship, Socio-Technological Imaginaries, Media

1. INTRODUCTION

Social innovation has a strong focus on the social *values* of innovative products. Products that are the outcomes of design processes for social innovation are expected to mediate desired social values at scale. Often, the values are related to issues of social inclusion and bridging of social divides. For technology to mediate such values successfully and mitigate social challenges it tackles, it needs to have an impact on socio-technological ecologies. However, once an innovative technology is finished and launched as a commercial product, it is hard to make changes to the product that influence its implications for these ecologies. At the same time, before the product is broadly available, it is difficult to predict its social impact. The 'goodness' (positive impact) of social innovations is not a given (Godin, 2015), and issues around responsibilities for the ethical and social concerns related to such innovations arise (Stilgoe, Owen, & Macnaghten, 2013). These challenges are not relevant for industries only, but also the academic research (Ribeiro, Smith, & Millar, 2017).

With technology-based Social Entrepreneurship (SE) coming of age, it is timely to consider how academic research can recognize and pursue opportunities that collaboration with SE offers. SE seeks alternate ways to solve real-life social problems by combining technology, creative thinking and making, good social causes, values beyond profit, and different means of funding projects. It builds on social networking and use of social media for connecting, advertising, sharing, and crowdfunding. A research collaboration with SE introduces a set of opportunities and challenges for Human-Computer Interaction (HCI) research. In particular, since media engagement is an integral part of SE and essential for its success, academic HCI research can also get into the media spotlight. This paper discusses the implications of media and public interest in academic HCI research.

Heightened focus on social implications of design is evident in Interaction Design and HCI, where Research through Design (RtD) (Gaver, 2012; Höök et al., 2015; Pierce, 2014; Zimmerman & Forlizzi, 2014), tangible, and ubiquitous computing (Ishii, 2008; Weiser, 1993) have been increasingly turning the outcomes of their research and design practice into innovative products. Researchers also turn their attention to implications for adoption of such outcomes, e.g., (Lindley, Coulton, & Sturdee, 2017). Recently, in (Odom et al., 2016), the authors have articulated the concept of a *research product* through the practice of RtD. Research products, as described in their paper, have key interrelated qualities. They are *research inquiry-driven, finished* (in the sense that they represent the actuality of the design artefact, and not its potential, as is commonly the case with prototypes), *independent* (do not require the presence of the researcher to be used in the actual settings for which the product was intended), and *fit* (relates to the lived experience with the artifact, how it fits in everyday lives of those using it). Research products, thus, can be viewed as boundary objects between everyday life and research and design practice (see Figure 1a). They make it possible for researchers and designers to engage in inquiries on social implications and possible futures of commercial products. This opportunity extends a set of questions that can be asked beyond traditional studies, which rarely shift focus from developed prototypes of new technologies to socio-cultural entanglements that the product would be a part of, and into the realm of responsible design.

One of the long-term challenges of high relevance for responsible innovations is known as the Collingridge dilemma (Collingridge, 1980). The heart of this dilemma focuses on the questions of when and how to explore the consequences of new technologies. In the early stages of design and development, when changes to the design are easier to make, knowledge related to real-life experiences with the product is lacking. When the technology becomes a part of the socio-technological ecology as a commercial product, the social implications are more readily available, but it is often too late to make any design changes. In (Kudina & Verbeek, 2018; van der Duin, 2018), the authors propose the concept of technology mediation as a way to address the dilemma, and build on the dynamics of the interactions between technologies and human values and inquiry into how technologies mediate perceptions, actions, and interpretations, and shape moral frameworks that affect moral actions, and decisions (Verbeek, 2011).

In this article, we position RtD and research products as a way to engage in field explorations as part of the collaboration with SE before product commercialization. The focus on commercialization of a research product is in contrast with previously published RtD research, where research products were not made toward commercialization, but for research purposes only, e.g. (Chatting et al., 2017; Odom et al., 2016). We draw on a particular set of experiences with a AV1 (stands for Avatar 1), see Figure 1b, and imageries created by the media with AV1 as a research product, and later, a commercial product (see Figure 1c – the commercial product has a more polished look).

Figure 1. a) Research products as a boundary between the real world and the research b) AV1 as a research product used in this work - the headline reads *"Sick children learn through robots"* [1] c) AV1 as a commercial product launched by No Isolation, the headline reads: *"An entirely Norwegian invention helps sick children to take part in education"* [2]

From the start of the collaboration with the SE startup No Isolation, the media attention has been massive. This was, in part, due to the importance of the underlying social cause that AV1 addresses – reducing isolation among children and youth who due to an illness cannot live an ordinary life. The fact that the research product was in actual use with seriously ill children, made our research more relatable to the media than the usual ways of dissemination of academic research and design, e.g., press releases, project websites or published articles. We collected both print and online media articles. However, for the purposes of this paper, we excluded social media and all advertisements and direct marketing by No Isolation. These have also had a huge impact, as they should in SE. However, we focus on the independent media coverage only.

The paper contributes to further understandings of how the media portrays HCI research. We argue that media discourse facilitates visibility of technological innovations, and in a case of social entrepreneurship and products such as AV1, opens for deeper public discussions and shaping of imaginaries. Our findings indicate

[1] In Norwegian, at https://www.utdanningsnytt.no/magasin/2016/juli/syke-barn-larer-via-roboter/
[2] At https://www.dinside.no/data/helnorsk-oppfinnelse-hjelper-syke-barn-til-a-delta-pa-skolen/61924788

that although heavily outnumbered, critical opinions have had the most influence on the shaping of the product and on the business model, while the positive coverage had both positive and negative consequences for research, researchers and participants, strengthening sensitivities towards media engagement in HCI research.

2. CONTEXT AND RELATED WORK

To contextualize our research collaboration with No Isolation, we provide a brief background. Based on our prior research involving vulnerable children, we were approached by one of the startup founders, and asked to participate in their project with social relevance – to use technology to reduce social isolation among children and youth with long-term health challenges. They were to make a simple networked artefact, in the shape of a small robot. We took part in the process of turning this idea into a research product, carried out field work with it, and followed AV1's initial deployment as a commercial product. The collaboration period with No Isolation lasted approximately two years. After some months of development and planning for deployment, we received the first ten robots made and used them to inquire into fit in everyday lives of children with health challenges, including AV1's role in education (Børsting & Culén, 2017) and social connectedness (Culén, Børsting, & Odom, 2019). Research products, such as AV1, can challenge the existing social and cultural practices, as they are so new that there are no established regulations, conventions, or moral implications around them.

During the initial phase of the collaboration with SE startup No Isolation, AV1 existed as a research product only. Later, it was launched as a commercial product. This transition between non-commercial and commercial allowed for insights on how the public discourse changed. At that time, advertisements and video commercials in social media, movie theatres, city-wide digital displays, etc. became abundant, making AV1 into a familiar artefact nation-wide, something that everyone could have an opinion about. Thus, we chose discourse analysis to understand the socio-technological imaginaries and how people think, expect, and imagine the effects of technologies such as AV1 on the way we live. We focused on conceptions, images, stories, social expectations, and other notions shared by groups of people (Jasanoff & Kim, 2015; Lockton & Candy, 2018; Taylor, 2002).

Next, we present related work, divided into two themes: 1) previous work on RtD and the media and 2) commercialization of HCI inventions.

2.1 RtD and the Media

Media attention can enable researchers to communicate their research to local, national and international communities. Prior research that engaged the media often entailed writing press releases on a research project. Sometimes, research findings unexpectedly generated media attention (Vines et al., 2017, 2013). Regardless of the way in which the media gets engaged, researchers have been concerned that making their research public through media outlets can represent their work in skewed, interpreted or construed ways that are not in line with the expectations from the research community. Vines et al. (2013) describe such issues, but also argue that "*misinterpretation could be considered useful as it provides a gauge for the political and emotional context of the work beyond the often homogenous, self-selected and motivated individuals that may participate in the research*" (p.1879). The focus in our paper is somewhat similar, but extends to understand the social imaginaries created by the increased visibility of research products in the wild. The imaginaries open for inquiries into broader concerns regarding research product's positioning and entanglements with the socio-cultural context in the real world.

The design research project iFloor is an example of a research artefact that received a generous amount of media attention. Similar to AV1, it was seen by the members of the royal family (always a media attractor), reported to international audiences, and awarded prizes for being innovative (Koskinen, Zimmerman, Binder, Redström, & Wensveen, 2011). The authors, however, do not address the implications of the media attention on the research, but highlight the importance of placing the research artefacts in the real world: *"If designers participate in dialog about the meaning of their work, it is not only curators, critics, and media who define it. A degree of control can be gained this way"* (ibid., p.98).

However, there are known accounts where media misrepresented research products and prototypes. For example, Auger's Audio Tooth Implant (Auger, 2013), a speculative prototype, has been described by Time Magazine as one of the best inventions of 2002. Other research artefacts misrepresented by the media as future commercial products include BinCam and Digital Cheques described in (Vines et al., 2013). In particular,

Digital Cheques, a fictive product, was referred to by tabloid newspapers as 'Granny nav', causing public reactions regarding the offensiveness of the name given by the media.

As our research involves vulnerable user groups, we explored similar cases of research with vulnerable user groups and startup collaboration that gained media attention. In (Vines et al., 2017), the authors report that the media focus on their research with Google Glass as a self-care technology for people with Parkinson's made the participants express overly positive views regarding the technology, before actually using it. They highlight ethical dilemmas to consider when working with vulnerable users and the media. Another relevant example is the case of the Prayer Companion (Gaver et al., 2010), where reporters[3] contacted the nuns who were using the research product (made to identify possible things that nuns could pray for). Although the nuns stated that they were ok with the media attention in this case, the attention conflicted with their monastic life and wows of seclusion.

In the case of our research, No Isolation generated media attention for marketing and fundraising purposes. The initial media focus on our research was a consequence of collaboration with No Isolation and forthcoming product commercialization. It was an unusual position. In line with other researchers who worked with the media, we recognized the importance of ethical concerns regarding the media coverage of AV1 and its users.

2.2 Commercialization of HCI Inventions

Concerns have been raised that great technology research innovations are too rarely developed into commercial products (Chilana, Ko, & Wobbrock, 2015b; Isaacs et al., 1996). This concern is the driving force behind an increased focus on how to approach technology exchange of research innovations to successful commercial products (Chilana et al., 2015a). Adoption-centered design and implications for adoption are examples of approaches that connect research innovations to commercialization. Adoption-centered design (Chilana et al., 2015b) focuses on a process of building an understanding of, and designing for, adopters and stakeholders of the product. The approach usually utilizes in-depth case studies of how a particular technological research innovation transitions into a commercial product, e.g., LemonAid, peer-to-peer help tool called that evolved into a startup from a research project or AnswerDash that lets users find precise answers quickly on websites, financed by venture capital and serving as a hybrid between the academic research and entrepreneurship. Implications for adoption (Lindley et al., 2017) highlights the role of DIY (Do-It-Yourself) and maker movements (Grimme, Bardzell, & Bardzell, 2014; Ratto, 2011; Tanenbaum, Williams, Desjardins, & Tanenbaum, 2013), and advocates the use of design fiction as world-building to form speculations related to research innovations to scrutinize and explore the implications and requirements associated with a research-to-product transition in the future.

3. METHODOLOGY

We choose discourse analysis as the analytical tool of media coverage of AV1. Discourse analysis is a research method that provides systematic evidence about social processes by examination of speech, writing and other forms of communication in the media (Talja, 1999; Wortham & Reyes, 2015). While common in social sciences, discourse analysis is not used that frequently within other research fields. In part, because it does not aim to capture participants' intentions, needs, meanings, or experiences, but cultural and social understandings. As mentioned in the introduction, we aim to uncover socio-technological imaginaries regarding AV1 as a new technology that made the presence of robots in everyday lives very concrete for the Norwegian population.

3.1 Discourse Analysis

The basis for the analysis, as shown in Table 1, were 170 media articles published during our collaboration with No Isolation, and separated into the first year when AV1 was a research product, and the second year when it became commercial. The articles examined, appeared in local newspapers, national and international newspapers, magazines and books, and online coverage of conferences or other arrangements (such as the Oslo Innovation week, technology fairs, concerts, TV-shows, etc.) where AV1 was featured. The articles were then

[3] At https://www.yorkpress.co.uk/news/8265632.nuns-of-poor-clares-in-york-embrace-technology-to-help-them-pray/

divided into four main a-priory decided on categories: positive discourse (technology positivism, but also other positive attitudes), neutral (descriptive and factual), balanced (reflecting on both positive and negative implications of the new technology, even if the coverage was not equal), and negative coverage, see Table 2.

Table 1. Types of Media Coverage

Coverage of AV1	*Local News*	*National/International*	*Magazine/Book*	*Conference/Social events*
Year 1	4	29/1	12/2	11/3
Year 2	11	30/26	12/0	27/2
Total:	15	86	26	43

Table 2. Discourse Analysis Results

Coverage of AV1	*Positive*	*Neutral*	*Balanced*	*Negative*
Year 1	61	0	1	0
Year 2	102	0	3	3
Total:	163	0	4	3

Table 2 shows that AV1 was never described purely in terms of facts, or in a neutral language. It also shows a clear prevalence of positive attitude towards this new technology (163 articles). Most coverage, especially during the first year, focused on how AV1 could mitigate long-term negative effects of being ill in regards to education, or wellbeing, see Figure 2. The second year, after the commercialization, sees a slight increase in balanced and negative coverage, but still, a huge majority of positive articles.

Within the positive category, the discourse followed technology positivist way of telling the story, social positivism or it portrayed positive experiences with the research product in use. We exemplify these in turn: *"The robot can make the everyday life better for cancer-affected, ME-sick or others who for various reasons must be away from school over time", "Seriously ill children are often isolated from school and friends. A new robot changes that now"* (technology positivist view, where the robot changes the situation), *"Children affected by serious illness often have to live their lives either at home or in the hospital. It can be difficult to participate in leisure activities, birthdays, or just attend school. But now five Norwegian entrepreneurs have spent four months developing something that gives hope, which can change these children's lives completely", "for the sick children and their families, it is usually not the illness that is experienced as the worst. It is the social isolation and absence from friends, classrooms and everyday events that is the hardest", "The reason why we have invested in No Isolation is that they want to contribute positively to the world"* (social positivist view where the robot is replaced by 'something that gives hope' and the focus is on entrepreneurs changing people's lives), *"... is looking forward to have his own robot that he can send to the school to keep in touch with his friends - It will be very nice. It's a fantastic invention, the ten-year-old smiles", "A robot that can be in the classroom changed the lives of many users. Emil in the ninth grade says: 'Thanks to the robot, I have been able to attend more school in a week than the whole year combined. And, I've been with my friends"* (positive experiences from robot users).

Examples of discourse categorized as negative reject the idea of the robot being the replacement for people *"I am only saddened by the advertisements showing children carrying the robot instead of the classmate being there with them. I think it will contribute to a more intense feeling of loneliness"*, or express concerns with privacy *"I find it worrisome that the outside world should have a peephole into where students are learning and failing, being educated and shaped"*. An example categorized as balanced *"The robots are cherished for the opportunities they give sick children to participate in teaching and social contexts, but they are not necessarily unproblematic in use"* try to point out both positive and negative issues regarding the topic.

We discuss next the imaginaries regarding connectedness, SE and gender, critical voices and governance.

Figure 2. The figure points to divisions concerning AV1: is it an educational help or an artefact that reduces isolation and improves the quality of life for sick children? a) In *"Robot going to school for sick children"* [4] AV1 is about education. b) In *"A good helper if one is long-term ill"*[5] and c) *"New technological reality for cancer patients"* [6] AV1 is about wellbeing

3.2 Imaginaries

3.2.1 Social Connectedness

Many articles discussed how chronically, or long-term ill children and youth can now be socially connected: *"This robot can save children with long-term illness from loneliness"*[7] or *"Robot breaks the isolation"*[8], Figure 3a. In this imaginary, technology is a powerful weapon capable of reducing isolation. To bring forward these powerful images and expectations related to the 'new connected reality', the media often uses individual stories. Among articles that addressed connectedness, nine were written at the start of our research and featured participants in our research (unsolicited by researchers) with youth with ME (Myalgic Encephalomyelitis). Children and adolescents with other illness at risk of isolation, such as cancer, were also portrayed in articles.

Figure 3. a) News article *"Robot breaks the isolation"*[8], b) Innovation Norway's article *"Record numbers of female entrepreneurs will invest internationally"*[9], c) Norway's Crown Princess trying AV1 robot at Oslo innovation week[10]

3.2.2 Gender and Social Entrepreneurship

When No Isolation was founded, the oil prices were falling and the unemployment numbers raising. Subsequently, many of the published articles focused on social entrepreneurship. The articles in this group told the public about No Isolation founders, or opportunities for startups that opened with the growing DIY and maker movements, see Figure 2a, daring to take a leap into social innovation with products like AV1.

[4] Available (in Norwegian) at https://framtida.no/2016/02/27/robot-skal-ga-pa-skulen-for-sjuke-barn
[5] At https://samfunnsviteren.no/2017/06/07/en-god-hjelper-dersom-man-er-langtidssyk/
[6] At https://ungkreft.no/blog/2016/06/07/ny-teknologisk-virkelighet-for-kreftpasienter/
[7] At http://www.frambu.no/Article1.aspx?NodeId=DFF8DCEF-A3CB-4F12-B192-1ED61D112912
[8] At https://www.handikapnytt.no/robot-skal-bryte-isolasjonen/
[9] At https://www.innovasjonnorge.no/no/om/nyheter/2016/rekordmange-norske-grunderkvinner-vil-satse-internasjonalt/
[10] At https://www.nrk.no/vestfold/moter-kronprinsparet-via-robot-1.13182768

A large media attractor was the fact that one of the No Isolation founders was female. She was one of the finalists for the Female Entrepreneur award in 2016, and as such, featured in several articles. She represented the image of a young, creative women in mid-twenties, with stories that include other startups already behind her, and other social entrepreneurship projects in front of her (reducing isolation among elderly, as one example). Among these, one article talked about female entrepreneurs investing abroad, see Figure 3b, featuring the female CEO from No Isolation.

In October 2016, several papers talked about AV1's presence at Oslo Innovation Week. One of the newsworthy points was that Norway's Crown Princess showed an interest in social entrepreneurship and AV1. She used AV1 to talk to one of the chronically ill children, see Figure 3c. A special notice on this was also featured at the website of the Royal House of Norway, showing the photo of the princess with AV1.

3.2.3 Critical Voices

Although much fewer in numbers (only 7 out of 170), the articles with more critical voices helped to create other imaginaries. They expressed opinions that AV1's does not act as an enabler of social connectedness, cannot satisfy demands for education or that it presents privacy risks. As can be seen from Table 2, apart from one, these imaginaries appeared only post-commercialization, and represent the change in perception of AV1.

Figure 4. a) News article *"Does not replace active participation"*[11], b) article *"It is problematic with a robot in the classroom"*[12], c) news article *"Will school robots be checked for privacy"*[13], d) article *"We need a robot law"*[14]

One of the national newspapers published an article arguing that AV1 is not an optimal alternative for person-to-person contacts. The article also forwards the view that attending school through AV1 cannot give its users the education they need after long-term absence from school due to their illness: *"A robot cannot replace or compensate for physically meeting teachers and schoolmates. If this is seen as a reasonable solution for facilitating teaching and attending to the student's demands for education, it becomes difficult to support such a technological development and cheer on the robot into the classroom"*[11].

Another article was more balanced in the discussion of AV1, concluding with "[The presence through the robot] *is far worse than being physically socially present, but certainly a little bit better than being entirely absent*"[14].

In 2017, a national newspaper article with a headline *"Problematic with a robot in the classroom"* [12] was published, see Figure 4b. The article states that several schools contacted the Norwegian Data Protection Authority (DPA) because they were uncertain whether the robot in the classroom violates the Personal Data Act. The article states that one of the things that these schools fear is that someone can see what is happening in the classroom. The long-term ill child or youth are expected to have the access, but there is no way for the school to ensure that others are not having access to AV1 and, thus, the classroom. The article provides a reply from the DPA stating that the robots constitute a privacy risk, and schools must find out what risks they can accept, and whether there are measures that reduce the risks.

Another local newspaper, with a headline: *"Should we allow video surveillance in Norwegian schools?"*[15] writes: *"I saw the television advertisement for the robot that is supposed to attend classes at school as a*

[11] At https://www.pressreader.com/norway/varden/20170621/281874413403873
[12] At https://www.p4.no/nyheter/--problematisk-med-robot-i-klasserom/artikkel/689010/
[13] At https://www.nrk.no/sorlandet/vil-personvern-sjekke-skoleroboter-1.13327572
[14] At https://agendamagasin.no/kommentarer/vi-trenger-en-robotlov/
[15] At https://www.dagbladet.no/kultur/skal-vi-tillate-videoovervaking-i-norske-skoler/66922647

substitute for students with long-term absence. Had the date been April 1, I would clearly consider this as an April fool's joke. But oh, no! It turns out that the robots have infiltrated Norwegian classrooms, long before schools, school professionals, trade unions, county governors and others who should have a principled attitude to the matter have managed to do anything"[15].

In addition, the article questions the motives of the SE: *"I see that the forces behind this invention are pushing a long-term ill or disabled child in front of them in the debate about whether school surveillance should be allowed or not. So, instead, parents and teachers who see this madness will get the 'blame' and appear as heartless"*[15].

3.2.4 Economic and Governance Challenges

Initially, some of the participants' parents in our study (who received AV1 for free, and got to keep the research product until it became commercially available) stood out in the press and told their positive experiences with the artefact, but also expressed concerns about pricing and their desire for AV1 to be easily available and affordable for all others, when it becomes commercial. This imaginary became something that influenced the startup to change their planned business model and lower the price of the commercial product.

After privacy issues related to the use of the robot in schools were presented in news articles, politicians came forth in the press stating that the government had started a formal process of reviewing the use of AV1 at schools, see Figure 4c. Following this process schools were given legal guidelines regarding how to use AV1 while adhering to privacy laws.

The media's discourse, presenting AV1 as either an aid for education or a wellbeing artefact, influenced later decisions at the governance level regarding who regulates the use of the robots, the Ministry of Education and Research or the Ministry of Health and Care Services. The process of regulating AV1 was difficult and time-consuming, and still ongoing, since different legal paragraphs apply for educational tools and wellbeing ones. As the product that can support both education and wellbeing, AV1 falls between these governance bodies and their different regulations.

4. DISCUSSION

We found that the positive imaginaries, especially at the start of our research, created more opportunities for field engagement of AV1. The media coverage made AV1 broadly familiar and people curious about the research product, creating willingness to engage in discussions about this new technology. The more critical views, on the other hand, affected both our research and No Isolation more directly, e.g., prompting re-thinking of the SE's business model (see 3.2.4) and bringing forth ethical aspects regarding our research. Exemplifying the latter, we point to the privacy issues regarding the parents of our participants, or others who could use the robot to observe the classroom. This led to asking the parents to sign a formal document attesting that only the participant would use the robot to participate in classroom activities. The parents signed the document after discussing privacy and concerns that classmates' parents had, in line with the media. Although we do not discuss design implications in this paper, we wish to mention that to protect the privacy needs of classmates, we suggested that No Isolation installs an off-button in case that sensitive situations in the classroom emerge and that AV1 needs to be turned off.

We ongoingly made critical and ethical judgments to protect our participants' identities from the media. However, some of our participants and their families decided to come forward and engage with the media on their own, seeing it as an opportunity to bring attention to health issues and other needs. Similar to (Gaver et al. 2010), we found out that researchers cannot protect the participants from the implications of the visibility given by the media. It was easy to understand that the visibility could be appealing and provide some relief from the feeling of being forgotten. Sometimes, the effects of appearing in the media were positive. However, researchers need to be sensitive to such appearances and discuss the implications before the media attention.

4.1 Discourse Analysis Findings

Initial media coverage was exclusively positive, with exception of the one balanced article that was published during the first year. This overly positive coverage is in line with results from previous research on HCI in the media, see Vines et al. (2017). The robot shape of AV1, see Culén et al. (2019), was perceived as cool by adolescents at the risk of isolation, and this alone easily made their expectations high. Together, positive press and high expectations did influence the participants in our research. On the other hand, a more critical view of AV1 as a hindrance to person-to-person presence is also skewed, and misses the point of the complex real-life situations of research participants (who do not have a choice to engage in person due to their illness). For participants in our research, the choice was often between AV1 or no presence at all. Looking critically at the media coverage, it mirrors difficulties when working with complex social issues and socio-cultural problem-solving, risking over-simplification and being overly optimistic.

Criticality (not criticism) is an important part of research that aims to reveal the unintended consequences of new technological products for the real world. Thus, the points of criticism that the media coverage brought up in post-commercialization phase were not new for us. We were already acutely aware of challenges with AV1 in everyday lives of our users. For instance, from the start of the research project privacy was a key concern for both researchers, participants, and for No Isolation. In the course of the research nuanced perspectives regarding AV1 and privacy emerged, but remained invisible in media coverage that focused only on the 'peephole' aspect of AV1's streaming.

When we chose to look for imaginaries created through the media coverage, we also hoped to find some clues regarding the Collingridge's dilemma. More specifically, we were curious if the public portrayal of the research and social innovation focus of AV1, would allow us to gain early knowledge on how the research product affects the society. The indications of social implications could then be used to inform the design as a step towards doing responsible innovation. This seemed relevant to explore especially in light of research collaborations with SE, and seeing how commercial products are too often first launched and then later the social implications investigated. However, from sixty-two news articles from the pre-commercialization stage, only one article had a more balanced view regarding the social presence through AV1[14]. Seeing how the first year of media attention projected high levels of technological determinism, it did not reveal real-world implications of the technology. When more critical voices appeared, the product was already a commercial one. Thus, the window for the media attention to facilitate responsible innovation through early research inputs on social implications was already closed, with one exception, related to the economic challenges for users that surfaced in the second year and that actually brought about changes in the SE's business model.

However, we remain hopeful that for the future products, a combination with ethical research, social innovation and media coverage could yield a better insight into the implications of new technologies.

4.2 Implications and Opportunities from Media Interest on Research

The media influenced the study participants and others related to the project, such as school principals and teachers, so it is reasonable to ask if it did influence us as researchers, leading to biased research. Additionally, collaboration with SE, in part because of the media coverage could also lead to biased research. Being aware of this, we made a contract with No Isolation regarding independence of our research, and sent the contract for approval to the Ethical Review Board, which subsequently was approved. No Isolation and its marketing, advertising, and fundraising were entirely separated from the research. On the other hand, in line with (Chilana, et al., 2015b), we found out that, even though there are challenges, collaboration between researchers and social entrepreneurship offers a huge opportunity to increase the visibility of research and design at large, perhaps also opening different research paths from the traditional research related to technology deployment and acceptance.

At the beginning of the study, people found robots placed in classrooms to provide sick adolescents and children with a remote social presence closer to science fiction than reality. The media publicity did make it easier for people to relate to this new technology, which in turn, affect our field work positively. The perceived newness of the technology was initially a barrier when talking to people about its real-world social implications. However, after the massive media attention, the robot became a frequent topic of conversations everywhere, making the entire society familiar with the product, reducing the novelty and perceived strangeness of the technology.

The pre-commercialization media attention and the public engagement that followed, got also those with governance and political decision-making power involved. Drawing in such stakeholders may be one of the most essential aspects when doing social innovation design work. The illness has made the participants in our research belong to a socially vulnerable group at risks of isolation and reduced access to education, among others. These issues are a matter of social governance, decisions made by such stakeholders have a power to influence participants' social worlds. For instance, new laws and regulations need to be made for the commercial version of the research product to be legal to use at schools – for the reasons of privacy protection. The legal issue is not that the current privacy laws forbid the use of AV1, but that AV1 represents a new technology, and as such, it is not covered by existing privacy laws regulating the use of technology at schools.

Finally, although these are initial steps in looking into the social innovation and collaborations with research products with SE, we find that the media engagement had impact and potentially, can be a way to engage with the social implications of new technology artefacts to facilitate responsible innovation.

5. CONCLUSION

This paper argued that research products in collaboration with SE could be potentially a useful and novel approach to improving and transforming innovation outcomes before they become real-world products, that is, research products intended for commercialization can be a way of engaging with the social implications of new technology artefacts and facilitate responsible innovation. Our research, as a consequence of the collaboration with the SE startup received a considerable amount of media attention. Our findings regarding the influence of the media attention show that AV1 became familiar to the broad public, raising the curiosity about the robot and facilitating our access to schools as part of the field work. In general, people could easily make up their minds about how they experience or think about AV1, helping us to access and explore the social, cultural and ethical impacts of this new technology design artefact before and just after commercialization.

Using discourse analysis to explore the way that media addressed AV1, we identified imaginaries related to social connectedness, social entrepreneurship and gender equality as positive social impacts. Also, the critical voices influenced large groups of people and raised concerns regarding the quality of education through the robot, the quality of social contacts, privacy risks, and economic and governance challenges around AV1. The critical voices had substantial impact, for example, by influencing politicians and policymakers to make changes in guidelines and regulations regarding AV1. Moreover, media coverage allowed for public discourse beyond our own research on how AV1 as a commercial product could affect its users and the society at large.

ACKNOWLEDGEMENT

No Isolation has our sincere gratitude for a wonderful collaboration and for the opportunity to engage in HCI research with AV1 as a research product intended for commercialization and as social innovation.

REFERENCES

Auger, J. (2013). Speculative design: crafting the speculation. *Digital Creativity,* 24(1), 11–35.

Børsting, J., & Culén, A. L. (2017). Experiences with a Research Product: A Robot Avatar for Chronically Ill Adolescents. In T. Issa, P. Kommers, T. Issa, P. Isaías, & T. B. Issa (Eds.), *Smart Technology Applications in Business Environments* (pp. 159–183). Hershey: PA: IGI Global.

Chatting, D., Kirk, D. S., Durrant, A. C., Elsden, C., Yurman, P., & Bichard, J. A. (2017). Making Ritual Machines: The Mobile Phone as a Networked Material for Research Products. *Proceedings of the 2017 CHI Conference on Human Factors in Computing Systems,* 435–447.

Chilana, P. K., Czerwinski, M. P., Grossman, T., Harrison, C., Kumar, R., Parikh, T. S., & Zhai, S. (2015a). Technology Transfer of HCI Research Innovations: Challenges and Opportunities. *Proceedings of the 33rd Annual ACM Conference Extended Abstracts on Human Factors in Computing Systems - CHI EA'15,* 823–828.

Chilana, P. K., Ko, A. J., & Wobbrock, J. (2015b). From User-Centered to Adoption-Centered Design: A Case Study of an HCI Research Innovation Becoming a Product. *Proceedings of the 33rd Annual ACM Conference on Human Factors in Computing Systems - CHI '15,* 1749–1758.

Collingridge, D. (1980). *The social control of technology.* New York: St. Martin.

Culén, A. L., Børsting, J., & Odom, W. (2019). Mediating Relatedness for Adolescents with ME: Reducing Isolation through Minimal Interactions with a Robot Avatar. *Proceedings of the 2019 ACM Conference on Designing Interactive Systems (DIS '19).* https://doi.org/10.1145/3322276.3322319.

Gaver, W. (2012). What should we expect from research through design? *Proceedings of the 2012 ACM annual conference on Human Factors in Computing Systems - CHI '12,* 937–946.

Gaver, W., Blythe, M., Boucher, A., Jarvis, N., Bowers, J., & Wright, P. (2010). The prayer companion: openness and specificity, materiality and spirituality. *Proceedings of the 28th international conference on Human factors in computing systems - CHI '10,* 2055–2064.

Godin, B. (2015). *Innovation Contested: The Idea of Innovation Over the Centuries*. London and New York: Routledge.

Grimme, S., Bardzell, J., & Bardzell, S. (2014). "We've conquered dark": shedding light on empowerment in critical making. *Proceedings of the 8th Nordic Conference on Human-Computer Interaction: Fun, Fast, Foundational - NordiCHI '14,* 431–440.

Höök, K., Bardzell, J., Bowen, S., Dalsgaard, P., Reeves, S., & Waern, A. (2015). Framing IxD knowledge. *Interactions,* 22(6), 32–36.

Isaacs, E. A., Tang, J. C., Foley, J., Johnson, J., Kuchinsky, A., Scholtz, J., & Bennett, J. (1996). Technology transfer: so much research, so few good products. *Conference companion on Human factors in computing systems common ground - CHI '96,* 155–156.

Ishii, H. (2008). The tangible user interface and its evolution. *Communications of the ACM,* 51(6), 32–36.

Jasanoff, S., & Kim, S.-H. (2015). *Dreamscapes of modernity: Sociotechnical imaginaries and the fabrication of power*. Chicago, IL: University of Chicago Press.

Koskinen, I., Zimmerman, J., Binder, T., Redstrom, J., & Wensveen, S. (2011). *Design research through practice: From the lab, field, and showroom.* Amsterdam, Netherlands: Elsevier.

Kudina, O., & Verbeek, P.-P. (2018). Ethics from Within: Google Glass, the Collingridge Dilemma, and the Mediated Value of Privacy. *Science, Technology, & Human Values,* 44(2), 291–314.

Lindley, J., Coulton, P., & Sturdee, M. (2017). Implications for Adoption. *Proceedings of the 2017 CHI Conference on Human Factors in Computing Systems - CHI '17,* 265–277.

Lockton, D., & Candy, S. (2018). A Vocabulary for Visions in Designing for Transitions. *Proceedings of Design Research Society Conference DRS 2018: Catalyst,* 908–926.

Lubberink, R., Blok, V., Van Ophem, J., & Omta, O. (2017). Lessons for Responsible Innovation in the Business Context: A Systematic Literature Review of Responsible, Social and Sustainable Innovation Practices. *Sustainability,* 9(5), 1–31.

Odom, W., Wakkary, R., Lim, Y., Desjardins, A., Hengeveld, B., & Banks, R. (2016). From Research Prototype to Research Product. *Proceedings of the 2016 CHI Conference on Human Factors in Computing Systems - CHI '16,* 2549–2561.

Pierce, J. (2014). On the presentation and production of design research artifacts in HCI. *Proceedings of the 2014 conference on Designing interactive systems - DIS '14,* 735–744.

Ratto, M. (2011). Critical Making: Conceptual and Material Studies in Technology and Social Life. *The Information Society,* 27(4), 252–260.

Ribeiro, B. E., Smith, R. D. J., & Millar, K. (2017). A Mobilising Concept? Unpacking Academic Representations of Responsible Research and Innovation. *Science and Engineering Ethics,* 23(1), 81–103.

Stilgoe, J., Owen, R., & Macnaghten, P. (2013). Developing a framework for responsible innovation. *Research Policy,* 42 (9), 1568–1580.

Talja, S. (1999). Analyzing Qualitative Interview Data. *Library and Information Science Research,* 21(4), 459–477.

Tanenbaum, J. G., Williams, A. M., Desjardins, A., & Tanenbaum, K. (2013). Democratizing technology: pleasure, utility and expressiveness in DIY and maker practice. *Proceedings of the SIGCHI Conference on Human Factors in Computing Systems - CHI '13,* 2603-2612.

Taylor, C. (2002). Modern Social Imaginaries. *Public Culture,* 14(1), 91–124.

van der Duin, P. (2018). Toward "Responsible Foresight": Developing Futures that Enable Matching Future Technologies with Social Demands. *World Futures Review,* 11(1), 69-79.

Vines, J., McNaney, R., Holden, A., Poliakov, I., Wright, P., & Olivier, P. (2017). Our Year with the Glass: Expectations, Letdowns and Ethical Dilemmas of Technology Trials with Vulnerable People. *Interacting with Computers,* 29(1), 27–44.

Vines, J., Thieme, A., Comber, R., Blythe, M., Wright, P. C., & Olivier, P. (2013). HCI in the press: online public reactions to mass media portrayals of HCI research. *Proceedings of the SIGCHI Conference on Human Factors in Computing Systems - CHI '13,* 1873-1882.

Weiser, M. (1993). Some computer science issues in ubiquitous computing. *Communications of the ACM,* 36(7), 75-84.

Wortham, S. E. F., & Reyes, A. (2015). *Discourse analysis beyond the speech event.* London and New York: Routledge.

Zimmerman, J., & Forlizzi, J. (2014). *Research through design in HCI.* Ways of Knowing in HCI. New York, NY: Springer.

A FITNESS BIKE MAINTENANCE TRAINING SYSTEM WITH THREE-DIMENSIONAL COMPUTER GRAPHICS

Takayuki Fujiwara[1], Shintaro Tsuchiya[1], Norihisa Komoda[2] and Toru Fujiwara[2]
[1]Research & Development Division, Hitachi Systems, Ltd. 1-2-1, Osaki, Shinagawa, Tokyo, 141-8672, Japan
[2]Graduate School of Information Science and Technology, Osaka University,
1-5, Yamadaoka, Suita, Osaka, 565-0871, Japan

ABSTRACT

This article describes a fitness bike maintenance training system using 3D computer graphics. The proposed system provides customer engineers with a 360-degree view and enables interactive manipulation. The system has three training modes: learning mode, examination mode, and positional relation check mode. Flashing CG objects and interactive manipulation are used so that engineers can readily understand the maintenance work. Test usage by customer engineers, managers, and training instructors has resulted in several positive comments including praise for the clearly indicated instructions and good instructions for handling the bike in 360-degrees.

KEYWORDS

Maintenance, Training, CAE, 3D, Fitness bike, E-learning

1. INTRODUCTION

Fitness bikes are widely used for exercise. These are installed in sports and fitness clubs nationwide. They require not only periodic maintenance to prevent faults but also fixing failure. Customer engineers working at numerous maintenance bases have to learn the structure, disassembly procedures, and troubleshooting skills for these bikes. Traditionally, the training is generally done by reading manuals or watching video tutorials. Training with actual machines is not always used because of two reasons. The first reason is that actual machines are not provided at all maintenance bases. Engineers at some maintenance bases cannot receive maintenance training with actual machines. Another reason is that engineers do not have enough time for training because they are constantly being sent out to fulfill maintenance requests. Additionally, the instruction pictures or figures in the training materials are always shown from single angle, such that engineers sometimes confuse the positions and viewpoints. Therefore, it is difficult to develop specific images of the corresponding machine and parts. Furthermore, both training methods do not include user manipulation for training but just reading or watching. They also do not include a method for confirming understanding of procedures and precautions.

To solve these problems, Computer Aided Engineering (CAE) is effective. Three-dimensional computer graphics (3DCG) of the fitness bike are effective in grasping an image of the corresponding machine. 3DCG has been studied for product design (Kuang, 2014), and has been adapted for assembly simulation (Flavien, 2012), and assembly training (Zhilong, 2013; Terasa, 2010). 3DCG and Augmented Reality based maintenance training system has also been studied (Francesca, 2011; Sabine, 2011; Michele, 2014). However, engineers need actual machines to use these AR-based maintenance training systems. 3DCG and virtual reality-based maintenance training systems have also been studied (Sportillo, 2015). However, since engineers need high performance PC, VR headsets, tracking devices, and large spaces, it is difficult for all customer engineers to prepare devices and spaces because they are usually busy with maintenance service calls.

In this paper, we propose a tablet or laptop PC based system using 3DCG for fitness bike maintenance training. Then, the effects of the combination of 3DCG and instructional text, and the proposed user interface are evaluated through testing.

2. MAINTENANCE TRAINING

2.1 Fitness bike

Fitness bikes are installed at sports clubs nationwide for health enhancement. When a bike has a problem, clubs ask maintenance personnel to repair it.

Figure 1. Overview photo of the target fitness bike

A fitness bike shown in Figure 1 is our target fitness bike. It consists of more than twenty parts including electronic parts. Customer engineers are stationed at several maintenance bases. They must learn how to disassemble the bike, how to make a failure diagnosis, how to fix the bike, and how to re-assemble the bike before engaging in any bike maintenance tasks.

2.2 Traditional training Methods for Fitness Bike

Fitness bikes are only prepared on a limited basis. Therefore, traditionally, printed manuals and video are used for maintenance training of the fitness bike. Manuals show how to disassemble the bike and precautions so that parts are not damaged. However, it is not always easy for engineers to understand it because some instructions do not include pictures or figures. The manual of the fitness bike has over 50 pages with 70 pictures. It is not sufficient because it does not include all troubleshooting instructions.

Video tutorials teach disassembly procedures with the instructor's movements. These movements are effective in getting engineers to understand the disassembly procedures. However, video tutorials also present difficulties for engineers in understanding positional relations. For example, when a video tutorial describes how to replace a circuit board in the fitness bike, it zooms in on the board or instructor's hands. Engineers sometimes become confused as to whether the board is set on left or right side. Furthermore, just watching videos is a monotonous and time-consuming work as the videos are a few hours long. It is difficult to learn all troubleshooting instructions with such a monotonous learning method.

2.3 Requirements of Maintenance Training System for Fitness Bike

Engineers have already used tablets or laptop PCs for maintenance work. Therefore, the training system should also run on these devices. By usage of hardware used in daily maintenance work, the engineers can learn during their fragmented free time such as while travelling or waiting.

From the viewpoint of software, engineers should be able to check target machines from all angles. If engineers read an instruction "Remove the left cover", they might be confused about to which "left" it actually refers. Engineers should also be able to check maintenance procedures through their own actual handling of the bike. With only boring reading manuals or watching videos, it is difficult to understand the procedures.

3. MAINTENANCE TRAINING CONTENT FOR FITNESS BIKE

3.1 User Interface of the System

The main display of the training content is shown in Figure 2. The display is segmented into three area in order to easily understand the training process.

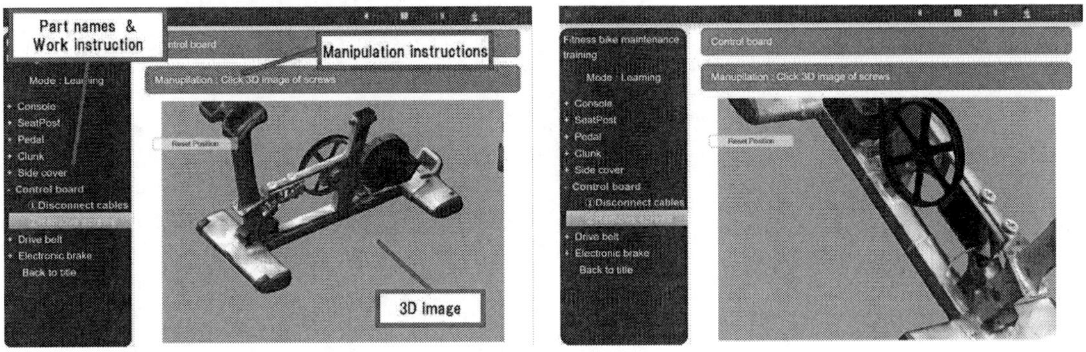

(a) An example of control board disassembly

(b) An example of another angle

Figure 2. Main screen shots of the content

(1) Part names and work instructions area

The left area of the display is for part names and the work instruction area shown in Figure 2(a). All part names of the machine and all work instructions are displayed here. The fitness bike parts are a pedal, saddle, cover, console panel, belt, etc. The tree-view index has been designed according to the requests of engineers. For example, when engineers click the part name of "Control board", work instructions such as "(1) Disconnect cables" and "(2) Remove screw" are displayed.

(2) Manipulation instructions area

The upper right area of the display is a manipulation instructions area as shown in Figure 2(a). The messages displayed in this area are manipulation instructions for each step. Engineers can readily understand maintenance procedures through virtual manipulation just by following the instructions. The area is also designed based on engineers' requests. Clear manipulation instructions are required because engineers are not familiar with the maintenance training system.

(3) 3D image area

The large area at the lower right is the content area. A 3D image of the fitness bike is displayed shown in Figure 2(a). In the area, parts that engineers should select flash in yellow. Engineers can see the fitness bike from a 360-degree angle by using the mouse or screen-touch. For example, when engineers rotate and zoom the fitness bike, the resulting image is displayed in this area as shown in Figure 2(b).

3.2 Training Modes

The training modes are classified as (1) learning mode, (2) examination mode, and (3) positional relation check mode from the results of an analysis of training manuals and videos.

3.2.1 Learning Mode

Engineers should learn step by step how to disassemble the machine, the positions of parts, and precautions. In learning mode, engineers can check every disassembly step with clear instructions. The main screenshot and sequence are shown in Figure 3.

As shown in Figure 3(a), a text instruction message flashes in the first step. In the example of replacing a drive belt in Figure 3(b), the first message is "(1) Loosen the screw of belt tension". After engineers click the text, the 3D image of the three screws flashes. Clicking the screws causes them to rotate and move. When the second message "(2) Loosen the belt pulley" in Figure 3(b) is clicked, a wrench approaches the three screws. When the third message "(3) Remove the drive belt" in Figure 3(b) is clicked, a warning dialog box is displayed as shown in Figure 3(b). Engineers must learn the precaution messages for some parts. For example, when replacing a drive belt of the fitness bike, engineers might have their fingers pinched between the wrench and belt if distracted. In learning mode, the procedures cannot advance without manipulation on the part of the engineer. Through their step-by-step clicking and confirmation, engineers can easily and deeply understand the maintenance procedures. They can learn each operation and the corresponding important points and precautions.

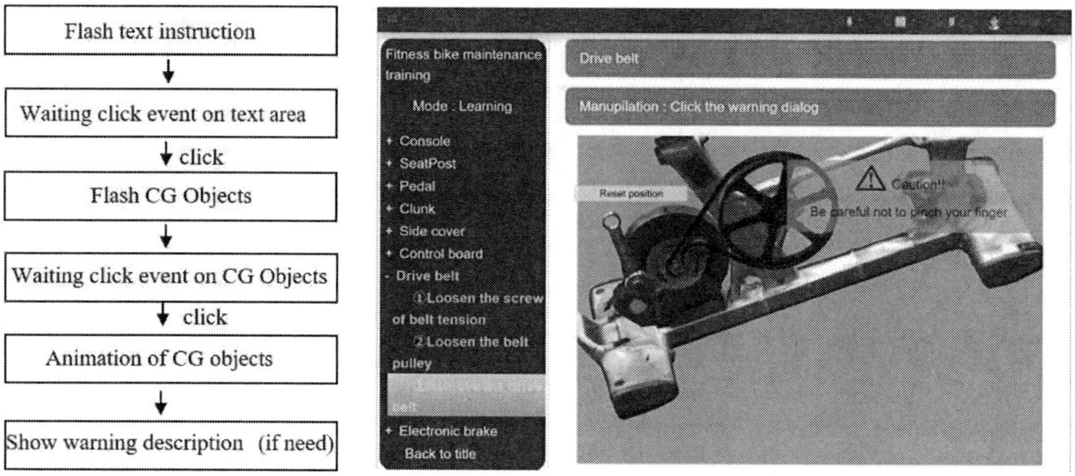

(a) Main sequence of learning mode (b) An example of warning description

Figure 3. Main sequence and screenshot of learning mode

3.2.2 Examination Mode

Engineers should confirm their comprehension of the machine itself and corresponding maintenance procedures. In examination mode, engineers take comprehension tests about the corresponding parts, positions, and directions. The example screenshot and sequence are shown in Figure 4.

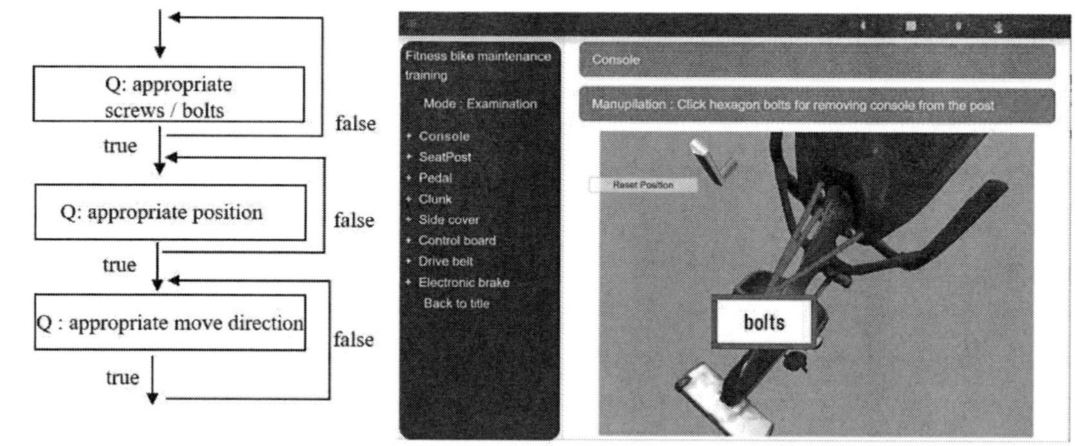

(a) Main sequence of examination mode (b) An example of appropriate bolts

Figure 4. Main sequence and screenshot of examination mode

As shown in Figure 4(a), engineers select the appropriate screws or bolts, and they click or tap the appropriate 3D images of bolts in Figure 4(b). If the answer is wrong, they must try again. After engineers select the appropriate bolts, the 3D image of the hexagonal wrench is rotated, and the bolt is removed.

When removing a console panel from a fitness bike's post, engineers must prop the console panel against a grip of the bike. They must not remove the console panel completely because it has several electronic cables. Engineers must be careful to protect the grip of the bike when propping up the console panel. Propping up the panel might scratch the grip. As shown by the "appropriate position" in Figure 4(a), engineers select the appropriate propped position. In this example, it is correct when they click or tap the area marked by the red square as shown in Figure 5(a). After engineers click or tap the appropriate position, the protective covering sheet moves close to the grip.

Engineers must be careful to remove parts gradually. In the example of the console panel removal, it must be removed in two steps. As shown by the "appropriate move direction" in Figure 4(a), engineers select the appropriate direction in the first step as shown in Figure 5(b). All directional objects are 3D image. If engineers correctly click or tap in the up direction in the 3D image, the 3D image of the console panel is moved up to lean against the grip of the bike.

This step-by-step checking of appropriate parts, positions, and movement directions checks whether the costumer engineers understand how to disassemble parts.

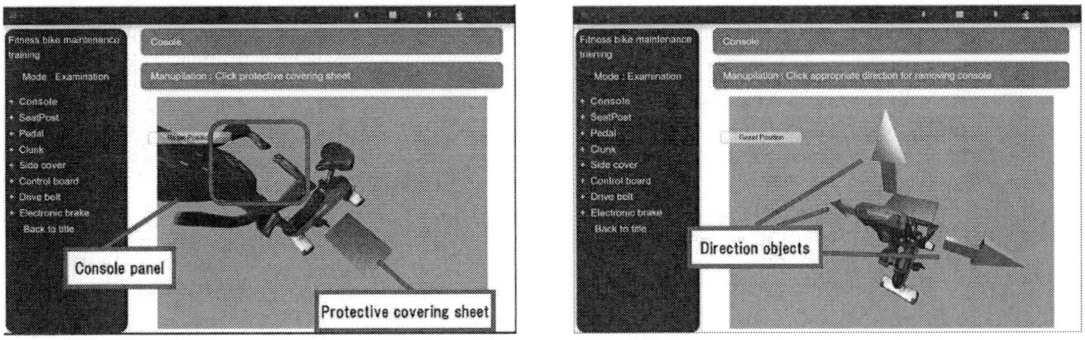

(a) An example of selecting appropriate position (b) An example of selecting appropriate direction

Figure 5. An example of selecting direction test

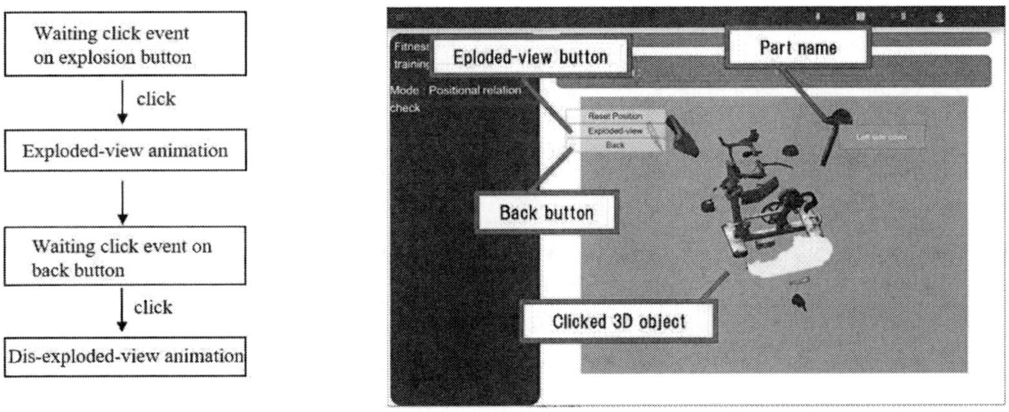

(a) Main sequence of positional relation check mode (b) An example view of positional relation check mode

Figure 6. Main sequence of check mode

3.2.3 Positional Relation Check Mode

Engineers should learn positional relations and part names of the machines. In the positional relation check mode, engineers check an exploded-view animation for all parts that provides engineers with the positional relation of each part. The main screenshot and sequence are shown in Figure 6.

As shown in Figure 6(a), the engineers click or tap the exploded-view button. The result is shown in Figure 6(b). All parts are spread out radially, and engineers can check all parts from a 360-degree angle. The color of a clicked 3D object is changed to yellow and the name is shown in a blue square. For example, the clicked object in Figure 6(b) is the left cover. When engineers click the back button, all parts return to their initial positions. Use of this clearly indicated exploded-view animation allows engineers to intuitively understand the positional relations of parts.

4. SYSTEM STRUCTURE

The software system structure of the training system is shown in Figure 7. Training content is consisted of program, data definition files, and media data. Files in data definition files define content data as 3D models, sequence, and instruction text. Media data includes 3D model. Common parts in the data are tools or parts that used at maintenance work commonly. A driver, wrench, and spanner are example of the tools. A screw, bolt, and nut are example of the parts. Program parses data definition files and displays the content. A layout file in the program defines content layout as shown in Figure 2.

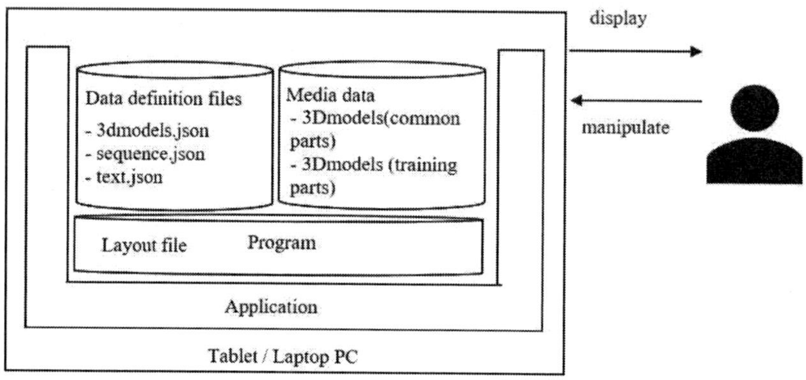

Figure 7. System structure

A simple example of the relation between data definition and display are shown in Figures 9, 10, and 11. Areas (1) to (11) in Figure 8 consist of (1) to (11) in Figures 10 and 11. Figure 8 shows maintenance training for the drive belt. The training has three sequences. Figure 8(a) shows the third sequence as "(3) Remove the drive belt" shown in Figure 8. In the third sequence, a warning message "Be careful not to pinch your finger" is overwritten on the 3D image in the content area. When engineers click the caution box, the dialog disappears. Then, the next and forth sequence is displayed on devices as shown in Figure 8(b).

These sequences are managed by the data definition files. All of the data definition files as shown in Figures 10(a), (b), Figure 10(a), and (b) consists of JSON (JavaScript Object Notation). JSON is a format to manage data using keys and values (ECMA, 2017). For example, "workItemAreald" in Figure 9(a) is a key, with "wi7" being a value. (1), (2), and (3) in Figure 9(a) define the text of the content. (4) and (5) in Figure 9(b) define the sequence number and conditions of proceeding on to the next sequence. Each segment of (4) and (5) defines each sequence.

"clickedText_id" of (4) in Figure 9(b) is a condition for proceeding to the next sequence. "clicked3dObject_id" of (4) in Figure 9(b) is not a condition because the value is blank. A layout file as shown in Figure 9(c) has attribute IDs. Each ID is related to an ID in "sequence.json" as shown in Figure 9(b). The tags as "workItemArea", "manipulationArea", and "3DimageArea" in Figure 9(c) are all rendered by the program in Figure 7. "clickedText_id" of (4) in Figure 9(b) is "mA7-3w". "mA7-3w" is the same as (2) in Figure 9(a). Therefore, the content is changed from (a) to (b) in Figure 8 when engineers click the warning text dialog of (2) in Figure 8(a). (5) in Figure 9(b) shows that "clickedObject_id" is "tp-7". "tp-7"is an identifier of the 3D model. An example definition of the 3D model by JSON is shown in Figure 10. (6) in Figure 10(a) defines a 3D wrench object. It is an example of common parts. Common parts include tools such as screwdrivers and wrenches." objFilePath" in Figure 10 is a path to the file in OBJ format, a commonly used 3D data format. It includes vertex, and surface information of a 3D object. "mtlFilePath" indicates is a path to the file in MTL format, a support format of OBJ. It manages the texture path and color information of the OBJ file. Figure 10(a) manages position, rotation and scale of the 3D wrench object. (7) in Figure 10(b) defines the body of the 3D object of the fitness bike. (8) in Figure 10(b) defines the 3D drive belt object of the fitness bike. These are training parts.

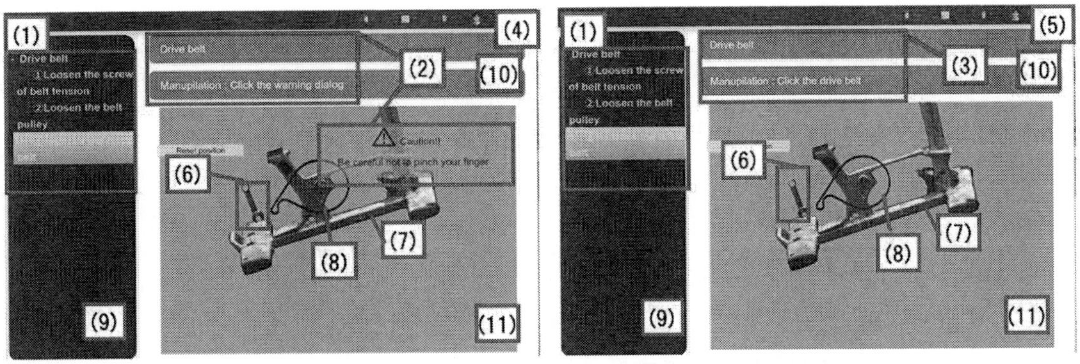

(a) An example of sequence 3 (b) An example of sequence 4

Figure 8. Example of display of sequence 3 and 4


```
{"workItemAreaId":"wi7","work name":"Drive belt",          (1)
"instructionItem": {
  "id":"1","text":"(1)Loosen the screw of belt tension"},
"instructionItem": {
  "id":"2","text":"(2)Loosen the belt pulley"},
"instructionItem": {
  "id":"2","text":"(3)Remove the drive belt"}}
```

```
{"manipulationAreaId":"mA7-3",                              (2)
"Work item name": "Drive belt",
"inductionText": "Manipulation:Click the warning dialog",
"clickedArea":{"clickedText_id":"mA7-3w",
"warningText":"Caution!! Take care not slamming your
finger"}},
```

```
{"manipulationAreaId":"mA7-4",                              (3)
"Work item name": "Drive belt",
"inductionText": "Manipulation:Click the drive belt",
"clickedArea":{"clickedText_id":"", "warningText":""}},
```


(a) An example of work item and instruction in text.json


```
{"sequenceNo":"3",                                          (4)
"workItemAreaId":"wi7",
"manipulationAreaId":"mA7-3",
"clickedText_id":"mA7-3w",
"clicked3dObject_id":""},
```

```
{"sequenceNo":"4",                                          (5)
"workItemAreaId":"wi7",
"manipulationAreaId":"mA7-4",
"clickedText_id":"",
"clicked3dObject_id":"tp-7"}
```


(b) An example of sequence.json


```
<workItemArea id=""></workArea>                             (9)
<manipulationArea id=""></manipulationArea>                 (10)
<3DimageArea id=""></3DImageArea>                           (11)
```


(c) An example of layout file

Figure 9. Example of data definition files

5. EVALUATION

Several customer engineers, mangers and training instructors carried out trial operation of our prototype system. We provided the content with through use of their laptop PC and tablet.

With our proposed system, examinees can learn each training content in less than 10 minutes. It is much more effective than the traditional training method. They can easily check any parts or instructions they want to know. Generally, they said that flashing objects and interactive manipulation enabled them to easily understand how to disassemble the fitness bike. Major comments on each mode were as follows:

(1) Learning mode

In learning mode, engineers can learn step-by-step assembly work by text instruction and flashing parts. Engineers said these instructions are highly effective in understanding what to do next. Instructors said that warning messages promote an understanding of maintenance training.

(2) Examination mode

Engineers said that examination mode is highly effective in making them remember the appropriate tools, part positions, and warning messages. Managers said that they can utilize the results of examinations for skills

management of the engineers.

(3) Positional Relation Check mode

Engineers' instructors said that positional relation check mode is a simple and good feature to check positions and parts names.

Some of them said difficult manipulation demotivated them to use such a CAE-based system, but our proposed system requires only simple manipulation on a laptop or tablet, and therefore it can be used easily by engineers. It was an important fact to adapt to our proposal for maintenance training.

```
"cp-1": {                                          (6)
"type":"common parts"
"name": "wrench",
"objFilePath":
 "/model/commonParts/wrench.obj",
"mtlFilePath":
 "/model/commonParts/wrench.mtl",
"position":
 {"x": -0.43,"y": 0.8,"z": 0},
"rotation": {"x": 1.57,"y": 0,"z": 0},
"scale": {"x": 1,"y": 1,"z": 1}}
```

(a) An example of common part in 3dmodels.json

```
{"tp-1": {                                              (7)
"type":"training parts"
"name": "bike base",
"objFilePath": "/model/fitnessBike/driveBelt.obj",
"mtlFilePath": "/model/fitnessBike/driveBelt.mtl",
"position": {"x": 0,"y": 0,"z": 0},
"rotation": {"x": 0,"y": 0,"z": 0},
"scale": {"x": 1,"y": 1,"z": 1}}},
```

```
{"tp-7": {                                              (8)
"type":"training parts"
"name": "driveBelt",
"objFilePath": "/model/fitnessBike/driveBelt.obj",
"mtlFilePath": "/model/fitnessBike/driveBelt.mtl",
"position": {"x": 1.2,"y": 0.2,"z": 0.8},
"rotation": {"x": 0,"y": 0,"z": 0},
"scale": {"x": 1,"y": 1,"z": 1}}}
```

(b) An example of training parts in 3dmodels.json

Figure 10. Example of 3dmodels.json

6. CONCLUSION

We developed a maintenance training system using a 3D model for a fitness bike. The system has the three training modes of learning, examination, and positional relation check. Each mode contains intuitive and interactive manipulation and shows step-by-step instructions. The system can easily exchange sequences, text messages and 3D objects with data management in the JSON format. Simple evaluation tests clearly indicated that the proposed maintenance training is effective and useful for training in fitness bike maintenance.

REFERENCES

Boussuge F. et al, 2012. An analysis of DMU transformation requirements for structural assembly simulations, *Proceeding of International Conference of Engineering Computational Technology (ECT)*, Dubrovnik, Croatia, pp. 1-22.

Chang K, 2014. *Product Design Modeling using CAD/CAE*. Academic Press, Cambridge, USA.

European Computer Manufacturers Association (ECMA), 2017. The JSON Data Interchange Syntax, Standard ECMA -404, Geneva, Switzerland, pp 1-7.

Fiorentino M, et al, 2014. Augmented reality on large screen for interactive maintenance instructions, *Computers in Industry,* Vol. 65, No. 2, pp 270-278.

Francesca D, et al, 2011. Augmented Reality for Aircraft Maintenance Training and Operations Support, *IEEE Computer Graphics and Applications,* Vol. 31, No. 1, pp 96-101.

Gutierrez T. et al, 2010. IMA-VR: A multimodal virtual training systems for skills transfer in Industrial Maintenance and Assembly tasks, Proceeding of International Symposium in Robot and Human Interactive Communication, Viareggio, Italy, pp. 428-433.

Liu Z. et al, 2013. Design and Implementation of Virtual Disassembly and Assembly Training System of Plunger Pump, Proceeding of IEEE International Conference of Virtual Reality and Visualizations, Shaanxi, China, pp. 289-292.

Sportillo D. et al. 2015. Training in VR: A Preliminary Study on Learning Assembly/Disassembly Sequences, *Proceeding of International Conference of Augmented and Virtual Reality (AVR),* Lecce, Italy, pp 332-343.

Webel S, et al, 2011. Design Criteria for AR-Based Training of Maintenance and Assembly Tasks, *Proceeding of International Conference on Virtual and Mixed Reality,* Orlando, USA, pp 123-132.

CLINICAL DECISIONS SUPPORT SYSTEM FOR CHOOSING THE TREATMENT COURSE CHILDREN WITH ENDOCRINOPATHIES

Olga V. Marukhina[1], Olga G. Berestneva[2] and Nina P. Stepanenko[3]
[1,2]Tomsk Polytechnic University, Russia, 634050, Tomsk, Lenina av., 30
[1,2]Tomsk State University, Russia, 634050, Tomsk, Lenina av., 36
[3]Institute of balneology and physiotherapy, Russia, 634050, Tomsk, Rosa Luxemburg st, 2a

ABSTRACT

The object of this research is the problem in children and teenagers overweight. The subject of the study is clinical and laboratorial parameters of the patients. The topicality of the research consists of creation of clinical decision support system to avoid many diagnostic mistakes. It is based on following aspects: the "Modernization of medical health care organization processes with use of information technologies" project is started by the Russian Federation government; there is an important goal to stabilize the part of Russian population with obesity; there are a lot of medical data that should be processed promptly. The novelty of the research is creation of decision-making algorithm for choosing the trajectory of treatment for children with endocrinopathy based on clinical and laboratorial parameters analysis. Clinical decision support system is being operated on the basis of Tomsk Research Institute of Health Resort Study and Physical Therapy.

KEYWORDS

Decision Support System, Medical Multidimensional Dataset

1. INTRODUCTION

The healthcare computerization creates opportunities to the clinical decision support system development. In the course of diagnosis, doctor manipulates a considerable amount of data and makes a decision in the context of uncertainty basing upon the first-hand experience and knowledge. IT-solution development for clinical purposes is one of the most promising and efficient ways to prevent these effects. That is why the efforts of many IT specialists are directed to the doctor's heuristics simulating software or expert-based medical decision-making algorithms development. Thus, the objective of this study is to develop clinical decision support system in the choice of treatment tactics (for children with endocrinopathies). One of the most common pathologies of endocrinopathy is obesity.

In 2014, the Government of the Russian Federation declared the list of top-priority research missions that require engaging all available resources. Currently, medical problems can be solved with help of actively developing information technologies. The technologies are covering almost all aspects of medical organizations activities, including management of resources, treatment and medical care. One of the most perspective direction is the development of clinical decision support systems (CDSS). CDSS serve as a basis for fundamentally new approaches creation. The approach solves traditional healthcare tasks such as monitoring a patient, consulting, deciding on further treatment. Studies in this field have been carried out in various directions [Kupeeva I.A. et al, 2015, Greenes R.A. 2007, Litvin A.A. el al, 2014, Ravodin R.A. et al, 2013, Zaripova G.R. et al., 2016, Latypov A.I. et al, 2002, Karpov O.E. et al, 2016, Berner E. S. 2007, Garg A.X. et al. 2005, Kawamoto K. et al. 2005, At'kov, O.YU. et al, 2013, Litvin, A.A. et al, 2016] for 30 years. According to e-Library, the amount of publications on this subject is constantly growing in our country, mostly in the last two years.

Clinical decision support systems serve as a basis for creating fundamentally new approaches to solving traditional problems in health care, such as patient observation, consultation, decision-making on further treatment [Chesnokova I.V. et al, 2007, Nikitina M.I., 2014]. The analysis of scientific publications on this topic revealed that the development and research in this area are conducted worldwide and in various directions [At'kov, O.YU. et al, 2013, Najdanov CH.A., 2015, Usov V.YU., 2017, Andersson B., 2011].

Among the Russian developments, the most well-known expert systems are: DIN (emergency recognition) and DIAGEN (diagnosis of hereditary diseases in children). According to the articles, the systems are created for different medical directions. One of the main aspects while working with decision support system data is to decrease the n-dimension attribute space. To solve this problem, the indexes must be selected with respect to their informative value assessment.

The analysis showed that in general, the systems are developed to solve problems related to a specific disease or medical direction. We want to develop a system for selecting a treatment pathway for any disease, provided that there are accumulated statistics on this disease before and after treatment. According to the articles, the systems are created for different medical directions. In this article we will consider the implementation of the system on the example of the problem of treatment of children with endocrinopathy (overweight).

2. METHODS AND RESULTS

2.1 Research Task Description and Solution

Tomsk Research Institute of Balneology and Physiotherapy provided the following data sets: clinical findings, cardiovascular systemindicators, physical efficiency, lipid metabolism, blood biochemistry, hormonal state, immunological status, blood plasma oxidation capacity and kininogenase system status (fig. 1). The data were received during the clinical studies from 2006 to 2013 and describes 464 children at the ages from 10 to 15 years suffering from obesity. Depending on the degree of obesity, the patient is prescribed a treatment complex (5 complexes in total).

The problem can be solved based on the given data that contain the following groups of basic parameters:

1. Clinic.
2. Cardiovascular system.
3. Physical performance.
4. Lipid metabolism.
5. Blood biochemistry.
6. Hormonal status.
7. Immunological status.
8. The state of the kallikrein-kinin system.
9. Oxidative ability of blood plasma.
10. Immunological Status

In addition to the above indicators, the dataset contains information on the patient's belonging to the treatment group (1-5). To solve the problem, it is necessary to build such a system that could determine for the newly arrived patient the path of treatment for him, that is, one of 5 groups, based on his primary clinical and laboratory indicators.

Mentioned indexes were studied twice: before and after the treatment, as well as their differences and changes were described.

As a result of the research, an algorithm was developed to support the adoption of medical decisions for the choice of treatment tactics for children and adolescents with endocrinopathy (figure 1).

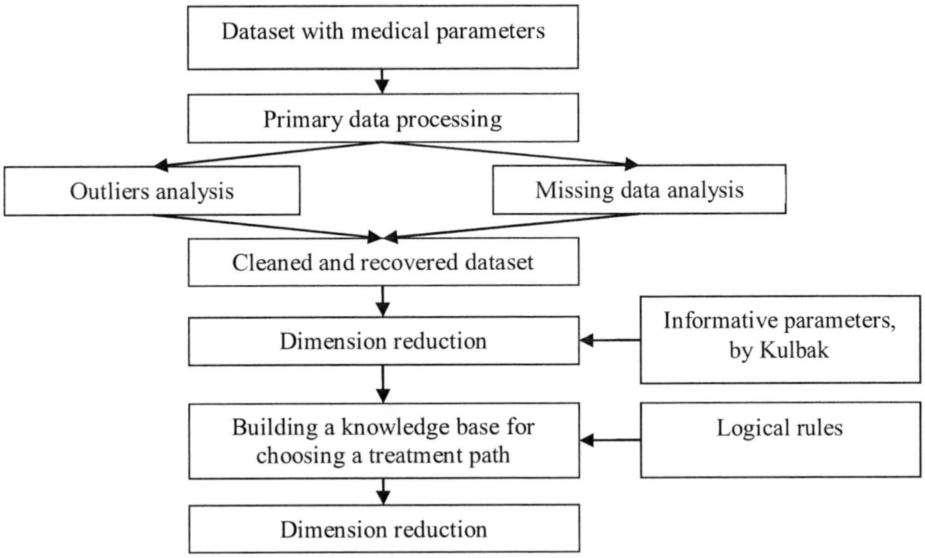

Figure 1. Algorithm for choosing a treatment path

The algorithm consists of the following steps:

1. Array of data. The Tomsk Research Institute of Balneology and Physiotherapy provided baseline data - clinical and laboratory parameters of children and adolescents with endocrinopathies.

2. Primary data processing. Next, data was cleared by analyzing the emissions in the RStudio software product and analyzing the missing values using the mean values method.

3. Reduction dimension. To reduce the size of the data, we chose the Kuhlbak informativeness calculation; from the set of features, the most informative in each treatment group were selected.

4. As a result of data cleansing and dimension reduction, a training and test sample was formed to form a knowledge base. As a method for building a knowledge base, a method of building a decision tree was chosen.

5. The decision tree is built in the Rapid Miner software product, on the basis of which we obtained logical rules.

2.2 Analysis and Imputation the Missing Data

Missing values and outliers are frequently encountered during the data collection phase of observational or experimental studies conducted in all fields of natural and social sciences. Too many missed values are the problem for further processing and analysis of data. Usually, 15% from the entire data extraction is the maximum percentage value of missed data. If the amount of percentage value exceeds 15%, it should discard this indicator.

Imputation involves replacing missing values with substituted values obtained from a statistical analysis to produce a complete data set without missing values for analysis. Imputations can be created by using either an explicit or an implicit modeling approach. The explicit modeling approach assumes that variables have a certain predictive distribution and estimates the parameters of each distribution, which is used for imputations. It includes different methods of imputation by mean, median, probability, ratio, regression, predictive-regression, and assumption of distribution. The implicit modeling approach focuses on computing an algorithm required to generate accurate imputation values, if possible. Common implicit modeling methods include hot-deck imputation, cold-deck imputation, and substitution. A combination of explicit and implicit modeling methods is also used.

Identification of missing data is the only unambiguous step. The analysis of the missing data depends on an understanding of the processes that reproduce the experimental information. The function *aggr()* from the package *mice* for R graphically displays the number of observations for each individual variable and for each combination of variables.

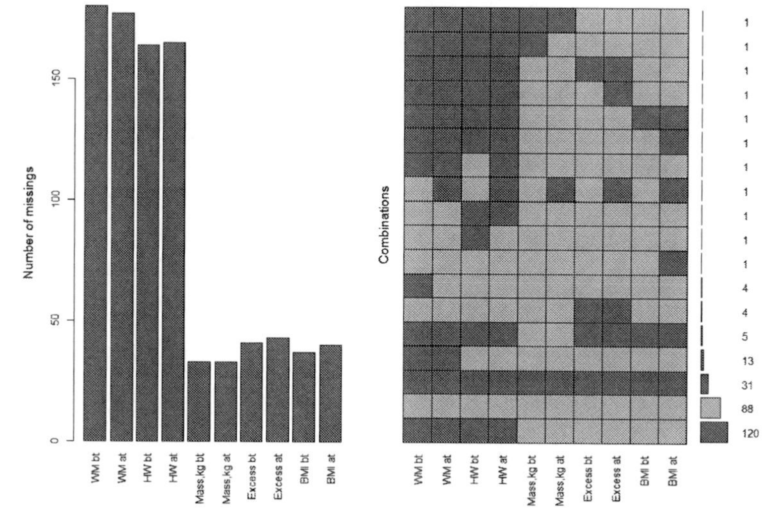

Figure 2. The function aggr() results for dataset which contains the results of the examination of children

Fragment at figure 2 shows that the most missing values are contained in the Waistline before treatment.

The idea of multiple recovery of missing data is well implemented in an R package like *mice*. The *mice()* function (multivariate imputation by chained equations) uses the original data table with missing values, and returns an object containing several complete data sets (five by default). Each such complete data set is obtained by restoring the missing data of the original table. There is a random component in the data recovery algorithm, so all derived complete data sets are slightly different from each other.

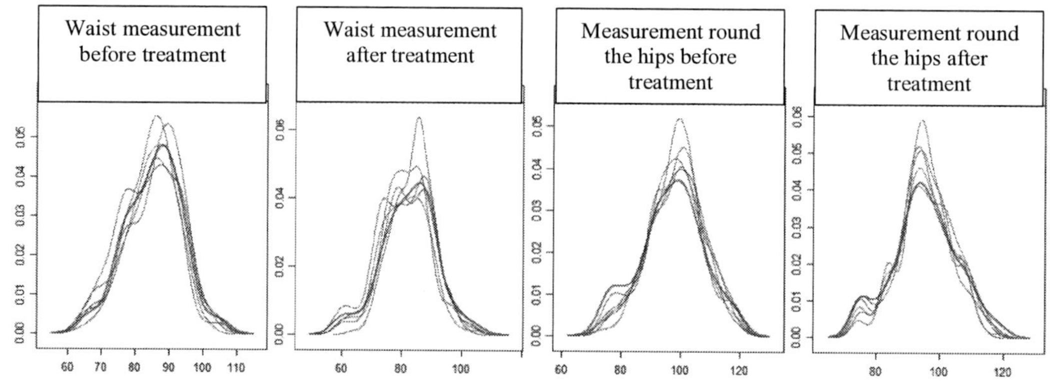

Figure 3. Accuracy evaluation the recovered data

Replacing the missing values is done using Gibbs samples. By default, the values of each variable containing missing values are predicted from the values of the remaining variables. The resulting equations are used to replace the missing data with suitable values.

The user can select the type of predictive model for each variable and define the variables that will be included in it. By default, the correspondence method, the predicted average is used to replace the missing values of continuous variables, and logistic or polynomial logistic regression is used for dichotomous (factor with two levels) or polynomial (factor with more than two levels) variables, respectively.

The result of the function *mice()* is the base with the restored values. To assess the accuracy of the recovered data, a *densityplot(imp)* graph was built (figure 3). The density of imputed data for each imputed set is shown in red, and the density of observed indicators is shown in blue. Based on this, we can conclude that the distribution of the recovered data coincides with the original.

2.3 Clinical Parameters Informativeness

Kulback method [Gubler E.V., 1978.] is used to assess the informative value. In medicine, it is possible to deal with the diagnosis issues, establishing diagnosis and medical condition definition only when the informative indexes typical to the patient are obtained and analyzed. Thus, it is necessary to determine the most informative indexes that characterize the patients psychophysical condition. The diagnosis depends on a kind of datamining based on these indexes. There are various techniques to assess the informative value, e.g. Shannon method and the cumulative frequency method, but let us concentrate on Kulback method of informative value assessment.

Indexes informational content depends entirely on how much this index helps to differentiate the object state. The more informative index corresponds to the greater distance between the random variables. The most widespread informative value for these distances is Kulback measure.

In 1948, a logarithmic measure was proposed by N. Wiener and K. Shannon as a way to define the amount of information. They offered the formula that was recognized as information quantitative measure. There is one measure that was introduced by Jeffreus in 1964 and was studied in detail by Kulback as an informative value $J(1,2)$, a measure of discrepancies between statistical distributions 1 and 2. For discrete distributions, this formula is as follows:

$$J(x_i / A_1, x_i / A_2) = \sum_j \lg \frac{P(x_{ij} / A_1)}{P(x_{ij} / A_2)} \left[P(x_{ij} / A_1) - P(x_{ij} / A_2) \right] \tag{1}$$

where A_1, A_2 – state classes; i –sign number; j – number of i-th sign range; $P(x_{ij} / A_k)$ – probability of object hitting belonging to A_k class in the j sign range.

In different groups, treatment has different effects on the physiological systems of the body, which has resulted in different informative signs in groups [Marukhina, O.V. et al, 2018].

2.4 Decision Trees

One of the methods for representing the knowledge base used in statistics is the decision tree. Decision trees are one of the most popular methods for solving many practical problems, due to the following reasons:

1. Decision trees allow us to obtain very easily interpreted models, which are a set of rules of the form "if..., then...". Interpretation is facilitated, in particular, by the possibility to present these rules in the form of a visual tree structure.
2. Because of their design, decision trees allow you to work with variables of any type without the need for any pre-preparation of these variables for input into the model (for example, logarithm, conversion of categorical variables into indicator ones, etc.).
3. The researcher does not need to explicitly define the form of the relationship between response and predictors, as is the case with conventional regression models. This is particularly useful when working with large amounts of data whose properties are not well known.
4. Decision trees, in fact, automatically select informative predictors and take into account possible interactions between them. This in particular makes decision trees a useful tool for exploratory data analysis.
5. Decision trees can be effectively applied to data with missing values, which is very useful in solving practical problems where missing values are a rule rather than an exception.
6. Decision trees apply equally well to both quantitative and qualitative dependent variables.

To solve the problem of building a knowledge base, a method of building a decision tree was chosen as one of the most popular and giving a good result. To construct a decision tree, we used only informative features, the change of which was the greatest after treatment. The initial data for the construction of a decision tree are informative features obtained as a result of calculating the information content. The percentage of attribution of an object to a particular group is 96.88% (figure 4).

accuracy: 96.88%

	true group1	true group2	true group3	true group4	true group5	class precision
pred. group1	21	0	0	0	0	100.00%
pred. group2	2	9	0	0	0	81.82%
pred. group3	0	0	14	0	0	100.00%
pred. group4	0	0	0	13	0	100.00%
pred. group5	0	0	0	0	5	100.00%
class recall	91.30%	100.00%	100.00%	100.00%	100.00%	

Figure 4. Classification assessment

As a result, we obtained a decision tree with the following structure:

- 10 branches. A branch is the rule by which subtrees are obtained;
- 10 subtrees. Subtree - a set of objects obtained from a certain rule.
- 6 leaves. Leaves represent some decision rule regarding the target parameter.
- 5 knots. A node – the place where a tree branching into subtrees occurs; at the time of creating nodes, it is decided how much and how the tree will be expanded.

The decision tree description is presented at figures 5 and 6.

Tree

```
TMT > 13.200
|   ObRabotos > 150
|   |   NO > 3.500: group3 {group1=0, group2=0, group3=46, group4=0, group5=0}
|   |   NO ≤ 3.500: group4 {group1=0, group2=0, group3=0, group4=42, group5=0}
|   ObRabotos ≤ 150
|   |   Leptin > 58.100
|   |   |   Leptin > 62.550: group1 {group1=5, group2=1, group3=0, group4=0, group5=0}
|   |   |   Leptin ≤ 62.550: group2 {group1=0, group2=28, group3=0, group4=0, group5=0}
|   |   Leptin ≤ 58.100: group1 {group1=71, group2=1, group3=0, group4=0, group5=0}
TMT ≤ 13.200: group5 {group1=0, group2=0, group3=0, group4=0, group5=18}
```

Figure 5. The decision tree description

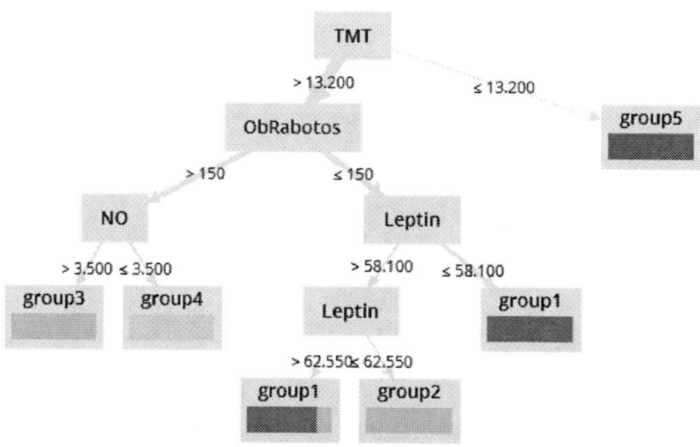

Figure 6. Graphical decision tree view

3. CONCLUSION

Development of systems to support medical decision-making is relevant due to frequent diagnostic errors and incorrect prescriptions of doctors. Mass computerization of health care makes it extremely promising to create systems for algorithmic and information support of medical decisions.

The relevance of our research is due to three aspects:

- the government of the Russian Federation prioritizes the project of the Russian Federation "Improvement of the processes of medical care organization based on the introduction of information technologies»;
- the importance of solving the problem of stabilizing the proportion of the population of Russia with obesity, this is especially important for children and young people;
- a large amount of medical data requires rapid processing.

Based on this, we set and solved the following tasks:

1) we got the dataset of clinical and laboratory parameters of the main physiological systems of the body in conditionally healthy children and adolescents, as well as with various forms of obesity before and after treatment; the problem is solved under the supervision of the Tomsk Research Institute of Balneology and Physiotherapy;

2) informativeness assessment of the main indicators physiological body systems according to the survey results;

3) we constructed the new algorithm for the choice of treatment tactics;

4) unique knowledge base about treatment outcomes based on processing a large amount of data collected at the Research Institute of Resort Medicine and Physical Therapy for several years;

We will continue our research and set ourselves new tasks:

5) building a prognostic model of treatment outcomes depending on the chosen trajectory, forming a knowledge base.

6) the creation of appropriate software, which in the aggregate is an intelligent system with the possibility of its implementation in any medical center conducting such research.

Our system will easily adapt for the decision of tasks of choice of individual course of treatment for any disease subject to the availability of databases of clinical and laboratory parameters before and after treatment. The system will be self-learning, as the database of treatment outcomes will be constantly updated. Another advantage of the system is its convenient use for a medical specialist who is not a specialist in the field of it - it will be an additional electronic assistant for the doctor. On the basis of scientific cooperation, we plan to implement the system in medical institutions free of charge, this is a significant difference from the systems listed in the review at the beginning of this article.

ACKNOWLEDGEMENT

The study was carried out with the partial financial support of the Russian Foundation for Basic Research (RFBR) within scientific project No. 18-07-00543.

REFERENCES

Andersson B., 2011. Prediction of severe acute pancreatitis at admission to hospital using artificial neural networks. *Pancreatology*, 2011. – Vol. 11. -№ 3. – P. 328 -335.

At'kov, O.YU. et al, 2013. Sistema podderzhki prinyatiya vrachebnyh reshenij. *Sistemy podderzhki prinyatiya vrachebnyh reshenij*. №6, pp. 67-75.

Berner E. S. 2007. Clinical Decision Support Systems. N. Y.: Springer.

Chesnokova I.V. et al, 2007. Sistema podderzhki prinyatiya vrachebnyh reshenij na dogospital'nom ehtape v terapii arterial'noj gipertenzii. *Sistemnyj analiz i upravlenie v biomedicinskih sistemah*. № 3, pp. 675–679.

Garg A. X. et al. 2005. Effects of Computerized Clinical Decision Support Systems on Practitioner Performance and Patient Outcomes: A Systematic Review. *Journal of the American Medical Association*, Vol. 293, № 10, pp. 1223-1238.

Greenes R.A. 2007. *Clinical decision support: the road ahead* / R.A. Greenes. Boston: Elsevier Academic Press.

Gubler E. V., 1978. Vychislitel'nye metody analiza i raspoznavaniya patologicheskih processov – MEDICINA, Russia.

Karpov O.E. et al. 2016. Primenenie intellektual'nyh sistem v zdravoohranenii. *Sovremennye naukoemkie tekhnologii*, № 7-1, pp. 38-43.

Kawamoto K. et al. 2005. Improving Clinical Practice Using Clinical Decision Support Systems: A Systematic Review of Trials to Identify Features Critical to Success. *British Medical Journal*, Vol. 330, № 7494, pp. 765-768.

Knyshov G.V. et al, 2014. Osobennosti proektirovaniya medicinskoj informacionnoj sistemy podderzhki prinyatiya reshenij, osnovannoj na intellektual'nom analize dannyh. *Kibernetika i vychislitel'naya tekhnika*. № 3, pp.79–87.

Kupeeva I.A. et al, 2015. Razrabotka intellektual'noj sistemy podderzhki prinyatiya vrachebnyh reshenij v dermatovenerologii. *Problemy medicinskoj mikologii*. Vol. 17, № 3, pp. 27–31.

Kupeeva I.A. et al, 2016. Ocenka ehffektivnosti intellektual'noj sistemy podderzhki prinyatiya vrachebnyh reshenij. *Vestnik Sankt-Peterburgskogo Universiteta*. №10, pp. 62–68.

Latypov A.I. et al, 2002. Nechetkaya logika v differencial'noj diagnostike stomatologicheskih zabolevanij. *Informacionnye tekhnologii v zdravoohranenii*, № 8-10, pp.19-21.

Litvin A.A. et al, 2014. Sistemy podderzhki prinyatiya reshenij v hirurgii. *Novosti hirurgii*, Vol. 22, № 1, pp. 96–100.

Litvin, A.A. et al, 2016. Sistemy podderzhki prinyatiya reshenij v diagnostike i lechenii ostrogo pankreatita. *Problemy zdorov'ya i ehkologii*. №2 (48), pp.10-17.

Marukhina, O.V. et al, 2018. Basic physiological systems indicator's informative assessment for children and adolescents obesity diagnosis tasks. *Journal of Physics: Conference Series*. 1015(3), 032091.

Najdanov CH.A., 2015. Sistema podderzhki prinyatiya reshenij dlya preduprezhdeniya riskov vozniknoveniya kriticheskih sostoyanij. *Al'manah sovremennoj nauki i obrazovaniya*. № 8(98), pp.92–95

Nikitina M.I., 2014. Trekhurovnevaya sistema podderzhki prinyatiya reshenij perinatal'nomu monitoring. *Obrazovatel'nye resursy i tekhnologii*. Pp. 151–156.

Ravodin R.A. et al, 2013. Intellektual'nye sistemy podderzhki prinyatiya reshenij kak instrument profilaktiki vrachebnyh oshibok. *Mediko-biologicheskie i social'no-psihologicheskie problemy bezopasnosti v chrezvychajnyh situaciyah*, № 1, pp. 27–31.

Usov V.YU., 2017. Struktura medicinskoj informacionnoj sistemy podderzhki reshenij, ispol'zuyushchej algoritmy intellektual'nogo analiza dannyh. *Vestnik Voronezhskogo instituta vysokih tekhnologij*. № 2, pp. 122–126.

Zaripova G.R. et al, 2016. Sovremennye modeli ehkspertnyh sistem podderzhki prinyatiya vrachebnyh reshenij v prognozirovanii operacionnogo riska v hirurgicheskoj praktike. *Tavricheskij mediko-biologicheskij vestnik*, Vol. 19, № 4, pp. 140–145.

THE INFLUENCE OF MEDIUM CREDIBILITY TOWARDS INFORMATION ADOPTION IN INDONESIA STOCK INVESTMENT VIRTUAL COMMUNITIES

Hardyin Alexander Hutapea, Achmad Nizar Hidayanto, Fatimah Azzahro
and Widijanto Satyo Nugroho
Faculty of Computer Science, Universitas Indonesia
Kampus UI Depok, Indonesia

ABSTRACT

This study aims to analyze the influence of medium credibility towards information adoption through information credibility and perceived usefulness. The context of this study is virtual communities dedicated to stock investment. Based on the survey obtained from 333 respondents, our analyses show that medium credibility positively influences information credibility and perceived usefulness. Meanwhile, information credibility and perceived usefulness are the antecedents of information adoption. Additionally, information credibility positively influences perceived usefulness. In particular, it can be concluded that in the context of stock investment virtual communities, medium credibility can influence information adoption through information credibility and perceived usefulness. The theoretical and practical implications of this study, and its limitations are also discussed.

KEYWORDS

Information Adoption, Information Credibility, Medium Credibility, Perceived Usefulness, Stock Investment Virtual Communities

1. INTRODUCTION

The capital market can drive macroeconomic turnover in a country and has potential to improve one's living standards (OECD, 2018). However, in Indonesia, the capital market is the least utilized financial sector due to low capital market literacy (Otoritas Jasa Keuangan, 2016). The index of capital market literacy in Indonesia is only 4.4%. In other words, among 1000 people, only 44 people have sufficient knowledge on capital market. In order to improve the literacy index, the Financial Services Authority (OJK) launched the National Strategy for Financial Literacy in 2017. One of its initiatives is to encourage the use of information technology-based media in financial education. As the number of internet users in Indonesia continually increasing, the internet-based media such as virtual communities is expected to be the most efficient way to improve the index of capital market literacy in Indonesia (We are social, 2018).

Virtual communities are online social networks where people with the same interests, goals or activities interact to share information and knowledge (Chiu, Hsu and Wang, 2006). In Indonesia, the popularity of virtual communities is increasing along with the rapid development of social media and instant messaging users. The convenience provided by virtual community to share and search information is among the reasons that motivate people to join virtual community. This also applies to stock investors that continuously need to find the most updated information to improve their portfolio performance. As social media and instant messaging become the two of the most widely used applications by internet users in Indonesia, stock investment virtual communities are often formed through social media (i.e. Facebook and Instagram), as well as instant messaging applications (e.g. WhatsApp and Telegram group). Additionally, there is also a social media that specifically serve stock investors, Stockbit.

Virtual community is often used by investors to exchange information about capital markets. In the capital market, investors who are able to get credible information earlier may secure greater profits. Thus, stock investors experience the fear of missing out (FOMO) and consider information as important commodities. The urgency of information has encouraged stock investors to search for up-to-the-minute information, including through virtual communities. However, despite its ability to spread information quickly, not all virtual communities circulating trustworthy information. In a study conducted by Bates and Annette, 85% of journalists stated that, in general, the information available on social media was less credible than conventional media due to lack of validation, verification and reporting standards (Bates and Annette, 2009).

Numerous studies have documented that medium credibility is the antecedent of information credibility (Kang, 2010; Westerman, Spence and Van Der Heide, 2012). Audience tends to assess the credibility of a medium before assessing the credibility of information distributed through it. On the other hand, several studies have documented the positive effects of information credibility on information adoption (Wathen and Burkell, 2002; Bates and Annette, 2009). However, there have not been many studies that discuss whether medium credibility can influence information adoption. To fill the gap, this study tries to evaluate whether medium credibility can also influence users' decision to adopt information through information credibility and information usefulness.

The rest of the paper is organized as follow. In the following section, we review the relevant literature on medium credibility, information credibility, and information adoption. Additionally, our proposed model and hypotheses development are also presented in the literature review section. We then describe our methodology and present our results, ending with a discussion and conclusion of our findings, including our theoretical implication, practical implications, and research limitations.

2. LITERATURE REVIEW AND HYPOTHESES DEVELOPMENT

2.1 Medium Credibility as Antecedent of Information Credibility and Perceived Usefulness

According to Metzger et al., (2003), medium credibility defines users' perceived level of trust towards a specific media. Medium credibility focus on the channel through which content is delivered rather than the content itself. To measure medium credibility, prior research used medium interfaces and features, which only represent the technical ability of medium to deliver information. However, the past approach is unable to represent users' phycological factors in evaluating medium credibility. Therefore, this study adopted the medium credibility theory developed by Li and Suh that combined both the technical and psychological aspects of users in assessing media credibility (Li and Suh, 2015).

Based on Li and Suh theory, medium credibility is defined as a second-order construct that consists of medium dependency (psychological aspects), interactivity, and medium transparency (technical aspect). First, medium dependency is defined as the extent to which users rely on a particular virtual community to find information about stock investment (Ito *et al.*, 2008). Meanwhile, interactivity is defined as media ability to increase user involvement. This includes the media interface, features, and its ease of use that help users to connect with each other (Li and Suh, 2015). Lastly, medium transparency refers to the ability of media to support the exchange of information between individuals candidly (Yang and Lim, 2009). According to Yang and Lim, medium transparency is the key to building relational trust. For example, blogs are considered more credible than conventional media because it provides more independent and transparent information (Andrews, 2003).

In the context of stock investment virtual communities, each virtual community has its own characteristics which lead to different credibility assessment from its users. Previous research found that medium credibility influences information credibility (Westerman, Spence and Van Der Heide, 2012; Li and Suh, 2015). Although people tend to have dependency to get information from their favorite media, they do not always feel that their most preferred media was the most credible. This also the case for stock investors which rely heavily on information to make decision. Hence, before deciding whether information from a specific virtual community is credible, one often assess the credibility of medium beforehand. If the virtual community does not provide good interactivity and transparency, then, users may find themselves to distrust the provided information. Based on these explanations, the authors draw the hypothesis:

H1: Medium credibility has a positive effect on information credibility.

Several researchers found that medium credibility also influences information credibility (Li and Suh, 2015; Hajli, 2018; Madli *et al.*, 2018). Media with high interactivity may provide rich and relevant information for users. In the context of stock investment virtual community, if the virtual community provides features and interface that encourage their users to interact and share information, it will build up the relevant content for its users. Hence, when users consider a virtual community as a credible media, for example having good interactivity and transparency, they will likely believe that the information provided by the media is useful for them. Based on this, it was concluded that:

H2: The credibility medium has a positive effect on perceived usefulness.

2.2 Information Credibility as Antecedent of Perceived Usefulness and Information Adoption

Information credibility is defined as the extent to which information can be trusted by the recipient, thus can influence the recipient to take certain actions (McKnight and Kacmar, 2007). Meanwhile, information adoption is defined as a process of involvement to use information that is intentionally carried out by information recipients (Yan *et al.*, 2016). In virtual community, adopting behavior is often performed (Cheung, Lee, and Rabjohn, 2008). For example, buyers in e-commerce platform often look for reviews from other users and ask questions to others before making purchases (Sussman and Siegal, 2003; Pitta and Fowler, 2005). This also happens in the context of stock investment virtual community. The member of stock investment virtual community often evaluates the credibility of information before deciding whether they will adopt the information. The process of adopting information itself starts when user agreeing to the information, following the suggestion, and/or making decisions based on that information (Sussman and Siegal, 2003). Several previous studies found that information credibility significantly influences information adoption (McKnight and Kacmar, 2007; Cheung *et al.*, 2009; Yan *et al.*, 2016). Therefore, the authors propose the following hypothesis:

H3: Information credibility has a positive effect on information adoption.

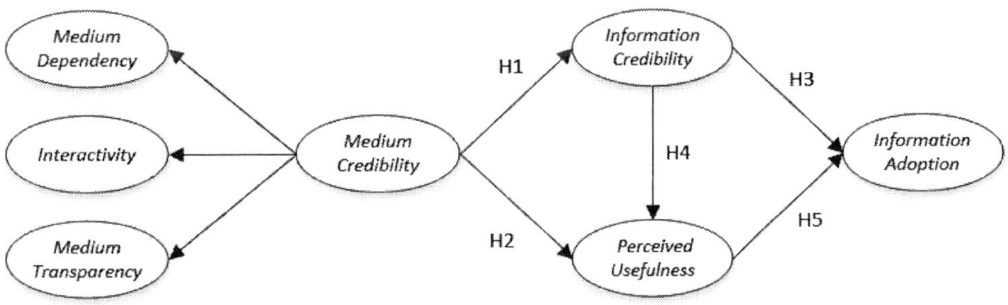

Figure 1. Research Model

In this era of data, there is abundance of information available every day. However, not all information is trustworthy and useful. Although information credibility can influence information adoption, only useful and relevant information will be adopted by people. On the contrary, useful information can predict users' intention in adopting information. However, untrustworthy information will reduce the usefulness or even increase the risk of information, especially in the context of stock investment which has direct impact on one's finances. Therefore, information credibility is a very important factor to determine whether information is useful or not. The argument is supported by several previous studies which showed a positive relationship between information credibility and perceived usefulness (Ko *et al.*, 2005; McKnight and Kacmar, 2007; Hajli, 2018). Therefore, the authors propose the following hypothesis:

H4: Information credibility has a positive effect on perceived usefulness.

According to Hussain et al, information adoption behavior is essential for consumers before making a decision regarding the quality of a product or service, especially in an online environment (Hussain *et al.*, 2018). Thus, information usefulness is considered to be essential to predict whether further adoption of information will happen. In the context of stock investment, information is considered useful when it can help improve one's performance in stock investing. When someone considers information useful to them, they will tend to adopt that information to benefit from it (Erkan and Evans, 2016; Hussain *et al.*, 2018). Therefore, the authors propose the following hypothesis:

H5: Perceived usefulness has a positive effect on information adoption.

3. METHODOLOGY

We tested the proposed hypotheses (Figure 1) using an online survey distributed to stock investors that also members of stock investment virtual communities. The questionnaire contains four measures addressing the research questions. First, medium credibility and information credibility construct are adopted from Li and Suh (2015). Next, perceived usefulness construct is adapted from (Tseng and Wang, 2016). Lastly, information adoption construct is adopted from Sussman and Siegal (2003). Responses to all the item measures were captured using six-point Likert-type scales. We avoid using odd number Likert scale due to respondents' tendency to choose the median or neutral statement. Since the research is conducted in Indonesia, each item on the questionnaire is translated from English to Bahasa Indonesia to facilitate respondents' understanding.

We received completed responses from 406 stock investors that are members of at least one stock investment virtual community. The virtual communities are mostly based on instant messaging or social media, with WhatsApp, is the most popular platform. After deleting unmatched and/or missing cases, the final sample consisted of 333 matched questionnaires. Table 1 summarizes the demographic data of our respondents. According to F. Hair Jr *et al.* (2014), the ideal sample size should be at least ten times the number of indicators. Since this study are measured by using 22 indicators, the minimum sample is reached.

Table 1. Demography of Respondents

Variable	Items	Frequency	Percentage
Sex	Male	260	78,08%
	Female	73	21,92%
Age	< 20	67	20.12%
	21-25	144	43,24%
	26-30	49	14,71%
	31-35	28	8,41%
	35-40	21	6,31%
Income (in IDR per month)	< IDR1 million	75	22,52%
	IDR1- 5 million	103	30.93%
	IDR5 - 10 million	84	25,23%
	> 10 million	71	21,32%
Duration of becoming a member of stock investment virtual community	< 1 year	168	50.45%
	1-2 year	96	28,83%
	2-3 year	38	11,41%
	4-5 year	12	3,60%
	> 5 year	19	5,71%

4. RESEARCH RESULTS

4.1 Measurement Model Evaluation

The measurement model was assessed to ensure the appropriate use of instruments, including its convergent validity, discriminant validity, and reliability. To assess the reliability of construct, the authors ensure that the composite reliability values are greater than 0.70 as suggested by Robinson et al (1991). Table 2 summarizes the loading ranges, AVE, and composite reliability for all items. Meanwhile, to ensure construct validity, all measures were adapted from existing validated scales whenever possible. Additionally, the convergent validity is measured by using loading factors and AVE. While the loading factors must be greater than 0.60. the AVE value must be greater than 0.50. Lastly, Table 3 shows that the square root of the AVE for each construct is higher than correlations between constructs, suggesting that the measurement model have good discriminant validity.

Table 2. The Results of Reliability and Validity Testing for the Constructs.

Factors	Items	Loading Factor	AVE	CR	Factors	Items	Loading Factor	AVE	CR
MT	MT1	0.68				I1	0.75		
	MT2	0.641	0.501	0.716	INT	I2	0.855	0.610	0.861
	MT3	0.706				I3	0.821		
IC	IC1	0.874				I4	0.686		
	IC2	0.862			MD	MD1	0.758		
	IC3	0.895	0.704	0.877		MD2	0.691		
PU	PU1	0.86				MD3	0.729	0.507	0.860
	PU2	0.804				MD4	0.685		
	PU3	0.852				MD5	0.654		
IA	IA1	0.795	0.673	0.861		MD6	0.75		
	IA2	0.808							
	IA3	0.857							

MT: Medium Transparency, IC: Information Credibility, PU: Perceived Usefulness,
IA: Information Adoption, INT: Interactivity, MD: Medium Dependency, MC: Medium Credibility

Table 3. Correlations between constructs

	IA	PU	IC	MC
IA	**0.820**			
PU	0.763	**0.839**		
IC	0.743	0.782	**0.877**	
MC	0.666	0.664	0.671	**0.856**

4.2 Structural Model Evaluation

For all hypotheses, we then conducted an evaluation on the structural model using AMOS 24. All proposed hypotheses were fully supported with significance level $p = 0.05$ (Table 4). Medium credibility is proved to be the antecedent of both information credibility and perceived usefulness (*p*-value for H1 & H2 are less than 0.05). Next, information credibility significantly influences perceived usefulness (*p*-value of H3 <0.05). Lastly, H4 and H5 show that both predictors appeared to significantly predict information adoption: information credibility (*p* 0.017) and perceived usefulness (*p* 0.003). Additionally, the R^2 value was used to assess the coefficient of determination. R^2 for information adoption, perceived usefulness, and information credibility are, respectively, 0.661, 0.649, and 0.473. R^2 value for information adoption from stock investment virtual communities is 0.473 suggesting that 47.3% of the variance in information adoption of stock investment virtual communities can be explained by factors in the research model.

Table 4. Hypothesis Testing Result

Hypothesis	Path	Estimate	*p*	Results
H1	Medium Credibility → Information Credibility	0.688	0.007	Accepted
H2	Medium Credibility → Perceived Usefulness	0.275	0.005	Accepted
H3	Information Credibility → Perceived Usefulness	0.591	0.004	Accepted
H4	Information Credibility → Information Adoption	0.298	0.017	Accepted
H5	Perceived Usefulness → Information Adoption	0.559	0.003	Accepted

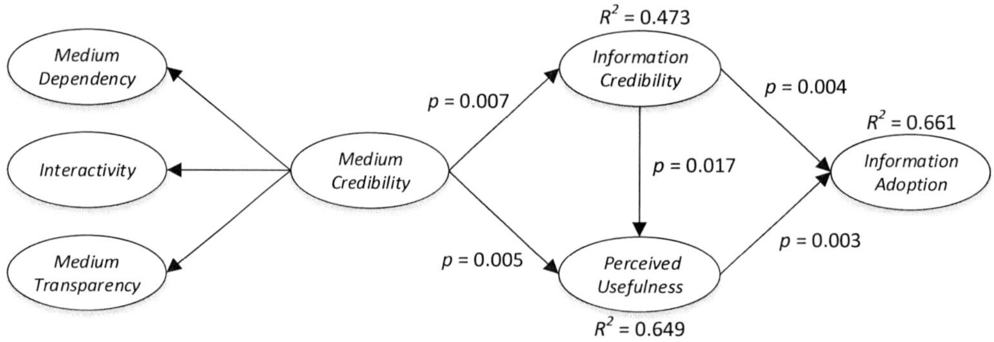

Figure 2. Research Result

5. DISCUSSION AND IMPLICATIONS

In light of the approval of H1 (medium credibility influence information credibility), we extended existing findings from Li and Suh (2015). Additionally, our result establishes an expansion of the existing findings from Eysenbach, (2008) in the now context of stock investment virtual communities. Our study also found that information credibility influences perceived usefulness. This finding also strengthens the findings of mobile word-of-mouth study by Erkan and Evans, (2016) and adopting information in food products purchase by Hussain *et al.* (2018). Through this research, the author further strengthens the theory of information credibility with information usefulness, as discussed by Hajli, (2018) and Ko *et al.*, (2005). This study also found that users of stock investment virtual communities tend to adopt credible information. The process of adopting information in this study is characterized by users agreeing to information, then users follow the suggestions contained in information, and users are encouraged to make decisions based on information. Therefore, it can be concluded that before adopting stock information the user usually considers the information credible. This finding supports the research of Cheung *et al.*, (2009) which concluded that the credibility of information affects the adoption of information. Finally, perceived usefulness also affects information adoption. Users will tend to adopt stock information if they feel the information is useful to them. In addition to assessing its credibility, the user also assesses whether information is useful to him before he adopts the information.

This study offers both theoretical and practical implication. First, through this research, the author proves that the medium credibility influences information adoption through perceived usefulness and information credibility. Several previous studies have indeed discussed the relationship of medium credibility with information credibility as well as the relationship between information credibility and information adoption (Cheung et al., 2009; Li and Suh, 2015). However, not many studies have discussed how the credibility of a communication medium influences the adoption of information by its users.

Based on the results of the analysis, the authors found that the credibility medium has a direct correlation with perceived usefulness. Several previous studies that discussed the usefulness of information in virtual communities usually linked it to information credibility and the quality of arguments (Huang and Kuo, 2014; Erkan and Evans, 2016; Hussain *et al.*, 2018). Therefore, the results of this study are expected to provide a new perspective on the relationship between the credibility and perceived usefulness medium. This study also confirms the dimensions of the medium credibility outlined by Li and Suh (2005). Previous research on the credibility medium generally discussed the medium credibility attribute based on the features or design of a communication medium and not many focused on discussing medium credibility from the user's point of view.

On the practical level, our findings suggest that stock investors can assess the medium credibility, or in this context, the credibility of virtual communities to improve the possibility of getting credible and useful information. One can evaluate the interactivity of medium, along with the medium dependency and medium transparency. Additionally, as this study shows that interactivity is part of medium credibility, social media that focus on stock investment such as Stockbit can improve their interactivity to ensure achieving better information credibility. By providing features that encourage users to interact with each other, the information credibility and perceived usefulness will improve. Thus, increasing the information adoption in investors.

6. CONCLUSION

This paper concludes that; medium credibility influences information credibility and perceived usefulness. This indicates that the more credible a virtual community is, the information distributed in the virtual community will be perceived as more useful and credible by users. Additionally, this study also found that medium credibility has more influence towards information credibility than perceived usefulness. Meanwhile, information credibility affects perceived usefulness with a level of correlation that can be categorized as strong. Thus, it can be concluded that credible information will be considered more useful for users of stock investment virtual communities. Lastly, information credibility and perceived usefulness influence information adoption behavior, with perceived usefulness having a more significant influence compare to information credibility. Thus, it can be concluded that in adopting information in stock investment virtual communities, users are more concerned with the use of information than the credibility of the information.

This study also has several limitations. Firstly, the number of respondents who filled out this questionnaire were 330 respondents. Meanwhile, the number of stock investors in the Indonesian capital market has reached around 851,662 as of December 2018 (KSEI, 2018). Thus, the number of samples that are relatively small compared to the total population may not reflect the behavior of all stock investors in Indonesia. Additionally, the author suggests for future study to compare several social media or instant messaging applications that have different characteristics while using medium credibility theory.

ACKNOWLEDGMENT

We would like to thank Direktorat Riset & Pengabdian Masyarakat for their support through Grant PIT9 (Grant No. NKB-0005/UN2.R3.1/HKP.05.00/2019).

REFERENCES

Andrews, P, 2003. *Is Blogging Journalism?* Available at: https://niemanreports.org/articles/is-blogging-journalism/ (Accessed: 2 April 2019).

Bates, D. and Annette, A, 2009. *How the press uses and values public relations and other media resources and journalists*. Washington, DC. Available at: www.cision.com (Accessed: 2 April 2019).

Cheung, C. M. K., Lee, M. K. O. and Rabjohn, N, 2008. The impact of electronic word-of-mouth: The adoption of online opinions in online customer communities. *Internet Research*, Vol. 18, No. 3, pp 229–247. doi: 10.1108/10662240810883290.

Cheung, M. Y. *et al,* 2009. Credibility of Electronic Word-of-Mouth: Informational and Normative Determinants of On-line Consumer Recommendations. *International Journal of Electronic Commerce*, Vol. 13, No. 4, pp 9–38. doi: 10.2753/JEC1086-4415130402.

Chiu, C. M., Hsu, M. H. and Wang, E. T. G, 2006. Understanding knowledge sharing in virtual communities: An integration of social capital and social cognitive theories. *Decision Support Systems*, Vol. 42, No. 3, pp 1872–1888. doi: 10.1016/j.dss.2006.04.001.

Erkan, I. and Evans, C, 2016. The influence of eWOM in social media on consumers purchase intentions: An extended approach to information adoption. *Computers in Human Behavior*, Vol. 61, pp 47–55. doi: 10.1016/j.chb.2016.03.003.

Eysenbach, G, 2008. Credibility of Health Information and Digital Media: New Perspectives and Implications for Youth, in *Digital Media, Youth, and Credibility*. pp 123–154. doi: 10.1162/dmal.9780262562324.123.

F. Hair Jr, J. *et al,* 2014. Partial least squares structural equation modeling (PLS-SEM). *European Business Review*, Vol. 26, No. 2, pp 106–121. doi: 10.1108/EBR-10-2013-0128.

Hajli, N, 2018. Ethical Environment in the Online Communities by Information Credibility: A Social Media Perspective. *Journal of Business Ethics*, Vol. 149, No. 4, pp 799–810. doi: 10.1007/s10551-016-3036-7.

Huang, L.-T. and Kuo, F.-J, 2014. A Study on Travel Information Adoption Intention in the Online Social Community: The Perspectives of Customer Experience and Information Adoption Model. in *PACIS 2014 Proceedings*, pp 1–13. Available at: http://aisel.aisnet.org/pacis2014/84/.

Hussain, S. *et al,* 2018. Consumers online information adoption behavior: Motives and antecedents of electronic word of mouth communications. *Computers in Human Behavior*. Pergamon, Vol. 80, pp 22–32. doi: 10.1016/J.CHB.2017.09.019.

Ito, M. *et al,* 2008. Living and Learning with New Media: Summary of Findings from the Digital Youth Project. *Digital Media*. doi: 10.1111/j.1548-1379.2010.01107.x.

Kang, M, 2010. Measuring Social Media Credibility: A Study on a Measure of Blog Credibility. *Institute for Public Relations*, pp 59–68. doi: 10.1136/bmj.g5133.

Ko, D. *et al,* 2005. Antecedents of Knowledge Transfer in enterprise to clients consultants System Implementations. *MIS Quarterly*, Vol. 29, No. 1, pp 59–85.

KSEI, 2018. *21 Tahun KSEI: Inovasi Untuk Kenyamanan Transaksi di Pasar Modal*. Jakarta. Available at: http://www.ksei.co.id/files/uploads/press_releases/press_file/id-id/156_berita_pers_21_tahun_ksei_inovasi_untuk_kenyamanan_transaksi_di_pasar_modal_20190111170001.pdf.

Li, R. and Suh, A, 2015. Factors Influencing Information credibility on Social Media Platforms: Evidence from Facebook Pages. in *Procedia Computer Science*, pp 314–328. doi: 10.1016/j.procs.2015.12.146.

Madli, F. *et al,* 2018. *Identifying the Factors Influencing Information Usefulness and Information Adoption in Promoting Organ Donation through Social Media. Journal of Media and Information Warfare*. Available at: https://jmiw.uitm.edu.my/images/Journal/C3V112.pdf (Accessed: 3 April 2019).

McKnight, D. H. and Kacmar, C. J, 2007. Factors and effects of information credibility, in, p. 423. doi: 10.1145/1282100.1282180.

OECD, 2018. *OECD Economic Survey of Indonesia 2018*. Available at: http://www.oecd.org/eco/surveys/Indonesia-2018-OECD-economic-survey-overview.pdf (Accessed: 5 April 2019).

Otoritas Jasa Keuangan, 2016. *Survei Nasional Literasi dan Inklusi Keuangan 2016*. Jakarta.

Pitta, D. A. and Fowler, D, 2005. Internet community forums: An untapped resource for consumer marketers. *Journal of Consumer Marketing*, Vol. 22, No. 5, pp 265–274. doi: 10.1108/07363760510611699.

Sussman, S. W. and Siegal, W. S, 2003. Informational influence in organizations: An integrated approach to knowledge adoption. *Information Systems Research*, Vol. 14, No. 1, pp 47–65. doi: 10.1287/isre.14.1.47.14767.

Tseng, S.-Y. and Wang, C.-N, 2016. Perceived risk influence on dual-route information adoption processes on travel websites. *Journal of Business Research*. Elsevier, Vol. 69, No. 6, pp 2289–2296. doi: 10.1016/J.JBUSRES.2015.12.044.

Wathen, C. N. and Burkell, J, 2002. Believe it or not: Factors influencing credibility on the Web. *Journal of the American Society for Information Science and Technology*, Vol. 53, No. 2, pp 134–144. doi: 10.1002/asi.10016.

We are social, H, 2018. *Indonesia Digital Landscape, Special reports digital in 2018: worlds internet users pass the 4 billion mark*. Available at: https://wearesocial.com/blog/2018/01/global-digital-report-2018.

Westerman, D., Spence, P. R. and Van Der Heide, B, 2012. A social network as information: The effect of system generated reports of connectedness on credibility on Twitter. *Computers in Human Behavior*, Vol. 28, No. 1, pp 199–206. doi: 10.1016/j.chb.2011.09.001.

Yan, Q. *et al,* 2016. E-WOM from e-commerce websites and social media: Which will consumers adopt? *Electronic Commerce Research and Applications*, Vol. 17, pp 62–73. doi: 10.1016/j.elerap.2016.03.004.

Yang, S. U. and Lim, J. S, 2009. The effects of blog-mediated public relations (BMPR) on relational trust. *Journal of Public Relations Research*, Vol. 21, No. 3, pp 341–359. doi: 10.1080/10627260802640773.

DEFYING THE CERTIFICATION DIPLOMA FORGERY WITH BLOCKCHAIN PLATFORM: A PROPOSED MODEL

Meyliana[1], Yakob Utama Chandra[1], Cadelina Cassandra[1], Surjandy[1], Henry Antonius Eka Widjaja[1], Erick Fernando[1], Harjanto Prabowo[2], and Charles Joseph[3]

[1]*Information Systems Department, School of Information Systems, Bina Nusantara University Jakarta, 11480, Indonesia*
[2]*Computer Science Department, BINUS Graduate Program – Doctor of, Computer Science, Bina Nusantara University Jakarta, 11480, Indonesia*
[3]*Bloocys Foundation, Pte. Ltd. 079903, Singapore*

ABSTRACT

In the University setting, part of management recorded all education transaction since the students register until they graduate. In this point, the transaction raises several new and crucial challenges. At a closer look, the concerns appeared due to no data integration, verification, and validation from parties both inside or outside of the university. In this respect, the data is not centralized or integrated. As this backdrop, this causes repeated data confirmation, and no one can authenticate the data validity when distributed to other parties. In this point of entry, the diploma certification forgery has become one of the significant issues in education in Indonesia. As a framework that enables the data integration, Blockchain contains verified data on every single of a transaction, so the data is trustworthy. With this in mind, this paper aims to discuss the best blockchain model for the university level. This study is qualitative-based research. As a result, McRhys model is introduced as a potential and implementable blockchain model in university in Indonesia.

KEYWORDS

University, Blockchain, McRhys Model, Qualitative Research

1. INTRODUCTION

Amid the excitement, people are now experiencing a myriad of technologies enhancement in this digital era. In this context, technology adoption in a different culture transforms people's profession and routine. Bearing this in mind, people interact with a thousand of data and information around the world on daily based. As one of the agents of changes, education institution should offer a creative and distinctive way for all stakeholders to be empowered with technology. With this lens, people talk about data integration for decades. However, the fact recorded that not all information was integrated. In particular, people required data confirmation repeatedly to obtain valid information. In this direction, it spans organizations and people with open opportunities to have solely trusted information media and can be used widely for various purposes should the concept of data integration applied properly. Furthermore, the internet and technology have performed the best mission, not only storing information and communication but also enabling people to start thinking about something innovative invention with a bigger impact. For this voice, we are closer to blockchain concept (Tapscott and Tapscott, 2017) if we think about data-distributed, data-integration, higher security platform, ledger, database, storage, sharing data and connecting people with a real data, unmanipulated, and trustworthy eventually.

Equally important, the blockchain concept is close to the distributed open ledger. With a distributed open ledger, verified stakeholders (Government and industry) will validate all transaction and documents such as diploma certificate and transcript. In the validation and verification stage, the data is more accurate and trustworthy.

Among the researchers, blockchain phenomenon was published by Satoshi Nakamoto (Nakamoto, 2008) in 2008. In his publication, Nakamoto introduced some findings on Proof of Work, Distributed Open Ledger. In that regards, the technology of Blockchain has been used as a popular application presently, and Bitcoin cryptocurrency is the first manifestation (Devecchi *et al.*, 2017). The successful of blockchain framework technology has led many Big Companies such as Intel, IBM, Microsoft, to commence the research on blockchain.

Based on the blockchain research recently, blockchain technology can be used in near sectors of the industry due to some values provided by blockchain such as "immutable", "unchangeable", "validated", "shared & open". The concept of blockchain is very acceptable to support the collaboration, not only for bitcoin, but the blockchain is also widely studied for construction management (Turk and Klinc, 2017). In this perspective, blockchain is close to what we called as identity; every person requires a valid identity and recognition/approval from the government, university, industries, bank, and other relevant sectors. In particular, Blockchain could also be used in the education area. In common practice, the data for educational purpose is not integrated among the stakeholders; no one can approve and recognize your data unless you got certificated and reported. Because of these reasons, blockchain is very suitable to be applied in the education sector or university. Several previous studies researched to implement blockchain in the library process (Hoy, 2017) and also for study loan process (Gazali *et al.*, 2017).

Blockchain is an appealing topic of discussion among industries. In this corridor, the research focused on university blockchain in term of the use of blockchain for Diploma Certificate Issue, which on the certificate contains elements of immutable (cannot be replaced and valid all the time). In a specific context, this research is conducted to overcome the increasing number of forged diplomas abuse (Agriesta, Dheri, 2017). In 2015, the Ministry of Education in Indonesia reported 187 working bogus diploma owner in government (Linggasari, Yohannie, 2015). These issues were crucial, not only involving students but also the government staff (Andi Saputra, 2017), (Nur Aditya, 2017). In other words, this old issue (bbc.com, 2015) is still happening until at present. With this background, these phenomena demand a solution to prevent the issue in the future. In the public sector, The Ministry of Research, Technology and Higher Education has established a team to evaluate this diploma forgery issue (*Independensi*, 2017).

In university, blockchain model can be described as a collaboration among Government, Corporate/Industry, Institution of Certification, and the University itself that has the same interest to the data of student, alumni, lecturer, or teaching assistant. Based on university desideratum, the researchers create a new proposed blockchain model for university level, which called a "McRhys model" in Indonesia.

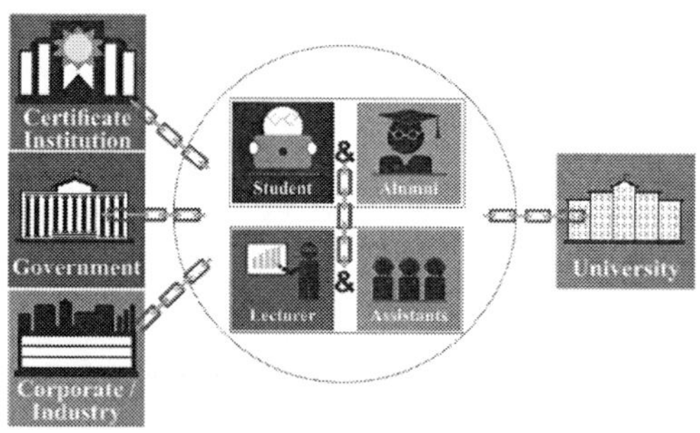

Figure 1. McRhys New Proposed Blockchain Model for University in Indonesia

McRhys is a model to record and integrate all activities in university with blockchain concept. McRhys model emphasizes on "Distributed Open Ledger". The data inside the blockchain is open to all stakeholder of the same interest with the data and information provided by the university. The transaction is validated peer to peer and verified.

The objectives of McRhys is to answer the problems because of a lack of data transparency, validity, and reliability of the score transcript. This score transcript is also used by industry to check the competency of their applicant and workers. Moreover, the industry requires less or no confirmation to the university if the concept of blockchain is applied appropriately. The industry accesses the data with ease to validate the employer.

At this stage, this study proposes two ways of identifying diploma certification fraudulent, namely illegal institutions issuing certificates or official institutions with data counterfeit (student never registered and followed the teaching and learning process, but received a diploma certificate). Based on this background, Blockchain represents a framework that can be used to surmount the problem of diploma certification forgery in education platform. At this line, qualitative research is used on this research to answer the question of

"How blockchain framework can be implemented to eradicate diploma certification forgery in university?". Moreover, the purpose of this study contributes to promoting the university in ensuring the data reliability and validity of the diploma certification and minimizing the misused information of diploma certification.

2. LITERATURE REVIEW

2.1 Blockchain

Blockchain is a new technology platform published by Satoshi Nakamoto (Nakamoto, 2008) and is used for almost one decade for cryptocurrency named Bitcoin. The success of Bitcoin drives other company to find the other way to implement blockchain in different industry and business. The concept is a financial transaction but without a financial institution. Bitcoin has become famous recently; there are many other examples of the success of bitcoin such as Litecoin, Peercoin, Ripple, and Ethereum Cryptocurrencies (Hoy, 2017).

Blockchain can also be implemented in the health industry (hospital) (Ahram, Sargolzaei, Sargolzaei, Daniels, & Amaba, 2017; Azaria, Ekblaw, Vieira, & Lippman, 2016; Hoy, 2017; Fanning & P. Centers, 2016; Karafiloski & Mishev, 2017), Education (Bdiwi, Runz, Faiz, & Cherif, 2017; Hoy, 2017), Manufacturing (Ahmed, Selena; Broek, 2017; Ahram et al., 2017), Financial (Treleaven, Brown, & Yang, 2017; Al-Saqaf & Seidler, 2017; Singh & Singh, 2016), Government (Hou, 2017), etc. In Education, commonly, blockchain is used for teaching and learning process (Bdiwi, Runz, Faiz, & Cherif, 2017) and also other research shows that blockchain is possible for the library (Hoy, 2017).

2.2. How Blockchain works

Blockchain draws a sequence transaction such as General Ledger. (Zheng *et al.*, 2017). In this frame, every block of blockchain has a hash or layered encryption. Validated data will be arranged in sequence order to be a chain and then distributed (distributed open general ledger).

Furthermore, the Blockchain concept also implements a Proof of Work concept. In this side, Proof of Work is also used in Bitcoin Network (Nakamoto, 2008). Proof of work is needed to validate each activity and create "hash key" in cryptography to ensure the security level for each level of the transaction.

2.3 Blockchain for University

Referring to the blockchain's ability to validate data and provide accurate information such as ledgers and their possible use in various fields, this reinforces the role of the blockchain that can be adopted at universities. (Tapscott and Tapscott, 2017). At a closer look, every transaction such as financial and other transaction such as teaching and learning, borrowing books, scoring, certification, can be recorded in the blockchain framework (Grech and Camilleri, 2017)

3. RESEARCH METHODOLOGY

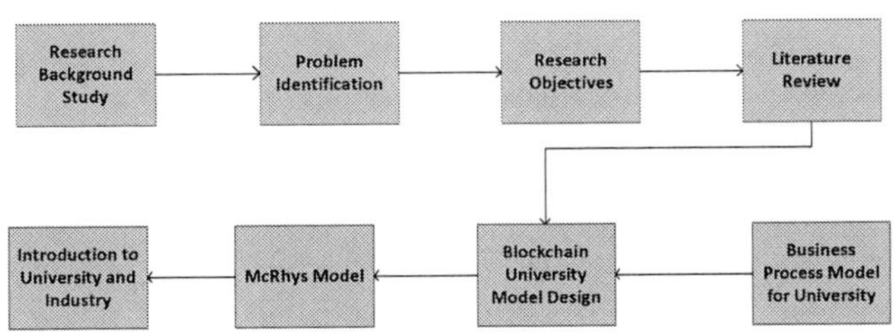

Figure 2. Research Methodology

3.1 Research Background Study

At the initial stage, the researchers found a phenomenon of diploma certificate forgery and highlighted a focal point of discussion and contemporary issue in Indonesia. The problem is not only from the illegal institution but also from the university that has a chance to publish a bogus certificate. In this setting, this is because of no valid verification from another key partner. As a result, a forged certificate leads to fake information and data accuracy. This issue drives the researcher to find the appropriate framework and model to be implemented.

3.2 Problem Identification

The research identified the increasing number of forged diploma certificate. In this line, people can obtain or purchase a certificate without joining the teaching and learning process. As described, this forgery symbolized a criminal act, and therefore, the government is required to cease it. It directs the research to find a method, a framework, and an idea on how to issue the real and verified certificate.

3.3 Research Objectives

In this part, the researchers defined the research objectives following the specific problem. At the same time, researchers figured out what the need is to solve the problem. The objective of this research is to provide open data and information which is auditable, valid, and reliable so that the students' portfolio and credentials are proven. For another counterpart, this also will help the industry to find the best talent for the company by using this blockchain model.

3.4 Literature Review

In this section, a literature review is conducted to help researchers finding the same interest in the topic to support this research. This research centres on blockchain implementation in university. The literature review will be the foundation of the blockchain model for the university.

3.5 Business Process Model for University

In this topic, the researchers also delved in and proposed the appropriate business process model for University. At the next level, the researchers decided the best solution for designing the model. As stated, the Business Process Model for University is obtained from the research. The research involved a survey of 58 universities in Jakarta. In this case, it reflects the formulated business model as a result (Meyliana, 2015; Meyliana, Hidayanto, & Budiardjo, 2015). The researchers applied the BPM model as the foundation for university blockchain.

3.6 Blockchain University Model Design

Based on all literature and business process models, Blockchain University Model Design was proposed to describe the overall process in universities and identify entities of each block.

3.7 McRhys Framework for University

McRhys Framework is a framework of blockchain for university. The framework shows the data integration and interaction of all stakeholders in the framework. With this framework, the reputations of the parties become indelibly. The research shows that data is always valid and verified for every block. Data is also can be used by other parties without confirming repeatedly. The process of issuing a diploma/bachelor certificate will always be validated, and certification forgery is eliminated because of the blockchain implementation. From the lesson, the industry and government will also access data easily.

3.8 Introduction to Universities and Industries

Based on the research, it confirmed the implementable state of McRhys Model in 24 universities in Jakarta as respondents. The respondents of selected universities represented top 100 rankings of universities in Indonesia from the Ministry of Research, Technology and Higher Education of the Republic of Indonesia and Webometrics. In this context, the researchers invited the respondents for this socialization stage to introduce the McRhys model.

4. RESULT AND DISCUSSION

Based on the business process model and discussion, the study concluded the process into one value chain of core business process in education. Figure 3 described the whole process of the value chain, which leads to the blockchain concept.

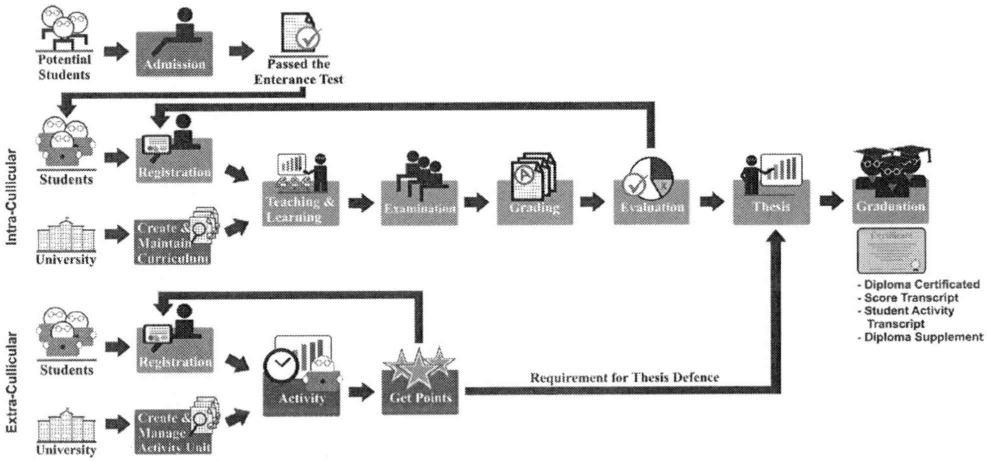

Figure 3. Value Chain of Core Business Processes in Education

4.1 Intra-curricular

After the graduation and selection of the intended university for higher education level, high school graduates must follow the registration process to become a university student. On the student side, the student completes all document required to Admission Front Office at first. After all fulfilled requirements, the candidate will take part in the entrance test. The entrance test might be different among universities. It depends on the stipulated standard. The student is required to re-register to become the active student as the candidate passes the test. The student data will be distributed from admission to the Student Registration and Scheduling Center, and the Student Services unit. Following that, the unit schedules the new student into Student Preparation Program. This program is to introduce the university closer to the student.

On the University side, Student Registration and Scheduling Unit creates a Lecture Scheduling by mapping the Lecturers, Students, Venue, and Time. While Academic Supporting Unit creates a curriculum for the faculty department, the faculty department will maintain the academic resources to be distributed to students every semester after the curriculum is published.

During the Teaching and Learning process, the Academic Operation Unit monitors the process and ensures everything is running on the right track. The Academic Operation Unit also records the attendance of lecturers and students. The examination reflects the evaluation process. Usually, the university runs the Mid Term Exam and the Final Exam to evaluate student comprehension holistically. After scoring the examination, lecturers input the student score on the Learning Management System provided by the university. Following the process, the Academic Operation Unit and Student Advisory Unit evaluate the score. The result of the score evaluation will determine the student eligibility for graduation. The ministry of higher education will receive the report of the scores and test results every semester through the Rectorate Unit. This process will be repeated every semester until the students graduate from the University.

At the final semester, students are required to take the thesis or final assignment and opt for a supervisor who guides them during the thesis supervision. Student Registration and Scheduling Unit also monitors the process of thesis submission and ensures all of the fulfilled requirements. The requirement such as Grade Point Average (GPA), credit passed, and student activity transcript. Once the student fulfils all the requirement, Student Registration and Scheduling Unit creates a Schedule for thesis defence and chooses examiner panellist who checks and verifies the student comprehension of the thesis. The panellist submits the score to Student Registration, and Scheduling Unit and the unit inputs the score into Learning Management Systems provided by the university.

At the next stage, Academic Operation Unit finalizes all student's score. This result determines the students' eligibility status to receive the graduation document, including Diploma Certificate, Score Transcript, Student Activity Transcript, and Diploma Supplement. The National Government issues a great number of diploma/bachelor certificates, and every student receives a unique code printed on the certificate. The government also receives the report of all eligible student through Rectorate Unit.

4.2 Extra-curricular

University manages and recommends student clubs or student association that bring students with the same interest to join activities for self-development in a different context. University facilitates the activities as long as the activity and group are registered and managed well. A student may choose the clubs to join based on the preference. The student accumulates the activity points by joining the activities. The Student Activity Unit evaluates the students and provides a point for students. The authorized centre calculates, inputs the point into the Learning Management System and the Student Activity Transcript as one of the requirements for a student to register for a thesis in the final semester.

4.3 McRhys Blockchain Student Registration and Course Registration Process

Figure 4 epitomized the detail of McRhys Model as the recommendation for University Blockchain.

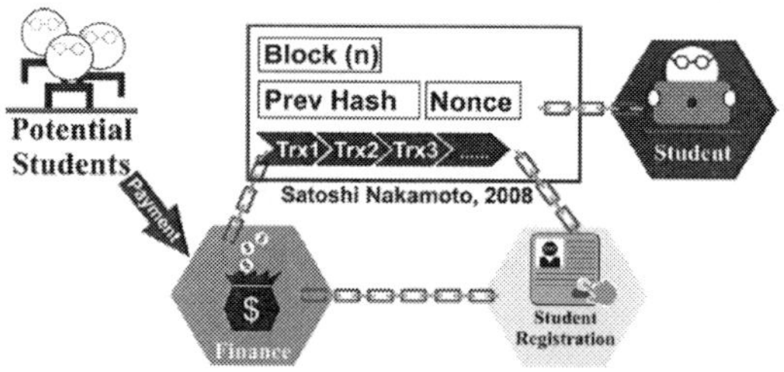

Figure 4. McRhys Blockchain Student Registration and Course Registration

"Genesis Block" or the first block is created when a student is registered and pays the settlement fee. After registration, all parties can access the new student. In this aspect, the parties consist of Marketing, Finance, SRC (Student Resource Center), and Academic Operation.

4.4 McRhys Blockchain University Scoring List Student Document

After a student is registered, all transaction will be recorded inside the blockchain such as courses, attendance, lecturer, venue, class, examination, and score. By using this concept, the forged diploma certificate is possible to be reduced because all of the transaction is validated and transparent, immutable, and unchangeable. The following process exhibits the detail of process on how McRhys model will help in fighting diploma certificate forgery issue. Figure 5 summarized the scoring based on McRhys Model.

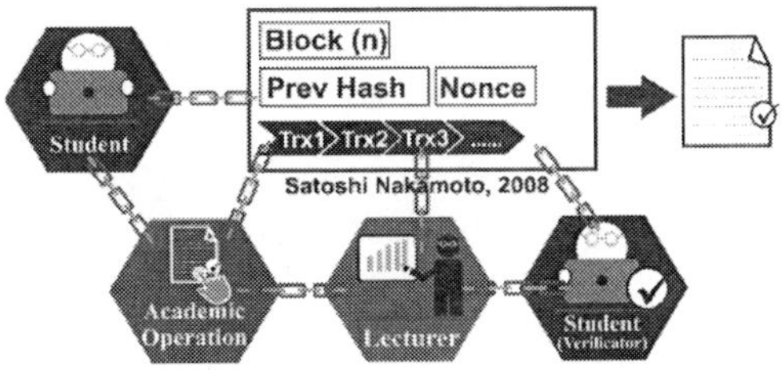

Figure 5. McRhys Blockchain University Scoring List Student Document

4.5 McRhys Blockchain University Diploma Certification

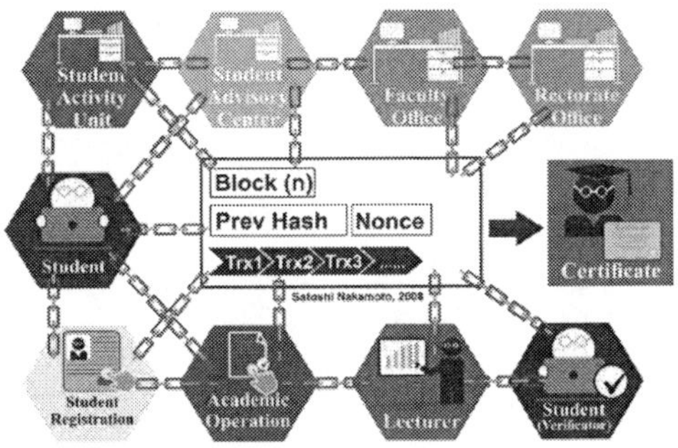

Figure 6. McRhys Blockchain University Diploma Certification

After a complete transaction, this step determines the eligibility of graduation. All decisions that will be permanently recorded and cannot be altered will be distributed to all related persons within this community. The use of blockchain in the education industry is possible because of the Immunity concept. The number of diploma certificates and the score transcripts are recorded in the certificate.

Figure 7 exhibits all transactions captured on the block and verified by the counterpart. For instance, the finance and student registration will verify student payment of the tuition fee and the transaction. The student will verify the courses schedule provided by the academic operation. For another example, when the student attends the class, the transaction will be verified by another student (verification) in the class (prefect) and the lecturer. Thus, figure 7 shows all the student transactions in the university that will be distributed to all parties after verification, validation, and the data is immutable. Therefore, the blockchain university transaction list can produce evidence of student attendance in the course. It means that the reliability and validity of university scoring list document can fight the forged data of diploma certificate. After students enrol in the last semester, the data of students will be submitted to the government, and they receive the registered number of diploma certification. The registered number will be published when students fulfil all requirements. All the transaction will be recorded to the blockchain university transaction.

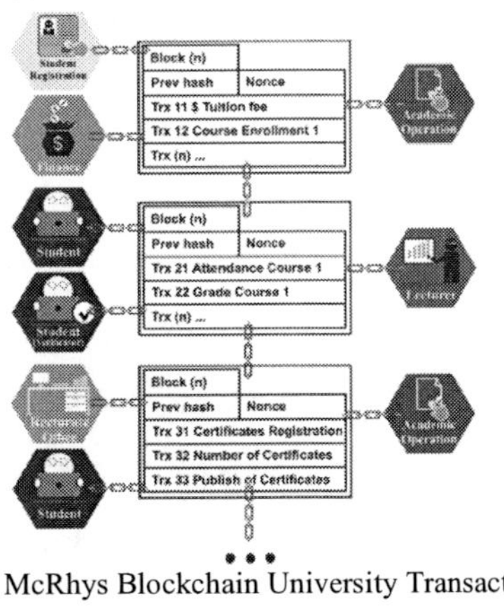

Figure 7. McRhys Blockchain University Transaction List

5. CONCLUSION

New proposed McRhys blockchain model is created based on the value chain of core business process in 58 universities in Indonesia. The data integration and centralized information offered by blockchain are similar to open data and general ledger. In this context, stakeholders can access the same data, and the data can be validated real-time. At the same time, this condition will keep the data up-to-date, validated, verified and accurate.

This concept of blockchain can solve the problem such as diploma certificate forgery which is an important contemporary issue nowadays in Jakarta. Because of no data validation, this provides an opportunity for a criminal to make a bogus diploma certification and sell it to people who requested. Not only illegal institution can provide this certification, but the universities can also publish diploma certification forgery. To anticipate this, McRhys model is proposed, which is driven by the blockchain model. In this scope, it offers data integration. It reflects that this concept is crucial for the university to keep the data validity and support the government to eradicate the diploma certification forgery.

6. IMPLICATION

In this research, the implication of this model will assist the university in Indonesia to obtain data validity without re-confirming the data repeatedly. This model is also bolstering the industry easier and more convenience in acquiring the background of their applicant and undertaking the verification. In this vein, the industry can hire an employee based on their preference and authorized data as well as repudiate data counterfeit.

7. LIMITATION AND FUTURE RESEARCH

This research is focusing on how blockchain can solve the problem of fake diploma certification. The result is an integrated value chain of core business processes, which allows the implementation of the blockchain model. Importantly, blockchain can solve many problems more than the diploma certificate issue. It highlights that future research should identify the different point of view of this research, elaborate more issue because of the novelty of this research area in education. In the future, blockchain technology and integration should be designed and implemented to provide evidence of data integration for university.

ACKNOWLEDGEMENT

This work is supported by the Directorate General of Strengthening for Research and Development, Ministry of Research, Technology, and Higher Education, Republic of Indonesia as a part of Penelitian Terapan Unggulan Perguruan Tinggi Research Grant to Binus University entitled "Implementasi Blockchain Platform untuk Menciptakan "Good Governance" pada Perguruan Tinggi" or "The Implementation of Blockchain Platform to Create "Good Governance" in Higher Education" with contract number: 12/AKM/PNT/2019 and contract date: 27 March 2019.

REFERENCES

Ahmed, Selena; Broek, N. ten, 2017. Blockchain Could boost food security. *Nature*, 550(7674), p. 43. DOI: 10.1038/550043e.

Ahram, T. *et al.*, 2017. Blockchain technology innovations. *2017 IEEE Technology and Engineering Management Society Conference, TEMSCON 2017*, (2016), pp. 137–141. DOI: 10.1109/TEMSCON.2017.7998367.

Al-Saqaf, W. and Seidler, N, 2017. Blockchain technology for social impact: opportunities and challenges ahead, *Journal of Cyber Policy*. Taylor & Francis, 0(0), pp. 1–17. DOI: 10.1080/23738871.2017.1400084.

Azaria, A. *et al.*, 2016. MedRec: Using blockchain for medical data access and permission management. *Proceedings - 2016 2nd International Conference on Open and Big Data, OBD 2016*, pp. 25–30. DOI: 10.1109/OBD.2016.11.

Bdiwi, R. *et al.*, 2017. Towards a New Ubiquitous Learning Environment Based on Blockchain Technology. *2017 IEEE 17th International Conference on Advanced Learning Technologies (ICALT)*, pp. 101–102. DOI: 10.1109/ICALT.2017.37.

Devecchi, C. *et al.*, 2017. Blockchain Educational Passport Blockchain Educational Passport: Decentralised Learning Ledger (DLL) Preceding white papers Proof-of-Concept: Authors. *Development Heads: Sajin Abdu (Technology)*, (Dll).

Fanning, K. and P. Centers, D,2016. Managing financial risk. *Australian Journal of Pharmacy*, 85(1011), pp. 440–441. DOI: 10.1002/jcaf.

Gazali, H. M. *et al.*, 2017. Re-inventing PTPTN study loan with blockchain and smart contracts. *ICIT 2017 - 8th International Conference on Information Technology, Proceedings*, pp. 751–754. DOI: 10.1109/ICITECH.2017.8079940.

Grech, A. and Camilleri, A. F, 2017. Blockchain in Education. *JRC Science for Policy Report*. DOI: 10.2760/60649.

Hoy, M. B, 2017. An Introduction to the Blockchain and Its Implications for Libraries and Medicine. *Medical Reference Services Quarterly*. Taylor & Francis, 36(3), pp. 273–279. DOI: 10.1080/02763869.2017.1332261.

Agriesta, Dheri, 2017. Menristek Dikti Minta Seluruh Pembuat Ijazah Palsu Ditangkap. medcom.id. 12 August 2017 [online]. Available at https://www.medcom.id/nasional/hukum/zNPdxngN-menristek-dikti-minta-seluruh-pembuat-ijazah-palsu-ditangkap (Accessed: 1 December 2018)

Karafiloski, E. and Mishev, A, 2017. Blockchain solutions for big data challenges: A literature review. *17th IEEE International Conference on Smart Technologies, EUROCON 2017 - Conference Proceedings*, (July), pp. 763–768. DOI: 10.1109/EUROCON.2017.8011213.

Nur Aditya, 2017. *Kasus ijazah palsu, ketua lembaga pendidikan di Samarinda ditangkap. merdeka.com.* 20 October 2017[online]. *Available at* https://www.merdeka.com/peristiwa/kasus-ijazah-palsu-ketua-lembaga-pendidikan-di-samarinda-ditangkap.html (Accessed : 1 December 2018)

Saputra, Andi, 2017. *MA Makzulkan Bupati Mimika karena Kasus Ijazah Palsu. detik.com.* 26 November 2017[online]. *Available at* https://news.detik.com/berita/d-3743651/ma-makzulkan-bupati-mimika-karena-kasus-ijazah-palsu (Accessed : 1 December 2018)

Linggasari, Yohannie, 2015. *Menteri Nasir: 187 Pemilik Ijazah Palsu Punya Jabatan Penting.* cnnindonesia.com. 27 May 2015[online]. *Available at* https://www.cnnindonesia.com/nasional/20150527145913-20-56045/menteri-nasir-187-pemilik-ijazah-palsu-punya-jabatan-penting (Accessed : 1 December 2018)

Meyliana (2015) *Social CRM in Higher Education: Model, Process, Channel Preference, and Critical Success Factors (Doctoral Dissertation)*. University of Indonesia.

Meyliana, Hidayanto, A. N. and Budiardjo, E. K, 2015. Evaluation of social media channel preference for student engagement improvement in universities using entropy and topsis method. *Journal of Industrial Engineering and Management*, 8(5), pp. 1676–1697. DOI: 10.3926/jiem.1652.

Nakamoto, S, 2008. Bitcoin: A Peer-to-Peer Electronic Cash System. *Www.Bitcoin.Org*, p. 9. DOI: 10.1007/s10838-008-9062-0.

bbc.com, 2015. *Praktek ijazah palsu perlu 'pengawasan ketat.* bbc.com. 4 June 2015[online]. *Available at* https://www.bbc.com/indonesia/berita_indonesia/2015/06/150603_indonesia_ijazah_palsu (Accessed: 1 December 2018)

Singh, S. and Singh, N.,2016. Blockchain: Future of financial and cybersecurity. *Proceedings of the 2016 2nd International Conference on Contemporary Computing and Informatics, IC3I 2016*, pp. 463–467. DOI: 10.1109/IC3I.2016.7918009.

Tapscott, D. and Tapscott, A., 2017. The Blockchain Revolution and Higher Education. *EDUCAUSE Review*, pp. 10–24. DOI: 10.1038/308683b0.

Independensi, 2017. *Tim Evaluasi Kemendikti Pastikan Jual Beli Ijazah di Universitas Negeri Jakarta. Independensi*.com. 22 September 2017[online]. *Available at* https://independensi.com/2017/09/22/tim-evaluasi-kemendikti-pastikan-jual-beli-ijazah-di-universitas-negeri-jakarta/ (Accessed: 1 December 2018)

Treleaven, P., Brown, R. G. and Yang, D., 2017. Blockchain Technology in Finance. *Computer*, 50(9), pp. 15–17. DOI: 10.1109/MC.2017.3571047.

Turk, Ž. and Klinc, R., 2017. Potentials of Blockchain Technology for Construction Management. *Procedia Engineering*. The Author(s), 196(June), pp. 638–645. DOI: 10.1016/j.proeng.2017.08.052.

Zheng, Z. *et al.*,2017. An Overview of Blockchain Technology: Architecture, Consensus, and Future Trends. *Proceedings - 2017 IEEE 6th International Congress on Big Data, BigData Congress 2017*, pp. 557–564. DOI: 10.1109/BigDataCongress.2017.85.

EDUCATION ON DIGITAL FORENSICS FOR WORKING PEOPLE AND GRADUATE STUDENTS IN JAPAN

Ryoichi Sasaki
Tokyo Denki University, 5 Senju- Asahi-Cho, Adachi-Ku, Tokyo, 120-8551 Japan

ABSTRACT

Security is becoming a very important technology for ICT, society and human beings. The importance of digital forensics, one of the security technologies has been recognized in Japan; however, in 2014, lectures on digital forensics were not offered at Japanese universities, and the shortage of experts in the field became a problem. Therefore, the authors planned to introduce digital forensics lectures at Tokyo Denki University for working people and graduate students. Lectures on digital forensics began in 2015 as part of a course called Cyber Security Studies Special Course for Working People and Graduate Students (CySec) with the support of the Ministry of Education, Culture, Sports, Science and Technology. This paper describes the needs, objectives, syllabus and other aspects of the lectures. We also discuss the results and student satisfaction with the lectures 4 years after their introduction.

KEYWORDS

Digital Forensics, Education, Japanese University

1. INTRODUCTION

Security is becoming a very important technology for ICT, society and human beings. The importance of digital forensics, one of the security technologies has been recognized in Japan; however, in 2014, lectures on digital forensics were not offered at Japanese universities, and the shortage of experts in the field became a problem.

Therefore, the authors decided to introduce digital forensics lectures for working people and graduate students at Tokyo Denki University. At that time, the Ministry of Education, Culture, Sports, Science and Technology (MEXT) was recruiting themes for graduate school programs for sophisticated education in advanced human resource development. Therefore, Tokyo Denki University proposed a special course on cyber security consisting of six subjects, including digital forensics. Our proposal was approved and lectures on digital forensics started in 2015 with financial support from MEXT. Although financial support from MEXT ended in March 2017, we have continued to offer these lectures.

In this paper, we first describe the history and current situation of digital forensics in Japan. Next, we discuss the needs of the digital forensics field, the purpose of the lectures, the lecture syllabus and the selection of lecturers and lecture contents. Finally, the trends in the number of students enrolled in the lectures over the 4 years since their introduction and the results of student satisfaction surveys are provided.

2. SHORT HISTORY OF DIGITAL FORENSICS IN JAPAN

In 1996, the National Police Agency started to deal with digital forensics issues in response to the Tokyo subway sarin gas attack conducted by Aum Shimrikyo cult members. The first company specializing in digital forensics was established in Japan in 2003. From that time on, the use of digital forensics in police work and in the private sector spread.

In 2004, the Institute of Digital Forensics (IDF) (IDF Homepage (n.d.)), a non-profit organization that aims to promote digital forensics and contribute to the realization of a healthy information technology society, was established. IDF members consist of security researchers, digital forensics engineers, people concerned with the law and digital forensics users. Both individual and group membership in IDF have increased constantly, as shown in Figure 1, and the number of digital forensic technology applications have also increased. The author of this paper has been a member of IDF since its foundation and served as chairman from 2011 to 2017.

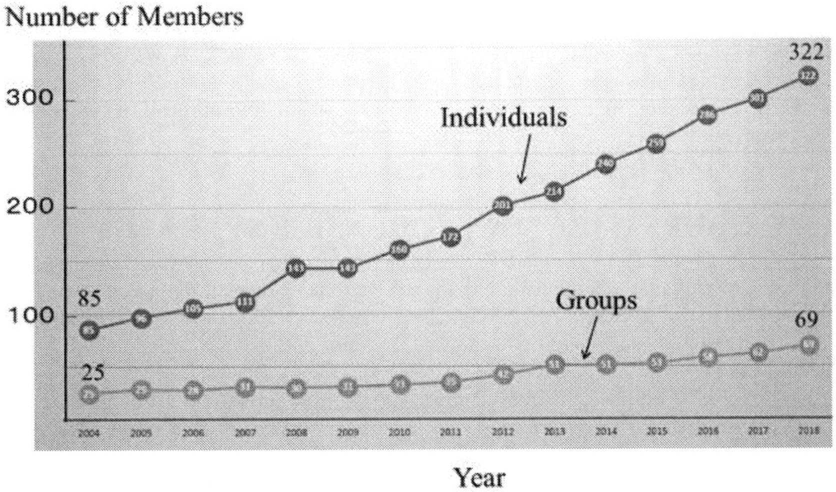

Figure 1. IDF Membership

From 2005 to 2007, a Japan-United States collaborative investigation on digital forensics was undertaken by Tokyo Denki University and Michigan University for encouraging research activities in Japan. In 2005, digital forensics was selected as one of the most important security technologies in a report published by the Japanese Cabinet Secretary. In 2006, the Encyclopedia of Digital Forensics was circulated by the publisher Nikka Giren under the supervision of IDF. The Fourth Digital Forensic International Conference, hosted by IFIP TC11, was held in Japan in 2008.

Until 2008, digital forensics education focused on self-study and on-the-job training within digital forensics companies. From around 2010, exercises and other activities were held at companies specializing in digital forensics and security education; however, due to the financial burden of such activities, the number of people receiving digital forensics education was limited.

Even as recently as 2014, digital forensics education at the university level was not available in Japan. To the best of our knowledge, Tokyo Denki University introduced the first digital forensics lectures in Japan in 2015.

3. OVERVIEW OF CYSEC COURSE

From 2015, Tokyo Denki University started a course in cybersecurity called CySec (CySec Homepage (n.d.)). CySec was designed for working people and graduate students with the support of MEXT. This course aims to nurture human resources to fulfill the position of Chief Information Security Officer (CISO). At the same time, we made it possible to provide students with practical experience in conducting simple security correspondence. CySec consists of the following six subjects:

1) Cyber Security Basics: This subject is in compliance with Certified Information Systems Security Professional which is an international information security and professional certification organized by International Information Systems Security Certification Consortium ((ISC)2 Homepage (n.d.)).

2) Cyber Defense Practical Exercise

3) Security Intelligence, Psychology, Ethics and Law

4) Digital Forensics

5) Information Security Management and Governance

6) Secure System Design and Development

When the course began, each lecture was 90 minutes and there was a total of 15 lectures for each subject. The lectures for the six subjects are held in both the spring and fall semesters, with lectures for three of the subjects held on evenings and weekends in both semesters.

Student may take lectures for all six subjects or only one. Since the course was financially supported by MEXT in its first two years, the tuition for all 15 lectures was 16,000 yen. After financial support from MEXT ended in 2017, tuition increased to 32,000 yen. However, the cost of the course is still considered affordable.

In order to offer the highest quality lectures, we recruited lecturers not only from academia, but also from experts in the private sector. We received much praise from instructors at other universities regarding our selection of lecturers.

4. CYSEC COURSE: DIGITAL FORENSICS SYLLABUS

In determining the syllabus, we investigated the educational contents of universities in the United States (Strzempka, K. (2010)) (Erbacher, R. (2003)) (Srinivasan, S. (2009)). We also conducted a questionnaire survey of prospective students, related government agencies and private companies to determine what topics should be included.

As shown in Table 1, Purdue University found that multiple topics should be included in digital forensics lectures.

Table 1. Model Course Proposed by Purdue University

Required Courses	Electives (Specialized Courses)
Introduction to Digital Forensics	Network Forensics
Advanced Digital Forensics	Mobile Device Forensics
Research in Digital Forensics	File System Forensics
Digital Forensics Capstone Course	Anti-Forensics
Thesis or Directed Project	Incident Response
	Digital Law
	Malware Forensics

We examined the syllabus of various overseas universities and selected 16 candidate items for lectures in each topic (Table 2). Here, to describe the procedure of digital forensic, the terms shown in Figure 2 as defined in Ref. (NIST SP 800-86 (2006)) are used.

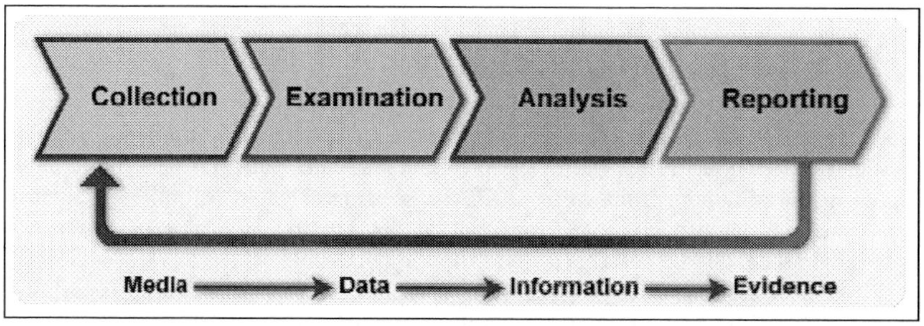

Figure 2. Digital forensics process

In addition, we conducted a questionnaire survey on candidate items with the following two participant groups:

(1) Students and university faculty, such as members of security-related academic societies and people enrolled in lectures on security at other universities (n=61).

(2) Superiors in private organizations who want their staff to receive digital forensics training (n=7).

The results are as shown in Table 2. The maximum score for each item was 4 points with higher scores indicating that the item is more desirable. Scores for SCADA (Supervisory Control and Data Acquisition) forensics and AI application items for E-Discovery were the lowest; therefore, these topics were not included in the lectures.

Table 2. Questionnaire results for candidate lecture items

No.	Lecture Item	Lecturer candidate	Dispatch source to lecture
1	Introduction to digital forensics	3.4	4.0
2	Hard disk structure, file system	3.1	3.9
3	Operating System for Digital Forensics	3.0	3.7
4	Basics of forensic work for hard disks	3.4	4.0
5	Data recovery technology	3.4	3.9
6	Data recovery tool exercise	3.3	3.5
7	Analysis technology of collected data	3.3	3.7
8	Digital Forensics Exercise	3.4	4.0
9	Forensic for SSD	3.2	3.7
10	Memory Forensics	3.4	3.6
11	Network forensics	3.5	3.7
12	Smartphone (mobile) forensics	3.3	3.6
13	Cloud forensics	3.3	3.7
14	SCADA Forensic	2.8	2.4
15	Legal literacy and court correspondence	3.0	3.4
16	Machine learning for E-Discovery	2.7	3.1

Considering these results, we created the following original syllabus. Here, lecturer names are given in parentheses.

1. Introduction to digital forensics (Prof. Sasaki)
2. Hard disk structure, File system technologies (Prof. Uehara)
3. Windows for forensics (Prof. Uehara)
4. Forensic work basics (Mr. Nozaki)
5. Forensic work, Data collection (Mr. Nozaki)
6. Forensic work, Examination including data recovery (Mr. Shirahama)
7. Forensic work, Analysis (1) (Mr. Shirahama)
8. Forensic work, Analysis (2) (Mr. Nozaki)
9. Forensic work exercise (Mr. Nozaki, Mr. Shirahama)
10. Network forensics (Prof. Yamaki)
11. Network forensic exercise (Prof. Yamaki)
12. Application of digital forensics (1): Case study of survey on intrusion (Mr. Nozaki)
13. Application of digital forensics (2): Case study of fraud accounting, E-discovery (Mr. Shirahama)
14. Law literacy and handling court (Mr. Sakuraba)
15. Future direction of digital forensics (Prof. Sasaki)

The titles and specialties of the above lecturers are as follows:

(1) Prof. Sasaki (Prof. of Tokyo Denki Univ.), Digital Forensics and Risk Analysis
(2) Prof. Uehara (Prof. of Ritsumeikan Univ.), Digital Forensics and Information Science
(3) Prof. Yamaki (Prof. of Tokyo Denki Univ.), Network and Artificial Intelligence
(4) Mr. Sakuraba (Lawyer), Civil Procedure Act and Digital Forensics
(5) Mr. Shirahama (Forensic Expert), Application of digital forensics
(6) Mr. Nozaki (Forensic Expert), Digital forensics in general

5. LECTURE IMPLEMENTATION AND EVALUATION

5.1 Current Syllabus

Over time, the syllabus was revised as described below to incorporate student feedback and new developments in the field.

From 2015 to 2016

(1) Because there was repetition in the "Introduction to digital forensics" and "Forensic work basics", these topics were combined into "Introduction to digital forensics".

(2) With increased smartphone use, student interest became stronger; therefore, we added "Mobile forensics".

(3) Application of digital forensics was combined into one lecture.

(4) We increased the number of digital forensics exercises from one to two.

From 2017 to 2018

In 2018, the university changed the time allocated for one subject from 15 90-minute lectures to 14 100-minute lectures throughout the university. Along with this change, we made the following additional changes.

(1) One of the two digital forensic exercises became a mobile forensic exercise.

(2) We decreased the number of lectures on data analysis from two to one.

Therefore, the current 2018/2019 academic year syllabus is as described in section 5.3.

5.2 Trends in Enrollment

The number of both working people and graduate students enrolled in the CySec course has changed over time, as shown in Table 3. The initial expected number of students was 20 working people and 20 graduate students; therefore, the number of students who are working has been larger than expected.

Table 3. Trends in the number of students enrolled in the CySec course

Fiscal Year	Workers	MSc Student	Total
2015	39	20	59
2016	36	20	56
2017	38	17	55
2018	35	14	49

As of 2018, there were many working students who were engaged in security at a vendor company and were trying to acquire more advanced security technology knowledge, as well as members of a Computer Security Incident Team (CSIRT) at user companies who require security knowledge and correspondence ability.

Though few students have been professionally engaged in digital forensics, four students involved with police organizations and public prosecutor offices have been engaged in digital forensics and wanted to upgrade their technical capabilities. The ratio of males to females in the lectures is 45 to 4. Most students are in their 30s, followed by students in their 20s, 40s, 50s and 60s.

5.3 Outline of Lectures at Present

Lectures are conducted using the book "Fundamentals and Practice of Digital Forensics" written by the lecturers and published in March 2017 (Sasaki, R (edited), 2017). The outline of each of the lectures is presented below.

(1) Introduction to digital forensics (Prof. Sasaki)

Here, the students can grasp the whole picture of digital forensics and are given the background knowledge necessary to learn about the topic in more detail. The following topics are introduced.

(a) What is digital forensics?

(b) Background of how digital forensics became important.

(c) Main procedures of digital forensics including examples.

(d) Terms related to digital forensics, such as network forensics and mobile forensics as illustrated in Figure 3.

(e) Digital forensics classification axis: Classification by subject using digital forensics, Acts subject to litigation, Types of litigation, and Operation form of information systems.

(f) Digital forensics technology corresponding to the procedure: Summary of prevention and detection technologies of falsification of logs and file recovery technologies.

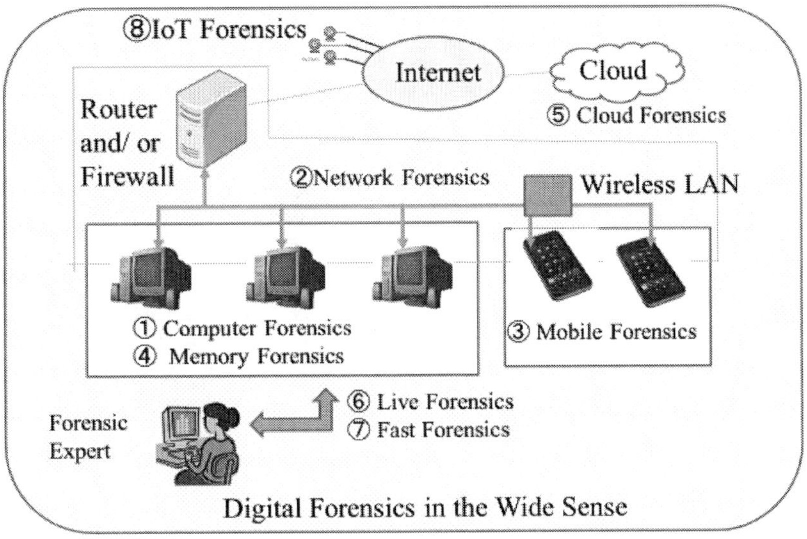

Figure 3. Forensics-related terms

(2) Hard disk structure, File system technologies (Prof. Uehara)

In order to develop concrete correspondence behaviors related to digital forensics, this lecture explains hard disk structure, flash memory structure and function, and file systems beginning with the fundamentals. In addition, somewhat more detail is provided about the type of erasure and the restoration methods that will be introduced in future lectures.

(3) Windows OS for forensics (Prof. Uehara)

Here, Windows is the target OS. In order to better understand digital forensics, a lecture on the fundamental functions of file systems, memory control, process control and data representation is given.

(4) Forensic work, Data collection (Mr. Nozaki)

As a method of gathering data for digital forensics from the target device, the lecturer introduces the advantages and disadvantages of using hardware, boot software and other software. In addition, the lecturer explains in a bit more detail how to deal with security settings. At the same time, the "Chain of Custody" is explained.

(5) Forensic work, Examination including data recovery (Mr. Shirahama)

Here, a concrete method of recovering data mainly using Autopsy (Autopsy homepage (n.d.)), which is an open source digital forensic tool, is explained. At the same time, the lecturer also describes the method of erasing data and a data concealment method using Alternative Data Stream (ADS).

(6) Forensic work, Analysis (Mr. Nozaki)

In this lecture, the lecturer mainly describes the analysis method using Autopsy. In order to aid understanding, we also define what a registry is, the difference in timestamps in the file system, the method of hash analysis, and various search methods.

(7) Forensic work exercise (Mr. Nozaki, Mr. Shirahama)

In this exercise, students learn how to recover deleted data and perform various kinds of searches using Autopsy. Figure 4 shows the results of recovering deleted jpeg files using Autopsy in the exercise.

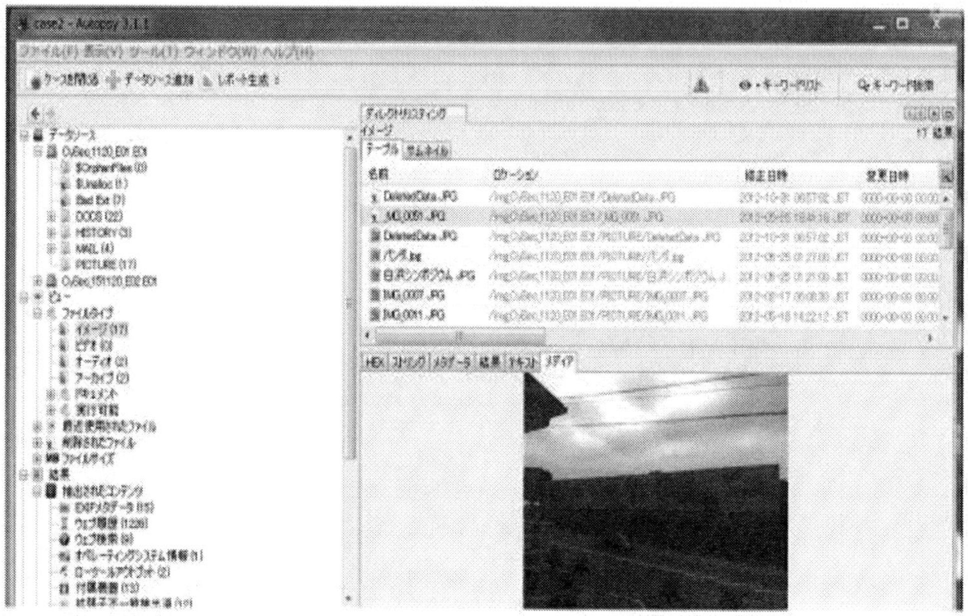

Figure 4. Recovered Picture Using Autopsy in Exercise

(8) Network forensics (Prof. Yamaki)

The lecturer explains network forensics, which refers to the capture, recording, and analysis of network events in order to discover the source of security attacks or other problem incidents.

(9) Network forensic exercise (Prof. Yamaki)

In this exercise, students learn concrete methods of grasping packets using Wireshark. At the same time, we allow students to analyze types of injustices based on the network log.

(10) Mobile forensics (Mr. Nozaki)

First, the lecturer gives background information on how mobile forensics for smartphones and other mobile devices has become important. Then, the difference between mobile forensics and forensics for personal computers is described. Next, the lecturer explains concrete data collection methods from the iOS terminal and Android terminal.

(11) Mobile forensics exercise (Mr. Nozaki)

In this exercise, students perform specific data collection from the Andoroid terminal.

(12) Application of digital forensics (Mr. Shirahama)

Examples of application to illegal entry into digital forensic servers and accounting fraud are described. In addition, methods of writing description reports are explained.

(13) Law literacy and handling court (Mr. Sakuraba)

First, the lecturer outlines trial mechanisms and digital forensics. Next, a simulated court as shown in Figure 5 is opened, and lawyers role play as judges, prosecutors, and digital forensic engineers. This exercise shows how a digital forensic engineer testifies in cases of taking confidential information.

Figure 5. Landscape of simulated court

(14) Future direction of digital forensics (Prof. Sasaki)

This lecture explains new and future directions of digital forensics. In 2017, the lecturer explained the trends of utilization of artificial intelligence for digital forensics and introduced the tool "LIFT", which we developed for intelligent network forensics (Sasaki, R. et al, 2018). In 2018, after the lecturer briefly introduced recent trends in digital forensics, a member of the CSIRT of a private company introduced the background of fast forensics and how it has become important, the tool they developed for that purpose, and concrete activities for fast forensics.

5.4 Trends in Student Satisfaction Surveys

In the first year of the CySec course, we conducted a student satisfaction questionnaire to determine whether the lecture contents were too easy or too difficult for working people and graduate students. The results showed that working people found the contents suitable, whereas graduate students found them somewhat difficult. Therefore, we decided to maintain the level of the lectures with the expectation that graduate students could study harder.

The results of student satisfaction surveys for each year are shown in Table 4. The maximum score for each item was 5 points. Since student satisfaction rose a little in the second year, it has remained high.

Table 4. Results of student satisfaction surveys

	2015	2016	2017	2018
Did your interest in digital forensics increase during this lecture?	4.2	4.7	4.6	4.4
Was a high level of expertise obtained?	4.2	4.6	4.5	4.5
Were you satisfied with this lecture?	4.4	4.6	4.7	4.6

Full score is 5 points.

The following comments were received from the students.

(1) This subject has a very orderly structure.

(2) The simulated trial was very good because it was possible to understand how digital forensics are used in court.

(3) My understanding greatly deepened by doing exercises such as the digital forensic exercise, network forensic exercise and mobile forensic exercise.

(4) By listening to Professor Sasaki's introduction to digital forensics, the whole picture can be grasped.

(5) By listening to Professor Uehara's lecture, the foundation was strengthened, and my understanding of the previous lecture deepened.

In addition to these high evaluations, we also received feedback on possible improvements.

(a) Students would like more exercises so that they can practice digital forensics work.

(b) Students want to learn more about memory forensics, live forensics, network forensics and other types of digital forensics.

To implement these changes, it is necessary to increase the number of subjects included in the lectures. In order to respond to request (a) above, Tokyo Denki University created a general foundation called CySec-Pro (CySec-Pro Homepage (n.d.)) and setup a digital forensic analyst course at the University in 2018. This is a digital forensics exercise-centered course consisting of 15 180-minute classes. Methods of responding to request (b) above are currently under consideration.

6. CONCLUSION

This paper described the needs, objectives, syllabus, implementation results, and student satisfaction with digital forensic lectures that we have been offering at Tokyo Denki University for the past 4 years.

Since these lectures have a good reputation, we would like to continue offering them in the future. At the same time, because there are very few universities in Japan that offer digital forensics education, we would like to contribute to the enhancement of digital forensics education in Japan.

ACKNOWLEDGMENT

I would like to express my gratitude to all of the digital forensics lecturers. I would also like to thank President Hiroshi Yasuda, Associate Professor Tomohide Ohkochi, and Associate Professor Yoshiro Kakizaki for their efforts to launch and continue CySec.

REFERENCES

(ISC)2 Homepage. Retrieved from https://www.isc2.org/. last accessed 2019/2/3.

Autopsy homepage (n.d.). Retrieved from https://www.sleuthkit.org/autopsy/, last accessed 2019/2/3.

CySec Homepage (n.d.). Retrieved from https://cysec.dendai.ac.jp/ (in Japanese). last accessed 2019/2/3.

CySec-Pro Homepage (n.d.). Retrieved from https://cysec-pro.org/course/, (in Japanese) last accessed 2019/2/3.

Erbacher, R (2003). Computer Forensics: Training and Education. Retrieved from https://www.researchgate.net/publication/2557555_Computer_Forensics_Training_and_Education. last accessed 2019/2/3.

IDF Homepage (n.d.). Retrieved from https://digitalforensic.jp/ (in Japanese). last accessed 2019/2/3.

NIST SP 800-86 (2006). Guide to Integrating Forensic Techniques into Incident Response. Retrieved from https://csrc.nist.gov/publications/detail/sp/800-86/final, last accessed 2019/2/3.

Sasaki, R (edited), 2017. *Fundamentals and Practice of Digital Forensics*, (in Japanese) Tokyo Denki University Publishers, Tokyo, Japan.

Sasaki, R. et al, 2018. Development and Evaluation of Intelligent Network Forensic System LIFT Using Bayesian Network for Targeted Attack Detection and Prevention. *International Journal of Cyber-Security and Digital Forensics*, Vol.7, No.4, pp 344-353.

Srinivasan, S (2009). Digital Forensics Curriculum in Security Education. Retrieved from https://dl.acm.org/citation.cfm?id=1940985. last accessed 2019/2/3.

Strzempka, K (2010). The Development of a Standard Digital Forensics Master's Curriculum. Retrieved from http://docs.lib.purdue.edu/techmasters/8/. last accessed 2019/2/3.

SOCIAL INCLUSION OF BRAZILIAN PEOPLE WITH DISABILITIES THROUGH THE LENS OF CRITICAL THEORY OF TECHNOLOGY

Patricia da Silva Leite and Leonelo Dell Anhol Almeida
Postgraduate Program in Technology and Society (PPGTE)
Research Group Xuê: Participation, Interaction and Computing
Federal University of Technology - Paraná (UTFPR) - Brazil

ABSTRACT

Technology is one of the sources of power more relevant in modern society. For that reason, technology is a social battlefield and a resource under power disputes. Technology is created and adapted to reproduce and incorporate society values as social groups who control technology creation. Thus, none technology is neutral or detached of a context. Instead, technology is an instrument used to change our society, at the same time that is reassembled by us. Considering that, critical theorist Andrew Feenberg elaborated the "Critical Theory of Technology" which discusses issues about technology in our society and the relationship between these two interrelated entities. Based on that, this paper critically analyzes the relationship of people with disabilities movements and technology and society changes, particularly with examples from the Brazilian context. We finish this research emphasizing the need for discussions and critical analysis about the democratization of technology and how this can provide a more equal and inclusive society.

KEYWORDS

Democratization of Technology, People with Disabilities, Social Inclusion, Critical Theory of Technology

1. INTRODUCTION

Technology, such as other systems and artifacts on our society act as instrumental support to reach objectives or impose wills, and with that, technology is an instrument of power in several segments as social, cultural, historical, political and economic. Thus, technology and decision related to its design and development became a social battlefield and a place of power disputes in our society (Feenberg, 2010; Neder, 2013).

Considering these topics, critical theorist Andrew Feenberg proposes the "Critical Theory of Technology". That theory is based on discussions of previous generations of "Critical Theory", with theorists such as Jürgen Habermas and Herbert Marcuse, among others, and approaches issues about values incorporated in technologies and how the democratization of its development process could result in a better society to people.

According to Feenberg (2013), modern society is organized surrounding technology, which indicates that changing the values embedded in technologies, and their producing processes could result in society shifts. This statement is also valid when we consider that society changes also perform technologies changes and all this occurs because technology and society are intrinsically related (Feenberg, 2010).

Feenberg's theory indicates that social groups excluded from technology development's decision process protests and do movements to express their dissatisfaction with the sociotechnical status. These movements indicate the possibility to expand the decisions about technologies to a more comprehensive scale, in which non-dominants groups concerns could also be considered in technology redesign (Feenberg, 2005). These actions may culminate in an increase in the social interests (Feenberg, 2010), and then the democratic transformation of technology could bring about economic, social, cultural, political, and historical changes.

With the discussion of social transformations through technological changes and as a means to strengthen his theoretical proposal, Feenberg presents examples of how non-dominant groups exert political pressure on society to have their demands recognized and, in some cases, reached. Examples include situations such as the criminalization of child labor in 19th century England, changes in technologies such as Minitel in France in the 1980s, and others.

Our focus in this paper are people with disabilities movements regarding democratization of technology such as war veterans with physical disabilities protests for environments free of locomotion barriers in 1950-1960 in the United States; books written with people with disabilities concerning technologies development in 1998, presenting examples of how incorrect projects hinder people with disabilities' locomotion; among others. And we choose to use the "Critical Theory of Technology" since this theory act as lenses to tint or fade objects (Halverson, 2002; Rogers, 2012), and in this paper, such tinted objects are discussions on the relationship between society and technology. Furthermore, this theory already was used to analyze cases about that relationship, as Feenberg and other authors present, without focusing on people with disabilities examples.

Feenberg's theory approaches (1) the technologies creation and its relation with the social context; (2) the fact that social inequality in decisions on technology projects contribute to social injustice; and (3) examples to show how public involvement in technology design makes a difference in the sociopolitical context. Based on these points, Feenberg elaborates two primary theses (Cupani, 2017; Feenberg, 2002):

1. Technological development is overdetermined by both technical and social factors, so that it can branch in several directions, according to the values and power of the dominant groups;
2. Social groups adapt to technological development, and the adaptation process is reciprocal. Thus, technology changes according to its production context, at the same time it influences the production context.

From the points proposed by Feenberg's Critical Theory of Technology, it is possible to accomplish discussions about how non-dominant groups, particularly people with disabilities, can have their demands satisfied through social protests and mobilizations that culminate in changes in technology and more democratic practices related to technology. Thus, this paper aims to discuss Feenberg's theory regarding examples about the rights of people with disabilities movement and how their results or related actions can perform changes in technology and society. Our focus are examples of these movements regarding Brazilian contexts, particularly cases related to internet use and governmental regulations, though we present examples of other movements occurred in other countries. The instrument used in this paper to analyze these examples, are the two hermeneutic dimensions proposed in Feenberg's theory.

This paper is organized as follows: the second section presents important details of Feenberg's Critical Theory of Technology; the third section presents our discussions on how people with disabilities movements can be articulated with Feenberg's theory and examples of these connections; finally, the last section presents our final remarks and further research appointments.

2. FEENBERG'S CRITICAL THEORY OF TECHNOLOGY

In addition to critically extending discussions held by the early generations of critical theorists such as Max Horkheimer, Theodor Adorno, Walter Benjamin, Jürgen Habermas, and Herbert Marcuse, Feenberg bases his theory on the critical discussion of various theories that advocate technology dependence in modern society; theories that use as argument forms of technological determinism. From this critical analysis, Feenberg elaborates his non-deterministic theory of modern society, the Critical Theory of Technology, which emphasizes contextual aspects of technology that are ignored by the dominant view (Feenberg, 2010).

As a starting point to discussing the possibility of democratization of technology, Feenberg (2010) presents his reason to refute the fundamental argument against industrial democracy[1], which is based on Max Weber's theory of rationalization, a theory followed by intellectuals such as Heidegger and McLuhan. The argument of this theory indicates that rationalization plays a fundamental role in the increasing control of social life in order to imposes an authoritarian social hierarchical structure, in a context of apparent autonomy of technology. Feenberg argues that there must be other alternatives to rationalizing society so that it is more democratic and holds other values such as liberty and individuality. In addition, he argues that the examples used against industrial democracy are identified with specific technologies created in the last century in the West, so that can not be related to an entire universal dimension of modernity (Feenberg, 2010).

From this discussion about the possibility of a new rationality of society, more democratic and participative, Feenberg analyzes three theories of technology (technological determinism, social constructivism, and

[1] Feenberg's reference to Karl Marx studies, about the democratization of the work domain as well as political domain.

indeterminism) to articulate his theoretical proposal. He points out the need to change the definition of technology, so that it "can no longer be considered as a collection of devices nor, more generally, as the sum of rational means" (Feenberg, 2010, p. 13). With this new definition of technology's concept, he argues that technology must be understood as a social object that is subjected to interpretation as any cultural artifact so that it is not possible to ignore the connections between technology and society (Feenberg, 2010).

Feenberg's interpretation of the technical object admits two hermeneutic dimensions: the social meaning and the cultural horizon. Social meaning is related to functional logic of technology, which may have a conflict of use interpretations, or have different definitions according to the characteristics of its components that contribute to attribute meaning to objects. Thus, "differences in the way social groups interpret and use technical objects are not merely extrinsic but make a difference in the nature of the objects themselves" (Feenberg, 2010, p. 15). This point is very important in the critical theory of technology by refuting arguments of technological determinism, which indicates that social groups need to adapt to technologies, particularly by believing that they are universal structures, argument refuted by Feenberg.

The cultural horizon, the second hermeneutic dimension of the technical object, is related to the fundamental forms of social hegemony. The conception adopted to form the cultural horizon refers to the configuration of the social power of a society, which has its base and strength in culture (Feenberg, 2010). This dimension of the technical object contributes in Feenberg's discussion to expresses the possibility to create different technologies, with different values, from the moment they are based on new rationality of society; such as an inclusive and democratic society.

With the two hermeneutic dimensions of the technical object, Feenberg elaborates the argument that the social and technical aspects of technology are inextricably involved in the same object (Feenberg, 2010). By analyzing technology in this way, it is possible to understand its power in society, since technologies are selected and designed based on the interests of specific groups that, through cultural and political power, define the cultural horizon under which technology will act. From the moment a technology is introduced into society, it begins to act as a material validation of the cultural horizon and consequently of the values that it incorporates (Feenberg, 2010). Moreover, these dimensions indicate the ability of social groups to adapt to technological development, at the same time that technologies are adapted to social changes, meaning a process of reciprocal modification (Cupani, 2017; Feenberg, 2010).

Based on the points presented to substantiate the Critical Theory of Technology, Feenberg argues that it is the perception of these possibilities of changes and deformations in the technologies that foment political movements towards the transformation of technology and society (Cupani, 2017). Feenberg's argument is based on the fact that the dominant groups of the technical code do not have enough strength to silence or erase the groups and communities that mobilize themselves to make their opinions and desires known. Examples of non-dominant groups movements and actions regarding technology are:

- Protests against the implementation of nuclear power plants next to urban areas (Feenberg, 2010);
- E-mail's changes over the years; which was introduced by skilled users and was not part of the designers' plans to be used as a worldwide communication tool (Feenberg, 2006);
- Child labor criminalization in the 19th century in England (Feenberg, 2010);
- Minitel transformation into a communication and entertainment tool (Feenberg, 2010);
- The case of the United States steamboat boilers in 1852, which represented the first technology that the US government subjected to regulation (Feenberg, 2010);
- AIDS patients' dispute in the 1980s who required participate in the new drugs tests to treat that disease (Feenberg, 1995; 2010);
- The movement of people with physical disabilities in the 1970s in the United States who protested against the adoption of technologies (machines, instruments, roads, sidewalks, transportation facilities, among others) that did not contemplate their disabilities, constraining their autonomy and independence (Cupani, 2017).

The Critical Theory of Technology discussions are based on examples such as those presented before to indicate a tendency for people participation in decisions of technology design and development. That kind of openness can expand into areas in which only experts and technicians have the power to decide about the developed technologies (Feenberg, 2006). Feenberg's perspective is that this tendency will reach larger spheres, in which population involvement in decisions about the technical structure influences the ways of life of society so that it would result in a better world (Feenberg, 2006). However, it is important to note that the society's shift toward the democratization of technology is replete of tensions and power disputes. That is the reason to

Feenberg's argument on the need to talk about more modestly of democratic interventions into technology, not a utopian democracy of techniques (Feenberg, 2006).

Finally, it is important to emphasize that the Critical Theory of Technology has other elements and particularities not approached in this article. However, we expect the content discussed in this paper presents sufficient points to consider the use of the Feenberg's theory in contexts and examples different from those shown by the theoretician and from this to foment discussions about the technology development and its democratization.

3. CRITICAL THEORY OF TECHNOLOGY AND SOCIAL INCLUSION OF PEOPLE WITH DISABILITIES

Feenberg's Critical Theory of Technology and the examples and questions presented previously contribute to the study of other political and social movements related to technologies. One of these is the rights of people with disabilities movement.

Events related to the rights of people with disabilities have taken place over the years in several regions of the world. Examples of these movements are:

- The case of war veterans with physical disabilities who protested for environments without locomotion barriers in the decade of 1950-1960 in the United States, that resulted in the first American norms of accessibility in buildings (Sassaki, 2011);
- The discussion on the inadequacy of the medical model of disability in South Africa, in the 1980s, culminating in the elaboration of the motto "Nothing about us, without us" and in the future amendment of United Nations (UN) documents on the medical model of disability (Sassaki, 2011);
- The publication of books with people with disabilities' participation in the development of technologies in 1998, such as *Nothing about us without us: developing innovative technologies for, by and with disabled persons* (David Werner, 1998), as a means of presenting examples of how incorrect projects are detrimental to the lives of people with disabilities (Sassaki, 2011);
- Madrid Declaration presentation in 2002, which explicitly indicated the need to adequately represent people with disabilities in media (Sassaki, 2011);
- The creation of one of the most important documents for the rights of people with disabilities, the Convention on the Rights of Persons with Disabilities (CRPD), presented in 2006 with the signature of 158 countries in its opening. It describes and codifies the rights of people with disabilities and outlines how they might be achieved (Ladner, 2014).

Based on global rights of people with disabilities movement, we focused on some examples of the Brazilian context as our discussion context in the following sections.

3.1 The Brazilian Context

Among the results of the rights of people with disabilities movement is the Brazilian Inclusion Law (LBI), considered as one that instigates clearer and more objective technological changes in Brazil. The law has been in conception for 15 years, and in addition to being compatible with the terms presented in the CRPD, explores issues such as access to information and communication technology (ICT), which were previously not mandatory or were not specified in detail (Brasil, 2015; Gabrilli, 2015).

While Article 21 of the CRPD declares that Nations that have signed the convention should "encouraging the mass media, including providers of information through the Internet, to make their services accessible to persons with disabilities" (United Nations, 2019), LBI, in its article 63, makes this action mandatory. Thus

accessibility is obligatory on websites maintained by companies with headquarters or commercial representation in the country or by government agencies for people with disabilities use, ensuring access to the available information, in accordance with best practices and accessibility guidelines adopted internationally.

This and the other modifications proposed in the LBI, related to CRPD or other regulations, stimulate changes in the technologies of our society. In the specific case of LBI's article 63, the changes can already be perceived in official documents to facilitate a standardized web accessibility implementation, such as "Accessibility Model in Electronic Government" (eMAG) – a guideline to development and adaptations of the government digital content (Brasil, 2014). Websites of public institutions, as indicated in the law, are also in the process of being updated for implementing accessibility features. Some cities such as São Paulo established a partnership with "Permanent Commission for Accessibility"[2] to organize a digital accessibility certificate to identify websites that comply with guidelines and recommendations such as eMAG and WCAG (Junior, 2018; Prefeitura de São Paulo, 2018). The movement "Web for all", a response to LBI, proposes a meeting point for institutions, developers and people with disabilities in order to mobilize society for debate about digital accessibility, and to help to transform the Brazilian web into an inclusive environment for all (WPT, 2019).

The cases of explosive boilers in the United States in 1852 and the criminalization of child labor in 19th century in England (Feenberg, 2010) are references to analyze the relationship between the discussions proposed by Feenberg and the movement of people with disabilities, such as the LBI and the technical changes triggered in websites accessibility. In this case, we understand that changes were made in society through people with disabilities protests and their participation in circumstances such as LBI formulation. Following we highlight some examples of these changes:

- Changes in public and private websites for implementation of accessibility features, resulting in technological and cultural changes;
- Architectural, cultural, or political changes that are influenced by changes in technologies such as the creation of access ramps for people with physical disabilities or mobility constraints;
- Ensuring the inclusion of people with disabilities at the university, culminating in structural, cultural, and political changes in universities, that need to adapt their environments and services to attend this public.

Thus, technological changes promoted by the LBI, which was created in response to protests by non-dominant groups, reinforce Feenberg's arguments by indicating the existence of technical and social aspects in the technologies, and how they can be adapted by society. Furthermore, the LBI changes can provide web accessibility to 57% of Brazilian with disabilities, who access the Internet daily (NIC.br, 2017).

3.2 LBI and the Two Hermeneutic Dimensions of the Critical Theory of Technology

Specifically, in the case of web accessibility motivated by LBI, it is possible to consider that the social meanings, the first hermeneutic dimension of Feenberg's theory, of accessible websites can be:

1. Created by people with disabilities who have access to information, citizenship, culture, and entertainment websites;
2. Interpreted by people without disabilities who can understand the importance of implementing accessibility features, even if they do not need to use them;
3. Interpreted by professionals who create or apply accessibility features on websites: (a) they have the opportunity to understand their role as citizens and seek ways for more people to have access to information; (b) according to the Brazilian Internet Steering Committee (2015), professionals can understand that action as an opportunity to bring new consumers for their products.

Regarding the cultural horizon, second hermeneutic dimension of Critical Theory of Technology, it is important to highlight the involvement of several groups in the LBI definition (politicians, people with disabilities, general society members, among others); and other groups work in the implementation of accessibility features of websites (programmers, designers, advertisers, journalists, testers, among others) (Gabrilli, 2015). With these groups' involvement and despite tensions and disputes, their main goal and values were aligned during the discussion of LBI concepts or to the creation of accessibility resources, which in this case are values and objectives related to the social inclusion of people with disabilities through ICTs. In this sense, the change in rationality discussed by Feenberg is shown to be possible, reinforcing elements pointed out in the Critical Theory of Technology by the theoretician. In LBI's case, the rationality was the social inclusion of people with disabilities, and these values are reflected on LBI as well.

Another example of web accessibility, but not directly related to LBI, is the use of hashtags #ToBlindSee, #Accessibility, #TimelineAccessible, among others, as a mechanism to provide alternative text for images or events description in social networks like Facebook and Twitter and thus complement the caption of a post, particularly postings whose subject matter refers to images (Pagani, 2018). The use of these hashtags is a way that people in Brazil have found to include a feature that these social networks did not provide in their original project (Pagani, 2018).

---

[2] A public organization of São Paulo City that works combined with the Secretary of the Person with Disabilities of São Paulo (SMPED) and is composed of representatives of several public agencies, and civil society.

This type of action is remarkable for people with disabilities, who are also social networks users, to have access to information and content of several sources, such as entertainment, science, education, journalistic communication, among others (Souza; Siqueira, 2017). In addition, these actions indicate the recognition of people with disabilities as an intended audience of content, web resources and technologies, since these actions introduce ways for people with disabilities to access, understand and interact with online content (Souza; Siqueira, 2017).

It is important to emphasize that the actions of several groups and companies by using the hashtags could result in a technological change in social networks. We understand this because Facebook and Twitter did not have options to include image alternative text until 2016 (Anderson, 2016; Todd, 2016), and the use of hashtags was proposed in 2012 in Brazil (Braille, 2012). In this way, we understand that social networking technology changed, as well as in the e-mail example and Minitel (Feenberg, 2000), what reinforces Feenberg's argument about technology adaptations initiated by society; and the use of hashtags reinforces the society's change as well as a technological change. Nevertheless, even whether people reassemble the technology to accomplish their needs, we cannot assure the adjustments on those social networks is exclusively related to the the hashtags case, for the reasons that this affirmation demand more investigations on the process and causes for technology modification.

Related to one of the two hermeneutic dimensions elaborated by Feenberg, we consider that the social meaning of the hashtags use can be interpreted by the rights of people with disabilities movement as a way of denouncing the technological problems and a way to present the agenda of real and important problems in society, especially related to information access, with other groups (web developers, public and private institutions, among others) mobilized to attempt to solve the problem (Souza; Siqueira, 2017). People with disabilities who use social networks are also benefited by the hashtags use, for the reason that they can be connected with their friends and family and have a channel for social interaction, through social networks, as well as access to information (Souza; Siqueira, 2017).

Related to the cultural horizon, Feenberg's second hermeneutic dimension, it is possible to highlight two power configurations at different moments. One configuration in the use of the hashtag and another in the technology adaptation of social networks.

The groups involved in the use of hashtags in social networks has as its members people from non-dominant power groups, who wish to have their demands listened and satisfied, which characterizes the cultural horizon with the values of social inclusion of people disabilities that are incorporated into technologies through the use of hashtags. This activity leads to technological change that is controlled by, as Feenberg (2010) calls, the "masters of technical systems" (corporate and military leaders, and professional associations of groups such as physicians and engineers), which in response to the use of hashtags, modifies the social networks technologies and incorporates in it values of social inclusion of people with disabilities. In this way, the actions performed by the people using the hashtags induced adaptations in the technology and in the values incorporated in it. This illustrates the inextricability of technical and social aspects of technology, as Feenberg affirms, and also exposes the possibility that by democratizing the design of technologies, they incorporate more human values and influence the accomplishment of a more inclusive society.

Although Feenberg's two hermeneutic dimensions can be used as an instrument to analyze social movements that demand technological changes, it is important to emphasize that there are relevant points in such analyzes, which are not considered in such analysis. An example of this may be associated with the technical object development that, although it may be related to the two hermeneutic dimensions, is not addressed particularly by any of them. Thus, in addition to considering the way the object is interpreted in society (the first hermeneutic dimension) and the social configuration that incorporates its values in the structure of the object (second hermeneutic dimension); can be relevant to consider the development process of that object, the people involved and the decisions of this process that resulted in the artifact used in society. In considering this other aspect of the technical object, it may be possible to understand in greater depth unfoldings of it in society, as well as the possibilities of modifications made later. Furthermore, by investigating the technology development process, through Feenberg's hermeneutic dimensions, we can also contribute to thinking about how the inclusion of people with disabilities can take place in projects that are defined as inclusive from the beginning.

4. CONCLUDING REMARKS

Considered a part of society, technology can be modified to propitiate changes in society, since, according to Cupani (2017), this constitutes the "material structure" of modern society. Based on this relationship between society and technology, Feenberg elaborates his Critical Theory of Technology that, as presented throughout this paper, proposes discussions about the power exerted through technology in modern society and how it causes changes in the society that consumes and produces it, at the same time that it is changed by the society. In this sense, Feenberg declares that technology incorporates values and interests from the dominant classes that determine how technologies are so that these values are engraved in the technologies' designs and procedures (Cupani, 2017). In this way, technology cannot be understood as a neutral instrument in society, but rather an artifact involving disputes of power and social control (Cupani, 2017; Feenberg, 2010).

In order to achieve social and technological changes, Feenberg understands that it is necessary the processes of technologies development be more democratic, so non-dominant social groups have their demands and values considered and inserted in the technologies design. In this way, both society and technologies can reach more coherent values to the people needs and well-being.

Based on Feenberg's theory propositions, we were able to analyze and discuss how social groups can mobilize themselves to bring changes in society through technology or changes in technology that culminate in social changes. Examples of this are presented by Feenberg to verify his theoretical proposal, as well as to refute theories that advocate for technological determinism. In this sense, the objective of this paper was to discuss how some actions related to the rights of people with disabilities movement in Brazil opened space for changes in technology and society.

The examples presented in this paper on some questions about web accessibility to meet the needs and demands of people with disabilities indicate how it is possible to base the concepts presented in the Critical Theory of Technology for analytical evaluations or actions regarding accessibility and social inclusion aspects related to technology and its development. In this sense, these examples contribute to highlight the means to produce and redesign technologies with more inclusive values so that people with and without disabilities have access to the same contents and opportunities, providing a more democratic and inclusive society.

It is important to emphasize that the examples presented and discussed in this paper are still an initial step towards the social inclusion of people with disabilities and the democratization of technology and that can not be limited to what has been achieved, even if they exemplify courageous actions in our society. Thus, there is an opportunity to rely on these examples and on the critical theory of technology to discuss other mechanisms and schemes used by the dominant groups to maintain their power, and through these examples and theories, to discuss social and technological changes in favor of more democratic, responsible and inclusive society.

Finally, it is important to recognize that the technical object may present other dimensions or points to be discussed that are not addressed by Feenberg's hermeneutic dimensions. In this way, future analyzes might consider the theory's gaps and present other perspectives of the democratization of the technology.

ACKNOWLEDGEMENT

To Fundação Araucária, CAPES and PPGTE. This study was financed by the Coordenação de Aperfeiçoamento de Pessoal de Nível Superior - Brasil (CAPES) - Finance Code 001.

REFERENCES

Anderson, S., 2016. *Social media now using alternative text for images*. Thomas Pocklington Trust, accessed 25 February 2019, <https://www.pocklington-trust.org.uk/social-media-now-using-alternative-text-images/>

Braille, P., 2012. *Pra Cego Ver: uma proposta de descrição de imagens para o Facebook*. Blog da Audiodescrição, accessed 25 February 2019, <http://www.blogdaaudiodescricao.com.br/2012/06/pra-cego-ver-uma-propostade-descricao.html>

Brasil, 2014. *eMAG: Modelo de Acessibilidade em Governo Eletrônico*. Ministério do Planejamento, Orçamento e Gestão – Secretaria de Logística e Tecnologia da Informação, accessed 25 February 2019 < http://emag.governoeletronico.gov.br/>

Brasil, 2015. *Lei Brasileira de Inclusão da Pessoa com Deficiência - Lei nº 13.146, de 6 de julho de 2015*. Presidência da República - Casa Civil - Subchefia para Assuntos Jurídicos, accessed 25 February 2019 <http://www.planalto.gov.br/ccivil_03/_ato2015-2018/2015/lei/l13146.htm>

Brazilian Internet Steering Committee – CGI.br, 2015. *Cartilha Acessibilidade na Web - Fascículo II*. Ebook, accessed 25 February 2019, <http://www.w3c.br/pub/Materiais/PublicacoesW3C/cartilha-w3cbr-acessibilidade-web-fasciculo-II.pdf>

Cupani, A., 2017. *Filosofia da tecnologia: um convite*. Florianópolis: Editora da UFSC, 3. ed.

Feenberg, A., 1995. *Alternative modernity: The technical turn in philosophy and social theory*. Univ of California Press.

Feenberg, A., 2000. From essentialism to constructivism: Philosophy of technology at the crossroads. In *Technology and the good life?*, pp. 294-315, University of Chicago press.

Feenberg, A., 2002. *Transforming technology: A critical theory revisited*. Oxford University Press.

Feenberg, A., 2005. Critical Theory of Technology: An Overview. *Tailoring Biotechnologies,* Vol. 1, Issue I, pp. 47-64.

Feenberg, A., 2006. What is philosophy of technology?. In *Defining technological literacy*, pp. 5-16. Palgrave Macmillan, New York.

Feenberg, A., 2010. *Between reason and experience: Essays in technology and modernity*. MIT Press.

Gabrilli, M., 2015. *LBI- Lei Brasileira de Inclusão*. Accessed 26 February 2019, < http://maragabrilli.com.br/wp-content/uploads/2016/03/Guia-sobre-a-LBI-digital.pdf>.

Halverson, C. A., 2002. Activity theory and distributed cognition: Or what does CSCW need to DO with theories?. *Computer Supported Cooperative Work (CSCW)*, *11*(1-2), 243-267.

Junior, I., 2018. *Acessibilidade WEB e o desafio do Selo Acessibilidade Digital*. Mãos em movimento Libras e Educação Especial, accessed 25 February 2019 <http://www.maosemmovimento.com.br/selo-de-acessibilidade-digital/>

Ladner, R., 2014. The impact of the united nations convention on the rights of persons with disabilities. *Communications of the ACM*, v. 57, n. 3, pp. 30–32, mar. 2014. ACM, New York, NY, USA.

Neder, R. T., 2013. O que (nos) quer dizer a teoria crítica da tecnologia? In *A teoria crítica de Andrew Feenberg: racionalização democrática, poder e tecnologia*. Brasília: Observatório do Movimento pela Tecnologia Social na América Latina. pp. 7–23.

NIC.br, 2017. *Web para Todos quer acabar com as barreiras de navegação na Internet no Brasil*. Accessed 25 February 2019, <https://www.nic.br/noticia/releases/web-para-todos-quer-acabar-com-as-barreiras-de-navegacao-na-internet-no-brasil/>

Pagani, T., 2018. *Trabalhando com texto alternativo de imagens em redes sociais: Saiba com inserir texto ALT no Facebook e Twitter*. Ux.blog, accessed 25 February 2019, <https://uxdesign.blog.br/trabalhandocom-texto-alternativo-de-imagens-em-redes-sociais-a22fa214ee6>

Prefeitura de São Paulo, 2018. *Selo de Acessibilidade Digital*. Accessed 25 February 2019, <https://www.prefeitura.sp.gov.br/cidade/secretarias/pessoa_com_deficiencia/selo_de_acessibilidade_digital/>

Rogers, Y., 2012. HCI theory: classical, modern, and contemporary. *Synthesis lectures on human-centered informatics*, *5*(2), 1-129.

Sassaki, R. K., 2011. *Nada sobre nós, sem nós: Da integração à inclusão*. Bengala Legal, accessed 25 February 2019 <http://www.bengalalegal.com/nada-sobre-nos>

Souza, J. B.; Siqueira, J. M., 2017. Redes sociais: tecnologias assistivas para a inclusão e a cidadania. *Revista Periferia: Educação, Cultura e Comuniação*, v. 9, n. 1, pp. 112–129.

Todd., 2016. *Accessible images for everyone*. Blog Twitter, accessed 25 February 2019, <https://blog.twitter.com/official/en_us/a/2016/accessible-images-for-everyone.html>

United Nations, 2019. *Article 21 – Freedom of expression and opinion, and access to information*. United Nations – Disability: Department of Economic and Social Affairs, accessed 25 February 2019, <https://www.un.org/development/desa/disabilities/convention-on-the-rights-of-persons-with-disabilities/article-21-freedom-of-expression-and-opinion-and-access-to-information.html>

WPT, 2019. *Web para todos*. Accessed 25 February 2019, <http://mwpt.com.br/>

DESIGNING A ROADMAP FRAMEWORK FOR HEALTHCARE SYSTEMS ADOPTION

Sinte Mutelo[1] and Suama Hamunyela[2]
[1]*Ms.*
[2]*Dr.*
Namibia University of Science and Technology
13 Jackson Kaujeua Street, Windhoek, Namibia

ABSTRACT

Developing country healthcare industry have policies and procedure to regulate health information systems (HIS) both in private and public sector. The Healthcare institutions as part of the government with the help of Non-Governmental Organisation (NGOs) have implemented information systems (IS) within its different directorates to maximise the quality of care. However, HIS benefits may not be recognised by the healthcare organisation and stakeholders when systems implementation and adoption of policies and procedures are not backed up by roadmap to archive HIS goals. Thus, the need for healthcare roadmap to guide the development of HIS is important to the future development of a product. A roadmap development needs different stakeholders to participate. Therefore, this study, propose a roadmap that will provide guide for planning, selection, implementation, and adoption of HIS to produce quality healthcare services in Namibia. The study adopted a qualitative research method, because of its suitability to assist the research answer the research questions in order to meet the research objectives. Data was collected using three different techniques, semi-interviews, documents analysis and questionnaire. A questionnaire was used to collect data about the applicability, usability, and the importance of roadmapping. Then data collected was interpretively analysed. Based on the interpretations and the findings from the analysis of data, the healthcare industry roadmap was developed.

KEYWORDS

Roadmap, Healthcare, Health information systems (HIS), Adoption

1. INTRODUCTION

Healthcare industry is slow to adopt technology compared to other industries, due to a number of reasons including lack of HIS experts to implement and to utilise the technology. Health information systems is the planned delivery of health services to individuals by healthcare professionals (Beam, & Kohane, 2018).

Health Information Systems (HIS) are interrelated systems designed to manage healthcare data, these handle data related to activities of providers and health firms (Sayles (2012). The systems with integrated efforts, maximise advantage to improve patient results, inform research, and influence policy-makers and decision-making stakeholders (Andargoli, Scheepers, Rajendran, & Sohal, 2017). In most developing countries, the Ministry of Health is responsible for implementing the National Health Information System (NHIS) but health information systems are under-utilised. HIS assist healthcare to gather, process and disseminate information within the firm and their stakeholders (Wang, Kung, & Byrd, (2018). Therefore, adopting of HIS is a challenge facing the health sector in developing countries as a result of technology changes, system implementation issues, and isolated systems. A roadmap towards HIS adoption is a proposed answer to alleviate the challenge and enforce the use of HIS in healthcare for quality data (Cetindamar, Phaal & Probert, 2016).

This means that if it is properly developed, a roadmap will support sustainable ICT implementation. Technology roadmap offers power and flexibility in terms of technology implementation (Zamberlan, 2015). The roadmaps have been used to guide focus the organisation strategic plans efficiently. It assists various stakeholders to reach organisational goals. In addition, roadmapping is the most commonly used technique for supporting the strategic management of technology.

Renals, et al., 2014 stated that "roadmapping is a process to communicate the development and integration of science and technology, and their incorporation into products or services to address business or societal opportunities" (p.41).

Therefore, roadmapping provides important details that determine the technical requirements and new ways of research and development.

Furthermore, a roadmap stipulates opportunities in ways to enlighten research groups of the upcoming and re-engineering the clinical research technologies (Managements, 2014). Implementation and system restructuring involving all stakeholders are important for changing the healthcare systems and improving health quality in the country (Jin, Jeong & Yoon, 2015).

Despite a variety of efforts to embrace technologies within the health sector, adoption and usage of Health Information systems in developing healthcare industry remain problematic without strategic plans, policies to determine current, present and future technologies.

Thus, a roadmap towards HIS adoption is a solution to alleviate some of the challenges and enforce the use of HIS in health for quality healthcare. The purpose of this paper is to identify the importance of roadmap for improving the quality of healthcare when applied organisation.

The objective of this paper is to develop a roadmap towards HIS adoption in the health that can guide the health sector delivery quality services. The roadmap will provide a guide for planning, selection, implementation, and adoption of HIS to produce quality healthcare services in any context. This paper provides view of HIS stakeholders and roadmap experts on the HIS adoption roadmap. The main question addressed in this paper is: ***How can a Health Information system adoption roadmap be developed to enhance the quality of health?***

2. OVERVIEW OF HEALTH INFORMATION SYSTEMIN HELATHCARE

Despite a variety of efforts to embrace technologies within the health sector, adoption and usage of Health Information Systems in developing countries is ongoing. Studies show a positive implementation of HIS has been ongoing, impacting the health service delivery in some developing countries (Karon, 2015). Ongundaini (2016) claims that there are limitations in terms of usability, functionality and peculiar social-technical factor; these systems are not user-friendly and not integrated. Most existing implementation of HIS techniques does not support or enhance quality healthcare services.

The developing countries health sector for example has no clear roadmap for HIS adoption. Though the health industry responsible for healthcare services has gone on board to accelerate the HIS process under the founded stakeholders, there is still no significant change in terms of HIS adoption. The absence of HIS strategic plan or policies may hinder HIS adoption. One of the assessments done in the health industry found that "much of the effort to date has been uncoordinated and directed mostly to isolated technical aspects of the HIS and not to institutional, coordination, and other behavioural aspects" (Khan & Edwards, 2012, p.15).

Furthermore, the report stipulated that "there is as yet no mechanism to effectively engage the leadership of the Healthcare-A and other national agencies in this process, and there is currently no up-to-date HIS strategic plan or policy" (Khan & Edwards, 2012, p.15). To deal with the complexity of HIS adoption concrete planning approach must be in place, a systematic approach that guide the health organisation to establish their HIS objectives and translate them to functional and technical requirements as well as identification of resources to implement HIS. Thus this study propose the components for consideration in the development of healthcare roadmap.

3. LITERATURE REVIEW

A roadmap is a plan that enables organisation to be able to align its technologies and business goals (Cetindamar, Phaal, & Probert, 2016).

Roadmapping (TRM) has been widely used as a strategic management device to help governments and private sectors in effectively recognising potential services for the future, determining proper technology alternatives and mapping them with resource allocation plans (Carvalho, Fleury & Lopes, 2013). Aleina,

Viola, Fusaro, and Saccoccia (2017) argued that technology planning is important for decision makers considering the competitive problems that many organisations are facing.

Literature review revealed that for HIS adoption to take place in healthcare organisations, the organisations needs support from higher decision bodies such as its government that support by allocation sufficient resources and employing skilled professionals. Stakeholder involvement is one critical part when considering system development, adoption and implementation.

Accordingly Piña, Cohen, Larson, Marion, Sills, Solberg and Zerzan (2015) said that healthcare system needs to be redesigned, and that huge task must be composed with key healthcare stakeholders including doctors, nurses, administrators, health information managers and policymakers, and as well as with patients. For the functionality of HIS, an information systems, need all IS components complete. Sayles (2012) specified "an IS consists of data, people, and work processes and a combination of hardware (machines and media), software (computer programs), and communications technology (computer networks) known as information technology (IT)" (p.850).

Based on the papers reviewed, the most important factors affecting the adoption of HIS in the health sector are governance, stakeholder involvement, IT skills, IS Infrastructure.

Different technology adoption model were reviewed by the research. The following theories were noted; Innovation Diffusion Theory, technology acceptance model (TAM), Concerns-Based Adoption Model (CBAM), unified theory of acceptance and use of technology (UTAUT) and DeLone and McLean IS success Model.

Rogers' Innovation Diffusion Theory, one of the most popular theories for studying adoption of information technologies (IT) and understanding how IT innovations blow-out inside and amongst communities. To Zhang, Yu, Yan, and Spil (2015) this theory, innovation is an idea, process, or a technology that is perceived as new or unfamiliar to individuals within a particular area or social system.

Atkin, Hunt, and Lin, (2015) debated that "the technology acceptance model is a widely used theoretical framework originating from information sciences to conceptualize technology adoption. The model provides an ungenerous and straightforward approach to studying how users accept and use a technology" (p.631).

On the hand, the concern–based model, the model finds and provides ways to assess seven stages of concern. Haines (2018) in this article noted, one model for change in individuals is the Concerns-Based Adoption Model, it applies to anyone experiencing change, that is, policy makers, teachers, parents even students. The UTAUT suggests that four core constructs (performance expectancy, effort expectancy, social influence and facilitating conditions) are direct elements of behavioural intention and ultimately behaviour, and that these constructs are in turn moderated by gender, age, experience, and voluntariness of use (Williams, Rana, & Dwivedi, 2015).

On the other hand, information systems success model (DeLone and McLean IS success model) theory which provides a comprehensive understanding of IS success by identifying, describing, and explaining the relationships among six of the most critical dimensions of success along which information systems are commonly evaluated. IS success model is considered one most powerful theories in contemporary information systems research. These models have been researched and found fit to other situation but not in this case.

4. METHODOLOGY

The study adopted a qualitative research method, because of its suitability to assist the research answer the research questions in order to meet the research objectives. To Silverman (2013), the reason for using the qualitative method is that the method is particularly important in the behavioural sciences where the aim is to realise the underlying motives of human behaviour.

Healthcare-A is a case studied in this paper. Mutelo and Jere (2017) defined case study as a tool of examination found in several field, in which research brings out an in depth analysis of the case. Hesse-Biber and Leavy (2011) pointed out that the uniqueness of a case study approach is that it provides the researcher with a complete understanding of a phenomenon within its social context.

Data was collected through three different techniques, semi-interviews, documents analysis and questionnaire. Questionnaires, documents, and interviews were used to collect data about the case studies. The interviewees involved systems users, top managers, and HIS implementers from the organisations. This was to ensure that interviewees were knowledgeable and skilled in discussing the areas pertaining to their positions. During the interviews, the researcher used a predefined set of questions. These sets of questions were of significance to the researcher as they were used as a guide for sustaining consistency of the questions asked to the interviewee. A questionnaire was used to obtain qualitative data about the applicability, usability, and knowledge of developing a technology roadmap from different HIS and IT roadmap experts.

5. RESULTS

5.1 Interview Findings

Healthcare-A will not function properly without policies to govern and manage its activities in achieving its planned goals and objectives. Without policies and strategic plans to guide and regulate the use of HIS, the Healthcare-A would have various types of HIS not needed for their business processes.

The policies regarding IT in Healthcare-A were formulated and developed by the IT department at the government level together with the IT directors and other management from the various government offices. According to one of the participants within Healthcare sector A mentioned, it is a good idea developing a roadmap for HIS adoption for the healthcare industry, because it will help align all plans within the organisation.

Therefore, one can conclude to say users of HIS have the interest to adopt HIS, but are held backward by existing processes and policies and a lack guide. This showed the support of employees

5.2 Questionnaire Findings

5.2.1 Health Information System Adoption Roadmap Development Stakeholder

Experts who were engaged in the research were asked to determine who should be part of the development of the HIS adoption roadmap. Five categories of some of the stakeholders were given to choose from: Policy makers; HIS users; HIS software developers; the entire Healthcare-A's directorates and health practitioners.

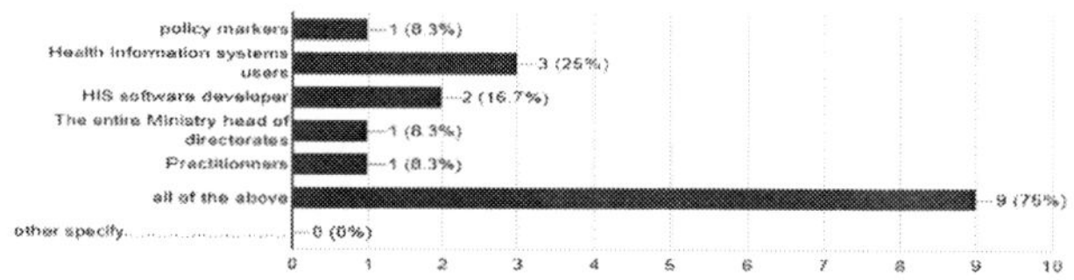

Figure 1. HEALTH information system adoption roadmap development and stakeholder

The questionnaire data shows the categories of stakeholders who can be part of the HIS development team. Most respondents choose all categories.

5.2.2 The Relationship between HIS Roadmap and Quality Healthcare (QH)

Health Information System roadmap aims to improve the healthcare services activities and processes in the country. The healthcare sector is very sensitive by nature as it involves people's lives and any errors can lead to serious damages such as loss of life. Thus, the HIS roadmap can be viewed as an approach that can guide the policy development and implementation across the country healthcare services. In turn, the policies developed to guide the healthcare professionals, patients, and management on how they should interact in the provision of quality healthcare services. As a result, there is a link between effective HIS roadmap and quality healthcare services. According to one of the respondents that was in support of an effective HIS roadmap, they stated that;

"A good HIS roadmap facilitates HIS technology adoption and use, which in turn contributes to the provision of quality healthcare" (RS2, pg7, 18).

The findings clearly shows that there is a link between healthcare services and HIS roadmap is an indication that quality healthcare services are not offered in isolation, but rather there is a need for the integration of various components such as technologies and people.

5.2.3 Technologies to Enhance Quality Health

Figure 2. shows the different technologies used to enhance quality health to sustain the implemented HIS in the health sector of Healthcare-A in developing country.

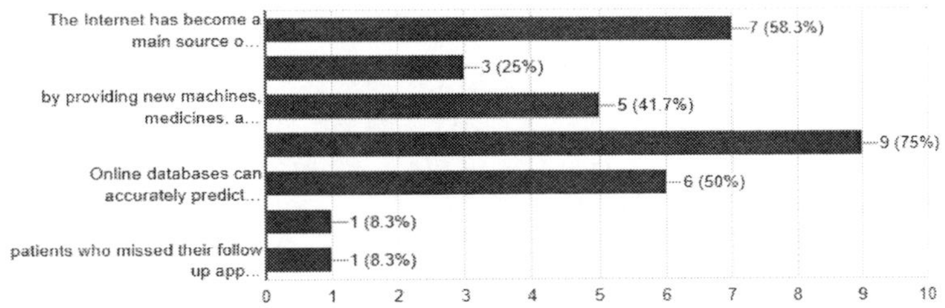

Figure 2. Technologies to enhance Quality Health

Experts and stakeholders of Healthcare-A have different knowledge and experience in information technology. Since the stakeholders are from different specialisations, this question was asked to find out the different technologies which could best suit the utilisation of HIS or are in use in the Healthcare-A to enhance quality health.

5.2.4 General Understanding of Technology Roadmap by Experts

The reason for studying the understanding of technology roadmap within the healthcare institutions and its stakeholders is to measure the level of expert knowledge. Figure 3 shows in detail that the term technology roadmap is not a very well knowledge strand within the expert Healthcare-A stakeholder. Employees and stakeholders, IT experts of Healthcare-A had different levels of technology roadmap understanding. Participants understanding was informed by their area of specialisation in the field of IT.

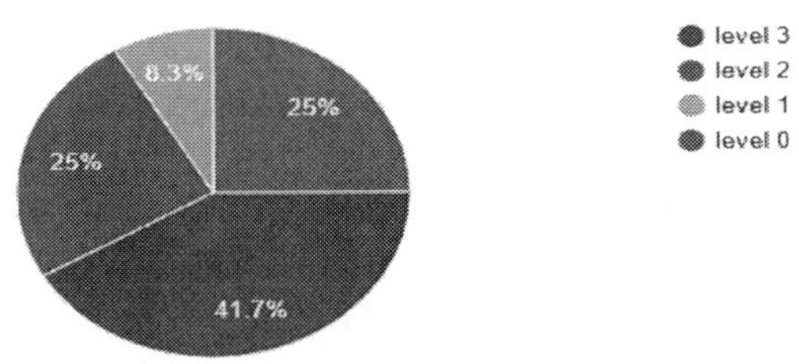

Figure 3. Technology roadmap level of understanding

To assess respondents' level of understanding four (4) categories level were created as follows. The results show that a big number of experts know what a TRM is and could define technology roadmap it.

5.2.5 Roadmap Development for the Developing Healthcare

The main objective of this research is to showcase a proposed HIS adoption Roadmap framework for healthcare institutions in order to have quality healthcare. Relevance of a roadmap framework was again confirmed in findings from questionnaires, where majority of respondents indicated that it is relevant.

Therefore, the majority feels it is important to develop a roadmap for the Healthcare-A.

5.2.6 The Relationship between Health Information System Roadmap and Quality Health

HIS Roadmap aims to improve the healthcare services activities and processes in the country. The healthcare sector is very sensitive by nature as it involves people's lives and any errors can lead to serious damages such as loss of life. Thus, the HIS roadmap can be viewed as an approach that can guide the policy development and implementation across the healthcare industries. Result show that the link between healthcare services and HIS roadmap is an indication that quality healthcare services are not offered in isolation, but rather there is a need for the integration of various components such as technologies and people.

6. ROADMAP DESIGN

Developing a HIS adoption roadmap is a challenge thus identification of key HIS technology has to be outlined that enhance quality healthcare. The roadmap framework is based on current HIS technologies, future HIS technologies and the roles stakeholders in healthcare industry. The developed roadmap framework was designed based on the interpreted data and research findings. The different components of the framework were discovered ad confirmed from literature review as some of the factors which affects the adoption of HIS in healthcare institutions.

6.1 Designing Health Information System Adoption Roadmap

Based on the findings and expert of health sector engaged, the following framework is developed. The developed roadmap framework was developed from the findings of the research studies. Policy makers and Healthcare-A management could use the presented design to guide HIS adoption. The design shows four factors which affects HIS adoption based on the findings. The design shows the factors which the ministry should consider when adopting HIS, they are; Governance, stakeholder, expert skills development and IS/IT technologies and Infrastructure.

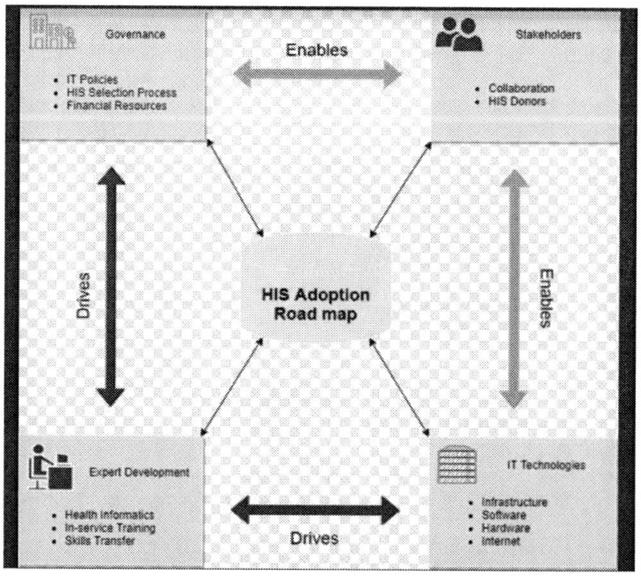

Figure 4. HEALTH Information System adoption roadmap

6.1.1 Governance

Wang and Guo (2015) noted that governance recognises the capacity to get things done without relying on the power of the government to command or use its power. He further emphasised that, in modern society, the government is moving its responsibilities to private sector organisations and NGOs groups, which are undertaking responsibilities that were formerly in the hands of the government. The management and governance of HIS via the IT directors may be an obstacle to the adoption of HIS in the Healthcare. Thus, an employee within the Healthcare-A felt that the process is long and decisions may exclude the users of systems. Again, people dealing with the selection HIS issues may lack knowledge of all systems. As a result, some decisions were not made for the best interest of the whole organisation but rather to serve personal interests. Employees in government health institution feel politics has more power in the development of HIS systems this holds the HIS adoption from the users side. The HIS adoption lacks management support and empowerment from top leadership. Thus, this research finds that proper support is vital during HIS planning and adoption. This concept relates to the non-technical actors, withholding the development of HIS adoption.

6.1.2 Health Information System Stakeholder

Stakeholders include government agencies, hospitals, physicians, dentists, nurses, pharmacies, labs, insurers/payers, a variety of associations, and consumer interests (Pradhan, & Das, 2017). This research records that the Healthcare-A has started with stakeholder engagement in the HIS division. The solo systems were a result of not engaging stakeholders. Until the new directorate was created, there was no single body to lead and coordinate the HIS emphasised one respondent. Stakeholders are actors that will bring and share different ideas toward the enhancement of the HIS and stakeholders are actually those who are most interested in solving the problem (Andriof & Waddock, 2017).

6.1.3 Health Information System Technologies

This concept represents HIS technology that needs to be in place to embark on HIS adoption. Healthcare institutions is affected by a lack of HIS infrastructure because of low resources affecting the budget. It was observed during the interviews that the division of HIS has been moving from different offices and documents were still packed in boxes with other computers. In order for the Healthcare institutions to successfully adopt and yield quality healthcare with HIS. They require proper HIS equipment is such a database, instead of depending on web application systems. The HIS assessment records that the infrastructure for both local and wide area information and communication technology (ICT) for health institutes is either inadequate or very absent, and a lack of required hardware and software. HIS technologies stand between service management and technology to prove repeatable processes and to provide a suitable operating environment for HIS users. Deployment of wireless technologies and mobile technologies to connect HIS with ICT will be a best option for the developing healthcare industries.

6.1.4 Health Information System Experts Development

This concept represents qualified experts who can use HIS technologies to enhance quality healthcare. Information technology (IT) has proven an effective instrument when utilised by people with IT knowledge. Advanced technology and people with IT knowledge are key to the utilisation of HIS. The Healthcare-A needs the best IT solutions to manage its HIS. In order to run HIS smoothly the organisation will need to acquire IT infrastructures such as fast computers, client server networks computers, hardware and software suitable for HIS platforms. The framework shows that the government and stakeholder are the enablers of the HIS adoption, the involvement of the stakeholder in developing roadmap for HIS enables Healthcare-**A** to successfully adopt the HIS.

7. CONCLUSION

This paper discussed the advantages of using a roadmap in healthcare. Roadmapping process that involve stakeholders is the approach organisation take to manage high-level and future requirements. Roadmap will help the health sector define their strategic plan at hand by placing the product into focus, it will keep the organisation in the know of the time and costs. The developed roadmap on HIS adoption is only for healthcare but it can be appropriate to other industries. The most important outcome is that before the actual roadmap is applied, there is need for more research to be done involving, health sector stakeholders, HIS developers, users and decision makers. This is the reason for focusing on the importance of roadmap in developing healthcare.

REFERENCES

Andargoli, A. E., Scheepers, H., Rajendran, D., & Sohal, A. (2017). Health information systems evaluation frameworks: A systematic review. *International journal of medical informatics*, *97*, 195-209.

Andriof, J., & Waddock, S. (2017). Unfolding stakeholder engagement. In *Unfolding stakeholder thinking* (pp. 19-42). Routledge.

Beam, A. L., & Kohane, I. S. (2018). Big data and machine learning in health care. *Jama*, *319*(13), 1317-1318.

Carvalho, M., Fleury, A., & Lopes, P. (2013). An overview of the literature on technology roadmapping (TRM): Contributions and trends. *Technological Forecasting and Social Change*, *80*(7), 1418-1437.

Cetindamar, D., Phaal, R., & Probert, D. (2016). *Technology management: activities and tools*. Macmillan International Higher Education.

Cho, Y., Yoon, S. P., & Kim, K. S. (2016). An industrial technology roadmap for supporting public R&D planning. *Technological Forecasting and Social Change*, *107*, 1-12.

Das, L. (2017). *Role of Data in Improving Care within a Health System* (Doctoral dissertation, PARDEE RAND GRADUATE SCHOOL).

Haines, K. (2018). Professional development for new classroom spaces: extending the concerns-based adoption model.

Li, M. F., & Feng, J. (2017). Healthcare Road Map to Modernization in Clouds Healthcare Forum for Healthcare Professionals, Medical Device Manufacturers, Pharmaceutical Companies and Average People on Virtual Private Clouds. *Accumulated Computer Machinery [ACM]*, 247-248.

Managements, C. (2014). Roadmapping and related publications. *Journal of Innovation and Technology Management*, *9*(3), 1-19.

Merriam, S. B., & Grenier, R. S. (Eds.). (2019). *Qualitative research in practice: Examples for discussion and analysis*. Jossey-Bass.

Pradhan, K., & Das, R. (2017). Exploration and interpretation of women stakeholders' overall involvement in women led agricultural innovation system (AIS). *Indian Research Journal of Extension Education*, *17*(3), 74-81.

Renals, S., Carletta, J., Edwards, K., Bourlard, H., Garner, P., Popescu-Belis, A., Sabbah, Y. (2014). Roadmap for Conversational Interaction Technologies. *Accumulated Computer Machinery [ACM]*, 39-42.

Tang, A., de Boer, T., & van Vliet, H. (2011). Building Roadmaps: A Knowledge Sharing Perspective. *Accumulated Computer Machinery (ACM)*, 13-20.

Wang, Q., & Guo, G. (2015). Yu Keping and Chinese intellectual discourse on good governance. *The China Quarterly*, *224*, 985-1005.

Wilbon, A. D. (2012). Interactive planning for strategy development in academic-based cooperative research enterprises. Technology Analysis & Strategic Management, 24(1), 89-105.

Williams, M. D., Rana, N. P., & Dwivedi, Y. K. (2015). The unified theory of acceptance and use of technology (UTAUT): a literature review. *Journal of Enterprise Information Management*, *28*(3), 443-488.

Zhang, X., Yu, P., Yan, J., & Spil, I. T. A. (2015). Using diffusion of innovation theory to understand the factors impacting patient acceptance and use of consumer e-health innovations: a case study in a primary care clinic. *BMC health services research*, *15*(1), 71.

E-BUSINESS ADOPTION BY NON-PROFIT CULTURAL INSTITUTIONS

Gabriel Antão[1] and Pedro Isaías[2]
[1]*Universidade Aberta, Portugal,*
Rua da Escola Politécnica, 141, 1269-001 Lisboa
[2]*The University of Queensland, Australia,*
Building 17, Level 3, Room 317, The University of Queensland, St Lucia Qld 4072

ABSTRACT

Technological adoption by traditional performing arts institutions is not taken for granted, and being one of the authors a musician in a professional symphony orchestra, many opportunities were perceived where more efficiencies could be achieved through technological adoption, specially regarding e-business. Even though orchestras and other cultural institutions could benefit from e-business adoption, it was not clear why it is not widely implemented by such organizations. In fact, we intended to know how cultural institutions evaluate e-business adoption, why they did (or not) adopt it and how it could benefit them.

From our multiple case study we ca affirm that institutions can fight against the compounded costs through a higher perceived value, both focusing on their artistry and audience development. In fact, e-business enhances the communication with audience, suppliers and clients, while also enabling higher efficiencies and returns. Cultural institutions therefore consider technology, in general, and e-business, in particular, very positive for their performance, and benefiting all stakeholders.

KEYWORDS

e-Business, Cultural Institutions, Cost-Disease, Technology, Audience Development

1. INTRODUCTION

The adoption of technology in traditional performing arts institutions is not certain. Institutions such as orchestras are often secular organizations that rely on their long tradition as their best presentation card. Notwithstanding, cultural institutions consider technology, in general, and electronic business, in particular, very positive for their performance, and benefiting all stakeholders: audience, management, artists and (production) offices. The existence of such paradox (benefits are acknowledged, yet not adopted) triggered the need for further investigation. Therefore, we wish to determine to what extent is important for non-profit cultural institutions to implement an e-business model. Hence, this main question should allow us an understanding of the perceived benefits of adopting an e-business model, as well as the emerging difficulties to its adoption.

Engaging in a multiple case study, we aimed to address the issue through open interviews, supported with quantitative data from questionnaires that would make the comparison between organizations more direct. This research is more vertical than horizontal, which might be a flaw from the perspective of generalization. However, this approach enables an analytical generalization instead of a statistical generalization.

We can affirm that institutions can fight against the compounded costs (cost-disease) through a higher perceived value, both focusing on their artistry and audience development, since an enthusiastic audience cannot be ignored. In fact, we understand that electronic business can not only enhance the communication with audience, suppliers and clients, but also enables higher efficiencies and returns. However, the costs inherent to e-business adoption are relevant for such non-profit organizations, which do not generate profit in order to reinvest in the organization.

In the next sections we will discuss the literature related to the topic (Theoretical Frame) that will help to understand the boundaries of our research, explain our approach to the research topic (Methods of Research), and subsequently we present the Results, followed by a Discussion and Conclusion.

2. THEORETICAL FRAME

Hansmann (1981) affirms that the performing arts are mainly – and nowadays – non-profit cultural institutions, in contrast to the paradigm they faced at the beginning of their foundation (especially orchestras), when they could generate income. Among the many different types of cultural institutions, symphony orchestras appear to be the most significant in the western culture (Brodsky, 2006). On the funding level of cultural institutions – and specially on orchestras - there are striking differences among countries, and we can find in the United States a system of low public funding, dependent on patronage/sponsors, and an almost exclusively public funding in Germany, with the highest density of orchestras and theatres (Krebs and Pommerehne, 1995). Hence, the management of institutions across the globe might differ substantially. Cultural institutions have (usually) a factor in common, in that almost the total of their funding is spent in salaries from artists and managers (Walter, 2015), therefore fixed costs, and that these costs might be better spread over a higher number of concerts (Leslie, 2004). We assume that orchestras cannot survive by their selves, and public funding is needed, thus justified by the public service orchestras offer to the communities. However, orchestras should try to have the highest returns out of their activity, so that their efficiencies and returns justify further funds. Some of the possibilities rely on the price discrimination available in the concert venues (Rushton, 2011). Other important costs might include storing, maintaining or replacing materials/parts, which are usually high for both theaters and publishers, and that may have in data banks a future cost-saving solution (Bellini et al., 1999). Orchestras are forced to spare, and also to reduce costs, but this might not lead to greater efficiencies, since in order to maintain or develop artistic quality – and to maintain the best artists, conductors and guests – there is a need for compounded investment (Goldfarb, 1984). Also, orchestras depend on their continuing exchanging surroundings, since they are not closed systems and need a flow of resources form the outside (Heimovics et al., 1993). But we could also consider the arts in a broader market scope, and treat them all as entertainment, considering the arts thus a competitive market (Heilbrun and Gray, 2004). Hence the fact that orchestras are considered, in the first place, as non-profit organizations, they are often compared to large profit-media-arts and other sorts of entertainment, such as sports (Seaman, 2005), making their survival more complicated. Furthermore, orchestras operate in a stable model, often conflicting with the creativity associated with music making, their core activity (Mauskapf, 2012). In fact, orchestras have an above average amount of creative people working within them, but very few creative solutions arise from the organization. In other words, musicians could be asked to participate in the management (corporative management) in order to find new solutions (Starr, 1997). In addition, Bertero (2001) affirms that cultural institutions should not persistently stick to models that have always worked in order to survive (upon a Darwinian model), because they might not be the best solution. Sometimes, it takes a positive (occasionally radical) change to achieve greater benefits and strategic advantages.

When we talk about cost reduction for cultural institutions, we must deal with the concept of cost-disease. First used by Baumol, it describes an economic activity whose costs tend to rise continuously and faster than the economy's rate of inflation (Baumol, 1996), meaning compounding pressures on its economic activity. The author (Baumol, 1967) also believes that there is no enthusiasm or determination that can provide more than a temporary relief, since its consequences are certain in the long run. These pressures are due to the low effect that technology has on productivity and efficiency for non-progressive industries, such as the performing arts and universities. In the other hand, progressive industries might compensate the inflation rate with higher productivity and efficiency rates, therefore reducing costs. Usually, scale and scope economies are possible since orchestral musicians share common knowledge and practice (Malhotra, 1981), and due to the growing level of professionals in the arts sector. In spite of that, the arts do not benefit from the same rates of growing productivity that progressive industries do from technology.

From the audience side, Boiarsky (2003) reveals that the new "Nintendo Generation" has a high visual and kinaesthetic acuity that unconsciously expects more from an "entertaining" performance, leading to symptoms of boredom and low interest for such special performances as from symphony orchestras.

Performing arts organizations should indeed rethink their approach to technology in order to reach new audiences. In addition, Botstein (1996) considers that we are probably living beyond the golden age of the orchestra and its repertoire, since we are not giving continuity to contemporary life and culture, and more than often just working as a live museum. Nevertheless, there are authors such as Mauskapf (Mauskapf, 2012), who believe that orchestras have never enjoyed a better moment, since music has been made more music and at a higher level than ever, guaranteeing its future. Also, Felton (1994) argues that some reports are exaggerated on their critics over orchestras' deficits, giving a false perception of the real case. Thus, for financial value to be created from the experiences of others, efforts should be made to attract and retain customers, while recruiting new ones (Tschmuck et al., 2013). There are indeed signs of good practices and results, like the audience for opera which is enthusiastic, relatively young and growing in numbers (Botstein, 1994), however, this enthusiasm lies on the inversion of expectations that the audience has concerning the opera role, specially in the way we confront artifice and reality.

Nowadays, orchestras face growing challenges, because in order to focus on artistic quality and on getting the desired stability, they should not seek profits (Boyle, 2007). In fact, they are very unlikely to have any profits at all, since measures focused on the quality are usually non-profitable (Guillard, 1985). However, despite not being profitable-firms, they are often forced to act as such (Olson et al., 2005), striving for more efficiencies and returns, a purpose we believe could be facilitated by the adoption of electronic business.

Electronic business may be defined as undertaking organizational processes as buying, selling, transferring, or exchanging products, services, or information through electronic means as computers and the Internet (Rainer et al., 2014), as part of a greater economic paradigm which brought significant transformations in businesses, namely on the technological level of networks and communications (Matsuo and Colomo-palacios, 2013). We must refer to the benefits of information systems as usually not recognizable in traditional measures as returns on investment, and other financial measures, hence the importance of this investigation to understand the perception of managers beyond financial data. The reaped benefits can be acknowledged through a strategical analysis to the organization, on the efficiency and productivity levels, and eventually in higher financial returns (Isaías and Issa, 2015).

3. METHODS OF RESEARCH

We decided to engage in case study research, because it focus on the gathering of data concerning a particular person, social setting, event or group, in order to understand how it operates or works (Berg, 2001). Despite the fact that case study research has been widely criticized, we believe it can be of great value when understanding specific situations, as the one we are studying concerning the e-business in cultural institutions. Hence, the case study must demonstrate its reliability and validity, which is difficult due to the uniqueness of situations (Cohen et al., 2007). Also, the strength of the conclusions from a single case study might not be very high, thus the use of multiple cases can add strength to the conclusions.

In order to study the case, we tried to persuade several institutions to participate, having found three (3) institutions, from two (2) different countries and in two (2) different cultural areas, who wished to contribute under anonymity. In order to gather new data, we decided to apply both open interviews and questionnaires, thus qualitative and quantitative approaches, respectively. As affirmed by Saunders, Lewis and Thornhill (2009), researches often require a combination of primary and secondary data in order to answer the research questions and fulfill the objectives. We indeed pursue our research recurring to mixed methods, thus believing they could provide the most significant data for our research question and objectives.

Concerning the open-ended interviews, they provide a solution that combines structure and flexibility (Legard et al., 2003), enabling us to cover all the important topics in depth and explore eventual new subjects during the interview. In order to analyse the great amount of data obtained, we used the software *nVivo* so we could reap greater benefits from our data. The interviews covered important topics, describing the institutions and their activity, their relationship with technology and how it affects their core activity – specifically the adoption of technological tools, its benefits and impact in the daily life of the institution - and the e-business topic, namely if it is known by the institutions and which are the perceived benefits and difficulties of its adoption.

The questionnaires lead to a descriptive research (Saunders et al., 2009) and represent a valuable complement to the interviews. This is particularly important in order to engage in triangulation, which includes the use of different approaches, methods or sources to validate conclusions drawn from the data obtained (Richtie and Lewis, 2003). Still concerning the questionnaires, we aim for discrete data, essentially numeric and category data, organized upon Likert scales. The questionnaires covered a detailed description of the organization, a full description of technological adoption and how its impact is perceived by the institution, an extended description of the difficulties to the implementation of e-business, as well as the expected benefits from its use. The questionnaires should be helpful on answering our research objectives – namely the specific benefits and difficulties of adopting an e-business model -, and the open interviews are tailored for deep and rich information, enabling us to understand the impact of e-business in cultural organizations.

4. RESULTS

We found that the concept of electronic business is not fully understood by cultural institutions, although importance has been given to technological adoption. Despite the fact that the concept of e-business is not clear yet, these institutions already work with many of its tools on a daily basis. We must say that one (out of the three) institution does fully understand the concept, and has a global strategy in order to implement and reap greater benefits of its use. Most of the institutions consider themselves in a low level of technological adoption, but confirm the adoption and daily use of electronic commerce. They also consider positive the use of technology to automatize processes. In fact, these institutions reveal that online ticket selling is a core activity and that they have ambition of adopting further technological tools and innovations.

Not every institution uses specialized software, but its use has been highlighted as generating several benefits at many levels: management, production offices and audience. We do find a logic between the use of specific software within the institution and its dimension: the use of specific (usually expensive) software only makes sense for bigger organizations. Also, the non-profit and non-progressive character of these institutions makes them less likely to get such advantages as higher productivity and efficiency rates through the use of technology. In addition, the absence of profits makes it harder to (re)invest in such expensive assets as technology. For small cultural organizations, these problems are more evident, since the amount of available resources and expected returns on investment are reduced.

Artistic product (and its quality) is the most important objective for cultural institutions, which might be enhanced by technology. Furthermore, technological developments should only serve the purpose of highlighting the artistic product of the institution. However, the interviewees did not mention any kind of technological benefits in the artistic production itself. Considering Art as communication, it can naturally be enhanced by technology. Henceforth, websites should be knowledge based content platforms, with dynamic contents which motivate to purchase a ticket or simply to generate interest (and discussion) about the institution, its artists and programs. The institutions have special interest in sharing videos online (due to its interactivity) and in social networks. However, they are conscious of the difficulties of getting it to work as they want, since these networks are open spaces, where both compliments and critics are expected. It is clear the need for social networks policies/strategies within the organization, so that its image and values are preserved over the internet mediated platforms. The institutions' website is a key component of their technological activity: electronic commerce is already a daily business for them and a significant share of the tickets being sold online. Henceforth, capabilities as secure page, online payments and information about the programs and the institutions are widely available on their websites. Among the institutions studied, only one had a website optimized for mobile platforms, but other meant to follow this step soon. One institution affirmed their intention of turning their website into a content exhibitor, aiming not only a better communication with the audience, but also extend the life of the products/services, using materials for educational purposes and interactive platforms.

Benefits from technology are unanimous. It enhances productivity and returns, especially for bigger organizations, where the investments in technology are more significant. In general, institutions believe that a higher degree of technological adoption promotes more efficiencies, reduces costs and gives more room for budget planning. They even affirm that technology is crucial for their future, specially concerning possibilities related to social networks and reaching audiences. Not only communication and cost reduction are boasted, also the communication with the client becomes interactive, fast, personalized and – of highest importance – measurable. In addition, in order to fight the effects of the cost-disease, the interviewees cited the collaboration between cost-disease affected institutions (cultural institutions and universities) so that chances of both sides can be enhanced.

The institutions recognize their activity as a public service, focused on the artistic quality and on audience development and education, a way of justifying public funding. As a public service, we cannot avoid the topic of price policies. We found that the same programs in smaller cities (venues) offer usually lower prices, when compared to denser populated areas. In addition – and concerning price discrimination - we were noticed that there are limits imposed to the institution (either from the State or City) for minimum and maximum prices, giving less room for price discrimination. Concerning market competitiveness, the Portuguese institutions affirmed to perform within a competitive market, but the third institution – this from a central Europe metropole – mentioned to be in a very competitive market.

There are several limitations to the institution's success: limited budgets (and funding), the almost non-existent rise in productivity, the costly consumer information management, and the adoption of information and communication technologies. Associated with technological adoption is the need for special skills and knowledge. Institutions might offer extra courses to its employees or employ new skilful ones, in order to face the technological challenges. Furthermore, in order to take greater advantage of data, institutions might turn either to external services or recruitment. One of our interviewees makes an interesting statement on this matter: technological adoption does not mean more workload; thus, the number of employees should not rise in order to fulfil the technological requirements. Technology should indeed simplify and clarify processes, and the rich information generated will enable the management to perform better and efficiently. Other difficulties are the projects planned with amateur cultural institutions, because it may represent a step backwards concerning efficiencies on the communication and production levels. When cultural institutions have a certain level of digital adoption, working on less technological-efficient levels (used by amateur institutions) might be frustrating and shows no benefits from the investments in technology. In other words, greater benefits await when everyone adopts technology. The institutions also mention the sponsoring as a way of getting financial flexibility, although this might mean some compulsory programs or image rights usage. Another curious topic, is that the recording market (audio cd's, or video) is not a profitable investment anymore for most cultural institutions, as predicted long ago by Tapscott (2015). However, orchestras and other institutions are forced to have some presence in this market in order to show activity and their level of artistry. We found that instead of investing solely in traditional channels, orchestras might choose modern ways of distribution, such as exclusively digital platforms, in order to avoid greater costs.

5. DISCUSSION

The fact that the institutions already use many components of the e-business but do not understand completely the concept, might lead to the conclusion that cultural institutions tend to adopt technological tools separately, and not as a global strategy for the organization. The interviewees did not mention any kind of technological benefits in the artistic production itself, but we believe that the efficiencies obtained on the communication and management level leave more room and time to dedicate to the artistic production. In other words, technological adoption might indirectly serve the artistic production within the organization, as time savings and online document access in order for the artists to prepare themselves, just to mention a daily example. Despite being assumed in the questionnaires that technological adoption had no significant impact on reducing production costs or getting competitive advantages, through the interviews we found evidence that costs in the artistic production were reduced indirectly by technological adoption. Furthermore, if institutions affirm that B2E brings them benefits, then we should strongly consider benefits for employees, namely on arts production. In fact, taking in consideration that the e-business subject was not fully understood by all institutions - and that the interviewees probably never reflected about the topic – some answers might not be consistent with their practices. We believe that triangulation through mixed methods helped to solve this question, and reinforced our choice for this research strategy.

Another question relates to external pressures for technological adoption. In a context of market competition - which might exist, according to our interviewees -, when technological adoption is widely accepted by all the stakeholder, cultural institutions might feel the pressure to follow the trend. However, the opposite might also occur, since adopting edge technology in traditional environments might not lead to more efficiencies, because one can only take full advantage of technology if it is adopted by the whole circuit of stakeholders. We usually take the adoption of new technology as a source of competitive advantage, and therefore justifying its acquisition. For cultural institutions, that might not be the case, since most of them have the monopoly over their market, or in other words, their community.

Considering Art as a form of communication, technology can automatically enhance its reach and effectiveness. On the communication level, new streaming possibilities are arising, but we must consider image rights and permissions, which might dissipate apparent cost reduction. Benefits of technological adoption at the communication level seem to be similar to cultural institutions as for other organizations. However, on measuring data and communication, cultural institutions are granted with valuable data and information that can represent one of their unique sources of strategic planning. With detailed data about their audience, institutions are better equipped to improve segmentation and communication.

The institutions mentioned that they try to show their social side, namely sharing backstage work/life from artists, an informal way to communicate, in order to reduce the gap between audience and artists. Social networks open up new possibilities, but require specialized knowledge and policies. However, we might ask about the real purpose of all the new electronic possibilities (like live streaming): might they become a substitute product? We believe that the most striking experience is witnessed in the concert all, and that technology cannot (yet?) capture the whole live experience, but could indeed be an ideal tool to extend the life span of the product (concert), either for advertisement, documenting or educational purposes.

If the performing arts represent a public service, should they consider broadening their focus to children and seniors? We find it logical that in order to get higher returns on their investment, these institutions focus on the segments which can pay the highest price. However, reaching a broader spectrum of the population might better justify their funding or grants. In addition, children should be a particularly important focus, since future audiences should be addressed early on. We can conclude that in denser metropolitan areas, cultural institutions have more room for programming since they have a larger audience, thus the possibility of filing the venues with high quality (less popular programs). The question of financial resources is still important in the metropolitan areas, since popular programs might help to finance quality programming.

Assuming that the institutions make a great amount of online ticket sales, the website as a commercial platform means easiness for the client on purchasing his ticket, but also benefits for the institutions, since valuable data is provided to the institution. Available data for analysis means possibilities of segmentation and price policies and discrimination. Relatively to price policies, we found that the same programs in smaller cities (venues) offer usually lower prices, when comparing to denser populated areas. We believe these differences might lie in the fact that in metropoles, institutions have a larger audience base which could attend the concert, while in smaller areas, institutions might struggle to sell the show completely. Having to follow State/City ticket-price policies, it becomes difficult for the institutions to discriminate prices, losing one of their most valuable tools to generate higher returns. Even if it is understandable that anyone would pay the price correspondent to the real cost of the show, we also agree that a minimum fee should be charged in order to give value to the product/service. However, having similar price policies for both quality and popular programs might reduce the possible financial returns from the organization.

The central Europe institution performs in a very populated area, it probably performs among many other cultural institutions, and eventually some from the same nature. This means that this institution might not only face competition from others of the same nature, as it could face competition from other "entertainment" organizations. Concerning the two Portuguese institutions, we believe that the monopoly situation they have is likely to be maintained, since there is no room for profits, and the limits concerning price policies deny institutions the possibility to reap higher returns from price discrimination.

The partnerships between cost-disease affected organizations was introduced to us as a solution that makes sense within this paradigm. We can find cultural organizations that request studies from universities about their performance or audience rates and development, or even as a mean (help) to implement technological innovation (in the case of technological departments). In the other hand, universities see in cultural institutions an opportunity for their students to make use of their knowledge and expertise in real-life situations. Cultural institutions face new challenges when dealing with the adoption of new technology, since they either must request external services and give additionally formation to its employees, or even employ individuals with knowledge and expertise to deal with the technologies desired. Some frequent errors on this matter concern the misplacement of employers into new technological positions without the skills or expertise required. This might lead to slower rates of work, and eventually the need for external services (help), meaning that technological adoption results in no benefits concerning efficiencies and returns.

Sponsors are nowadays valuable sources of income for organizations. Notwithstanding, this financial help is usually part of a deal which consists in image selling, direct publicity, or even compulsory programs, which may not fit the objectives of the institution. Therefore, cultural institutions should balance the sponsorship with their artistic objectives in order to keep track of their principal function, the artistic product.

6. CONCLUSION

Despite all the mentioned problems concerning the life – and death - of symphony orchestras (and cultural institutions in general), Botstein (1996) believes that they have a brilliant future due to the uniqueness and irreplaceability of its performance and audience. The author compares the (better) situation of symphony orchestras with the Yiddish language which has still to die, but whose death has been announced for over a thousand years. Orchestras can work has a museum of the past and a platform for the modern art/music, and should turn their challenges into opportunities for their advantage.

Concerning our research question, there is an ever-growing importance for e-business implementation in cultural institutions. We understand that electronic business can not only enhance the communication with audience, suppliers and clients, but also enables higher efficiencies and returns, and its impact might be proportional to the size of the institution. Although most cultural institutions have a monopoly over their market, e-business should also be beneficial, since they will not seek for competitive advantages but higher efficiencies and cost reduction. At the communication level, it enables such dynamic institutions to shape their image differently (not rooted in traditional acoustic sound experience), reaching out to new audiences through various channels and multimedia possibilities. In fact, cultural institutions might be able to reshape their image, attain more efficiencies and reach broader audiences, always giving that funds for e-business adoption are within their budget, or when expected cost reduction and higher efficiencies justify and pay off the investment made. The new technological developments set new challenges to cultural institutions but equally as many opportunities. One of the most important lessons from our research is resembled in the words of Douglas Dempster (in Mauskapf, 2012), that institutions affected by the cost-disease should not seek growth through greater productivity but through perceived value. Only controlling the latter, institutions are able to keep pace with the inflationary costs of the economy (Douglas Dempster in Mauskapf, 2012). In order to control such measures as value, institutions must engage with their communities, broaden their audience base, and engage in new technological platforms and practices, namely in educational activities. Also, institutions should seek efficient processes and higher returns despite being usually in a monopoly position in their markets. In fact, due to the ticket price limitations imposed by state or municipality, institutions can hardly engage in price discrimination strategies, but should instead turn their selves to segmentation, which is enhanced by e-business adoption, namely on the data acquired through digital platforms. Cultural institutions consider technology, in general, and electronic business, in particular, very positive for their performance, and benefiting all the stakeholders: audience, management, artists and (production) offices.

REFERENCES

Baumol, W.J., 1996. Symphony Orchestra Economic: The Fundamental Challenge. *Harmony Forum Symphony Orchestras*. Inst. 2, 52–54.

Baumol, W.J., 1967. Performing Arts, The Permanent Crisis. Economic Analysis indicates possible extinction. *Business Horizon*. 10, 47–50.

Bellini, P., Fioravanti, F., Nesi, P., 1999. Managing Music in Orchestras. *IEEE Press* 32, 26–34. https://doi.org/10.1109/2.789748

Berg, B., 2001. *Qualitative Reserach Methods for the Social Sciences*, 4th ed. Allyn and Bacon, Boston, USA.

Bertero, C.O., 2001. Orquestras Sinfônicas: uma metáfora revisitada. *Revista Administração de Empresas*. 41, 84–88.

Boiarsky, C., 2003. This Is Not Our Fathers' Generation: Web Pages, the Chicago Lyric Opera, and the Philadelphia Orchestra. *Journal of Popular Culture*. 36, 14–24.

Botstein, L., 1996. The Future of the Orchestra. *Music Quarterly,* 80, 189–193.

Botstein, L., 1994. The Opera Revival. *Music Quarterly*, 78, 1–8.

Boyle, S., 2007. Single serve or package deal? A study of regular attendees to symphony orchestra concerts. *International Journal of Nonprofit and Voluntary Sector Marketing*. 12, 127–134. https://doi.org/10.1002/nvsm

Brodsky, W., 2006. In the wings of British orchestras: A multi-episode interview study among symphony players. *Journal of Occupational and Organizational Psychology*. Br. Psychol. Soc. 79, 673–690. https://doi.org/10.1348/096317905X68213

Cohen, L., Manion, L., Morrison, K., 2007. *Research methods in education*, 6th Edition. ed. Routledge, New York, USA. https://doi.org/10.1080/19415257.2011.643130

Felton, M.V., 1994. Evidence of the existence of the cost disease in the performing arts. *Journal of Cultural Economics*. 18, 301–312. https://doi.org/10.1007/BF01079761

Goldfarb, R.S., 1984. A Davis-Bacon Musicale : Symphony Orchestras as Migrant Labor. *Journal of Labor Research*. V, 427–433.

Guillard, J.-P., 1985. The Symphony as a Public Service: The Orchestra of Paris. *Journal of Cultural Economics*. 9, 35–47.

Gustafsson, J., 2017. *Single case studies vs. multiple case studies: A comparative study*. Halmstad, Sweden.

Hansmann, H., 1981. Nonprofit Enterprise in the Performing Arts. *Bell Journal of Economics*. 12, 341–361. https://doi.org/10.2307/3003560

Heilbrun, J., Gray, C.M., 2004. *The Economics of Art and Culture*, 2nd ed. Cambridge University Press, New York, USA. https://doi.org/10.1017/CBO9781107415324.004

Heimovics, R.D., Herman, R.D., Coughlin, C.L.J., 1993. Executive Leadership and Resource Dependence in Nonprofit Organizations: A Frame Analysis. Public Adm. Rev. 53, 419–427.

Isaías, P., Issa, T., 2015. high Level Models and Methodologies for Information Systems. Springer-Verlag, New York, USA.

Krebs, S., Pommerehne, W.W., 1995. Politico-economic interactions of German public performing arts institutions. *Journal of Cultural Economics* 19, 17–32. https://doi.org/10.1007/BF01074430

Legard, R., Keegan, J., Ward, K., 2003. *In-Depth Interviews, in: Qualitative Research Practice - A Guide for Social Science Students and Researchers*. Sage Publications, London, UK, pp. 138–169.

Leslie, P., 2004. *Price discrimination in Broadway theater. RAND Journal of Economics*. 35, 520–541.

Malhotra, V.A., 1981. The social accomplishment of music in a symphony orchestra: A phenomenological analysis. *Qualitative Sociology* 4, 102–125. https://doi.org/10.1007/BF00987214

Matsuo, T., Colomo-palacios, R., 2013. *Electronic Business and Marketing: New Trends on Its Process and Applications*. Springer.

Mauskapf, M.G., 2012. *Enduring Crisis, Ensuring Survival: Artistry, Economics, and the American Symphony Orchestra*. The University of Michigan.

Olson, J.R., Belohlav, J.A., Boyer, K.K., 2005. Operational, economic and mission elements in not-for-profit organizations: The case of the Chicago Symphony Orchestra. *Journal Opera Management*. 23, 125–142. https://doi.org/10.1016/j.jom.2004.07.008

Rainer, R.K., Prince, B., Cegielski, C., 2014. *Introduction to Information Systems: Supporting and Transforming Business*, 5th Editio. ed. Wiley, New York, USA.

Richtie, J., Lewis, J., 2003. *Qualitative Research Practice: A Guide for Social Science Students and Researchers*. Sage Publications, London, UK.

Rushton, M., 2011. Pricing the Arts, in: Towse, R. (Ed.), *A Handbook of Cultural Economics*. Edward Elgar, Cheltenham, UK, pp. 350–355.

Saunders, M., Lewis, P., Thornhill, A., 2009. *Research Methods for Business Students*, 5th ed. Prentice Hall Financial Times, Essex, Uk.

Seaman, B.A., 2005. *Attendance and Public Participation in the Performing Arts: A Review of the Empirical Literature* (No. 06-25). https://doi.org/10.2139/ssrn.895099

Starr, S.F., 1997. Symphony Orchestras: How Did We Get Here? Where Are We Going? *Harmony Forum Symphony Orchestras*. Inst. 5, 73–88.

Tapscott, D., 2015. *The Digital Economy Anniversary Edition: Rethinking Promise and Peril in the Age of Networked Intelligence*, 2nd ed. McGraw-Hll Professional, USA.

Tschmuck, P., Pearce, P.L., Campbell, S., 2013. *Music Business and the Experience Economy: The Australian Case*. Springer-Verlag, Berlin-Heidelberg.

Walter, C., 2015. *Arts Management: An Entrepreneurial Approach*. Routledge, New York, USA. https://doi.org/10.1017/CBO9781107415324.004

SOCIOCULTURAL INFORMATION URBAN SPACE CONSTRUCTION

Olga Kononova[1], Dmitry Prokudin[1,2], Vitalina Karachay[1] and Daria Pilysova[1]
[1]*St. Petersburg National Research University of Information Technologies, Mechanics and Optics (ITMO University) 197101, St. Petersburg, Russia*
[2]*St. Petersburg State University 199034, St. Petersburg, Russia*

ABSTRACT

The construction of information urban space allows effectively improve the management quality and the sociocultural development of cities. In this paper the concept of Sociocultural Information Urban Space considered as logical development both Smart city infrastructure and social machine concepts, proposed for studying and understanding the features, possibilities, base information flows of the smart city sociocultural face. The Sociocultural Information Urban Space idea helps to recognize or improve the ordinary data driving city concept because of smart and gamification technology use so that greater range of digital services related to the sociocultural city facets can be provided to different stakeholders. Suggested smart city architecture, models, as well as St. Petersburg cases illustrate the approach, structure, and core implementation steps of the urban space. Two application scenarios allow discussing how processes of sustainable development and self-regulation mechanisms of Sociocultural Information Urban Space can be used to meet the factual needs of citizens and decision-making.

KEYWORDS

Smart City Architecture, Sociocultural Information Urban Space, Social Machine, Smart Technology, Gamification

1. INTRODUCTION

Modern urbanization process and urbanism have been basically conditioned by technological changes and by the organization of the city and society as a media-sphere (Wakabayashi, 2002). In this regard, the issue of description and feature characteristics determination of sociocultural information space and the study of motivation mechanisms identification for citizens' participation in the decision-making processes in urban development domain among the proposed intellectual smart cities solutions become relevant.

Generally, the concept of the Sociocultural Information Urban Space can be briefly identified as the complex of the information flows and sources of urban and Internet data that are peculiar to sociocultural urban space, including such elements as data aggregation, using the methods of search and explication of contextual knowledge, the life situations description, web services design, providing the intellectual support for socially oriented solutions, and implementation of the gamification technologies at the stage of service design. In regard to citizens, these services perform some specific functions. Providing the feedback by means of these information resources and services, citizens might be involved in the process of the sociocultural environment formation; therefore, they can actively influence this space.

Based on the analysis of academic resources on the issue of Sociocultural Information Urban Space, it is reasonable to note, that there is a lack of researches, concerning the approaches to the use of technologies of the intellectual support of socially oriented solutions in the context of the social and cultural space of the city. Moreover, it can be stated that there is the absence of the complete deterministic concept of sociocultural service oriented information space of the modern city, describing its information resources, information flows, and information needs of the population. Big data, reflecting the various aspects of the social activity, demonstrates a great potential to the support of the socially-oriented decisions adoption, however, the practice of its use is still limited by single pilot projects and is still far from a unified standard.

Thereby, the research problem, which the current study is aiming to solve, consists in the development of the methodology of intellectual support of socially oriented solutions of sociocultural service oriented information environment of the modern city. It is proposed to apply the complex approach to the use of intellectual/smart technologies and gamification technologies, taking into account the cross-functional nature and complex multi-layered structure of sociocultural information urban environment. It should be noted that the relevance and scientific significance of the research problem is determined by the lack of a deterministic concept of sociocultural service oriented information urban space, describing its information resources, information flows, and information needs of the population, as well as complex approaches to monitoring, collection, and analysis, clustering and aggregation of data from heterogeneous information flows, generated in the media saturated dynamically changing sociocultural information space of the modern city. Moreover, the scientific novelty of the research problem is to offer a methodology for intellectual support of socially oriented solutions of sociocultural service oriented information space of the modern city, including the design of models, methods and services, and the description of life situations and the creation of sustainable channels of interaction and orientation in urban space.

The methodology provides a complex use of gamification- and smart technologies, urban information resources, and new sources of big data that reflect different aspects of social activity (social networks data, citizens' petitions, traffic flows, economic activity of citizens, mobile applications, etc.), Internet texts and media materials, produced by individual Internet users and Internet communities in order to develop the cognitive, educational, creative interests, the formation of sociocultural needs of the urban community, providing these needs with appropriate web services, increasing the accessibility of the city and its sociocultural space for visitors, promoting the cultural interpenetration.

2. RELATED WORKS

It should be noted that the progress in information and communication technologies (ICT) solutions enables not only the public and private sector, but also offers the potential for the information space of sociocultural urban environment. In this regard, the essential research issues are increasing the citizen participation via tailored efficient service provision and democracy instruments, and economic development with smart joining sustainability as a key factor of the dynamic modern city promotion. In urban planning and development sphere, the ICT concept refers to the set of urban infrastructures, architectures, applications, systems, and computational and data analytics capabilities (Bibri, 2018). Many attempts to conceptualize the information space in sociocultural urban area have been made. A considerable number of investigations have been conducted in this domain. In particular, the information environment can be viewed as the intercultural communication space. Although the availability of modern information technologies by themselves does not facilitate the intercultural communication, however, it promotes mutual recognition among peoples and their cultures (Drotianko and Yahodzinskyi, 2017).

Technical (or resource) approach to the information environment defines it via the information, stored and circulating within this environment. Whereas the sociocultural concepts of the information environment refers to the space of social communications, and identifies it as an integral part of the culture. According to the Belon et al. (2015), sociocultural environment is a complex, dynamic construct that encompasses the community's social and cultural context that shapes beliefs, values, and practices, which, in turn, may foster or inhibit individual efforts to participate in physical activity. Besides, in the field of Human Computer Interaction (HCI), the sociocultural information space can be considered focusing on studying the interactions and the relationships between humans and computers (Sharma and Mehta, 2016). Masucci et al. describes the information space as the environment where information is handled in order to navigate through the city. Despite that, wider applications of these smart ICTs are indispensable to make infrastructure systems more interdependent and interconnected (Masucci et al., 2014). In regard to the cultural heritage domain, the exchanged and produced data can be opportunely exploited by a set of applications and services in order to transform a static space into a smart environment (Chianese and Piccialli, 2016). In this case, environments defined as intelligent and pervasive identify places where there is a wide spread use of embedded devices, sensors, mobile applications and services. Such an environment enables the creation of a dynamic ecosystem where a large amount of data is constantly produced and captured. Thereby, there is the necessity of relevant mechanism of data and service delivery. The problem of evaluation and care of cultural heritage through smart city enabling technologies examine in the research of Castiglione et al. (2018). The authors note that the corresponding information systems for cultural environments should possess the following technical features: capability to gather information from distributed and heterogeneous data sources (Social Media Networks, Digital Libraries and Archives, Multimedia Collections, Web Data Services, etc.); advanced data management techniques and technologies; ability to provide useful and personalized data to users based on their preferences and context; advanced information retrieval facilities, data analytics and other utilities/services. Despite the number of advanced digital participatory platforms (DPPs) in the information space, there are some issues and challenges that local governments face in fostering online and offline citizen engagement (Falco and Kleinhans, 2018). The authors consider the DPPs as a specific kind of collaborative social media. They argue that there are contextual, technological, and organizational factors influencing the citizen engagement. Depending on the context, they can act as challenges, making the citizen engagement limited or ineffective. Thus, the most important factor for innovative communication is a genuine understanding (at the management level) of the benefits that could be gained through DPPs and social media in general.

Based on the issue that the general goal of smart cities is to improve sustainability with help of technologies, Ahvenniemi et al. (2017) recommend use the term “smart sustainable cities” instead of “smart cities”. Authors argue that as urban sustainability frameworks contain a large number of indicators measuring environmental sustainability, smart city frameworks lack environmental indicators while highlighting social and economic aspects. However, the current large gap between smart city and sustainable city frameworks suggests that there is a need for developing smart city frameworks further or re-defining the smart city concept. Digital urban spaces have the following features: to automate the process of data acquisition, storage, organization and analysis with the help of the Internet of Things, cloud computing and other technologies; to show the city’s real-time performance from different perspectives; to dynamically select and integrate smart data for providing intelligent urban information services. Digital urban spaces can comprehensively integrate data resources of urban physical, social and cyber spaces to form an urban data service system, covering the entire process of data collection, organization, analysis and management (Yaxue Ma et al., 2018).

Exploring the issue of the Sociocultural Information Urban Space within the framework of smart city concepts, which consider the smart city or smart infrastructure initiatives, launched by the governments to improve the quality of citizens’ life and help city managers/planners optimize the operation and management of urban infrastructures (Thomas et al., 2017). However, it should be noted that most of the concepts do not consider the Sociocultural Information Urban Space as a point of application of efforts and technologies and do not include the methods and information models for citizen engagement in its formation. Moreover, the interests and needs in involvement into dynamic activity on use and social and cultural city environment development of the categories of “temporary” citizens (labor migrants, tourists, etc.) are not considered. Another significant research problem, recognized by scientific community, but is not studied enough in academic studies, is the lack of mechanisms to motivate the citizens’ participation in the decision-making processes in urban development sphere among the proposed intellectual smart cities solutions, thus, there is the absence of maximal satisfaction of the urban community needs in quality services.

Therefore, the conducted research is aimed at filling indicated gaps by preparation and theoretical justification of the concept of sociocultural service oriented information space of the modern city as an interactive form of communication between the subjects of urban space, focused on the supplementation of existing forms and types within the framework of traditional social and cultural institutions (school, club, museum, university, theater, library etc.), on the development of intellectual and creative activities of people, based on their interactions, both in real and virtual space. The preparation of the concept includes the identification of the stakeholders and analysis of their needs, and of the basic information flows and sources of urban data. Moreover, the study can be considered as a source of knowledge and facilitates the better urban design, making it more functioning and more sustainable; optimize the use of limited resources and make better decisions in Sociocultural Information Urban Space.

3. THE CONCEPT AND THE ARCHITECTURE

Sustainable cities face many challenges that can be alleviated through the construction of smart cities. Smart city is a set of technical solutions and organizational activities aimed at achieving the highest possible quality of the urban management. Smart technologies reveal wide opportunities for the development of the urban environment, which becomes smarter when the infrastructure of the city's ICTs providing most of the city's functional needs. Smart city can be related to data-driven cities (DDC) which characterized by the ability of city authorities to use data collection, processing and analysis technologies to improve the social, economic, environmental situation and enhance the living standards of residents. DDC core components are urban data in all its diversity, data processing technologies, decision-making systems. Key stakeholders, government, business, and city residents are sources and recipients of data. The balance of stakeholders' views enhances the legitimacy, support, and effectiveness of projects smart city. However, there is another smart city component, the sociocultural, which also is important for its formation and development. Modern smart city focusses not only on certain technology packages, such city is a way to form a new society; the city solving sociocultural problems, which limit the life of the urban community, define a breakthrough into the future.

The global experience of creating information systems in various spheres of human activity, recorded in the methods of the world largest consulting companies, says that any initiative to create a smart city (building from scratch or transforming an existing model) should be accompanied by a set of basic documents and materials. The smart city architecture occupies important place (Robinson, 2012; Narmeen et al., 2015). The author's metamodel of the Smart City architecture based on the Open Group TOGAF 9.2 standard is demonstrated in Figure 1.

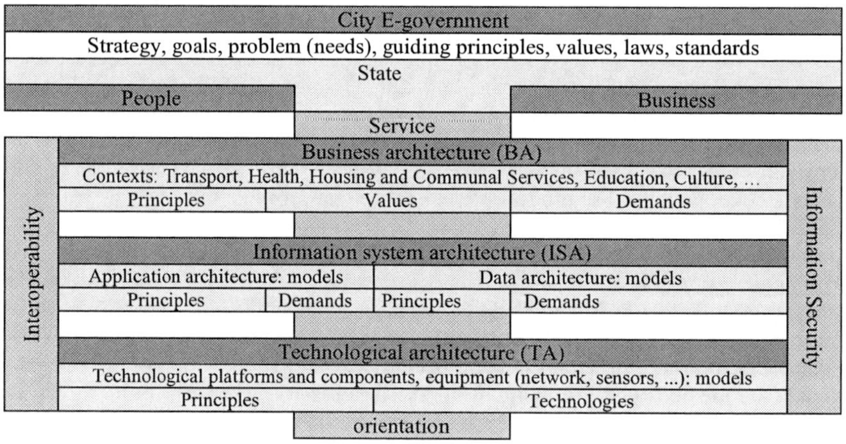

Figure 1. Metamodel of Smart City Architecture

The architecture metamodel takes a city-wide perspective and focuses on city contexts and architectural elements of every domain (Kartman et al., 2015). The metamodel helps to build the logical bridge between the definitions 'Smart City' and 'Information Urban Space' (IUS). There are several base common term-concepts for such mental migration that define every city domain content: 'Information Process', 'Application', 'Information resources', 'Big Data', 'Smart Technology'. The composition of space contexts depends on IUS type (set of urban spheres of activity). According to the authors' opinion, the Sociocultural Information Urban Space contains three base contexts, presented in Figure 2.

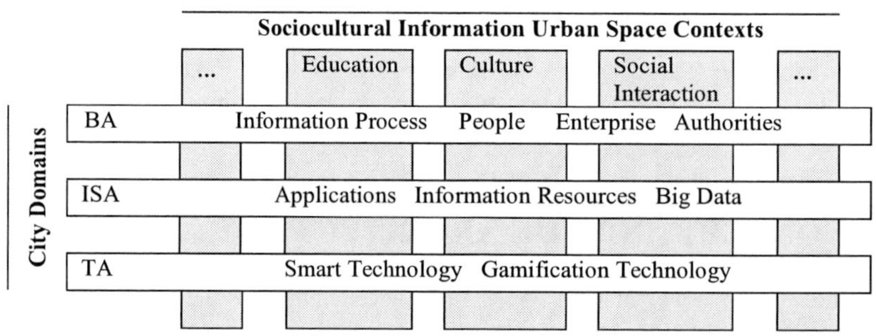

Figure 2. Domains and Contexts of Sociocultural Information Urban Space

With the growing importance of independent social interactions gamification technologies become an important public motivation mechanism in e-government and city management, as well as self-organization, self-development one (Feng et al., 2018; Mueller et al., 2018; Vanolo et al., 2018; Zica et al., 2018; Hassan et al., 2019).

There are many IUS definitions. None of the concepts gives a complete picture of the complexity and features of the Sociocultural Information Urban Space allowed to form structure and precise description of the space. The most constructive approach took into account social aspect. The Concept of digital urban space, proposed by Chinese researchers (Ma et al., 2018), based on the conceptions and technologies of CPSS, Digital Twin, and data science proposes to use urban big data sensed and acquired from urban Cyber- Physical- Social spaces by transformation into smart data to meet the needs of urban management and operation. This approach is a kind of pragmatic and utility, however, does not sufficiently take into account the concept of social machine, corresponding with sociocultural aspects of city realities, social communications, and initiatives, sophisticate city cultural connections and interactions because of the authors seek exclusively to further activate the value and realize the use of urban data. In order to clarify the understanding of the structure and composition of the Sociocultural Information Urban Space, the authors have reviewed and compared two initial concepts associated with Smart City: information system, social machine. Information system is a system, with the associated organizational resources (human, technical, financial, and others), that provides and distributes information (ISO/IEC 2382-1:1993). In a sociotechnical perspective, information systems are composed by four components: task, people, structure (O'Hara et al., 1999).

A social machine is an environment comprising humans and technology interacting and producing outputs or action, which would not be possible without both parties present (Berners-Lee and Fischetti, 1999). Researchers (Shadbolt et al., 2019) regard social machines are co-created by their human participants and their technological components. The associative term 'co-creation' in context of social machines means – there is no simple dividing line between the human and the technological, and from the point of view of the social machine it may be irrelevant whether a particular function is performed by a person or a computer. Social machines bring people together, using technology to enable communication and cooperation at scale (Shadbolt et al., 2019). It should be noted those researchers, who consider games and gamification as examples of social machines, as the players, possibly using avatars or alternative identities, interact both with each other and with programmed machine features and AI in a synthetic environment (Castronova, 2005). The common features of the concepts presented are obvious. The authors' point of view on the development of the conceptual base is reflected in Figure 3.

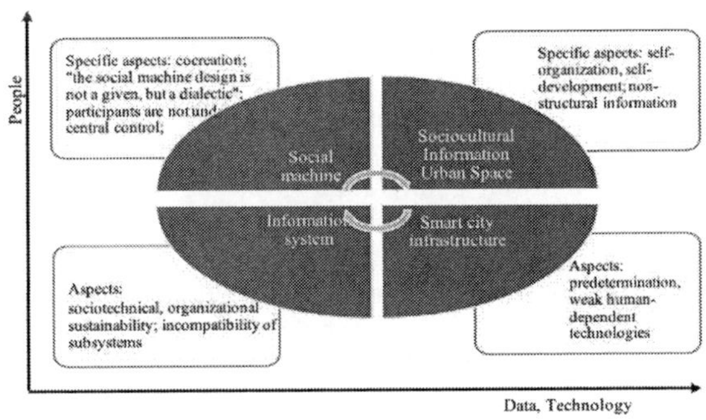

Figure 3. Sociocultural Information Urban Space Development

So, Sociocultural Information Urban Space is an evolutionary development of concepts presented with a focus on the socio-cultural development of the city. It has unique feature – the ability to self-organization and self-development, the most important for the smart city sustainability. Therefore, it is necessary to investigate and design such a space, using two scenarios at once: top-down design (purposeful planning view — city authorities, government structures, business) and bottom-up design (entropy view – personal initiatives).

Based on the construction of city profile's ideas, generalized and outlined by Ma et al. (2018), it is possible to propose specific approach to the Sociocultural Information Urban Space formation, represented as one of the components of Smart Living (Giffinger et al., 2010). There are following main components of the

Sociocultural Information Urban Space in the electronic network environment: Internet sites; service-oriented Internet portals; social network. Besides, the components are divided into several main levels: administrative; organization-oriented level; commercial; socially oriented level. There are the different information flows between the components at different levels, which define vertical links between the levels (Figure 4). On the one hand, they are determined by the power and business impact on the person (from up to bottom): regulations, cultural policy, control (level 1); citizens involvement into the Sociocultural IUS, provision of services (levels 2, 3, 4); formation of cultural needs and its satisfaction, formation of demand (levels 3, 4). On the other hand, people themselves actively influence the formation of Sociocultural IUS in accordance with their spiritual world and individual and collective needs (from the bottom up): collective communication in social networks, cultural events discussion, individual and collective preferences formation (level 4); impact on the upper levels for the development of the Sociocultural Information Urban Space through the feedback mechanisms; impact on the cultural policy formation (levels 1-4); correction of business supply through the financial flows while services purchasing (level 3).

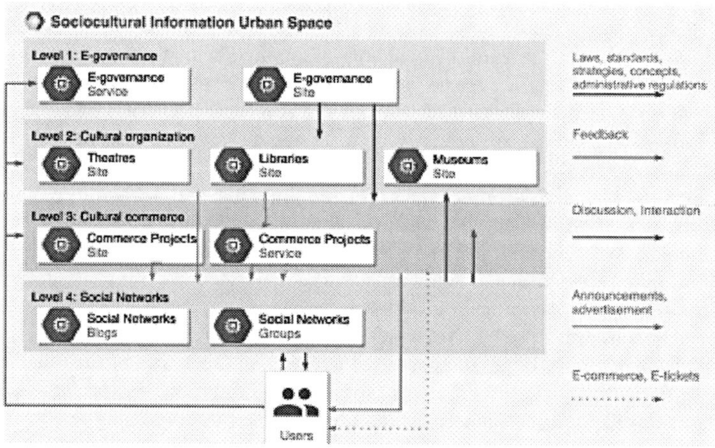

Figure 4. Architecture of Sociocultural Information Urban Space

It is obvious that the development processes of the Sociocultural Information Urban Space are possible only with a comprehensive account of all the information flows. At the same time, the city residents' involvement in active interaction within the Sociocultural Information Urban Space is the determining development factor, because the urban environment exists for the citizens and it cannot develop without their participation. In this situation, the study of information flows and its cultural contexts is a necessary condition for the cultural urban space analysis and for the operational decision-making at the level of state and municipal government. In turn, the information flows monitoring and the analysis of its contexts is a powerful analytical tool for business, which can affect the operational adjustment of the commercial offer for the cultural needs of citizens. The technique allows forming thematic collections of materials (contexts, which are relevant to the research topics). A thematic collection is a result of the peer review of paragraphs obtained sequentially with the relative, and then with thematic queries.

4. ST. PETERSBURG CASE

St. Petersburg (the cultural capital of Russia) have been chosen for studying the cultural information urban space. It contains all the diversity of Russian culture and the development of information infrastructure allows to identify the main components of the Sociocultural Information Urban Space. Various network information resources, which represent the different levels of the developed architecture, were considered in accordance with the approach to the formation of the Sociocultural Information Urban Space, proposed in this study. The interconnected components and the defined information flows between them were revealed by means of expert method. Special attention was paid to the gamification implementation in that components. Besides, the gamification function and the connection of information and real cultural space were also determined. To illustrate the pilot study, some examples are given below. Based on the analysis of the relationships between the components of the given examples, the formation of a sustainable developing Sociocultural Information Urban Space, which is one of the elements of Smart City, is concluded.

For example, several local information spaces were investigated: Anna Akhmatova Museum in the Fountain House (level 2); Museum of the history of Kronshtadt (http://visitkronshtadt.ru/) and commercial projects for the sale of tickets for cultural, sports and other events in Russia Afisha (level 3, https://www.afisha.ru). All the considered examples are characterized by the related components at both its levels, as well as at level 4. There are information flows between the levels that implement similar functions. Next, consider the implementation of the information space of Anna Akhmatova Museum in the Fountain House (level 2). The Museum has a website (https://akhmatova.spb.ru). It performs several functions: information (Museum activities, schedule, exhibitions, announcements of events, etc); educational (additional materials, description of projects and programs for different ages); motivational (by means of the theatre project "Theatre + Museum» and gaming programs for children); feedback (guest book). Using the aggregator (https://radario.ru/hosts/4994) Anna Akhmatova Museum distributes the information about the events, sells the e-tickets for events. Besides, there is Museum group on the social network Vkontakte (https://vk.com/akhmatova.museum), which includes more than 13 000 participants. The Museum publishes in the group the announcements of events and the additional cultural information, related to the theme of the Museum's exhibitions, which are discussed by the group members. There are also various documents, poems by Anna Akhmatova and by the related with Akhmatova poets, photos and videos of past events. This creates a media space of the Museum and performs a motivating function for attraction the visitors. The other thematic groups, related with this one, are the following: Information and analytical portal Brodsky.online (https://vk.com/brodsky.online) - 231 participants; Anna Akhmatova (https://vk.com/ahmatova_akuma) – more than 72 000 participants; "The American Cabinet of Joseph Brodsky" (https://vk.com/brodsky.kabinet) – 1 421 participants; Museum-Apartment of Lev Nikolaevich Gumilev (https://vk.com/lngumilevmuseum) – 842 participants; Project "Museum + Theatre in the Fountain House" (https://vk.com/museumplustheater) – more than 4 000 participants. These groups constitute a unified information and cultural space, engaging the people in the dialogue, as well as involving the participants into its real space.

5. CONCLUSION

The proposed approach to the formation and study of sociocultural IUS allows concluding the following items: sustainable development of IUS is possible with maximum consideration of information flows: the sustainability is provided by information flows " from above "(formed by public and municipal authorities, cultural institutions and business); development is provided by information flows "from below" (people' initiatives and needs expressed in their activity in the Sociocultural Information Urban Space); creative activity (Social Machines) and initiatives in sociocultural IUS should be supported by citizens presence and activity at all levels of architecture; for active residents' involvement in constructive and creative activity it is necessary to use various motivational mechanisms, particularly gamification.

The study also revealed a number of prospective interdisciplinary research areas at the intersection of sociocultural IUS and gamification (including the interdisciplinary research area "Social and ethical aspects of the Digital Economy: gamification in the social, scientific and educational subject domains"), and expanded the terminological landscape. Further study development involves the development of methods for information flows monitoring between the levels and components of the Sociocultural Information Urban Space and its contexts extraction.

ACKNOWLEDGEMENT

The reported study is funded by RFBR according to the research project "The integrated approach elaboration to the analysis of the terminological base of the developing interdisciplinary research in distributed network environment" № 18-011-00923, 2018-2020.

REFERENCES

Ahvenniemi, H. et al, 2017. What are the Differences Between Sustainable and Smart Cities? *In Cities*, Vol. 60, pp. 234-245. DOI: 10.1016/j.cities.2016.09.009

Belon, A. P. et al, 2015. Community Lenses Revealing the Role of Sociocultural Environment on Physical Activity. *In Am J Health Promot.* Vol. 30, No. 3, pp. e92–e100. DOI: 10.4278/ajhp.140428-QUAL-169

Berners-Lee, T. and Fischetti, M., 1999. Weaving the Web: The Original Design and Ultimate Destiny of the World Wide Web by its inventor. Britain: Orion Business. ISBN 978-0-7528-2090-3.

Bibri, S. E., 2018. A Foundational Framework for Smart Sustainable City Development: Theoretical, Disciplinary, and Discursive Dimensions and Their Synergies. *In Sustainable Cities and Society,* Vol. 38, pp. 758-794. DOI: 10.1016/j.scs.2017.12.032

Castiglione, A. et al, 2018. CHIS: A Big Data Infrastructure to Manage Digital Cultural Items. *In Future Generation Computer Systems,* Vol. 86, pp. 1134-1145. DOI: 10.1016/j.future.2017.04.006

Chianese, A. and Piccialli, F., 2016. A Smart System to Manage the Context Evolution in the Cultural Heritage Domain. *In Computers and Electrical Engineering*, Vol. 55, pp. 27-38. DOI: 10.1016/j.compeleceng.2016.02.008

Drotianko, L. and Yahodzinskyi, S., 2017. Information Environment as the Intercultural Communication Space. *In MATEC Web Conf.*, Vol. 106. 01006. DOI: 10.1051/matecconf/201710601006

Falco, E. and Kleinhans R., 2018. Beyond Technology: Identifying Local Government Challenges for Using Digital Platforms for Citizen Engagement. *In International Journal of Information Management*, Vol. 40, pp. 17–20. DOI: 10.1016/j.ijinfomgt.2018.01.007

Feng, Y. et al., 2018. Gamification artifacts and crowdsourcing participation: Examining the mediating role of intrinsic motivations. *In Computers in Human Behavior*, Vol. 81, pp. 124-136. DOI: 10.1016/j.chb.2017.12.018

Giffinger, R. and Gudrun, H., 2010. Smart cities ranking: an effective instrument for the positioning of the cities? *In ACE: Architecture City & Environment*, Vol. 6, No. 12, pp. 7-26. DOI: 10.5821/ace.v4i12.2483

Hassan, L. and Hamari, J., 2019. Gamification of E-Participation: A Literature Review. *Proceedings of 52nd Hawaii International Conference on System Sciences (HICSS'52)*, At Maui HI, USA, pp. 3077-3086.

Castronova E., 2005. *Synthetic worlds: the business and culture of online games.* University of Chicago Press, Chicago.

Kartman, G, Sandnes, A., Smit, G., 2011. Creating municipal ICT architectures. A reference guide from smart cities. https://joinup.ec.europa.eu/document/eu-creating-municipal-ict-architectures-reference-guide-smart-cities.

Ma, Y. et al., 2018. City profile: using smart data to create digital urban spaces. *ISPRS Ann. Photogramm. Remote Sens. Spatial Inf. Sci.*, Vol. IV-4/W7, pp. 75-82. DOI:10.5194/isprs-annals-IV-4-W7-75-2018

Masucci, P. A. et al, 2014. Exploring the Evolution of London's Street Network in the Information Space: A Dual Approach. In Phys. Rev. E, Vol. 89, No. 1, 012805. DOI: 10.1103/PhysRevE.89.012805

Mueller, C., Klein, U., Hof, A., 2015. An easy-to-use spatial simulation for urban planning in smaller municipalities. Computers. *In Environment and Urban Systems,* Vol. 71, pp. 109-119 DOI: 10.1016/j.compenvurbsys.2018.05.002

Narmeen, Z. B. and Jawwad, A. S., 2015. Smart City Architecture: Vision and Challenges. *In International Journal of Advanced Computer Science and Applications*, Vol. 6, No. 11, pp. 246-255. DOI: 10.14569/IJACSA.2015.061132

O'Hara, M., Watson, R., Cavan, B., 1999. Managing the three levels of change. *In Information Systems Management.* Vol. 16, No. 3, pp. 63-70. DOI:10.1201/1078/43197.16.3.19990601/31317.9

Sharma, S. and Mehta, V., 2016. Socio-Cultural Context of Human Computer Interaction (HCI) in Online Shopping Environment. *In Apeejay-Journal of Management Sciences and Technology*, Vol. 4, No.1, pp. 26-36. URL: https://apeejay.edu/aitsm/journal/docs/issue-oct-2016/ajmst040103.pdf

Shadbolt, N., O'Hara, K., De Roure, D., Hall, W., 2019. *The Theory and Practice of Social Machines*. Springer Nature Switzerland AG, Switzerland. DOI: 10.1007/978-3-030-10889-2

Thomas, S. et al, 2017. A Master Data Management Solution to Unlock the Value of Big Infrastructure Data for Smart, Sustainable and Resilient City Planning. *Creative Construction Conference 2017, CCC 2017, 19-22 June 2017, Primosten, Croatia. Procedia Engineering,* Vol. 196., pp. 939-947.

Wakabayashi, M., 2002. Urban Space and Cyberspace: Urban Environment in the Age of Media and Information Technology. *In International Journal of Japanese Sociology*. Vol. 11, No. 1, pp. 6-18. DOI: 10.1111/1475-6781.00014

Vanolo, A., 2018. Cities and the politics of Gamification. *In Cities,* Vol. 74, pp. 320-326. DOI: 10.1016/j.cities.2017.12.021

Zica, M. R., Ionica, A. C., Leba, M., 2017. Gamification in the context of smart cities. *International Conference on Applied Sciences (ICAS2017), 10–12 May 2017,* Hunedoara, Romania. *Materials Science and Engineering. International Conference on Applied Sciences*, Vol. 294, 012045. DOI: 10.1088/1757-899X/294/1/012045

LACK OF POPULARITY IN AUGMENTED AND VIRTUAL REALITY APPLICATIONS FROM THE PERSPECTIVE OF USERS, POTENTIAL USERS AND NON-USERS

Guilherme Daguir[1] and Fábio Campos[2]
Federal University of Pernambuco, Recife, Brazil

ABSTRACT

This study provides evidence on the possible barriers that affect the massification of solutions based on virtual reality (VR) and augmented (AR). To gather this evidence, nine sessions of Focus Groups were held with 43 people in total. Users of VR or AR applications, potential users and non-users were involved. The evidence obtained shows a plurality of entry barriers to decrease the lack of value perception related to applications using VR and AR. The majority of the sample shows a strong relation with theses technologies only with leisure and entertainment. Also some biases and less value of an immersive virtual reality for daily experiences or activities. However, AR was received better to daily purposes it was also not well connected with urban people routine in their perspective.

KEYWORDS

Perception, Feeling, Virtual Reality, Augmented Reality, Users

1. INTRODUCTION

With the popularization of the internet and increased processing power of desktops and laptops (desktops, notebooks and smartphones), easy access to a form of virtuality was achieved. However, familiarity with completely virtual worlds, through equipment with greater immersion potential (such as VR goggles), did not have the same popularity.

The virtuality has been studied and implemented for several decades. It is a matter of understanding reality with several steps up to a totally virtual world (VR). It is like a continuous line, where one end is however the real and physical world as it is now known, and along it points of interference of virtual elements, moving to the other end containing an artificially created reality by computer (Jason, 2016).

Virtual reality is defined to be a computer-generated digital environment that can be experienced and interacted through any sensory stimuli as if that environment were real (Jason, 2016). Augmented Reality (AR) is the mixing of virtual reality elements upon our everyday reality, usually done through a display, like a smartphone display.

Since 2008 augmented reality has been listed as one of ten technology that would change the way humans relate to computers (Trends, 2008). And the diminishing strangeness of systems that support these interactive formats in urban societies around the world is noticeable. However, augmented reality (AR) can be perceived in synchrony with virtual reality (VR) at this point of lack absorption by society (Erra, Malandrino, Pepe 2018). Both are not popular, routine and common in applications beyond casual entertainment.

Participatory design (or co-design), which involves the relationship with the user (Canina, 2011), it is also expressed here by the technique used (the Focus group) to get knowledge from the users perspective. The results from these experiments should help to power this way of problem exploration in the design process. It means to relate this phase of designing as a relationship with users in order to know about their perspective before constructing any project to them.

---

[1] gui.daguir@gmail.com
[2] fc2005@gmail.com

This document proposes to investigate this lack of familiarity of people with these technologies. The research carried out offers points of discussion that can lead some evidence on how to improve the interaction within this area, beyond the former goal of understanding what causes non-use of AR eVR in different groups.

2. INSIGHTS AND PERCEPTION

The applied research strategy was the use of the Focus Group qualitative technique. The Focus Group was chosen because of its flexibility of application and the ability to generate insights about the subject.

Focus group is a qualitative method often used in the design process in the phase of exploration of the problem or in analysis of solutions and prototypes. It is a dynamic created by a small group of well-chosen people, when guided by a skilled moderator, can provide deep insight into themes, patterns, and trends. This moderator guides the dialogue between the participants in order to maintain the discussion and achieve the objectives of that meeting. Participants in turn are free to discuss the proposed topics without fear of being judged is diminished. Participants are more likely to share experiences, stories, memories, perceptions, wants/needs, and fantasies, expectations, opinions, feelings (Martin, Hannington, 2012).

When analyzing focus group data, is recommended to pay particular attention to stories people tell, the metaphors and analogies they use, and how they describe their experiences, preferences, and memories. By looking for recurring topics and themes that produces strong responses, that can be analyze for trends and patterns (Martin, Hannington, 2012). This responses can be called insight, a popular word in design area related to some accurate or deep intuitive understanding of a target. Results from focus groups should never be extrapolated for how a whole population is or feels. It should be integrated with other qualitative or quantitative methods that can be realized in further experiments.

The study performed here, used the application of this technique to seek to understand the perspective of people divided in three groups. First group is the ones who often have contact and use of VR or AR applications (which we consider "users"). The second group are the ones who had some episodic contact with the technology and consider accessing it in the future (those we consider "potential users"). The third group have never experienced VR or AR (consider as "non-users").

The "user" group was composed of developers or early adopters of VR and AR applications (gamers, IT and design staff involved in the development of VR and AR solutions, content producers for VR and AR, etc).

The "potential users" group was composed of people who have already had the opportunity to use a VR or AR application in some situation and who are open to eventually reusing those technologies (several users who have experienced VR or AR at a trade show , for example, or in a game console of some known).

The "non-users" group was composed of people who had never experienced the use of VR or AR solutions. Some of them were not interested and other were open to experiencing the use of such solutions some day.

The following sections describes the experiment performed, detailing each session of Focus Groups.

3. HOW THE FOCUS GROUP WERE PERFORMED

The experiment was conducted this way, a group of volunteers undergraduate student designers that applied the focus group technique in a volunteer groups of participants invited by the designers. The total number of groups and focus group sessions were 9. The designers were organized in a way they could engage in the experiment, and were disposal for one week to deal it. Could be happened more sessions in this time but no more participants appeared or setted an appointment .

Characterizing the groups, the designers were about 20, between 1 and 4 years of experience in the area, were undergoing training. All of them received that month previous explanatory and practical training in relation to technique. Each team counted with at least 1 moderator, and the data were recorded through audio and video for further analysis. When the group had more than a person, the rest of the designers helped in the recording activity, prepare the room and write down the saved content, being helpful to quickly delivery of the data. As fewer the group fewer the speed.

The participant group were gather by the designers, they announcing the event to relatives, colleagues, in tourism spots and in front of university departments linked to the area of technology (computer science, engineering and design). The participating professions were in the areas of: Computer science, biology, architecture, physical education, dancers, physicians, teachers, self-employed professionals, students of computer science and design, electronics and computer technicians.

No gender or age specification was required for this activity. The designers asked the invited people about their relationship with VR and AR, and only if there were one of each group (users, potential users and non-users) this could be considered a session for the experiment. The concept of virtual reality and augmented reality considered for this article, holded by the designers and participantes, are explained in the introduction chapter one of this paper.

The total sample were 43 participants ranging from 8 to 65 years. One child, one 16-year-old adolescent, three elderly aged 60-65 years old, two middle-aged participants, one in 46 other in 55 years old, and 36 participants aged 18-30 years. A brief of all the evolved in the experiment can be readed in Table 1.

The focus groups occurred in 2018, in the city of Recife, Pernambuco, without the need for participants to be born in that city, but only native showed. A confidence interval and level were calculated by the Research System (Creative Research System, 2018), in order to compare how the discussion provided through this activity is reflected in level of fidelity in the Brazilian population. On this experiment we have a confidence interval of 15 and 95% confidence level reached.

The confidence interval is also called margin of error. The confidence level tells you how sure you can be. It is expressed as a percentage and represents how often the true percentage of the population who would pick an answer lies within the confidence interval. The 99% confidence level means you can be 99% certain. Most researchers use the 95% confidence level (Creative Research System, 2018).

Who was available at the time and date marked were gone to the focus group events were available in the three shifts of the day, for a period of 7 days, these sessions not happened sequentially, each group has a particular hour to begin.

The experiment purposed was carried out in person. Exception for one group that applied it remotely due to request of all participants involved in that specific session. The procedure was conducted in the same way for all groups, so even the one which occured in online video chat had the same steps. All the session were analyzed in the same way here. Maybe further experiments could be realized in order to map variables and compare if answers provided from online way have different results.

In the first moment of the focus group the participants were advised about the recorder, and informed that activity will occur as a simple conversation and the review of the meaning of VR and AR has been said. The moderator started a conversation with the participants about VR and AR, and conduct them to talk about these topics below in the following order. If the groups starts to diverge, the moderator should bring them back naturally without instruct it. The reason for it is making all participants feel in a free environment to express their thoughts, as a casual chat. The guiding topics were:

1. Knowledge and general use of VR and AR;
2. Problems in the use of these technologies, and general technologies;
3. Applications and services that use VR and AR.

Table 1. Distribution of participants in the focus group experiment

ID Group	A	B	C	D	E	F	G	H	I
Designers evolved	6	3	2	1	2	1	1	2	2
Total number of subjects in the sample group	7	4	4	4	5	3	6	5	5
Range age of subjects per group	15-21	18-65	8-49	21-26	21-40	28-46	21-29	18-65	19-28

This study relied on data collection by undergraduate design students. The acquired data were punctuated in commented topics, that occurred with the proposed dialogue with the focus group participants, it can be seen in the next chapter (table 2). These topics were extensively described at the outset. And they were later reorganized into larger categories called here as "clustering topics".

These clustering topics received scores equivalent to length of groups that raised those point of argument in the focus group session. That is, many questions emerged and each one counted as one, even when discussed twice or more within a single group.

A parallel between the clustering topics and theirs score, were made based on likert scale scores of importance (Vieira, Dalmoro, 2008).

Therefore,

0% - 20% Unimportant

21% - 40% Little important

41% - 60% Reasonably important

61% - 80% Important

81% - 100% Very important

Through this, none of the categories fitted as "unimportant" nor as "very important."

4. RESULTS

As explicated in the last chapter the talk between the participants in the focus group was conduct in the three major questions. These questions resulted in insights called here as "commented topics", each one have been ascertained by the designers team and these were organized in relation to group that they come from, and are reported in Table 2.

Table 2. Topics resultant from application of focus group

ID Group	Commented Topics
A	• Addiction in virtual reality. • Not practical. • Aversion to technologies. • Fears of misuse of people with the unfolding of technology.
B	• Aversion to immersive virtual reality • Belief that technological evolution is always associated with future dystopic. • Utility for entertainment only. • Virtual reality would deepen social divisions.
C	• Rejection of this type of technology for daily use. • Low usability of VR devices (headsets) for everyday use. • Consider immersive only applications that require a headset, disregarding AR. • Identifying AR as a possibility to be used daily by not associating this with peripherals or headsets.
D	• Excitement for using VR and AR daily with banal activities (eg snacking). • Ease of adaptation to AR because it is less immersive, and more useful for routine activities.
E	• Perceive AR and VR just as entertainment. • Realize the negative points of the headsets as weight, and possibility of headache • Identify AR as easier for adaptation and day-to-day situations. • VR would be useful only for long-term experiences.
F	• See in the AR and VR the future of technology. • Never used VR arguing, relating this to the need for a specific device. • Rejection to these technologies for fear of damage to health. • Understand that VR does not apply to routine activities, only at very specific moments in life.

G	• Participants commented on the use of these technologies for serious purposes (education, training etc) but in their daily lives perceived AR and VR only as entertainment possibilities. • AR and VR should be encouraged for training more often. • VR without utility for daily use. • Understand the peripherals (controls and headsets) as a fact of breaking in the immersion experience. • Participants never researched the cost of devices that supported AR and VR technology, but argued that their high cost was a deterrent. • Fear of health damage caused by VR immersion with headset.
H	• Little interactivity in AR applications on screens. • High cost of VR devices and no daily applicability. • AR and VR are only consistent for entertainment purposes.
I	• Understand in AR and VR the future of technology, but not financially accessible at all. • Realize advantages in VR and AR applications for serious purposes. • Relate VR to teleportation and holograms. • Punctuate the evolution of AR and VR only in the universe of games.

5. DISCUSSION

The themes discussed were grouped into general categories in an attempt to understand the data in a quantitative perspective. These categories involving the topics discussed are detailed in Table 2, also in this tabulation is the relation of the quantity of groups of the experiment that approach this topic.

Using a Likert scale application (Vieira, Dalmoro, 2008) the categories were distributed according to the length of times that they were discussed. A category with more discussions per group was considered more important than another with less groups talked about it.

It is worth remembering that these categories and scores may prove different in new samplings. Further studies are encouraged with different subjects.

Table 3. List of emerging focus group topics

Clustering topics	Length of groups that addressed	Percentage in total number of sampling groups	Impact on the sample
Exclusive relationship with leisure	6	66%	Important
Relation to serious purposes	5	55%	Reasonably important
Futuristic perception, not applied to the contemporary	4	44%	Reasonably important
Little applicability in everyday urban routine (For questions of usability or system issues)	4	44%	Reasonably important
Cost-benefit of adaptation	3	33%	Little important
High investment	3	33%	Little important
Damage to health (physical and mental, eg headaches and addiction)	3	33%	Little important
Impact on social inequality (being accessible to select groups of society)	2	22%	Little important
Uselessness	2	22%	Little important

A strong relationship can be perceived regarding the connection of exploited technologies with entertainment, being related in 6 of the 9 studied groups.

What can be understood as pejorative, due to the use of terms that may classify the use of this technology as inferior when not used for serious purposes. Or it can be understood as a way for penetration and expansion of AR and VR in the population masses as it happened with other technologies.

Games such as Pokemón Go that uses augmented reality may contribute to the argumentation of the market impaction related to this technology encourage the increase of access to similar application. Also facilitate people to recognize this technology when it became usual in serious purposes.

There are many causes of bad VR. Some failures come from the limitations of technology, but many come from a lack of understanding perception, interaction, design principles, and real users. However, creating compelling VR experiences is an incredibly complex challenge (Jason, 2016).

Issues such as adaptation and applicability have emerged that can be used by the field of design as an incentive to the exploration of VR and AR. Web systems and mobile apps have been translated into punctual solutions, adding value to solving problems and popularizing these technologies worldwide. Opportunities for optimizing the usability and interaction issues surrounding the theme here are also open.

In a lower degree of impact, AR and VR technologies were underestimated from the point of view of this sampling, and related to damage in health, social hierarchy and loss of money. These topics have already been judged many times according to the literature and some are not total true. As an example, the relationship between virtual reality and health detriment, whose evidence has shown ways to circumvent this correlation (Jason, 2018). This evokes further study in order to get validated answers.

The dystopian perspective could be correlated with the lack of popularization of the real possibility of VR and AR and the lack of discussion about them. Similar to access to the Internet through personal computer and mobile that it has optimized the communication and sharing of data and information, resulting in a social improvement, with access to education and the vascularization of the economy. Once these technologies and devices were also associated with future tragedies. In fact one of the biggest points demonstrated through sample is that people cannot accept AR and VR with the contemporary reality. Delaying getting used with something that is already here.

6. CONCLUSION

This study served its purpose of exploration on the topic of the lack of popularity of technologies, applications and devices, involving virtual and augmented reality, from the point of view of users, potential users and never users.

Through this experiment can be seen some popular thoughts and a strong aversion to adopting immersive technologies as virtual reality. Some rely in reasons that are not supported by literature and market as damage in health, high prices, lack of usability and low appliance in everyday urban routine. This perception can be either biases or lack of perception of practical value. In fact the second option is near truth due to high levels of connection between AR and VR with leisure and entertainment purposes. Both technologies are identified mostly not as tools but as support for entertainment.

Applications that use non-immersive at all as augmented reality receive less criticism, likely to be involved in people's daily lives through other devices or media, and connection with daily challenges. This instructions can be used to conduct the industry in the spread of this technology.

The results obtained also evokes relevance of participatory design techniques. User involvement seems to be a new valuable way to consider the user in subjects that are going to affect them further. Participatory path of project support ask user not exclusively a theoretical exercise, but a new way of thinking, as basic requirement to develop solutions able to meet desires of real people (Canina, 2011).

Other point this article claims is collaborating in evidences that helps validate results from qualitative techniques as the "focus group". This method is often used in Design field and brings good insights from user perspective.

The resolutions shows the perception of local society, which has its own culture and perspective characteristics related to digital artifacts. This experiment could be replicated in order to generate similar and contrasting data. Also comparing the difference results from online and presencial sessions, and different public.

REFERENCES

Canina, Marita; Coccioni, Elisabetta. *Creating Participatory Design Tools: a Didactic Experience.* INDACO Dept, Politecnico di Milano. ICORD 11: Proceedings of the 3rd International Conference on Research into Design Engineering, Bangalore, India, 2011.

Creative Research System. *Sample Size Calculator.* Avaliable in 2019 on https://www.surveysystem.com/sscalc.htm

Jerald, Jason. *Human-Centered VR Design.* IEEE Computer Graphics and Applications, 2018.

Jerald, Jason. *The VR Book: Human-Centered Design for Virtual Reality.* Association for Computing Machinery and Morgan & Claypool Publishers, 2016.

Martin, Bella; Hanington, Bruce. *Universal Methods of Design – 100 Ways to Research Complex Problems, Develop Innovative Ideas, and Design Effective Solutions.* Rockport Publishers, 1° edition, United States of America, 2012.

Trends, G. E. *Technologies roadshow.* Gartner Identifies Top Ten Disruptive Technologies for 2008 to 2012, 2008.

Ugo Erra, Delfina Malandrino & Luca Pepe. *Virtual Reality Interfaces for Interacting with Three-Dimensional Graphs.* International Journal of Human–Computer Interaction, 2018. DOI: 10.1080/10447318.2018.1429061

Vieira, Kelmara Mendes; Dalmoro, Marlon. *Dilemas na Construção de Escalas Tipo Likert: o Número de Itens e a Disposição Influenciam nos Resultados?* XXXII Encontro da ANPAD, Rio de Janeiro, RJ, 2008.

THE EFFECTS OF PERSONAL TRAITS AND GAME FACTORS ON IMMORAL GAME BEHAVIOR: FOCUSED ON <LEAGUE OF LEGENDS>

Sungje Lee, Jeonyoung Kong, Meiying Piao and Euijun Jeong
Dept. of Culture Contents,
Konkuk University, 120 Neung Dong-Ro,
Gwang Jin-Gu, Seoul
South Korea

ABSTRACT

As digital games have become popular, the number of incidents and the degree of damage caused by immoral game behavior (such as "flaming", "trolling") are on the rise. But few studies have been conducted to explore the antecedents to such flaming and trolling. Therefore, this study empirically examined the effects of aggression and self-esteem, and game factors (game moral positioning, game motivations, gaming time) on immoral game behaviors with participating game players of <League of Legends>. Results showed that game moral positioning (i.e., a tendency to choose evil characters or activities) and advancement motivation (i.e., focus on competition and growth) positively affect immoral game behaviors. While "fun/interest" motivation has a negative effect on immoral game behaviors. In addition, gaming time did not affect flaming and trolling. These results show that preference of an evil moral identity or competitive motivation in a game could affect immoral game behaviors. These results show that moral preference of an evil identity or competitive motivation in a game could affect immoral game behaviors. And it could impede delectable game experience. Furthermore, meanwhile, aggression increase immoral game behaviors. But self-esteem did not affect immoral game behaviors. Finally, moral positioning moderates the impact of aggression and advancement motivation on immoral game behaviors. Consequently, digital games that solicit moral deviations should seek ways to offer unique entertainment, and to encourage game users not to put an obstacle to the other game users' positive gaming experience due to their excessive immersion in evil characters or identities. As suggested, game producers must offer diverse types of gaming systems or to organize special game modes than those promoting excessive competitiveness for the pleasure and enjoyment of various types of users.

KEYWORDS

Immoral Game Behavior, Game Moral Positioning, Game Motivation, Aggression, Self-Esteem

1. INTRODUCTION

As digital games have become popular, the number of incidents and the degree of damage caused by immoral game behavior are on the rise. Such behaviors obstruct others' comfortable gaming experience and the spirit of fair competition (Fragoso, 2016), thus requiring an urgent study on the prevention and eradication of immoral game behavior. In particular, flaming and trolling have led to difficult situations as these occur more often than match-fixing or the use of illegal programs, resulting in considerable displeasure.

To address these issues, game developers are restricting abusive language and trolling in games by using various internal and external measures. For example, Riot Games, the developer of the globally sensational game, <League of Legends>, has developed its own slang detection system and is running a jury system in the game to deter abusive language in the South Korean server (League of Legends, 2016; Kou & Nardi, 2013). Despite such efforts, however, flaming and trolling in digital games still pose grave concerns (Seo, 2015).

Flaming is an actual phenomenon that frequently occurs in the environment of computer-mediated communication (CMC) (Hwang et al, 2016; Lea et al, 1992). It is categorized as a negative behavior that expresses hostility toward others or subjects indifferent to oneself by using vicious language (Moor, 2010).

Previous studies have reported that flaming stems from self-esteem (Suh, 2012; Brewer & Kerslake, 2015), game motives (Alonzo & Aiken, 2004; Chu et al, 2013; Bishop, 2014), and social identification (Lee, 2005).

Trolling is a type of behavior that intentionally dismisses cooperating with a user or carries out certain actions repetitively to provide advantages to the user's competitors. Recently, trolling has often been used as an online language with the aim of intentionally making others angry (Thacker & Griffiths, 2012). According to previous studies, trolling is affected by personal factors like aggression (Buckels et al, 2014; Lee et al, 2016; Patchin & Hinduja, 2010), game motives like enjoyment (Graham & Gosling, 2013) and the structural characteristics of digital games where loose regulations are applied (Seo, 2015).

As one of the antecedents to game behaviors, game motivation is believed to play an important role in the use of flaming and trolling behaviors. The use and gratification theory says that game users are clearly aware of their motives, which they must satisfy and for which they actively use media. Thus, specific motives for the use of media affect the users' media use or behavioral patterns, including gaming behaviors (Stafford et al, 2004; Zhang et al, 2011; Yee, 2006a; Yee, 2006b; Kim & Park, 2007). Billieux et al. (2013), for example, conducted research that focused on "World of Warcraft," and showed that motivations, such as advancement and escapism, affected immoral behaviors, like illegal player killing (PK).

As personal traits, self-esteem and aggression have also been reported to affect immoral (Brown et al, 2011; Donnellan, 2005; Kaplan, 1982; Berkowitz, 1993). Self-esteem is the degree of awareness of one's affection for oneself or the degree of one's positive evaluation of oneself (Larson, 1992) Donnellan et al. (2005) reported in their longitudinal study that low self-esteem is related to anti-social behavior. In line with this study, similar research also pointed out that low self-esteem is a key factor in cyber bullying and misdeed (Kaplan, 1982). Aggression refers to all forms of behavior that aim to damage others physically or psychologically (Berkowitz, 1993), which has been used as a parameter for predicting anti-social behavior or of deviant behaviors like misdeeds or crimes (Jung, 2011; Olweus, 1979; Thomas, 2006). Regarding immoral behaviors in video games, Lee et al. reported that high levels of aggression lead to trolling behaviors (Lee et al, 2016).

Furthermore, moral positioning by players during gaming (i.e., game moral positioning) may play a key role in explaining in-game immoral behaviors. Moral positioning means an individual under social conflict is using moral context and moral tendencies to understand the moral identity and meaning of the subject and object (Sammut & Gaskell, 2010). Individuals, when facing conflicts, refer to other viewpoints or to the roles of the other members, and, through this process, they verify their position or pursue a specific behavioral objective (Triberti et al, 2015). In this context, it is believed that moral positioning is a process in which one judges his or her position or behavior by referring to moral identity, even in the online space. Triberti et al., for example, argued that moral positioning may affect the occurrence of aggressive behavior in online games.

However, there have been few studies that attempted to use the players' game motivations and moral positioning with regards to immoral behaviors in multi-user online games. Therefore, this study empirically examined the effects of moral positioning, game motivations, and personal traits (i.e., aggression and self-esteem) on immoral behaviors with the controls of the users' gaming habits and demographic variables.

2. METHOD

<League of Legends (LOL)>, a PC-based, multi-user online game, has been distributed globally and is a top game in South Korea. A survey was conducted with the participants recruited from "League of Legends Inven" (lol.inven.co.kr) and "League of Legends Hungryapp" (leagueoflegends.hungryapp.co.kr), the top two LOL communities in Korea.

A total of 401 study participants joined. The data from 343 participants, excluding those with missing values, were selected for analysis. They included 299 males (87.1%), whose average age was around 26 years old. The average daily gaming hours was 1.54 hrs. (SD =54 min.).

Based on previous studies (Lee, 2003) six questions were adapted to measure FT (flaming and trolling) behaviors. Flaming items (α=.862) included curses and mockery (e.g., "I curse when I don't like the playing style of the other game users," "I mock or ridicule the other game users to make them feel bad"). Trolling items (α=.859) covered intentional negligence or behavior that intentionally put one's ally in danger (e.g., "I do not participate in the game or let my competitor kill my character when I don't like the playing style of the other game users").

In terms of game motivations, 17 items from the game use motive scale (Motivations for Playing Online Games) were used (Park & Song, 2010). The sub-scale items were social relationship (α=.872), acquisition (of unique personality) (α=.775), escapism (α=.738), advancement (of competitive game skills) (α=.805), and fun/interest (α=.847).

To measure self-esteem and aggression, Rosenberg's Self-Esteem Scale (Rosenberg, 1965) (α=.862, 10 items) and The Short-Form Buss-Perry Aggression Questionnaire (α=.882, 12 items) were used, respectively (Diamond et al, 2005). Finally, in terms of game moral positioning, modified scales by Triberti et al. were used (Triberti et al, 2015). The 5 items included preference for evil roles and characters (e.g.,"I tend to choose evil game roles," "I prefer to make evil choices.", α=.908).

3. RESULT

The variables that had significant positive relations with flaming and trolling were aggression (r=.509; p<.001), game moral positioning (r=.466, p<.001), and motivations such as social relationship (r=.133, p<.05), escapism (r=.314, p<.001), advancement (r=.297, p<.001). Fun/interest (r=-.203, p<.001) showed a negative relationship. In the regression analysis, moral positioning demonstrated positive effects on flaming and trolling (see Model1, Table 1). In the game motivations, advancement of competitive game skills showed a positive effect (β =.199, p<.001) whereas fun/interest had a negative effect on immoral behaviors (β =-.214, p<.001).

In terms of control variables, there were no significant effects on gaming time and age on the behaviors. In terms of personal traits, aggression had a positive effect (β =.384, p<.001), while self-esteem had no significant effect.

Game moral positioning showed interactive effects with aggression and advancement motivation (see Figure 1). In the group of higher preference for evil-role characters, a higher level of aggression increased the level of immoral behaviors while there was no significant change for the lower group. Likewise, in the higher group, higher level of advancement augmented the degree of immoral behaviors.

4. DISCUSSION

Game moral positioning played a key role in the degree of flaming and trolling. Moral positioning increased the level of immoral behaviors and showed interactive effects with aggression and advancement motivation. Though the levels of aggression and advancement strongly increased the level of flaming and trolling, moral positioning moderated the effects. These results proved that preference of an evil moral identity in a game could affect one's in-game immoral behaviors, such as verbal hostility and anti-user behaviors, which could impede fair competition and gaming pleasure. They also implied that the moral preferences of the narrative or playing style in the system might cause malicious and rude tendencies (Happ et al. 2013; Hollingdale & Greitemeyer, 2013).

In terms of game motivations, the advancement of competitive game skills had a positive effect on immoral behaviors. In line with the competitive playing environments of <League of Legends>, the obsessive pursuit of winning might cause aggressive language and behaviors. For example, obsessive competition might lead one to coerce his or her team members more than it would be necessary, or to slight others who have fallen behind. Thus, it is expected that the experience of failure in a competition could cause immoral game behaviors under the guise of "enjoyment," in which users hide their disappointment and misery.

Fun/interest, however, was shown to have a negative effect on flaming and trolling. This means that game users who are more interested in leisurely pursuits tend to manifest less immoral behaviors in a game. Furthermore, it implies that, from the perspective of game content design, a comfortable game environment can be established by offering diverse types of entertaining contents than stressing excessive competitiveness.

Aggression had a positive effect on flaming and trolling. This result showed that, in the real world, game users' aggression might lead to immoral behavior in online games, and offered interesting research implications on the relation between digital gaming and aggression. On the other hand, self-esteem had no significant effect. This result implied that positive self-evaluation affected digital game behavior, which might be closer to online efficacy than to organic self-esteem. Because online/offline self-efficacy affects each other (Jeong & Kim, 2011), even with higher levels of organic self-esteem, if one has lower online (or game) self-efficacy, one may become more easily agitated or frustrated under stimulating circumstances within a game.

Table 1. Regression Analysis

	Model 1		Model 2	
Variables	β	SEB	β	SEB
Controls				
Gender	-.085*	.093	-.100*	.089
Age	-.075	.006	-.063	.006
Gaming Time (Daily gaming hours)	.022	.026	-.004	.025
Moral Positioning				
Game Moral Positioning (GMP)	.243***	.033	-	-
Personal Traits				
Aggression (AG)	.384***	.050	.691***	.095
Self-esteem (SE)	.002	.049	-.017	.048
AG x GMP			.352**	.035
SE x GMP			.049	.008
Motivation				
Relationship	.058	.037	.054	.036
Acquisition	-.053	.041	.014	.040
Escapism	.028	.047	.019	.045
Advancement (AD)	.199***	.036	.404***	.066
Fun/interest (FN)	-.214**	.038	-.228***	.052
AD x GMP			.332***	.024
FN x GMP			-.072	.016
R^2	.501		.551	
F-value	27.175***			28.182***

Note. Dependent variable: Flaming & Trolling.
Due to high collinearity (VIF= 34.593), GMP was not used in Model2
P*<.05, p**<.01, p***<.001

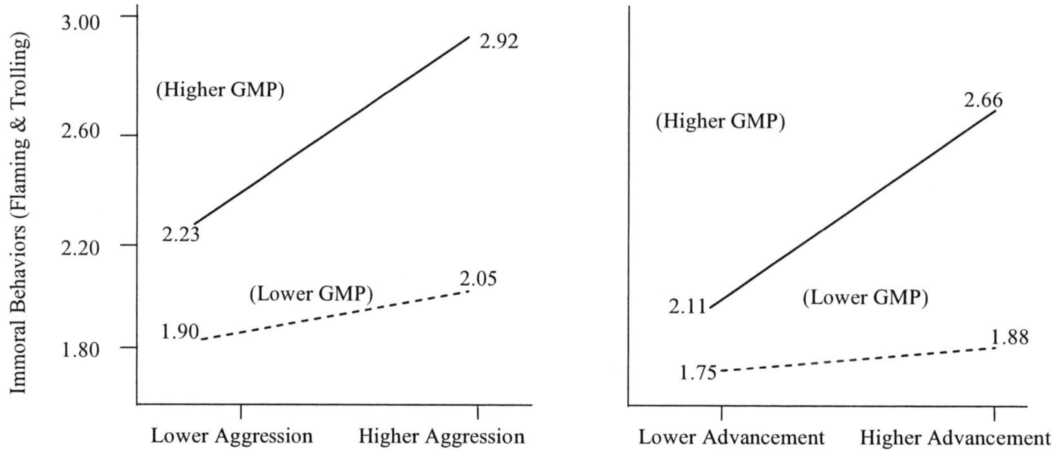

Figure 1. Interaction Effects of Game Moral Positioning with Aggression and Advancement

It is interesting to note that gaming time did not affect flaming and trolling. This result is consistent with that of a trolling study on Korean gamers. The results supported the argument that playing games for a long time does not necessarily increase immoral game behavior. Consequently, in the research on immoral game behavior, it is necessary to consider diverse variables like structural traits of games and individuals' internal factors rather than the hours devoted to gaming.

This study has several limitations. First, this study does not guarantee causal relationships. Further research must be conducted, including a longitudinal study, to determine causality. Next, empirical data were collected from just one country. Future studies may replicate this study from a global perspective to include diverse cultural environments.

In conclusion, this study showed the important roles of moral positioning and game motivations in multi-user online games. Those results imply that, in a multiplayer gaming environment, users are not forced to immerse themselves in immoral behaviors only because these digital games are "virtual." The competitive environment that entices users' motivation to become more competitive can make other players uncomfortable since one, especially for those who are highly aggressive, can assume an evil identity to remain motivated. Consequently, digital games that solicit moral deviations should seek ways to offer unique entertainment, and to encourage game users not to put an obstacle to the other game users' positive gaming experience due to their excessive immersion in evil characters or identities. As suggested, game producers must offer diverse types of gaming systems or to organize special game modes than those promoting excessive competitiveness for the pleasure and enjoyment of various types of users.

REFERENCES

Alonzo M, Aiken M. Flaming in Electronic Communication. Decision Support Systems 2004; 36:205–213.

Berkowitz L, 1993. *Aggerssion: Its causes, conseqiences, and control*. philadelphia : Temple University Press.

Billieux et al, 2013. Why do you play World of Warcraft? An in-depth exploration of self-reported motivations to play online and in-game behaviors in the virtual world of Azeroth. *Computers in Human Behavior*, 29, 103–109.

Bishop J, 2013. The effect of de-individuation of the internet troller on criminal procedure implementation: An interview with a hater, *International Journal of Cyber Criminology*, 7, 28–48.

Brewer G & Kerslake J, 2015. Cyberbullying, self-esteem, empathy and loneliness. Computers in Human Behavior, 48, 255–260.

Brown J et al, 2001. From the top down: Self-esteem and self-evaluation. *Cognition and Emotion*, 15, 615-631.

Buckels et al, 2014. Trolls just want to have fun. *Personality and Individual Differences*, 67, 97–102.

Chu K et al, 2013. A Study on Factors Influencing on Flaming Behavior in Cyberspace. *Journal of Cultural Industry Studies*, 13, 47–57.

Diamond P et al, 2005. Factor structure of the Buss-Perry Aggression Questionnaire (BPAQ) with mentally ill male prisoners. *Criminal Justice and Behavior*, 32, 546-564.

Donnellan et al. 2005, Low self-esteem is related to aggression, antisocial behavior, and delinquency, *Psychological Science,* 16, 328–335.

Fragoso S, 2016. HUEHUEHUE I ' m BR : spam, trolling and griefing in online games. *Revista FAMECOS : mídia, cultura e tecnologia,* 22, 147–164.

Graham L & Gosling S, 2013. Personality profiles associated with different motivations for playing World of Warcraft, *Cyberpsychology, Behavior, and Social Networking,*16, 189-193.

Happ C et al, 2013. Superman vs. BAD man? The effects of empathy and game character in violent video games. *Cyberpsychology, Behavior and Social Networking,* 16, 774-778.

Hollingdale J & Greitemeyer T, 2013. The changing face of aggression: The effect of personalized avatars in a violent video game on levels of aggressive behavior. *Journal of Applied Social Psychology,* 43, 1862–1868.

Hwang J et al, 2016. Cyber neutralisation and flaming. *Behaviour & Information Technology,* 35, 210–224.

Jeong E, Kim D, 2011. Social activities, self-efficacy, game attitudes, and game addiction. *Cyberpsychology, Behavior and Social Networking,*14, 213–221.

Jung Y, 2011. Early Adolescents' Changes in Aggression and Delinquency According to Using Computer Games: Latent Growth Curve Modeling, *Journal of Cybercommunication Academic Society*, 28, 89–125.

Kaplan H. 1982. Self-esteem and deviant behavior. *Journal of Youth and Adolescence*, 4, 175-188.

Kim Y & Park S, 2007. A Study on the Online Game Use Influences in Game Flow and Addiction: Focusing on the Uses and Gratifications Approach. *Korean Journal of Journalism & Communication Studies*, 51, 355–377.

Larson J, 1992. Anger and aggression management techniques through the think first curriculum. *Journal of Off ender Rehabilitation*, 18, 101-117.

Lea M. et al, 1992. Flaming in computer-mediated communication: Observations, explanations, implication. In: M. Lea, eds. *Contexts of Computer-mediated communication*. London: Harvester Wheatsheaf.

League of Legends, 2016, *Korean slang sanctions system*. League of Legends News. http://www.leagueoflegends.co.kr/?m=news&cate=notice&mod=view&schwrd=&p=1&idx=253132#.WBt7X5v_rIU

Lee C, 2004. A Study for Flaming in Virtual Community, *Korea Marketing Review*, 18, 3-30.

Lee E, 2004. Effects of Visual Representation on Social Influence in Computer-Mediated Communication. *Human Communication Research*, 30, 234–259.

Lee J et al, 2016. The Relationship between Players' Characteristics and Trolling Behavior: Focused on < League of Leagend >. *Journal of Korea game society*, 16, 63-72.

Moor P. et al, 2010. Flaming on YouTube. *Computers in Human Behavior*, 26, 1536–1546.

Olweus D, 1979. Stability of aggressive reaction patterns in males: A review. *Psychological Bulletin*, 86, 852–875.

Park J & Song Y, 2010. College Students' Motivations for Playing Online Games and Experiential Satisfaction. *Korean Journal of Journalism & Communication Studies,* 54, 131–154.

Patchin J & Hinduja S, 2010. Cyberbullying and self-esteem. *Journal of School Health,* 80, 614-621.

Rosenberg M, 1965. *Society and the Adolescent Self-Image.* New Jersey: Princeton University Press.

Sammut G & Gaskell G, 2010. Points of View: Social Positioning and Intercultural Relations. *Journal for the Theory of Social Behavior,* 40, 47-64.

Seo S & Kim C, 2015. Recognition of the Type and Cause of < League Of Leagend > Trolling. *Journal of Korea Game* 15, 93–110.

Stafford et al, 2004. Determining Uses and Gratifications for the Internet. *Decision Sciences*, 35, 259-288.

Suh A, 2012. The Factors Affecting Individuals' Flaming Behavior in Virtual Communities: Theoretical Exploration and Empirical Analysis. *The e-Business Studies*, 13, 89–114.

Thacker S & Griffiths MD, 2012. An Exploratory Study of Trolling in Online Video Gaming. *International Journal of Cyber Behavior, Psychology and Learning,* 2, 17–33.

Thomas A, 2006. Moral Positioning: A formal theory. *Grounded Theory Review : An International Journal,* 6, 30–31.

Triberti S et al, 2015. Moral positioning in video games and its relation with dispositional traits: The emergence of a social dimension. *Computers in Human Behavior*, 50, 1-8.

Yee N, 2006. Motivations for Play in Online Games. *Cyber Psychology & Behavior*, 9, 772–775.

Yee N, 2006. The demographics, motivations, and derived experiences of users of massively multi-user online graphical environments. *PRESENCE: Teleoperators and Virtual Environments*, 15, 309-329.

Zhang Y et al, 2011. Gratifications, collective self-esteem, online emotional openness, and traitlike com- munication apprehension as predictors of Facebook uses. *Cyberpsychology, Behavior, and Social Networking*, 14, 733–739.

THE ANALYSIS OF USER'S INTENTION IN USING MOBILE PAYMENT: A CASE OF YAP!

I Gede Adi Surya Atmajaya, Putu Wuri Handayani, Ave Adriana Pinem and Fatimah Azzahro
Faculty of Computer Science, Universitas Indonesia, Depok, Indonesia

ABSTRACT

This study discusses the acceptance of mobile payment in Indonesia using the case study of mobile payment YAP. The model used in the research is TAM (Technology Acceptance Model) and the analysis process uses SEM-PLS (Structural Equation Modeling-Partial Least Square). This research is a quantitative research by using analysis of primary data in the form of questionnaires distributed to all of YAP users. The results of the study show that a person's main factor in using the YAP mobile payment services is influenced by one's experience in using mobile payment services (at least toward using) and social influence from other person (perceived social influence). The expected experience is supported by the perception of benefits from the mobile payment services. This perception of benefits is influenced by the level of ease and degree of conformity of a person's habits in making payment transactions. This can be used by mobile payment service providers to create services with applications that are easy to use, convenient, and have the power of interest for users such as giving a gimmick to certain payment transactions.

KEYWORDS

User Acceptance, Mobile Payment, Yap!, TAM

1. INTRODUCTION

The use of mobile payments in the millennial era grows rapidly. Millennial consider mobile payment services as an innovative payment alternative. YAP (Your All Payment) mobile payment is a non-cash payment tool issued by one of the largest listed state-owned banks in Indonesia (BNI). The YAP application runs on a mobile device with the Android or IOS operating system. The YAP payment process uses a scan QR code model. This QR code is a standard code in the form of a two-dimensional matrix containing black and white squares in an irregular position (Li, et al., 2015). Merchants are required to have a unique QR code to ensure that there is cooperation between merchants and BNI. One of the advantages of YAP and BNI customers is that there is no need to do a top up process for the application wallet. This is because the source of this wallet connected to BNI savings, credit card and wallet products. This YAP can be used as an online payment, offline payments at YAP merchants, debit transactions, credit cards, and money withdrawals. Based on BNI Corporate Plan 2014-2018, BNI will strengthen the consumer business in collaboration with business partners and provide financial transaction solutions with a focus on e-commerce and millennial generation. The process to achieve this goal is to provide digital payment services to support customer transaction needs such as mobile payment.

The organization of electronic money and electronic wallets in Indonesia is regulated by Bank Indonesia. Based on data from Bank Indonesia as of September 26-2018, there are 32 companies that have obtained electronic licenses (Bank Indonesia , 2018). Several companies compete to provide the best electronic-based payment services with their respective products. Based on interviews with operational manager of BNI Bank who handle YAP, it was disclosed that management targeted users of YAP application to be 2 million users and the number of merchants participating in YAP network reached 1 million merchants by the end of 2018. Based on the BNI's internal data as of September 2018, the number of users as many as 355,229 and the number of merchants is 314,265. These show that the target of management is still far to be achieved, because the users only reached 17% and 31% merchants respectively.

Research on the acceptance of mobile payment is increasingly popular along with the growing development of the e-commerce industry and the use of mobile cellular technology. This is also the case in

Indonesia. A study on the investigation of receipt of mobile payments, shows that there are users in Indonesia motivated to use mobile payment (Hunafa, et al., 2017). A significant factor in motivating to use mobile payment is perceived usefulness and perceived ease to use. Perceived ease to use is influenced by social influence, while perceived usefulness is influenced by personal innovativeness and perceived ease to use. The desire to use the system can be determined by the analysis of behavior and profiles of the users or potential users (Jia, 2014). There are many methods for making predictions to analyze the level of system adoption, including mobile payment technology. The most widely used method is TAM (Technology Acceptance Model).

Based on the facts presented, a strategy is needed to increase (Bank Indonesia , 2018) the acceptance of mobile payment applications to pursue the company targets. This research will raise the issue of "What factors can influence the acceptance of mobile payments with YAP case study?" This study is expected to provide information about factors influencing the acceptance of mobile payments and play a role in the process of implementing mobile payment in Indonesia. Organizations can get recommendations for the process in developing a mobile payment therefore it can be used more widely, and it is expected to achieve the goals of the organization in developing business processes. This paper has 7 sections namely theoretical background, conceptual model, methodology, results and analysis, discussion, implications as well as conclusion.

2. THEORETICAL BACKGROUND

2.1 Mobile Payment

According to Bank Indonesia regulations, the term of mobile payment is generalized into digital financial services (DFS), which defined as payment system and financial services activities carried out in collaboration with third parties and using mobile or web-based technology tools and equipment to support inclusive finance. This definition from Bank Indonesia is also in line with the opinion of (Dahlberg, et al., 2015) who define mobile payment as a means of payment for goods, services, and bills with a wireless mobile device and other communication technologies. Based on the two definitions of mobile payment, we can conclude that mobile payment is a mean of payment for goods, services, and bills by using applications on mobile devices issued by third parties. YAP is a payment tool stored in a mobile application. The source of funds used in YAP are comprises of savings, credit cards, and electronic money. Since it was introduced in January 2018, YAP can be used to process payments to offline and online merchants/merchants. The payment process at offline merchants can be done by scanning the merchant's QR code, while online merchants can be done by choosing an online payment method through YAP. The ease of the payment process is in a more flexible funding source facility for various customers, especially for BNI customers who do not need to top up because the source of fund can be taken from savings or credit card facilities.

2.2 Technology Acceptance Model (TAM)

Technology Acceptance Model (TAM) is a study of the acceptance of a technology for the users of these technologies. This theory was introduced by Davis in 1989 regarding the acceptance of someone to accept or reject information technology. The TAM theory uses 2 important variables in determining the acceptance of a technology namely perceived usefulness (perceived use) and perceived ease of use. There are several information technology acceptance theories such as technology acceptance model (TAM), a unified theory of acceptance and use of technology (UTAUT), and diffusion of innovation (DOI). In this study TAM will be used as a research model for the acceptance of mobile payment technology. The use of TAM is considered very suitable to provide more informative conceptual predictions with various variables that can be adjusted to the main research to analyze the behavior of users of mobile payments (Jia, 2014).

3. CONCEPTUAL MODEL

This study is the result of a combined research model from (Ma, et al., 2018) (Cabanillas, et al., 2015) (Karjaluoto, et al., 2017) (Mun, et al., 2017) (Hossain & Mahmud, 2016). Previous researches discussed the factors that influence the use of mobile payment services. These factors are also called research variables, then these variables are formed into indicators of research that will be tested against several respondents. The research model can be seen in Figure 1.

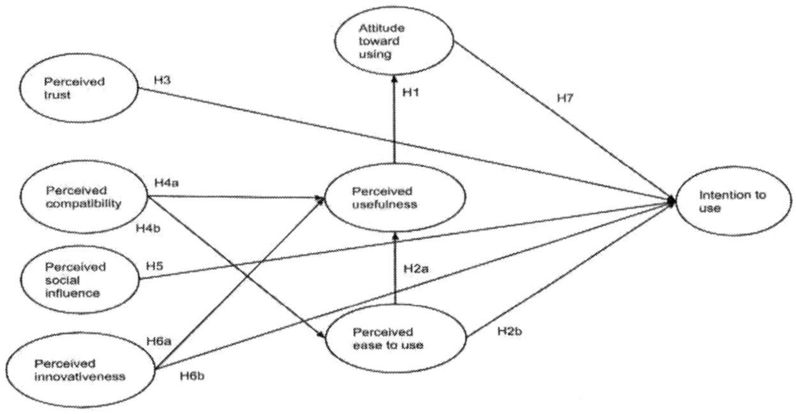

Figure 1. Proposed Model

Research by (Davis, 1989) mentions two factors that influence a person's desire to use a system, namely, perceived usefulness and perceived ease of use. Perceived usefulness is defined as the level of how much someone believes that the use of a system will improve performance (Davis, 1989). Research by (Cabanillas, et al., 2015) (Davis, 1989) state that perceived usefulness has a positive impact on attitude toward to use. Mobile payment is one of the uses of technology to assist in the payment process. If an individual considers mobile payment technology to be useful, it will be a pleasure to use. Mobile payment can provide convenience and comfort in making payments, and people are no longer bothered with carrying lots of cash. Relationships that can be formed from perceived usefulness are:

H1: Perceived usefulness influence positively on attitude toward to use mobile payment.

Perceived ease of use is one of the significant factors in the acceptance of a technology (Davis, 1989). Perceived ease of use is defined as a person's level of trust in using a system with minimal effort. Perceived ease to use has a positive impact on intention to use and perceived usefulness (Ma, et al., 2018). The studies by (Cabanillas, et al., 2015) and (Davis, 1989) resulted that strengthen perceived ease to use has an impact on perceived usefulness. The study by (Mun, et al., 2017) also results in perceived ease to use having an impact on the intention to use. If the user feels easy in transacting using a mobile payment, then it can increase the frequency and nominal of the transaction using mobile payment. Relationships perceived ease to use with perceived usefulness and intention to use hypotheses can be formed as follows:

H2a: Perceived ease to use influences positively on the perceived usefulness in using mobile payment.

H2b: Perceived ease to use influence positively the intention to use an individual in using mobile payment.

Research by (Ma, et al., 2018) says perceived of trust affects the intention to use. Trust is a person's belief to use a mobile payment transaction in accordance with expectations. Trust is still important in ecommerce transactions. If a person's level of trust increases, the desire to use mobile payment will also increase. The relationship of perceived of trust and mobile payment can be written with the following hypothesis:

H3: Perceived of trust influences positively on intention to use

Research by (Ma, et al., 2018) says that perceived compatibility affects perceived ease to use. Someone who is accustomed to shopping online will be more easily interested in mobile payment. The results of the study by (Cabanillas, et al., 2015) states that perceived compatibility affects perceived usefulness. The payment process can be accommodated by YAP by making offline payments through scanning a QR code on a mobile device and for payment online with payment notifications that must be made on the online transaction activities that have occurred. If someone has a transaction behavior related to online payments, they will be more interested in using mobile payment. The perceived compatibility relationship can be written as a hypothesis as follows:

H4a: Perceived compatibility influences positively on perceived usefulness

H4b: Perceived compatibility influences positively on perceived ease to use

Researches by (Cabanillas, et al., 2015) and (Mun, et al., 2017) give results that social influence influences intention to use. In addition, research by (Cabanillas, et al., 2015) says that personal innovativeness to IT influences perceived ease to use and intention to use. Evaluation of technology acceptance cannot be separated from decisions that consider social environmental conditions. The social environment is an individual's perception of how important a system is used. The relationship between perceived social influences can be written as a hypothesis as follows:

H5: Perceived social influence influences positively on intention to use

Personal innovativeness is a form of desire from individuals to use new technology (Cabanillas, et al., 2015). This is in line with the research conducted by (Karjaluoto, et al., 2017) which uses the personal nature of individuals to have an impact on the level of adoption of a system. (Cabanillas, et al., 2015) says that innovative personal can influence the level of individual acceptance to use technological innovations. Personal innovativeness is also influenced by perceived usefulness and intention to use. (Karjaluoto, et al., 2017) has the aim of research that describes the acceptance of the value of technology. The value is also influenced by personal innovativeness. This form of value describes the benefits and experience in using a technology. The relationship between perceived innovativeness on mobile payment can be written with the following hypothesis:

H6a: Perceived innovativeness influences positively on perceived usefulness

H6b: Perceived innovativeness influences positively on intention to use

Attitude toward to use is a positive or negative feeling to use a new system. Research by (Cabanillas, et al., 2015) states that attitude toward using affects intention to use. The same thing is also supported by research by (Hossain & Mahmud, 2016) which says that attitude toward using affects intention to use. If someone has a sense of wanting to use a mobile payment, it will give a positive boost to using the mobile payment. The attitude relationship toward to use can be written with the following hypothesis:

H7: Attitude toward to use influences positively on intention to use

4. METHODOLOGY

4.1 Research Method

The approach in this study uses a quantitative approach. This research uses a case study research method and the data collection method uses an online survey. Stages of research carried out include the process of problem identification, study of literature, primary data collection (preparation of quantitative data collection instruments, readability test of questionnaires, distribution of questionnaires), data analysis, and conclusion. Before conducting questionnaires, readability testing needs to be performed for the purpose to provide information on how much the readability of the questionnaire by respondents. Questionnaires that have been prepared are disseminated through Twitter social media, Instagram and communication channels. The analysis process will be carried out using SEM-PLS (Structural Equation Model) by utilizing SmartPLS 3.0. The selection of SEM-PLS is based on the advantages of the data sample that does not have to be normally distributed, the number of samples is small, and does not have to meet the criteria of goodness of fit.

4.2 Instruments

The questionnaires filled out by the respondents are divided into 3 parts. The first is the use of mobile payment products that have been used. Second is fill in with respondents' identity such as age, gender, education level, occupation, frequency of mobile payment usage, and e-mail address. Third is the set of questions of user acceptance of mobile payment. The questionnaire uses a 5 Likert scale where scale 1 is strongly disagree and scale 5 strongly agrees.

5. RESULT AND ANALYSIS

5.1 Respondents Demographics

The research questionnaire data was collected with a period of 1 month (151 respondents). The summary of the respondents' demographics in the study can be shown in Table 1. The data meets the minimum requirements where more than 30 respondents are required to conduct research (Roscoe, 1975). The summary of the respondents' demographics in the study can be shown in Table 1.

Table 1. Respondent Profile Demographic Summary

Characteristics		Number of Respondents	Percentage	Characteristics		Number of Respondents	Percentage
Gender	Men	75	50%	Education	Junior High School	4	3%
	Women	76	50%		High School	4	4%
Age	<18 years	2	1%		Bachelor	113	75%
	18-24 years	31	20%		Master/Doctoral	29	19%
	25-34 years	95	63%		Others	1	1%
	35-44 years	16	11%	Duration of Use	<= 3 months	25	17%
	45-54 years	7	5%		> 3 - 6 months	31	20%
	55-64 years	0	0%		>6 - 12 months	33	22%
	>=65 years	0	0%		>1 - 2 months	35	23%
					>2 - 4 months	17	11%
					> 4 months	10	7%

5.2 Analysis using SEM-PLS

The phase analysis of the outer model is a process of testing reliability and testing validity. Reliability testing is seen in the Composite Reliability (CR) value and the value of Cronbach's Alpha (CA). Based on Table 2 shows that the composite reliability value of all latent variables is above 0.7, so that it can be said that all latent variables qualify for the next process. The testing process after fulfilling the reliability requirement test is testing the outer loading. Outer loading is used to check indicators that meet the requirements of a latent variable. The outer loading value is said to qualify if the value is more than 0.7 (Hair, et al., 2014). Testing the value of the outer loading shown has met the conditions where the outer loading value for each indicator used above 0.70 so that the process is continued with a validity testing process. Convergent validity testing is used to ensure that all domains used in the construct are relevant and are covered by existing indicators. Convergent validity test is acceptable if the average variance extracted (AVE) value is greater than 0.50 (Hair, et al., 2014). The results of convergent validity testing with AVE values can be shown in Table 2 where all latent variables have met the requirements. The AVE value of each latent variable is above 0.5.

Table 2. CA, CR and AVE Values

Variables	CA	CR	AVE	Variables	CA	CR	AVE
attitude toward using	0.823	0.883	0.655	perceived innovativeness	0.718	0.798	0.676
intention to use	0.905	0.933	0.778	perceived social influence	0.890	0.932	0.820
perceived compatibility	0.828	0.897	0.743	perceived trust	0.844	0.883	0.640
perceived ease to use	0.850	0.899	0.692	perceived usefulness	0.841	0.896	0.822

Based on the results in Table 3 it can be shown that the results of hypothesis testing are based on the value of the path coefficient and the value of t-statistics with an error rate of 5%. The hypothesis is accepted if the path coefficient value is greater than 0.05 and the t-statistics value is more than 1.96. The results of the analysis show that there are 6 accepted hypotheses and 4 hypotheses rejected (Figure 2).

Table 3. Results of Hypothesis Test

Hypothesis	Path Coefficient	t-statistics	p-value	Results
H1	0.730	12.736	0.000	Accepted
H2a	0.396	3.797	0.000	Accepted
H2b	-0.088	0.830	0.406	Rejected
H3	0.033	0.358	0.720	Rejected

Hypothesis	Path Coefficient	t-statistics	p-value	Results
H4a	0.415	3.777	0.000	Accepted
H4b	0.617	10.119	0.000	Accepted
H5	0.343	2.214	0.027	Accepted
H6a	-0.005	0.057	0.954	Rejected
H6b	-0.032	0.446	0.655	Rejected
H7	0.575	4.605	0.000	Accepted

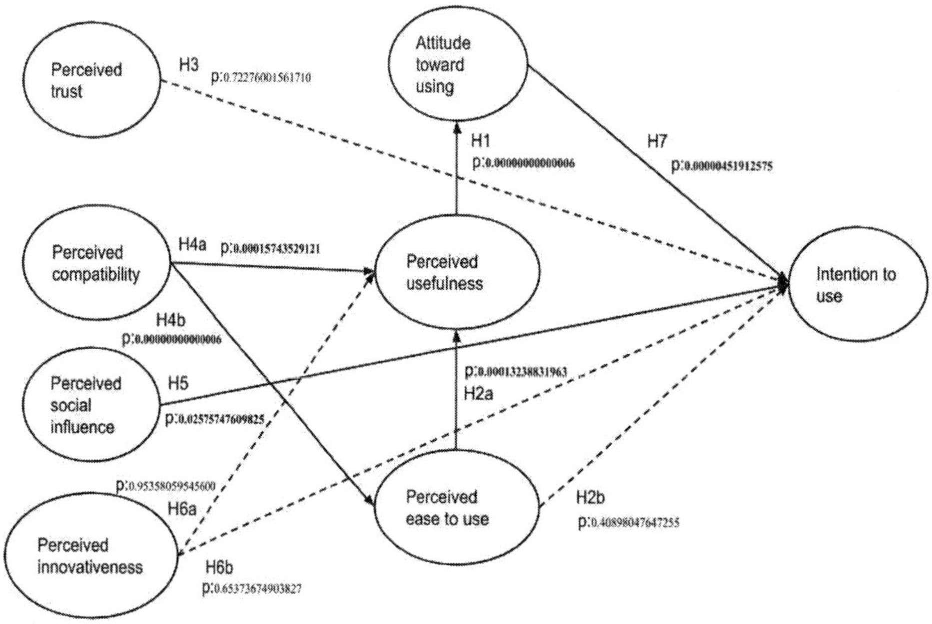

Figure 2. Research Model After the Hypothesis Testing

6. DISCUSSIONS

In the study shows that the H1 perceived usefulness test has a significant impact on the personality toward using the users to use the mobile payment services. It can be interpreted that if the user gets the benefit of the mobile payment services, it is possible for the user to have the drive to continue using the mobile payment services. In other words, to get encouragement for users to use mobile payment services, mobile payment services providers can provide benefits to the ease of transacting on payments that are usually done every day. This is in line with research by (Cabanillas, et al., 2015) which states that the perception of benefits is positive in determining one's experience in using a QR-based mobile payment system.

Then, the factor perceived ease to use has a significant impact on the perceived usefulness of the use of mobile payment services. This can be interpreted that the user feels the ease of use of the mobile payment application can provide more encouragement to explore the mobile payment service. In other words, mobile payment service providers can improve the user experience in interacting with easy applications, so that the benefits of mobile payment services can be felt more by mobile payment users. Ease of use can be produced by providing face-to-face forms that are easy to operate and provide a nuance of beauty that matches the mobile device.

In H3, the relationship perceived easy to use does not have a positive influence on the intention to use for the case of using the mobile payment services. The ease of use of the application is not a priority for payment transaction users to switch to the mobile payment services. This is contrary to research by (Cabanillas, et al., 2015) and (Mun, et al., 2017) which says that perceived ease has a positive impact on someone's interest in using mobile payment services. This happens because mobile payment services in China and Malaysia are already mature enough and the readiness of its users has been formed to accept the mobile payment model. This condition cannot be formed in the environment of mobile boom users who have just boomed.

In addition, a person's belief in mobile payment services do not have a positive impact on someone's interest in using mobile payment services. A person's interest to switch or try mobile payment services to accommodate payment transactions compared to the aspects of benefits and suitability expected by users or prospective users. This finding contrasts with research by (Ma, et al., 2018) which says that the perception of trust has a positive influence on interest in using mobile payment. This happens because the mobile payment services providers in China have gained trust from its users because its service providers are trusted international companies, namely WeChat, Alipay, and Baidu Wallet. In addition to international service providers, the Chinese community also believes in services released from the country because of the national soul that has been instilled by the Chinese government.

In addition, the results of the H5 test indicate that perceived compatibility has a significant impact on the perceived usefulness of using the mobile payment services. It can be interpreted that the trend or lifestyle of a person in making a payment transaction is very influential to bring about the desired benefits on the mobile payment services. For mobile payment services providers, to maintain and increase mobile payment users, it can provide the benefits expected by users. These benefits can be encouraged by providing payment services that were previously used by users to switch to mobile payment services. Giving a gimmick can also be a stimulus for people to use. This finding is in line with research by (Cabanillas, et al., 2015) which states that the perception of conformity positively determines the perception of the benefits of a QR-based mobile payment system.

The perceived compatibility relationship has a significant impact on perceived ease to use the use of mobile payment services. It can be interpreted that the trend or lifestyle of users of payment transaction services can encourage increased ease of use of mobile payment applications. In other words, if the mobile payment service provider can provide a stimulus for the use of mobile payment services for various payment transactions that have been widely used, it will encourage people to try using the mobile payment application. Types of transactions that can be provided in the form of purchases of goods and services through online media or direct cash transaction media. The ease of use of the mobile payment application turned out to be not only influenced by the design of face-to-face applications that are good and interactive, but also driven by the desire of users to try the application due to the commonly used payment transaction model. This finding is also in line with research by (Ma, et al., 2018) which says that perceptions of conformity have a positive impact on perceived ease.

The H7 test results perceived social influence have a significant impact on the intention to use on the mobile payment service. This can be interpreted that the social influence of one's experience in using a mobile payment service provides moral support for others to try to do things that are considered beneficial for others, especially in using mobile payment services. For mobile payment services providers to be able to increase someone's desire to use mobile payment services, they can provide a marketing model, one of which focuses on the experience, benefits, and convenience of users of mobile payment services. This marketing model can be used to build positive thinking for everyone involved with payment transactions, so that they start trying out mobile payment services and move from the old payment method (cash, debit cards and credit cards). This finding is in line with research by (Mun, et al., 2017) which says that social influence has a relationship with consumer interest in using mobile payment services. This is also supported by research by (Cabanillas, et al., 2015) which says that the perception of how important a system is from users positively determines the interest in using a QR-based mobile payment system.

7. IMPLICATIONS

The results showed that there were 6 variables involved in the desire of users to use the mobile payment service. There are 5 significant variables related to user desires, namely perceived compatibility, relative to using, perceived usefulness, perceived ease to use, and intention to use. One influential variable was also perceived social influence. The results of the study show that a person's main factor in using the mobile payment service is YAP influenced by one's experience in using mobile payment services and social influence from someone. If someone has a pleasant experience with a mobile payment service, it is highly likely that the person will continue to use the mobile payment services. The social environment factors of a person also have a big role for someone to continue to use mobile payment services or influence new people to start trying mobile payment services. This social environment can be in the form of the opinions of people around, people who influence others, or through social media. Social media can be used to show the benefits and convenience felt by using a mobile payment service. This usage experience is influenced by the perception of benefits, where these benefits are supported by perceptions of ease and conformity in one's habits in making payment transactions.

8. CONCLUSION

The results of the study show that a person's main factor in using the mobile payment services is influenced by one's experience in using mobile payment services (attitude using toward) and social influence from someone (perception social influence). A pleasant experience with mobile payment services, provides a higher possibility for someone to continue to use the mobile payment services. Supporting factors for generating such experiences are perceived usefulness and perceived ease to use. The social environmental factor of a person (perceived social influence) also has a big role for someone to continue to use mobile payment services or influence new people to start trying mobile payment services. This social environment can be in the form of the opinions of people around, people who influence others, or through social media. Social media can be used to show the benefits and convenience felt by using mobile payment services. This usage experience is influenced by the perception of benefits, where these benefits are supported by perceptions of ease and conformity in one's habits in making payment transactions.

REFERENCES

Bank Indonesia , 2018. *Informasi Perizinan Penyelenggara dan Pendukung Jasa Sistem Pembayaran.* [Online] Available at: https://www.bi.go.id/id/sistem-pembayaran/informasi-perizinan/uang-elektronik/penyelenggara-berizin/Pages/default.aspx [Accessed 8 October 2018].

Cabanillas, F. L., Luna, I. R. & Ríos, F. J., 2015. User behaviour in QR mobile payment system: the QR Payment Acceptance Model. *Technology Analysis and Strategic Management,* 27(9), pp. 1031-1049.

Dahlberg, T., Guo, J. & Ondrus, J., 2015. A critical review of mobile payment research. *Electronic Commerce Research and Applications,* 14(5), pp. 265-284.

Davis, F. D., 1989. Perceived Usefulness, Perceived Ease of Use, and User Acceptance of Information Technology. *MIS Quarterly,* 13(3), pp. 319-340.

Hair, J. J. F., Sarstedt, M., Hopkins, L. & Kuppelwieser, V. G., 2014. Partial least squares structural equation modeling (PLS-SEM) An emerging tool in business research. *European Business Review,* 26(2), pp. 106-121.

Hair, J. J., Hult, G. M., Ringle, C. M. & Sarstedt, M., 2014. *A Primer on Partial Least Squares Structural Equation Modeling (PLS-SEM).* California: SAGE Publications, Inc.

Hossain, R. & Mahmud, I., 2016. *Influence of cognitive style on mobile payment system adoption: An Extended Technology Acceptance Model.* s.l., s.n.

Hunafa, K., Hidayanto, A. N. & Sandhyaduhita, P., 2017. *Investigating Mobile Payment Acceptance Using Technological- Personal-Environmental (TPE) Framework: A Case of Indonesia..* s.l., IEEE.

Jia, L. H., 2014. *The effect of technology usage habits on consumers' intention to continue use mobile payments.* s.l., s.n.

Karjaluoto, H., Shaikh, A. A., Saarijärvi, H. & Saraniemi, S., 2017. How perceived value drives the use of mobile financial services apps. *International Journal of Information Management.*

Li, L., Qiu, J., Lu, J. & Chang, C.-C., 2015. An Aesthetic QR Code Solution Based on Error Correction Mechanism. *The Journal of Systems & Software,* Volume 116, pp. 85-94.

Ma, L. et al., 2018. *What Drives the Use of M-payment ? An Empirical Study about Alipay and WeChat Payment.* s.l., s.n.

Mun, Y. P., Khalid, H. & Nadarajah, D., 2017. Millennials' Perception on Mobile Payment Services in Malaysia. *Procedia Computer Science,* Volume 124, pp. 397-404.

Roscoe, J.T. 1975. *Fundamental research statistics for the behavioral sciences, 2nd edition.* New York: Holt Rinehart & Winston.

CRGOURMETCOFFEE.COM: USING E-COMMERCE TO MITIGATE THE COFFEE PARADOX IN COSTA RICA

Francisco J. Mata[1] and Irene Hernández Ruiz[2]
Escuela de Informática, Universidad Nacional-Costa Rica, Heredia, Costa Rica

ABSTRACT

We present the background and the design and development considerations for an electronic platform to sell Costa Rican roasted coffee through e-commerce, referred to as crgourmetcoffee.com (https://www.crgourmetcoffee.com). This system is proposed as a solution to mitigate the coffee paradox −phenomenon that makes the coffee prices received by famers in developing countries to be increasingly lower, despite a growing demand for this product. In this regard, crgourmetcoffee.com is aimed at enabling Costa Rican coffee farmers to sell directly its coffee to final consumers in developed countries, eliminating intermediaries in an effort to allow producers to obtain higher price margins.

KEYWORDS

E-commerce, Coffee, Costa Rica, Coffee Paradox

1. INTRODUCTION

Costa Rica began producing coffee since the XIX century. Until the decade of 1970, the country´s economy heavily depended on this product; however, the economic importance of coffee has diminished over time −giving way to other agricultural products like banana and pineapple and to medical devices. According to the Costa Rican Export Promoting Agency PROCOMER (2017), coffee exports represented 3 percent of total exports of the country, in economic terms, for 2017.

Coffee, like most agricultural products that are distributed through agro-chains, is at the mercy of fluctuations in international markets. As explained by Daviron and Ponte (2005), these fluctuations −evidenced in the form of large variations in prices− affect mainly the producers of this product, which are characterized by being small farmers located in developing countries. These authors refer to this phenomenon to as the coffee paradox. This situation is a major factor for the continuous decrease of coffee producers in Costa Rica. In the last decade, this number has decreased in more than 10 thousand producers, from 53,086 (2006-2007 harvest) to 43,035 (2016-2017 harvest) (ICAFE, 2017).

As a result of this condition, many lands with coffee vocation in the country are becoming properties for real estate developments. This is notorious in several parts of the Central Valley −where most of the country's population is concentrated. Likewise, knowledge for coffee production −traditionally passed down from generation to generation− is being lost.

On the other hand, Costa Rican coffee continues to be recognized for its quality worldwide. In the 2018 edition of the Cup of Excellence (https://allianceforcoffeeexcellence.org/cup-of-excellence/) −competition held in several countries to reward coffee quality−, one of the participating coffee samples in Costa Rica reached the extraordinary price of US$300.09 per pound in the auction held as part of this international competition. This price exceeded the record of US$130.20 per pound, previously obtained in 2017 by Brazil in this same competition. As a reference, the price of coffee in 2018 in the international market was just US$1.15 per pound (Otey, 2018).

[1] fmata@una.cr
[2] irene.hernandez.ruiz@una.cr

In this regard, Mata et al (2016) have proposed the development of an electronic commerce system to allow the direct sale of roasted coffee from producers to consumers as a solution to the coffee paradox. This mechanism would eliminate intermediaries in the global value chain of coffee, making it possible to producers to receive the price paid for roasted coffee by the final consumers.

This system is envisioned as an innovative tool to promote social and economic change, and it is being developed and implemented by the Universidad Nacional (UNA) in Costa Rica (http://www.una.ac.cr).

In the following sections, we discuss the background, and the design and development considerations for this e-commerce system, known as crgourmetcoffee.com (https://www.crgourmetcoffee.com). In addition, we present the results of this project to date and the further steps being taken to convert the existing prototype into a fully operational e-commerce platform.

2. BACKGROUND

2.1 The Coffee Paradox

The coffee paradox has been studied by Daviron and Ponte (2005) and Fitter and Kaplinsky (2001a, 2001b). This phenomenon is characterized by the increasingly lower prices that farmers receive for their coffee, even though the demand for this product has been growing. This is due to the entry of new countries in coffee production −such as, Vietnam, Indonesia and Uganda−, which has increased the world production of this product. Currently, around 70 countries −more than a third of the existing in the world− produce coffee (ICO, 2014).

In this regard, it is important to note that most of the coffee consumed in the world behaves as a primary commodity −for which the quality of the product is not adequately recognized[3]. For this reason, coffee roasters can modify the mix of beans they use in order to produce their roasted coffee products, taking advantage of the price obtained from different countries (Daviron and Ponte, 2005).

However, with the advent of specialty coffee −which differs by flavor (gourmet coffee), origin (coffee with denomination of origin) or process (organic coffee, trade-fair coffee, etc.)− possibilities are arising for the de-commodification of this product, providing options to cope with the coffee paradox (Kaplinsky and Fitter, 2004).

2.2 The Global Value Chain (GVC) for Coffee

As Mata et al (2016) claim, the structure of the global value chain (GVC) for the mainstream-coffee market is greatly responsible for the coffee paradox. Seven major actors can be identified in this chain: farmers, processors, export agents, global traders, roasters, retailers, and consumers (see Figure 1).

Coffee farmers in developing countries grow coffee trees, which produce coffee cherries. After being harvested, the coffee cherries need to be processed to separate the beans from the skin and pulp and reduce their humidity. This process produces what is referred to as "green coffee" and is usually done in large processing plants. Since small farmers commonly do not count with such facilities[4], they sell their harvested cherries to coffee processing plants. As a result of this processing, beans from different producers are mixed, losing the coffee its traceability to the producer.

Most of the green coffee produced is exported, although a small part remains in the producing country for local consumption (see Figure 1). This is due since green coffee lasts longer than roasted coffee. Exporting of green coffee is done through export agents, which act as intermediaries between the processing plants and the global traders and roasters in consuming countries. As already explained, roasters usually blend different types of green-coffee beans, prior to roasting them to release their aroma. Roasted coffee (ground or in whole bean) is later packed in vacuum-sealed bags, to be finally sold by retailers −mainly supermarkets− to consumers.

[3] Coffee sold under this condition is said to be traded in the mainstream market.

[4] However, some small farmers have begun to process their own coffee in micro-mills.

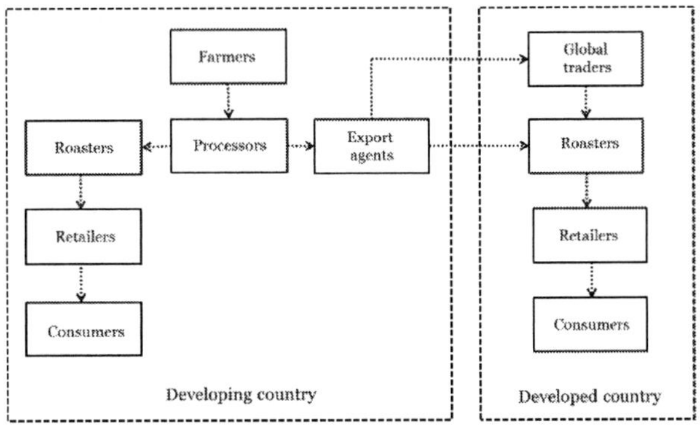

Figure 1. Global value chain for coffee (Mata et al, 2016)

The distribution of rents between actors in developing and developed countries regarding coffee has been a matter of discussion for long time (see Daviron and Ponte (2005), Fitter and Kaplinsky (2001a, 2001b), Kaplinsky and Fitter (2004) and Fairtrade Foundation (2012)). Although each of the activities in the GVC for coffee described before add value to the coffee purchased by the final consumers –and therefore, this value is reflected in the price paid by such consumers–, it is claimed that oligopolistic conditions existing in this chain allow international roasters to extract rents –that is, a compensation beyond the value-added. For this reason, coffee farmers are able to receive only 7 to 10 percent of the price paid by final consumers (ITC, 2011), even though it is widely recognized that the main determinants of coffee quality come from its cultivation and processing (species and variety of coffee cultivated, type of soil, altitude and climate of the plantation, and type of processing for the beans) (Brown, 1991) –that is, from value added by local, and not international, actors.

Furthermore, different from other agricultural products, it is the international roasters –and not the retailers, as usually occurs in other agriculture products– which enjoy a privileged position in the GVC for coffee (Daviron and Ponte, 2005). Therefore, the governance of this GVC –which relates to authority and power relationships among actors in the chain– rests on international roasters, particularly those with a large market share (e.g., Nestlé, Mondelēz –formerly Kraft Foods–, and Sara Lee Corp. (López Porras, 2014)).

2.3 E-commerce Systems used to trade Coffee in Costa Rica

As previously indicated, there are five intermediaries between coffee farmers in developing countries and final consumers in developed countries (processors, export agents, global traders, roasters, and retailers). In addition to the physical activities for production, processing and distribution that these intermediaries perform –previously discussed–, these actors also carry out informational functions aimed at matching buyers and sellers, facilitating the transactions, and providing institutional infrastructure (see the work of Bakos (1998) about these functions). This is because coffee farmers traditionally have not been able to perform these informational activities, due to *lack of economies of scale*, *expertise*, or *contact networks* (Mata et al, 2016). However, given the communication and brokerage effects of information and communication technologies (ICT) –postulated by Malone et al (1987) –, these technologies are able to reduce search costs and to handle complex products –as it is the case with gourmet coffee. Therefore, ICT can be used to overcome these limitations, favoring the creation of electronic markets. These effects are very well epitomized in modern e-commerce systems.

In the case of Costa Rica, Mata et al (2016) identified two electronic commerce systems used for trading coffee: 1) the Cup of Excellence and 2) the electronic commerce systems developed by Costa Rican roasters. Both systems support the de-commodification of coffee and focus on the sale of gourmet coffee.

The Cup of Excellence –already mentioned– has been developed by the Alliance for Coffee Excellence (https://allianceforcoffeeexcellence.org/), a not-for-profit organization aimed at rewarding quality in coffee. The system facilitates the direct sale of green coffee –through an electronic auction– from farmers in selected developing countries to international roasters. Therefore, this is a B2B e-commerce system.

Different from coffee offered in the mainstream market, this system offers coffee from a single farmer ("single-estate" coffee), allowing its traceability back to the producer.

Although the Cup of Excellence can benefit coffee farmers −allowing them to obtain better prices, and thus mitigating the effect of the coffee paradox− its impact is very limited for at least two reasons. First, the system requires that farmers prepare samples of exceptional quality (known as micro-lots) −a process which is expensive for the farmers. Second, the coffee samples presented by farmers need to be cupped several times by experts to assess their quality −which is cumbersome. For these reasons, the number of coffee farmers that can benefit from the Cup of Excellence is reduced, and the quantities of coffee that can obtain higher prices thanks to this system are minimal. Furthermore, there is evidence that although farmers can obtain higher prices, international roasters can get even higher prices from selling the award-winning coffees (Daviron and Ponte, 2005).

The limited scope of the Cup of Excellence to mitigate the coffee paradox can be explained using the analysis of GVCs (see the seminal work on this field by Gereffi et al (1994)), since this system does not change the geographical location of the agents in the GVC for coffee (territoriality), neither does it change the authority and the power relations between the actors involved in this chain (governance) (Mata et al, 2016).

The other e-commerce systems found in Costa Rica to trade coffee are the systems developed by Costa Rican roasters. Different from the Cup pf Excellence, these are B2C systems. Mata and Quesada (2015) found that almost 30 percent of the roasters in Costa Rica had developed such systems and that most of them are intended to sell roasted coffee abroad. Although such systems can benefit Costa Rican roasters by obtaining higher prices, this advantage does not necessarily is transferred to the farmers. By allowing domestic roasters to sell roasted coffee directly to final consumers in developed countries, this type of systems displace roasters in developed countries −upgrading the first their position in the GVC for coffee−, and thus, letting the roasters in developing countries to reach the same advantageous situation that their homologous, in developed countries, have. Therefore, although this second type of system allows a change in territoriality in the GVC, governance in this chain remain the same (Mata et al, 2016).

As a result of the above, Mata et al (2016) conclude that the key for an e-commerce system to address the coffee paradox rests in its ability to establish a direct connection between coffee farmers and consumers. This is supported by Pelupessy's (2001) remark that at present there is not a market that allows these two actors to relate. Due to the structure of GVC for coffee, consumers connect with roasters in a "roasted-coffee market", whereas farmers deal with roasters in a "green-coffee market" (see Figure 2), being roasters in developed countries the common denominator in both markets.

Furthermore, roasters tend to make farmers invisible to consumers. In part, this is due since in the mainstream-coffee market is not possible to trace the coffee beans back to their producers, serving the roasters as the guarantors of their quality. Therefore, Mata et al (2016) postulate that by including meaningful information on coffee farmers in an e-commerce system, consumers can relate better to their practices and endowments, which in the end influence the quality of coffee −as already explained.

Figure 2 shows the differences among the connections provided by the Cup of the Excellence, the Costa Rican roasters' e-commerce sites, and the proposed e-commerce system aimed to mitigate the coffee paradox in Costa Rica.

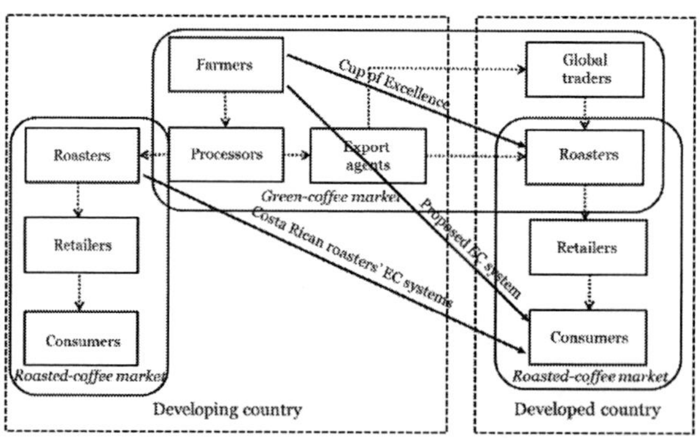

Figure 2. Connections for different e-commerce systems for coffee in Costa Rica

3. DESIGN AND DEVELOPMENT CONSIDERATIONS FOR CRGOURMETCOFFEE.COM

3.1 Methodology

We started the design of crgroumentcoffee.com in the middle of 2016. At the beginning, we thought this system could be designed with the participation of the coffee farmers in Costa Rica, using a "design thinking" methodology (Brown and Wyatt, 2010). However, we early discovered that coffee producers in Costa Rica were not well versed in e-commerce. Therefore, we switched the design approach to one based on benchmarking. In this regard, we considered e-commerce sites belonging to the following three categories: 1) international roasting companies, 2) Costa Rican roasters, and 3) Costa Rican farmers.

3.1.1 E-commerce Sites from International Roasters

Although most international large coffee roasters have websites for their coffee brands[5], they are mainly informational –not transactional– sites. This is because these roasters are large consumer product companies, which rely on retailers to sell their products to final consumers. Other specialized roasters, however, have e-commerce sites. Among them, the site of Intelligentsia (https://www.intelligentsiacoffee.com) –a company selling specialty coffee– proved to be useful. This site provides information for farmers, whose coffee is sold through the site. Nevertheless, despite this company promotes coffee from selected coffee farmers worldwide (single-estate coffee), it acts as an intermediary selling the coffee "on behalf" of the producers. That is, it buys green coffee from selected coffee farmers, roast it and sell the resulting product through e-commerce.

3.1.2 E-commerce Sites from Costa Rican Roasters

As previously mentioned, many Costa Rican roasters have developed e-commerce systems to sell their roasted coffee. These systems barely mention coffee farmers. The most successful of such systems is the one operated by Café Britt (https://www.cafebritt.com), owned by Grupo Britt –a multinational company based in Costa Rica (Mata and Quesada, 2015). This site does not only sell Costa Rican coffee, but also coffee from Colombia and Peru.

3.1.3 E-commerce Sites from Costa Rican Farmers

A handful of Costa Rican farmers have developed e-commerce site to sell their own roasted coffee. Among them, we found interesting the following sites: Brumas del Zurquí (https://www.cafebrumasdelzurqui.cr) and Monte Copey (https://montecopeycoffee.com) –both owned by farmers highly ranked in previous editions of the Cup of Excellence of Costa Rica. Although, these sites have merits, they have several limitations. First, it is difficult for these sites to position themselves on the Internet based on search engine criteria. Second, these sites offer a reduced number of products, which are limited to the available coffee varieties grown by the respective farmers. Finally, although the sites are owned by the same farmers, the amount of information provided about them is very scarce, which does not allow these sites to establish a meaningful connection with final consumers. The first two limitations are related to the need of developing a national platform to facilitate marketing and promotion of roasted coffee in Costa Rica, as proposed by López Porras (2014).

3.2 Site Structure

The site for crgourmetcoffee.com has been designed as an electronic platform, consisting of different webstores, having them front-stores for each farm owned by a participating famer, and a corresponding back-store for this farmer. The store-fronts are public and have a catalog of roasted coffee products and offer all the expected e-commerce functionality. In addition, there is a general administration module used to enable and disable webstores and control the operation of the platform (see Figure 3).

[5] See for example htttp://www.nescafe.com part of Nestlé and http://www.jacobsdouweegberts.com part of Mondelēz.

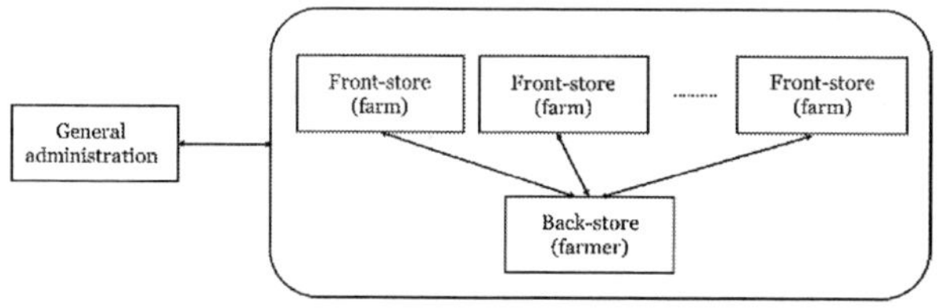

Figure 3. Site structure for crgourmetcoffee.com

3.3 Graphic Design

Several iterations were used to come to the graphic design for crgourmetcoffee.com. The following criteria were used for this design: 1) a minimalist approach, 2) use of colors and images related to coffee[6], and 3) styles for the pages able to be displayed responsively in different devices (desktops, tablets, and mobile phones). Figure 4 shows the design of the homepage for the site.

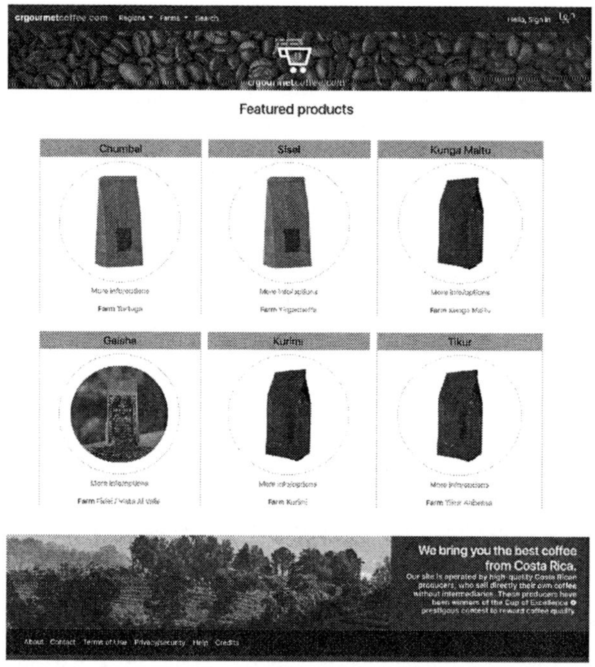

Figure 4. Graphic design for crgourmetcoffee.com (homepage)

3.4 Farm Information

In order to achieve an effective communication between farmers and users (potential consumers), a page with information about the farm and its products have been developed (see Figure 5). This page will be complemented with a page containing information about the famer, which is currently being designed.

It is important that most coffee farms in Costa Rica are owned by families, which have been inherited through several generations. This situation lends to the use of storytelling to connect the consumer to the farmer. Storytelling has been proposed as useful way for marketing (see Woodside et al (2008)). Following Picard's (1997) influential work, we plan to use affective computing –that is, "computing that relates to,

[6] These colors cannot be appreciated in the figures, since they are presented in black and white.

arises from, or deliberately influences emotions (p. 3) – to develop the page with information about the farmer. Storytelling and affective computing will support relationship marketing, which "is based on the notion that on top of the value of products and/or services that are exchanged, the existence of a relationship between two parties creates additional value for the customer and also for the supplier or service provider" (Grönroos, 2004, p. 99). Such type of marketing has been proposed by Daviron and Ponte (2005) for coffee in the form of "relational coffee", or coffees for which consumers establish a direct relationship with actors in coffee-producing countries. This marketing strategy has been successfully used by Café Britt in Costa Rica (Mata and Quesada, 2015).

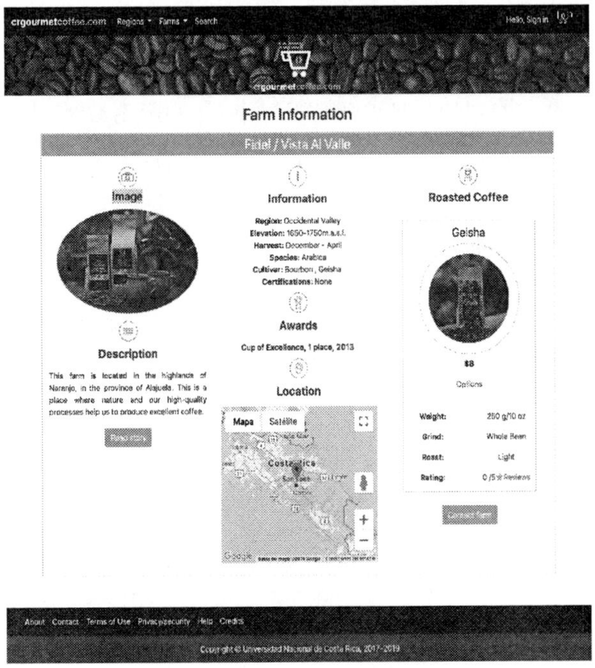

Figure 5. Example of the information for a farm

3.5 Software Considerations

A LAMP[7] software stack has been used to develop crgourmetcoffee.com. We originally planned to use an open-source e-commerce package based on PHP to develop the site. For this purpose, we considered the following options: Drupal/Ubercart (https://www.drupal.org/project/ubercart), Magento (https://magento.com/), osCommerce (https://www.oscommerce.com/), and Zen Cart (https://www.zen-cart.com/). However, only Drupal/Ubercart offered a free multi-vendor solution, by adding a module known as Ubercart Marketplace (https://www.drupal.org/project/ubercart_marketplace).

After reviewing this last solution, we found it difficult to implement with this package the functionality required for the proposed site for two reasons. First, although Ubercart Marketplace allows different vendors to manage their own products, all the products appear in the same webstore. Second this package is designed so all payments go to the operator of the site, and not directly to the different vendors. We considered important to separate the technical operation of the site from its financial procedures, to isolate the operator of the site from possible legal disputes that may arise from the transactions being executed, as later discussed.

Changing the code for Drupal/Ubercart Marketplace to create different webstores for farmers and allow producers to receive directly their own payments was deemed more difficult than to develop the system from

[7] Linux (operating system), Apache (web server), MySQL (database management system), PHP (programming language).

scratch. For this reason, we selected Symfony (https://symfony.com) –a PHP-based framework implementing the model-view-controller architectural pattern– to develop the e-commerce site.

In addition, we used the bootstrap front-end framework (https://getbootstrap.com), to make the site responsive. This eliminates the need to have apps for using it with mobile devices.

4. RESULTS TO DATE

We have successfully completed a prototype for crgourmetcoffee.com. A usability test of this site was conducted in November 2018, using the System Usability Scale (SUS) (Brooke, 2013) and relying on professors and students at UNA. This test provided encouraging results, as well as suggestions for further improvement of the system.

We also have presented the prototype to several coffee farmers in Costa Rica, who have expressed much interest in using it. According to them, the fact that this system provides the opportunity to create a national platform to market and sell gourmet coffee is a major advantage, since it simplifies its use –not having the farmers to deal with technical aspects–, as well as it provides better opportunities to position the site on the Internet.

Terms of use for the system are being developed, as well as security and privacy policies, for the platform. Such policies consider the General Data Protection Regulation (GDPR), approved by the European Union (EU, 2018).

Furthermore, contractual terms with the Costa Rican farmers –that will be using crgourmetcoffee.com– are been finalized. In this contractual agreement, UNA legally will be only the facilitator of the platform. This means that the university will not be responsible for any of the transactions occurring through the platform.

5. FURTHER STEPS AND MAJOR CHALLENGES

We are in the process of making the prototype for crgourmetcoffee.com into an operational e-commerce platform. In this endeavor, we are offering crgourmetcoffee.com to selected coffee farmers –that have been highly ranked in the previous editions of the Cup of Excellence– without cost until the end of 2021. After that period, we will reevaluate the way the system will be provided. At the long term, the ideal will be to license the software to an "association" of gourmet-coffee producers. Although, this association does not exist, we believe crgourmetcoffee.com could lead the way for creating it.

For implementing crgourmetcoffee.com, we are in the process of seeking the collaboration from key government agencies in Costa Rica, such as the Ministry of Science, Technology and Telecommunications (MICITT), the Ministry of Agriculture and Livestock (MAG), the Ministry of Foreign Trade (COMEX), the Export Promoting Agency of Costa Rica (PROCOMER) and the Coffee Institute of Costa Rica (ICAFE). These organizations are key to develop a national platform for trading roasted coffee.

We are also looking for funding for this project. Although, most of the labor and operational costs needed to launch this platform are being covered by UNA, additional funding will be instrumental to promote the platform on Internet and to improve the farmers' capabilities to sell roasted coffee.

In order to provide a consistent framework for handling payments and providing the necessary logistics services, we are in the process of selecting a company to provide the electronic-payment services and another to offer the shipping services needed for this system. Logistics is a major challenge for a platform like this, since shipping many small orders –as it is necessary in B2C– is a complex and expensive process (Turban et al, 2012). Furthermore, coffee farmers are accustomed to export green coffee –which is a large volume process–, therefore, selling small packages of roasted coffee will demand farmers to develop new processes and skills.

Training coffee farmers to use the system and operate its back-store facility also presents challenges, since many of them are not well acquainted with IT. However, we have found that children of such producers are very knowledgeable in IT –some of them even have university education. Therefore, training efforts will focus on this group.

Finally, securing the quality of the coffee sold through the system is paramount. Coffee quality is guaranteed by two basic mechanisms: organoleptic and non-organoleptic (Daviron and Ponte, 2005). Organoleptic mechanisms rely on the human senses, and they are associated with coffee characteristics such as acidity, aroma, body and taste. For this purpose, coffee samples are cupped by experts and assessed based on such characteristics (ITC, 2011). This is a cumbersome and expensive mechanism, which is used in the Cup of Excellence. On the other hand, non-organoleptic mechanisms rely on subjective attributes of coffee. The most commonly used of such mechanisms is the creation of brands, which is mainly used by roasters. International roasters invest heavily in advertisement related to their brands, for example, Nescafé, Folgers, and Maxwell House.

A combination of both mechanisms is planned to be used in crgourmetcoffee.com. In this regard, the system will be offered only to farmers that have been ranked as producers of specialty coffee by the Cup of Excellence of Costa Rica. This guarantees that the participating farmers have already the endowments (coffee trees, agro-climatic conditions, etc.) and knowledge about coffee cultivation, harvesting and processing to produce high-quality coffee. Furthermore, through marketing methods −such as relationship marketing, previously mentioned− and the name that Costa Rican coffee has worldwide, we plan to create a reputation for the platform. Creating such a reputation will overcome the limitation of positioning on the Internet individual farmers' websites −as already mentioned−, since participating farmers would be able to rent the reputation from the platform (see the pioneering work on economics of e-commerce by Choi et al (1997)). This last mechanism (reputation) will be complemented by a rating system for each of the coffee products offered through crgourmetcoffee.com, which is currently under development.

6. CONCLUSION

Although e-commerce is growing in Costa Rica, as in most Latin American countries (Visa, 2016), this growth is mainly due to the use of foreign platforms, such as Amazon, E-Bay or AliExpress. In addition, most
e-commerce efforts in the country has focused on creating sites for the local market; however, the reduced size of the country (roughly 5 million inhabitants) makes this market off-putting.

Instead of thinking inwards, efforts to develop e-commerce sites in Costa Rica should look abroad. In this process, using products where Costa Rica has a competitive advantage −such as coffee− is key. Cafe Britt, as already mentioned, illustrates well this approach. According to Mata and Quesada (2015), this company sold approximately 18 percent of its coffee through e-commerce in 2013.

The platform crgourmetcoffee.com is been designed and developed with this principle in mind: focus on the foreign market with coffee, a product in which Costa Rica excels. In this way, this platform is aimed at mitigating the coffee paradox, and thus encourage Costa Rican farmers that produce gourmet coffee to continue in the business.

Furthermore, we believe this platform might encourage new generations to get involved in the coffee activities of their parents, favoring to pass down the coffee tradition and knowledge from generation to generation. Adding a technological component to coffee production and marketing can make it more attractive to the farmers' children to get involved in the coffee activities of their families.

Although crgourmetcoffee.com has the potential to become a tool for social and economic change, still several challenges must be faced −as previously discussed− to achieve this purpose.

REFERENCES

Bakos, Y., 1998. The Emerging Role of Electronic Marketplaces on the Internet. *In Communications of the ACM*, Vol. 41, No. 8, pp. 35–42.

Brooke, J., 2013. SUS: A Retrospective. *In Journal of Usability Studies*, Vol. 8, No. 2, pp. 29-40.

Brown, J.G., 1991. *Agro-Industry Profiles: Coffee.* World Bank,Washington, DC, USA.

Brown, T. and Wyatt, J., 2010. Design Thinking for Social Innovation. *In Development Outreach*, Vol. 12, No. 1, pp. 29-43.

Choi, S. et al, 1997. *The Economics of Electronic Commerce*. Macmillan Computer Publishing, Indianapolis, IN, USA.

Daviron, B and Ponte, S. 2005. *The Coffee Paradox: Global Markets, Commodity Trade and the Elusive Promise of Development.* Zed Books, London, UK.

EU, 2018. *Regulation (EU) 2016/679 of the European Parliament and of the Council of 27 April 2016 on the Protection of Natural Persons with Regard to the Processing of Personal Data and on the Free Movement of Such Data, and Pepealing Directive 95/46/EC (General Data Protection Regulation)* [online]. Available at: https://eur-lex.europa.eu/legal-content/EN/TXT/PDF/?uri=CELEX:32016R0679&from=EN.

Fitter, R. and Kaplinsky, R., 2001a. Can an Agricultural Commodity Be De-commodified, and If So Who Is to Gain? *In IDS Bulletin (discussion paper 380).* Institute of Development Studies, University of Sussex, Brighton, UK.

Fitter, R. and Kaplinsky, R., 2001b. Who Gains from Product Rents as the Coffee Market Becomes More Differentiated?: A Value-Chain Analysis. *In IDS Bulletin*, Vol. 32, No. 3, pp. 69-82.

Fairtrade Foundation, 2012. *Fairtrade and Coffee.* Fairtrade Foundation, London, UK.

Gereffi, G. K. et al, 1994. Introduction: Global Commodity Chains. In Gereffi G. and Korzeniewicz, M. (eds.). *Commodity Chains and Global Capitalism.* Praeger Publishers, Westport, CT, USA.

Grönroos, C., 2004. The Relationship Marketing Process: Communication, Interaction, Dialogue, Value. *In Journal of Business & Industrial Marketing*, Vol. 19, No. 2, pp. 99-113.

ICAFE, 2017. *Informe sobre la Actividad Cafetalera en Costa Rica.* Instituto del Café de Costa Rica, San José, Costa Rica.

ICO, 2014. *Exports of All Forms of Coffee to Exporting Countries: Calendar Years 2000 to 2013.* International Coffee Organization, London, UK.

ITC, 2011. *The Coffee Exporter's Guide.* 3rd ed.. International Trade Centre, Geneva, Switzerland.

Kaplinsky, R. and Fitter R., 2004. Technology and Globalisation: Who Gains when Commodities Are De-commodified? *In International. Journal of Technology and Globalisation*, Vol 1, No. 1, pp. 5–28.

López Porras, K., 2014. *El Mercado Mundial de Café Tostado.* Promotora del Comercio Exterior de Costa Rica, San José, Costa Rica.

Malone, T.W., Yates, J. and Benjamin, R.I,, 1987. Electronic Markets and Electronic Hierarchies. *In Communications of the ACM*, Vol. 30, No. 6, pp. 484-497.

Mata, F. J. and Quesada, A., 2015. E-Commerce and Coffee in Costa Rica: Case Studies of Costa Rican Roaster Companies. *Proceeding of the 2015 Latin American Computing Conference (CLEI)* [online]. Avaliable at https://doi.org/10.1109/CLEI.2015.7359997.

Mata, F.J., Quesada, A., and Mata-Marín, G., 2016. Can E-commerce Provide a Solution to the Coffee Paradox?: The Case of Costa Rica. In Mata, F.J. and Pont, A. (eds). *ICT for Promoting Human Development and Protecting the Environment.* Springer International Publishing, Switzerland.

Otey, J., 2018. "Café de Costa Rica Rompió Récord de Precios", CrHoy, 10 July [online]. Available at: https://www.crhoy.com/economia/cafe-de-costa-rica-rompio-record-mundial-de-precios/.

Pelupessy, W., 2001. La Crisis de Mercado en Cadenas Globales del Café. *In Perspectivas Rurales*, Vol. 5, No. 1, pp. 57-71.

Picard, R., 1997. *Affective Computing.* MIT Press, Boston, MA., USA.

PROCOMER, 2017. *Anuario estadístico 2016.* Promotora de Comercio Exterior de Costa Rica, San José, Costa Rica [online] Available at: https://procomer.com/downloads/estudios/estudio_estadistico_2016/Capitulo3.pdf.

Turban, E., King, D., Lee, J., Liang, T. and Turban, D., 2012. *Electronic Commerce 2012.* New Jersey: Pearson Education, Upper Saddle River, NJ, USA.

Visa, 2016. Latin America e-Readiness Report by Visa. Visa [online]. Available at: https://www.visa.com.bs/pay-with-visa/ereadiness.html.

Woodside, A., Sood, S., and Miller, K.E., 2008. When Consumers and Brands Talk: Storytelling Theory and Research in Psychology and Marketing. *In Psychology & Marketing*, Vol 25, No 2, pp. 97-145.

INCLUSION THROUGH DIGITAL ARTS: CREATING A COMMUNITY OF PRACTICE

Ana Barata[1], Paula Escudeiro[2], Valérie Duarte[3] and Jadir Lino[4]
ISEP; GILT
Rua Dr. António Bernardino de Almeida, 4314249-015 Porto, Portugal

ABSTRACT

To communicate is the deepest will of every human being since their very first minute of existence, as communication is what makes human beings really feel part of a whole. One of the most transversal, barrier-dropper, and universal ways of communicating is creating art. Having that assumption in mind, this paper introduces a proposal for combining technology and arts production using an online educational Community of Practice aimed at encouraging communication and collaboration between blind/low vision individuals and deaf/hearing impaired individuals having the creation of digital artworks using a technologically developed collaborative environment. To provide a framework for this challenge, this study provides a review of concepts and examples related to the art practices from an inclusive point of view, to inclusive design, and to the essential features of reliable Communities of Practice. Furthermore, the proposal for developing a collaborative environment for creating digital artworks, combining the best practices and features of the analyzed examples, targeting at the blind and deaf communities is described as well as the evaluation model – the Quantitative Evaluation Framework – to be used to assess this creative learning and communication environment.

KEYWORDS

Collaboration, Community of Practice, Digital Arts, Inclusive Design, QEF

1. INTRODUCTION

The technological development, and the improvement of digital systems have revolutionized the way human beings interact not only with each other but also with the world around, they interfere with people's work habits, with the education environments, and have opened the path for a wide set of communication possibilities in myriad contexts. Being able to communicate is what makes human beings feel, and really be, part of a whole (Gomes 2009). Interacting, understanding, sharing, feeling and being integrated are unquestionable conditions for belonging to a community, regardless of abilities, disabilities, origin or condition, and one of the most fascinating, transversal, barrier-dropper, and universal means of communication is creating art.

In this paper we propose to combine the already long and close relationship between the arts and technology (Paul 2003), (Greene 2004), (Chung 2006), (Barata 2014) with the learning and challenging potential of online Communities of Practice (CoP), introducing a proposal for developing an inclusive collaborative learning and creative environment aimed at allowing blind and deaf individuals to produce digital artworks together. This project derives, on the one hand, from the authors' experience in working with assistive technology and interaction projects (P. Escudeiro et al. 2013; B. P. Marques et al. 2017; P. M. Escudeiro et al. 2018), and on the other hand from the strong interest the authors have in contributing for diversifying and for the further development of various means and environments that may propel inclusive learning, working to tear apart barriers and to enrich human-human interaction. This way, the authors wish to put the technological innovation at the service of inclusion.

[1] abt@isep.ipp.pt
[2] pmo@isep.ipp.pt
[3] 1171493@isep.ipp.pt
[4] jadirlino@gmail.com

To better address our proposal, and to clearly framework it, this paper starts by reviewing the field of digital arts, focusing especially on art practices, experiences and productions that can be embraced as inclusive and/or produced by blind or deaf artists, once the deaf and the blind are our primary target audiences. Then, an overview of inclusive design concepts, purposes and practices is presented to scaffold the essential background that is being studied to build an appropriate learning and creative environment. Afterwards, the demands and features of CoPs are detailed, followed by our concept proposal of an inclusive collaborative environment, which is going to be assessed with the Quantitative Evaluation Framework (P. Escudeiro and Bidarra 2006), and tested with deaf and blind people.

2. DIGITAL ARTS TOWARDS INCLUSION: PERSPECTIVES

The arts have an already long and close relationship with technology, dating from the 20th century's 60s the first references to scientific and technological work within the arts field (Greene 2004), (Barata 2014). Nam June Paike, David Medalla, Roy Ascott are only few of the first artists who started exploring the potential of the by-then new media and tools, opening the path for what became known as the Experiments in Art and Technology Group, which gathered artists and engineers working together on the same creative projects (Barata 2014, 1).

That was when "inclusion" from an inter-and-multidisciplinary perspective started within the arts. Moreover, the social and educational role played by the arts became more accessible and recurrent following the requirements set by the advances in computing, and by the publics' participation (Popper 2007, 1975). Art, in particular digital art, started being present at homes, cybercafes and any public or private space with internet access, mobile, wireless, or local (Wands 2006, 8). Accessing as well as experiencing and producing art became easier and more flexible, authors started adopting interactive and collective strategies, embracing a wide variety of spaces, perspectives and formats (Barata 2014, 10–38). Therefore, referring to an artwork as "digital" implies that it was created using digital tools, software, or any technological means, therefore it "can be described as an electronic series of zeros and ones" (Lieser and Morbey 2009). These technological means are used either to explore or to create artworks, sometimes they are the artwork itself like the Pinokio Lamp, created with Arduino, and OpenCV (Zhou, Ben-Dror, and Doggett 2012; Ben-Dror 2012). Motion, immersion, smell, and sound "communicate simultaneously on four levels: sensory, emotional, mental and spiritual. It is this multiple synchronicity of body, mind and intellect that helps to define our complex reactions to art, as well as to the everyday world," states Wands (2006). People experience through their senses, that is what makes human-beings unique. Digital artworks appeal to all the senses, individually or simultaneously, thus they cannot be perceived as objects but as concepts, information, perspectives that reflect an author's or a collective of authors' views on specific issues. There is no "object" (Chierico 2016), but an experience, the way the audience interacts, feels, reacts to, i.e., how the audience experiences the digital artwork is the artwork itself. The dominant senses depend on each individual's characteristics. Vision, movement, vibration, tactile experiences are essential senses for a deaf person. Movement, tactile experiences, smell, touch, taste, sound are essential senses for a blind person, and essential for experiencing contemporary art.

In Pittsburgh, the Andy Warhol Museum launched a guide to Warhol's artworks aimed at enabling the blind to have a direct experience of contacting with the works, hence making both the author's life and work accessible to people who cannot see them, which includes not only an audio guide called Out Loud but also tactile reproductions of a number of Warhol's works (The Andy Warhol Museum 2019).

Art Beyond Sight: A Resource Guide to Art, Creativity and Impairment, Art education for the Blind, published by the American Foundation for the Blind, already in 2002, was one of the first books to analyze the arts education perspective for blind/low vision people, focusing on how blind/low vision people create art, and on how they experience, interact with it and enjoy it. Blind people who are given the opportunity to experience art are able to understand it, including form, depth, and perspective (Axel 2003).

It is our belief that the polyform possibilities, immersive experiences and countless interconnections made available by digital technology, make the digital the best field to explore and integrate in an environment intended to widen communication, engagement, creativity and inclusion of blind and of deaf people through collaborative artistic performance. Next section handles inclusive design concepts and examples, focusing on the essential assets for creating an inclusive, user-friendly web environment, essential to our aims.

3. UNDERSTANDING INCLUSIVE DESIGN

Before embracing Inclusive Design, it is essential to understand what inclusion and exclusion mean. Going back to its Latin origin, "inclusion" means *to shut in* while "exclusion" means *to shut out*. Considering inclusivity as a circle holding inside all that should be included, exclusivity, as its antonym, keeps everything out of that circle. Hence, people usually tend to promote inclusivity as they believe in the possibility of being in a large circle in which almost everything fits. Known as "Design for All" in Europe, and as "Universal Design" in the USA, the history of Inclusive Design goes back to the beginning of the European social ideals materialized after the World War II, which include healthcare and housing for everyone (John Clarkson and Coleman 2015). In early approaches, its focus was in designing for disabled and elderly people. In 2000, the UK Government defined Inclusive Design as products, services and environments that include the needs of the widest number of consumers (Brand and Brooker 2015). However, as part of recent international trends towards inclusion, Inclusive Design goes beyond targeting at older and disabled people to also focus on so far excluded groups, including the blind and the deaf.

Most recently, Microsoft expanded the concept of Inclusive Design by defining it as a methodology, born out of digital environments, which enables and draws on the full range of human diversity. Most importantly, this means including and learning from people with myriad perspectives. Microsoft also presents two distinctions. The first refers to universal design as strong at describing the qualities of a final design, specifically as to the nature of physical objects. The second, originally from Treviranus, points out that universal design is one-size-fits-all while inclusive design is one-size-fits-one (Microsoft 2018).

Accessibility criteria are the foundation of integrity for any inclusive solution (Holmes 2018), in which inclusive design has to be considered. The resulting designs, though for people with permanent disabilities, are often beneficial for a larger number of people. For example, automatic doors were created for the visually impaired community and for people with mobility issues, but they also benefit people with situational limitations such as an arm injury, or a parent holding an infant. Inclusive design does not imply always designing products to address the entire population's needs. Instead, it implies devising an appropriate design response to diversity in the population. The Persona Spectrum used by Microsoft to understand related mismatches and motivations across a spectrum of permanent, temporary, and situational scenarios is a useful easy-to-use tool that helps foster empathy, providing a possible scalable audience scenario in inclusive design thinking. Table 1 exemplifies that Persona Spectrum we are applying to develop the collaborative creative learning platform.

Table 1. Persona Spectrum providing permanent, temporary and situational targeted scenarios

Scenarios	Permanent	Temporary	Situational
Vision	Blind Color blindness Farsightedness Partially visually impaired	Cataract Looking at a bright light Eye injury	Distraction When driving a car
Hearing	Deaf Hearing impaired	Middle ear infection Being exposed to a loud sound/noise Excess of earwax	Bartender Music performer

After recognizing and accepting that different people have different needs for accessibility, it is easier to allow people to choose how they want to interact with an experience. The pyramid model of diversity (Figure 1) can be used to show how inclusive design aims at extending the target audience to include those with some kind of disability, while accepting that specific solutions may be required to satisfy the needs of those at the top of the pyramid (Engineering Design Centre 2017).

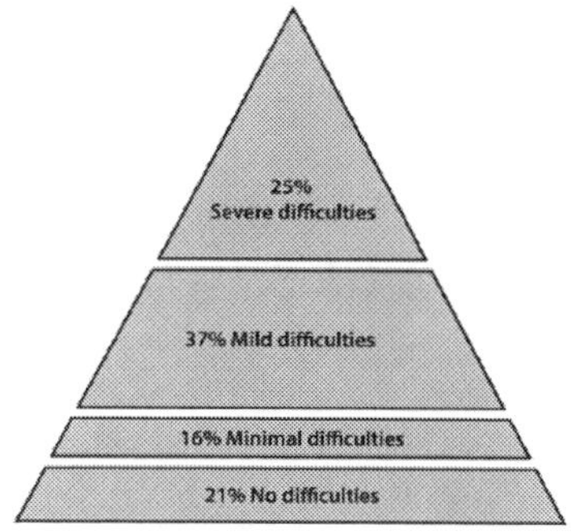

Figure 1. Pyramid Model of Diversity (Engineering Design Centre 2017)

On the other hand, co-design is a collaborative design process. It is often considered an inclusive method deployed to gather data by recognizing the participant as a partner not only during the data gathering phase, but also during implementation, delivery, and validation (Steen, et. Al., 2011). Collaborative sessions or workshops are the main platform where participants cooperate with researchers. These sessions differ based on both context and needs; nevertheless, three basic stages are present in almost all participatory design research: Initial Exploratory Work; Discovery process, Prototyping. The last stage involves using a variety of techniques for interactively shaping artifacts. These techniques can include, among others, mock-ups and paper prototyping. The best practice in inclusive design is to create the objects or environments with the participation of people with disabilities, or who have experienced any accessibility issue.

In the early 19th century, Pellegrino Turri, a skilled mechanic from Italy, built the first working model of a typing machine and invented carbon paper, which served as the machine's ink, inspired by his affection for the Contessa Fantoni, a childhood friend who was blind. Being blind, the countess was unable to write letters in private and autonomously, so Turri decided to create a mechanical solution to allow her to communicate with the world (Dictionary.com 2019). The result was a typing machine that associated a letter with a specific key that could be tapped to imprint on carbon paper, making writing accessible to blind people. Centuries later, modern keyboards and mobile devices are in use. The touch-sensitive imaging technology grew out of Wayne Westerman's UD doctoral thesis. He developed the revolutionary computer interface technology with John Elias, who was at the time a UD professor in the College of Engineering. Wayne had tendonitis which motivated him to tinker with different types of input technology. After some testing, he noticed that his hands had more endurance with zero-force input like optical buttons and capacitive touch pads than with force-actuating keys and buttons. Later, his company, the FingerWorks, created the first prototype of a touchpad for each hand to replace the keyboard, which was popular among people with hand disabilities and with temporary hand injuries. His work was so relevant that culminating in Apple buying the rights to the technology which was used for developing the first gesture-controlled multi-touch interface for the iPhone (Roberts 2014). These are only two examples that people tend to think in numerous creative ways to do what they enjoy or value, and work to develop the means they need. Designing environments to be inclusive impacts positively on individuals, on businesses, on society. Inclusive environments promote independence, empower the population and foster accessibility to content. These benefits lead exclusion and friction to be put aside and enable positive emotional contexts to blossom. This is also our motivation to develop a collaborative learning and creative environment that enables blind and deaf people to produce digital artworks.

Once personal computers and currently mobile devices as well have enormously enhanced the autonomy and the communication abilities of people with diverse disabilities, those are the devices where our environment will be accessed from. We aim at an adequate user interface design which will have high impact on the users' social lives. Approaching the creation of this collaborative environment user interface, focusing on a collaborative process during all the phases of its design, implies including blind and deaf people (our target primary users) in a user centered design methodology. It is not about creating "one thing for all people", it is about creating diverse ways for people to participate with a sense of belonging. In our proposal, inclusive design expands with the audience, i.e., our development model for the environment interface embraces the users' feedback, evolves considering their perspectives along with our views. Our User Centered Inclusive Design Model represented in Figure 2 considers our target audience (user-centered), our purpose (to be inclusive), the way we act and perceive development (cooperatively), and our output (design).

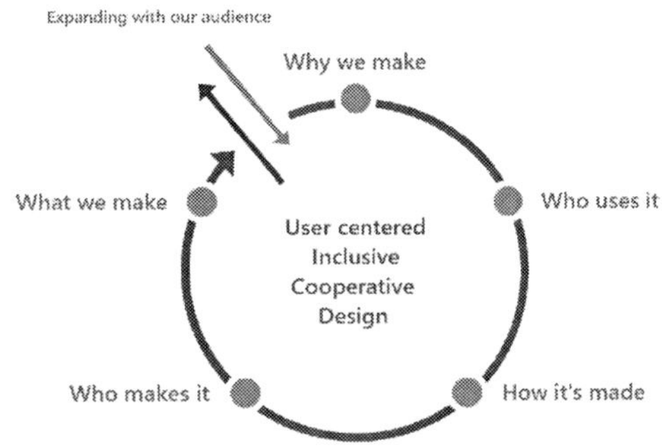

Figure 2. Representation of our model: Inclusive design expanding with the audience

4. ENGAGEMENT TOWARDS INCLUSION IN A COP

Etienne Wenger and Jean Lave theorized that the learning process does not rest in the individual but in a social process, given the culture and communities where the individual interacts and learns. The concept of Communities of Practice (CoP) directly emerges from that theory, as it can be described as a group of individuals that gather together in communities, around a common topic or shared concern, passion or something they want to learn in any given domain of our society. However, not all communities are CoPs and some CoPs may not be intentionally focused on the learning process. For instance, a neighborhood might be called a community but it is not usually a CoP; however, a group of nurses that have lunch together every day and who might dive into sharing information about their individual practices during the job, thus expanding their base knowledge in a daily basis, may be considered a non-intentional CoP.

A CoP has therefore three crucial characteristics: the Domain, the Community and the Practice (Farnsworth, Kleanthous, and Wenger-Trayner 2016), whereas the Domain is a group of people who are committed to each other and, consequently, share competences that distinguish their members from other people. The Community refers to the members' engagement in joint activities and discussions over subjects of their interest. Nevertheless, having the same job does not structure a CoP unless there is an effort to interact and learn from each other. The practice is what makes any community a real CoP, a community with a domain is not a CoP unless practitioners of their field develop a repertoire of experiences, stories, and ways to address recurring problems. According to Wenger, it is a common mistake to try to engage all members of the community in an equal level of participation (Wenger, McDermott, and Snyder 2002). Given the different levels of interest, the members can be divided into three groups: the main group, the active group, and the periphery group. The main group is often the one guiding the CoP for being more engaged in the activities, it represents 10% to 15% of the members. The active group, around 15% to 20% of the members, are people who attend meetings, and take part in the forum discussions but are not as engaged as the main group. Most members lay in the peripheral body, 65% to 75%, those are the ones that rarely take part in the activities but watch the group's interactivities. However, these members are not as passive as they might seem, they have their own insights of the discussions, and practice putting those to good use (Wenger, McDermott, and Snyder 2002).

Community-based art is a creative expression that emerges from communities of people working together to improve their individual and collective circumstances (Schwarzman, 2006). Following this statement, the aim of the Inclusive Digital Arts Practice Community conceptualized in this paper is to be an online inclusive environment fostering communication, collaboration, education, learning, integrative knowledge, and creativity, in which the virtual learning environment plays a major role. Focusing on the blind and deaf people, this CoP integrates both in a single environment. Taking into account their particular capacities, we are creating a multimedia environment that aims to translate the perspective and understanding of one community environment to the other in a feasible way, through a multi-modal interactive interface where it is possible to create digital artworks in both sound and image formats, allowing for blind and deaf to communicate during the process, devising in such a way a piece of digital art perceived by both. For this it is essential to consider the sound-colour correspondence, following the studies performed by (Ward, Huckstep, and Tsakanikos 2006; Bischin 2018).

5. QEF – THE ASSESSMENT METHODOLOGY

A simple question for any educational social network or CoP should be: "Can this educational environment really do what it is supposed to?" This simple question may lead to many beguiling features. It requires the evaluator to recognize his/her own view of the way users learn, to relate that view with the learning objectives and to determine how and whether those objectives are carried out in the online and self-standing platform. This is even more challenging and demanding when an inclusive social network is being considered.

The application of QEF, which has already been successfully applied in controlling the quality of several products with very positive results (P. Escudeiro 2007), (B. Marques et al. 2018), throughout the development life cycle of an inclusive social network highlights the flaws present in the version at the time of evaluation, allowing the development team to focus on those flaws, and guiding them through the improvement process to achieve the desirable requirements. Moderating the development of an inclusive social network with QEF assures the quality of the results (P. Escudeiro 2015). QEF enables evaluating the inclusive educational social network quality in a three-dimensional space, each of which aggregates a set of factors. The quality of a given system is, hence, defined in our three-dimensional Cartesian quality space and measured, in percentage, relatively to a hypothetically ideal system represented in our quality space by the coordinates (1, 1, 1). The coordinates of a given system in our quality space may be obtained through the application of one of several aggregation forms. These coordinates will be computed as the average of the factors contributing to it. The average is simple and gives the same relevance to all factors.

The quality space is defined by the content expert. In our present proposal this is the expert in digital arts. Regarding the inclusive social network, the definition of the Cartesian quality space will be settled on the following dimensions: Pedagogical, Ergonomic, and Technical – each of these dimensions aggregates a set of factors for which it is important to determine our proposed system's performance degree. In this case, a factor is an element that will represent the performance of the digital content in the system, according to predetermined criteria (P. Escudeiro 2015). For our quality scenario, two factors were added in the Pedagogical dimension: The Learning Factor and the Evaluation Factor. The Ergonomics dimension is the aggregation of three factors: Usability, Video/Audio, and Text. The Technical domain reflects the digital content quality regarding the functional factors. This dimension includes adaptability and content management. Through them we can measure to what extend the scenario and the system content are effective – whether they are focused on and able to present different instructional design theories and different learning environments in a common platform, i.e., if they interconnect fluently. However, in the scope of our present proposal, we want to evaluate a very specific network based on inclusion. We wish to promote the quality of an inclusive social network that involves digital arts collaborative production. Having this in mind, we need to create a new specific quality space for the inclusive social network. The dimensions or aspects of our Cartesian quality space are the Technical Domain, the Ergonomic Domain and the Pedagogical Domain.

The Technical Dimension reflects the characteristics of the digital content regarding operational aspects. This dimension adds the following factors: adaptability and content management, as included in Table 2.

The Ergonomic Dimension is related to the scientific knowledge, the design and development of tools that guarantee the overall performance of a given educational environment and can be used easily and safely, (Wisner, Fialho & apud Santos 1995), i.e., the aspects that directly affect the work that must be done in their technical, ergonomic and social aspects: Usability, Video/Audio, and Text, as considered in Table 3.

The Pedagogical Dimension is based on the teaching/learning process supported by the learning criteria. Learning is determined by various factors involving the interrelationship between individuals. Therefore, we believe evaluation to be a tool of a teaching/learning environment that leads us to technological procedures supported by educational issues (Bloom, 1983, Bloom 1964): cognitive, affective, psychomotor (Table 4).

Table 2. Technical Domain Characteristics

Id	Technical Domain
F1	Adaptability
F2	Content management

Table 3. Ergonomic Domain Characteristics

Id	Ergonomic Domain
F3	Usability
F4	Video/Audio
F5	Text

Table 4. Pedagogical Domain Characteristics

Id	Pedagogical Domain
F6	Learning
F7	Evaluation

There are considerable differences in the learning criteria between the Ergonomic dimension and the Pedagogical dimension. The Ergonomic dimension refers to the way of learning how to operate the system (usability) while the Pedagogical dimension refers to the way of learning with a system (learning). Both domains, however, human and computer, are closely connected, enabling the cooperative and collaborative development of digital artworks, straightening human-to-human communication within the inclusive social network or CoP. This way, it is possible to develop an evaluation system addressing fundamental assessment properties for evaluating the quality of digital learning content.

6. CONCLUSION

This paper introduced a proposal for developing an inclusive collaborative learning and creative educational environment focused on enabling blind and deaf individuals to create digital artworks together. This project contributes to foster inclusive learning, and human-to-human interaction by means of technological innovation. A short review of digital arts concepts, especially highlighting practices involving deaf and blind communities was included. The overview on inclusive and cooperative design enabled to conceive the inclusive design model we are following to design the collaborative environment considering our target audience, our purpose, the way we act and perceive development, and our output. The evaluation methodology ensures the environment's consistence, robustness and effectiveness. The direct collaboration of associations for the deaf as well as associations for the blind are collaborating in the concept of this transversal inclusive environment for fostering communication, engagement, learning, creativity and interaction between blind and deaf people.

ACKNOWLEDGEMENT

The authors thank to the R&D group GILT, and to the Portuguese National Funding Agency for Science, Research and Technology (FCT) for the funding of the ACE-Assistive Communication for Education Project, in which scope this research is being developed.

REFERENCES

Axel, Elisabeth Salzhauer. 2003. *Art Beyond Sight: A ResourceGuide to Art, Creativity, and Visual Impairment.* Edited by Elisabeth Salzhauer Axel and Nina Sobol Levent. 1st ed. New York: American Foundation for the Blind Press. https://books.google.pt/books?id=B4ioCFic7m0C&printsec=frontcover&hl=pt-PT&source=gbs_ge_summary_r&cad=0#v=onepage&q&f=false.

Barata, Ana. 2014. 'Despertar Consciências: Activismos e Artes Digitais'. Lisboa: FCSH-Universidade Nova de Lisboa. http://hdl.handle.net/10362/13086.

Ben-Dror, Adam. 2012. 'Pinokio'. indexhibit. 2012. http://ben-dror.com/pinokio/.

Bischin, Maria-Roxana. 2018. 'Music and the Sound: A Philosophy of Perception'. *Brolly, Journal of Social Sciences* 1 (2): 83–91. https://www.journals.lapub.co.uk/index.php/Brolly/article/view/65.

Brand, Johan, and Jamie Brooker. 2015. 'Inclusive Design - a People Centered Strategy for Innovation'. 2015. http://www.inclusivedesign.no/ict/kahoot-article172-261.html.

Chierico, Alessio (interviewer). 2016. 'Media Art and Art Market: An Interview with Wolf Lieser • Digicult | Digital Art, Design and Culture'. 2016. http://digicult.it/news/media-art-art-market-interview-wolf-lieser/.

Chung, Sheng-Kuan. 2006. 'Digital Storytelling in Integrated Arts Education'. *The International Journal of Arts Education* 4 (1): 33–50. http://ed.arte.gov.tw/uploadfile/Periodical/1320_arts_education41_033050.pdf.

Dictionary.com, LLC. 2019. 'Typewriters Were Originally Created to Help the Blind'. Dictionary.com, LLC. 2019. https://www.dictionary.com/e/is-this-goodbye-to-the-typewriter-learn-the-love-story-that-helped-create-the-typewriter/.

Engineering Design Centre. 2017. 'Inclusive Design Toolkit: What Is Inclusive Design?' Cambridge University. 2017. http://www.inclusivedesigntoolkit.com/whatis/whatis.html.

Escudeiro, Paula. 2007. 'Avaliação de Conteúdos Digitais [Evaluation of Digital Contents]'. In *E-Conteúdos Para E-Formadores [E-Contents for E-Trainers]*. Braga: TecMinho/Gabinete de Formação Contínua 2015. 'Unidade Curricular-CAMUL'. P.Porto.

Escudeiro, Paula, and José Bidarra. 2006. 'X-TEC: Techno-Didactical Extension for Instruction / Learning Based on Computer - A New Development Model for Educational Software'. In *WEBIST 2006, Proceedings of the Second International Conference on Web Information Systems and Technologies: Society, e-Business and e-Government / e-Learning*. Setúbal.

Escudeiro, Paula, Nuno Escudeiro, Rosa Reis, Maciel Barbosa, José Bidarra, Ana Bela Baltazar, and Bruno Gouveia. 2013. 'Virtual Sign Translator'. *International Conference on Computer, Networks and Communication Engineering (ICCNCE 2013)*, no. Iccnce: 290–92. https://doi.org/10.2991/iccnce.2013.72.

Escudeiro, Paula Maria, Tiago Oliveira, Nuno Escudeiro, and Fernando Maciel Barbosa. 2018. 'ACE Assisted Communication for Education: Architecture to Support Blind & Deaf Communication'. In *2018 IEEE Global Engineering Education Conference (EDUCON)*, 1015–23. Tenerife: IEEE. https://doi.org/10.1109/EDUCON.2018.8363341.

Farnsworth, Valerie, Irene Kleanthous, and Etienne Wenger-Trayner. 2016. 'Communities of Practice as a Social Theory of Learning: A Conversation with Etienne Wenger'. *British Journal of Educational Studies* 64 (2): 139–60. https://doi.org/10.1080/00071005.2015.1133799.

Gomes, Maria do Céu. 2009. 'O Ensino Do Português Num Contexto de Educação Bilingue'. *Revista Diversidades*, no. 25: 10–14.

Greene, Rachel. 2004. 'Internet Art'. *Art Book* 6: 224. http://www.amazon.com/dp/0500203768.

Holmes, Kat. 2018. 'The No. 1 Thing You're Getting Wrong about Inclusive Design'. 2018. https://www.fastcompany.com/90243282/the-no-1-thing-youre-getting-wrong-about-inclusive-design.

John Clarkson, P., and Roger Coleman. 2015. 'History of Inclusive Design in the UK'. *Applied Ergonomics* 46 (PB): 235–47. https://doi.org/10.1016/j.apergo.2013.03.002.

Lieser, Wolf, and Helena (translated by) Morbey. 2009. *Arte Digital*. Königswinter: Tandem Verlag GmbH h.f.ullmann.

Marques, Bertil, Ana Barata, Piedade Carvalho, Ana Silva, Patrícia Queirós, and Paula Escudeiro. 2018. 'Applying the Quantitative Evaluation Framework Model for Ensuring the MOOC Quality'. In *MCCSIS 2018 - Multi Conference on Computer Science and Information Systems; Proceedings of the International Conferences on e-Learning 2018*. Vol. 2018-July.

Marques, Bertil P., Piedade Carvalo, Paula Escudeiro, Ana Barata, Ana Silva, and Sandra Queiros. 2017. 'Post Graduations in Technologies and Computing Applied to Education: From F2F Classes to Multimedia Online Open Courses.' In *International Association for Development of the Information Society*, edited by Miguel Baptista Nunes and Maggie MacPherson, 55–62. Lisbon: International Association for the Development of the Information Society. e-mail: secretariat@iadis.org; Web site: http://www.iadisportal.org. https://eric.ed.gov/?id=ED579389.

Microsoft. 2018. 'Inclusive Design'. 2018. https://www.microsoft.com/design/inclusive/.

Paul, Christiane. 2003. *Digital Art*. London: Thames & Hudson.

Popper, Frank. 1975. *Art, Action, and Participation*. New York: New York University Press 2007. *From Technological to Virtual Art*. Cambridge, London: The MIT Press.

Roberts, Karen B. 2014. 'Tech Pioneers UD Inventors of Touch Imaging Interface Technology Inducted as NAI Fellows'. Edited by University of Delaware. UDaily. University of Delaware. 2014. http://www1.udel.edu/udaily/2014/may/nai-fellows-052714.html.

Schwarzman, Mat, and Community Arts Criticism. 2006. 'Community-Based Art for Social Change', 9–10.

The Andy Warhol Museum. 2019. 'Out Loud + Tactile Art Reproductions'. The Andy Warhol Museum. The Andy Warhol Museum. 2019. https://www.warhol.org/accessibility-accommodations/.

Wands, Bruce. 2006. *Art of the Digital Age*. Thames & Hudson.

Ward, Jamie, Brett Huckstep, and Elias Tsakanikos. 2006. 'Sound-Colour Synaesthesia: To What Extent Does It Use Cross-Modal Mechanisms Common to Us All?' *Cortex* 42 (2): 264–80. https://doi.org/10.1016/S0010-9452(08)70352-6.

Wenger, Ethiene, Richard Arnold McDermott, and William Snyder. 2002. *Cultivating Communities of Practice: A Guide to Managing Knowledge*. Boston, Massachussetts: Harvard Business School Practice.

Zhou, Shanshan, Adam Ben-Dror, and Joss Doggett. 2012. *Pinokio Lamp*. New Zealand: Victorian Wellington University. https://vimeo.com/52366512.

EMPIRICAL INVESTIGATION OF FACTORS THAT IMPACT E-GOVERNMENT ADOPTION IN NIGERIA

Joshua Chukwu, Marc Conrad and Tess Crosbie
University of Bedfordshire, Luton Campus, UK

ABSTRACT

This paper is a review of the impact of data protection/privacy, website usability and culture on e-government adoption. Along with Hofstede's cultural dimensions and technology acceptance theory, the paper uses these two theories to analyse the highly anticipated era of electronic government, an aspect through which government communicates with agencies and business organisation through information communication technology. We examine the adoption process, its challenges and difficulties, especially in developing countries like Nigeria considering fundamental deficiencies in basic infrastructure, human capacity, political and cultural constraints. This paper can help Nigerian government policy and decision makers develop strategies to adopt e-government services and improve the further development of these services. The paper does not only provide empirical support to previous research, but it validates and improve the results of similar studies in the field.

KEYWORDS

e-Government, Usability, Culture, Adoption, Nigeria, Data Protection/Privacy, Technology Acceptance, Hofstede

1. INTRODUCTION

E- Government is a driving force that has the power to shape public policies at a global level, at time when both political and business leaders around the world are embracing e-government leadership that can be seen working effectively in public and private sectors (Ciborra 2009). The electronic approach dwells on the integration of different public services and other organisational functions, some examples are e-payment, e-learning, e-security, and e-commerce (Carter and Belanger, 2005). The implementation of e-government ensures productive relationships between the government and other stakeholders such as government agencies, citizens and business organisations (Mundy and Musa 2010; UN 2018). According to Ciborra (2009), e-government is a significant reason policy reform is taking place in public sectors around the world. However, it appears to be difficult for developing countries to conceptualise a situation where all government activities and interaction can be done through one platform 24 hours a day and seven days a week without going through a third party or waiting in lines or bribing someone (Dada, 2006). UN e-government Survey (2018) found that Nigeria is ranked 143 in the world out of 192 countries in terms of e-government, that is, since 2016 there has not been any change. The e-participation index which highlights the degree of application of ICT and participation by governments to enhance their services have seen a constant reduction of -42 since 2012 when Nigeria was ranked 75. Several studies have revealed that culture is a major factor as it affects both data protection/ privacy and e-government usability. This paper seeks to understand how culture impact e-government adoption, the influence of data protection/privacy and website usability on Nigerians. To answer this question, we will refer to Hofstede dimension theory and technology acceptance will be used to examine the correlation between culture and E-government adoption. Four out of six Hofstede dimension will be used *(power distance, individualism, short term orientation and uncertainty avoidance).* The reason behind this is that the rest of the dimensions have no direct impact on technology acceptance used to analyse e-government in Nigeria in this paper.

2. RELATED WORK

2.1 e-Government Adoption

The application of information communication technology is transforming government services in terms of speed, accuracy and efficiency (Atzori et al., 2010). In the view of Kumar et al. (2007) and Ciborra (2009), the transformation is the reason both the public sector and organisations are reforming their policies. More so, Gubbi et al. (2013) believe that various government organisations have realised the benefits of e-government, hence want to leverage it to offer citizens easy access to government information and increase the quality of government services. There is a push at various government levels to adopt electronic means of providing government services to citizens. It is an agenda of many governments in Africa to benefit from this technology in order to replace paperwork with electronic means for effectiveness and quality service delivery to citizens (Lee, Chang and Berry 2011; UN, 2018). However, E-government initiatives look very promising but appears to be difficult to implement in developing countries like Nigeria (Dada, 2006), According to a substantial study by Heeks (2002), most implementations of e-government projects in developing countries fail with 35% considered total failure and 50% abandoned as a result of undesired results. On the other hand, some other countries like South Korea, Austria, New Zealand and the Netherlands are doing well in e-government services (Stier, 2015). e-government adoption as research is fragmented. However, recent studies are beginning to use theories to explore major factors that impact e-government adoption, the importance of this technique is that the integration of theories can correct the limitation of an individual approach (Carter and Belanger, 2005). The theory of e-government adoption according to Gilbert et al., (2004) characterised attitude based on the design of diffusion of innovation theory and Theory of Reason Action in relation to service quality using Technology acceptance model. This approach is supported by behavioural theory which has direct impact on user intention. The theory variable is dependent on the willingness of citizens to use e-government services. The perceived usefulness includes the reducing physical contact, cost, time and convenience. Its disadvantages are the lack of usability, reliability, data protection/privacy and ease of use. (Davis 1989).

2.2 e-Government in Developing Countries

According to the recently concluded UN e-government survey 2018, none of the African countries emerged in the top 50 of the e-government development global index (UN 2018). To understand these factors that impact e-government adoption, Colesca (2009) proposes a model which has a solution to reduce e-government related risk. The model is characterised with determinant of trust in e-government such as perceived usefulness, perceived quality, risk perception, trust in technology, privacy concern and education. Her recommendation revealed that a younger generation is more responsive to e-government than the older generation. Lean et al. (2009) emphasised that technological acceptance and diffusion of innovation theory can be used to capture individual perception of technology. This framework was used to analyse factors influencing user's intention on e-government services in Malaysia. The findings suggest that perceived usefulness, perceived relative advantage have more impact on citizens towards using e-government. However, these models have mixed variables and are really narrow in their scope, they tend to focus on limited factors impacting e-government adoption. Few researchers have considered data protection/privacy, website usability and culture in their proposed frameworks. The overall benefits of e-government are enormous, it is not just Government to citizen, Government to Government transactions, but also efficiency and effectiveness in government service delivery (Jaeger 2003). The recently concluded UN e-government survey 2018 emphases that transparency and accountability of government business improve utilisation and enhances the democratisation process. Nevertheless, e-government initiatives represent a high risk for developing countries. There are risks of digital a divide and marginalisation for countries that fail to embrace information communication technology tools for entering the global market and addressing development needs (Ndou, 2004). However, according to Heeks (2002), the potential benefit of e-government includes reduction in corrupt practices, electronic means of communication, equal opportunity and elimination of bureaucratic governance.

3. DEFINITIONS AND RELEVANT FACTORS

3.1 e-Government Definition

United Nations (2018) defines e-government as the use of information technology by government organisations and agencies to provide effective electronic interaction, transaction and exchange of information between the government and the citizen. The World Bank sees e-government as a process of implementing cost-effective models for citizens, government organisations, agencies and other stakeholders to transact business online and access government information (World Bank, 2017). Fang (2002) proposed that e-government is a transformation of public sector internal and external relationships with electronic means in order to effectively improve government service delivery. Halchin (2004) argues that e-government lacks a comprehensive definition that is accepted globally. However, the use of information systems to improve the effectiveness and efficiency in delivering government services constitutes the concept of e-government. Ihmouda et al. (2014) and Ihmouda and Alwi (2006) see e-government as a form of the structure through which government information is delivered electronically to the public, which could either be the citizens or businesses organisations. The various e-Government types are government to citizens (G2C), Government to business (G2B), Government to employee (G2E) and Government to Government (G2G). From the recently concluded UN e-government survey 2018, we can observe that after 2 years Nigeria ranking is still in one position. The study of Dada (2006) concluded that the degree of e-government adoption in developing countries like Nigeria is driven by individual government and not a long-term government system. The projects are presented as political evidence. The political nature makes e-government adoption in Nigeria slow and often abandoned (Heeks 2002). It also shows that Nigeria is not among the top ten countries on the Africa e-government global development index. Several studies have revealed that culture is a major factor as it affects both data protection/ privacy and e-government usability. The following section discusses in detail the factors as they relate to e-government adoption in Nigeria.

3.2 Hofstede

The six-dimension theory developed by Geert Hofstede is a model that explains different culture across countries, suggesting pattern of business carried out in different cultures. The framework differentiates between different national cultures, their dimensions and impacts on the members of the society (Hofstede 2001). Hofstede (2001), defines culture as a collective way of life, beliefs that differentiate a group of people from another. Different theories try to analyze cultural differences (Dickson et al., 2003; Inglehart and Welzel, 2005) but among them Hofstede six dimension is the most widely used. This is despite criticism of Hofstede theory by Baskerville (2005) who reveals various disparity in both theory and methodology, hence caution researchers against unfussy reading of Hofstede's cultural dimensions. The assumption of equating nations with culture and the status of the observers outside the culture was criticised by Baskerville (2005). However, Hofstede's approach appears to be relevant as it involves the West African region which includes Nigeria and is well cited within the technology acceptance domain (Hasan and Dista, 1999). Nigeria has an average score of 55% uncertainty avoidance, 80% on power distance, 30% on individualism, 13% on long term orientation and 60% on masculinity. The six dimensions shows substantial diversity within citizens in a particular country and similarities among people from a different country (Hofstede, 1983). In this paper, we will limit our study to four out of six Hofstede dimensions *(power distance, individualism, short-term orientation and uncertainty avoidance)* as these are directly relevant to the adoption of e-government.

3.2.1 Power Distance

Power distance index is used to measure the extent to which a particular society or members of an organisation accept equal distribution of power. In countries with high power distance, leaders are unquestionable, and they decide what information is to be shared with the public (Hofstede and Hofstede, 2005). Countries with a high score of power distance struggle with innovative technology because technology appears as a threat to bureaucratic and corrupt leadership.

3.2.2 Uncertainty Avoidance

Uncertainty avoidance deals with cultural values on future predictability. According to Hofstede and Minkov (2005), it is the magnitude to which members of a culture feel vulnerable to unknown situations. Nigeria has an average score of 55% on Uncertainty Avoidance which does not show a clear preference (Hofstede, 2005).

3.2.3 Individualism/ Collectivism

Individualism versus collectivism is a dimension that represents personal decision against integrated groups. Personal differences do not matter as people tend to seek for freedom to practice and do what they like without control. Cultures high on individualism promote personal decision over group. (Hofstede and Minkov 2005). Nigeria is considered a collectivistic country (Hofstede, 2005), where people are loyal to each other and tend to be in groups.

3.2.4 Short/Long Term Orientation

According to Hofstede (2005), term orientation is classified into short-term and long-term orientation of people in a particular society, this dimension represents some characteristics of social and ethical philosophy (Gong et al. 2007). Every long-term oriented culture is characterised by values with priority for the future goal and result. With respect to technology acceptance, members from a short orientation cultural structure are associated with immediate perceived usefulness.

3.3 Technology Acceptance (TAM)

According to Davis (1989), TAM suggests that Behavioural intention of an individual depends on the attitude towards the behaviour. It is measured with two major factors.

I. **Perceived Usefulness (PU)**
This refers to the degree to which an individual believes that the use of a particular technology would enhance his or her job performance.

II. **Perceived Ease of Use (PEOU)**
Davis refers to this as the degree to which an individual believes that the use of a particular technology would be free from personal effort.

TAM explains user acceptance of information system technology with clearer understanding on various behaviour surrounding technology acceptance (Shareef, 2011). The model has been cited by thousands of professionals in the information system field and has demonstrated its effectiveness beyond organisational and geographical contexts. Surendran (2012) linked TAM and information behavioural model to explain the relevance of an information system. Also, Pikkarainen et al. (2004) used TAM to understand the acceptance of online banking in Finland and the role played by perceived usefulness in online banking.

3.4 Usability

"In a fair society, all individuals would have equal opportunity to participate, or benefit from the use of computer resources regardless of race, sex, religion age, disability, national origin or other similar factor" (Shneideerman, 2000). Buie and Murrary (2012) state that usability is the capacity to communicate, learn and use new products and services and obtain a positive result. According to Gant et al. (2002) and Casalo et al. (2005) Usability demonstrates how easily users can access and navigate government websites. Some research work believes that this demonstration depends on different features of usability such as effectiveness, efficiency, satisfaction, learnability, error tolerance and memorability (Nielsen, 2006; Abran et al., 2003; Casalo et al., 2008).

4. APPLYING HOFSTEDE AND TAM TO THE CASE OF NIGERIA

4.1 Data Protection and Privacy in Nigeria

Data protection and privacy concerns, according to Wimmer and Bredow (2002), are Secured transactions, protection against unauthorised access to government information, major attacks from hackers. The sharing of government information in real-time has increased the popularity of e-government since it has been used to break administrative barriers and enable citizens to have access to government information from the comfort of their home. However, it has created a major security challenge (Hui and Hayllar, 2010). Data protection is a security process of safeguarding important information from corruption, compromise or loss. The UN e-government survey report (2018), emphasised that privacy is a great influence on e-government adoption. Small and big business organisations in Nigeria recognise this challenge in their electronic transaction services (Okifo and Igbunu, 2015). In the Nigerian perceptive it is a right and control over their information according to the Constitution (1999), as amended. However, the right of privacy stated in section 37 of the Nigerian 1999 constitution does not protect online personal data in this present day of online communication. There is no comprehensive law that provides Nigerians online data protection unlike countries like the United Kingdom, United States of America or Germany that favour a comprehensive regulatory approach to data protection (Aliyu, 2016). Therefore, to achieve data protection and privacy and encourage usability, it is important for the Nigerian Government to reassess data protection/ privacy framework. Given the challenges of online services with the abundance of data, it is essential to reassess and develop effective legal infrastructure for data protection and privacy. After all, e-government is not an automatic solution, rather a combination of technical, social and cultural shifts which need a data protection legal framework. Effort must be made to ensure that people's information is secured and protected (Kesar, 2011).

4.2 Usability of E-Government Websites in Nigeria

With reference to Gant et al., (2002) and Casalo et al. (2005), in section 3.4, usability shows the level users can interact and navigate web interphase without difficulties, as well as considering speed and efficiency. A developing country like Nigeria and some other West African countries are confronted with vast gaps between demand and supply of e-government services. (Adeyemo 2011; and Moon, 2002) revealed that insufficient development of e-government results in failing to meet users' real needs and expectations. Full e-government adoption depends on its usability according to Chan et al., (2018), citing Nielsen's research work on user's behaviour on the web. Sometimes users give time to observe if the website is slow with download time or have an unstable design, or it takes users few times to understand the function of a website and decide how it will meet their needs. However, the basic element relevant to users is the ability of the website to solve their problems effectively (Thompson, 2003). Users will abandon a website and consider it unusable when it cannot solve their problems. Therefore, using a case study in Kenya on e-government website user experience, e-government Usability in Nigeria can overcome barriers like bureaucratic processes, lack of accountability and transparency, digital division, poor management and legal barriers (Kamau et al., 2016).

4.3 Technology Acceptance and Hofstede in Nigeria

As referenced in this paper, Hofstede's dimension theory has been used to measure and quantify Nigerian culture, values and behavioural pattern. In our review, we used Hofstede four of dimension's which were developed from the concept of IBM as well as his estimation for countries that were not in the IBM survey (Hofstede, 2001). The four dimensions are power distance, uncertainty avoidance, individualism-collectivism, and short/long term orientation. Each of these represent a cluster of related values. According to Al-adawi et al., (2005), who extended the TAM model by identifying factors that improve citizen trust and reduce risk in e-government, e-government adoption in Nigerian lacks confidence in the infrastructure of the internet especially with the regular outcry of problems of data protection/privacy, online fraud and security attacks. These factors directly affect behavioural intention to use e-government (Ridwan 2015). Some countries place different values on e-Government adoption, although national culture is seen as a major factor that affects the acceptance of e-Government but research in this direction appears to be limited (Zhao 2011). The possible impact of Hofstede's dimension theory on e-Government can be analysed through the characteristics and interaction of TAM.

4.3.1 Power Distance

According to Hofstede (2005), Nigeria has a score of 80 for this dimension compared United Kingdom with (35), Germany (35), and Austria as low as (11). Heeks, (2005) emphasised that even when a new technology is adopted the people in power still control the system and they determine what information to be shared. Using Hofstede dimensions theory, Nigerian culture is characterised by a high level of power distance (Hofstede, 2005), people respect leaders and tend to accept hierarchy which makes followers loyal to their leaders. The culture encourages obedience. People grow up in an atmosphere of not questioning their leaders. However, despite the level of power distance in Nigeria culture, citizens accept e-government services based on perceived ease of use and perceived Usefulness (Shareef, 2011). The acceptance of e-government services contradicts Hofstede dimensions in the Nigerian context. The behavioural intention is based on technology acceptance (Zhao 2011).

4.3.2 Uncertainty Avoidance

Uncertainty avoidance is a cultural determinant of e-government adoption, and it decides how convenient citizens see e-government services. According to Hofstede and Minkov (2005), it is the magnitude to which members of a society feel vulnerable by an unknown situation. In a high uncertainty avoidance society, people are generally more resistant to innovations, risk-averse and less responsive to change (Gong et al., 2007). The bureaucratic system in Nigeria makes individuals consider e-government services an option to eliminate prolonged delays and third-party system that has to do with a traditional applicational process of government services; e-government services are appreciated in Nigeria with an average score of 55% on uncertainty avoidance index.

4.3.3 Individualism Versus Collectivism

Individualism describes the relationship between groups and individuals. In a low collectivism society, people are concerned about themselves (Gong et al., 2007). In Nigerian context where collectivism is high, people use the group as a primary source for approval and support; this predisposes a culture that rejects innovations like e-government because online services could stop the group's face to face interactions (Hofstede and Minkov 2005). Reviews from the researchers (Gong et al., 2007; Kovacic, 2005; Bagchi et al., 2004) argue that ICT adoption is high among individualistic cultures because the members of an individualistic society have more freedom to express themselves and try new things base on their own opinion. On the other hand, in a collectivistic society, an individual depends on group approval (Gong et al., 2007; Kovacic, 2005). Therefore, everyday features of information technology, such as social media platforms, internet mails and phones calls, are perceived as a threat to face-to -face interaction by members in collective society like Nigeria (Bagchi et al., 2004).

4.3.4 Short-term Orientation

According to Hofstede (2005) as a result of short-term orientation culture, people's perception towards e-government results tend to be different. This dimension is about the traditional cultural values and how society members relate with their past and future (Gong et al., 2004; Erumban and Jong 2006). Cultures with short term orientation like Nigeria are characterised by immediate benefits and quick results; more attention is given to past events and traditional stability. Gong et al. (2007) consider long term orientation society to be characterised by persistence and perseverance. They are more focused on future occurrences, and this makes them preserve the importance of long-term benefits of ICT.

5. RECOMMENDATIONS AND CONCLUSION

Our novel approach to contextualise Hofstede's six dimensions with TAM shows that culture has a direct impact on data protection/privacy and e-government Usability in Nigeria. Some of the points are as follow: firstly, to ensure e-government adoption government needs to take a citizen-centric approach to understand the cultural values that support technology acceptance. In Nigerian society, culture can influence values and expectations of people in accepting e-government. Secondly, it is paramount to put in place a legal framework to enhance online data protection/privacy. Addressing the issue of e-government through legal framework is critical not only to safeguard online transactions, but also to encourage e-government service usability.

This paper has shown that understanding cultural impact, and good legal formulation for data protection/ privacy are enablers of e-government adoption in Nigeria as well as Government website usability. Using Hofstede's dimensions and TAM within the context of e-government adaption we recommend the reassessment and development of effective legal infrastructure for data protection in Nigeria as the most suitable way forward. As there is an indication of partial failure of e-government adoption already it requires an immediate addressing following the understanding of cultural characteristics of technology acceptance used in the study. Further research will focus on how national culture delays e-government adoption specifically and how the legal framework can be implemented.

REFERENCES

Abran, A., Khelifi, A., Suryn, W. & Seffah, A. (2003). "Usability Meanings and Interpretations in ISO Standards". Software Quality Journal, Volume 1(4), pp. 325-338.

Adeyemo, A.B., (2011). E-government implementation in Nigeria: An assessment of Nigerias global e-gov ranking. Journal of Internet and Information Systems, 2(1), pp.11-19.

Al-adawi, Z., Yousafzai, S. and Pallister, J., (2005), September. Conceptual model of citizen adoption of e-government. In *The Second International Conference on Innovations in Information Technology (IIT'05)* (pp. 1-10).

Aliyu, A.S., (2016). The Nigeria Data Protection Bill: Appraisal, Issues, and Challenges. *Peer-reviewed academic journal Innovative Issues and Approaches in Social Sciences*, p.1961.

Atzori, L., Iera, A. and Morabito, G., (2010). The internet of things: A survey. *Computer networks*, *54*(15), pp .2787-2805.

Bagchi, K., Hart, P. and Peterson, M.F. (2004) National culture and information technology product adoption. *Journal of Global Information Technology Management*, *7*(4), pp.29-46.

Baskerville-Morley, R.F., (2005). A research note: the unfinished business of culture. *Accounting, Organizations and Society*, *30*(4), pp.389-391.

Buie, E. and Murray, D. eds., (2012) Usability in government systems: User experience design for citizens and public servants. Elsevier

Carter, L. and Bélanger, F., (2005). The utilization of e-government services: citizen trust, innovation and acceptance factors. *Information systems journal*, *15*(1), pp.5-25.

Casaló, L., Flavián, C. and Guinaliú, M. (2005) "The role of accessibility and commitment in the development of an e-government strategy", eGovernment Workshop "05 (eGOV05), Brunel University, West London, UK

Casaló, L.V., Flavián, C. and Guinalíu, M., (2008). The role of satisfaction and website usability in developing customer loyalty and positive word-of-mouth in the e-banking services. International Journal of Bank Marketing, 26(6), pp.399-417

Chan, W., Nasrudin, M.F. and Mohamed, I., (2018). A study on the security impact of the web services implementation in the Malaysian government's online applications. *International Journal of Advanced Intelligence Paradigms*, *11*(1-2), pp.159-175.

Ciborra, C.U., (2009). Interpreting e-government and development: Efficiency, transparency or governance at a distance?. In *Bricolage, Care and Information* (pp. 90-110). Palgrave Macmillan, London.

Colesca, S.E. (2009) Increasing E-trust: A solution to minimize risk in e-Government adoption. *Journal of applied quantitative methods*, *4*(1).

Dada, D., (2006). The failure of E-government in developing countries: A literature review. *The Electronic Journal of Information Systems in Developing Countries*, *26*(1), pp.1-10.

Davis, F. D., Bagozzi, R. P. and Warshaw, P. R. (1989) 'User acceptance of computer technology: a comparison of two theoretical models'. Management science, 35 (8), pp. 982-1003.

Dickson, M.W., Den Hartog, D.N. and Mitchelson, J.K. (2003), "Research on leadership in a cross-cultural context: making progress, and raising new questions", The Leadership Quarterly, Vol. 14, pp.

Erumban, A.A. and De Jong, S.B. (2006) Cross-country differences in ICT adoption: A consequence of Culture?. *Journal of world business*

Fang, Z., (2002) E-government in digital era: concept, practice, and development. *International journal of the Computer, the Internet and management*, *10*(2), pp.1-22

Federal Government of Nigeria (1999), Constitution of the Federal Republic of Nigeria 1999.

Gant, J.P and Gant, D.B. (2002) "Web Portal Functionality and State Government E-Services", Proceedings of the 35th Hawaii International Conference on Systems Sciences.

Gong, W., Li, Z.G. and Stump, R.L., (2007) Global internet use and access: cultural considerations. *Asia Pacific Journal of Marketing and Logistics*, *19*(1), pp.57-74.

Gubbi, J., Buyya, R., Marusic, S. and Palaniswami, M., (2013). Internet of Things (IoT): A vision, architectural elements, and future directions. *Future generation computer systems*, *29*(7),

Halchin, L. E. (2004) 'Electronic government: Government capability and terrorist resource'. *Government Information Quarterly*, 21 (4), pp. 406-419.

Hasan, H. and Ditsa, G., (1999). The impact of culture on the adoption of IT: An interpretive study. Journal of Global Information Management (JGIM), 7(1), pp.5-15.

Heeks, R., (2002). e-Government in Africa: Promise and practice. *Information polity*, *7*(2, 3), pp.97-114.

Hofstede, G., Hofstede, G.J. and Minkov, M. (2005). *Cultures and organizations: Software of the mind* (Vol. 2). New York: Mcgraw-hill.

Hui, G. and Hayllar, M.R., (2010). Creating public value in e-Government: A public-private-citizen collaboration framework in Web 2.0. *Australian Journal of Public Administration*, *69*, pp.S120-S131

Ihmouda, R., Alwi, N.H.M. and Abdullah, I., (2006). Successful factors on e-government security social-technical aspect.

Ihmouda, R., Alwi, N.H.M. and Abdullah, I., (2014). A Systematic Review on E-government Security Aspects. *International Journal of Enhanced Research in Management and Computer Applications*.

Inglehart, R. and Welzel, C. (2005), Modernization, Cultural Change, and Democracy: The Human Development Sequence, Cambridge University Press, New York, NY.

Kamau, G., Njihia, J. and Wausi, A., 2016, May. E-government websites user experience from public value perspective: Case study of iTax website in Kenya. In *2016 IST-Africa Week Conference* (pp. 1-8). IEEE.

Kesar, S., (2011), Is cybercrime one of the weakest links in electronic government. *J. Int'l Com. L. & Tech.*, *6*, p.243.

Kovacic, Z.J. (2005) A brave new e-world? An exploratory analysis of worldwide e-government readiness, level of democracy, corruption and globalization. *International Journal of Electronic Government Research (IJEGR)*, *1*(3), pp.15-32.

Kumar, V., Mukerji, B., Butt, I. and Persaud, A., (2007). Factors for successful e-government adoption: A conceptual framework. *Electronic Journal of E-government*, *5*(1).

Lean, O.K., Zailani, S., Ramayah, T. and Fernando, Y., (2009). Factors influencing intention to use e-government services among citizens in Malaysia. *International Journal of Information Management*, *29*(6), pp.458-475.

Lee, C.P., Chang, K. and Berry, F.S., (2011). Testing the development and diffusion of e-government and e-democracy: A global perspective. *Public Administration Review*, *71*(3), pp.444-454.

Moon, M. (2002) The Evolution of e-government among municipalities: rhetoric or reality. Public Administration Review 62 (4), 424-33

Mundy, D. and Musa, B., (2010). Towards a framework for egovernment development in Nigeria. *Electronic Journal of E-government*, *8*(2), p.147.

Nielsen, J., Loranger, H. (2006) "Prioritizing web usability", New Riders, Berkeley, California

Ndou, V. (2004). E-government for developing countries: opportunities and challenges. The Electronic Journal on Information Systems in Developing Countries 18 (1), 1-24.

Okifo, J. and Igbunu, R., (2015). Electronic Payment System in Nigeria: Its Economic Benefits and Challenges. *Journal of Education and Practice*, *6*(16), pp.56-62.

Ridwan, S.M., (2015), Electronic Government and the Future of Digital Age: A Road Map of Nigerian Government (Prospects and Challenges). *American Scientific Research Journal for Engineering, Technology, and Sciences (ASRJETS)*, *11*(1), pp.42-50.

Saunders, M., Lewis, P. and Thornhill, A., (2009). Research methods for business students. Pearson education

Shareef, M.A., Kumar, V., Kumar, U. and Dwivedi, Y.K., 2011. e-Government Adoption Model (GAM): Differing service maturity levels. *Government information quarterly*, *28*(1), pp.17-35.

Shneiderman, B., (2000). Universal usability. Communications of the ACM, 43(5), pp.84-91

Stier, S., (2015). Political determinants of e-government performance revisited: Comparing democracies and autocracies. *Government Information Quarterly*, *32*(3), pp.270-278.

Thompson, K. M., McClure, C. R. and Jaeger, P. T. (2003) "Evaluating federal websites: Improving eGovernment for the people", In J. F. George (Ed.), Computers in society: Privacy, ethics, and the Internet, Upper Saddle River, NJ: Prentice Hall.

United Nations Survey (2018). Mobilizing e-government to build resilient societies: Preconditions and enabling environment, New York, pp. 1-25.

Wimmer, M. and Von Bredow, B., (2002), A holistic approach for providing security solutions in e-government. In *System Sciences, 2002. HICSS. Proceedings of the 35th Annual Hawaii International Conference on* (pp. 1715-1724). IEEE.

World Bank, (2011), Definition of E-Government, [online] available from http://go.worldbank.org

Zhao, F., (2011), Impact of national culture on e-government development: a global study. *Internet Research*, *21*(3), pp.362-380.

PREDICTIVE SUCCESS FACTORS IN SCHOOL PERFORMANCE: AN ANALYSIS OF THE LARGE-SCALE ASESSMENT IN BRAZIL

Ivonaldo Vicente da Silva[1], Márcia Terra da Silva[2] and Saturnina Alves da Silva Martins[1]
[1]*Me.*
[2]*Dra.*
Paulista University, Dr. Bacelar Street, 1212 - 4th Floor - Vila Clementino - São Paulo - SP – Brazil - Cep: 04026-002

ABSTRACT

With the advent of new technologies and the strengthening of the concept of Industry 4.0, it becomes important to observe the issue of the need for more qualified and up-to-date professionals concerning the labor market. Thus, there is a need to investigate the level of school performance, especially among high school graduates, who will be the ones who will most quickly enter the labor market. In order to compose the research data, the results of the SAEB large-scale evaluation of the year 2015 in the Portuguese Language and Mathematics proficiency were used. The data were collected, standardized and the results presented in groupings by levels, obeying a scale of 0 to 10. RapidMiner software was used for data mining and decision tree construction. The central objective was to identify the best predictive factors for students' performance equal to or greater than 350 points (level 6). The results showed that there is a significant percentage of students with scores lower than 225 points in the two proficiencies analyzed, considered by the government as a concern, since these students did not learn the necessary minimum. The decision trees demonstrated that the level of schooling of the parents or guardians of students can be considered important and fundamental factors for school performance

KEYWORDS

School Performance, SAEB, Data Mining

1. INTRODUCTION

In Brazil, the young person who wishes to complete a higher education course must pass through all the basic education cycles, composed of Elementary and Middle School. The Elementary School consists of a cycle of nine grades and the High School for three. In some states, the fourth grade of high school is already being tested.

Based on the need for better monitoring of the quality of education, the government created an indicator called the Basic Education Performance Indicator (IDEB) and established it through the National Education Plan - PNE (MEC, 2014). One of the goals of the PNE is that the IDEB index for national education should be 6.0 by the year 2022. Each Brazilian state has its proportional target, but that converges to the national target set for 2022, however in 2015 no state has reached its goal for high school

The IDEB index is composed of data from the School Census and the performance in the large-scale evaluation of the Basic Education Evaluation System (SAEB). This system evaluates students graduating from Elementary and High School (INEP, 2018a).

Each year the labor market receives several individuals, high school graduated, looking for occupation and professional development. A large proportion of these individuals do not yet have professional qualifications, but they need to start their careers.

It is known that the Brazilian educational system suffers from several deficiencies, as its structure, teaching training, safety, access to technological means among other factors. However, several authors corroborate the fact that preparing the young, and future professionals for the job market requires a model of education based on quality and directed towards the changes of this market (Castro and Carvalho, 2013; Alves and Silva, 2013 ; Ferraz and Abreu, 2015; Hypolito and Hypolito, 2015).

Some studies point out that family participation can be a crucial factor in students' school performance, because when there is better monitoring and interest, especially parental participation, in the school routine of children and young people, it is observed that school performance (Nogueira et al. 2015, Gomes, 2016; Zafani and Omote, 2016; Mato et al, 2017; Silveira and Brittes, 2017).

With the advent of the so-called Fourth Industrial Revolution, the labor market starts to demand more skills and abilities from the new professional. Competencies and Skills based on communication, technological knowledge and abstraction power to understand the environment based on logical and mathematic reasoning, become basic prerequisites for the individual ables to maintain and design his professional career (Sátyro et al. 2018)

The high school graduate, usually still without much qualification, needs support and guidance in order to address the labor market, since on the one hand there is a lack of experience and on the other a labor market that seeks increasingly qualified professionals (Comazzetto et al. 2016). It is important to note that the individual with the highest educational level and professional qualification is more likely to evolve professionally. (Sabóia et al. 2016; Messias and Santos, 2018)

Based on a scenario that places on the opposite sides the young person with no professional experience and the highly selective labor market, it is necessary to investigate the level of school performance of high school graduates and identify the factors that contribute or influence their performance. The population universe was composed of the results of the proficiencies in Portuguese Language and Mathematics of the students participating in the SAEB evaluation of the year 2015.

The results of this work will can to contribute with greater knowledge regarding the difficulties of learning in each proficiency analyzed and the factors that contribute to better performance in large scale evaluation, so that the government and society can adapt the public policies, in order to strengthen the work in these predictive factors and in others that are directly related to the school performance.

2. BODY OF PAPER

2.1 Methodological Path

In order for the researcher to be able to conduct his or her work in a targeted manner and to mitigate possible failures, both in data collection and in interpretations of results, it is necessary to define the entire methodological course, including method, techniques and, in particular, researcher creativity, always observing the objectives one wishes to attain.

Firstly, for the development of this study, bibliographic research was carried out in databases such as Scielo, Google Scholar and Web of Science in order to identify the predictive factors of school performance.

Next, SAEB2015 data were collected on the website of the National Institute of Anísio Teixeira - INEP, including complementary documents such as data dictionaries, proficiency scales, among others (INEP, 2018b). The results range from 0 to 500 and are organized in a range of 25 points, with the lowest, from 0 to 225, being considered as level zero. 70698 students participated in this edition, 39326 girls and 31373 boys.

Table 1 presents the results for the proficiencies in Portuguese Language and Mathematics organized by level and gender of the students. The groupings were performed according to the performance of each proficiency, that is, in each level was described the total number of students who had a final grade within the analyzed range. Ex: Level 1> = 225 and <250 points.

After this phase, in order to try to identify important factors in the prediction of good results in the SAEB evaluation, some attributes were separated, according to Tanle 2, for the construction of Decision Trees with support of the data mining technique. The software used for data mining was RapidMiner. The results will be analyzed in the topic Analysis of Results.

Table 1. Number of students in each SAEB 2015 Proficiency

Scale	Girls				Boys			
	PORT	% PORT	MAT	% MAT	PORT	% PORT	MAT	% MAT
Level 0 < 225	6555	16,669	6863	17,452	7476	23,829	4829	15,392
Level 1 225 < 250	5394	13,716	8987	22,853	4470	14,248	5679	18,102
Level 2 250 < 275	6122	15,568	8155	20,737	4736	15,096	5627	17,936
Level 3 275 < 300	6376	16,214	5437	13,826	4419	14,085	4128	13,158
Level 4 300 < 325	5778	14,693	3444	8,758	3902	12,437	3184	10,149
Level 5 325 < 350	4747	12,071	2499	6,355	3278	10,448	2594	8,268
Level 6 350 < 375	2937	7,469	1907	4,849	2078	6,624	2139	6,818
Level 7 375 < 400	1208	3,072	1159	2,947	846	2,697	1577	5,027
Level 8 400 < 425	208	0,529	631	1,605	168	0,535	999	3,184
Level 9 425 < 450			213	0,542			505	1,610
Level 10 >=450			30	0,076			112	0,357
Total...:	**39325**	**100,00**	**39325**	**100,00**	**31373**	**100,00**	**31373**	**100,00**

Note: In Portuguese Language (PORT) Level 8 includes all students with a mark above 400

Source: Developed by the Author (2018)

2.2 Analysis of Results

It is observed a high percentage of students in level 0, (see Table 1), considered by the government as a worrying factor because at this level, the student did not learn the minimum necessary for the proficiency. In Portuguese Language, the total number of girls at level zero was 16.67% and boys 23.83%, whereas, in math, 17.45% of the girls and 15.39% of the boys have this low evaluation.

If the scale used for analysis is Level > = 6 of the scale for proficiency, in Portuguese language the total number of girls was 11.07% and boys 9.86%. In Mathematics, the total number of girls was 10.02% and boys 17.0%. Both the large number of students at level zero and the low number of students at the level>= 6 are worrisome. The differences in performance in Mathematics and Portuguese Language, among boys and girls, have already been observed in the studies of (Laros and Marciano, 2008; Laros et al. 2010), in studies involving high school students in the SAEB 2001 edition.

Then the predominant factor was verified so that the students obtained better performances in this evaluation. In this way it was necessary to use the data mining technique.

Data mining can be used to discover patterns in databases, and from these standards generate sufficient and necessary knowledge in support of decision-making (Silva et al. 2016; Provost and Fawcett, 2016).

The variables/attributes were chosen and prepared based on the forms applied to the students and the data/responses for each variable/attribute were collected from the results available by INEP (INEP, 2018b). The variables/attributes used for this study are described in Table 2.

Table 2. Variables/Attributes used for the Decision Tree

Description	ShortName
What is your gender?	SEX
Have your mother, or the woman responsible for you, studied untill what grade?	MOTHER_STUDY
Have your father, or the man responsible for you, studied untill what grade?	FATHER_STUDY
Do your parents or guardians encourage you to study?	PARENTS_ENCOURAGE_STUDY
Do your parents or guardians encourage you to do homework or school tasks?	PARENTS_ENCOURAGE_HOMEWORK

Do your parents or guardians encourage you to read?	PARENTS_ENCOURAGE_READ
Do your parents or guardians encourage you to go to school or not miss classes?	PARENTS_ENCOURAGE_GOTOSCHOOL
Do your parents or guardians talk to you about what happens at school?	PARENTS_TALK_ABOUTSCHOOL
Do you like to study Portuguese Language?	LIKE_PORTUGUESE
Do you do your homework of Portuguese Language?	DO_HOMEWORK_PORTUGUESE
Does the teacher correct homework in Portuguese Language?	TEACHER_CORRECT_PORTUGUESE
Do you like to study Mathematics?	LIKE_MATHEMATHICS
Do you do Mathemathics homework?	DO_HOMEWORK_MATHEMATHICS
Does the teacher correct Mathematics homework?	TEACHER_CORRECT_MATHEMATHICS
Do you use your school's library or reading room?	USE_LIBRARY
Level of Proficiency (Level <6; Level> = 6)	LEVEL_PROFICIENCY

Source: Developed by the Author (2019)

Data normalization process was performed so that there was no inconsistency and variable/attribute with no response. In this way, all the data that were duly completed were used.

RapidMiner software was used and the technique used was classification. Data were separated into two groups one for training and one for testing. From these groups the decision trees were created, one with data for proficiency in Portuguese Language and another for Mathematics. The results were grouped using level 6 of the proficiency scale as a parameter, so the label parameter of analysis was the level on the proficiency scale (Level< 6 or Level>=6), with the objective of identifying the predominant factors for students to perform better. The results are described in Tables 3 and 4. The accuracy percentage for Portuguese Language was 89.04% and for Mathematics 86.42%.

Table 3. Decision Tree for Proficiency Portuguese Language

```
MOTHER_STUDY = <5th grade Elementary School: <Level6 {<Level6=6412, >= Level6=128}
MOTHER_STUDY = >=5th grade Elementary School e <9º Ano: <Level6 {<Level6=6385, >= Level6=293}
MOTHER_STUDY = >=9th grade Middle School e <High School: <Level6 {<Level6=5169, >= Level6=387}
MOTHER_STUDY = >=High School e <College degree: <Level6 {<Level6=14346, >= Level6=1958}
MOTHER_STUDY = >=College degree
| FATHER_STUDY = <5th grade Elementary School: <Level6 {<Level6=352, >= Level6=29}
| FATHER_STUDY = >=5th grade Elementary School e <9º Ano
| | PARENTS_ENCOURAGE_STUDY = No: <Level6 {<Level6=4, >= Level6=3}
| | PARENTS_ENCOURAGE_STUDY = Yes
| | | PARENTS_ENCOURAGE_GOTOSCHOOL = No: <Level6 {<Level6=9, >= Level6=0}
| | | PARENTS_ENCOURAGE_GOTOSCHOOL = Yes
| | | | PARENTS_ENCOURAGE_HOMEWORK = No
| | | | | PARENTS_TALK_ABOUTSCHOOL = No
| | | | | | TEACHER_CORRECT_PORTUGUESE = Sometimes: <Level6 {<Level6=6, >= Level6=0}
| | | | | | TEACHER_CORRECT_PORTUGUESE = Never or almost never: <Level6 {<Level6=1, >= Level6=1}
| | | | | | TEACHER_CORRECT_PORTUGUESE = Teacher does not give homework to do at home: >= Level6
{<Level6=0, >= Level6=2}
| | | | | | TEACHER_CORRECT_PORTUGUESE = Always or almost always: <Level6 {<Level6=8, >= Level6=3}
| | | | | PARENTS_TALK_ABOUTSCHOOL = Yes: <Level6 {<Level6=12, >= Level6=1}
| | | | PARENTS_ENCOURAGE_HOMEWORK = Yes: <Level6 {<Level6=572, >= Level6=61}
| FATHER_STUDY = >=9th grade Middle School e <High School: <Level6 {<Level6=759, >= Level6=153}
| FATHER_STUDY = >=High School e <College degree: <Level6 {<Level6=2924, >= Level6=781}
| FATHER_STUDY = >=College degree: <Level6 {<Level6=3667, >= Level6=1636}
| FATHER_STUDY = Never attended a school: <Level6 {<Level6=43, >= Level6=4}
| FATHER_STUDY = I don´t Know: <Level6 {<Level6=736, >= Level6=98}
MOTHER_STUDY = Never attended a school: <Level6 {<Level6=1191, >= Level6=14}
MOTHER_STUDY = I don´t Know: <Level6 {<Level6=3206, >= Level6=87}
```

Source: Developed by the Author (2019)

Only for didactic purposes, we will use the term SUCCESS for the level of proficiency equal to or greater than 6 (Level> = 6), both for Portuguese Language and Mathematics.

It can be observed that, in the Portuguese Language case, the most critical factor presented in the decision tree is the MOTHER_STUDY. The positive variation of the mothers' schooling provides an increase of percentual of the students' success. The first four rows of the decision tree indicate that this variable alone can be used to predict the percentage of SUCCESS of the group of students.

For the condition MOTHER_STUDY="Finalized the College degree" the percentage of SUCESS reaches 30%, the greater percentual among all, when the condition FATHER_STUDY="Finalized the College degree" is also true.

To complete, if the condition MOTHER_STUDY="Never Studied" the percentage of SUCCESS reaches 1.6%, and if MOTHER_STUDY="Not Finalized 5th grade Elementary School" to 4.38%, thus reinforcing the importance of the schooling level of mother or woman responsible for the student.

Some variables/attributes were not relevant to the point of appearing in the decision tree, some of which could initially have been considered as factors for school performance, such as if the student enjoys Portuguese Language (LIKE_PORTUGUESE) and uses the school library (USE_LIBRARY). From the results presented, it can be assumed that these factors are not essential for good performance in Portuguese Language proficiency.

Based on the results presented, it is clear that the schooling of the mother or woman responsible for the student is fundamental for the school performance, a fact already observed by some authors (Luiz, 2006; Gerard and Booth, 2015; Benner et al. 2016; Lobo, 2017; Fantinato and Cia, 2017)

Then the decision tree for mathematical proficiency will be analyzed.

Table 4. Decision Tree for Mathematical Proficiency

```
LIKE_MATHEMATHICS = No: <Level6 {<Level6=21310, >=Level6=1465}
LIKE_MATHEMATHICS = Yes
|  FATHER_STUDY = <5th grade Elementary School: <Level6 {<Level6=3860, >=Level6=214}
|  FATHER_STUDY = >=5th grade Elementary School e <9º Ano: <Level6 {<Level6=3492, >=Level6=383}
|  FATHER_STUDY = >=9th grade Middle School e <High School
|  |  MOTHER_STUDY = <5th grade Elementary School: <Level6 {<Level6=320, >=Level6=8}
|  |  MOTHER_STUDY = >=5th grade Elementary School e <9º Ano: <Level6 {<Level6=503, >=Level6=52}
|  |  MOTHER_STUDY = >=9th grade Middle School e <High School: <Level6 {<Level6=674, >=Level6=88}
|  |  MOTHER_STUDY = >=High School <College degree: <Level6 {<Level6=928, >=Level6=189}
|  |  MOTHER_STUDY = >=College degree
|  |  |  TEACHER_CORRECT_MATHEMATICS = Sometimes: <Level6 {<Level6=42, >=Level6=18}
|  |  |  TEACHER_CORRECT_MATHEMATICS = Never or almost never: >=Level6 {<Level6=6, >=Level6=10}
|  |  |  TEACHER_CORRECT_MATHEMATICS = Teacher does not give homework to do at home: <Level6
{<Level6=14, >=Level6=7}
|  |  |  TEACHER_CORRECT_MATHEMATICS = Always or almost always: <Level6 {<Level6=297, >=Level6=107}
|  |  MOTHER_STUDY = Never attended a school: <Level6 {<Level6=25, >=Level6=2}
|  |  MOTHER_STUDY = I don´t Know: <Level6 {<Level6=47, >=Level6=2}
|  FATHER_STUDY = >=High School <College degree
|  |  MOTHER_STUDY = <5th grade Elementary School: <Level6 {<Level6=272, >=Level6=26}
|  |  MOTHER_STUDY = >=5th grade Elementary School e <9º Ano: <Level6 {<Level6=506, >=Level6=73}
|  |  MOTHER_STUDY = >=9th grade Middle School e <High School: <Level6 {<Level6=635, >=Level6=148}
|  |  MOTHER_STUDY = >=High School <College degree: <Level6 {<Level6=3160, >=Level6=896}
|  |  MOTHER_STUDY = >=College degree
|  |  |  TEACHER_CORRECT_MATHEMATICS = Sometimes: <Level6 {<Level6=172, >=Level6=120}
|  |  |  TEACHER_CORRECT_MATHEMATICS = Never or almost never: <Level6 {<Level6=34, >=Level6=23}
|  |  |  TEACHER_CORRECT_MATHEMATICS = Teacher does not give homework to do at home: >=Level6
{<Level6=29, >=Level6=54}
|  |  |  TEACHER_CORRECT_MATHEMATICS = Always or almost always: <Level6 {<Level6=1120,
>=Level6=570}
|  |  MOTHER_STUDY = Never attended a school: <Level6 {<Level6=22, >=Level6=2}
|  |  MOTHER_STUDY = I don´t Know
|  |  |  PaisIncetivamEstudar = No: >=Level6 {<Level6=1, >=Level6=2}
|  |  |  PaisIncetivamEstudar = Yes: <Level6 {<Level6=124, >=Level6=10}
|  FATHER_STUDY = >=College degree
|  |  MOTHER_STUDY = <5th grade Elementary School: <Level6 {<Level6=47, >=Level6=6}
```

```
| | MOTHER_STUDY = >=5th grade Elementary School e <9º Ano: <Level6 {<Level6=96, >=Level6=32}
| | MOTHER_STUDY = >=9th grade Middle School e <High School: <Level6 {<Level6=173, >=Level6=78}
| | MOTHER_STUDY = >=High School <College degree: <Level6 {<Level6=918, >=Level6=602}
| | MOTHER_STUDY = >=College degree: >=Level6 {<Level6=1499, >=Level6=1585}
| | MOTHER_STUDY = Never attended a school: <Level6 {<Level6=8, >=Level6=2}
| | MOTHER_STUDY = I don´t Know
| | | TEACHER_CORRECT_MATHEMATICS = Sometimes: >=Level6 {<Level6=3, >=Level6=6}
| | | TEACHER_CORRECT_MATHEMATICS = Never or almost never: >=Level6 {<Level6=1, >=Level6=2}
| | | TEACHER_CORRECT_MATHEMATICS = Teacher does not give homework to do at home: <Level6
{<Level6=2, >=Level6=1}
| | | TEACHER_CORRECT_MATHEMATICS = Always or almost always: <Level6 {<Level6=42, >=Level6=9}
| FATHER_STUDY = Never attended a school: <Level6 {<Level6=1070, >=Level6=26}
| FATHER_STUDY = I don´t Know: <Level6 {<Level6=3485, >=Level6=261}
```

Source: Developed by the Author (2019)

The results for mathematical proficiency have shown that the main condition is whether the student likes Mathematics (LIKE_MATHEMATHICS). When the condition LIKE_MATHEMATHICS= "No" the percentage of SUCCESS reaches 6.43%. Already when the condition LIKE_MATHEMATHICS="Yes" the tree shows other important conditions, one of them is the question if the father studied (FATHER_STUDY).

When the condition LIKE_MATHEMATHICS="Yes" and FATHER_STUDY="Finished College degree", the percentage of SUCCESS reaches 51.4% when the condition MOTHER_STUDY= "Finalized the College degree" is answered and 39.6% in the case of the condition MOTHER_STUDY="Finalized the High School, but not the College ". Both situations reinforce the assumption that parents 'or guardians' schooling significantly influences school performance.

Another important factor in the student's school routine is the teacher's participation. It is clear that the acting teacher can provide greater motivation and better student performance (Oliveira, 2016). In the conditions LIKE_MATHEMATHICS="Yes", FATHER_STUDY="Finished High School, but not College degree" and MOTHER_STUDY="Finalized the College degree" the percentage of SUCESS reaches 33,73% when the condition TEACHER_CORRECT_MATHEMATHICS="Always or almost always "is true.

Finishing when the condition FATHER_STUDY="I do not know" the percentage of SUCCESS reaches 6.97%.

The observed conditions are in line with some studies on the subject of learning in Mathematics by the students, where they also reinforce that the presence of the family becomes essential for the evolution of school performance (Laros et al. 2010; McNeal, 2015; Ross, 2016).

3. CONCLUSIONS

The objective of this study was to analyze the students 'performance in the SAEB 2015 large scale evaluation and to identify predictive factors of success in relation to students' performance in Portuguese Language and Mathematics proficiencies.

Initially the proficiency results showed that there is a high percentile of students, (reaching 23.8% in Portuguese Language, for boys), who presented performance compatible with level zero in both proficiencies. Likewise, the small number of students who reached a performed above level 6 is also worrisome.

In this way, it becomes necessary to have a more judicious view that can identify the deficiencies in the educational environment that may impair the performance of the students, and from that, propose changes in the educational plans and even in public policies that can offer better conditions for the learning at all levels of education (Oliveira, 2010; Oliveira and Waldhelm, 2016).

After the phases described in the methodological course, the results presented in the decision trees indicate that the level of education of parents or guardians of students is a primary factor and influences school performance. When looking at the decision trees, the results indicate that the family's role in accompanying the student's school routine may be preponderant so that the student has condition to develop and projetct his professional career.

The labor market, more and more selective, requires skilled and updated professionals, especially in relation to new technologies and innovations, so it is necessary that the young graduates of High School have a minimum of condition, in terms of knowledge, to work in these companies. What has been observed is that the level of proficiency presented mainly in Mathematics becomes worrisome because it may be that this egress is not minimally prepared to face professional challenges that require a higher level of logical reasoning and mathematical calculations. In an environment in constant technological change, factors related to mathematical and logical reasoning may be fundamental for the maintenance of the individual in the labor market. Inclusive the level of performance presented may be an influential factor in the choice of profession (Araujo et al. 2018).

The results found may contribute to future research in the area of education, principally in the sense of improving public policies aimed at education and the participation of the family in the student's school routine. As a limitation, there is the question of the population universe of this edition of the SAEB, with the suggestion that this study can be replicated in other large-scale evaluations, including other educational levels, such as the 5th year of Elementary Education or international like PISA.

ACKNOWLEDGMENT

This work was carried out with the support of the Coordination of Improvement of Higher Level Personnel - Brazil (CAPES) - Financing Code 001.

REFERENCES

Alves, T. and Silva, R.M. da 2013. Estratificação das oportunidades educacionais no Brasil: contextos e desafios para a oferta de ensino em condições de qualidade para todos. *Educação & Sociedade* 34(124), pp. 851–879.

Araújo, A.J.N. et al. 2018. Ensino profissionalizante, desempenho escolar e inserção produtiva : uma análise com dados do ENEM. *http://ppe.ipea.gov.br* . Available at: http://repositorio.ipea.gov.br/handle/11058/8353

Castro, J.A. de and Carvalho, C.H.A. de 2013. Necessidades e possibilidades para o financiamento da educação brasileira no plano nacional de educação. *Educação & Sociedade* 34(124), pp. 829–849. doi: 10.1590/S0101-73302013000300010.

Comazzetto, L.R. et al. 2016. A Geração Y no Mercado de Trabalho: um Estudo Comparativo entre Gerações. *Psicologia: Ciência e Profissão* 36(1), pp. 145–157.

Fantinato, A.C. and Cia, F. 2017. Envolvimento parental, competência social e o desempenho acadêmico de escolares. *Psicologia Argumento* 29(67). Available at: https://periodicos.pucpr.br/index.php/psicologiaargumento/article/view/20401

Ferraz, R.R.N. and Abreu, J.S. 2015. Quando a Culpa do mau Desempenho Escolar não é Exclusivamente do Aluno. *UNILUS Ensino e Pesquisa* 12(28), pp. 96–100.

GIL, A.C. 2010. *Métodos e técnicas de pesquisa social*. 6th ed. São Paulo: Atlas.

Gomes, J.A.M. 2016. Os Recursos do Ambiente Familiar e a Influência no Rendimento Acadêmico. *Revista Lugares de Educação* 6(12), pp. 103–124.

Hypolito, Á.L.M. and Hypolito, Á.L.M. 2015. Trabalho docente e o novo Plano Nacional de Educação: valorização, formação e condições de trabalho. *Cadernos CEDES* 35(97), pp. 517–534. doi: 10.1590/CC0101-32622015150376.

INEP 2018a. IDEB - SAEB. Available at: http://portal.inep.gov.br/web/guest/educacao-basica/saeb

INEP 2018b. INEP - Microdados. Available at: http://portal.inep.gov.br/web/guest/microdados.

Lakatos, E.M. and Marconi, M. de A. 2017. *Fundamentos de Metodologia Científica*. Edição: 8ª. Atlas.

Laros, J.A. and Marciano, J.L. 2008. Índices Educacionais Associados à Proficiência em Língua Portuguesa: Um Estudo Multinível. *Avaliação Psicológica.* p. 19. Available at: http://pepsic.bvsalud.org/scielo.php?script=sci_abstract&pid=S1677-04712008000300010&lng=en&nrm=iso&tlng=pt

Laros, J.A. and Marciano, J.L.P. Moura, J.A 2010. Fatores que Afetam o Desempenho na Prova De Matemática do SAEB: Um Estudo Multinível. *Avaliação Psicológica*, p. 14. Available at: http://www.redalyc.org/resumen.oa?id=335027283004

Lobo, G.D. 2017. Avaliação do Desempenho Escolar dos Estudantes da Região Nordeste que Realizaram o ENEM: Uma Análise com Modelos Hierárquicos. *Revista Espacios* 38, p. 13.

LUZ, L.S. 2006. Os Determinantes do Desempenho Escolar: A Estratificação Educacional e o Efeito Valor Adicionado. *XV Encontro Nacional de Estudos Populacionais, ABEP* Caxambu-MG

Matos, D.A.S. et al. 2017. Impactos das práticas familiares sobre a proficiência em Língua Portuguesa e Matemática no Ensino Fundamental. Available at: http://www.repositorio.ufop.br/handle/123456789/9797.

MEC 2014. PNE - Plano Nacional de Educação - Plano Nacional de Educação - Lei n° 13.005/2014. Available at: http://pne.mec.gov.br/18-planos-subnacionais-de-educacao/543-plano-nacional-de-educacao-lei-n-13-005-2014

Messias, J.F. and Santos, O.S. dos 2018. O Déficit Educacional e a Exclusão Tecnológica no Mercado de Trabalho Brasileiro. *Brasil Para Todos - Revista Internacional* 6(1). Available at: https://ojs.eniac.com.br/index.php/Anais_Sem_Int_Etn_Racial/article/view/536

MINAYO, M.C. de S. (or). 2010. *Pesquisa social: teoria, método e criatividade*. 29th ed. Petrópolis/RJ: Vozes.

Nogueira, R.K.S. et al. 2015. Família e Escola: Relação que Promove o Bom Rendimento Escolar dos Alunos de Duas Turmas do Ensino Fundamental em uma Escola da Região Arapiraquense. *Anais do Congresso de Inovação Pedagógica em Arapiraca* 1(1). Available at: http://www.seer.ufal.br/index.php/cipar/article/view/1916

Oliveira, A.C.P. de and Waldhelm, A.P.S. 2016. Liderança do diretor, clima escolar e desempenho dos alunos: qual a relação? *Ensaio: Avaliação e Políticas Públicas em Educação* 24(93), pp. 824–844.

Oliveira, J.A.P.F. 2016. O Que É Um Bom Professor, na Visão do Aluno: um estudo de caso em uma Instituição de Ensino Superior em Oliveira-MG. *Revista Acadêmica FEOL* 1(2), pp. 47-67–67.

Oliveira, L.M. de 2010. Políticas educacionais na formação da professora dos anos iniciais do ensino fundamental em cursos de licenciatura. *Ensaio: Avaliação e Políticas Públicas em Educação* 18(67), pp. 235–252.

Provost, F. and Fawcett, T. 2016. *Data Science para Negócios*. Rio de Janeiro: Alta Books.

Sabóia, A.L. et al. 2016. Adolescentes e jovens no Brasil: escolarização e inserção no mercado de trabalho. *Anais*, pp. 1–17.

Sátyro, W.C. et al. eds. 2018. *Indústria 4.0: Conceitos e Fundamentos*. Edição: 1ª. Blucher.

Silva, L.A. da et al. 2016. *Introdução à Mineração de Dados*. Rio de Janeiro: Elsevier. Available at: https://www.loja.elsevier.com.br/introducao-a-mineracao-de-dados-9788535284461.html.

Silveira, R.B. and Brittes, L.R. 2017. A Participação da Família Na Escola: Desdobramentos Sobre a Evasão Escolar e a Educação Profissional E Tecnológica Na Lógica Neoliberal. *Educação Básica Revista* 3(1), pp. 29–46.

Sousa, M. de. 2017. Eficácia escolar e o desempenho de meninos e meninas. *Aleph* , p. 55 f.

A PERCEPTIONAL STUDY ON THE ROLE OF DEVELOPMENT AGENTS AND GLOBAL LEADERS IN LEVERAGING TECHNOLOGY FOR SUSTAINABLE DEVELOPMENT

Luís de Castro and Vìtor dos Santos
Nova Information Management School, Portugal

ABSTRACT

Over the past decades Technology shaped the modern world we live in, consequently, it became an increasingly discussed topic in the Global Agenda for Sustainable Development. On the turning point from the Millennium Development Goals to the Sustainable Development Goals, new challenges and opportunities arise, where Development Agents and Global Leaders have to determine new directions and guidelines to successfully use and deploy this tool for sustainable development on a 2015 post-agenda context. The present multidisciplinary study was conducted on the context of the World Summit on Information Society, where 16 experts' in the fields of Development and Technology were interviewed to further analyze their opinions on what the role of Development Agents and Global Leaders is in leveraging technology for sustainable development.

KEYWORDS

Sustainable Development, Technology, SDGs, Global Leaders, Development Agents, WSIS

1. INTRODUCTION

To achieve Sustainable Development societies will have to transform, in order to, on the one hand, keep the pace of human progress and on the other assure global sustainability. The United Nations (2016) believe that Technology has shaped society, economy and the environment, and only now we are truly unlocking the power of technology to help solve the 21st-century challenges. It is, therefore, a potential tool to be used in order to achieve a new sustainability paradigm. National and international action plans and roadmaps should be developed for achieving the SDGs individually and together, including the participation of the UN and its organizations, governments, private-sector, academia and civil society United Nations (2016). Based on these premises, the main goal of this study was to answer the question: what are the role of these Development Agents and Global Leaders in leveraging technology for sustainable development?

Technology is increasingly becoming a major tool to transform economies and increase the well-being of nations while creating new opportunities and challenges for humankind and its relation with the environment (Hazboun, 2014).

A Global call-to-action to gather, not only nations but also entities from every sector to collaborate and discuss the role of technology to achieve Sustainable Development, "We are at a historic crossroads, and the directions we take will determine whether we will succeed or fail on our promises" (United Nations, 2014, pp.3). Based on this shifting moment marked by the transitioning from the Millennium Development Goals to the Sustainable Development Goals, it is crucial to reflect on the next steps to be taken in a post-2015 agenda context.

The international community early on recognized the potential of technology for development and encouraged Development Agents and Global Leaders who are represented by International Organizations such as the UN and NGOs, Governments, Private-Sector, Academia and Civil Society to define strategies and roles as an integral part of national development plans to achieve the SDGs (UNCTAD, 2014).

2. STUDY METHOD

Face-to-face interviews were conducted with field experts on Development and Technology. The type of interview script created was semi-structured to meet both validation requirements and specifications which followed a storyline created based on the research undertaken: starting with a general approach to the perceived role of Technology in the context of Development, then moving into the specific question regarding the role of Global Leaders and Development Agents.

Openness to dialogue, express personal points of view and experience sharing was given making the nature and flow of the interviews neither too formal and structured nor too informal and conversational (Mann, 2016). According to Blaxter et al. (2006, as cited in: Alshenqeeti, 2014), interviews offer researchers the possibility to uncover information that would not be possible accessing using other techniques, such as questionnaires not to mention the fact that data coming from interviews can be recorded and reviewed different times helping the reporting and results to be more accurate (Alshenqeeti, 2014).

2.1 Validation

This study was validated by field experts, global leaders and development agents, all participants of the World Summit on Information Society (WSIS), a conference dedicated to the topic of Technology and Development, held in Geneva, 2018.

The conference served as the physical place to conduct a series of interviews with experts on the fields of Development and Information Systems with the goal to Understand their opinion on the role of technology to achieve the SDGs and the respective role of Development Agents and Global Leaders.

A total of 16 interviewees (11 males and 5 females) from 11 different countries, backgrounds, and sectors gave their contribution to the present study:

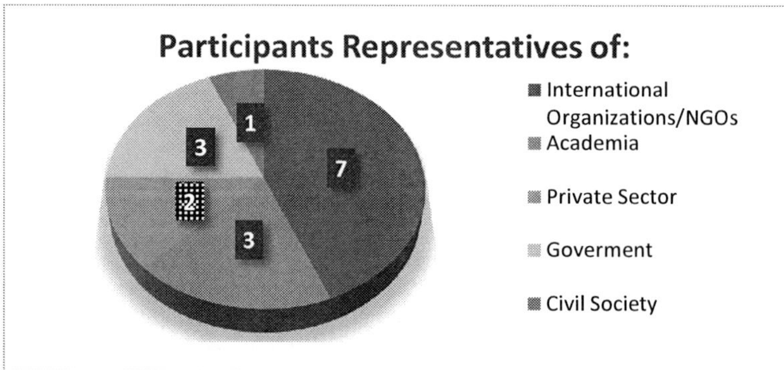

Figure 1. Interviewees Representing: International Organizations, Academia, Private Sector, Government and Civil Society

Before and during the WSIS 2018, the sixteen interviewees were invited to participate in the series of interviews undertaken with the aim to help address the study main questions. All the interviewees attended the WSIS, and their invitation to participate in the study was based on their demonstrated academic and professional background relevancy for the research context, either in Development and Technology fields and within a position of leadership. Consent for publishing the results was given by the study participants.

The Interview Script was created with the intent to explore the interviewee's perception on the role of technology to achieve the SDGs and what the role of Development Agents might be in leveraging technology for sustainable development, and the questions asked were:

1. Do you consider sustainable human development dependent or independent upon technology?
2. What other variables do you believe to be crucial?
3. According to your experience and opinion, what might be the main role of Technology to achieve the Sustainable Development Goals?

4. What is in your opinion the role of development agents and global leaders (governments, NGOs, private-sector and civil society) in leveraging technologies for sustainable development?

The Duration of the interviews varied approximately from 15 minutes up to 1 hour. From the 16-total number of interviews, 14 were conducted face-to-face at the WSIS, while the remaining 2 were conducted via Skype. From the 16 interviews, only one was not allowed to be recorded. The qualitative analysis of the interviews was conducted by the researcher and the following process based on the work of Blair (2015) was adopted:

1. Audio Transcription;
2. Underlining answers sections according to relevancy, scope, and extent;
3. Revise the audio interviews to complement and add any missing relevant content;
4. Creating general and specific categories within given answers;
5. Correlating and interpretation of the answers' categories with researched literature.

3. RESULTS

The first part of the study focused on the broader topic of Technology for Development followed by the experts' opinion on the role of Development Agents and Global Leaders.

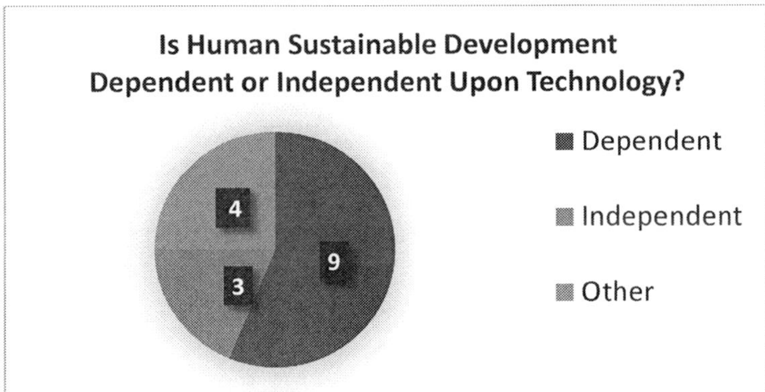

Figure 2. Results: Experts opinions on Human Sustainable Development dependency on Technology

Nine experts believe that Human Sustainable Development is dependent upon technology. Three participants believe its achievement is not dependent on technology, while the remaining four offered a more nuanced point of view and approach in answering the question: the two main arguments given were that (1) development can be enabled by technology without being fully dependent on it and (2) in the form of a criticism to the viability of the SDGs programme, which will be further addressed in the discussion section of this study.

According to the experts, the following variables are crucial to the successful achievement of Human Sustainable Development:

- Diverting resources and national budgets for sustainable development purposes;
- Reducing inequalities;
- Collaborating and partnering with stakeholders;
- Personal behavior and the ability to learn from past experiences;
- National ownership and agenda alignment between International Organizations and National Governments;
- Governance and access to education;
- Understanding the needs at the local level;
- Having a sustainable development approach in businesses;
- Technology and education for all;

- ❖ Capacity for critical thinking and developing digital literacy skills;
- ❖ Creating the right incentives and assertive policies;
- ❖ SDGs implementation and monitoring guidance;
- ❖ Taking action.

When exposed to the question "what might the main role of Technology be in achieving the Sustainable Development Goals by 2030?", the following answers were given:

- ❖ It is an enabler and connector of problems to solutions for sustainable development;
- ❖ It has the role of empowering the economy, education, and equal access;
- ❖ It has the role of improving efficiency and timeliness in achieving the SDGs;
- ❖ It plays the role of a facilitator and mediator of the development process;
- ❖ It has the role of an accelerator, providing services faster and at a more accessible price;
- ❖ It helps make the usage of resources more efficient;
- ❖ Technology has to be accessible, understandable and usable for development;
- ❖ Technology should not look how we want it to look like, but instead reflect the world we want, how we define sustainable development and how we use technology for this purpose;
- ❖ Technology helps make use and sense of the large amount of data produced every day, for development purposes;
- ❖ Technology enables the inclusion and makes it possible and easier to achieve the SDGs
- ❖ Technology currently has the role of enhancing economic growth rather than reducing poverty.

According to the study participants, the main challenges and issues faced by development agents and global leaders in their quest to leverage technology for sustainable development are:

- ❖ The alignment of global agenda with nation-specific priorities. For instance, in a certain country, X, a specific technology can play an important role for development purposes, which might not happen in country Y, with different social, economic, and environmental contexts. Therefore, technology development, commercialization, and use must account for these specific characteristics and local needs;
- ❖ Correctly understanding and applying the Information and Communication Technologies for Development (ICT4D).
- ❖ Over the past years the massification of technology production, dissemination and use are making the concept of ICT4D blurred, with it increasingly becoming Development for ICTs (D4ICT) – which doesn't have human sustainable development at its core, but rather commercial purposes and interests, meaning that far too often the private sector, governments and civil society are using the concept of development to further their ICT interests while it should be the other way around. ICT4D entails the production and use of technology to truly serve the interests of the poor, minorities and marginalized, therefore reducing poverty and inequalities
- ❖ Creating the right incentives and ecosystem around science, technology and innovation (by enabling, for example, free and open access to information on a global scale, or by introducing policies that attract and allow businesses to give their contribution in leveraging technology for sustainable development), while fostering an environment of trust among stakeholders of different social sectors through the use of regulatory and governance best practices to ensure fair competition in the technological sector;
- ❖ Creating a balanced regulatory environment while at the same time addressing security management (cybersecurity) and the capacity building issue is necessary to make legislation and regulation work for both digital and technological markets.

Finally, according to the results, different roles could be identified for each society sector represented in the study as far as their ability to help solve the aforementioned challenges:

International Organizations/NGOs:

- ❖ The United Nations should spread the best practices worldwide regarding how technology can be deployed to achieve the SDGs;

  NGOs have the role of conducting research at the local level and engaging locally with the communities.

Governments:

- Employing technology, science, and innovation to help society achieve better outcomes;
- Empowering communities and creating an innovation ecosystem for entrepreneurs to develop new meaningful technologies, which will have a positive impact on people's lives;
- Creating incentive policies and encourage people to take action, changing mentalities and behaviors through funding and collaborative initiatives within society;
- Regulating markets and their competition by cutting down unnecessary expenses, increasing investment and offering services at lower prices, while enforcing fair taxes to the private sector and enabling the creation of new businesses with sustainable models;
- Fostering inclusion through technological innovation and providing access to affordable and modern technology tools, mainly in developing countries.

Private Sector:

- Collaborating and engaging with governments for development purposes;
- Providing emerging markets with new alternatives and solutions to achieve the SDGs, not only the developed countries;

Academia:

- Preparing future leaders for sustainable development;
- Giving young minds the know-how, skills, and tools to achieve the SDGs.

Civil Society:

- Cooperating with other sectors in addressing local challenges;
- Giving voice to the poor and most marginalized.

4. DISCUSSION

The current globalized world we live in reflects what technology has enabled in recent years. Technology is now an integral part of most human activities as we know them, and it affects our everyday lives. Neither the Millennium Development Goals (MDGs) nor presently the SDGs could be achievable without the contribution of science, technology, and innovation (Ely, Zwanenberg, and Stirling, 2011). This is also the opinion of more than half of the study experts, who believe human Sustainable Development to be dependent on technology.

The main arguments given were that despite the known merits of technology in this context, there are other ways to achieve the SDGs such as educating people for sustainability and having the right mindset not to allow technology to become the end of development itself. Also, the participants emphasized the importance of defining Sustainable Development and its purpose, and then putting it into practice through proper regulation and policies. As an example: the "eco-social policies", which stipulate that economic growth from a sustainability point of view must also be "green", allow for the creation of employment and reduction of environmental damage by shifting behaviors or providing the right incentives for a sustainable management of resources and adaptive capacities of individuals and communities (UNRSID, 2017).

Technology can be a tool and enabler for development without development being fully dependent on it. According to one of the experts, the discussion around the SDGs goes deeper to its founding roots, purpose and programme architecture, which from the start might have compromised any achievement of the SDGs. Different factors can help address this point of view, ranging from thexz transparency of the international funding addressed by Denney (2012), the fact it was a top-down exercise and left out many countries in the process, namely in Africa, which was covered in detail by Transparency International (2012) and Easterly (2009), or the lack of alignment between international and national level goals, as mentioned by McArthur and Rasmussen (2017). Despite the improvement on some of these limitations in the transition to the SDGs, there still remains among skeptics the opinion that not enough is actually being done to truly bring extreme poverty and world hunger to an end or to reduce inequalities, goals which are at the core of the SDGs.

According to Asah (2015) there are inconsistencies in the architecture of the Development Agenda and its guiding principles such as the different conceptualizations and viewpoints on what Sustainable Development entails (which, according to Du Pisani (2006), has been the case throughout history) and the higher relevance given to western worldviews and constructs of the Sustainable Development concept than to the issues and debates around the social, economic and environmental needs of the so-called Global South.

From a strategic point of view, country ownership, leadership, and a supportive international environment is crucial for an effective mobilization of resources according to the United Nations (2014a). Each country must be responsible for its own Development while the international community's role is to provide the necessary support and an enabling environment; this will then lead to a second stage, where government policies are at the core of a robust SD financing strategy. These public policies will, in turn, allow all the other sectors to operate within this framework guided and strengthened by effective policymaking and its resulting policies, transparency, accountability and good governance (United Nations, 2014a).This way, synergies can be maximized between financing streams such as private and public finance - and their respective investment decisions – and the creation of new mechanisms and instruments at the national level to give answer to social

Understanding local level needs and empowering local communities by providing them with the necessary tools, such as education and the 21st-century skills, will allow societies to be more ready to face not only local but also global challenges in the future (Filho, Mifsud & Pace, 2018).

This new 21st-century paradigm for educational change entails not only formal education but also non-formal and informal education. The European Council (2006) created a recommendation on key competencies for lifelong learning, which then started to be used and implemented by governments, from learning foreign languages and developing digital competencies to developing a sense of initiative, entrepreneurial spirit, cultural awareness, and expression. (Filho et al., 2018).

The alignment of International, National and Local levels, combined with the lifelong learning approach to education for Sustainable Development and the effective contribution of each one of the society sectors (International Organizations/NGOs, Governments, Private-Sector, Academia and Civil Society) can help pave the way to dignity and the subsequent achievement of the Sustainable Development Goals.

Despite the technological progress undertaken over these past few years, namely in the field of Development, "a related painful paradox is that despite the ongoing technological revolution the majority of the world population still lives in abject poverty" (Vergragt, 2006, pp.1). This reality is in part based on the premise that development is a process of structural changes that will require a series of historic steps that the developing nations have to follow in order to reach the present levels of mass consumption of the developed world (Brito, 2014; mentioned in Hazboun, 2014). While technology has been recognized by the 2030 agenda as an important means for implementing the SGSs according to the UNDP (2017), technology has not yet been sufficiently addressed regarding its conception, creation and implementation for development purposes as well as who should be responsible for it (Vergragt, 2006).

At a Global level, the United Nations and other international and non-governmental organizations, have the role of spreading best practice worldwide on how technology can be deployed to achieve the SDGs. And according to Evans (2012), they also have the role to gather and share data and knowledge, support Intergovernmental decision making and finance and support country-level implementation of the SDGs.

Being the adopters of the SDGs, governments have the responsibility to take the lead in collectively tackling the world's most pressing Sustainable Development challenges, however, the range of possible contributions of the business sector shows that public and private roles and responsibilities are increasingly becoming intertwined (Agarwal, Gneiting, & Mhlanga, 2017).

According Agarwal et al. (2017), the private-sector has increasingly demonstrated its interest and commitment to Sustainable Development by supporting policy development that matches their actions while looking to even the odds and overcome the competitive disadvantages of unilateral sustainability actions.

Companies should focus not only on what the SDGs can do for them but also what they should do for the SDGs, by looking at how core commercial practices such as wages and taxation either detract from or enable a world with reduced inequalities, through the exploration of new sustainable business models or by removing barriers to sustainable business behavior (Agarwal et al., 2017).

Civil Society has the role of giving and raising the voice of the poor and most marginalized. It should advocate for the application of human rights conventions and bridge the communication gap between society and remaining sectors, mainly the private sector and governments, in order to mobilize resources and work towards local development.

Education has been introduced in this section as one of the major drivers for Sustainable Development, and the preparation of the present and future generations; goal 4 of the SDGs, reflects the importance attributed to Academia's contribution in achieving the SDGs and leveraging technologies for this purpose.

Academia has been playing a crucial role in advocating and promoting innovation through advancing technological research and sharing their findings with the public (Vidican, 2009). Universities have the role of contributing to community development and coherence by advocating their core ethical values of equity and transparency. Through their interaction with the local government they can develop programmes that involve and engage young people and the local community in general in SDGs-related activities. Finally and according to UNDESA (2015), to realize the potential contribution of each and every society sector in facing the 21st century challenges, the international community has increasingly recognized the importance of embracing a Global Partnership to deliver on all of the SDGs and facilitate an intense global engagement, bridging the path of cooperation between the International, National and Local levels and among Development Agents and Global Leaders, and, together, walk the road to dignity 2030.

5. CONCLUSION

The transition from the MDGs to the SDGs brought new challenges and opportunities for international development in an increasingly globalized world, where alignment and collaboration between developed and developing countries is now a key variable to achieve the Sustainable Development Goals.

Technology is, according to both the revised literature and the experts who participated on this study, one of greatest hopes for humankind to effectively address the 21st Century Challenges. However, technology alone will not be sufficient to solve the problems and challenges we face. In order to successfully expand and enable the potential of these tools for development, several other variables have to be brought together by Development Agents and Global Leaders such as:

- Governments to effectively mobilize financial and natural resources according to Sustainable Development practices. Through technology, it might be possible to effectively improve resource management, avoid waste and reuse materials in an efficient way;
- Regulations that foster Science, Technology and Innovation through the implementation of flexible policies that create incentives and explore new technological solutions, as well as creating policies that ensure fair competition, the security of data and information and encourage businesses to adopt sustainability best practices. Regulations can and should also play a crucial role in making technologies more accessible and affordable, through taxation policies on the private sector.
- Education Programs for Sustainable Development, as a way to provide the current and future workforce with the 21st Century skills necessary for success, such as digital literacy, critical thinking, flexibility and adaptability, allowing people to rapidly adapt to new working environments and to be able to effectively use technological tools not only for professional purposes but also in their everyday lives.
- Engage citizens and local communities in SDGs and technology related activities; this will lead to the rapid dissemination of sustainability best practices alongside and greatly increase awareness on technology can be used for the good of society and to improve people's lives, mainly those of the poor and marginalized in remote communities.

Technology is considered by both the relevant literature and study participants a powerful tool and enabler of development, but only by gathering international, national and local efforts toward Sustainable Development best practices can it help overcome barriers such as the digital divide, while preparing the present and future generations to effectively keep up with the rapid world progress and technological change we are facing today, and effectively use these tools to tackle the 21st century global challenges and simultaneously improve the economy, the environment and society.

REFERENCES

Agarwal, N., Gneiting, U., & Mhlanga, R. (2017). Raising the bar: Rethinking the role of business in the Sustainable Development Goals. *Oxfam Discussion Papers*, (February), 1–32. Retrieved from www.oxfam.org

Alshenqeeti, H. (2014). Interviewing as a Data Collection Method: A Critical Review. *English Linguistics Research*, *3*(1), 39–45. https://doi.org/10.5430/elr.v3n1p39

Asah, S. T. (2015). Post-2015 Development Agenda: Human Agency and the Inoperability of the Sustainable Development Architecture. *Journal of Human Development and Capabilities*, *16*(4), 631–636. https://doi.org/10.1080/19452829.2015.1103712

Blair, E. (2015). A reflexive exploration of two qualitative data coding techniques. *Journal of Methods and Measurement in the Social Sciences*, *6*(1), 14–29. https://doi.org/10.2458/jmm.v6i1.18772

Denney, L. (2012). Security: The missing bottom of the Millennium Development Goals?, (August). Retrieved from http://dev.odiorg.chaptermediadevelopment.com/sites/odi.org.uk/files/odi-assets/publications-opinion-files/7788.pdf

Du Pisani, J. A. (2006). Sustainable development – historical roots of the concept. *Environmental Sciences*, *3*(2), 83–96. https://doi.org/10.1080/15693430600688831

Dugarova, E., & Gülasan, N. (2017). GLOBAL TRENDS: Challenges and Opportunities in the Implementation of the Sustainable Development Goals. *Undp-Unrisd*, 1–101. Retrieved from www.undp.org

Easterly, W. (2009). How the Millennium Development Goals are Unfair to Africa. *World Development*, *37*(1), 26–35. https://doi.org/10.1016/j.worlddev.2008.02.009

Ely, A., Zwanenberg, P. Van, & Stirling, A. (2011). New Models of Technology Assessment for Development.

European Council. (2006). Recommendation of the European Parliament and the Council on key competencies for lifelong learning. *Official Journal of the European Union*, (March 2002), 10–18. Retrieved from http://eur-lex.europa.eu/LexUriServ/LexUriServ.do?uri=OJ:L:2006:394:0010:0018:en:PDF

Evans, A. (2012). *The UN's Role on Sustainable Development. Center on International Cooperation.*

Filho, W. L., Mifsud, M., & Pace, P. (2018). *Handbook of Lifelong Learning for Sustainable Development.*

Hazboun, E. (2014). *Technologies for Sustainable Development.* https://doi.org/10.1007/978-3-319-00639-0

Mann, S. (2016). *The research interview. London: Continuum International Publishing Group.* https://doi.org/10.1057/9781137353368

McArthur, J. W., & Rasmussen, K. (2017). Change of Pace. *Best's Review*, (chapter 7), 61.

Transparency International. (2012). Real lives, true stories: Health, 7.

UNCTAD. (2014). A Framework For Information and Communications Technology Policy Reviews: Helping Countries Leverage ICT for Development. Retrieved from http://unctad.org/en/PublicationsLibrary/dtlstict2013d6_en.pdf

UNDESA. (2015). *Partnerships for the SDGs: A legacy review towards realizing the 2030 Agenda. United Nations Department of Economic and Social Affairs.* Retrieved from https://sustainabledevelopment.un.org/sdinaction/publication/partnerships-a-legacy-review

United Nations. (2014a). Sustainable Development Financing, 68. Retrieved from http://www.un.org/esa/ffd/documents/ICESDF.pdf

United Nations. (2014b). United Nations The Road to Dignity by 2030 : Ending Poverty, Transforming All Lives and Protecting the Planet. In *Synthesis Report of the Secretary-General On the Post-2015 Agenda* (pp. 1–47). New York. Retrieved from http://www.un.org/disabilities/documents/reports/SG_Synthesis_Report_Road_to_Dignity_by_2030.pdf

United Nations (UN). (2016). Global Sustainable Development Report, 134.

UNRSID. (2017). Challenges and Opportunities in the Implementation of the Sustainable Development Goals. *District Nursing*, *12*(10), 194–196.

Vergragt, P. J. (2006). How Technology Could Contribute to a Sustainable World. *Great Transition Initiative: Towards a New Praxis Paper Series*, 1–26.

Vidican, G. (2009). The role of universities in innovation and sustainable development. *WIT Transactions on Ecology and the Environment*, *120*, 131–139. https://doi.org/10.2495/SDP090131

DIGITIZATION OF PUBLIC SERVICES IN RUSSIA: HOW A "MAN-MADE" REFORM GOES AHEAD AND SETS BACK AGAIN

Evgeny Alekseevich Mamay
Department of Constitutional and International Law, Nizhny Novgorod Academy of the MIA of Russia, 603144, Nizhny Novgorod region, Nizhny Novgorod, Ankudinovskoe highway, 3, Russia

ABSTRACT

Introduction: The government of the Russian Federation moves its services and other activities towards digitalization. The chosen path shows certain advantages and limitations of e-services in comparison with traditional («paper-based») forms of their provision. An adequate assessment of the current state and prospects for the development of this institution and further normative legal regulation is impossible without clear goals and indicators, which would allow evaluating all the parameters of reforms from the quantitative and qualitative points of view.
The purpose of the article is to assess the adequateness of the criteria and objective indicators for the evaluation of the development of e-government in Russia.
The research methodology is based on the application of logical, dialectical techniques and methods of scientific knowledge, comparative and juridical technique analysis of law texts and other documents.
Results: The article analyzes foreign scientific literature, international ratings, Russian legislation and strategic planning documents in order to establish the criteria for determining the stages of e-government in Russia and the effectiveness of the state policy in this regulatory sphere. The undertaken study leads to the conclusion that there is hardly any strategic vision for the e-government development in Russia, the indicators of e-government programs are imperfect and preliminary indicators obtained without proper justification may result in the manipulation of information and inefficient budget spending.
Conclusions. There is no holistic view on the prospects of digitalization of public services in Russia. Despite the fact that there are enacted Strategies which set the general directions for the development of e-government the subsequent federal legislation is often adopted haphazardly and does not constitute a comprehensive system of legal regulation. The bureaucratic style of governance, especially at the regional and municipal levels, hinders innovations, prevents the achievement of the planned goals and leads to manipulations lacking any factual basis. The author of the article believes that the solution to these problems lies in the definition of the essence of public (state and municipal) services, the establishment of a clear system of normative criteria and law-implementing regulation.

KEYWORDS

e-Services, Public Services, Service State, State and Municipal Services, e-Government

1. INTRODUCTION

The late 1980s and early 1990s saw the growing interest of international communities and states in building an information society and the prospects for the development of an electronic state. At that time, the governments of several European countries established working groups to develop common principles and standards for the use of information technologies in public administration.

By the beginning of the 2000s, individual states reached the stage of practical implementation of e-government principles: they introduced tools for electronic identification, signed relevant agreements between governments (at the national, regional and municipal levels) and created necessary telecommunication networks. At the same time basic criteria for the digitization of public administration were in the process of formulation. Thus, in 2001, the United Nations developed the initial criteria for ranking the UN member states in ensuring equal access to e-services through the implementation of Information and Communication Technologies (ICT) in public administration (United Nations Division for Public Economics and Public Administration, 2002).

Over the years, as the reforms in the field of public administration have progressed, Russia's ratings in various global ratings have remained stable or gradually improved. So, the United Nations in 2012 e-Government Development Rating put Russia in the 27th position, in 2016 it was ranked 35th, in 2018 - 32nd. In 2007 according to the Information Society Development Rating compiled annually by the International Telecommunications Union Russia was in 50th place in the list of 154 states, and in 2017 it was ranked 45th in the list of 176 countries (ITU, 2017). The "Doing Business" rating of 2013 placed Russia at the 112th position in the list of 185 countries, and in 2018 it was already at 35th place (from 190 countries covered by the rating) (International Bank for Reconstruction and Development, The World Bank, 2018).

The experience of foreign countries and the daily practices of administration in the Russian Federation show a significant inertia in the formation of e-government at various levels of state and municipal administration. The world experience testifies to the strategic advantage of small economically developed states in the sphere of e-government and ensuring equal access of citizens to its results.

In this context, it seems interesting and scientifically grounded to look into the criteria for the formation of an e-Government, the effectiveness of the implementation of e-services and the objective possibility to achieve the planned goals in the modern Russian state.

2. DEVELOPMENT OF E-GOVERNMENT IN RUSSIA

2.1 Setting of Common Benchmarks for e-Government Development

The development of electronic governance is an evolutionary process. This statement took shape a long time ago and was confirmed by many facts in previous research devoted to the theoretical problems of digitalization of public administration as well as governmental practices described in scientific literature. Tapscott et al. (1998) outlined the similarity of the evolutionary path of an electronic state and electronic commerce. The state, as well as businesses, follows the path of development from the simplest stage of translation through the subsequent stages of interaction and transactions - to the integration stage. Wagner et al. (2003) give the following description of the named development stages of the electronic state. At the broadcasting stage, electronic government is limited by mere presence on the Internet, the pages are static and simply provide information. At the interactive stage websites of public bodies allow the exchange of information with citizens, and consumers can themselves receive some information resources from the database-backed websites. At the transactional stage the function of financial transactions becomes available for citizens at the websites of government departments (for example, paying fines, taxes, other fees, etc.). This stage implies a high level of information processing, reliability and security of payment terminals. Finally, e-government reaches the integration stage, when all departments and offices of public administration in the state effectively interact, duplication of functions is excluded, and as a general rule, all e-services of the state are accessed through a single (unified) portal.

It should be noted that in the above-mentioned ranking of the UN member states, the key criteria are based precisely on the assessment of the stages of e-government development: the official presence of the authorities on the Internet; type of service provision through the sites: basic or informational support, interactive cooperation (stage of information exchange) and transactional interaction (the possibility of payments and other operations through official websites); implementation of services in five critical areas (education, health; employment; social and financial services); the use of single contact points (portals of public services); following strategic plans for the development of e-government (United Nations Division for Public Economics and Public Administration, 2002).

Despite the fact that the listed criteria are evaluating in character and largely dependent on the methodology and skills of experts, the rating itself is quite indicative. According to this study, in 2001 only 169 countries out of 190 the UN Member States had websites of departments, about half of this number (84 states) did not have any government websites, except the sites of central government, only 36 countries had uniform information portals, and only 17 countries had web-sites that provided the possibility of financial transactions through them. The UN rated the potential of Russia as average, the indicator being 1.92 points, with the average global indicator of 1.62 points, the leading one was 3.11 and the closing one was 0.46 points. From the beginning of the 2000s Australia and New Zealand have topped the list and Denmark, South Korea, the UK, Sweden, Finland, Singapore, France and Japan have also been in the Top Ten countries.

Russia has a federal system of governance, and it is the Federal Government that takes responsibilities as a reform coordinator, including the reforms in the sphere of public services. For federal states it is common practice to initiate such changes from the "top" level of state administration. For example, in Austria it was the federal government that implemented plans for state digitalization by signing in 1998 corresponding agreements on cooperation in the IT-sphere with individual lands that are parts of the Austrian Federation (IT Cooperation Agreement, Die Kooperation von Bund und Ländern), and since 2003 it initiated the implementation of the plans and principles of e-Government.

2.2 Legislative Framework of e-Government: Steps Forward and Back Again

In Russia the first political documents and legal acts that led to a wide range of administrative reforms were enacted about two decades ago. So, the former President of Russia Boris Yeltsin in his message to the Federal Assembly of Russia in 1998 noted: "*It is impossible to ensure the rise of Russia without effective authority working on the principles of serving to the community, but not to itself*". In his speech about the necessity of an administrative reform, the President outlined the distinction between the functions of the administration itself and the functions of providing public services. As an outcome of the proclaimed intentions the President of Russia enacted the Decree № 730 "*On the measures to eliminate administrative barriers to the development of entrepreneurship*" (June 29, 1998), but unfortunately it was not implemented as a complex set of instruments neither at the federal level, nor at the regional level. As a result only several regional administrations established interdepartmental commissions to study administrative barriers for businesses (*Administrative barriers, 2001*).

The logic of reasoning by Boris Yeltsin was further continued by Vladimir Putin. In 2004 in his speech before his personal representatives during the election campaign he outlined the goal of the administrative reform: "*... every citizen will not only know, but will also be able to really demand the level and quality of services that he must be provided by specific levels of government. And, of course, it will directly influence the decisions that concern it* ".

The intentions expressed in the program documents of the beginning of the 2000s began to receive their real implementation together with other measures within the framework of a large-scale administrative reform. In 2004 the Russian Government attempted to review all functions and procedures carried out by state and municipal authorities. A total number of analyzed functions was 5634 out of which 1468 were recognized as redundant, 263 as duplicating each other, 868 as requiring changing (Order of the Government of the Russian Federation № 1789-p, 2005). Nevertheless, a potentially necessary result in the form of an appropriate Register of State and Municipal services (functions) has not yet been compiled.

In 2008 the President of Russia approved *the Strategy for the Development of the Information Society in the Russian Federation* (Strategy-2008), one of whose goals was to "*improve the efficiency of state and municipal administration, the interaction of civil society and businesses with public bodies, the quality and efficiency in the provision of public services*" (Decree № Pr-212, 2008).

For the appropriate assessment of Strategy-2008 this document set up a list of reference indicators for the period up to 2015, which included 16 positions (the place of Russia among leading countries in international ratings; the level of accessibility of basic telecommunication services for people; availability of personal computers in households; etc.). For the most part they have not been implemented. So, in none of the international ratings, be it the development of the information society or the availability of infrastructure, has Russia ever occupied a place above forty. The federal authorities failed to resolve problems with significant differences among Russian regions in the level of digital technology development. Subsequently, 100% of public services available in electronic form, as well as 70% of electronic document circulation between governmental bodies, were later recognized as baseless indicators. The greatest achievement implemented within the framework of Strategy-2008 were the introduction of electronic procedures in the field of public procurement (Federal Laws № 223-FZ, 2011, № 44-FZ, 2013), as well as the adoption of the federal law "On the organization of state and municipal services" (Federal law № 210-FZ, 2010), which started the implementation of e-services and "one-stop access" points in public administration. However, both laws since their enactment have been a subject for disputes.

In the general spirit of the ongoing reforms since November 2011 the updated list of state functions and services has been regularly published on the administrative reform website. Its volume continues to increase every year. Thus, the updated list on the website of the administrative reform as of September 29, 2018, included 878 positions (Ministry of economic development, 2018). Every month this list is supplemented by an average of ten new positions out of which "services" (in official terminology – «functions») related to control (supervision) make up almost a quarter (currently there are more than 200 control functions only at the federal level of governance). The relevance of control and supervisory functions of the authorities to the public services sector still leaves room for doubt.

Strategy-2008 ceased to be valid due to the adoption in 2017 of a new *Strategy for the Development of the Information Society in the Russian Federation for 2017-2030* (Strategy-2017), effective since May 2017. It is noteworthy that one of the basic principles of the newly adopted document was defined as the "*preservation of traditional and customary for citizens (other than digital) forms of receiving goods and services*," thereby emphasizing the need to provide public services in traditional ("paper") form familiar to a significant part of the society. This idea can be traced through the entire document. For example, in the sphere of social relations and public administration Stategy-2017 guarantees citizens the possibility of interaction with organizations and government bodies without the use of information technology.

2.3 "Man-made" Criteria and Indicators

Even the criteria defined in Strategy-2017 give grounds for discrepancies. Thus, according to the International Telecommunications Union the Russian Internet Audience amounted to 76 million people in 2017 (ITU, 2018), while in Strategy-2017 more than 80 million people were already identified as users of the Russian Internet segment at the end of 2016. Following the total number of Internet users defined in Strategy-2017, all indicators related to the effectiveness of the central information resource of the Russian e-government - the Unified Portal of State and Municipal Services (the Unified Portal, official abbreviation – EPGU) should be considered. It is noteworthy that already in *«The Concept for the Development of Mechanisms for the Provision of State and Municipal Services in Electronic Form»*, approved by the Decree of the Government of the Russian Federation № 2516-р on December 25, 2013, noted the low efficiency of the Unified Portal. So, in 2013 the possibility to obtain the results in electronic form was implemented only for 3.3% of services provided at the federal level and only for 1.1% of public services provided at the regional and municipal levels (Resolution of the Government № 313, 2014). Thus, the identified dynamic initially excluded the possibility to achieve the planned goals, in particular, by 2018 a 70% increase in the proportion of citizens using electronic services which was announced during the election campaign and proclaimed in the presidential decrees enacted in 2012 (Decree № 601, 2012).

Strategy-2017 itself also contains information that contradicts the official statistics of the Ministry of Communications and Mass Media. In particular, Strategy-2017 declared the creation of the Unified Portal within 2017 more than 34 million of Russian citizens were logged in. Earlier, at the end of 2016 the official report of the Ministry of Digital Development, Communications and Mass Media of Russia announced the achieved goal of 40 million people registered on the Unified Portal (2017). This number among other things does not fully match with the total number of Internet users in Russia that we have mentioned above. Since 80 million is equal to the total number of working-age population in Russia (men at the age of 16 to 59 and women at the age of 16 to 54) and even potential internet-users (men and women at the age of 14 to 55), it's hard to imagine the half of that number of people (40 million) to be users of the Unified Portal. In the same manner the figures of annual growth for previous years were quite controversial and had shown suspiciously positive dynamics: according to official statistics, in 2013 the total number of users was only 6.9 million people, in 2014 it achieved the benchmark of 13 million and in 2015 – already 22.5 million (a double-fold increase every year!).

According to the authors of the reform, the development of an electronic state in Russia should have led to a systematic reduction of inequalities in integral and other indicators between the regions of the Russian Federation. In this context, close attention is drawn to the results of the annual survey conducted by the Federal State Statistics Service of the Russian Federation (Rosstat) on the indicator «The proportion of citizens using the mechanism for obtaining state and municipal services in electronic form». The respondents who participated in this survey in 2017 were asked about the total number of state and municipal services received during the previous 12 months and the quality of their provision. The leaders of the rating showed that 86% of citizens received public services via the Internet (the Moscow Region, the Yamalo-Nenets Autonomous District) and the Tatarstan Republic - 80%. The lowest rates were shown during the survey of citizens in the Kostroma region (37%), the Jewish Autonomous Region (36%) and the Chukotka Autonomous Region (19%) (Expert center of e-government, 2018).

The optimistic picture shown by the Rosstat statistics is overshadowed by two factors, which, in our opinion, speak of the «man-made» nature of statistics coming from most regions of Russia. Firstly, it concerns a sharp increase demonstrated in 2017 by such regions as the Republic of Tyva (plus 49 per cent in comparison with previous year), the Krasnoyarsk Region (plus 48%), the Yamalo-Nenets Autonomous District (plus 46%), the Moscow Region and the Karachay-Cherkess Republic (42 per cent each). Secondly, it is a sharp contrast between the regions that demonstrate the highest rates and the capital cities (Moscow and Saint-Petersburg), which are traditionally above average Russian indicators on the use of digital technologies. For example, in March 2018 the Rosstat declared that 17 regions of the Russian Federation passed the 70% mark in the share of citizens over 14 years old registered on the Unified Portal. From our point of view, for some inexplicable reasons, the leaders of the rating became provincial regions remote from the central part of country: the Nenets Autonomous District (95.2%), the Republic of Tyva (93.5%), the Chukotka Autonomous Region (87.6%), the Khanty-Mansi Autonomous Region (85.2 %) and the Yamalo-Nenets Autonomous District (81.0%). All of them are significantly ahead of both St. Petersburg (49.2%) and Moscow (45.2%) (Expert center of e-government, 2018).

An indirect confirmation of our doubts is shown by the study "Digital life of Russian megacities", which in 2016 revealed certain imbalances in the penetration of digital technologies into the life of Russian regions. According to the survey more than 90% of the population in Moscow regularly used the Internet, while in Perm or Volgograd - a little more than 70% (Skolkovo Institute for Emerging Market Studies, 2016). In the same context, it is difficult to explain why, for example, the Chukotka Autonomous Region appears among the leaders in the number of citizens registered on the Unified Portal, but demonstrates the lowest figures in the number of citizens who received electronic public services.

3. CONCLUSION

The electronic government and the sphere of provision of public (state and municipal) services in electronic form, as a general rule, exclude the competition of the state with other participants of public relations (and service providers). The removal of the state from this sphere may entail large-scale negative consequences, however, the excessive regulation of this sphere also has a prolonged negative effect. Our analysis shows that in Russia the federal level of government bears special responsibility for the planned implementation of innovations. Following the previously mentioned classification of the stages of e-government (Wagner et al., 2003) we can conclude that the Russian e-Government has achieved the integration stage and the Unified Portal is intended to be a one-stop contact point for all e-services for citizens and businesses. It provides access to many public services, includes the possibility of payments and other transactions, but the range of available services continues to be very narrow. An absence of adequate statistics and open data makes it impossible to properly evaluate the present stage of development and real progress in e-government initiatives in Russia.

Under the present Russian political system the transfer of regulatory powers from the federal to regional and local levels of administration has negative consequences expressed in a fragmented state policy and manipulation of information to the detriment of the achievement of real indicators. According to the numerous studies the most significant differences are observed in the use of online services related to the interaction with local institutions – an appointment to see a doctor and public services in the housing sector - as opposed to paying fines, taxes and other services standardized at the federal level (Skolkovo Institute for Emerging Market Studies, 2016).

The Russian government takes certain actions and spends a vast amount of money to digitize public administration, but it still faces with general troubles related to a bureaucratic style of governance, especially at the regional and local levels. That is why authorities tend to concentrate regulatory powers, exercise coordinating functions, actively monitoring the execution of their decisions and ensuring adequate funding.

REFERENCES

International Bank for Reconstruction and Development, The World Bank. (2018). *Doing Business*. Retrieved from: https://www.doingbusiness.org/content/dam/doingBusiness/media/Annual-Reports/English/DB2018-Full-Report.pdf

International Telecommunication Union. (2017). *Measuring the information society report*. Retrieved from: https://www.itu.int/en/ITU-D/Statistics/Pages/publications/mis2017.aspx

International Telecommunication Union. (2018). *Percentage of Individuals using the Internet*. Retrieved from: https://www.itu.int/en/ITU-D/Statistics/Documents/statistics/2018/Individuals_Internet_2000-2017_Dec2018.xls

Tapscott, D., Lowy, A., Ticoll, D., & Klym, N. (1998). *Blueprint to the digital economy: creating wealth in the era of e-business*. NY: McGraw-Hill.

United Nations Division for Public Economics and Public Administration. (2002). *Benchmarking e-government: A global perspective*. Retrieved from: https://publicadministration.un.org/egovkb/Portals/egovkb/Documents/un/English.pdf

Wagner, C., Cheung, K., Lee, F., & Ip, R. (2003). Enhancing e-government in developing countries: Managing knowledge through virtual communities. *The Electronic Journal on Information Systems in Developing Countries*, 14(4), 1-20. https://doi.org/10.1002/j.1681-4835.2003.tb00095.x

Административные барьеры: опыт преодоления субъектами Российской Федерации. [Administrative barriers: the experience of overcoming by the regions of the Russian Federation]. (2001). Москва: Ресурсный центр малого предпринимательства / Moscow: Resource Center for Small Business. Retrieved from: https://rcsme.ru/library/df/3463/9842 [In Russian].

Государственная программа Российской Федерации "Информационное общество", Постановление Правительства РФ № 313 (15 апреля 2014). [*The state program of the Russian Federation "Information Society"*, Resolution of the Government of the Russian Federation № 313 (April 15, 2014)]. Retrieved from: http://www.szrf.ru/szrf/doc.phtml?nb=100&issid=1002014018020&docid=77 [In Russian].

Ельцин, Б.Н. [Yeltsin, B.N.] (1998). *Общими силами – к подъему России (О положении в стране и основных направлениях политики Российской Федерации)*, Послание Президента РФ Федеральному Собранию от 17 февраля 1998 года). [*By common forces - to the rise of Russia (on the situation in the country and the main directions of the policy of the Russian Federation)*, The message of the President of the Russian Federation to the Federal Assembly of February 17, 1998)]. Retrieved from the Official Internet Resources of the President of Russia: http://www.kremlin.ru/acts/bank/20941 [In Russian].

Институт исследований развивающихся рынков бизнес-школы СКОЛКОВО. [SKOLKOVO Institute for Emerging Market Studies]. (2016). *Цифровая жизнь российских мегаполисов: модель, динамика, примеры. [Digital life of Russian megacities: model, dynamics, examples]*. Retrieved from: https://iems.skolkovo.ru/downloads/documents/SKOLKOVO_IEMS/Research_Reports/SKOLKOVO_IEMS_Research_2016-11-30_ru.pdf [In Russian].

Министерство цифрового развития, связи и массовых коммуникаций Российской Федерации. [Ministry of Digital Development, Communications and Mass Media of the Russian Federation]. (2017). *На Едином портале госуслуг зарегистрирован каждый второй пользователь Рунета*. [*Every second user of the Runet is registered on the Unified Government Services Portal*]. Retrieved from: https://minsvyaz.ru/ru/events/36373/ [In Russian].

Минэкономразвития России. [Ministry of economic development of the Russian Federation]. (2018). *Перечень государственных услуг и функций* (28 сентября 2018). [*The list of public services and functions* (September 29, 2018]. Retrieved from: http://ar.gov.ru/ru-RU/document/default/view/522 [In Russian].

О закупках товаров, работ, услуг отдельными видами юридических лиц, Федеральный закон № 223-ФЗ (18 июля 2011). [*On the procurement of goods, works, services by certain types of legal entities*, Federal Law № 223-FZ (July 18, 2011)]. Retrieved from: http://www.szrf.ru/szrf/doc.phtml?nb=100&issid=1002011030000&docid=13 [In Russian].

О контрактной системе в сфере закупок товаров, работ, услуг для обеспечения государственных и муниципальных нужд, Федеральный закон № 44-ФЗ (8 апреля 2013). [*On the contract system in the field of procurement of goods, works, services for state and municipal needs*, Federal Law № 44-FZ (April 5, 2013)]. Retrieved from: http://www.szrf.ru/szrf/doc.phtml?nb=100&issid=1002013014000&docid=16 [In Russian].

О Концепции административной реформы в Российской Федерации в 2006 - 2010 годах, распоряжение Правительства РФ N 1789-р (25 октября 2005). [*On the Concept of Administrative Reform in the Russian Federation in 2006-2010*, Order of the Government of the Russian Federation № 1789-р (October 25, 2005)]. Retrieved from: http://www.szrf.ru/szrf/doc.phtml?nb=100&issid=1002005046000&docid=49 [In Russian]

О мерах по устранению административных барьеров при развитии предпринимательства, указ Президента РФ № 730, (29 июня 1998). [*On Measures to Eliminate Administrative Barriers to the Development of Entrepreneurship*, Decree of the President of the Russian Federation № 730, (June 29, 1998)]. Retrieved from the Official Internet Resources of the President of Russia: http://kremlin.ru/acts/bank/12570 [In Russian].

Об организации предоставления государственных и муниципальных услуг, Федеральный закон № 210-ФЗ (27 июля 2010). *On the organization of the provision of state and municipal services,* Federal law № 210-FZ (July 27, 2010). Retrieved from: http://www.szrf.ru/szrf/doc.phtml?nb=100&issid=1002010031000&docid=25 [In Russian].

Об основных направлениях совершенствования системы государственного управления, указ Президента РФ № 601 (7 мая 2012). [*On the main directions of improvement of the public administration system,* Decree of the President of the Russia № 601 (May 7, 2012)]. Retrieved from the Official Internet Resources of the President of Russia: http://www.kremlin.ru/acts/bank/35265 [In Russian].

Путин, В.В. (Президент России) [Putin, V.V. (President of Russia)]. (2004, February 12). *Выступление перед доверенными лицами* [Speech to proxies]. Retrieved from the Official Internet Resources of the President of Russia: http://www.kremlin.ru/transcripts/22393 [In Russian].

Стратегия развития информационного общества в Российской Федерации, указ Президента РФ № Пр-212 (7 февраля 2008). [*Strategy for the Development of the Information Society in the Russian Federation*, Decree of the President of the Russia № Pr-212 (February 7, 2008)]. Retrieved from: https://rg.ru/2008/02/16/informacia-strategia-dok.html [In Russian].

Стратегия развития информационного общества в Российской Федерации на 2017 - 2030 годы, указ Президента РФ № 203 (9 мая 2017). [*Strategy for the Development of the Information Society in the Russian Federation for 2017-2030*, Decree of the President of the Russia № 203 (May 9, 2017)]. Retrieved from the Official Internet Resources of the President of Russia: http://www.kremlin.ru/acts/bank/41919 [In Russian].

Экспертный центр электронного государства. [Expert center of e-government]. (2018). *Росстат посчитал долю граждан, получавших электронные госуслуги в 2017 году. [Rosstat considered the share of citizens who received e-government services in 2017]*. Retrieved from: http://d-russia.ru/rosstat-poschital-dolyu-grazhdan-poluchavshih-elektronnye-gosuslugi-v-2017-godu.html [In Russian].

Экспертный центр электронного государства. [Expert center of e-government]. (2018). *Рейтинг регионов по доле граждан, зарегистрированных в ЕСИА на 1 марта 2018 года. [Rating of regions by the share of citizens registered in the ESIA on March 1, 2018]*. Retrieved from: http://d-russia.ru/kolichestvo-regionov-preodolevshih-70-protsentnuyu-otmetku-po-dole-grazhdan-zaregistrirovannyh-v-esia-dostiglo-17.html [In Russian].

DESIGNING A NOVEL SMART HOME MONITORING SYSTEM WITH THE INTEGRATION OF BIM AND WSN

Mustafa Corekci[1], Ozgun Pinarer[1] and Sylvie Servigne[2]
[1]*Galatasaray University Ciragan Cad. No:36 34349 Istanbul, Turkey*
[2] *Univ Lyon, INSA-Lyon, CNRS, LIRIS, UMR5205, F-69621, Villeurbanne, France*

ABSTRACT

In the recent years, the Building Information Modelling (BIM) has become one of the hottest research area in computer science. It attracts many researchers from huge various research domains. Not only the researchers from computer science but also researchers from environmental health, archeology and cultural heritage started working in BIM and its integration with Wireless Sensor Networks (WSN). In this paper, we focus on the integration of BIM and WSN. We tackle one of the major challenges of this integration: how to manage sensor streams by using a digital model of the environment and how to integrate sensor data with the environmental data. Even there are few studies that manage multi sensor data streaming, these approaches are often fitted to a single application and mostly they are independent from the building model. To overcome this problem, we propose a novel real-time environmental monitoring system based on the BIM principles. In this study, we present a multi-application monitoring system architecture. As a testbed environment, the university campus is preferred and for the prototype chosen offices and classrooms are equipped with sensor devices. Real data are enriched with the simulated data to get a large database. The 3D digital model introduces the numerical model of the building and a sensor integration is achieved on the given digital model.

KEYWORDS

Pervasive environment, Building information modelling, Sensor technology, Sensor integration, Wireless sensor networks

1. INTRODUCTION

We live in an era where our lives are surrounded by highly advanced technological devices. In recent years, there has been a great trend to work on the field of Building Information Modelling (BIM) and the integration of wireless sensor networks (WSN) into digital model of a building. It is considered that to build a robust smart city, a well-connected smart building has a crucial role.

Over the last few decades, popular attention to smart building has increased. Smart building and sustainability are intertwined. Since traditional buildings are primary consumers of a significant portion of energy resources, we need smart buildings that are designed based on sustainable construction standards to consume less energy than traditional buildings and to minimize their impacts on the natural environment. Thus, smart buildings became one of the major application domains of smart environments such as smart cities. Smart building technology brings in some nice features such as security, comfort and accessibility. It can also enhance the energy consumption of the buildings.

Advanced technology based smart devices form an environment (the environment we live in) in which each device may interact with the other devices and with the human. This interaction opens a new era in the technology and a research domain so called Internet of Things (IoT). It is considered as the next wave in the era of computing [Gubbi, 2013]. A generic description commonly adopted by the researchers is that the IoT is the network of objects that surround us with the understanding that information and communication systems are invisibly embedded in the environment around us. Objects may embed various sensors, actuators, UI devices, etc. This invisible network covers smart connectivity, cloud computing, context-aware computation, etc.

We spend most of our life in the buildings and enhancing living environment through the use of smart technology has a crucial role to improve the ambience in buildings and also working environments. To reduce energy consumption, management of the building (monitoring via control based wireless sensor networks and actuators) is required [Wu, 2014], even taking into account energy consumption of the monitoring system itself [Pinarer, 2017].

BIM has become a powerful technology based on an object-oriented approach, which fulfills all the functions of traditional 3D CAD/CAM techniques. With BIM technology, a virtual building model is built numerically, which can be very useful for planning, design, pre-build and post-build processes [Azhar, 2012]. The BIM is generally visible in 3D, but it also includes data that can be used by other analysis applications, such as energy consumption simulation, cost estimation, natural lighting, etc. Figure 1 from a market report presents the possible market usage of BIM.

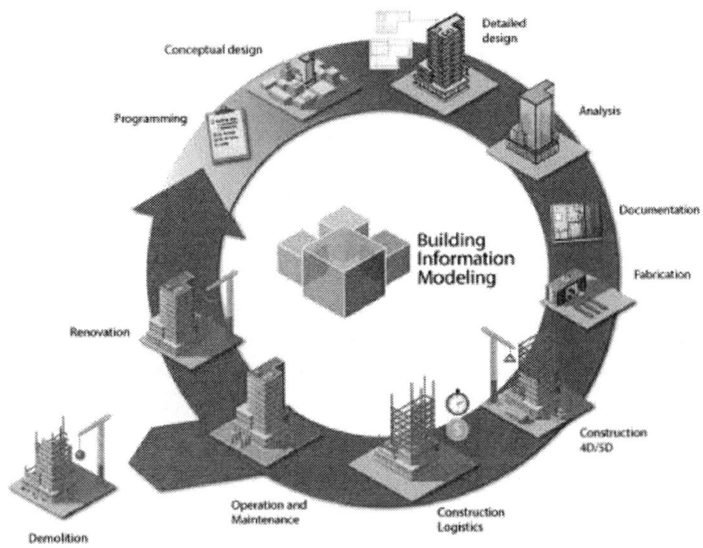

Figure 1. Product scope of BIM and Market Opportunities (Global Building Information Modeling (BIM) Market Report)

BIM is an emerging trend in the Architecture, Engineering and Construction (AEC) sector, which can be used to improve building life cycle performance and productivity throughout the design process, construction, operation and maintenance. BIM is an innovative methodology that can be used to improve the performance and productivity of an asset owner's construction, operation and maintenance processes. BIM provides a multi-collaborative platform for sharing semantic and geometric information within the project management team throughout the asset lifecycle. It allows us a standardized means of sharing and exchanging information about building data. It provides a virtual model of a building with all minor details prior to its physical construction. There are several definitions of BIM. The National Institute of Building Sciences of the United States (NIBS) defines BIM as "a digital representation of the physical and functional characteristics of an installation. [Eastman, 2011] defines BIM as a modeling technology and a set of associated processes for generating, communicating, and analyzing building models. [Isikdag, 2015] defines BIM as the digital representation of a building containing semantic information about building elements. BIM also defines an information management process based on the collaborative use of semantically rich 3D digital building models at all stages of the project and building lifecycle. A BIM is defined by its object model schema. IFC - Industry Foundation Classes is currently the most widely used BIM standard. According to [Azhar, 2012], BIM is one of the emerging developments in the architectural, engineering and construction industries.

In this study, we construct a 3D model of a building (a building of our university as a prototype) and deploy the wireless sensor devices in the offices and classrooms to acquire temperature, humidity, emission of CO_2, occupancy and luminosity data. A database system is constructed in order to register all stream sensor data into database. This database is served to other applications that require sensor data. We consider that every sensor device individually is a service provider (from the user point of view) serves physical measure (such as temperature, humidity etc.) All the deployed sensor devices are virtualized in the 3D model that called BIM. Via BIM, we can manage the locations of each sensor device. Afterwards, we developed a user interface to manage the BIM and the sensor environment. By using this interface, based on the user preferences on building-floor-room and available services in that room, a subscription to that sensor devices are made and sensor data stream is launched.

The remainder of this paper is organized as follows: related works are given in Section 2. Section 3 presents the architecture of the proposed real-time smart home monitoring system. Finally, we conclude in Section 4.

2. RELATED WORK

The literature review shows that there is a big trend on working on the integration of BIM and WSN and the existing works in this area are divided in three main sub researches: using BIM during the construction phase of a building, using BIM for the management of the smart home system and using BIM in cultural heritage.

2.1 Benefits of BIM in Early Stages of Construction

With the recent improvements in architecture, softwares and platforms specialized in architecture are now capable of integrating other systems such as sensor networks. This gives a huge opportunity to users to manage the area even during the construction phase of the building. In such systems, the researchers benefit the sensor technology to monitor the construction environment where the field is occupied by the workers. Such systems are called environmental health where the sensor data is used to get information about the environment such as temperature, humidity etc. Although many appropriate data acquisition technologies are available and used in other sectors, applications in the construction sector are not very common [Vaha, 2013].

[Riaz, 2014] offers a solution based on WSN and BIM for environmental monitoring in confined spaces. The authors propose a prototype titled Cosmos to monitor the physical condition and safety of operators. The presented system includes a notification mechanism to alert building supervisors and the responsible to take the necessary action if needed/in case of emergency.

[Kiani, 2014] introduces a prototype system for visualization of sensor data. It is used for the real-time environmental monitoring, visualization and reporting of the construction. The study uses the standard BIM software and modifies it to view and manage sensor data in real time in its native environment.

[Lee, 2012] highlights a major problem for tower crane operators. They often operate a tower crane with blind spots. To solve this problem, video camera systems and collision avoidance systems are often deployed. However, current video camera systems do not provide accurate distance and do not include the vicinity of the crane. A collision detection system provides location information only as digital data. The authors present a tower crane navigation system providing three-dimensional information about the building and its surroundings, as well as the position of the lifted object in real time, using various sensors and a BIM. The proposed system indicates the location of an object raised in the context of a built building and its surroundings, in the manner of an automobile navigation system, indicating the location of an automobile in the context of roads and of historic buildings.

2.2 Benefits of BIM in smart building management

Besides the construction phase, BIM mainly is used in smart home monitoring and management systems. The studies in this part focus on managing sensor data flows and the integration of BIM and the actuators in the environment.

[Liu, 2009] introduces that a digital model of a building provides a useful information about the spatial context information. The authors tackle the lack of integration of sensor information and BIM. Authors declare that all information about the environment can be achieved via analyzing sensor data and integration sensor metadata to building model.

[Park, 2016] offers a tracking system. The study proposes an integrated approach that merges information from Bluetooth beacons and motion sensors, extracts map knowledge information from a BIM, and integrates aggregated sensor data with map knowledge to estimate position of a target. The tracking system consists of three main components (BLE - Bluetooth Low Energy - sensors, motion sensors and BIM). BLE sensors were used to estimate real-time position information, motion sensors were used to obtain relative motion information, and a BIM was used as a geometric constraint. The BIM used in this study can detect and correct false movements, such as moving through a wall, and viewing the BIM on a mobile device. Building geometry and object information are extracted into an XML-readable file and imported into the system. This information serves as a geometric constraint. Relevant BIM data is converted to a format compatible with a mobile device and used for real-time visualization of the model.

[Hu, 2014] focuses on the advanced lighting system. Since improper sensor placement can compromise system performance, inconvenience occupants and reduce savings, the placement and orientation of occupancy sensors and photoelectric sensors are essential in these systems. Thus, the authors present a method for automating the deployment of the detection device. Since the BIM contains a detailed geometry of building elements, the proposed system can accept sensor parameters and user constraints for sensor placement. With all entries, code compliance and performance requirements are verified. The proposed approach is an optimization in which if the solutions are found to be non-compliant, the process goes backwards to evaluate alternative solutions.

[Kim, 2012] offers an energy management system called EnerISS (System for planning and integrated urban management of energy). The platform middleware retrieves geospatial data from a GIS database and data from each sensor installed on the city and provides the browser-based client with the appropriate hosted information to display the location-specific geolocation characteristics. respective energy. The study introduces a new urban data structure model for monitoring and visualizing aggregated and real-time reports of various energy uses.

2.3 Benefits of BIM for Cultural Heritage

In the area of architectural risk management, many cultural heritage organizations have conducted research on methods and tools for assisting conservation planning and management decisions. Risk management can be defined as the process of identifying, assessing and analyzing potential damage or establishing a strategy to reduce damage to cultural heritage. However, the risk management of architectural heritage is more complicated due to the combination of structural instability and component degradation. Thus, new methods and tools are needed to assess, analyze and implement a damage reduction strategy for architectural heritage risk management.

[Lee, 2019] proposes a new form of metadata and a framework for Risk management using historical building information modeling (HBIM) data in a virtual environment for architectural heritage risk management is suggested. To this end, it is important to share enriched data between those who monitor and diagnose inheritance and those who recognize the context of the information.

The existing studies in the literature propose a local solution for environmental health and monitoring. However most of the proposed approaches are not at level of being prototype and are not suitable for every environment. Besides, multi sensor data management are not handled in these studies and they are bounded by predefined building applications. Even there are few studies that manage multi sensor data streaming, these approaches are often fitted to a single monitoring application. In this study, we present a **multi-application monitoring system architecture** where multiple users are allowed to get served by multiple services.

3. ARCHITECTURE

3.1 Architecture

BIM is currently widely used in the design and engineering phases, but very little effort has been expended to consider the combination of sensor technology and BIM. A full integration of BIM and WSN is extremely required to real time smart home monitoring systems and to stay connected to the environment/ stay connected to other systems.

In this study, we construct a 3D model of a building (a building of our university as a prototype) and deploy the wireless sensor devices in the chosen offices and classrooms to acquire temperature, humidity, emission of CO_2, occupancy and luminosity data. Due to having limited electronic components, we enrich the real data with the simulated data. Thus, in database, a huge number of sampled data are obtained. A database system (using Open Source MySQL platform) is constructed in order to register all stream sensor data into database. It is a continuous sensor data streaming that each sensor device measures the physical measure periodically and sends to the sink (base station). This database is served to every application that requires sensor data. Once a database structure is well constructed, every sensor device individually becomes a service provider (from the user point of view) that serves physical measure. The architecture of our proposed system is illustrated in Figure 2.

We used Autodesk Revit software architecture platform to model the building and its environment. Since model of building gives a very detailed information about the environment, the descriptions of the deployed sensor devices and the locations are covered by the digital model as well. Thus, the XML file (export the model as a XML file) gives all the relevant information about the sensors. A XML parser is developed in Python 3 to read that file and understand the information about the sensor devices such as which sensor devices are located in which room, which services are available from each sensor etc.

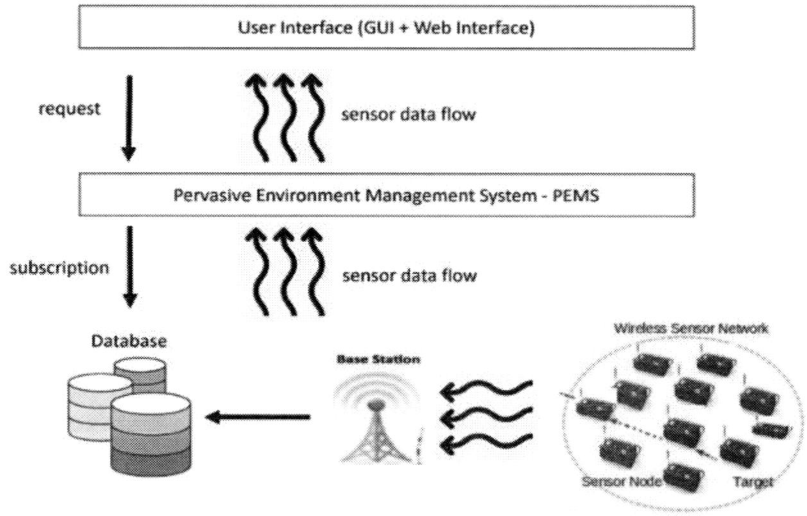

Figure 2. Architecture of The Proposed System

3.2 Hardware Setup and Implementation

For a prototype, chosen offices and classrooms are equipped with ESP8266 and relevant sensor devices. As sensor devices, temperature, humidity, emission of CO2, presence and luminosity sensors are used. The acquired data is sent to the base station via ESP8266 wifi module (by using MQTT). Another ESP8266 stands for a base station and gather all acquired data from all the sensor devices. Through a serial port, sampled and sent data are inserted to the database. Instead of using commercial sensor devices, we prefer to build our own electronic circuits to avoid having hardware constraints.

All the deployed sensor devices are virtualized in the 3D model that called the BIM. Via the BIM, the users are not obliged to have knowledge about the sensors or their locations. A user simply chooses the building-floor and the room form where he wants to get information (physical condition). Once the user submits his preferences, system based on the BIM and the sensor data stored in the model, proposes the available services from that room. Finally, the user chooses the available services from the list and the system makes the subscription to the chosen services. Here, the subscription stands for the retrieving the sensor stream data that goes to database in actual condition. The samples from the developed user interface (in Python 3) are represented in Figure 3.

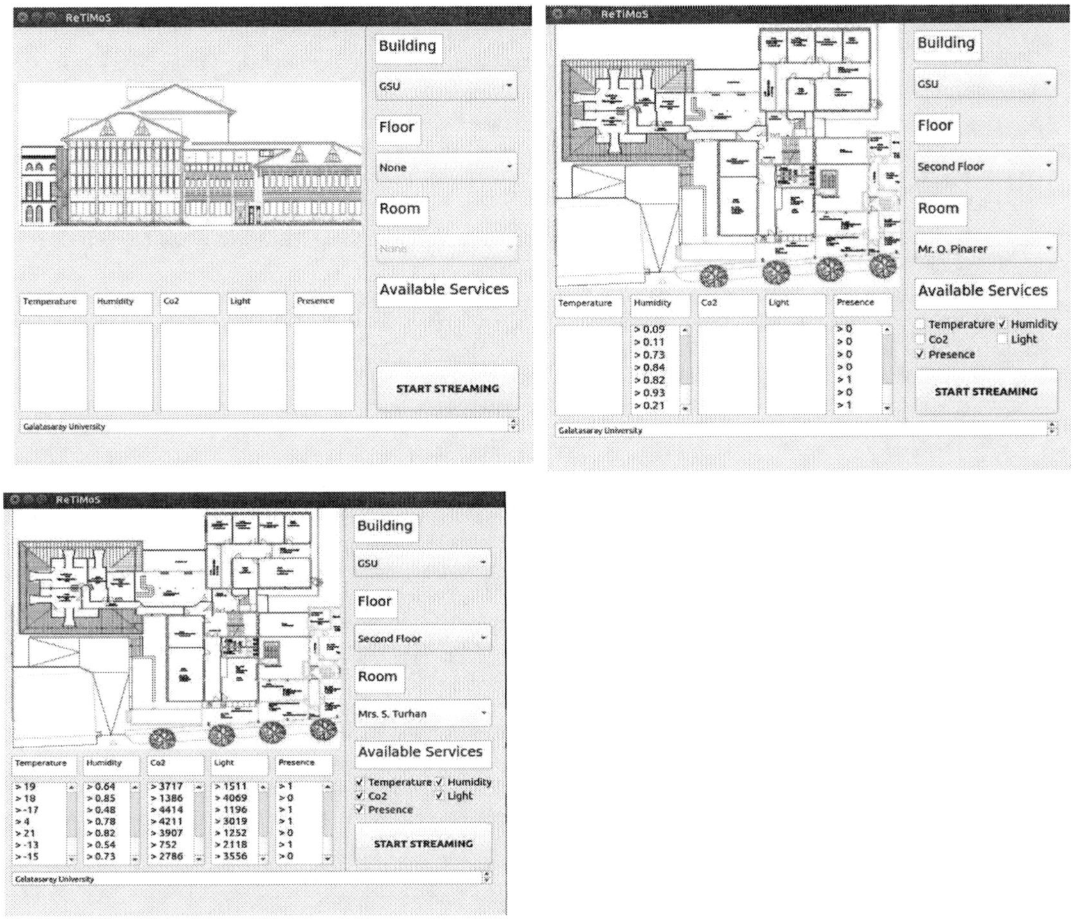

Figure 3. a. Choosing a building from the list. b. After choosing the building and a floor, a reliable plan of the floor is fetched to present the rooms on that floor. In the chosen room, presence and humidity services are available. c. Streaming data from the chosen services

4. CONCLUSION AND DISCUSSION

In this paper, we point at a major challenge of smart building monitoring systems: using the 3D model of the building to manage sensor network for real time monitoring systems. Here, we focus on the integration of BIM and WSN in smart home environments and connected systems. By relying on declarative PEMS principles, we present a sustainable declarative monitoring architecture to process massive raw data from sensors assisted by digital model of the building. In the further phases of this study, we are planning to integrate a continuous query structure to retrieve sensor stream data to fulfill user requirements successfully. Besides, the researchers in this domain have difficulties to find a working physical testbeds to run and test their approaches, algorithms. We are working on converting our system in a public testbed where users can connect remotely and deploy their novel approaches.

ACKNOWLEDGEMENT

This work is supported by Galatasaray University Research Foundation under the Grant No. 19.401.002 and Consortium of Galatasaray University.

REFERENCES

Azhar, S., Khalfan, M., & Maqsood, T. (2012). Building information modelling (BIM): now and beyond. Construction Economics and Building, 12(4), 15-28.

Eastman, C., Teicholz, P., Sacks, R., & Liston, K. (2011). BIM handbook: A guide to building information modeling for owners, managers, designers, engineers and contractors. John Wiley & Sons.

Gubbi, J., Buyya, R., Marusic, S., & Palaniswami, M. (2013). Internet of Things (IoT): A vision, architectural elements, and future directions. Future generation computer systems, 29(7), 1645-1660.

Hu, J., & Patel, M. (2014). Optimized Selection and Placement of Sensors using Building Information Models (BIM). In IES Annual Conference.

Isikdag, U. (2015). Building Information Models: An Introduction. In Enhanced Building Information Models (pp. 1-12). Springer, Cham.

Kiani, A., Salman, A., & Riaz, Z. (2014). Real-time environmental monitoring, visualization, and notification system for construction H&S management. Journal of Information Technology in Construction, 19, 72-91.

Kim, S. A., Shin, D., Choe, Y., Seibert, T., & Walz, S. P. (2012). Integrated energy monitoring and visualization system for Smart Green City development: Designing a spatial information integrated energy monitoring model in the context of massive data management on a web based platform. Automation in Construction, 22, 51-59.

Lee, G., Cho, J., Ham, S., Lee, T., Lee, G., Yun, S. H., & Yang, H. J. (2012). A BIM-and sensor-based tower crane navigation system for blind lifts. Automation in construction, 26, 1-10.

Lee, J., Kim, J., Ahn, J., & Woo, W. (2019). Context-aware risk management for architectural heritage using historic building information modeling and virtual reality. Journal of Cultural Heritage.

Liu, X. & Akinci, B. (2009). Requirements and evaluation of standards for integration of sensor data with building information models. In Computing in Civil Engineering (2009) (pp. 95–104).

Park, J., Cho, Y. K., & Ahn, C. R. (2016). A wireless tracking system integrated with bim for indoor construction applications. In Construction Research Congress 2016 (pp. 2660–2668).

Pinarer O., Gripay Y., Servigne S., Ozgovde A.& Baskurt A. (2017). Dynamic energy-aware sensor configuration in multi-application monitoring systems. Pervasive and Mobile Computing, vol. 41, pp. 192-204.

Riaz, Z., Arslan, M., Kiani, A. K., & Azhar, S. (2014). Cosmos: A bim and wireless sensor based integrated solution for worker safety in confined spaces. Automation in construction, 45, 96–106.

Vähä, P., Heikkilä, T., Kilpeläinen, P., Järviluoma, M., & Gambao, E. (2013). Extending automation of building construction—survey on potential sensor technologies and robotic applications. Automation in Construction, 36, 168–178.

Wu, W., Yang, X., & Fan, Q. (2014). Gis-bim based virtual facility energy assessment(vfea)—framework development and use case of california state university, fresno. In Computing in Civil and Building Engineering (2014) (pp. 339–346).

MOG - A SMART MOBILE SYSTEM FOR INTERACTIVE MUSEUM VISITS

Bruno Coitos, Carlos Serrão[1] and Nuno Garrido[2]
ISCTE – Instituto Universitário de Lisboa
[1]Information Sciences, Technologies and Architecture Research Center (ISTAR-IUL)
[2]Instituto de Telecomunicações (IT-IUL)
Ed. ISCTE, Av. das Forças Armadas, 1649-026, Lisbon, Portugal

ABSTRACT

In this work we propose an integrated system to manage and enhance the museums visiting experience for the general public, providing a more comfortable, intelligent and interactive way to visit multiple museums without the need for several mobile applications, whilst giving a tool to museum curators that allows them to easily manage and extend the content displayed to each individual visitor. For that purpose, our approach was to develop a single mobile application, a module to an open-source Content Management System (CMS), namely Drupal 8, and incorporate location information inferred by the capture of BLE's signals (beacons). The proposed prototype features an Android application that will be used by the visitors where they can access the available information about several museums, and combined with BLE's, will display information about the museum and spaces of the museum where the visitor is (or is planning to visit). This application gives the option to choose from several languages that are provided and managed by each museum.

KEYWORDS

Smart Museum, Smart places, BLE, Android, Beacons, Indoor Location System

1. INTRODUCTION

The increasing number of local and foreign tourists with multiple specific interests and contexts increases the need to provide personalized and interactive touristic information with multilanguage support. Museums are one of the main places that receive millions of foreign visitors each year - e.g. in Portugal, the museums had 15.5 million visitors, of which 6.7 million were foreigners, in 2016 (Lusa, 2017).

Nowadays, the usage of mobile devices (smartphones, tablets and others) to perform many of daily tasks is on the rise and tourism may benefit from the use of this type of technology. Tourists use their mobile devices to get more information about what they are visiting and what they plan to visit. Mobile devices are used to plan and prepare their visiting experience, but also to augment it.

Since there are a large number of museums and most of them offer their own mobile guiding application to the visitors, if a tourist wishes to visit multiple museums he needs to download several applications, with different functionalities and interfaces, to take advantage of their features. This is something that can bring discomfort and usability problems to the tourist, undermining the purpose of developing and offering a mobile application to enhance the museum visiting experience.

To provide interactive touristic information to visitors, we decided to use an Indoor Location System (ILS) taking advantage of IoT devices, namely Bluetooth Low Energy (BLE) beacons, which allows the system to detect when a visitor enters a zone of interest, making it possible to show more relevant and tailored information considering its current location. Also, to avoid the need to download multiple applications we developed an adaptable mobile application that provides a way for tourists to have access to information about several museums and exhibitions in a single application. In addition, we focused on the development of a low-cost prototype to financially satisfy a larger number of museums.

To enhance the tourist visiting experience, providing him with a smart, interactive and personalized visiting experience, we developed an integrated system that includes a mobile smart guide application named My Own Guide (MOG) integrated with IoT BLE devices and a Content Management System (CMS) module, that allows museums to dynamically create, modify and feed content to the mobile application users, based on their own visiting experience and queries, as well as providing museum curators with valuable information about the interaction of the visitors with the museum.

The next section presents a short state of the art overview including some existing methods of smart museum visits. The architecture of the prototype and the way each component interacts with the others is shown in the following section. In the last two sections, we compare the presented prototype with the available literature solutions and draw conclusions for future work that needs to be explored.

2. STATE OF ART

Throughout our research, we have found several approaches that present smart and interactive visiting experiences for museums. Alletto et al. (2016) presented a system where the visitor must install the museum mobile application and answer a questionnaire to generate a QR code. After that, when the user goes to the museum, he shows the QR code that is read by a wearable device (Odroid-XU). This device stays with the visitor recording the whole visit and when he enters a BLE zone the device detects the object observed by the visitor and along with the position of the visitor (obtained through the information sent by the BLE's) the object is identified, and the information is shown. This method besides being complex is very expensive for the museums.

Chianese and Piccialli (2014) proposed another system where beacons and Wi-Fi areas are used. In this method, one application connects to the Wi-Fi network and, together with the information from the beacons, generates information about the neighboring pieces of art. The application shows texts, audios, images and videos with relevant information but only in Italian.

In Bae, E.S. et al. (2013) approach is proposed that could be implemented a system with a single application that brings together a group of museums, in this case, a group of museums from the Jongno district, in South Korea. Each of them could contribute to the creation of a "Unified App" by providing information about themselves, and that could attract more visitors to these museums.

Another solution, but in this case applied to a Zoo was T. Ishida et al. (2016). In this study, one application was developed and notifies the visitor when the signal of a beacon is captured. Each beacon has an ID that matches with an animal ID and with that, the application shows the desired information. Moreover, there was also developed a tool to assist museum curators in the management of the contents shown to the visitors.

Lakmal G.K.U et al. (2016) also uses BLE technology and the mobile application provides a verbal guide to the visitors, suggestions based on the visitor information, like "National or Passport ID number, Name, Date of Birth, Occupation, Ambition, Time duration, Country" and allow the user to collect a copy of audio files used during the tour.

Besides those approaches, we also found proprietary products that seek to meet the needs mentioned before, such as *izi.TRAVEL Help* (2019) and *Locatify* (2019). The first consists of a mobile application that provides information in different formats, such as audio, video and text, and a CMS to help museum curators uploading information to the mobile application. This product instead of using IoT devices to turn the visits more interactive uses QR codes making it necessary for the visitor to read the codes placed physically in the museum. The second product, *Locatify*, is similar to the first but uses IoT devices to enhance the visiting experience and in the mobile application, it is possible to choose from two languages, English and Icelandic.

In order to make it easier to museum curators to manage their contents, is usual to use CMS's aimed at museums, so we explored and found three interesting systems. Two of them are proprietary, named *TMS* and *Proficio*, that are collection management systems, where the first is web-based and enables multilingual collections management, dynamic reports and forms, configurable design and secure access. *Proficio* is a software that has a set of available modules: collections module, library module and archaeology module.

Besides these two systems, we found the *Omeka* (2019), that is an open-source system, that allows the creation of Item objects that can have types, named Item Types, and associate them to Collections. *Omeka* also provides a REST API making possible to access the information from outside of the system.

After analyzing the state of the art, we realized that there were gaps in the systems available to museums and their visitors, not covering all needs. So, we decided to develop this prototype to cover the existing gaps and to be an easily adaptable and low-cost system for different museums.

3. SMART MOBILE SYSTEM ARCHITECTURE

As we mentioned in the previous sections, this system prototype has the objective of giving the museums a quick and easy way to manage and deliver their information to visitors enhancing their experience of visiting a museum or exhibition, but also giving the visitors a practical way to access information of several museums in just a single mobile application.

Figure 1 shows an overview of the architecture with all the elements that are relevant to the prototype, and how they are connected.

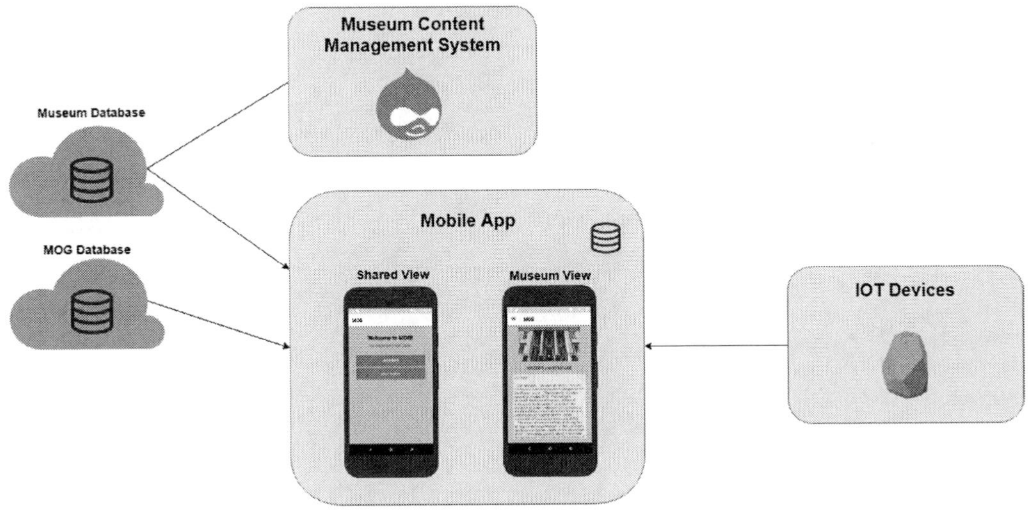

Figure 1. Smart Mobile System Architecture

The next sections describe each component and its role in the system as well as its relevance and connection with the other components.

3.1 Data Model

One of the main components of this prototype is the database. This prototype is built on top of the MOG main database, but for each museum have total control of their available contents, the prototype also uses a database for each museum. For the sake of easiness of development, we opted to use the Firebase (2019) storage services that enable a fast development solution for the prototype since it provides the required services, including a simple way to connect to different databases.

The MOG database is used to store information about the museums that are registered and available for the mobile application users, so the following information will be stored for each museum: Museum Id, Museum name, Museum address, Schedule, Price, Logo image, Location (link for Google Maps), Rating (calculated based on the different inputs made by the mobile application users), Default language and Museum database info (Database URL, Storage Bucket, Application Id, API Key).

On the other hand, the museum databases follow the data model depicted in Figure 2.

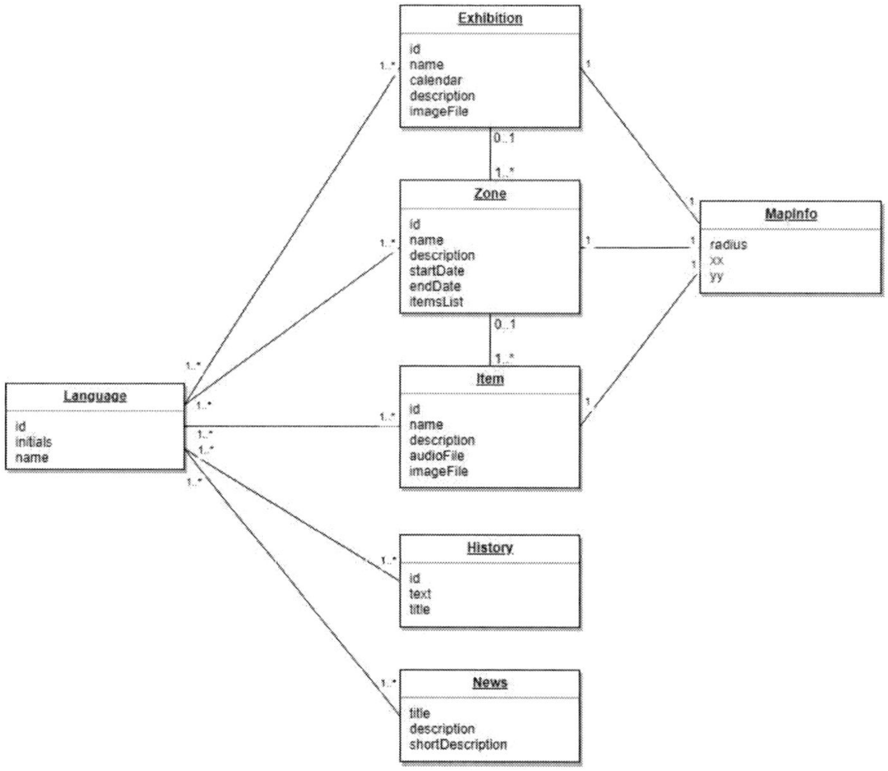

Figure 2. Data Model

This data model was based on existing museums CMS and was adapted to satisfy the needs that we identified previously, such as the multilinguistic needs of the museums' visitors. The most relevant information to a visitor, when inside a museum, is the Exhibition, Zone and Item, and each of these can have information about its location at the museum, meaning that if the museum wants to provide the possibility to see, e.g. a visited exhibition, then it should fill the MapInfo for that Exhibition specifying the pixel coordinates and radius which will be used to draw on the map. The History object is the information that will be shown on the main screen of the application and the News objects will be shown as a list. On the Mobile Application section, more details about how each of these objects is displayed to the visitor are presented.

3.2 Museum Content Management System (MCMS)

In this section, we explain with more detail the decisions made in the development of the Museum Content Management System (MCMS). As we mentioned previously, the museum curator needs a quick way to manage the information displayed to the visitors, so to make this possible while avoiding a big learning curve, we studied the applicability of some existing CMS. First, we researched CMS's aimed at museums, but most of them are proprietary systems, that would bring additional costs and our approach is to provide a prototype affordable for most of the museums, so we explored CMS's that are open-source and found the *Omeka* system, that is aimed at museums, and Drupal, that is a more generic CMS. Between these two systems, we opted by Drupal, since it is more customizable, flexible and has a huge support community.

This MCMS allows and assists the museum curators in the database configuration where the information displayed in the Android front-end application is stored, ensuring that all the information stored in the database, has the correct structure and that all the dependencies between them are coherent. This system will help to configure the available languages, museum map, beacons location (to draw in the map showed to the visitors), general information of the Museum, list of exhibitions and their synopsis, zones of each exhibition and items on display and relevant news for the visit.

Besides this configuration of the database, this MCMS will allow the Museum to see some detailed visitors' analytics such as the number of visitors per exhibition, the most visited exhibitions, zones and items, the total number of visitors, and much other detailed information. So, in the MCMS the museum curators will have three main options, "Manage App", "Back-Up" and "Statistics".

The option "Manage App" provides to museum curators a way to manage the content that is displayed in the mobile application. This option allows the deletion, creation and updates of the content, ensuring all the dependencies of the data model and those defined in the system. If a museum curator makes several changes and wants to revert to a previous version of the database, he can use the option "Back-Up". Here he can see the previous versions of the database and choose to what version he wants to revert. As we mentioned above, the museum curators can see museum performance through the MCMS using the option "Statistics, where is possible to see some performance indicators.

3.3 Mobile Application

To make possible to the visitor to access information about several Museums the mobile application scan for the IoT devices, so the user must enable the Bluetooth on the mobile device and give permissions to access Bluetooth and Location information, and, after that, the visitor will receive a notification whenever a BLE signal is intercepted. Otherwise, the visitor can use the application but will be limited to the general information and will not have access to exhibitions, zones and items information.

As we shown in Figure 1 the application has a Shared View and a Museum View, that we explain next.

3.3.1 Shared View

When the mobile application is opened, the visitor sees the Shared view, that is connected to the MOG database. In this view, the visitor has the possibility to see a list of museums that are available in the application but also the last visits realized, that is stored locally in the user mobile device.

The Museums available are listed with their schedule and address. After choosing one of them, is displayed more information such as price, schedule, address/location (opened in Google Maps), the rate of the Museum (0-5 stars) with the option to give a rate and option to open the Museum View.

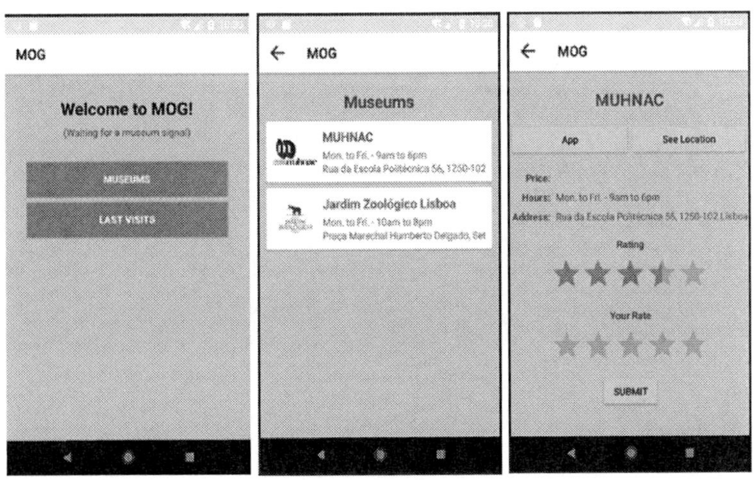

Figure 3. Shared View

3.3.2 Museum View

In this view the mobile application connects to the database of the chosen Museum and is possible to see the history, news and the museum map (see Figure 4: Museum View). The remaining information, like exhibitions, zones and items, will only be shown when the visitor intercepts a BLE signal (see Figure 5: Exhibition, Zone and Item screens).

The first time that a visitor accesses the Museum View of a museum, the mobile application will check if the language defined in the mobile device is one of the defined languages by that museum. If it is, the information of that museum will be shown in that language, but if the language is not one of the available, the mobile application will redirect the visitor to a screen where will be asked to choose from one of the available languages having the possibility to change it later.

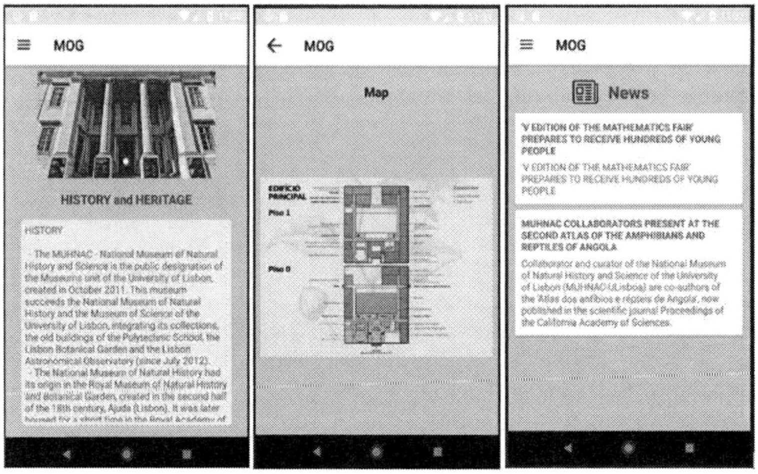

Figure 4. Museum View – General information

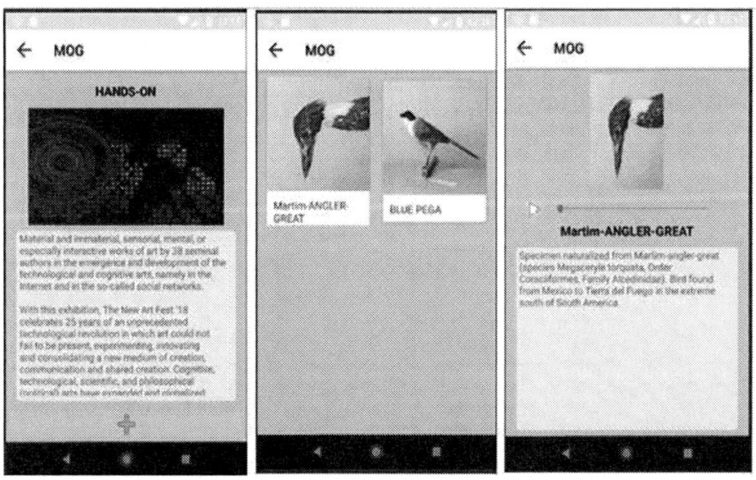

Figure 5. Museum View - exhibition, zone and item screens

3.4 BLE Devices

As mentioned in the previous sections, we used IoT devices to infer the location of the mobile application user through the BLE's signal to create a more interactive experience of visiting a museum. This signal contains keys that will be used to identify what the Beacon represents, this means, if the beacon is identifying an Exhibition, Zone or Item, and which of them, e.g. exhibition 'X'.

In our prototype, we defined these 3 possible "spaces" (exhibition, zone and item) to have a more flexible prototype since different museums have different needs. For example, if a museum has dozens of items displayed in a room, is much simpler and affordable to put one or two beacons in the room entries and configure them to identify that room instead of associate one beacon per item. In this example, if the beacons identify one room, the configuration of the beacon can be, for example, to represent one zone. In Figure 6: Beacon placement example is represented examples of beacon placement, which in room A we represent the example mentioned above, where two beacons were placed at the room entries, representing the same zone. The room B are representing a space where exists an exhibition, that is split into two zones, so the two beacons in the room entries identify an exhibition, and the other two beacons are zone identifiers. Room C shows an example where in a room are just one item, and in this case, one beacon represents one Item.

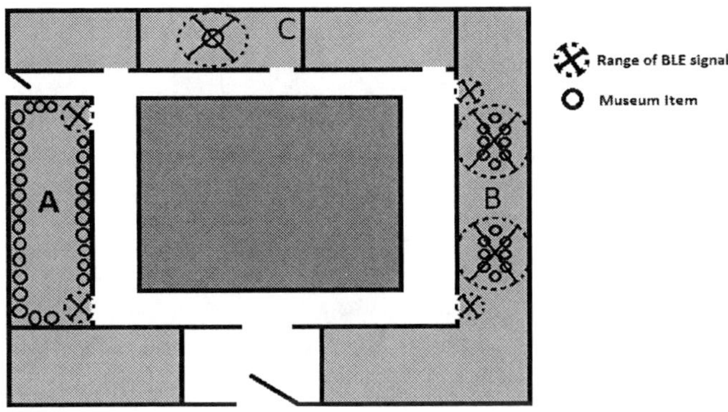

Figure 6. Beacon placement example

So, this makes that each Museum must analyze their needs as well as their budget to create a network of beacons that satisfy their needs and comply with the defined budget.

4. SYSTEM COMPARISON AND DISCUSSION

In this chapter, we will make a discussion and comparison between our approach and the ones mentioned in the state of art chapter.

Starting with the approach in Alletto et al. (2016), their approach brings some functionalities that our approach does not, such as communication to social networks, in this case, Facebook. However, it is a very complex approach for most museums and our objective was to create something simple and affordable, that every Museum could use in a simple manner.

On the other hand, the Chianese and Piccialli (2014) approach only provide information in Italian, while our solution brings to the visitor a way to choose from a set of languages defined by each Museum.

In our approach, one big difference is the centralization of information from different museums, allowing the users to plan their visits without the need to install several applications. This idea of centralization was already mentioned in Bae, E.S. et al. (2013) but was limited to a geographical area and since it was not developed we cannot make a comparison between the technologies.

Another approach mentioned was the T. Ishida et al. (2016), but it's specific to a Zoo and all the information is limited to one language. The last one was Lakmal G.K.U et al. (2016) that also take advantage of the use of BLE devices, but in our opinion have the disadvantage of needing personal information of the visitor to make suggestions, since this can bring discomfort to the visitor.

We also analyzed some products available in the market and the first mentioned was *izi.TRAVEL* but we consider a disadvantage the fact that does not use IoT devices to turn the visits more interactive. Another product is the *Locatify* that use BLE's but like the other product and technologies, is one application per each museum, bringing to the visitors the need to download one application per Museum that wants to visit.

Table 1 shows a summary of the comparison between the products and approaches considering the factors: Centralization – Capacity to centralize several museums information in one mobile application; Multiple Languages – Allow the user to choose from a set of languages; Simple and affordable – Does not bring many costs to museums and has a tool to help in the management; Indoor Location System – Support ILS for more interaction.

Table 1. Comparison between approaches and products

	MOG	Alletto et al. (2016)	Chianese and Piccialli (2014)	Bae, E.S. et al. (2013)	T. Ishida et al. (2016)	Lakmal G.K.U et al. (2016)	*izi.TRAVEL (2019)*	*Locatify (2019)*
Centralization	✔	-	-	✔	-	-	-	-
Multi-Language	✔	-	-	?	-	-	✔	✔
Simple and cheap	✔	-	✔	?	✔	✔	✔	✔
ILS	✔	✔	✔	?	✔	✔	-	✔

5. CONCLUSIONS AND FUTURE WORK

In this paper, we described the developed prototype whose main objective is making the experience of visiting museums more interactive for the visitors while keeping it simple and affordable. The prototype database design is aimed at flexibility so that it can easily adapt to different museums.

To help the museum curators upload data coherent with the defined data model, an MCMS module was developed. This module allows him to manage the contents displayed to the visitors through thc mobile application and provides statistics of the museum performance.

The prototype uses a single mobile application to interact with the visitor in a common interface design usable in various museums. The mobile application makes the visits more interactive since the information displayed on the device considers the location of the visitor near each particular item, zone or exhibition of each museum. It also allows the visitor to access additional relevant information complementary to the physically available in the visited museum.

ACKNOWLEDGEMENT

The authors would like to acknowledge the FCT Project UID/MULTI/4466/2016.

REFERENCES

Bae, E.S. et al., (2013). Smart museum based on regional unified app. International Journal of Software Engineering and Its Applications, Vol. 7, No. 4, pp. 157-166.

Beacons. (2019) *What is a beacon?* Available from: https://kontakt.io/beacon-basics/what-is-a-beacon/

Chianese, A. and Piccialli, F. (2014). Designing a Smart Museum: When Cultural Heritage Joins IoT. 2014 Eighth International Conference on Next Generation Mobile Apps, Services and Technologies, pp. 300-306.

Drupal 8. (2019) *Build something amazing.* Available from: https://www.drupal.org/8

Firebase. (2019) *Firebase helps mobile app teams succeed.* Available from: https://firebase.google.com/

izi.TRAVEL Help. (2019). [online] Available at: https://academy.izi.travel/help/production/cms-for-museums/

Lakmal G.K.U et al., (2016). Museum 360: Automated Guiding System for a Museum. International Journal of Scientific and Research Publications, Vol. 6, No. 11.

Locatify. (2019). Automatic Museum Guide. [online] Available at: https://locatify.com/automatic-museum-guide/

Lusa (2017). "Museus aumentam número de visitantes em 2016 com ajuda dos estrangeiros", *PÚBLICO*, 12 December.

Omeka. (2019) *Omeka provides open-source web publishing platforms for sharing digital collections and creating media-rich online exhibits.* Available from: https://omeka.org/

S. Alletto et al., 2016. An Indoor Location-Aware System for an IoT-Based Smart Museum. In IEEE Internet of Things Journal, Vol. 3, No. 2, pp. 244-253.

T. Ishida et al., (2016). Development of a Zoo Walk Navigation System using the Positional Measurement Technology and the Wireless Communication Technology. Journal of Internet Services and Information Security, Vol. 6, No. 4, pp. 65-84.

COMPARISON OF IOT DEVICES ARCHITECTURE IN HOME NETWORK

Takashi Murakami[1], Keiichi Teramoto[2], Ritsuko Kanazawa[3], Ryo Hasegawa[4], Tetsushi Matsuda[5], Kanji Mizuno[5], Dai Ando[6], Yasuo Sugawara[7], Yoko Masuda[7], Yudai Kawasaki[7], Yoichi Masuda[1], Moe Hamamoto[1], Hiroshi Sugimura[8] and Masao Isshiki[8]

[1]ECHONET Consortium / Panasonic Corporation, Shimbashi TS Bldg. 4F, 1-22-5 Nishishinbashi, Minato-ku, Tokyo 105-0003 Japan
[2]ECHONET Consortium, Shimbashi TS Bldg. 4F, 1-22-5 Nishishinbashi, Minato-ku, Tokyo 105-0003 Japan
[3]ECHONET Consortium / Hitachi, Ltd., Shimbashi TS Bldg. 4F, 1-22-5 Nishishinbashi, Minato-ku, Tokyo 105-0003 Japan
[4]ECHONET Consortium / Hitachi Appliance, Inc., Shimbashi TS Bldg. 4F, 1-22-5 Nishishinbashi, Minato-ku, Tokyo 105-0003 Japan
[5]ECHONET Consortium / Mitsubishi Electric Corporation, Shimbashi TS Bldg. 4F, 1-22-5 Nishishinbashi, Minato-ku, Tokyo 105-0003 Japan
[6]ECHONET Consortium / Nippon Telegraph and Telephone Corporation, Shimbashi TS Bldg. 4F, 1-22-5 Nishishinbashi, Minato-ku, Tokyo 105-0003 Japan
[7]ECHONET Consortium / Sharp Corporation, Shimbashi TS Bldg. 4F, 1-22-5 Nishishinbashi, Minato-ku, Tokyo 105-0003 Japan
[8]Kanagawa Institute of Technology, 1030 Shimoogino, Atsugi-city, Kanagawa 243-0292 Japan

ABSTRACT

Recently, the number of IoT devices has increased, and this trend has been extended to home appliances (e.g. air conditioners, washing machines, refrigerators, etc.) and equipment (e.g. storage batteries, photovoltaics, etc.). There are mainly two architectures regarding to IoT conversion of the appliances installed in these houses. Specifically, they are "IoT devices connect to a server on the Internet via a controller" and "IoT devices connect to a server on the Internet directly". In this paper, these architectures are compared and it is shown that what kind of usage each architecture is effective.

KEYWORDS

IoT, Architecture, Home Network, ECHONET Lite, Cloud, Service

1. INTRODUCTION

In recent years, as Internet technology and network technology have progressed, standard transmission media (Ethernet, Wi-Fi, Bluetooth etc.) that can be used for home networks has been spreading. Therefore, even in the home, home appliances and equipment (hereinafter referred to devices) that had been operating as standalone in the past have network functions installed and have become IoT devices. And home network (Biljana L. and Kire V., 2017), (Charlie, W. et al, 2014) can be built with IoT devices. Now that various services such as the home energy management system (HEMS) and remote control from outside the home etc. are being introduced.

It is important how to convert devices in home to IoT. Now there are roughly two possible architectures to convert each device in home into IoT. The first is that the device itself is not connected directly to the service on the Internet but is connected to the service on the Internet via the controller installed in the home to construct the system (Figure 1 (a)). At this time, standard communication specifications (e.g. ECHONET Lite (ISO/IEC 14543-4-3, IEC 62394) (ECHONET, 2019), KNX (ISO/IEC 14543-4-3) (KNX, 2019), ZigBee (ZigBee, 2019) etc.) or proprietary specifications are used as communication specifications between the controller and the devices. In this paper, home network is focused on and since it is common that a lot of people often use device of multiple vendors at each home, communication specifications between controllers and devices are considered to use standard communication specifications. The controller has a function of controlling each device and a function of monitoring each device, and connects to a server on the Internet. A server on the Internet can cooperate with various business operators and provide services to users. The second is that the device itself connects directly to the service on the Internet (Figure 1 (b)). In many cases, the device can be connected only to a server operated by a vendor that manufactures the device. As a connection method, there are a method of connecting to a server via a router installed in the house, a method of connecting via a communication network such as LPWA and LTE, and so on. Each vendor's server cooperates with service providers to provide services to users.

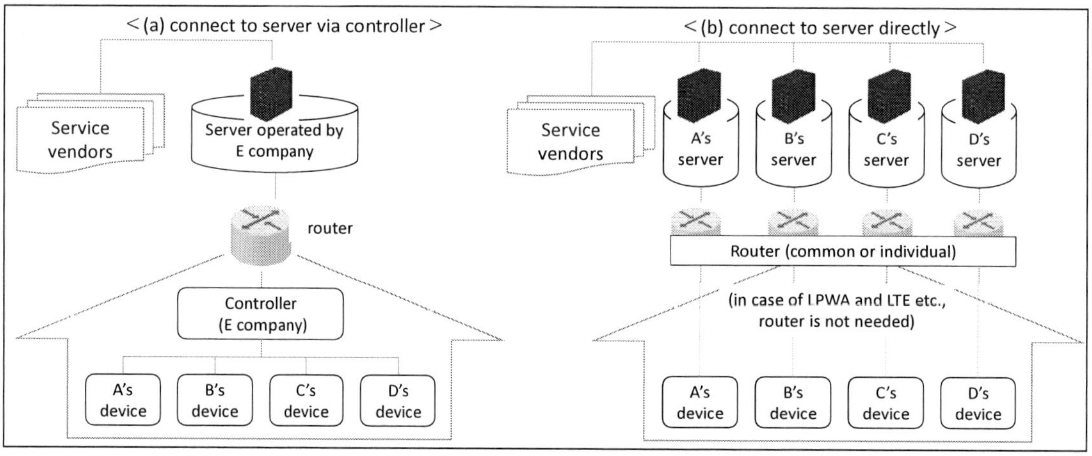

Figure 1. Architectures of home network

Depending on the services offered to users and the objectives of converting the devices to IoT, the architecture to be selected is different. In this paper, both architectures are compared from the viewpoint of realizing various services using home network system. There are various cooperation methods between servers on the Internet, such as WebAPI, MQTT and so on, but in this paper, in order to clarify the architecture of IoT devices as a main focus, the methods between servers are simply abstracted.

2. ARCHITECTURES OF HOME NETWORK

Particularly in Japan, home networks are spreading with HEMS as a trigger. From the perspective of further spreading in the future, the viewpoints of "system construction", "realization of various kinds of services", and "introduction / operation cost" are important. The evaluation of both architectures is summarized from these viewpoints.

2.1 System Construction

Items to compare architectures in system construction are shown in Figure 2, and outline of the comparison is shown in Table 1. As items to be compared, "Connection between service providers and server", "Introduction of controller", "Introduction of IoT device" can be mentioned.

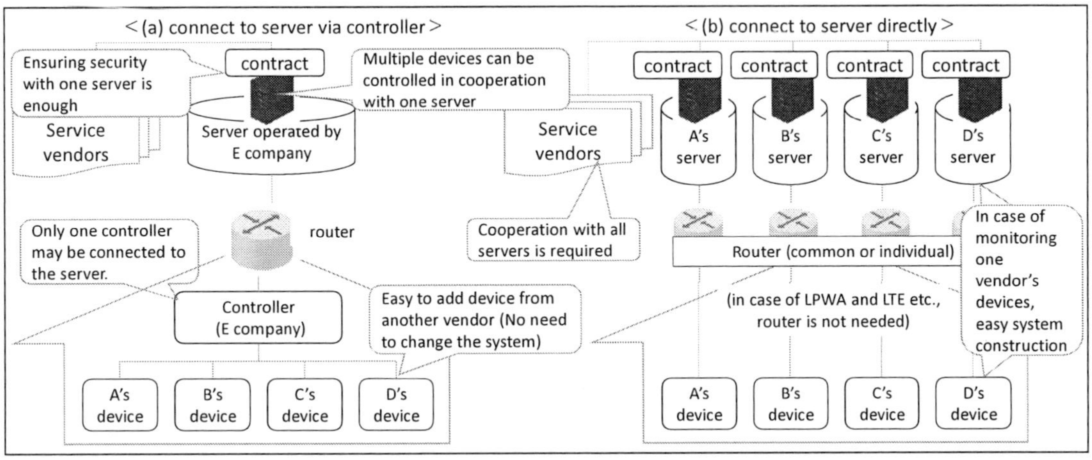

Figure 2. Comparison of architecture related to "system construction"

Table 1. Outline of comparison of architecture related to "system construction"

	(a) Connect to server via controller	(b) Connect to server directly
Connection between servi providers and server	For each house, the server and the service providers can establish a system with 1: N connection	For each house, the servers and the service providers can establish a system with M: N connection
Introduction of controller	Since the controller terminates the devices in the home, there is no need to replace the system such as the controller and the server in case of adding or changing the device.	No controller is needed. When device vendors monitor or control only their own devices, it is possible to construct a system without a controller.
Introduction of IoT devic	Since the controller and the devices are connected by the standard communication specifications, it is not necessary to change the system just by replacing the device.	Since devices and server are vertically integrated, changing the devices requires changing the server configuration

2.1.1 Connection between Service Providers and Server

In the architecture of "connect to server via the controller", the service provider can cooperate with one server, thereby making it possible to provide services by utilizing a plurality of devices bundled by the in-home controllers.

On the other hand, in the architecture of "connect to server directly", the service provider needs to cooperate with the servers each device vendor operates. Therefore, in the case of providing services utilizing a plurality of devices in home, a service provider is required to contract to use servers operated by a plurality of device vendors. However, if it is impossible to make a contract to use some servers operated by some device vendors, it will be impossible to provide services that control and monitor a part of the devices to the users. In addition, since standard specifications to cooperate between servers at the application level such as control commands do not exist, it is necessary for service vendors to comply with several cooperative specifications that each device vendor specifies.

Therefore, when providing services targeting multiple devices in the home, it is considered that the architecture of "connect to server via the controller" is easier to construct the system.

2.1.2 Introduction of Controller

The controller installed in the house keeps the function of aggregating the information of the devices in the home and coordinating with the server. In case of using the standard communication specifications common to the communication between the controller and each device, the controller can accommodate new devices even in the case of addition or exchange of devices of different vendors. Therefore, configuration of servers and controller are not needed to change. In addition, by introducing the controller, it is unnecessary for devices with small resources to directly connect to the Internet, thus the risk of being attacked from the outside is considered to be small.

In the case where a device vendor constructs a system for the purpose of controlling and monitoring only its own device, it may be easy to construct a system based on the architecture of "connect to server directly".

2.1.3 Introduction of IoT Device

In the architecture of "connect to server via the controller", since the controller that aggregates each device connects to a server on the Internet, even for devices that are difficult to mount the function of connecting to the Internet, it is possible to convert to IoT device by connecting to the controller in the home network. In addition, service providers can also provide services to users who are subject to control and monitor the devices that are difficult to connect to the Internet directly.

Since it becomes unnecessary for devices to install a communication function and a security function (Joseph Bugeja et al, 2016) for connecting to the Internet, it is also possible to reduce the cost for making the device IoT.

2.2 Realization of Various Kinds of Services

Even if the system can be constructed in the home network, unless the user can use various services, the home network will not be used. In realizing a wide variety of services, the comparison points of the two architectures are shown in Figure 3, and the outline of the comparison is shown in Table 2. The points to be compared are "ease of implementation of a service provider", "communication state on the Internet", "real-time property of device cooperation" and "device to be controlled and monitored".

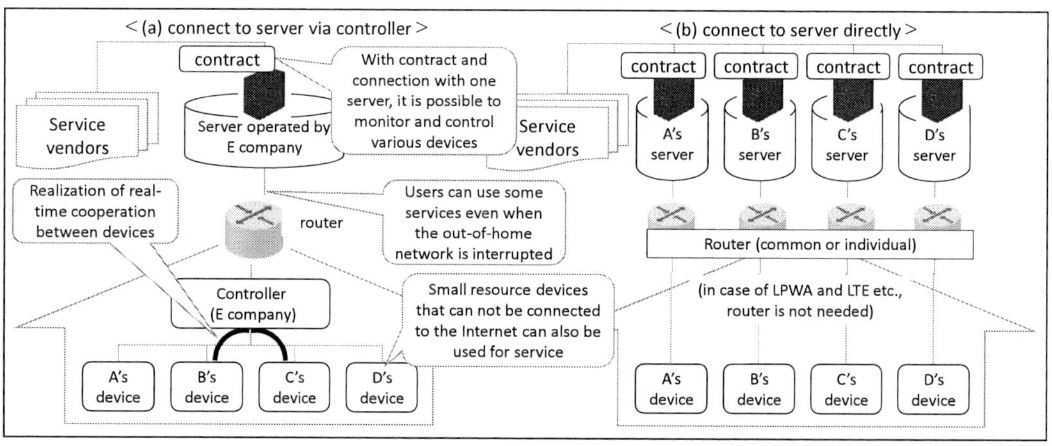

Figure 3. Comparison of architecture related to "Realization of various kinds of services"

Table 2. Outline of Comparison of architecture related to "Realization of various kinds of services"

	(a) Connect to server via controller	(b) Connect to server directly
ease of implementation of service provider	Each service provider can provide services to each house by connecting with one server	"Development to connect to multiple servers" and "contract with server operator" are required
communication state on th Internet	Even when the Internet is not in service, users can use some service functions held by the controller	At the time of Internet disconnection, the service using communication cannot be used by the user
real-time property of devi cooperation	Since the controller controls each device in the home network, cooperation between devices with low delay is possible	Cooperation between servers on the Internet is required, so equipment control at home is delayed
Devices subject to control and monitoring	Service providers can also use small resource devices that cannot connect to the Internet for services	Service providers can use only devices that can connect to the Internet for services

2.2.1 Ease of Implementation of a Service Provider

It is common to conclude a contract to connect between servers on the Internet. In the architecture of "Connect to server via controller", each service provider can provide a service to each user by linking with a server connected to the controller. On the other hand, in the architecture of "Connect to server directly", service providers need to cooperate with servers to which each device connects, and when a contract to connect with some servers cannot be made, service providers have to restrict a part of services provided to users.

At the present time, as a coordination method between servers, there is a standard method such as WebAPI, but standardization at the application level such as control command has not specified in actuality. Therefore, in the architecture of "Connect to server directly", service providers may need to implement multiple communication specifications in order to link with servers which each device vendor operates.

2.2.2 Communication State on the Internet

In the architecture of "Connect to server directly", when an external network such as the Internet network or mobile network is disconnected, all services provided by the service provider cannot be used. On the other hand, in the architecture of "Connect to server via controller", since the controller can control and monitor each device, it is possible to continue to use some services.

2.2.3 Real-time Property of Device Cooperation

First of all, the examples of "equipment cooperation at home" is shown below.

e.g. 1: When the controller detects that the power generation of photovoltaics is surplus, the controller sets the operation mode of the storage battery to the charge mode.

e.g. 2: When the controller acquires the electric power used from the smart meter and detects that the electric power is over the set value, the controller changes the state of the air conditioner.

In the architecture of "Connect to server via controller", it is the controller in the home that can monitor and control the devices. Since the controller can control the devices by using the home network after monitoring the state of the device and the measured value, it is possible to provide devices cooperation service with high real-time property. On the other hand, in the architecture of "Connect to server directly", since it is necessary to share the state of the device and control commands between servers, some delays occur in device control.

2.2.4 Devices Subject to Control and Monitoring

In the architecture of "Connect to server via controller", since the controller aggregates each device and connects to the server on the Internet, even in a device which is difficult to implement the function of connecting to the Internet, it becomes possible to realize IoT device by connecting to the controller in the home network. Therefore, even for service providers, it is possible to provide services to users as objects of control and monitoring for devices that are difficult to connect to the Internet. And since it is unnecessary to implement a communication function and a security function for connecting the device to the Internet, the cost for making the IoT devices can be lowered as well.

On the other hand, in the architecture of "Connect to server directly", implementing the function to connect to the internet may increase the cost. Also, for devices that do not have resources to implement the function for connecting to the Internet, they are out of control or monitoring objects.

2.3 Introduction / Operation Cost

Items to compare architectures in terms of the introduction cost at the time of system construction and the subsequent operation cost are shown in Figure 4, and outline of the comparison is shown in Table 3. As items to be compared, "Operation cost of servers", "Network line expenses", "IoT devices and controller introduction costs" can be mentioned.

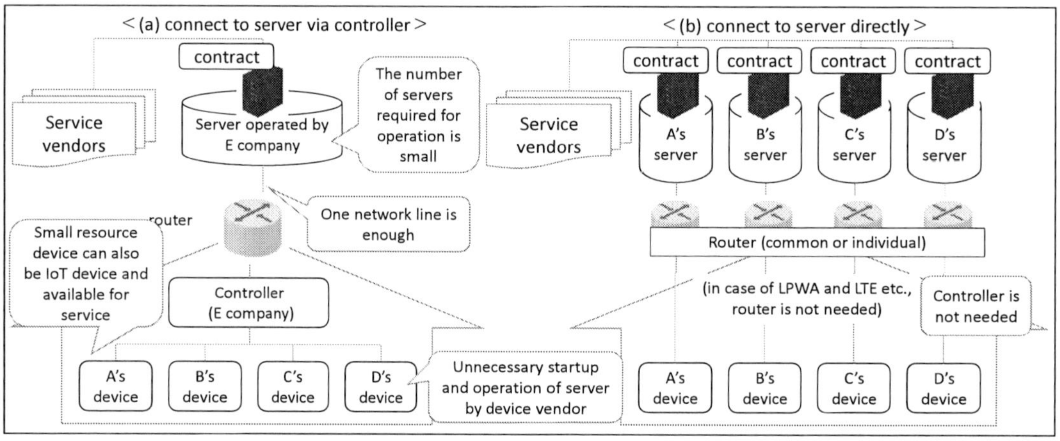

Figure 4. Comparison of architecture related to "introduction / operation cost"

Table 3. Outline of comparison of architecture related to "introduction / operation cost"

	(a) Connect to server via controller	(b) Connect to server directly
Operation cost of servers	One server to which the controller connects	Number of servers connected to each device at home
Network line expenses	Basically one network line is enough.	Depending on requirements, network lines may be required for each device
IoT devices and controller introduction cost	Since each device does not need to connect directly to the Internet, devices with small resources can also become an IoT device	Controller is not needed.

2.3.1 Operation Cost of Servers

In the architecture of "Connect to server via controller", a system is constructed by servers of each service provider and one server to which controller connects. On the other hand, in the architecture of "Connect to server directly", a system is constructed by servers of each service provider and a plural of servers which each device vendor operates. Assuming that the amount of data handled by each server is almost the same, the architecture of "Connect to server via controller" seems to be able to reduce the operation cost of the server because the number of servers to be operated is smaller.

2.3.2 Network Line Expenses

In case of the architecture of "Connect to server via controller", since only the controller connects to the Internet, if there is only one network line, the devices which connect to the controller can be made IoT devices, and the service provider can provide the service of the home network to the user. If users already have an Internet environment at home, users can build it without additional communication cost by using that environment. On the other hand, in case of the architecture of "Connect to server directly", similarly there are cases in which a system can be constructed with one network line. However, depending on the product, there are cases where the use of exclusive lines or independent networks is must. In addition, when introducing IoT devices using communication lines such as LPWA and LTE, the cost of communication lines may be required for each device.

2.3.3 IoT Devices and Controller Introduction Costs

In the architecture of "Connect to server via controller", each device only needs to implement a home network function for communicating with a controller in the home, and it is possible to become an IoT device at low cost. In addition, inexpensive devices with small resources that are difficult to install communication functions and security functions for connecting to the Internet can also be used as IoT devices. In the architecture of "Connect to server directly", since no controller is required, the cost of the controller is unnecessary. However, as described above, it is necessary to install a function of Internet connection, and only devices having a certain level of resources can be handled.

3. FEASIBILITY OF ARCHITECTURE VIA CONTROLLER

From the comparison of the architecture shown in Chapter 2, when providing various services to control and monitor a large number of devices in the home, it is necessary to construct a home network by converting the equipment into IoT in the architecture via the controller, it turned out that it is better to construct a home network by IoT device in the architecture of "Connect to server via controller" than in the architecture of "Connect to server directly".

For services that device vendors control and monitor only their own equipment, it can be realized with the architecture of "Connect to server directly". However, restrictions are large when trying to deal with a wide variety of services over the medium to long term.

In this chapter, the "standard communication specifications between controller and device in the home" which is important to realize the architecture of "Connect to server via controller" and the devices which is compatible with the standard communication specification are introduced.

3.1 ECHONET Lite which is International Standard Specifications

There are various international standard communication specifications such as ECHONET Lite (ISO/IEC 14543-4-3 / IEC 62394), KNX (ISO/IEC 14543-3) and ZigBee etc. in the communication specifications between the controller and the IoT devices. In this paper, ECHONET Lite is described as an example of standard communication specifications. The communication specification of ECHONET Lite is ISO / IEC 14543-4-3, and the control commands of devices is IEC 62394, both of which are international specifications.

Main features of ECHONET Lite are "Transport-free communication specifications that can use existing standard transmission media such as Ethernet, Wi-Fi, etc.", "Specify detailed control commands of more than 110 types of devices targeting general households, small and medium-sized buildings, and small and medium-sized stores", "High interoperability by specifying how to use concrete ECHONET Lite at the application level" (Takashi Murakami et al., 2016) and "A wide variety of services can be realized by architecture via controller". Numerous IoT devices and controllers compatible with ECHONET Lite are already on the market.

3.2 IoT Devices and Controller which complied with ECHONET Lite

Number of certification acquired is shown in Figure 5 (referred to https://echonet.jp/number-of-certification-acquired/). Since the launch of certification system of ECHONET Lite in 2012, more than 600 applications have been certified by the end of September 2018. In addition, the shipment quantity of ECHONET Lite devices is cumulative total of more than 17 million units. In Japanese smart energy meter, which is the key device to energy management, ECHONET Lite is installed in approximately 28 million smart energy meters as of March 2017 (finally 77 million smart energy meters).

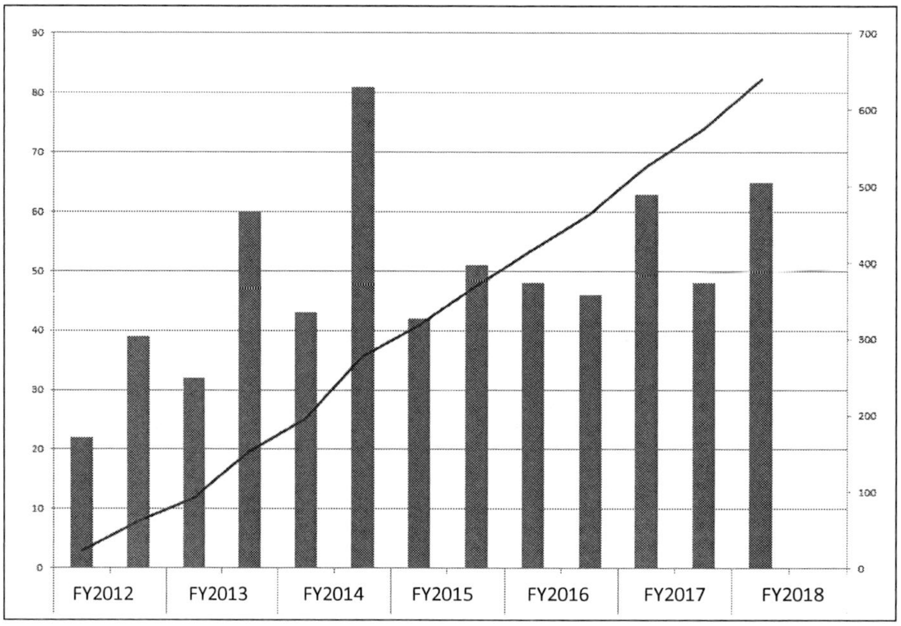

Figure 5. Number of certification acquired and shipment quantity

In addition, the controller certified by ECHONET Lite and shipped to the market are shown in Figure 6 and the devices certified by ECHONET Lite and shipped to the market are shown in Figure 7.

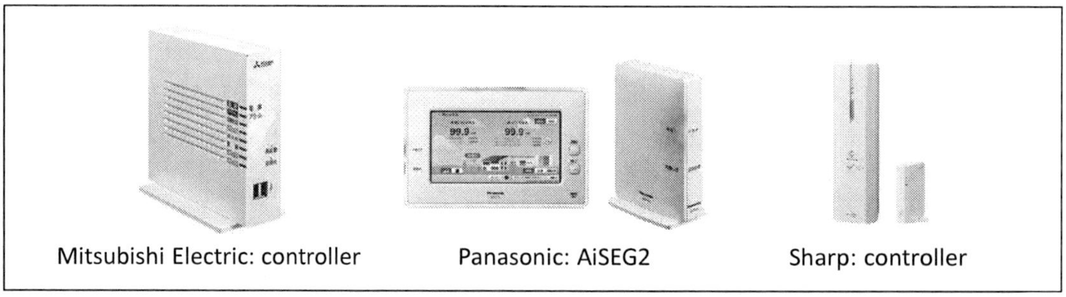

Figure 6. Examples of ECHONET Lite certified controllers

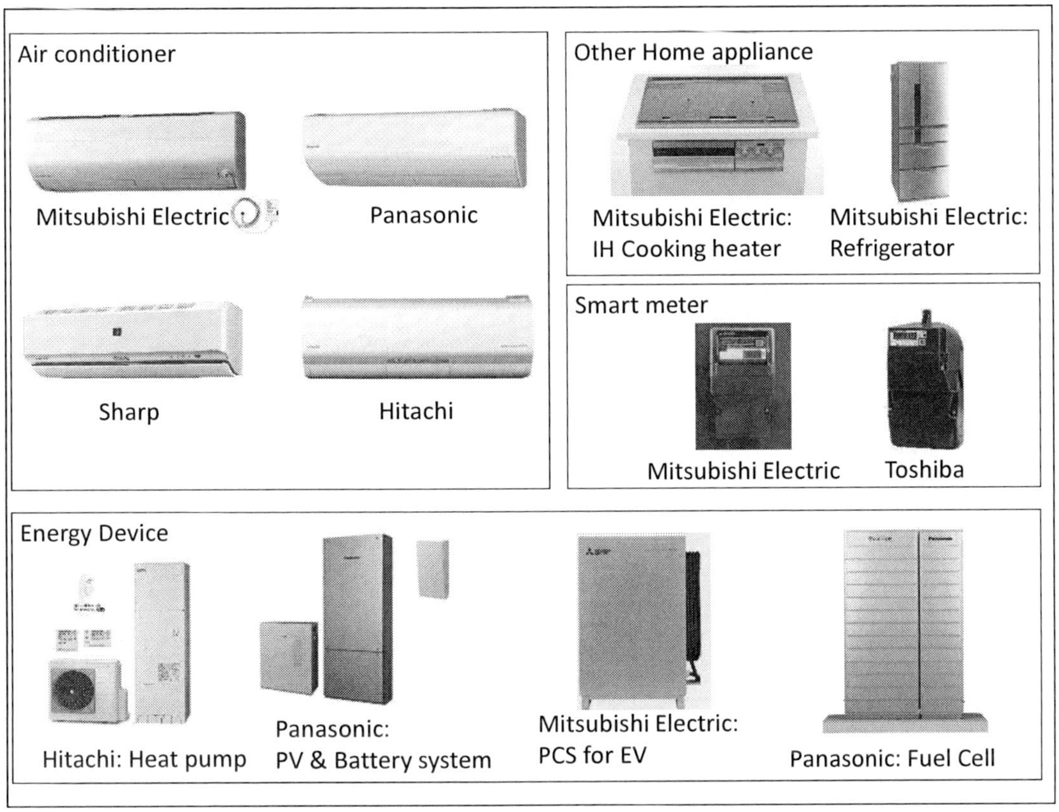

Figure 7. Examples of ECHONET Lite certified devices

4. CONCLUSION

The architecture of "Connect to server via controller" and the architecture of "Connect to server directly" have been compared from the viewpoint of the IoT devices in the home. As a result, it was confirmed that the architecture of "Connect to server via controller" can enjoy various merits in order to provide various services to users. In the architecture of "Connect to server directly", it is possible to easily construct a system to perform services targeting only monitoring and control of specific device. However, it is difficult to extend the system when providing services targeting the entire house to the user. Furthermore, in order to realize the architecture of "Connect to server via controller", commercialization of controllers and IoT device compliant with standard specifications becomes important. In fact, with the "Connect to server via controller" architecture, there are marketed services linked with Google Home, Amazon Alexa, etc. (Cu et al., 2018) And one example of IoT devices is devices and controllers implemented with the international standard ECHONET Lite (ISO / IEC 14543-4-3, IEC 62394).

ACKNOWLEDGEMENT

The authors would like to thank the ECHONET Consortium members for cooperating in the development of standard specifications, promoting standardization, and providing various data any time.

REFERENCES

Biljana L. and Kire V., 2017. A review of Internet of Things for smart home: Challenges and solutions. *Cleaner Production,* Vol. 140, Part 3, pp.1454-1464.

Charlie, W. et al, 2014. *Smart homes and their users: a systematic analysis and key challenges.* Springer-Verlag, London, UK.

Cu Pham, Yuto Lim, and Yao Tan, 2018. A Platform for Integrating Alexa Voice Service into ECHONET-Based Smart Homes, *2018 IEEE International Conference on Consumer Electronics-Taiwan*, Taichung, Taiwan, pp.1-5

ECHONET, https://echonet.jp/english/, (Accessed January, 2019).

Joseph Bugeja et al, 2016. On privacy and Security Challenges in Smart Connected Homes. *Proceedings of European Intelligence and Security Informatics Conference 2016*, Uppsala, Sweden, pp.172-175.

KNX, https://www.knx.org/knx-en/for-professionals/index.php, (Accessed January, 2019).

Takashi Murakami, Hiroshi Sugimura and Masao Isshiki, 2016. Application of ECHONET Lite which is open standard into energy management system. *2016 IEEE International Conference on Consumer Electronics*, Las Vegas, NV, USA, pp.493-496.

ZigBee, http://www.zigbee.org/, (Accessed January, 2019).

A FEDERATED LEARNING SYSTEM FOR OPTIMISED ENVIRONMENTAL CONTROL OF CONSECUTIVE AREAS

Robert Perry and Enda Fallon
Software Research Institute, Athlone Institute of Technology, Athlone, Ireland

ABSTRACT

Building management systems have led to artificially controlled environmental conditions. While new infrastructure will lead to a lower carbon footprint and a better working environment, the costs cannot justify the rewards at this present time. Ambient temperature regulation has the potential to mitigate excessive energy consumption. This work proposes an externally influenced environmental control Artificial Neural Network (ANN) implementation to optimise ambient temperature for a given specific area whether that be internal or external to the building. The approach uses a multi-aspect ANN. Two architectural components are introduced, an Agent ANN (A-ANN) and a Coordinating ANN (C-ANN). The Agent ANNs (A-ANN) are deployed to provide temperature control at the extremities of the open plan area. The A-ANN operates with a degree of autonomy. A Coordinating ANN (C-ANN) considers the optimal ambient temperature of the room and consequently effects the surrounding area(s). These A-ANNs have internal and external factors acting as effectors to the system such as outdoor environmental conditions and internally located effectors such as adjacent rooms. Results are presented which diagnose the effort applied by A-ANN instances in varying environmental conditions both internally and externally.

KEYWORDS

Artificial Neural Networks, Ambient Temperature Control, Building Management Systems

1. INTRODUCTION

Heating Ventilation and Control (HVAC) systems are contributing to the ongoing damage we inflict on our planet. In the United States of America, one of the highest pollution factors is from the industrial and commercial electricity sector of which HVAC units play a major part (Ueda, & Shimonaka, 2017; Edenhofer, et al, 2014). In many environments these systems are left on for extended periods of time or are increased to temperatures which make the room uncomfortable and at times unusable. Open plan areas are a common architectural construct. Recent adoption of work practices such as the "Agile Way of Working" in the software design sector has coupled the design of a building to the working methodology. Agile software methodologies introduce the concept of "Informative Workspaces". The tightly coupled relationship between building and methodology has resulted in the reconfiguration of older buildings towards physical open plan seating. The reorganisation of such spaces can lead to an imbalance in temperature profile, tenant discomfort and excessive running costs through higher gas and electricity consumption. Buildings are often reconfigured without consideration of air flow, solar gain or the revised meaning of temperature sensor readings.

This work proposes a federated ANN configuration with two new architectural components an Agent ANN (A-ANN) and a Coordinating ANN (C-ANN). The A-ANN operates with a degree of autonomy with some federated influence from the C-ANN. The C-ANN considers the optimal ambient temperature of the entire open plan area. Having previously created a theoretical model and simulated results (Perry, Fallon, Fallon, & Qiao, 2017) this work proposes an experimentally based evaluation of the architecture using a physical scaled model. The model enables the analysis of dispersion of heat between rooms in an office environment consisting of meeting rooms and a central open plan area. The work illustrates how a federated ANN approach consisting of both centralised and distributed intelligence can learn the optimal of HVAC actuators so as to optimise thermal flow throughout the office space.

This paper is organised as follows. Related work is discussed in section 2. An overview of ANN architectures is provided in Section 3. The system architecture of our approach is presented in Section 4. An experimental system evaluation is provided in Section 5. Finally, conclusions are described in Section 6.

2. RELATED WORK

In (Matta, Rehu, Tanner, & Kansala, 2017) the authors attempt to show the importance for both the control and monitoring of HVAC units with regard to the health and well-being of employees. Monitoring air quality is becoming an ever-increasing worry for most countries with many simply turning a blind eye to the damage that is happening with little action. Using a relatively new technology Bluetooth low energy, a range of monitoring devices were deployed as part of this research to ascertain the range of human effectors which are sometimes unconsciously present in an everyday commercial office building. Using temperature, humidity and air pressure metric sensing the research outlines a range of practically implemented points in a building that were monitored and the location of the HVAC unit associated with them. Updated on a minute by minute basis the research gains an accurate picture of what the environment most of us breath in and out in an office environment. Although this research only proposes future work in regard to the actual control of the environment the results show how the temperature and humidity variance in an office greatly increases and decreases dependant on the area being monitored at a given time. This research in similar in the way that monitoring the given environment is essential to gain an accurate picture of what this research plans to show. Air quality optimisation and HVAC control are problems that most advanced economies deal with on a daily basis and yet in most cases choose to ignore. It is the proposal of this research to find solutions to this extremely high drain on our energy consumption and show how we might increase the quality of the air that we breath concurrently, find other work which proposes to do the same and build upon existing infrastructure to try to solve inefficiencies.

In (Hsiung, & Lin, 2018) the authors present a cyber-physical system with user-optimized control strategy that trades off between power consumption and user-specific comfort for building energy management. The work differs from our approach as the consideration is the optimisation of power consumption rather than ambient temperature regulation. In adopting such an approach, the authors show how a predicated mean voting mechanism can be substituted in the absence of a set of weights where a seven-point thermal scale is used to predict the comfort levels of a particular set of individuals. The flaw that this research presents however is in the consideration of the thermal comfort of a particular subject and not the efficiency of adjacent areas combined with the assumption that the research data collected will be absent of human error. At a contrast the research outlined here will show how historical data will be collected on an ongoing basis to account for thermal comfort but also take into consideration the environmental factors that exist as a result.

Furthermore to (Hsiung, & Lin, 2018) , the authors in (Ardiyanto, Pipattanasomporn, Rahman, Hariyanto, & Suwarno, 2018) express how thermal comfort objectives are not being met in buildings and how employees do not feel they are adequately comfortable, hence a predictive mean system could be introduced to allocate the setpoint temperatures more efficiently throughout a building. the authors devise a practical solution powered by a raspberry pi using Radio frequency identification to detect the occupancy and hence allocate the setpoints throughout the building to different HVAC area controllers. Using the eQuest simulation tool the authors implement show the building plan of a system located in Alexandria showing an efficiency increase of 14.58% when compared with a system not using the mean voting system. The research in addition outlines additional criteria for which an additional 8.79% may also be met given times of occupancy being accounted for. In (Gopika, 2015) a more holistic approach to the measurement of metrics is attained with the discovery of the thermal and energy inefficiency of a building using real-time data logging from multiple sources adding a more historical element to that of (Hsiung, & Lin, 2018) or (Ardiyanto, et al, 2018). This approach shares convention with some existing smart controller HVAC systems and does not take the subjects comfort level as an input metric however this research does show how the application of neural network algorithm can improve performance and adaptability when studied from afar and excluding human decision factors and consequently human error.

Given the many advancements we have seen as part of artificial intelligence design in the software industry in recent years. The focus of this research should be to remove as much human control as possible and to let an algorithm decide based on historical data the optimal conditions that humans can thrive in based in minimal human influence negating as much human error as possible. In studying this research (Gopika, 2015), the resounding overall theme is similarly present notwithstanding the contrast being this paper proposes that we use the underlying infrastructure which may already be present in our building(s) in a more intelligent way while also factoring in human input and not discounting it completely. (Vatanparvar, Burago, & Abdullah, 2018) Accurately describes how a historical collation of user behaviour in conjunction with a neural network and user input absorption over an extended time period are used to gain a predictive behavioural analysis over driving characteristics that one may accomplish greater power efficiency in an electric vehicle. Similarly planned to be shown in this research metrics are collected and allocated weights given a pre-determined set of factors. This research shows how in the automotive industry similar research exists but is at an early stage ready to be improved upon, this is similar to the HVAC industry however in contrast that for a long time period without the need to increase battery saving techniques, the problem was left to exist, this was interesting in the way that it poses a question many devices outside of the automotive or HVAC industries today could probably be coded more efficiently if there was a need to reduce the energy consumed when not directly or indirectly connected to the power grid.

Finally, the work in (Kim, 2018) focuses on a similar challenge HVAC Systems in Multizone Office Buildings Considering Thermal Preferences of Individual Occupants. The work shows how occupants thermal preference, a neural network modelling algorithm, a grid tie strategy and variable speed heat pumps are used to enhance productiveness and gain a reduction in energy consumption, similar to this approach the research outlined plans to show the practical application of how monitoring information, a neural network, historical data and a reduced element of user input metrics might be used in a neural network to reduce power network drain and accurately pinpoint spikes in demand throughout the day at a given area hence reducing the cost to maintain existing infrastructure and reform transmission loses proportionately.

3. ARTIFICIAL NEURAL NETWORKS

ANN are data processing models which are based on the operation of the brain. The first work on ANN was presented by McCullock and Pitts in 1943. The work proposed a Threshold Logic Unit (TLU) which used weighted binary inputs. If the weighted sum of inputs exceeded a threshold value, the neuron fired. Many enhancements to the original model have been introduced. The first unsupervised learning approach, Hebbian Learning, was proposed in 1949. Classification of inputs was introduced by the perceptron model. The introduction of back propagation enabled the training of synaptic weights based on a desired output. Modern ANN consist of a large number of interconnected neurons working in parallel, typically used for pattern recognition and data classification.

Figure 1 illustrates a supervised learning ANN. Values X_0, X_1, X_2....X_n are provided as input to the neuron. The neuron has 2 modes of operation; training or trained. In trained mode, the neuron applies synaptic weights wk0, wk1....wkn which enhance or degrade the input values. These weighted values are summed and an activation function φ(.) is applied. φ(.) determines whether the neuron should "fire", producing an output yk which classifies the input pattern. Training mode can be implemented through supervised or unsupervised learning. In supervised learning the ANN will have an offline training phase in which neural outputs are compared against a training set. Alterations are made to the synaptic weights to limit the error in classification between the output yk and the training set dk. When the ANN correctly classifies the input pattern, the ANN operates in trained mode. Unsupervised learning has no external training patterns. In this mode the ANN self organizes data presented to the network and detects recurrent properties.

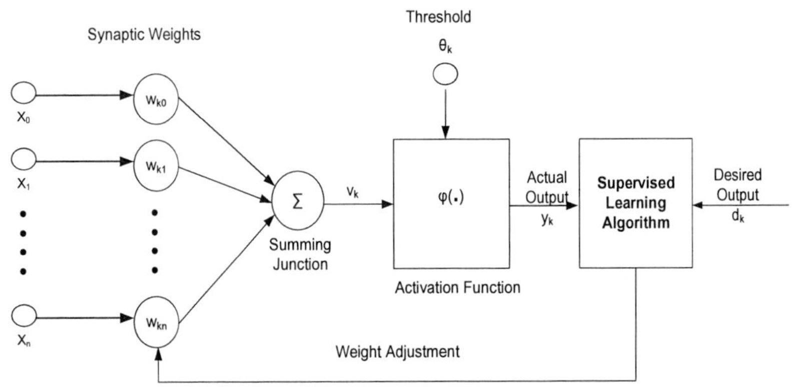

Figure 1. A Supervised Learning Neural Network

4. SYSTEM ARCHITECTURE

This section describes the architecture of our federated artificial neural network, building on research undertaken in Perry, Fallon, Fallon, and Qiao, 2017. We illustrate how the system may be implemented to practically monitor the metrics and control the actuation of heating the ventilation controls. The approach uses a multi-phase ANN. Two architectural components are introduced an Agent ANN (A-ANN) and a Coordinating ANN (C-ANN). The A-ANN operates with a degree of autonomy. The C-ANN considers the optimal ambient temperature of the entire open plan area and influences the decisions of individual A-ANN in order to achieve a collectively balanced temperature. Figure 2 represents multiple implementations of Figure 1 in an exploded format. Each declaration of R_n is a full implementation a learning network. The approach consists of X_0, X_1,... X_n neuron inputs corresponding to the performance metrics; outdoor temperature, Open Plan Area Temperature and Meeting Room 1 temperature. X_0R_0 corresponds to the current value of indoor temperature for meeting room R_0. W_0R_0 represents the synaptic weight applied to the current value of indoor temperature for meeting room R_0. Figure 2 illustrates the combined configuration of theses inputs with respect to their neural network allocated area. A-ANN neurons representing 3 meeting rooms affecting the temperature of the overall open plan area. While each A-ANN has a degree of functional autonomy each is coordinated by the C-ANN through the ancillary weight assessment. The C-ANN coordinates the ambient temperature for the main area within the open plan represented in Figure 2 as R_0. It weights the relative importance of the temperature contribution of each individual A-ANN to the overall ambient temperature, making each A-ANN an iterative consideration metric until a desired output is reached. The Scale of the experiment could be much larger in tune with the number of neurons that we see implemented, Figure 2 may expand in number without limit but also increasing the learning time required to exhaust a desired output. Each neuron is a threshold gate producing an activation value V_k. The larger the input values/synaptic weights the larger the activation value. O_y Is actuator control decision and is calculated as follows:

$$O_y = \begin{cases} \textbf{Heat High if } V_k \geq \theta * 2 \\ \textbf{Heat Med if } V_k \geq \theta * 1.5 \\ \textbf{Heat Low if } V_k \geq \theta \\ \textbf{Heat Off if } V_k < \theta \end{cases}$$

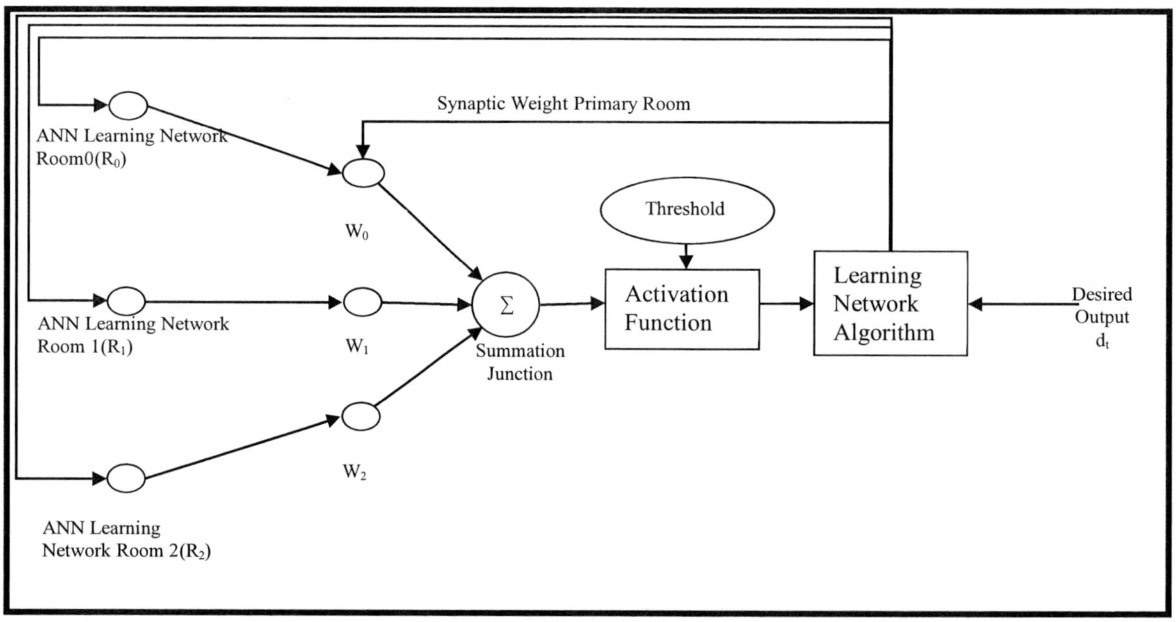

Figure 2. Synaptic Weight Adjustment

We calculate the rate of change, c, of a linear regression line for historic indoor temperature as follows:

$$c = \frac{\sum(x - x')(y - y')}{\sum(x - x')^2}$$

Using c we can determine the rate by which alterations to synaptic weights affect internal temperature. A positive c indicates that synaptic weight alterations have a beneficial effect on the delta in desired and actual temperature. A negative c indicates that synaptic weight alterations have a detrimental effect on the delta in desired and actual temperature. A large c (positive or negative) indicates numerous training cycles are required. A small c indicates that the selection of weights is close to optimal. In order to control the rate of learning we define a user configurable learning rate constant r. The selection of an appropriate learning rate is critical for the effective operation of the algorithm. If the learning rate is too low the network learns very slowly. If the learning rate is too high weights diverge, resulting in little learning. We define the error correction, ΔW, as the product of c and r.

5. SYSTEM EVALUATION

Using the proposed neural network architecture, a scaled test model was created consisting of Arduino prototyping software andesp8266 micro controllers with embedded Wi-Fi. JSON structured restful web programming interface calls provide a communication medium to push and pull information from the sensors. A relay was configured to actuate the heating and cooling system states. The intention is to recreate in scale for issues experienced as in (Gopika, 2015), (Vatanparvar, Burago, & Abdullah, 2018), (Kim, 2018) and (Ardiyanto, et al, 2018). Figure 3 illustrates the configuration of the scaled model. Figure 3 illustrates the configuration of the scaled model which consists of 3 areas:

Meeting Room 1 – This is the main area for evaluation by the experiment. There is no temperature actuation (heating/cooling) in this room. The temperature of this room is dependent on the ambient temperature from both the Open Plan Area and Meeting Room 2. The room has a temperature sensor which provides readings to the C-ANN. Meeting Room 2 – The temperature actuation for configuration is controlled in this room. The room temperature is controlled by A-ANN policy which actuates both a heater and window which can be opened or closed. The room also has a temperature sensor which provides readings to the C-ANN. Open Plan Area- This area is the main working area. From an ambient temperature viewpoint, it connects the temperature actuation of Meeting Room 2 and Meeting Room 1. The area also has a temperature sensor which provides readings to the C-ANN.

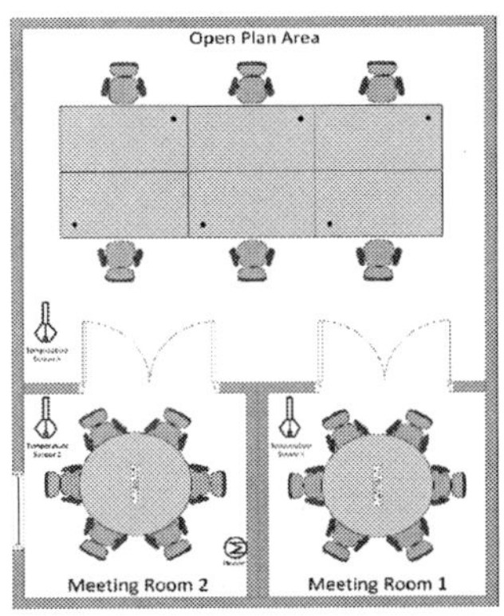

Figure 3. Scaled Office Configuration

In order to evaluate the operation of the approach 20 tests were undertaken. A sample representative test is described in detail to illustrate the operation of the approach. During the test the outdoor temperature ranged from a minimum of 17.06° to a maximum of 18.27°. The desired ambient temperature for all room was a minimum of 20° to a maximum of 27°. The A-ANN and C-ANN configurations are considered trained when the ambient temperature in all rooms was between the minimum and maximum values. The initial starting temperatures were Meeting Room 2=17.0°, Meeting Room 1=16.938° and an external temperature of 17.125 °.

The experiment has 3 phases (1) Initial Analysis (2) ANN based temperature optimisation (3) ambient temperature dispersal. In the initial phase the C-ANN and A-ANN configurations use a coarse-grained mechanism to obtain optimal configuration. Actuators (heater/window opening) are configured using a preliminary rules-based policy to achieve a general optimal temperature. In this configuration the internal room temperatures of 17.0° and 16.938° are below optimal. The temperatures are also slightly below the external temperature of 17.125°. In the initial phase both actuators are activated; window is opened and heater is turned on. Figure 4 illustrates the external temperature, open plan area temperature and Meeting Room 1 temperature. The results illustrate that after 8 minutes the temperature of both internal areas has risen above the external temperature. At this point the window is automatically closed. The results also illustrate the increasing variation in temperature between the open plan area at 18.31 ° and the Meeting Room 1 temperature of 17.188 °.

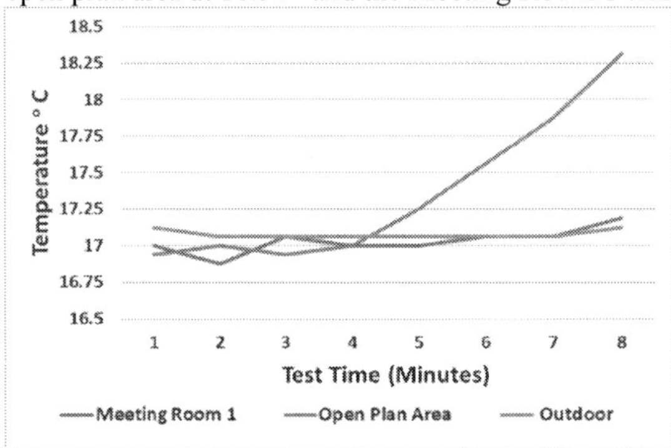

Figure 4. Test Phase 1 (0-8 Mins) Temperatures

In the second phase the external window has been closed and the C-ANN and A-ANN control the ambient internal temperature. The activation value controls the actuation of the heater. If the activation value is greater than 0 the heater is turned on. If the activation value is less than 0 the heater is turned off. Figure 5 illustrates the activation value during this test phase. Initially the activation value is 2.046 resulting in "Heater On". After 18 minutes the activation reaches its maximum value of 84.446. The activation value remains above 0 until 40 minutes when it achieves the value -3.486. As this is a negative activation value the heater is turned off.

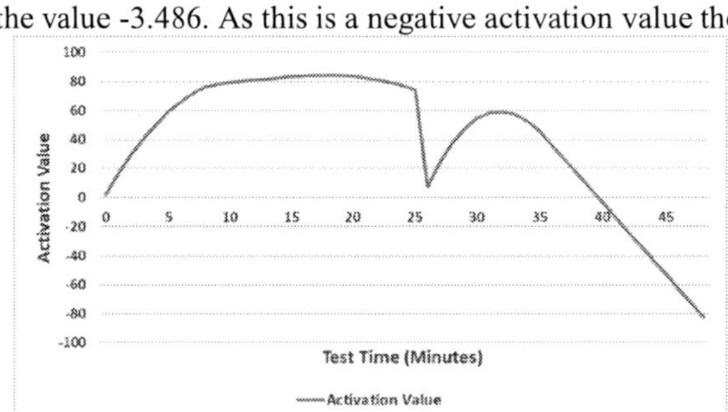

Figure 5. Test Phases 1 and 2 (0-50 Mins) Activation Value

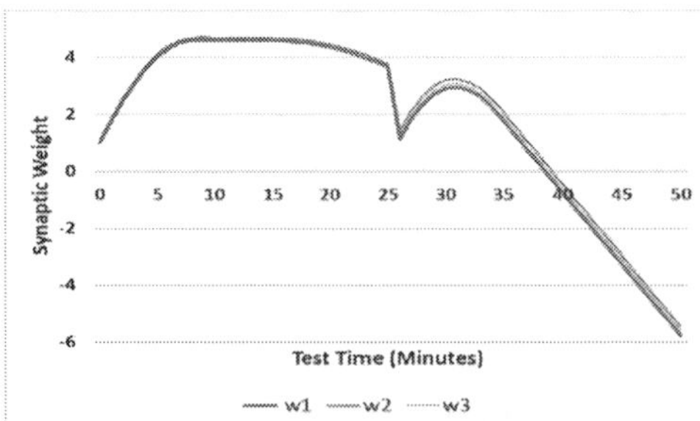

Figure 6. Test Phases 1 and 2 (0-50 Mins) synaptic Weights

Starting with initial synaptic weights w1 =0.997, w2=1.105 and w3=1.055 the weights increase significantly in the first 0-8 second period. Increasing weights produce a more aggressive reaction from the C-ANN and A-ANN meaning it is more likely the heater will be in state "On". The synaptic weights reach a maximum value of w1 = 4.608, w2= 4.692 and w3= 4.647 after 10 minutes, 9 minutes and 14 minutes respectively. There is a general decrease in all 3 synaptic weights until 25 minutes when there is a sudden reduction to w1 = 1.143, w2= 1.44 and w3= 1.289. In order to explain the sudden decrease in weight adjustment and resulting weights (Figure 6) we analyse the change in configuration temperature in Figure 7.

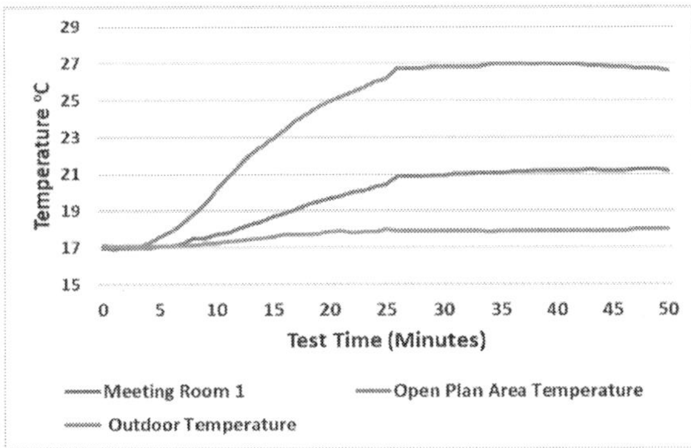

Figure 7. Test Phases 1 and 2 (0-50 Mins) Temperatures

Figure 7 illustrate that between 25 and 27 minutes there is a sudden increase in both the open plan area and meeting room 1 temperature. The open plan area room temperature increases from 20.3° to 20.9°. In the same interval the temperature increases from 25.68° to 26.8°. The C-ANN and A-ANN implementation react to the sudden increase in temperature by reducing the weight adjustment and thereby the weights. For the next 3 minutes the temperature of the open plan area and Meeting Room 1 remain constant at 20.9° and 26.8° respectively. As the temperature of Meeting Room 1 is below the required value the weigh increase is increased. After 40 minutes the activation value is reduced to a negative value and the heater is turned off. Figure 8 illustrates the external, open plan area and meeting room temperature for all the test phases.

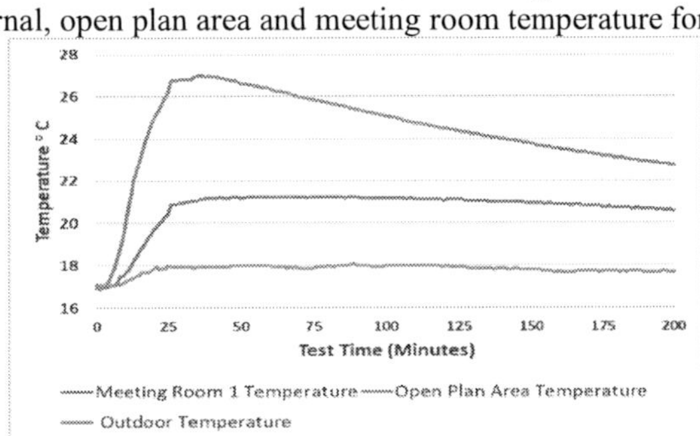

Figure 8. Complete Test Temperatures

In phase 1 (0-8 minutes) the window is open and the heater is on as the external temperature exceeds the internal temperature. After 8 minutes the window is closed as the internal temperature exceeds the external temperature. Between 9 minutes and 40 minutes the heater remains on as the activation value of the C-ANN and A-ANN configurations is greater than 0. After 40 minutes the activation value is negative and the heater is turned off. The temperature of the open plan area reduces from a maximum of 26.938°C at 42 minutes to 22.75°C at the end of the test. The temperature of Meeting Room 1 reduces from a maximum of 21.25°C at 43 minutes to 20.563°C at the end of the test.

6. CONCLUSION

This work proposes a federated ANN implementation which is influenced by environmental control factors to optimise ambient temperature within an office area. The configuration introduces two new architectural components an Agent ANN (A-ANN) and a Coordinating ANN (C-ANN). The A-ANN operates with a degree of autonomy with some federated influence from the C-ANN. The C-ANN considers the optimal ambient temperature of the entire open plan area. The work presents an experimentally based evaluation of the architecture using a physical scaled model. The model enables the analysis of dispersion of heat between rooms in an office environment consisting of meeting rooms and a central open plan area. The work illustrates how a federated ANN approach consisting of both centralised and distributed intelligence can learn the optimal of HVAC actuators so as to optimise thermal flow throughout the office space.

REFERENCES

Ardiyanto, D., Pipattanasomporn, M., Rahman, S., Hariyanto, N., & Suwarno, N., 2018. Occupant-based HVAC Set Point Interventions for Energy Savings in Buildings. *Green Energy for Sustainable Development*. pp.1-6

Edenhofer and S. Kadner, S. K. Seyboth, A. Adler, I. Baum, S. Brunner, P. Eickemeier, B. Kriemann, J. Savolainen, S. Schlömer, C. von Stechow, T. Zwickel and J.C. Minx. 2014. Climate Change 2014: Mitigation of Climate Change. *Cambridge University Press, Cambridge, United Kingdom and New York, NY, USA*. pp. 671-739.

Gopika, S., 2015. Agent Based HVAC Optimization Model for Building Energy Efficiency. *IEEE 9th International Conference on Intelligent Systems and Control (ISCO)*. pp.1-5.

Hsiung, P., &Lin, C., 2018. Cost optimization of electrical usage with customizable comfort considerations. *IEEE International Conference on Applied System Invention (ICASI)*, Chiba. pp.172-175.

Kim, Y., 2018. Optimal Price Based Demand Response of HVAC Systems in Multizone Office Buildings Considering Thermal Preferences of Individual Occupants Buildings. *IEEE Transactions on Industrial Informatics*, vol. 14, no. 11, pp. 5060-5073.

Matta, K., Rehu, J., Tanner, H., Kansala, K., 2017. Building Intelligence – Home operating system for smart monitoring and control. *IEEE Conference on Electro Information Technology (EIT)*. pp. 245-24.

Perry, R., Fallon, E., Fallon, S., & Qiao., Y. 2017. A Hierarchical Learning System for Ambient Environmental Control of Open Plan Buildings. *UKSim-AMSS 20th International Conference on Modelling & Simulation*. pp.21-27.

Priya Bhavesh, P. Karhade and Sulbha Rajkumar Hawa. 2016. Optimisation of HVAC system using programmable controllers and data acquisition. *International conference on Internet of things and Applications (IOTA). pp.254-258.*

Ueda, K., & Shimonaka, S., 2017.Quantitative Evaluation of Intellectual Productivity Considering Depth of Concentration.*IEEE International Conference on Systems, Man, and Cybernetics (SMC)*, Banff, Canada.pp. 758-763.

Vatanparvar, K., Burago, I., & Abdullah, M., 2018. Extended Range Electric Vehicle with Driving Behaviour Estimation in Energy Management. *IEEE Transaction on Smart Grid*, vol. 14, no. 8. pp.2959 - 2968

THE CHALLENGE OF SMART MOBILITY INTEGRATION IN THE EVOLVING SMART CITY CONTEXT; THE PARADIGM OF HERAKLION

Efthimios Bakogiannis, Maria Siti, Stefanos Tsigdinos, Georgia Christodoulopoulou and Christos Karolemeas
National Technical University of Athens, Heroon Polytechneiou 9, Zographos 15780, Greece

ABSTRACT

Contemporary cities face significant challenges, particularly due to climate change and the rapid urbanization. Therefore, a new concept has emerged, utilizing the striking technological progress. This paradigm is no other than the Smart City; a city that responds to the needs of its residents for managing assets and resources in a sustainable and efficient way through the use of information and communication technologies (ICTs). The smart cities' concept has six main areas: Government, Mobility, Environment, Economy, Living and People. Urban Mobility, although remaining one of the toughest challenges, is not always adequately integrated in Smart Cities' schemes particularly in Greece, where it is often undermined or completely forgotten. In this context, the paper aims at highlighting the importance of smart mobility as a fundamental element of Smart Cities. Moreover, it proposes a Smart Mobility Strategy along with its evaluation process for the city of Heraklion in Greece, which can be used as guide for other cities in the field. The research presents nine (9) grouped sets of policy interventions and measures as well as five (5) categories of evaluation indicators to be applied in cities with similar characteristics. The proposed actions and indicators can be integrated in the planning procedure towards smarter, more sustainable and more efficient cities.

KEYWORDS

Smart Cities, Smart Mobility, Policy Actions, Assessment Indicators, ICT Tools, Heraklion City, Greece

1. INTRODUCTION

Urban areas have been facing extremely serious challenges in recent years, especially due to the crucial consequences of climate change and the rapid process of urbanization (Papa et al., 2017; Caragliu et al. 2009). Environmental deterioration, traffic congestion, poverty, inadequate housing conditions, inequalities, accessibility deficiencies, constitute some of the serious issues that contemporary cities face (Jabareen, 2006, Dameri, 2017). This situation demands an effective and resilient planning and development perspective (Pickett et al., 2004). Therefore cities must now embark on a process of transformation by developing strategies to counter the negative impacts of urbanization and bring prosperity to the urban environment (Aleta et al., 2017). A new city development model that has emerged from the late 1990's (Neirotti et al., 2014) utilizing the notable technological process, is called the "Smart City" (Garau et al., 2016). According to Caragliu et al. (2009), a city is smart when 'investments in human and social capital and traditional (transport) and modern (ICT) communication infrastructure fuel sustainable economic growth and a high quality of life, with a wise management of natural resources, through participatory governance'. A smart city is defined by its efficiency and livability as well as by its use of innovative operational and information technology. One of the key issues determining the new era of cities, is the ability of gathering, using and leveraging a meaningful amount of data (stored or real-time) in order to improve services directed to their citizens, decrease costs in energy consumption etc. A Smart City should perform sufficiently in six (6) key fields of urban development, built on the 'smart' combination of endowments and activities of self-decisive, independent and aware citizens (Giffinger et al., 2007). These fields are smart economy, smart governance, smart living, smart people, smart environment and smart mobility (Caragliu et al., 2009).

Cities tend to compete regarding their positioning in the global rankings in order to alter or enhance their future development, identify strengths and weaknesses as well as take advantage of the existing good practices and transfer knowledge and practices. Research in smart cities has well adopted this competitive approach, while monitoring data in transportation terms became the norm for Sustainable Urban Mobility Plans and hence Smart Mobility'. There are plenty of ranking systems, such as the *Smart City ranking by Boyd Cohen*, the *European Smart Cities*, the *Juniper's Smart City Rankings*, the *Deloitte City Mobility Index*, the *Intelligent Community Forum* assessment as well as panels from global and European stakeholders (i.e. the World Bank, universities, UN Habitat representatives etc.), listing cities that perform well in one or more of the afore-mentioned sectors. These rankings can directly assist cities in global and regional recognition as they draw public attention as well as attract several investment and development funding. More and more projects are being implemented within the concept of smart cities with the formulation of partnerships and other entities participating in programs such as INTERREG, URBACT, HORIZON 2020, CIVITAS etc.

One the most significant pillars of Smart Cities is Smart Mobility (Vanolo, 2014) which refers to the transportation sector of an urban area (peoples or goods) aiming to go one step further by searching for innovative and sustainable ways to provide mobility for people in cities –by developing environmentally-friendly public transport fuels and propulsion systems supported by technology, and the proactive behavior of citizens (Neirotti et al., 2014). However, this particular field is not always adequately integrated in Smart Cities' schemes. Especially in Greece, Smart Mobility is often undermined or completely forgotten (Bakogiannis et al., 2017), and that undoubtedly constitutes a serious hindrance in the way towards the making of sustainable, just and functional cities.

The aim of this research is primarily to highlight the importance of smart mobility as a fundamental element of Smart Cities and propose a Smart Mobility Strategy along with its evaluation process for a specific case study. The case study of this research is the city of Heraklion in the island of Crete. Heraklion is the 4th largest urban formation in Greece, having approximately 175.000 residents and the past few years has carried out notable efforts in the Smart City case, recognized by the New York- based Intelligent Community Forum on the list of 21 smart cities in the world for the years 2012, 2013 and 2014. However, Heraklion remains insufficient on implementation of smart mobility policies and actions ranking, low on all relevant indicators.

2. SMART MOBILITY: DEFINITIONS AND PERSPECTIVES

Conventional urban and transport planning have dealt so far with practices that tend to meet demands by improving capacity through car-oriented approaches especially in cities where urbanization is rapidly growing. Typical solutions have led to car-favoring development patterns (Marshall, 2005), which also drive the land use patterns in unsustainable city forms. Numerous researchers and studies consider transport to be among the three most energy consuming activities, with the other two being the sectors of housing and food production (Schafer et al., 2009). Therefore, a complete shift to a sustainable and efficient transport system is urgent. Sustainable urban mobility is considered as an emerging field in transportation and environmental studies-particularly in the European transport Agenda- introducing policies and practices to face problems such as traffic congestion, air and noise pollution, road safety etc. The need for sustainable urban mobility has been distinctly described only after 2001 (CEC, 2001), with the Green Paper from the European Commission being finalized and issued in mid- 2007 entitled '*Green Paper- Towards a new culture for urban mobility*' (CEC, 2007). Later on, in 2011 the European Commission, via the White Paper *'Roadmap to a Single European Transport Area - Towards a competitive and resource efficient transport system'*, adopted a roadmap of 40 concrete initiatives for the next decade to build a competitive transport system that will increase mobility, remove major barriers in key areas and fuel growth and employment (CEC, 2011). Recently, the introduction of Sustainable Urban Mobility Plans (SUMPs) contributed significantly to the enhancement and promotion of sustainable mobility in urban areas. Even medium or small sized cities have now the possibility of recreating their urban environment towards efficiency, vitality and sustainability. A Sustainable Urban Mobility Plan is "*a strategic plan designed to satisfy the mobility needs of people and businesses in cities and their surroundings for a better quality of life. It builds on existing planning practices and takes due consideration of integration, participation, and evaluation principles*" (Wefering et al., 2014).

One of the key elements of sustainable mobility, which is also embedded in SUMPs, is the concept of Smart mobility. According to Vanolo (2014), smart mobility constitutes one of the main urban strategies to pursue city sustainability. Smart mobility uses ICT not only to collect, process and spread information about the traffic in city, but also to implement Intelligent Transport Systems (Dameri, 2017) and to promote sustainable means of transport (e.g. bicycles, eco-vehicles, car sharing) that respect the environment. The novelty is thus not so much the individual technologies, products or services but the *interconnection* and the *synchronization* of these and the systems they include, so that they can function in concerted action (Hojer and Wangel, 2015). Nevertheless, smart mobility is not solely a technological affair, but also a social and cultural approach (Benevolo et al., 2016). Furthermore, it should be noted that a smart mobility system requires a variety of infrastructure types, including physical infrastructure, operational and information technologies. Without any single component of this system, smart mobility products cannot meet their full potential to achieve operational efficiency and manage the users' demand (Schneider Electric, 2014). Dameri (2017) states that smart mobility is one of the most promising topics, as it could produce high benefits for the quality of life of almost all the city stakeholders. Through literature review, it is possible to gather the most significant smart mobility objectives (Ambrosino et al., 2015; Lawrence et al., 2006; Bencardino and Greco, 2014) which are summarized in the following six categories: 1. reducing pollution; 2. reducing traffic congestion; 3. increasing people safety; 4. reducing noise pollution; 5. improving transfer speed; 6. reducing transfer costs. Smart solutions in mobility terms consist of systems, applications, implementation of policies, designs and plans, indicator's assessment and many more. Some solutions can only be adopted by cities that have already implemented progressive transport planning including walking, cycling and public transport infrastructures parameters; while other solutions can support cities that are at a critical point in terms of tech industry revolution. Anyhow, smart mobility services are changing the way cities move, while at the same time "smart infrastructure" projects are becoming commonplace. More and more cities are implementing practices and policies related to intelligent transport systems (ITS) and many of them are investing in infrastructure that can assist in the transition to an up-to-dated 21st century urban mobility agenda. This agenda should place innovation at its core (CEC, 2011), thus including different technology- assisted services, alternative use of vehicles, introduction of the 'sharing' culture, innovative integration of traditional traffic calming tools, implementation of customized solutions and a communicative participatory approach for information and awareness raising.

Greek cities being formally obliged to follow European strategies have implemented several, however abstract, practices related to transportation and smart mobility. European Funds (Horizon 2020, Interreg etc.) have allowed the development of a number of strategies, projects, mobility practices and services related to the smart city concept in cities such as Athens, Piraeus, Thessaloniki, Thermi, Trikala, Heraklion and others. Innovations in smart mobility are more profound in Thessaloniki (project Intelligent Thessaloniki) as well as in the city of Trikala (project CityMobil2), where the first autonomous bus has completed its pilot application and tested in real traffic conditions, while also Piraeus (project CYCLECITIES, SMILE, MOBILITAS) has participated in a number of innovative mobility projects. Although several projects regarding mobility have been implemented, development has mostly focused on pilot services and the output data are *not* integrated in the future strategic municipal or regional planning. Similarly, the tools and innovative services developed by these projects do not seem to be upgraded in following schemes or applied in future technologies. Furthermore, public- private partnerships in Greece do not follow the European norms, and thus it is difficult to promote the concept of sustainable competitiveness as a driver of prosperity and long-term growth in terms of sustainable mobility. Initiatives are driven either by public entities (universities and research centers) or by businesses and project consultants whose interest is usually limited to the end of each program (Bakogiannis et al., 2017).

3. HERAKLION PARADIGM; INTEGRATING MOBILITY IN THE MUNICIPAL SMART CITY STRATEGY

Heraklion is a dynamic Mediterranean city of Greece and the largest city of the island of Crete. Urban development has been defined by sprawl, incohesive planning and car-dependency, however the public transport system has been improved in terms of services and operation management. Although there are numerous fruitful discussions and attempts which embrace sustainable urban mobility and promote smart mobility in the planning discourse, it is profound that there is still a long way to go in order to achieve an efficient level of human-centered mobility. The particularities in the urban environment, such as the narrowness of the street form, the lack of organized on and off street parking spaces, the short distances and the sense of enclosure in existed inner-city neighborhoods, provide an ideal environment for combined smart mobility tools. Policy directions as well as actions should involve a range of traditional and innovative research tools that would put an emphasis on participatory processes which can raise awareness and somehow motivate citizens' engagement.

3.1 Specification of Heraklion's Smart Mobility Strategy

Heraklion aims to be transformed into a sustainable, accessible and *truly smart city* in mobility terms. It will be a city not based solely on the automobile, but a place that promotes walking, cycling, collective and shared transportation through a functional network with well aware and informed commuters. The Strategy on Smart Urban Mobility consists of 9 sub-sections (according to SUMP principles): a) Walking, b) Bicycle, c) Collective Transportation, d) Traffic Management and Private Vehicle Circulation, e) Speed Management and Road Safety, f) Innovative Means of Transport & Shared City Concept, g) Clean Vehicles, Logistics & Supply Management and h) Education-Communication-Awareness. Each one of the aforementioned sections includes innovative and core actions, which are described briefly below, mentioning also issues about their social acceptance, the expense and funding possibility balance as well as their contribution to sustainable mobility.

Walking is the most free and independent way of travelling around the city. The programmed *innovative* actions include; a) pilot testing and installation of special ICT urban equipment (signs, benches, lighting, shelters, stops, information and/ or sale kiosks etc.), b) development of systems to measure pedestrian flows and identify the geography and patterns of most used routes, c) installation of smart and accessible bus stops and Taxi stops, d) electronic accessibility rehabilitation of the transport system for disabled people as well as other vulnerable users (i.e. ticket issuing) and e) upgrade of the existing municipal APP or new Application development for crowdsourcing data collection while walking in the city (incl. existing functions such as problem reporting, points of interest etc.). The *core* actions regarding **Walking** include; a) improvement of sidewalks and pedestrian crossings in the context of the contemporary legislation and the urban mobility principles, b) improvement of street junctions facing inadequate road safety features, particularly on areas around school complexes and areas with increased pedestrian flows, c) development of traffic calmed roads and traffic calming areas (e.g. in central and suburban neighborhoods d) development of Pilot Urban Mobility Neighborhoods (one per municipal unit), e) upgrade of the existing green routes and development of an Eco-Cultural Network along significant routes, f) special provisions for each different disability category (e.g. different requirements for blind people, people with reduced mobility etc.) and g) improvement of accessibility in Public Transport Stops and taxi stops and enhancement of multimodality between pedestrian-PT system, cyclists' -PT system, pedestrian-cyclist, private vehicle-PT, private vehicle-cyclist etc. (e.g. on the main city gates, crucial junctions etc.). The social acceptance of the aforementioned actions is medium to high due to several completed interventions, while the innovation and the smartness of the measures can attract many funding resources, thus minimizing cost issues. The contribution to sustainable mobility is great, as they enhance the smart dimension of mobility in Heraklion. The presence of the FORTH institute in the vicinity allows for several pilot testing and attraction of relevant funds. The first three *innovative* actions (a,b,c) are already funded, while the fifth action (e) is already in the development phase with ensured funds and high social consensus. Most of the *core* actions are programmed to be implemented through the SUMP funding, which is mostly confirmed by the municipal budget.

Cycling has similar benefits to walking, but can be easily used for long-distance travels. The *innovative* actions include; a) upgrading of the existing bike sharing system for citizens (residents and visitors) with a 24/7 dock less system and electronic application support, b) installation of an electronic system for dispensing shared bikes to citizens (residents and visitors) with 24/7 lending system and electronic application support either from specific delivery and receipt points (dockless with designated parking lot) either completely dockless, c) research on the utilization of electric scooters and segways as last mile alternative commuting modes, d) use of environmentally friendly electric bicycles (in passenger and freight transport), e) development of a smart bike flow measurement system to identify the geography of the most frequently selected routes, and f) development of an application with various data (or enhancement of existing apps) aiming at a readable and complete navigation system for cyclists. The *core* actions regarding **Cycling** include; a) development of a complete cycling network (cycle lanes, cycle corridors and mixed use streets) as well as bicycle parking stations, b) improvement of crossings with emphasis on the safe passage of pedestrians and cyclists c) promotion of public spaces and network integration for pedestrians and cyclists and d) improvement of accessibility in Public Transport Stops and taxi stops and enhancement of multimodality between pedestrian-PT system, cyclists-PT system, pedestrian-cyclist, private vehicle-PT, private vehicle-cyclist etc. (e.g. on the main city gates, crucial junctions etc.). Regarding the social acceptance of the above actions in terms of cycling, those that do not claim streetspace from the motor vehicles (i.e. core action a) have been already welcomed along with those promoting road safety (i.e. core actions b & c). The public-private cooperation in the field of bike sharing (incl. innovative actions a, b, c, e) allows for the feasibility of most actions to be high, while the cooperation of the municipality with renowned research institutes and local universities is already promoting innovative actions e and f. Lastly the recent public engagement meetings with public transport operators and taxi union's representatives show their eagerness to support multimodality (core action d) however only if financial incentives are provided for any conversions.

Public Transport should be the backbone of the city's transport infrastructure. The benefits to residents and visitors vary, with the most important being road safety, sociability and economic efficiency. The innovative actions include; a) research on the feasibility of developing a Light Rail Transit Network, b) utilization of clean electric buses and smaller vehicles with emphasis on routes serving the most congested areas (for example city center, University, Airport, Archeological site of Knossos, etc.), c) improvement of the installation of telematics system for passengers' information and interfacing through "DIMOTIS" application for remote information, d) construction of (electronic) accessible infrastructure for people with disabilities and vulnerable citizens' groups, e) research on the potential integration of a single electronic ticket for bus and taxi (and bus-tram in the future), f) development of efficient public transport management technologies, g) sensor installation on Public transport vehicles in order to enhance traffic and pollution monitoring in the urban area of Heraklion and h) installation of smart bus stops. The core actions regarding **Public Transport** include; a) reorganization of existing routes and development of new Public Transport connections, b) installation of new accessible stops and stations, upgrading of existing stops and reallocation of the Taxi stations in order to serve complementary to public transport network, c) enhancement of multimodality for better service of the system pedestrian-public transport, cyclist-public transport (bicycle dragging), taxi-pedestrian, taxi-public transport, taxi-cyclist, etc.), d) provision of exclusive road space for public transport (e.g. bus lanes in arterial roads) e) development of Park & Ride Infrastructure at the outskirts of the city and f) route enhancement, necessary route changes and development of a strategy to tackle seasonal variation of demand due to tourism activities through smart integration of Taxi and Public Transport. The aforementioned measures are characterized by medium to high social acceptance, although some of them are considered difficult to be accepted by the locals (e.g. innovative action a, core action d; Provision of exclusive road space for public transport) and they also present a medium to high level of cost- benefit equilibrium. The key weaknesses identified in the field that reduce the feasibility of several actions include the severe underfunding in public transportation that complicates innovative actions a and h as well as core actions e and f.

Private car is not only the leading factor in creating traffic congestion in cities, triggering traffic incidents, but also one of the most important causes of air pollution, Greenhouse effect and, in general, urban degradation. The motorcycle also operates towards the same direction; however it occupies significantly less space. It is therefore urgent to severely limit their dominance and improve their circulation in certain sectors. The innovative actions regarding **Traffic Management and Private Vehicles Circulation** include; a) establishment of Traffic Control Center (including connected vehicles management), b) development of a system for traffic data collection and provision of real-time navigation information, c) variable message system (VMS) installation, d) development of a smart system for controlling short-term parking and variable parking spaces in the city center and the densely populated suburbs or neighborhoods of the city, e) development of a smart system for preventing illegal parking at predetermined points (i.e. pedestrian crossings), f) development of a navigation and parking assistant application for mobile phones aiming at the prevention of unnecessary parking searching, g) improvement of traffic management with smart signaling and h) import of electric vehicles and their charging points at central places of the city. The core actions regarding **Traffic Management and Private Vehicles Circulation** include; a) road network classification and relevant policies, b) development of traffic calmed areas in combination with prevention of through traffic in neighborhoods, c) permanent or Temporary Interventions in order to prevent illegal parking, d) improvement of mobility conditions around school complexes by creating mobility plans to promote alternative modes of transport -school mobility plans (e.g. walking/ cycling bus, carpooling), e) improvement of mobility in organizations through the creation of mobility plans- work travel plans (e.g. Commuters to the University

Hospital of Heraklion, University, Companies located in the Industrial Area etc.) and f) development of Park & Ride Infrastructure at the outskirts of the city. The social acceptance of the above actions is high, the smartness of the measures has already attracted several funding resources – although few of them confirmed, thus tackling the large cost of particular measures (e.g. establishment of a traffic control center) and the contribution to sustainable mobility is great, as they enhance efficiency of the whole transport system.

Speed is one of the most important operating factors of an area's road network. High speed road networks are creating conditions of increased risk, resulting in more traffic accidents. The innovative actions referring to **Speed Management and Road Safety** include; a) development of a system for traffic data collection and provision of real-time navigation information, b) combination of ICT tools for monitoring of environmental and traffic issues, c) implementation of innovative ways for traffic monitoring and road maintenance (identification and improvement of dangerous points and systematic monitoring of driving behavior) and d) variable message system (VMS) installation in order to inform and warn drivers for speed limits, real-time network situation, etc. The core actions are; a) reduction of speed limits across the city at 40km/h and in the neighborhoods from 20 to 30km/h (in combination with case specific traffic calming interventions at crucial sites such as schools), b) traffic calming measures for enhancing vulnerable users' accessibility, c) redesign of junctions for road safety in key spots and d) redesign of traffic signs in conjunction with restrictions for through- traffic. The public perception of such measures is positive however lacks the extensive funding to cover the overall actions. The feasibility of several actions is high (innovative actions a, c, d and core actions a, b, c and d) due to completed traffic studies which are time-consuming and set the precondition for funding. The need to create sustainable, social and functional cities requires a shift to innovative modes of transport, which will be shared and allow public and collective use. The innovative actions regarding **Innovative Means of Transport & the Shared City Concept** include; upgrading of the existing bike sharing system for citizens (residents and visitors) with a 24/7 dockless system and electronic application support, b) installation of a new electronic system for dispensing 200 more shared e-bikes to citizens (residents and visitors) with automatic lending and support from an electronic application either from specific delivery and receipt points, either completely dockless, c) research on the utilization of electric scooters and segways (dockless or not) as an alternative last-mile commuting mode, d) integration of mini/ midi buses into the Public Transport System for developing on-demand services, e) research on the introduction of financial or other incentives for the enhancement of collective and shared modes of transport and f) support of private initiatives regarding car sharing. The high social acceptance of all the above measures due to the national trends in the sharing economy and the presence of private investors allows for the increased feasibility of the actions.

Emissions from conventional motor vehicles are considered the most serious drivers of greenhouse gas emissions, pollution etc., while the noise they produce generates significant nuisances in the urban environment and quality of life. Therefore, the shift to new clean vehicles is considered imperative and Heraklion aims to be at the forefront of such transformation. The innovative actions regarding **Clean Vehicles** include; a) promotion of gradual replacement of municipal vehicles' fleet (e.g. garbage truck, school buses etc.) with clean vehicles, b) promotion of gradual replacement of public transport vehicles' fleet with clean vehicles, c) installation of a functional e-mobility charging network, and d) research on the introduction of financial or other incentives for the integration of E-mobility in organizations & companies with large vehicle fleets. The aforementioned actions are expected to be welcomed by the local society as information and awareness for clean vehicles will be established in the area. National funding along with economic incentives can ensure the implementation of most actions while the participation of the private sector is expected to cover the various operational costs.

Logistics and Supply management is now seen as a key sector of any urban mobility strategy. Innovative actions proposed are; a) support of gradual implementation of cooperative transport systems in freight transportation, b) promotion of gradual replacement of the conventional supply vehicles (trucks and motorcycles) with green and shared vehicles, and c) combined management of supply chain activities and parking policies. Furthermore, the core action suggested is the development of Sustainable Urban Logistics Plan (SULP) in order to adopt a holistic and efficient approach of the issue. The feasibility of such actions depends highly on the reactions and adaptability of logistics' companies as well as on national policies. Although the social acceptance of such actions is positive, the feasibility of the actions is inextricably related to the maturity of the supply chain operators.

Substantial change in urban transportation and mobility behavior will not be managed if there is no change in the citizens' attitude and everyday choices. The innovative actions regarding **Education-Communication-Awareness Raising** are; a) the development of awareness raising campaigns for the role of technology in urban transportation and mobility and b) conducting of workshops aiming at familiarizing travelers in participatory planning and the use of crowdsourcing applications. The core actions are; a) information and awareness raising actions and campaigns on issues of transportation, urban mobility, accessibility and parking, and b) combined informative actions for children and the elderly (emphasis on target groups: children, elderly people, people with disabilities, etc.) on issues of mobility choices and road safety. Such actions are in place for Heraklion, which was awarded as the best big city in Greece for awareness raising activities during the European Mobility Week 2018, while future actions have ensured funding and are going to be completed with the participation of volunteers and various stakeholders.

The feasibility of measures (social consensus, cost-fund efficiency, contribution) has been examined thoroughly, but is not presented at this particular point due to the limited extent of the paper.

3.2 Monitoring of Smart Mobility. Challenges and Perspectives

A key element for the municipality's involvement in international city networks, partnerships in European and international programs, as well as an important parameter in the municipality's rating in official cities' ranking, that affect cities' funding and financial support, is the assessment and evaluation of the proposed actions through a proper set of indicators (Aleta et al., 2017). The selected indicators, which quantify attributes related to sustainable urban mobility, are used as benchmarking tools to monitor sustainable mobility in different urban areas (Pitsiava- Latinopoulou, 2012). The indicators selected in this particular study for Heraklion are 41 and they are related to the various objectives of the proposed strategy. Furthermore, they were classified into the following categories; Outcome indicators (15), transport activity indicators (11), output indicators (5), input indicators (3) and contextual indicators (7). It should be noted that this study not only suggests the appropriate evaluation indicators, but also forms a coherent table which includes the definition of the indicators, the implementation area, the data collection methods, the competent bodies as well as the financial resources. This holistic approach ensures the efficiency and the functionality of the suggested evaluation method and can contribute considerably in the improvement of the proposed strategy. A sample of this overall table is presented below.

Table 1. Sample of Indicators' Table

Indicator	Category	Definition	Application area	Data Collection	Competent bodies	Financial resources
Killed and seriousl injured by mode	Outcome Core Safety	Number of people killed or seriously injured in traffic accidents	City wide or on specific areas	Regular reporting from police or equivalent	Police Department of Heraklion/Traffic Police, Municipal Police	Own resources
Carbon emissions of traffic in the city	Outcome Core Environmental	CO_2 emissions of motorized traffic	City wide	Calculations based on vehicle km and emission factor, existing data from projects (RERUM)	Municipality of Heraklion (Technical service), University Institutions	Own resources, European Projects
Clean Vehicles Share	Contextual	Percentage of clean vehicles in total fleet	City wide	Reports from competent authorities	Municipality of Heraklion, Region of Crete	Own resources

As stated before, monitoring and evaluation of smart mobility actions and measures is a fundamental part of Smart Mobility in general. When a set of policy measures and actions is implemented, it is considered mandatory to examine the impacts, the benefits and the possible deficiencies it has. Therefore, this task requires a monitoring process to be carried out. Monitoring constitutes an ongoing process which gives feedback and draws attention to crucial issues. Furthermore, monitoring contributes to the classification of these crucial issues, prioritizing the most urgent to be dealt with. This specific process should be adopted and run by local authorities and not by external partners, in order to enhance their role and strengthen their independence in both assessment and problem solving. Possible cooperation in the early stages of the monitoring procedure is still beneficial, only if emphasis is placed on transferring the potential know-how to the municipalities. Local authorities ought to be adaptable in such a new scientific perspective and they have to utilize proper strategies and tools to solve independently the occurring traffic and transportation problems.

A basic tool for monitoring the municipality's efficiency level is the creation of a City Dashboard. City Dashboards are portals which represent Data and Information about several elements of a city often at real- time. The main features of a Dashboard are: a) Legibility and Readability, b) open-access of the data,

c) capability of combining different datasets, d) Innovative interface, e) Availability of different languages and f) Installation of City Dashboards in certain sites in the city. Certainly, Dashboards are one of the possible tools and strategies for monitoring. Heraklion has already a digital platform (https://smartcity.heraklion.gr/en/home/) which includes several features about the city such as weather condition, economical and demographical data etc. However, it is necessary to enrich these features, by adding public transport timetables and real-time traffic data as well as some of the aforementioned urban and transport indicators, thus improving the Smart mobility monitoring level of the city. Moreover, Heraklion city should not be limited solely to the Dashboard portal. Therefore, the introduction and adaptation of more functional tools will enlighten the way of the future aiming at efficiency, sustainability and economical effectiveness.

4. CONCLUSION

Sustainable urban mobility is fundamental to European and Mediterranean cities' social life and economy. In this context, SUMPs constitute a considerable opportunity for the cities' future, contributing to the enhancement and promotion of sustainable means and ways of transport in urban areas. Pleasant and affordable daily commuting, as suggested in SUMPs, is a key contribution to the quality of everyday life for citizens and can ensure accessibility, equity and increase of social cohesion. Smart solutions in the field of urban mobility aim to address these issues, while engaging citizens in action and removing obstacles in their communication. Smart mobility is an integral element of SUMPs, and Sustainable mobility in general, which requires a variety of infrastructure types, including physical infrastructure, operational and information technologies. Without any single part of this system, smart mobility cannot achieve an adequate efficiency level. On the one hand this paper has highlighted the significance of smart mobility as a principal element of Smart Cities and on the other the fundamentals of this importance; it has proposed a Smart Mobility Strategy along with its evaluation process for the city of Heraklion, which can be transferred to cities with similar characteristics and dynamics or needs. A set of categorized actions and indicators was presented, composing a plan which not only suggests new ways towards sustainable and efficient mobility, but also points out a monitoring procedure. Studying the experience of Heraklion in terms of its technological advances, its alignment to smart solutions in administrative level and the implementation of urban mobility projects has led to the conclusions that smart mobility parameters have to be studied and applied in accordance to the city's particularities and deficiencies.

The presented methodology, as applied through the case of Heraklion City, develops a creative *toolbox* with actions that can lead to smart paradigms of shifts in a daily commuting base as well as in the overall transportation culture of car-oriented cities. Moreover, the various indicators will contribute to examination and perhaps reconsideration of the suggested actions, contributing to the making of a more efficient Smart Mobility Plan. The crucial element in the suggested study remains the applicability and its potential outcomes in the future modal share. Critical issues raised from the above may also include the adaptability of local authorities in such a new scientific perspective along with their eagerness to adopt strategies and tools to solve long-established traffic and transportation problems.

Finally, the discussed issues within the overall concept of the smart city are expected to raise several research questions related to the role of mobility in cities, travel and mobility behavior, approaches in different age groups and different mobility attitude groups, as well as provide crucial outcomes in future transportation studies. This paper, as part of a series of ongoing research material, highlights the foundations of Smart Mobility Strategy and the way it is integrated to Sustainable Urban Mobility Plans, including both innovative and traditional policies and actions. Future interest in the field is addressing also actions for inclusion of various social groups, information and awareness as well as public engagement which shall allow for further exploration of innovative actions that involve the crowd in both problem solving and decision making.

REFERENCES

Aleta, N. et al., 2017. Smart Mobility and Smart Environment in the Spanish cities. *In Transport Research Procedia*, Vol. 24, pp. 163-170.

Ambrosino, G. et al., 2015. A method to assess and plan applications of ITS technology in public transport services with reference to some possible case studies. *In Case Studies on Transport Policy*, Vol. 3, No. 4, pp. 421-430.

Bakogiannis, E., 2017. Using Traditional and New Digital Technology Tools to Promote Sustainable Mobility: Current Trends in the Evolving Transformation of the Smart City. In Stratigea, A. et al. eds *Smart Cities in the Mediterranean: Coping with Sustainability Objectives in Small and Medium-sized Cities and Island Communities*. Springer, Cham, Switzerland, pp. 113-133

Bencardino, M. and Greco, I., 2014. Smart communities. Social innovation at the service of the smart cities. *In TeMA: Journal of Land Use, Mobility and Environment*, pp. 39-51.

Benevolo, C. et al., 2016. Smart Mobility in Smart City. In Torre T. et al. eds *Empowering Organizations*. Springer, Cham, Switzerland, pp. 13-28.

Caragliu, A., et al., 2009. Smart cities in Europe. *Proceedings of 3rd Central European Conference in Regional Science (CERS)*. Bratislava, Slovakia, pp. 45-59.

CEC, 2001. *European transport policy for 2010: time to decide (White paper)*. Brussels, Belgium

CEC, 2007. *Towards a new culture for urban mobility (Green paper)*. Brussels, Belgium

CEC, 2011. *Roadmap to a Single European Transport Area: Towards a Competitive and Resource Efficient Transport System (White paper)*. Publications Office of the European Communities, Luxemburg

Dameri, R. P., 2017. *Smart City Implementation*. Progress in IS. Springer, Cham, Switzerland

Garau, C. et al., 2016. Cagliari and smart urban mobility: Analysis and comparison. *In Cities*, Vol. 56, pp. 35-46.

Giffinger, R. et al., 2007. *Smart cities: Ranking of European medium-sized cities*. Centre of Regional Science, Vienna UT, Vienna

Hojer M. and Wangel J. 2015. Smart Sustainable Cities: Definition and Challenges. In Hilty, L. and Aebischer, B. eds *ICT Innovations for Sustainability*. Springer, Cham, Switzerland, pp. 333-350.

Jabareen, Y., 2006 Sustainable urban forms: their typologies, models, and concepts. In *Journal of Planning Education and Research*, Vol. 26, No. 1, pp. 38–52

Lawrence, F. et al., 2006. *Promoting public health through smart growth: Building healthier communities through transportation and land use policies and practices*. Smart Growth BC, Vancouver, Canada

Marshall, S., 2005. *Streets & Patterns*. Spon Press, Abingdon, UK

Neirotti, P. et al., 2014. Current trends in smart city initiatives–some stylised facts. *In Cities*, Vol. 38, pp. 25–36

Papa, R., et al., 2017. The evolution of smart mobility strategies and behaviors to build the smart city. *Proceedings of the 5th IEEE International Conference on Models and Technologies for Intelligent Transportation Systems (MT-ITS)*, Naples, Italy, pp. 409-414.

Pickett, S. et al., 2004. Resilient cities: meaning, models, and metaphor for integrating the ecological, socio-economic, and planning realms. *In Landscape and Urban Planning*, Vol. 69, pp. 369-384.

Pitsiava-Latinopoulou, M., 2012. Sustainable Mobility indicators in urban areas. *In Prospectus of Greek Transportations Engineers*, Vol. 182, pp. 13-17

Schafer, A. et al., 2009. *Transportation in a climate-constrained world*. Mit Press, Cambridge, Massachusetts

Schneider Electric, 2014. *Urban Mobility in the Smart City Age*.

Vanolo, A., 2014. Smartmentality: The Smart City as Disciplinary Strategy. In *Urban Studies*, Vol. 51, No. 5, pp. 883-898.

Wefering, F. et al., 2014. *Guidelines. Developing and Implementing a Sustainable Urban Mobility Plan*. European Commission, Brussels, Belgium

A MOBILE E-TICKET FRAMEWORK FOR BUS COMMUTERS: A MAURITIAN CASE STUDY

Darshini Gopaul, Sandhya Armoogum and Geerish Suddul
School of Innovative Technologies and Engineering, University of Technology Mauritius
LaTour-Koenig, Pointe-Aux-Sables, Mauritius

ABSTRACT

E-tickets and mobile tickets are widely used across the world for travel by air, trains and coaches. For daily commutes, smart cards are a popular mode of fare collection. These smart travel cards are re-usable and can be easily topped up but may involve a large investment which is hardly affordable in various developing countries. We therefore propose a mobile ticket-based framework which is more economically viable. Bus commuters can purchase their tickets through a mobile application which generates a unique Quick Response (QR) code. During their trip, the QR code is scanned and validated with a corresponding mobile application. This approach considerably reduces the investment in infrastructure as opposed to smart cards. The implemented solution is flexible as it allows the mobile tickets to be used by any bus operator in Mauritius.

KEYWORDS

Mobile tickets, Mobile Application, QR code, Fare Collection

1. INTRODUCTION

In Mauritius, public transportation mainly consists of a bus system, where the major bus operators are the National Transport Corporation (NTC), United Bus Service (UBS), Triolet Bus Service (TBS), Rose-Hill Transport (RHT) and Mauritius Bus Transport Ltd (MBT). Mauritius, being a small island, bus travel is a convenient and popular means of transport. The bus network is widespread with around 220 bus lines and roughly 900 bus stops (NTA, 2019). Only recently, due to the increasing demand for public transport in Mauritius, the Government of Mauritius has decided to implement mass rapid transit system in the form of light rail termed "Metro Express".

E-tickets and Mobile tickets are widely used across the world for travel by air, trains and buses. For daily commutes, smart cards are popular e.g. Oyster card in London, Opal cards in Sydney, and Octopus card in Hong Kong. In the context of Mauritius, the current payment for bus travel has not evolved since its first implementation in the 1980s. Two staffs are required to work in a bus while it is servicing a particular route: a bus driver and a bus conductor. The tickets are purchased from the bus conductor using cash-only after alighting the bus. Bus ticket prices are regulated by the Government of Mauritius and implemented by the National Transport Authority (NTA) which operates under the aegis of the Ministry of Public Infrastructure and Land Transport (NTA, 2019). This mechanism of purchasing travel tickets present several inconveniences. Firstly, bus commuters are required to carry small change cash for purchase of bus tickets while travelling. However, the use of debit or credit card for payment is widely used for general retail. Secondly, given that many people use the public transport, buses are often quite full especially during peak hours whereby many people will stand during the bus journey. In such circumstances, it is quite challenging for the bus conductor to navigate among the travellers for collecting payment and also quite inconvenient for travellers to handle cash in such circumstances. This onboard fare collection naturally involves a large number of cash transactions and thus, it is also highly susceptible to fraud (i.e. bus conductor does not report the exact amount of money collected on a journey) and even theft. Moreover, this form of paper ticketing system does not support the collection of data regarding travel patterns of travellers. Finally, this form of payment is also not in line with the country's efforts towards sustainability due to the use of printed paper tickets issued to travellers.

Very recently, since the 29th June 2017, the RHT bus operator has launched, on a pilot basis, the only contactless smart card system called "Filao" for bus ticket payment in Mauritius. The Government of Mauritius has eventually expressed interest towards a universal smart card for purchase of bus tickets with any bus operator, for the metro express as well as for taxis. It is also being debated that such a card can be used for payment of parking. As such, the Filao card can be purchased from two points (Victoria and Rose-Hill bus terminals) currently; and the card can be topped up at six points on the island using cash or debit/credit cards (TMSL, 2019). The Filao card needs to be tapped on the card reader in the bus when getting on the bus and has to be tapped again when getting off the bus. This automated bus fare payment system can definitely alleviate certain inconveniences regarding the ticket purchases as it is an easier and quicker way for purchasing tickets. However, currently the Filao smart travel card is only available on the RHT bus routes and travellers need to use one of the six top-up points to top up their card. Furthermore, a transaction statement regarding a card can only be obtained upon request by calling on a hotline number, after which the statement can be emailed to the user or collected at the card sales booths, which is not very convenient. Deploying, smart travel card systems at a national level will also involve significant investment in infrastructure i.e. all buses equipped with card readers, card sales and top-up points across the island with staff to operate the top-up points or automated top-up machines, and smart cards for the commuters amongst others. With limited financial support in developing countries, it is important to consider the use of technology for more cost-effective solutions. Thus, in this paper we describe a framework to use mobile e-tickets in the context of Mauritius for purchasing bus tickets based on a mobile application and the popular QR-code. In (Saidi Siuhi, 2016), several smart mobile applications in the area of transportations have been identified to be potentially beneficial.

This paper is organized as follows: in Section 2, we present the background study conducted which supports our proposed framework and related works. Section 3 describes the fare calculation system in Mauritius, while Section 4 describes our proposed framework and discusses its implementation. In Section 5, we discuss the benefits of the proposed framework as compared to the existing mechanism in place. In Section 6, a brief survey conducted to assess usability is presented. Section 7 concludes the paper and discusses the future work.

2. BACKGROUND STUDY

According to (Hootsuite, 2018), in 2018, two-thirds of the world's population have a mobile phone and more than half of the handsets in use today are "smart" devices. The mobile phone penetration in 2018 (68%) is actually higher than the Internet penetration (53%) and is on the rise. Furthermore, mobile internet users constitute 49% of the world's population. The mobile connectivity index of Mauritius is 62.7 (GSMA, 2016). Similarly, in January 2018, (Hootsuite, 2018) reported 143% mobile connections penetration and 63% internet penetration; 56% of the population of Mauritius are mobile internet users. This proliferation of mobile connectivity and technology has become a tool for a variety of activities in the developing world, especially given the low budget in such countries for development of services and infrastructure. Apart from its use for communication and social networking, it has several positive advantages such as contributing to the economic growth, employment, the reduction of the rural-urban differential across several developing nations around the world, to agriculture, to education and to health amongst others. As such, mobile has emerged as a platform of choice for creating, distributing and consuming innovative digital solutions and services.

The government and several companies in Mauritius have developed applications to make their products and services available online and accessible through mobile phones. Some notable examples include the Mauritius Airport App, Mauritius Traffic Alert, Smart Police Mauritius, Consumer Rights, and my.t Weather. Numerous mobile applications are also available regarding shopping in Mauritius. Mobile banking is also quite present on the island (Ramdhony & Munien, 2013). Unfortunately, there are currently no mobile services regarding the purchase of travel tickets in Mauritius. However, based on the above discussion, it is clear that Mauritius is ready for such an initiative. Mobile tickets are already popular for air tickets, sports and cultural events worldwide. For instance, Barcelona is in the phase of improving its public transport by the introduction of T-mobilitat chip card for contactless validation as well as supporting mobile app using NFC technology (T-Mobilitat, 2018). Similarly, many European countries - which are already using smart cards - are now also enhancing their services via mobile applications. In (Ferreira, et al., 2014), the authors also proposed a cost-effective public transport ticketing solution based on mobile devices such that minimal investment is incurred.

3. BUS FARE IN MAURITIUS

There are 305 bus routes in Mauritius which are serviced by the following bus operators/owners/co-operative societies: NTC, UBS, TBS, RHT, MBT, and Individual Operators (IO) (NTA, 2019). The bus ticket prices are regulated by the Government of Mauritius. Thus, bus tickets are the same irrespective of the bus operator and some bus routes are serviced by more than one bus operator. The bus fare is calculated based on distance travel in Mauritius, according to the number of fares stages travelled, where each fare stage is about 1.6 km. Each route consists of varying number of fare stages, which coincide with bus stops along the routes. A sample of the most recent bus fare as at August 2013 is shown in Figure 1 (a). As in most countries, there are concessionary fares for the following categories of passengers: (1) Children, and (2) Students. Pensioner or disabled person is issued a travel pass by the Ministry of Social Security, which authorize them to travel free of charge as from 15th August 2005. Figure 1 (b) depicts the stage information for the Route 1A which connects Port Louis (Victoria Square) to Rose-Hill (Market). The bus fare is simply computed by finding the number of fare stages travelled by the passenger i.e. disembarkation stage number minus the embarkation stage number, and then using the fare stage table. For example, a passenger travelling on Route 1A alighting the bus at the bus stop Brabant (SPAR) and disembarking at Rose Hill (Market), would have travelled 8 stages. Finding the passenger fare is just a simple lookup in the Bus Fare Stage table depicted in Figure 1 (a). The adult passenger fare would be Rs 30, while the fare for a child travelling the same journey would be Rs 16.

Stage No.	*Adult Rupees*	*Child Rupees*	*Student Rupees*
1	12.00	7.00	12.00
2	18.00	10.00	12.00
3	24.00	12.00	17.00
4	24.00	12.00	17.00
5	27.00	14.00	17.00
6	27.00	14.00	17.00
7	30.00	16.00	17.00
8	30.00	16.00	17.00
9	31.00	17.00	17.00
10	31.00	17.00	17.00
11	31.00	17.00	17.00
12	31.00	17.00	18.00

(a)

Fare Stage	*Locality*	*Average Journey Times in minutes*	*Fare Stage*
0	Port Louis (Victoria Square)		0
1	Brabant (SPAR)	6	1
2	G.R.N.W.	13	2
3	Coromandel (Sunray Hotel)	18	3
4	Belle Etoile (Tamil Social Hall)	21	4
5	Beau Bassin (Vinayak Mandir)	25	5
6	Beau Bassin (Serge Alfred Swimming Pool)	35	6
7	Hugnin Road (Rose Hill Transport Garage)	40	7
8	Boundary Road (St Patrick Church)	47	8
9	Rose Hill (Market)	50	9

(b)

Figure 1. (a) Extract of Bus Fare Stage for Adult, Child and Student as at 12th August 2013 (NTA, 2019)
(b) Bus Route 1A Port Louis (Victoria Square) to Rose Hill (Market) (NTA, 2019)

4. PROPOSED FRAMEWORK

4.1 Architecture and Design

The proposed framework aims to facilitate travelling by bus in Mauritius by introducing mobile tickets for bus travellers via the MoTicket mobile application. This mobile application allows travellers to buy their travel tickets before travelling, thereby avoiding the need to perform cash payment on the bus. The fare calculation is as per the government regulation as described in Section 3 and the mobile ticket can be used when travelling via any bus operator. Payment of tickets online can be done by debit/credit card, via mobile payment (e.g. MCB Juice, Orange Money) or by PayPal. Each individual ticket can be used once and, for flexibility, tickets bought have a validity period, after which the ticket is no longer valid. The proposed framework architecture is as depicted in Figure 2. Figure 3 shows a few user interfaces. The system consists of the following main components: a smart mobile device for the client side (used by traveller), a smart mobile device as ticket scanner (used in bus), a database server for storing information, and a web server for computing fare and for handling payment of tickets. The system administrator(s) can use a web browser to login to the server for entering/updating fare, route information, bus stop, driver information, ticket type, etc.

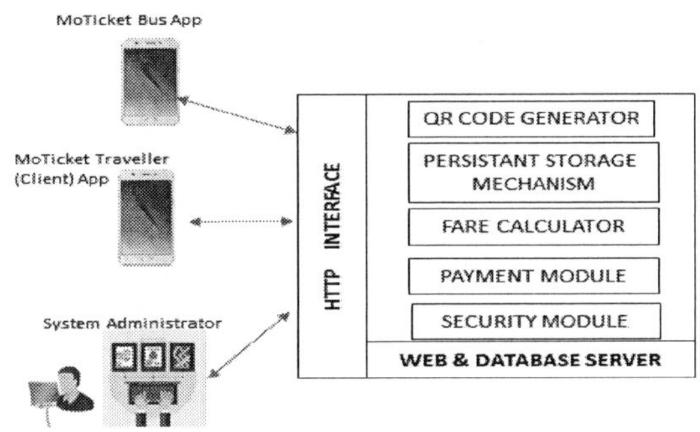

Figure 2. System Architecture

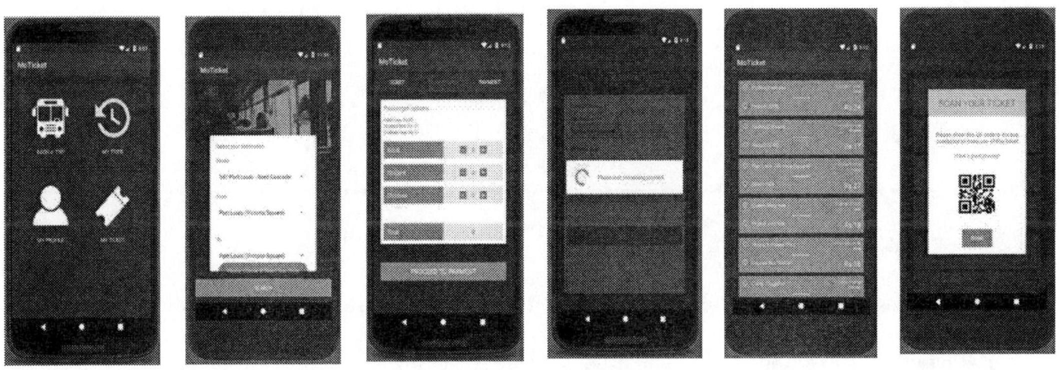

Figure 3. User Interfaces

4.2 QR Code for Securely Storing Information for the Mobile Ticket

Quick Response (QR) codes are widely used today as they provide faster and easy readability independent of their orientation than traditional barcodes. QR codes can also store a large amount of information in a compact fashion as compared to traditional barcodes, Near Field Communication (NFC) and RFID. They have error correction capability and are less prone to physical damages which make them more robust for storing information. QR codes can be used to store text, video, advertisement, personal information, URL, business card information or any type of digital information. As mobile technologies are booming, QR codes are being used for various purposes such as for accessing information on the web, for discount coupons, for interacting with social media, for mobile marketing, smart labelling (Ramalho, et al., 2018), for tickets (Kadge, et al., 2017), and for enhancing government service (Lorenzi, et al., 2014), amongst others. NFC is an alternative for contactless interaction (validation of tickets), however it may not be available on all smart phones. Moreover, NFC is known to have security issues such as eavesdropping whereby data from the mobile phone could be stolen, manipulation of data being transmitted, insertion of fake data, man-in-the-middle attack whereby the attacker acts as a middleman between two NFC devices to intercept the data, and denial of service attack whereby the attacker can disrupt the communication between two devices. In this proposed framework, QR code is thus used for implementing mobile tickets for bus payment. The mobile ticket consists of the data as shown in Table 1. All data components, excluding the status byte, are concatenated and the resulting output is hashed using the SHA512 algorithm. The hash value is then encrypted using the private key of the server to generate the signature of the ticket, which allows checking the authenticity and integrity of the ticket. All ticket data including the signature is to be encoded and stored as QR code for the mobile ticket.

Table 1. Mobile Ticket Data

Ticket Data	Data Type	Bytes	Remarks
TicketID	Numeric	1	Uniquely identifies the ticket
UserID	Numeric	1	Uniquely identifies the user who bought the ticket
TicketTypeID	Numeric	1	Indicates the type of ticket (Adult, Child, Student)
StartStopID	Numeric	1	Uniquely identifies the embarkation stop
EndStopID	Numeric	1	Uniquely identifies the dis-embarkation stop
No. of routes	Numeric	1	Indicates the no. of routes for which the ticket is valid.
Routes	Alphanumeric	10	Indicates routes on which ticket can be used
No. of Stages	Numeric	1	Indicates the number of fare stages of the journey
Fare	Numeric	1	Indicates fare amount paid for ticket
Expiry Date	Numeric	4	Day/Month/Year
Status	Binary/Byte	1	Unused ticket status 1, Used ticket status 0
Hash Value	Byte	128	SHA512 hash algorithm used. The hash value is stored as 128 hexadecimal numbers in the ticket
Signature	Byte	256	Hash value encrypted using private key of server (RSA Algorithm with a key of 2048 bit key) to generate the Signature

4.3 Creating QR Code

When encoding data into a QR code, three parameters have to be selected: the encoding mode, the version, and the error correction level.

Determining Encoding. A QR code usually encodes a string of text into a string of binary digits by using one of the following modes: (1) numeric, (2) alphanumeric, (3) byte or UTF-8, and (4) Kanji. The ticket information mainly consists of numeric data as shown in Table 1; except for the hash value and signature, which are non-numeric. In the proposed framework, the mobile ticket data is encoded using UTF-8, which is a variable width character encoding capable of encoding all 1,112,064 valid code points in Unicode using one to four bytes.

Determining Version. The size of the QR code is called the version. The smallest QR codes are 21x21 pixels (version 1), and the largest are 177x177 (version 40). Version 40 can carry the largest amount of information. Usually, the smallest version has to be determined for storing the data to be encoded. The storage capacity of QR codes however, also depends on the type of data being stored. Most of the ticket data are numeric values and can be effectively represented and stored as 1 byte of information as shown in Table 1. A particular journey may be undertaken on several bus routes if the path of one route overlaps partially and/or completely with the path of another route. In the proposed framework, it is assumed that the maximum number of routes which satisfy the overlap criteria for a journey is 5. Thus, the number of bytes for storing the routes for which the ticket is valid is assumed to be a maximum of 10 bytes (each route requiring a maximum of 2 bytes to store the information). The storage of the date requires 1 byte each for the storage of day and month respectively and 2 bytes for storing the year, thus a total of 4 bytes. For computing the hash value, the SHA512 hash algorithm is recommended. This algorithm generates fixed length hash values of size 512 bits, which is to be stored in the ticket as 128 hexadecimal numbers thus requiring 128 bytes. The signature is generated by encrypting the hash value with an RSA algorithm and key of 2048 bits, thus the signature size being 2048 bits, is equivalent to 256 bytes. The total amount of ticket information to be encoded is thus 407 bytes. The smallest version of QR code which can encode the ticket data is version 13 (69x69).

Determining Error Correction Level. QR codes provide error correction by means of the Reed-Solomon (RS) error correcting codes. This redundant data helps the QR reader accurately read the code even if part of it is unreadable. There are four levels of error correction: L, M, Q, H. The higher levels of error correction, the better the error detection and correction capability, however it also requires more redundant bytes resulting in a larger QR code. Version 22 (105x105) and onwards (till Version 40) could be used to encode the 407 bytes of ticket data with the *highest* error correction. The QR code being stored on the mobile phone (no major risk of damage e.g. torn, blurred,…), it is believed that a medium error correction level provides adequate recoverability. For scalability and flexibility (i.e. allowing for additional data if required in the future), the version 17 is used.

QR Code Generation. After payment has been received, the mobile ticket containing such a QR code is generated by the server and sent to the user's mobile device.

4.4 Validating the QR code/Mobile ticket

Usually, in countries making use of smart cards or mobile tickets, QR code readers are fixed in the bus or handheld QR code readers are used. But such hardware devices have some financial implications. Today, QR code reader apps are readily available on mobile phones. In the proposed framework, a smart mobile phone with the MoTicket Scanner Bus app is to serve as the QR code reader to validate the mobile ticket. Mobile tickets can also be verified visually, by the bus conductor, as application displays all the information which is encoded in the QR code. This solution is most economic and can be very quickly deployed. Such a mobile app scans the QR code and read the encoded data. Given that smart phones nowadays have good processing power and adequate storage capacity; the app is designed to validate the ticket locally to reduce the network dependence thereby reducing the cost of data connectivity. The MoTicket Bus Scanner mobile app also regularly connects to the server to update the tickets status information about the validated tickets such that such validated tickets cannot be re-used. Before starting to service a route, the bus conductor logs in and sets the bus operator and bus route, whereby the mobile application downloads all the bus stops (StopID) for the selected route from the server and saves this information on the mobile phone in a suitable data structure (e.g. SQLite on Android). The bus route information is required to allow the application to validate tickets.

5. POTENTIAL BENEFITS AND LIMITATIONS OF PROPOSED FRAMEWORK

The proposed framework for mobile bus ticketing in Mauritius offers numerous benefits as follows:

(1) Increased user satisfaction and convenience: Travellers do not have to handle monetary transaction while on the bus and they also have the flexibility of buying their tickets anytime and anywhere from their mobile phone unlike in the case of the Filao smart travel card system whereby the travel card can be topped up at specific points. Via the mobile application, local travellers and even tourists can quickly search for a bus route and find the cost of the bus tickets for any journey. Travellers have a "Wallet" where they can view valid tickets and a "Travel History" where they can view used tickets and journeys.

(2) Ease of validation of the mobile ticket by the bus conductor: The bus conductor using a smart phone can quickly scan and validate the mobile tickets as passengers' board the bus. The mobile ticket will most definitely drastically reduce the need to handle cash.

(3) Bus operator independence: Given that the cost of travel by bus is regulated by the government and is the same irrespective of the bus operator, the mobile app allows travellers to select their bus trip and to

buy tickets. Such tickets can be used on any bus operator. The system keeps track of the operator which validates the ticket and the payments received from the travellers transferred to the specific operator.

(4) Green and Cashless economy: The proposed framework promotes a cashless economy and provides a safer way for purchasing tickets and reduces fraud or theft. It also promotes a green economy due to the decrease of paper-based tickets.

(5) Scalable and quickly deployable: The proposed system is scalable and can accommodate the growing number of travellers in urban regions. Furthermore, once the mobile ticketing system is implemented, the mobile apps can be made available for download easily and instantaneously for use by bus travellers.

(6) Low Capital Expenditure (CapEx): Less investment in infrastructure in terms of hardware is required to implement the mobile ticketing. The use of smart phones for ticket validation by the bus conductor, a backend server, and a database server is the basic requirements.

(7) Better monitoring and reporting: The mobile ticketing framework as compared to the traditional ticket system, offers better insights regarding transportation statistics. Data collected from the system can be mined and be valuable to understand travel patterns. This analysis can be used for effective management when planning and scheduling new bus routes, and bus frequencies on different days and times. This can greatly help the bus operator optimize their running costs.

(8) Enhanced services to customers: The mobile application using the smart phone features can be extended to offer additional services such as real-time bus tracking via an interactive map, as well as other similar services.

However, the proposed framework for mobile bus ticketing in Mauritius also involves certain limitations such as the dependency on the mobile data network connection. The bus app needs to communicate with the server frequently to update information about validated bus tickets. However, there are certain small areas where the mobile connectivity may not be reliable. This can incur a delay in communication with the server. Moreover, the cost of mobile data connectivity is also an important Operational Expenditure (OpEx) consideration. The network operators may be reluctant to bear the cost of the data connection. Travellers are also required to have mobile connectivity for purchasing tickets.

6. SURVEY

An online survey was carried out to evaluate the acceptance of the proposed framework by university students of the age group 18-30 who travel by bus at least once a day, of which 63% were male and 37% were female. All respondents possessed a smart phone and had internet connectivity as follows: 85.2% use both Wi-Fi and Mobile data, while 14.8% use only Wi-Fi for internet connectivity. Thus, it can be concluded that users mostly have connectivity. Apart from the respondent themselves, 81.4% of the respondent reported that one or two persons from their home also uses the bus at least once daily. All the respondents were 100% positive about their intention to use the mobile app for buying their bus tickets and about the usefulness and ease of use of the application. They all agreed that the framework would make travel by bus easier and that the information provided regarding the costs of tickets was useful. Most respondents preferred the micro payment mechanism (MCB Juice and Orange Money) for purchasing bus tickets. Figure 4 summarizes the result of the a few questions in the survey.

In (Ferreira, et al., 2013), a more in-depth study, with a small sample of the population, was conducted for the mobile ticket system proposed for Porto City in Portugal to assess the user acceptance of system. The results indicate that users found the mobile app based ticket purchase and validation easy to use, useful, convenient and informative, while perceived risk and complexity was deemed low by respondents. Another, more recent study was conducted to assess the mobile payments adoption in public transport in the medium-sized metropolitan area of Porto as compared to the large metropolitan area of Beijing, China (Fontes, et al., 2017). It was observed that the mobile payment for purchase of public transport tickets was greatly accepted in both cities and has high potential market (30-68%), even though the Chinese people showed a higher motivation. These studies further support the acceptance of the proposed framework by travellers.

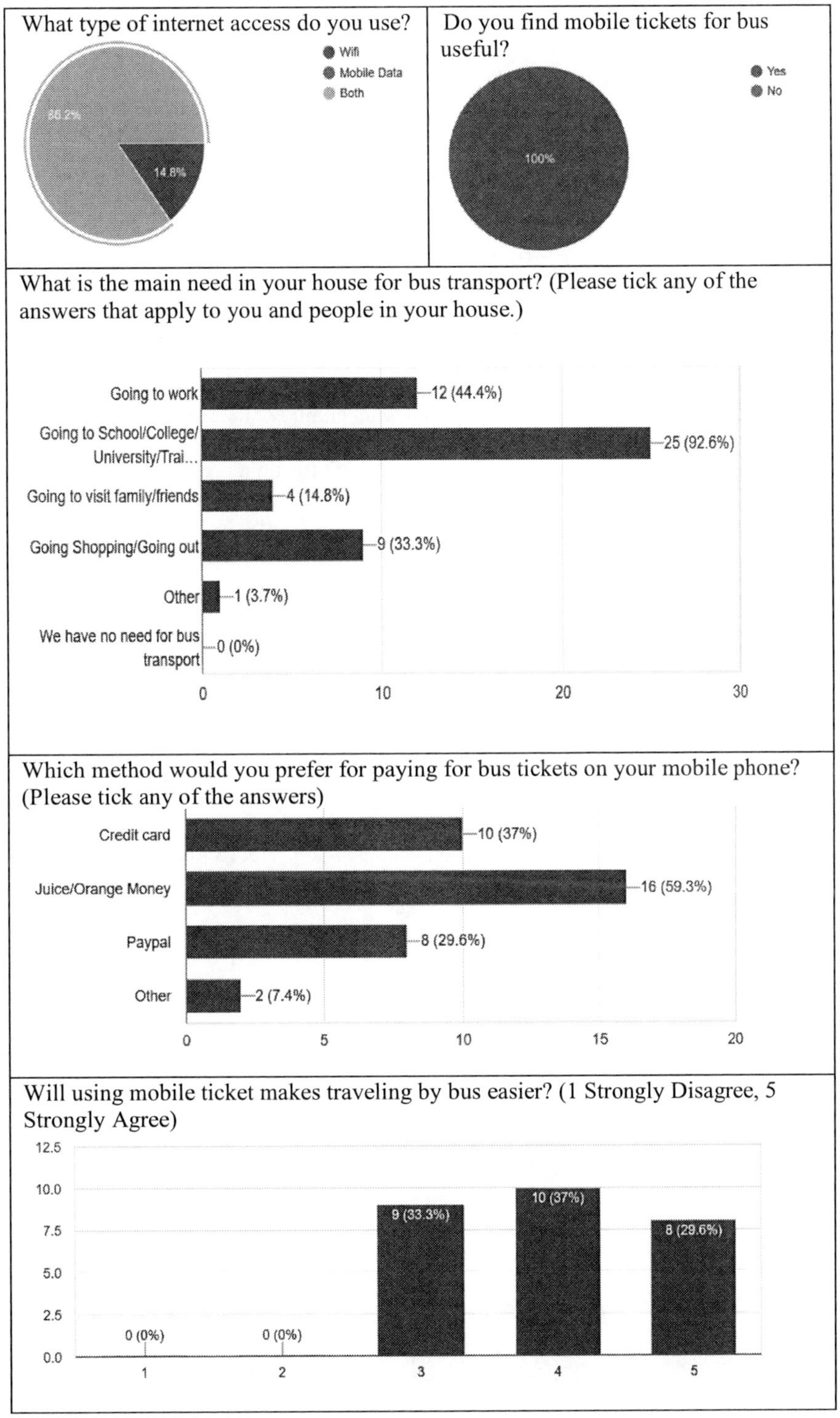

Figure 4. Survey Results

7. CONCLUSION

Currently, public transport in Mauritius has remained unaddressed until recently where the Metro Express project has been initiated by the government of Mauritius in 2018. Similarly, bus ticketing in Mauritius has not changed since its implementation until June 2017 where one bus operator has introduced smart travel card. Several developing countries in Asia and Sub-Saharan Africa are in a similar situation. The main motivation of the proposed framework has been to provide a new service offering in the form of mobile ticketing which may replace or complement the traditional public transport to provide efficient, economically feasible, easily deployable, and modern system to meet the mobility needs of people. The implemented prototype was showcased to a group of students who travel by bus on a daily basis and positive feedback was obtained. The adoption of e-services in Mauritius is on the rise where citizens are filing tax online, using the numerous government e-services, engaging in online shopping and actively participating on social media networks. Thus, the adoption of the mobile bus ticketing service by the general population is promising in Mauritius. Such a framework could be easily adopted by several developing countries in Africa to complement their existing fare collection system. Data inherently collected in the long run can be analyzed to help bus companies to enhance their policy regarding optimized organization of their bus fleet schedule.

Future work involves improving the proposed framework to add more flexibility such as the possibility of purchasing return tickets or a weekly travel ticket. For the payment of tickets, the use of existing traditional mechanism such as credit card payments seems overrated especially given that bus fares often involve small amount of money. More micro-payment mechanisms are to be investigated as the payment mode as well as extended services such as real-time bus tracking.

REFERENCES

Ferreira, et al., 2014. A proposal for a public transport ticketing solution based on customers' mobile devices.. *Procedia - Social and Behavioral Sciences,* Volume 111, p. 232 – 241.

Ferreira, M. C., Nóvoa, M. H. & Dias, T. G., 2013. A Proposal for a Mobile Ticketing Solution for Metropolitan Area of Oporto Public Transport. In: J. F. e. C. M. S. H. Nóvoa, ed. *Lecture Notes in Business Information Processing: Exploring Services Science.* Berlin Heidelberg: Springer-Verlag, p. 263–278.

Fontes, T. et al., 2017. Mobile payments adoption in public transport. *Transportation Research Procedia,* Volume 24, p. 410–417.

GSMA, 2016. *Mobile Connectivity Index.* [Online] Available at: https://www.mobileconnectivityindex.com/#year=2016&globalRankings=overall&globalR [Accessed 27 January 2019].

Hootsuite, 2018. *Digital in 2018.* [Online] Available at: https://hootsuite.com/pages/digital-in-2018_[Accessed 27 January 2019].

Kadge, S., Sayyed, S., Buwa, B. & Madraswala, B., 2017. M-Ticketing System using QR Codes for Mumbai Local. *International Journal of Computer Applications,* 162(11).

Lorenzi, D. et al., 2014. Enhancing the government service experience through QR codes on mobile platforms. *Government Information Quarterly,* 31(1), pp. 6-16.

NTA, 2019. *National Transport Authority (NTA) Bus Routes.* [Online] Available at: http://nta.govmu.org/English/Procedures/Documents/Bus-TimeTable_[Accessed 27 January 2019].

Ramalho, J. F. et al., 2018. Luminescent QR codes for smart labelling and. *Optics & Laser Technology,* Volume 101, pp. 304-311.

Ramdhony, D. & Munien, S., 2013. An Investigation on Mobile Banking Adoption. *World Journal of Social Sciences,* 3(3), p. 197 – 217.

Saidi Siuhi, J. M., 2016. Opportunities and challenges of smart mobile applications. *Journal of traffic and transportation engineering (English Edition),* 3(6), pp. 582-592.

T-Mobilitat, 2018. *Intelligent Mobility.* [Online] Available at: https://www.tmb.cat/en/abouttmb/ [Accessed 4 December 2018].

TMSL, 2019. *Introducing Filao Automatic Bus Fare Collection.* [Online] Available at: http://tmsl.mu/ [Accessed 27 Jan 2019].

PERFORMANCE EVALUATION OF AN ADAPTABLE inVANETS-BASED INTERSECTION TRAFFIC CONTROL

Hadeel A. Tabaza, Iman Saeed and Mourad Elhadef[1]
College of Engineering, Abu Dhabi University, Abu Dhabi, UAE
[1]Ph.D.

ABSTRACT

With the recent advances in intelligent vehicles ad-hoc networks (inVANETs), the traditional traffic control problem at intersections is being revisited to cope with the future intelligent transportation systems. In this paper, we introduce the performance evaluation of a centralized inVANETs-based intersection traffic control protocol. Extensive simulations have been conducted using various real traffic scenarios to evaluate the efficiency and the dynamics of the newly proposed traffic control approach that gives the intelligent vehicles full autonomous control of crossing intersections using vehicle-to-vehicle and vehicle-to-infrastructure communications. Simulation results using the tools OMNet++, VEINS, and SUMO showed that the new approach is a viable alternative and addition to the existing traffic control approaches.

KEYWORDS

Smart cities, Intelligent Transportation Systems, Intersection Traffic Control, Distributed Algorithms, Intelligent Vehicles ad-hoc networks (inVANETs)

1. INTRODUCTION

An important part of Intelligent Transportation System (ITS) is the intersection traffic control, as it needs to adapt to the increasing number of congestions as well as emergencies and accidents (Wei 2014), (Srinivasan 2006), (Baras et al. 2017). Many applications for ITS were proposed such as collision avoidance, traffic surveillance which make the way to the next generation of smart cities. Numerous solutions were proposed to control intersections automatically. The conventional solutions mostly concentrated on improving the scheduling of the traffic lights to reduce congestion as well as increasing the vehicles flow on the intersections, (Chen 2010). The new approaches focus on more intelligent scheduling of traffic lights depending mainly on computational intelligence for example like evolutionary genetic algorithm (Chen 2010), (Zhao 2012), machine learning (Gokulan 2010), fuzzy logic (Qiao 2011), (Lertworawanich 2011), (Gokulan 2010), and neural networks (Wei 2014), (Qiao 2011). For more details the readers can read this survey (Bhatt 2010), (Hassan and Elhadef 2018), (Saeed and Elhadef 2017).

The insufficiencies were shown by Wu et al (Wu 2014) in this approach such as deciding the optimal time for the green light knowing the subtleties of the flow of the traffic. Moreover, the algorithms of computational intelligence consume time thus aren't suitable for real time traffic control. Advanced communication and sensing technologies were proposed in (Srinivasan 2006), (Lee 2010), (Zhou 2010) which are being used to allow real time traffic response for green light traffic control that uses a type of control strategy deduced from preselected logic rules and traffic data to schedule traffic lights. Another approach was the trajectory maneuver has been discussed in (Lee 2010), (Zhou 2010), (Tubaishat 2009), (Glaser et al. 2010). This approach is built on an intersection controller that handles the trajectories of the vehicles knowing the conditions of the nearby vehicles to prevent any possibility for an overlap. In this approach, the vehicles are able to move without the need to stop, and this leads to enhancing the system's efficiency. Numerous ways have been studied in order to calculate the ideal trajectories, such as fuzzy logic (Raravi 2007), merging (Dresner 2008), cell-based (Bulgannawar 1995), scenario-driven (Milans et al. 2010), global adjusting, and exception handling (Srinivasan 2006). There are some insufficiencies in the trajectory maneuver approach such as the trajectory calculation complexity and being reliant on a centralized controller causes this approach to be costly, and likely to single point of failure.

In this paper, we are going to evaluate the proposed novel adaptable centralized intersection control for intelligent transportation systems, which relies on inVANETs. The intersection control algorithm that is based on inVANETs contains two tasks: the vehicleTask, and the controllerTask. The two tasks work with each other using the exchange of messages to let the vehicles cross an intersection with no conflicts at all. This work is based on the centralized algorithm that was developed in (Wu 2014) that considers the existence of traffic controller that its role to give the privilege of passing the intersection to the vehicles requesting to cross. The centralized approach considers that if the controller gives the passing to a queue of vehicles on the intersection, then it waits until the release message is received from the last vehicle in the queue, or in real life situations there might be a delay for vehicles due to bottleneck congestion, or accidents, which make using this centralized approach impractical. The traditional scheduling of traffic light overcomes the situation by changing the lights to red for a certain amount of time to allow the vehicles to pass while resolving the situation. The adaptable inVANETs work proposes a solution to solve the weakness in the original centralized approach, which adapts this approach to real scenarios. In the controller-based approach, an algorithm for locks is being used to give or reject access to the intersection the waiting vehicles can cross the intersection when the controller has locked the lanes that are conflicting successfully. When a vehicle reaches the queuing area, it sends a request to the controller to lock the conflicting lanes. The controller, which manages the locks, will reply to the vehicle with a message to give it access to the intersection. The objective of the controller is to guarantee the efficiency of the mutual exclusion as well as maximize the number of vehicles passing in the intersection simultaneously. The paper is organized in this approach. In Section 2, we discuss preliminary definitions, and explain the system model. In Section 3, we discuss the algorithm, the messages, and other details of the new adaptable inVANETs-based intersection control. In Section 4, we discuss the application of algorithm in Abu Dhabi, and in Section 5 we discuss the performance evaluation results. In Section 6, we conclude the paper.

2. PRELIMINARY

The adopted system model was developed by (Wu 2014). Consider this example of an intersection having four directions (Figure 1), and the lanes are numbered from l0 to l7. The *core area* is the area of the small dashed square, and the larger area is the one called the *queuing area*. Each vehicle will have the state of *CROSSING* in the core are, and the state will be either *WAITING* or *QUEUING* in the queuing area. The rules of the traffic intersection state that the vehicles having crossing paths such as l_0, and l_6 should pass the intersection mutually exclusively. These lanes are supposed to be *conflicting* and represented by $\propto$. The vehicles having non-crossing paths such as l_0, and l_4 can pass the intersection at the same time. These lanes are considered to be *concurrent* and represented by $\approx$. Using this definition, we have $l_0 \propto l_6$, and $l_0 \approx l_4$. In (Wu 2014) the concurrency and conflict relationships were represented using a graph, which can be used with any type of intersection.

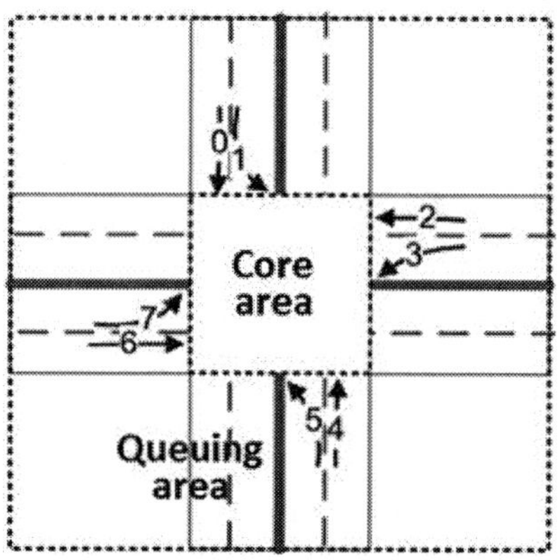

Figure 1. A Typical intersection

It is assumed that each vehicle has its own *ID* and is self-driven. The vehicles count on their sensors, and other devices for navigation, and collision avoidance. In addition, each vehicle is able to detect the core, and queuing areas' limits using the positioning system of the vehicle such as GPS, as well as sensors placed at the limits of the areas. Vehicles have devices for wireless communication that allow the vehicle to communicate in vehicle-to-infrastructure communication or vehicle-to-vehicle communication. In addition, the vehicles are equipped with wireless FIFO channels. It is assumed that the message transmission is reliable, and the range of transmission is larger than the length of the queuing area. Therefore, all the vehicles in the queuing area creating a one-hop ad-hoc network, which allows any set of vehicles to directly communicate.

In Figure 2 you can see the transition of states of the vehicle. Any vehicle will start in the *IDLE* state if it's outside of the intersection area. The state of the vehicle will change when it enters the queuing area to *WAITING*. When the vehicle is in this state, it will request the access to the core area from the controller and waits for the approval from the controller. When the controller gives the access the vehicle, the state of the vehicles changes to *QUEUING*. The vehicles having the *QUEUING* state cross the core area in a first-in-first-out fashion. The vehicles that are delayed and cannot cross the core area in a specified certain time, their state will change to *WAITING* again. Moreover, the vehicle that change its position to another lane which is conflicting while being the *QUEUING* state, its state will also change to *WAITING*. Then the vehicle needs to send the request to cross again to the controller to cross the intersection. The vehicle state is changed to *CROSSING* when it enters the core area. Finally, when the vehicle crosses the core area, and leaves, the state is changed to *IDLE*.

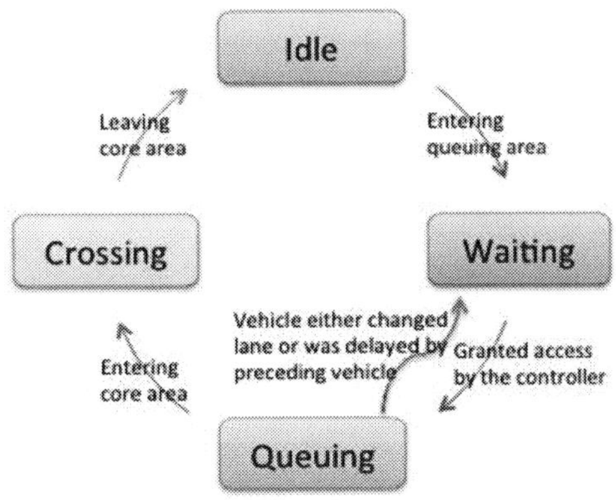

Figure 2. Vehicle State transition diagram

In (Wu 2014), they showed the intersection traffic control like a vehicle mutual exclusion for intersections (VMEI) problem, which says that at the intersection, each vehicle sends a request in whatever direction it desires. Therefore, the vehicles queue up at the equivalent lanes in the queuing area. The vehicles can pass the intersection in the same time if they are in the same lane or concurrent lanes. Also in (Wu 2014), the correctness properties are summarized in order to give any solution to the problem as in the terms of *safety*, *liveness*, and *fairness*, shown below.

Safety (mutual exclusion): at any given moment, in the core area, no conflicting vehicles can be in it. If there was more than one vehicle, these vehicles should be concurrent with each other.

Liveness (deadlock free): any vehicle in waiting state will be given the access to the core area in a finite time.

Fairness (starvation free): each vehicle should be able to pass, after a finite number of vehicles pass the intersection, and all the lanes share the same priority.

3. AN ADAPTABLE INVANETS-BASED INTERSECTION TRAFFIC CONTROL ALGORITHM

In (Wu 2014), the first algorithm that was developed to solve the VMEI problem was called the centralized algorithm. It considers the existence of a controller which its role to give privilege to requesting vehicles to pass the intersection. It is shown that the algorithm mentioned in (Wu 2014) does not satisfy the properties of safety, liveness, and fairness. There is an error in the locking mechanism that does not satisfy the safety property. This algorithm considers the existence of traffic controller that its role to give the privilege of passing the intersection to the vehicles requesting to cross. The centralized approach considers that if the controller gives the passing to a queue of vehicles on the intersection, then it waits until the release message is received from the last vehicle in the queue, or in real life situations there might be a delay for vehicles due to bottleneck congestion, or accidents, which make using this centralized approach impractical. The traditional scheduling of traffic light overcomes the situation by changing the lights to red for a certain amount of time to allow the vehicles to pass while resolving the situation.

The adaptable inVANET work proposes a solution to solve the weakness in the original centralized approach, which adapts this approach to real scenarios. In the controller-based approach, an algorithm for locks is being used to give or reject access to the intersection the waiting vehicles can cross the intersection when the controller has locked the lanes that are conflicting successfully. When a vehicle reaches the queuing area, it sends a request to the controller to lock the conflicting lanes. The controller, which manages the locks, will reply to the vehicle with a message to give it access to the intersection. The objective of the controller is to guarantee the efficiency of the mutual exclusion as well as maximize the number of vehicles passing in the intersection simultaneously.

The controller preserves one lock per lane, therefore, for the intersection shown in Figure 1 eight locks are going to be used. Since the safety property was not satisfied by (Wu 2014), the locking mechanism was improved and correcting, and still relies on the same idea of locking two conflicting lanes.

Table 1. The lane-locking scheme

Vehicle's lane	**0**	**1**	**2**	**3**	**4**	**5**	**6**	**7**
Lanes to be locked	0 5 7	1 3 6	1 2 7	0 3 5	1 3 4	2 5 7	3 5 6	1 4 7

The inVANETs-based intersection control algorithm consists of two parts: the *vehicleTask* and the *controllerTask*. The following representation $state_i$ which designate the state of the vehicle which has the state *IDLE*, when the vehicle is outside the area of intersection, the state *WAITING*, when the vehicle sent a request to the controller to cross the intersection and still waiting for the controller reply to cross, the state *CROSSING*, which shows that the vehicle is crossing the intersection area, and finally, the state *CROSSED* which shows that the vehicle crossed the intersection. $Lane_i$ represents the lane of the vehicle. *crossingLists* denotes the list of vehicles that the controller accepted their request message and is allowing them to cross the intersection. Any vehicle in that list can move and then cross the intersection area.

These five messages are exchanged between the *vehicleTask* and the *controllerTask*:

- <*REQUEST, i,* $lane_i$>: The vehicle *i* sends this message to the controller to indicate its lane and that it wants to cross the intersection.
- <*CROSS, lane, vehiclesList, duration*>: message sent by the controller to order waiting vehicles in *vehiclesList* to cross the intersection within the specified *duration.*
- <*DELAYED, i,* $lane_i$>: vehicle *i* sends this message to inform the controller that it failed in crossing the intersection within the specified duration.
- <*NEWLANE, i,* $lane_i$>: vehicle *i* moved into a new lane that conflicts with its old position.
- <*CROSSED, i*>: vehicle *i* informs the controller that it crossed the intersection.

3.1 *VehicleTask* Operations

In Figure 3 we show the main steps on the *vehicleTask* as it communicates with the *controllerTask.* When a vehicle *i* enters the queuing area it sends a request message to the controller <*REQUEST, i,* $lane_i$> to the controller to get permission to cross the intersection (Step 1.1), the vehicle *i* state updates to WAITING which means that the vehicle is waiting for the reply from the controller that gives the vehicle the access to the intersection. While the vehicle is waiting to get the access from the controller, the vehicle may transfer to another lane that is conflicting with the old position that was sent earlier to the controller, so in that case, the vehicle sends the message <*NEWLANE, i,* $lane_i$> to the controller to notify it about the change (step 1.5). Any vehicle *i* can be in the intersection area while crossing or outside of it after crossing or in the queuing area, and as a result of that, the vehicle state changes correspondingly.

When any vehicle *i* receives the message <*CROSS, vehiclesList*> and *i* is in the *vehiclesList,* only then the vehicle can cross the intersection. It was assumed in (Wu 2014) that when the controller grants the cross to a list of vehicles, the controller has to wait until it receives a message from the last vehicle in the list to confirm that every vehicle crossed which can lead to delays in real life scenarios if a slow driver is driving the vehicle or a congestion happened in the intersection. To solve this problem, a duration period was added, which is set by the controller after which the vehicles that are delayed will not get access to the intersection until the controller decides based on the waiting list. When this period elapses, any vehicle *i*, which was delayed and was not able to cross the intersection, this vehicle will receive the delayed message <*DELAYED, vehiclesList*> in order to be notified by the controller that this vehicle has been changed to the waiting state again. In addition, in order to solve the situation where a vehicle may have changed its lane to a conflicting one after sending the *REQUEST* message, in the *CROSS* message, the lane that was given access to the intersection was added.

In (Elhadef 2015), (Wu 2014), it was assumed that the last vehicle in the vehicles list to cross the intersection is the vehicle that will notify the controller by sending a message noted as *RELEASE*. When taking into consideration that the vehicles may get delayed and aren't able to cross the intersection in the specified period of time, the algorithm was changed to make the vehicle send the *CROSSED* message to the controller when it crosses the intersection (step 1.6), and in that way the controller will know which vehicles already crossed the intersection, and which vehicles were delayed because they will send the *DELAYED* message.

Algorithm 1 *VehicleTask*

```
Initialization //tasks performed by vehicle i
    State_i = IDLE; crossingList = ∅;
CoBegin
  1.1. Vehicle i enters the queuing area:
         Send (<REQUEST, i, lane_i>, Controller);
         oldLane_i = lane_i;
         State_i = WAITING; // wait for message CROSS from Controller

  1.2. Vehicle i's GPS position changed:
       if (i's position in IntersectionArea) State_i = CROSSING;
       else if (State_i = CROSSING & i's position out
                 IntersectionArea)
            State_i = CROSSED;

  1.3. Receive (<CROSS, vehiclesList>) from controller:
         if (State_i = WAITING & i ∈ vehiclesList) {
              State_i = QUEUING;
              crossingList = vehiclesList;
              Move and cross the intersection; }

  1.4. Receive (<DELAYED, vehiclesList>) from controller:
         if (State_i = QUEUING & i ∈ vehiclesList)
              State_i = WAITING;

  1.5. Lane change detected:
         if (State_i = QUEUING & oldLane_i ∝ lane_i) {
              Send (<NEWLANE, i, lane_i>, Controller);
              oldLane_i = lane_i;
              State_i = WAITING; }

  1.6. State_i = CROSSED //Vehicle i crossed the intersection:
         Send (<CROSSED, i>, Controller);
         State_i = IDLE;
CoEnd
```

Figure 3. The *vehicleTask* inVANETs-based intersection control algorithm

3.2 *ControllerTask* Operations

The *controllerTask* main steps are shown in Figure 4 $locks_i$ represents the set of lanes that are going to be locked for vehicle *i* (refer to Table 1) and *locked* represents the set of lanes that are already locked by the controller at any certain point of time. When the controller receives <*REQUEST, i, lane$_i$*> from the vehicle *i* which is sending a request in order to cross the intersection (step 2.1), first, the controller examines if the set of lanes to be locked for this vehicle are already locked by the controller then at that time *i* is added to the *crossingList* of vehicles which are given the access to the intersection, and then the controller broadcasts the cross message <CROSS, crossingList> to the vehicles in the *crossingList* to notify them that they are able to cross the intersection. However, if the controller didn't lock any lane then vehicle *i*, and the other vehicles on concurrent lanes with vehicle *i* can cross the intersection. Else, in that case, the controller adds vehicle *i* to the *waitingList*. The controller also sets the *crossingTimer* to certain duration, and hence giving the access to the intersection for a period that is limited. Also, the controller may receive the new lane message <*NEWLANE, i , newLane*> from the vehicle that changed its lane. Then the controller updates its information. If the vehicle sending this message changed its lane to a conflicting one with the old one, which has been granted access to the intersection and is in the *crossingList*, then the vehicle i is moved from the *crossingList* to the *waitingList*. (Step 2.2). When the controller receives the message crossed *<CROSSED, i>* which informs the controller that the vehicle *i* crossed the intersection, and after that the controller updates the information in the *crossingList*, and when it the *crossingList* becomes empty then the controller gives access to the intersection to the first vehicle in *waitingList*.

The controller uses the *crossingTimer* for the implementation of fairness property. The fairness property means that any vehicle will have the chance to cross the intersection after a finite amount of time (step 2.4). When the timer finishes, the controller examines first if there are waiting vehicles. If there is, the controller checks if the vehicles that were given access to cross the intersection crossed the intersection or not. If some of these vehicles were delayed the controller will send them the delayed message *<DELAYED, crossingList>* to notify these vehicles that they need to wait up until the next round. In order to manage the situation of a vehicle being currently in the intersection, then the timer waits for another *crossingDuration* before giving the access to other vehicles to cross the intersection. If there are no vehicles waiting then the controller extends the duration for crossing to delayed vehicles.

Algorithm 2 *ControllerTask*

```
Initialization //tasks performed by the controller
  crossingList = waitingList = locked = ∅;
CoBegin
  2.1. Receive (<REQUEST, i, lane_i>) from vehicle i:
      if (locks_i ⊂ locked ) {
        crossingList = crossingList ∪ {i};
        Broadcast (<CROSS, crossingList>);
      else if (locked = ∅) {
        locked = locks_i;
        crossingList = all vehicles in waitingList and on lanes  concurrent to lane_i;
        broadcast (<CROSS, crossingList>);
        SetTimer(crossingTimer, duration); }
      else waitingList = waitingList ∪ {i};

  2.2. Receive (<NEWLANE, i, newLane>) from vehicle i:
      if (i ∈ crossingList & lane_i ∝ newLane) {
        crossingList = crossingList - {i};
        waitingList = waitingList ∪ {i}; }
      Update lane_i in waitingList using newLane;

  2.3. Receive (<CROSSED, i>) from vehicle i:
      crossingList = crossingList – {i};
      if (crossingList = ∅) {
        Let j be the first vehicle in waitingList;
        locked = locks_j;
        crossingList = all vehicles in waitingList and on lanes concurrent to lane_j;
        Broadcast (<CROSS, crossingList>);
        ResetTimer(crossingTimer, duration); }

  2.4. Timeout of crossingTimer:
      if (waitingList ≠ ∅)
        if (crossingList ≠ ∅) {
            Broadcast (<DELAYED, crossingList>);
            Wait(crossDuration); }
        Let j be the first vehicle in waitingList;
        locked = locks_j;
        crossingList = all vehicles in waitingList and on lanes concurrent to lane_j;
        Broadcast (<CROSS, crossingList>);
        ResetTimer(crossingTimer, duration); }
      else if (crossingList ≠ ∅)
         ResetTimer(crossingTimer, duration);
CoEnd
```

Figure 4. The *controllerTask* inVANETs-based intersection control algorithm

4. APPLICATION OF AN ADAPTABLE inVANETS-BASED INTERSECTION TRAFFIC CONTROL ALGORITHM ON A REAL-LIFE INTERSECTION IN ABU DHABI

In this section, we will discuss the application of the algorithm on a real-life intersection in Abu Dhabi. Mainly, Abu Dhabi City has intersection has around 4 lanes in each road, so the intersection will have around 15 lanes, as seen in Figure 5, and Figure 6. Therefore, when applying the locks table, we will get this locks table for 16 lanes.

Figure 5. An intersection in Abu Dhabi

Each lane will lock its lane with 4 conflicting lanes, but we need to take in consideration that some of the lanes are *"twins"*, which means that these lanes are *identical* which means they are *concurrent* with each other, and concurrent with the same lanes, as well as conflict with the same lanes on the road. Referring to Table 2, In order to solve this issue, the twin lanes will have the same locks, and when 1 lane of the twin requests to lock it will mean the other twin lane is concurrent and shares the same locks. For example, when a vehicle *i* in l_0 requests the access to the intersection from the controller, and the controller locks l_0 locks, it means that it will allow a vehicle *j* on l_1 to cross as well since it shares the same exact locks with l0 which are l_{10}, l_{11}, l_{014}, and l_{15}. Similarly, like Table 1. If a vehicle *i* is concurrent with the lane that the controller already has its locks it will get access to the intersection, for example like $l_0 \approx l_2$. Also, if vehicle *i* is on a conflicting lane then the controller will request it to wait. For example, like $l_1 \propto l_4$.

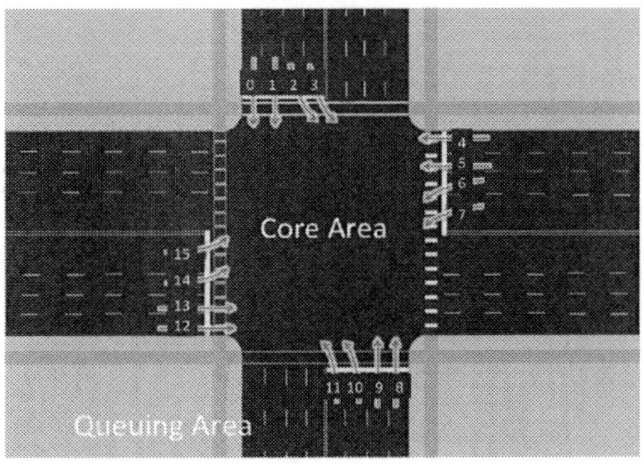

Figure 6. View of an intersection in Abu Dhabi

5. SIMULATION RESULTS

In order to check the performance of the developed algorithm, we analyzed simulation results generated on different metrics that depend on mainly on the traffic of vehicles in the simulation.

5.1 Simulation Environment

We developed our algorithm based on VEINS, an open source framework for the simulation of vehicular networks in which it uses Omnet++, and SUMO to simulate the vehicular networks. We used a map of a real intersection in the city of Abu Dhabi, and it was created using Open Street Map, which is a geographic data tool. In Figure 7, we can see the traffic in the simulation generated.

We ran our algorithm on nine simulations generated with different scenarios. In figure 8, we can see that the vehicles are distributed in an almost non-uniform fashion on four different roads.

Table 2. The lane locking scheme for an intersection in Abu Dhabi

Vehicle's lane	**0**	**1, 2**	**3, 4**	**5**	**6, 7**	**8, 9**
Lanes to be locked	0 6 7	(1,2) 13 14 18 19	(3,4) 8 9 16 17	5 11 12	(6,7) 3 4 18 19	(8,9) 1 2 13 14
Vehicle's lane	**10**	**11,12**	**13, 14**	**15**	**16, 17**	**18, 19**
Lanes to be locked	10 16 17	(11,12) 3 4 8 9	(13, 14) 6 7 18 19	15 1 2	(16, 17) 8 9 13 14	(18, 19) 3 4 11 12

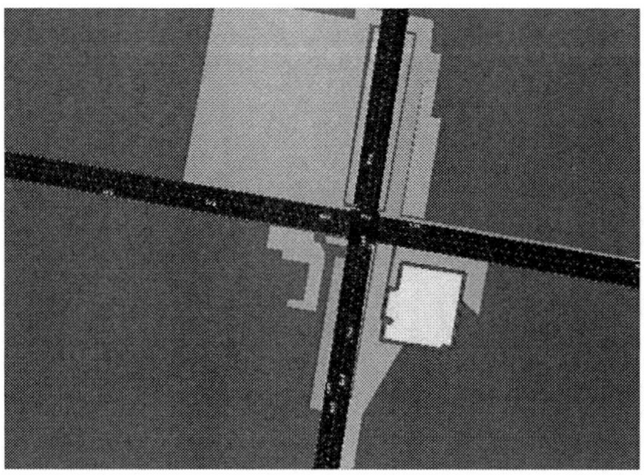

Figure 7. Simulation on Omnet++ and SUMO

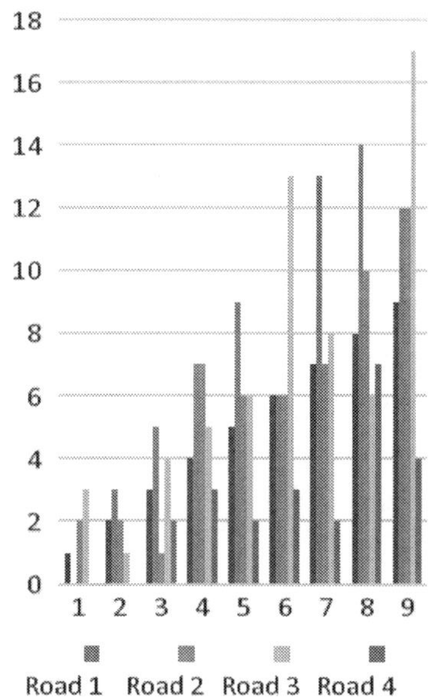

Figure 8. Distribution of vehicles on roads on scenarios

5.2 Simulation Metrics

The size of the intersection that we are using is 200m * 200m. The transmission reaches up to 510m, and we use IEEE 802.11p for the communication in the network since it is a wireless communication protocol environment that are vehicular. The algorithm was used on different scenarios having different numbers of vehicles ranging between 0 to 50. The simulation time varies depending on the number of vehicles as it is from the range of 51s to 150s. We will show the results based on these performance metrics:

- *Average message cost*: Average number of messages that is sent by each vehicle from the time it entered the queuing area till it crosses the intersection.
- *Average queue length*: Average number of waiting vehicles in queue area.
- *Average waiting time*: Average duration that each vehicle stays from the time it entered the queuing area till it crosses the intersection.
- *System throughput*: Number of vehicles that crosses the intersection in each minute.

5.3 Average Message Cost

In Figure 9, we can see the different messages sent on the network whether they are from the vehicles or the controller. Each vehicle is allowed to send one request message to the controller, and then the controller decides which vehicles that will get the permission to cross based on the locking mechanism and send a cross message to the vehicles who are allowed to cross based on that mechanism. The vehicles then cross the intersection and send the crossed message to the controller. In addition, the controller has a crossing timer that will allow the waiting vehicles to get a chance to cross the intersection; therefore, in that case, it will send the delayed message to the vehicles in order to give the permission to other vehicles to cross the intersection.

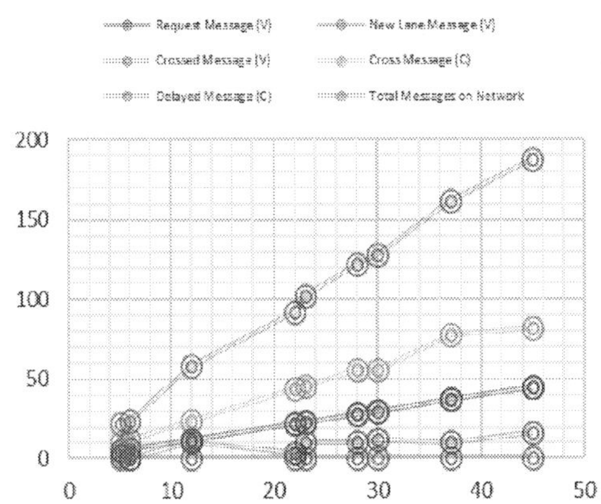

Figure 9. Messages on the Network

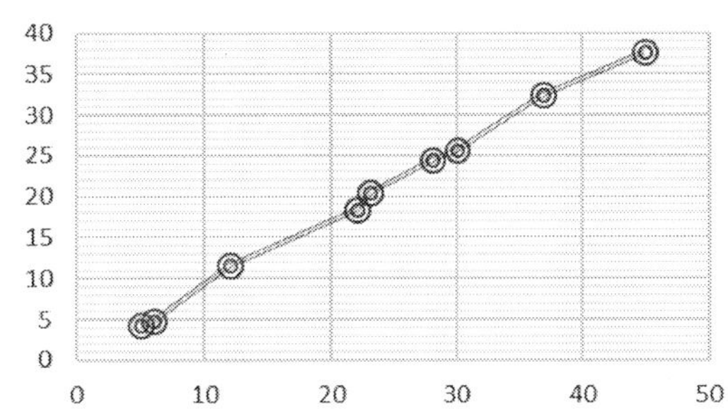

Figure 10. Average Message Cost

In figure 10, we can see the average message cost in the network, we can notice as we increase the number of vehicles in each simulation, the average messages increases steadily.

5.4 Average Queue Length

We can see in figure 11, the Average Queue Length, we notice that the queue length depends on the scenario itself, so we can see it might increase or decrease depending on the real traffic generated by the scenarios we have. We can notice that there is no steady increase in this figure.

5.5 Average Waiting Time

In figure 12, the simulation results show that the Average Waiting Time depends on the Average Queue length of the scenario, so if the scenario has a longer queue, the vehicles will have a longer waiting time, so the waiting time does not increase steadily, but instead increases or decrease based on the traffic generated by the scenario.

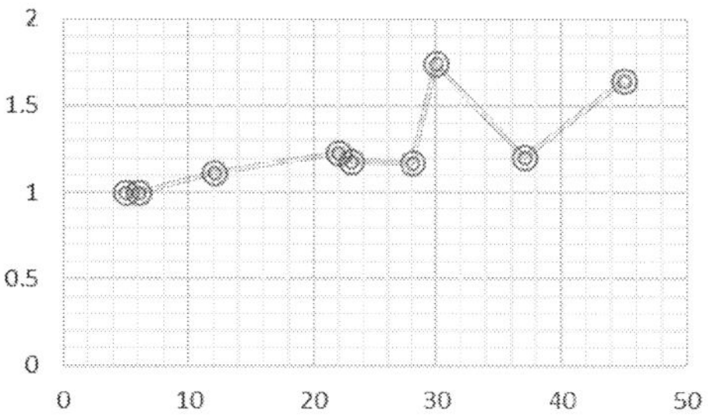

Figure 11. Average Queue Length

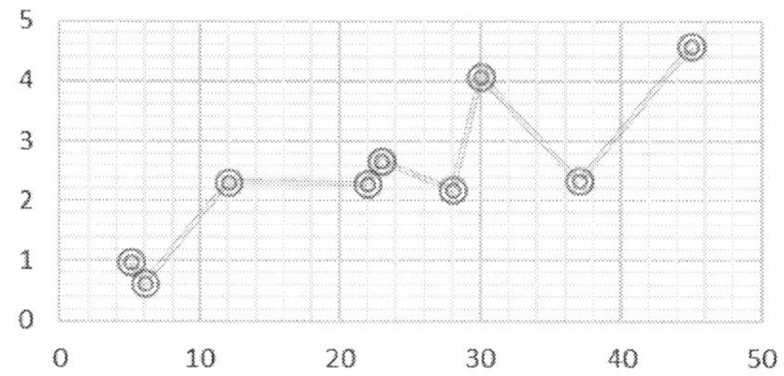

Figure 12. The Average Waiting Time

5.6 *System Throughput*

The simulation results shown in figure 13 display the system throughput throughout the different simulations we have generated. When we notice previous graphs, we can see that the throughput is in relation with the Average Queue Length and the Average Waiting Time, the scenarios that have longer queues, and waiting times have less system throughput, but in general there's an increase in the system throughput using the algorithm we created.

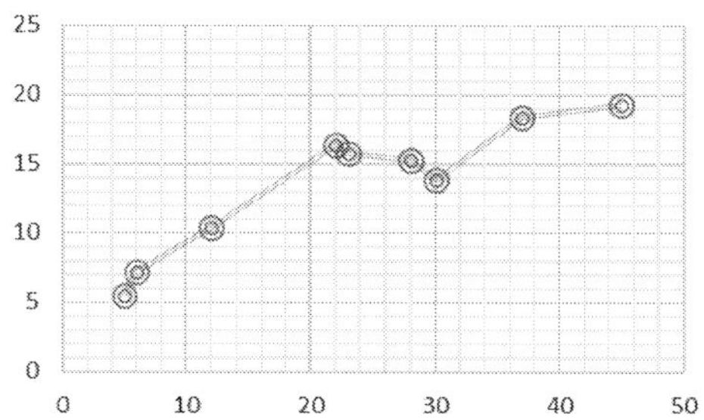

Figure 13. System Throughput 1/M

6. CONCLUSION

In this paper, we discussed developed novel adaptable centralized intersection control for ITS (Intelligent Transportation Systems) which depends on inVANETs (Intelligent Vehicular ad-hoc Networks). The intersection control based on inVANETs contains two main parts: the vehicleTask, and the controllerTask. These two tasks exchange message and cooperate to make the vehicles able to cross the intersection without suffering from any type of conflicts.

In addition, we also, applied the algorithm on an intersection in Abu Dhabi, and explained the improvements necessary in order to be applied with no issues, since the intersections in Abu Dhabi are much larger than the intersection proposed in the algorithm.

We also performed extensive performance evaluation of the algorithm and displayed the results for this evaluation. The traffic in the scenarios were in a non-uniform fashion, we showed statistics involving the message cost, the queue length, the waiting time, and the throughput in each scenario of these different scenarios.

ACKNOWLEDGEMENT

This work is supported by ADEK Award for Research Excellence (A2RE) 2015 and office of Research and Sponsored Programs, Abu Dhabi University.

REFERENCES

Bhatt V. (2010). "Group Mutual Exclusion in O(log n) RMR", Proc. 29th ACM SIGACT-SIGOPS Symp. Principles of Distributed Computing (PODC-10), pp.45 -54.

Bulgannawar S. (1995). "A Distributed K-Mutual Exclusion Algorithm", Proc. 15th Int. Conf. Distributed Computing Systems (ICDCS).

Chen X. (2002). "Real-Coded Genetic Algorithm for Signal Timings Optimization of a Signal Intersection", Proc. First Int. Conf. Machine Learning and Cybernetics, pp. 1245–1248. IEEE Press, Beijing.

Dresner K. (2008). "A Multiagent Approach to Autonomous Intersection Management", J. Artificial Intelligence Research, vol. 31, no. 1, pp.591 -656.

Elhadef, M. (2015). "An Adaptable inVANETs-Based Intersection Traffic Control Algorithm," IEEE Int. Conference on Computer and Information Technology; Ubiquitous Computing and Communications; Dependable, Autonomic and Secure Computing; Pervasive Intelligence and Computing, no. 6, pp. 2387 – 2392.

Gokulan B.P. (2010). "Distributed Geometric Fuzzy Multiagent Urban Traffic Signal Control", IEEE Trans. Intelligent Transportation Systems, vol. 11, no. 3, pp.714 -727.

Lee J. (2012). "Development and Evaluation of a Cooperative Vehicle Intersection Control Algorithm Under the Connected Vehicles Environment", IEEE Trans. Intelligent Transportation Systems, vol. 13, no. 1, pp.81 -90.

Lertworawanich P. (2011). "A New Multiobjective Signal Optimization for Oversaturated Networks", IEEE Trans. Intelligent Transportation Systems, Vol. 12(4), pp.967 -976.

Qiao J. (2011). "Two-Stage Fuzzy Logic Controller for Signalized Intersection", IEEE Trans. Systems, Man and Cybernetics-Part A: Systems and Humans, vol. 41, no. 1, pp.178 -184.

Raravi G. (2007). "Merge Algorithms for Intelligent Vehicles", Proc. GM R&D Workshop, pp.51 -65.

Srinivasan D. (2006). "Neural Networks for Real-Time Traffic Control System", IEEE Trans. Intelligent Transportation Systems, Vol. 7(3), pp.261 -272.

Tubaishat M. (2009). "Wireless Sensor Networks in Intelligent Transportation Systems", Wireless Comm. and Mobile Computing, vol. 9, no. 3, pp.287 -302.

Wei Ni (2014). "A Message Efficient Intersection Control Algorithm Based on VANETs," Internet of Vehicles - Technologies and Services, Lecture Notes in Computer Science Volume 8662, pp 31-41.

Wu W.G. (2015). "Distributed Mutual Exclusion Algorithms for Intersection Traffic Control," IEEE Transactions on Parallel & Distributed Systems, Vol.26 (1), pp. 65-74.

Zhao D. (2012). "Computational Intelligence in Urban Traffic Signal Control: A Survey", IEEE Trans. Systems, Man, and Cybernetics-Part C: Applications and Reviews, Vol. 42(4), pp.485 -494.

Zhou B. (2010). "Adaptive Traffic Light Control in Wireless Sensor Network-Based Intelligent Transportation System", Proc. IEEE Vehicular Technology Conf. Fall.

Milans V. et al (2010). "Controller for Urban Intersections Based on Wireless Communications and Fuzzy Logic", IEEE Trans. Intelligent Transportation Systems, vol. 11, no. 1, pp.243 -248.

Glaser S. et al (2010). "Maneuver-Based Trajectory Planning for Highly Autonomous Vehicles on Real Road with Traffic and Driver Interaction", IEEE Trans. Intelligent Transportation Systems, vol. 11, no. 3, pp.589 -606.

Hasan S. and M. Elhadef (2018). A Citywide Distributed inVANETs-Based Protocol for Managing Traffic. In Proc. of the *13th International Conference on Future Information Technology (FutureTech 2018)*, Salerno, Italy.

Saeed I. and M. Elhadef (2017). A Distributed inVANETs-Based Intersection Traffic Control Algorithm. In Proc. of the *9th International Conference on Computer Science and its Applications (CSA 2017)*, Taichung, Taiwan.

Baras S., I. Saeed, H. A. Tabaza, and M. Elhadef (2017). VANETs-Based Intelligent Transportation Systems: An Overview. In Proc. of the *11th Int. Conference on Multimedia and Ubiquitous Engineering*, Seoul, Korea.

INTEGRATED METHODOLOGICAL FRAMEWORK FOR SMART CITY DEVELOPMENT

Zineb Korachi and Bouchaib Bounabat
ALQUALSADI Team, ADMIR Laboratory Rabat Information Technology Center
ENSIAS/Mohamed V University in Rabat Rabat, Morocco

ABSTRACT

Making a city smart requires a strategy to meet the problems generated by the urban population growth and rapid urbanization. Many cities are treating projects of city transformation into a smart city as typical IT projects. In fact, there is a basic challenge of understanding the drivers behind city transformation and building a solid strategy planning to support and guide this transformation. To meet these challenges, this work proposes a methodology for defining and evaluating digital strategies for building smart cities. It presents how to develop and implement strategies for smart city development. Despite extensive and deep research on cities' successful transformation into smart cities, a gap exists on the methodology that the cities follow in transforming their services into digital services and making them smarter. This work builds on an integrative literature review of smart cities and digital strategies to propose an integrated methodology for smart cities development.

KEYWORDS

Digital Strategy, Smart City, Smart City Strategy, Key Performance Indicators (KPIs), Smart City Evaluation, City Dashboard

1. INTRODUCTION

Today, 55% of the world's population lives in urban areas, a proportion that is expected to increase to 68% by 2050 (UN DESA, 2018). This rapid urbanization is adding pressure to the existing resource base while increasing the demand for energy, water, sanitation, and public services such as education and health care (ITU-T FG-SSC, 2015a). To meet the growing needs associated with the increasing urban population, cities require an innovative strategy to achieve smart sustainable development, cities need transforming their services towards smart services.

Currently, the city's systems operate within silos and there is little or no cooperation between them (Budde, 2019). ICT (Information and Communication Technologies) can be the bridge between these silos which allow managing the city in a better way. ICT is able to create interoperability between silos via different technologies and frameworks like EAI (Enterprise Application Integration) and SOA (Service-Oriented Architecture Concept). The interrelationship between a smart city's core systems is taken into account to make them smarter (Chourabi et al., 2012). No system operates in isolation. In this sense, Kanter and Litow (Kanter and Litow, 2009) consider a smarter city as an organic whole—as a network, as a linked system.

Although there are several works on cities' successful transformation into smart cities, there is still not a clear and integrative methodology for smart city development. This paper attempts to start filling this gap by providing an integrated methodological framework for smart city development based on the exploration of an extensive array of literature from various fields such as smart cities, digital strategies, and smart city evaluation.

Strategy, not technology, drives digital transformation (KANE et al., 2015). Our framework addresses strategy, design, implementation, evaluation, and use of smart cities initiatives. It is used to characterize how to envision a smart city and to design and assess smart transformation strategy. This research presents a smart city integrated approach, which comprises a platform to support and monitor the building of a smart city. The methodology is consisting of three phases: strategic vision, action plan, and management strategy. The paper presents an interesting framework for smart city evaluation. This evaluation framework is based on a list of meaningful KPIs that helps a city assess its smart transformation. It is a continual process of improvement that scrutinizes the city's positioning in terms of its competitiveness, ICT capabilities and the quality of its smart services.

The paper is structured as follows: the next section explores related works, followed by a section describing the smart city methodological framework, followed by conclusion and suggestions for future research.

2. RELATED WORKS

2.1 Digital Strategy

A digital strategy is required for a successful city's transformation into a smart city. What makes digital transformation different for cities compared to organizations? There may be a difference between the two transformations, but there is certainly something in common between them. There have been relevant works related to the digital transformation of organizations that can help in cities' digital transformation.

Successful digital transformation is based on a common set of elements (Eder, 2017). Each is a lever you can use to initiate and drive digital transformation in your organizations. Leaders diagnose the potential value of existing corporate assets and build a transformative vision for the future. Then, invest in skills and initiatives to make the vision a reality. Fundamental to the transformation is effective communication, evaluation, and governance to ensure that your firm is moving in the right direction. These common elements are summarized in this work in the following three steps: strategic vision, action plan, and management strategy.

There are differences between digitalization and digitization (Gobble, 2018). In short, digitization is the conversion of atoms to bits (replacing paper with electronic files). Digitalization is the transformation of all those bits into value. Digitization may deliver some savings, most commonly through efficiency gains and reduced error rates, but it doesn't change how the company does business—how it thinks about, creates, and delivers value. Digitalization is what cities need for transforming into smart cities. That kind of transformation doesn't happen by accident (Gobble, 2018). Digitalization is a journey, and a journey needs a map—in this case, a clear roadmap driven by a digital strategy. This roadmap is well expressed in the methodological framework presented in this work.

2.2 Smart City Strategy

Some researchers have developed frameworks and guides to cope with the challenge of digital transformation. Worldwide health organization has developed a National eHealth Strategy that helps to implement ICT in the health system to make it smarter (WHO and ITU, 2012). This strategy is based on the common elements of the digital transformation; however, several objections may be raised to it: it allows the use of ICT only in the health system and it does not offer a tool to facilitate the definition or evaluation of digital strategies. Creative cities such as Montreal rely on community-based and private sector initiatives, living labs, and social entrepreneurship. However, such cities lack the ability to steer and coordinate fragmented efforts (Ben Letaifa, 2015). Small and independent initiatives often fail to grow due to the lack of resources and formal leadership (Ben Letaifa, 2014).

London, Barcelona, Stockholm, and Amsterdam are four major European cities in the process of developing or implementing a smart city strategy (Angelidou, 2016). These smart initiatives are organized around different key themes: innovation, open data, leveraging research technology and creative talent, enabling smarter infrastructure development, and seeking to forge an open environment for collaboration among government, industry, academia, and citizens. Several works have studied frameworks that help organizations in thinking about digital strategy, or technologies that accelerate a given sector digital transformation (e.g. e-Health). However, there is a lack of research of operationalized concepts and models that guide organizations in thinking about strategy formation for driving competitive advantage in the digital age (Boström and Celik, 2019). This work is conceived to fill this gap by providing a methodological framework for defining and evaluating digital strategies for building smart cities.

2.3 Smart City Evaluation

Transformation strategy should be revisited and evaluated on a regular basis and make sure that the action plan for implementing the strategy is on the right track. There are some city evaluation systems like DQSC-MM (Data Quality Driven Smart Cities Maturity Model) that focus on data quality for smart city evaluation (Korachi and Bounabat, 2018). Focusing on data in smart city assessment is very indeed important but not sufficient. A Real-Time Air Pollution Monitoring Systems has been implemented using Wireless Sensor Networks (Guanochanga et al., 2018). It is a very useful dashboard in case of air pollution but cities need an evaluation framework that takes into account all smart city dimensions. The most common smart city dimensions are smart economy, smart people, smart governance, smart mobility, smart environment, and smart living (Giffinger et al., 2007).

For an inclusive evaluation, smart cities can use real-time data. Smart city real-time data can be delivered on various platforms (Lange, 2018). How can cities take advantage of these indicators to monitor the progress of smart city initiatives? Real-time data can be used for smart cities ranking and benchmarking. They can be used by city dashboards to allow the city's users to get up-to-date information about a city and to help decision makers. A city dashboard consists of several modules, each of which contains a number of applications that display various data about the city (Mannaro et al., 2018). In this research, we have developed a smart city ranking system and a real-time dynamic dashboard that allows smart cities evaluation and monitoring.

3. FRAMEWORK FOR DEFINING AND EVALUATING DIGITAL STRATEGIES FOR SMART CITY DEVELOPMENT

In this section, we present a methodology for defining and evaluating digital strategies for building smart cities. This methodology allows establishing a digital strategy to effectively exploit the digital revolution for transforming the way people go about their everyday lives. The methodology consists of two frameworks. The first one is dedicated to defining the strategic plan for the city's smart transformation while the second is dedicated to assessing, ranking and benchmarking smart cities. The second one can evaluate transformation progress and identify the weaknesses and gaps in order to improve them in the next strategic planning.

3.1 Smart City Strategy Framework

The following figure (Fig.1) provides an overview of the phases and key components involved by the smart city strategy framework in the process of establishing a smart city strategic planning.

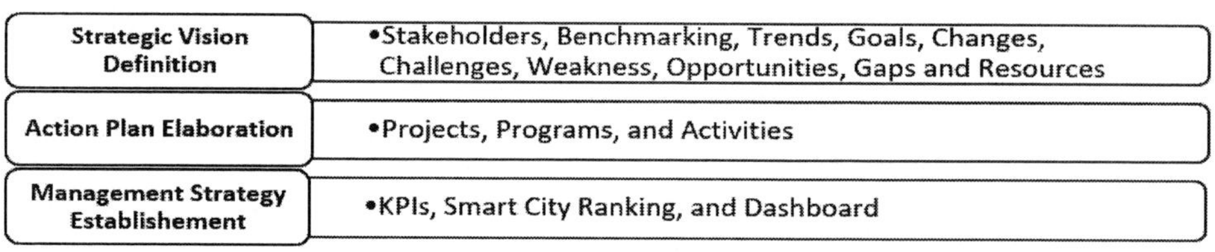

Figure 1. Smart City Strategy Framework

3.1.1 Strategic Vision Definition

The first challenge of the smart transformation is to develop the strategic vision: determine why the city needs to be transformed into a smart city, what are changes and desired outcomes of this transformation, and what are resources required to perform the smart transformation. The following diagram (Figure 2) illustrates the strategic vision development process.

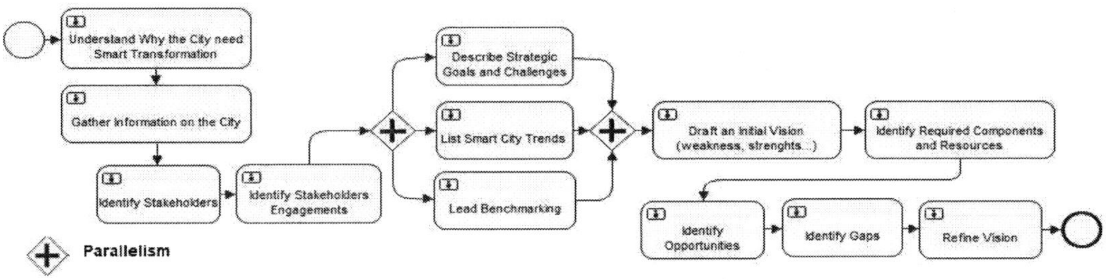

Figure 2. Strategic Vision Development Process

- ***Understand Why the City need Smart Transformation.*** Justify the contribution of ICTs in the city's transformation into a smart city and identify what are strategic objectives of the smart transformation.
- ***Gather Information on the City:*** Cities should study the existing system and the around environment to get a holistic view of the current state of the city and define the framework of the study and work.
- ***Identify Stakeholders and their Engagements.*** Successful stakeholder identification approaches initially require correct contextualization (Fritz et al., 2018). The stakeholders that are indirectly involved in the Smart City project are considered to be part of the operating environment (e.g., government agencies, local communities) and the broad environment (e.g., technological change, global political/legal forces) (Harrison and John, 1998).
- ***Describe Strategic Goals and Challenges.*** Describe in details smart city strategy goals and identify challenges that might face the smart transformation of the city. Example of challenges: cost, devices heterogeneity, diversity of technologies, interoperability, big data analysis, and information security.
- ***List Smart City Trends.*** learn from technologies and trends that have an impact on smart cities (Lea, 2017; Dodson, 2019): open data, e-participation, and smart technologies (e.g., internet of things, data analytics, cloud computing, artificial intelligence, city-wide digital platforms, greater real-time citizen interaction, linking autonomous vehicles with government sensors/networks, increased focus on human-centric technologies).
- ***Lead Benchmarking.*** Research into the experience of smart cities projects of other countries to learn from their successes and failures. Indeed, new smart cities are currently being developed such as (Pellicer et al., 2013; Anthopoulos, 2019): Songdo IBD in South Korea (Songdo.com, 2019), Meixi Lake in China (Madakam and Ramaswamy, 2016), Masdar city in Abu Dhabi (Alzaabi et al, 2018)(Masdar.ae, 2019), PlanIT Valley in Portugal, Skolkovo in Russia (Chudiniva and Afonina, 2018), Tampere (Business Tampere, 2019) and London (London City Hall, 2019).
- ***Draft an Initial Vision.*** The initial vision includes elements to focus on in building a successful smart transformation strategy. Steps to draft initial vision are: (1) determine city strengths and weaknesses, (2) identify the main components that will be introduced or strengthened through the transformation strategy (e.g., leadership, governance, investment, service, application, standard, interoperability, infrastructure, legislation, policy, compliance, workforce (WHO and ITU, 2012)), (3) define desired outcomes, changes, and impact of the smart transformation, (4) and identify required components for achieving desired goals and outcomes.
- ***Refine Vision.*** Identify opportunities and gaps, and refine the list of elements defined in the previous steps. To make a successful smart city, we need to be continually innovating and looking for opportunities.

3.1.2 Action Plan Elaboration

This section is intended to define the process for how a smart city action plan should be prepared to achieve the strategic vision. Strategic planning should be limited to the city as a whole, the businesses, and the important functions. A smart city action plan is a set of smart projects, programs, and activities.

A smart city action plan should determine success potentials. Determining success potentials is the main task of strategic planning (Grünig and Kühn, 2018). Strategic planning is not primarily concerned with optimizing success during the planning period itself. The focus is rather on determining the investments for maintaining existing success potentials and for building up new ones. Success potentials can be defined based on strategic vision elements (e.g. Do we have enough resources to implement the strategy?). The following diagram (Figure 3) presents the process to be followed to build an action plan for city transformation into a smart city.

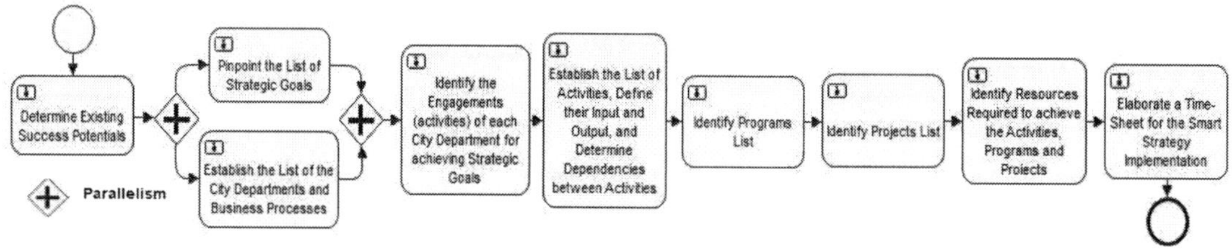

Figure 3. Action Plan Development Process

- ***Determine Existing Success Potentials.*** Existing success potentials should be defined in the strategy development phase whereas new success potentials are detected during strategy implementation.
- ***Pinpoint the List of Strategic Goals.*** This list is already defined in Phase1 (Strategic Vision Definition)
- ***Establish a List of City Departments and Business Processes.*** (e.g., Education and Environment).
- ***Identify the Engagements (activities) of each City Department for achieving Strategic Goals.*** Identify the expected engagements (activities) of each city business process in the achievement of strategic goals.
  Establish the List of Activities, Define their Input and Output, and Determine Dependencies between Activities. Dependencies between activities help to identify their logical sequence, expected duration, and it provides a basis for allocating management responsibility.
- ***Identify the Programs List.*** A program definition depends on the city and its context. A program can be a list of engagements per business processes or per strategic objectives.
- ***Identify the Projects List.*** A project is a set of programs. Based on the programs list identified in the step before, identify projects list and affect each program to the appropriate project.
- ***Establish the List of Resources Required to achieve the Activities, Programs, and Projects.***
- ***Elaborate a Time-Sheet for the Smart Strategy Implementation.*** Elaborate a time sheet containing planning for projects, programs and activities (short-term, mid-term and long-term).

3.1.3 Management Strategy Establishment

The strategy should not be a two-step process, where one team creates a plan and another implements it, with little interaction between the two (Eder, 2017). A strategy is a continual process that needs management and monitoring. To monitor the smart transformation strategy, cities need a management strategy. This section is intended to define the process for how a smart city management strategy should be prepared.

Key Performance Indicators are useful tools for guiding urban development, by efficiently monitoring the sustainable evolution of cities. In this regard, an appropriate set of relevant indicators must be established and properly evaluated (Picioroaga et al., 2018). A management strategy should define a list of indicators that include the perspective of stakeholders and allow to monitor the action plan progress, assess smart strategy results, make appropriate decisions, and perform smart cities ranking and benchmarking.

Goal Question Metric (GQM) is a suitable approach to define relevant KPIs. It is a well-known paradigm proposed by Basili for defining the software measurements (Basili, 1993). The GQM approach identifies three steps. As suggested by its name, the GQM Approach provides a method for defining Goals, refining them into Questions and then defining the Metrics to collect data. This approach has been applied successfully in several contexts (Mannaro et al., 2018; Akbar et al., 2014; Basili et al., 2014; Behkamal et al., 2014; Southekal, 2017) and it will be successful also in the context of this work. GQM defines a top-down approach based on three levels: a conceptual level (Goal); an operational level (Question); and a quantitative level (Metric). This method will help to exploit KPIs for assessing strategic goals defined in the strategic vision. The following process (Fig.4) helps cities develop a management strategy.

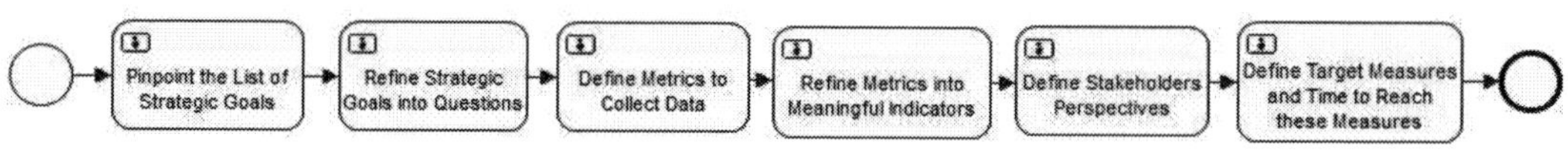

Figure 4. Management Strategy Development Process

3.2 Smart City Evaluation Framework

Appropriate metrics are required in order to assess the contribution that ICTs are making toward smart development of cities. They are needed to measure progress, that is to establish the contribution that ICTs are making to overall social and economic progress as well as to environmental advancements (Lombardi, 2011). These metrics can be used also to help a city understanding exactly where it stands in relation to other cities so that it can establish a starting point in its transformation (Nabil, 2015). Cities need an evaluation framework allowing to exploit these metrics to monitor the contribution of smart initiatives and to perform benchmarking. The proposed smart city framework offers an evaluation system that allows for monitoring strategy progress, performing smart city benchmarking, and identifying the improvements points to deal with in the next strategic planning.

3.2.1 Smart City Key Performance Indicators

Key Performance Indicators allow the city to monitor the outcomes of long-term investments and evaluate their overall impact (Picioroaga et al., 2018). They allow smart cities benchmarking in order to learn from the experience of other smart cities.

In smart cities, the focus is not only on the ICT infrastructure but is mainly on the role of human capital, economy, education, social, and environment. This paper proposes a list of KPIs that enables a holistic smart city evaluation, it allows assessment based on smart city dimensions: smart economy, smart people, smart governance, smart mobility, smart environment, and smart living. Each of these dimensions provides a separate view of progress and when reported together provide a holistic view of a smart city (United Smart Cities, 2019). The KPIs list proposed in this work has been selected from the literature review (ITU-T FG-SSC, 2015b; Lombardi et al., 2012; United smart sustainable cities, 2019; Vogt et al., 2013; ITU-T FG-SSC, 2015c). Selection of this list of KPIs is performed based on the following characteristics: relevance, comprehensiveness, comparability, availability, independence, simplicity, and timeliness. AHP (Analytic Hierarchy Process (Teknomo, 2006)) Model is adopted in order to select the most relevant KPIs. The criteria tree model used in the selection procedure is presented in the diagram below (Figure 5):

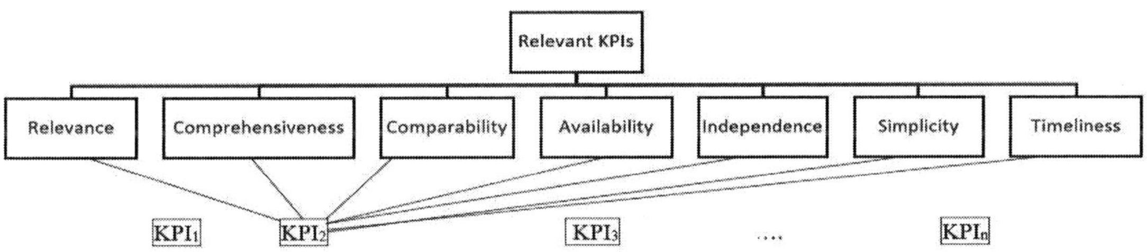

Figure 5. Relevant KPIs AHP Tree

Selected KPIs are presented in the following table (Tab.1) and they are classified according to smart city dimensions. The list cannot be regarded as final, it can be modified in line with policy and time changes and changes in availability, and/or cost-effectiveness of new measurement systems.

Table 1. Smart City KPIs

Dimension	Smart City Key Performances Indicators
Economy	**Network facilities:** Household Internet Access; Fixed Broadband Subscriptions; Wireless Broadband Subscriptions; Wireless Broadband Coverage; Availability of WIFI in Public Areas.
	Information facilities: Percentage of enterprises providing network-based services (e-commerce, e-learning, cloud computing); Proportion of business based on cloud computing; Proportion of business based on GIS (Geographic Information System); Percentage of smart devices by person; Ratio of children online protection; Level of cyber-security.
	Water and Sanitation: Smart Water Meters; Water Supply ICT Monitoring; Drainage Water System ICT Monitoring.
	Electricity Supply: Smart Electricity Meters; Electricity Supply ICT Monitoring; Percentage of renewable energy use; Electricity Saving; Electricity Production; Electricity Peak Response Capacity.

	Innovation : Percentage of hackathons organized per year for the development of the city; Number of Small and Medium-Sized Enterprises; Number of new Enterprises per year; Statistics of entrepreneurs; R&D (Research and Development) Expenditure; Patents; Ratio of knowledge-intensive enterprises; Revenue share of knowledge-intensive enterprise; SSC (Smart Sustainable City) new projects opportunities; Penetration of teleworking system; Improvement of traditional industry with ICT; Proportion of business based on Artificial Intelligence; Employment rate in knowledge-intensive sectors; Percentage of e-commerce transaction amount; Percentage of transaction by card
	Employment: Unemployment Rate; Youth Unemployment Rate; ICT Sector Employment
Living	**Convenience and comfort:** Satisfaction with online commercial and financial services; Satisfaction with environmental safety; Convenience of government services; Convenience of smart traffic information administration and service; Satisfaction with quality of public transport; Satisfaction with crime prevention and security control; Satisfaction with countermeasures against disaster; Satisfaction with food drug safety monitoring; Convenience of urban medical care; Convenience for citizens to access education resource; Perception of proof against risk of poverty; Satisfaction with housing conditions **Security and safety:** Accident prediction ratio; Penetration of ICT for disaster prevention; Publication rate of disaster alert; Penetration of city video surveillance; Natural Disaster Related Deaths; Disaster Related Economic Losses; Resilience Plans; Population Living in; Disaster Prone Areas; Emergency Service Response Time; Police Service; Fire Service; Violent Crime Rate; Local Food Production **Health care:** Percentage of archiving electronic health records for residents; Usage rate of electronic medical records; Sharing rate of resource and information among hospitals; Coverage rate of household e-health services **Education and training:** Effectiveness of hatching smart tech from knowledge centers (research centers, universities, etc.); Penetration of e-learning system; Percentage of courses downloadable from the internet
Mobility	Dynamic Public Transport Information; Traffic Monitoring; Traffic Fatalities
Environment	**Air** : Proportion of information published on environmental quality; Progress degree of ICT in the protection of city water resources; Effect of flood control monitoring by means of ICT measures; Proportion of water pollution control by means of ICT measures; Proportion of air pollution monitoring by means of ICT measures; Proportion of toxic substances monitoring by means of ICT measures; Proportion of noise monitoring by means of ICT measures
	Water and Sanitation: Drinking Water Quality; Water Consumption; Freshwater Consumption; Wastewater Treatment; Solid Waste Treatment; Solid waste disposal management with ICT measures
	Public Space and Nature: Green Areas; Green Area Accessibility; Protected Natural Areas; Recreational Facilities
	Energy: Proposition of Electricity Consumption; Proposition of Residential Thermal Energy Consumption; Improvement of civilian electricity usage (per capita) with ICT measures; Improvement of industrial electricity usage with ICT measures; Improvement of civilian water usage (per capita) with ICT measures; Improvement of industrial water usage with ICT measures; Improvement of fossil fuel usage with ICT; Improvement of rare metal/noble metal usage with ICT measures
Governance	Digital access to urban planning and budget document; Appliance of smart community services; Penetration rate of government online services; E-government usage by individuals; Percentage of government information open; Penetration of smart impediment removal (accessibility) system; No. of universities and research centers in the city; Proposition of open data
People	**Openness and public participation**: Penetration of e-learning system; Improvement of turnout at city hearings by means of ICT; Online civic engagement; Feasibility of appealing online; Atmosphere of free online comment; Contribution in increasing consciousness of citizenship and social coherence
	Education: Student ICT Access; School Enrollment; Higher Education Degrees; Adult Literacy
	Health: Electronic Health Records; Life Expectancy; Maternal Mortality Rate; No. of Physicians per citizen; In-Patient Hospital Beds per citizen; Health Insurance / Public Health Coverage
	Culture : Cultural Expenditure; Cultural Infrastructure
	Housing: Informal Settlements
	Social inclusion: Gender Income Equity; Rate of Poverty; Voter Participation; Child Care Availability

3.2.2 Smart Cities Ranking

To perform Smart Cities Benchmarking, we provide in this section a Smart Cities Ranking System. For calculating the rank (overall score) of a smart city the next steps have been followed:

1) Determine the Weights of Key Performance Indicators

The AHP model helps us calculating KPIs weights using a scale from 1 to 9 (Teknomo, 2006), and using the criteria tree model illustrated in figure 5. KPIs weights should not be assigned by each city, they should be assigned by experts which allow the framework to be useful for benchmarking.

Constructing the judgment matrix. The importance of KPIs can be scaled, using numeric values from 1 to 9. 1 is associated with equally important KPIs, 3 is accorded when KPI i is slightly more important than j, 5 when i is more important than j, 7 when i is strongly more important than j, and 9 when i is absolutely more important than j, while 2, 4, 6 and 8 are associated with intermediate situations (Teknomo, 2006). The pairwise comparison matrix, A=(aij)nxn, is structured as follows (Teknomo, 2006):

$$A = \begin{pmatrix} a_{11} & a_{12} & \cdots & a_{1n} \\ a_{21} & a_{22} & \cdots & a_{2n} \\ \vdots & \vdots & \ddots & \vdots \\ a_{n1} & a_{n2} & \cdots & a_{nn} \end{pmatrix} \qquad (1)$$

***n**: the number of KPIs to be evaluated; **aij**: the importance of the KPI I according to KPI j.*

Estimating the relative weights. Once the judgment matrix is constructed, the relative weights (priorities) of KPIs are estimated, computing the normalized Eigen Vector (W) of the matrix (Teknomo, 2006).

2) *City Rank*

City rank is the scalar product of the weight vector and the vector of values obtained by the city for each KPI.

$$R = \sum_{j=1}^{n}(Vj * Wj) \qquad (2)$$

***R**: the rank of the city; **Vj**: the value obtained by the city for KPI j; **Wj**: the associated weight for KPI j; **n**: the number of evaluated KPIs.*

3.2.3 Smart Cities Evaluation

To evaluate the progress of smart city projects and control the achievement of strategic goals, we should collect strategic goals identified in the previous steps (strategic vision) and adopt the GQM method to define a set of KPIs for each strategic goal. These KPIs will allow assessing and monitoring the achievement of the associated strategic goal using Control Theory in order to control the variation and development of KPIs measurements at any moment of time. The control theory studies the possibility of acting on a dynamical system dependent on the temporal variable in order to lead the state of this system to a given state at a given instant. The dynamical system in this work is R_{SgObj} vector, it is the ranking vector of KPIs, it provides a clear idea of the reality of achievement of the strategic goals at a specific moment in time.

$$\begin{pmatrix} R_{SgObj1}(t_0) \\ R_{SgObj2}(t_0) \\ \vdots \\ R_{SgObjn}(t_0) \end{pmatrix} \Rightarrow \begin{pmatrix} R_{SgObj1}(t) \\ R_{SgObj2}(t) \\ \vdots \\ R_{SgObjn}(t) \end{pmatrix} \Rightarrow \begin{pmatrix} R_{SgObj1}(t_1) \\ R_{SgObj2}(t_1) \\ \vdots \\ R_{SgObjn}(t_1) \end{pmatrix} \qquad (3)$$

As Is **To Be**

*$R_{SgObji} = \sum_{j=1}^{m}(Vj * Wj)$: Rank of KPIs associated to the strategic goal i; **n**: Number of strategic goals; **m**: Number of KPIs associated to the strategic goal i; **t_0**: The initial moment; **t_1**: Moment of reaching objective values of KPIs*

3.2.4 Smart City Dashboard

A city dashboard is a big data platform designed, on the one hand, to allow city's users to get up-to-date information about a city and, on the other hand, to give access to a wide range of datasets about the city to help decision makers (Mannaro et al., 2018). The design of a city dashboard needs a clear vision of the direction that public administrations intend to undertake, alongside an ability to build scenarios and analyze the results of experiments in the context of the changing urban variables.

We may differentiate between ways of displaying information on dashboards, via charts and graphs, diagrams or maps (Kitchin at al., 2015). Distinctions can further be made between indexical interfaces, with a direct reference to the measured object (e.g. an electricity meter), and symbolic interfaces that involve a further translation (e.g. an alarm light indicating an empty tank) (Mattern, 2015), between fixed and interactive visualizations (Kitchin at al., 2015), and between dynamically refreshing or cumulative ones. The evaluation framework proposed in this work offers a real-time dynamic smart city dashboard. It illustrates smart KPIs in the form of a smart city performance map. Each KPI is presented in the appropriate form depending on its signification (line chart, bar chart …). The platform will use network sensors to capture city KPIs measurement. Sensors are placed at the appropriate places in the city to capture real-time data. The architecture of the dashboard system includes network sensors, servers, internet and Remote Terminal Unit (Suakanto et al., 2013). RTUs are used to send data captured by sensors to servers via the internet.

4. CONCLUSION

Digital transformation is not about a digital department and a mobile strategist won't save your organization. It's a philosophy that all must adopt (Eder, 2017). Smart city strategy is needed to achieve the smart city strategic goals and advance the city's strategic vision.

This paper presents a smart city integrated approach, which comprises a platform and dashboard to support and monitor the building of a smart city. A list of KPIs is provided to help a city assess its transformation and perform benchmarking via calculating smart city ranking. These KPIs will be used in our next research to create customized maturity models for evaluating the maturity level of smart cities. To facilitate the use of the proposed smart city methodological approach, we started the development of a software framework supporting this methodology. This framework provides stakeholders the ability to establish a strategy for city transformation into a smart city. It helps to mind mapping, boost productivity, creativity, and memory to develop a digital strategy for building a smart city. The development of the framework is in progress and it will be used by Smart Agdal Region when it is completed.

Here we list several promising future research directions:

- Use the provided list of KPIs to create maturity models for smart city assessment.
- Use artificial intelligence to transform the smart city framework into a knowledge-based system.

REFERENCES

Akbar, M., Sukmana, H. T., & Khairani, D. (2014). Models and software measurement using Goal/Question/Metric method and CMS Matrix parameter (Case study discussion forum). In *2014 International Conference on Cyber and IT Service Management (CITSM)*(pp. 34–38). South Tangerang.

Alzaabi, M., Rizk, Z. and Mezher, T. (2018). Linking Smart Cities Concept to Energy-Water-Food Nexus: The Case of Masdar City in Abu Dhabi, UAE. *Smart Cities in the Gulf*, pp.85-106.; https://doi.org/10.1007/978-981-13-2011-8_6.

Angelidou, M. (2016). Four European Smart City Strategies. *International Journal of Social Science Studies*, 4(4); ISSN 2324-8033E-ISSN 2324-8041; doi:10.11114/ijsss.v4i4.1364.

Anthopoulos, L. (2019). *Smart utopia VS smart reality: Learning by experience from 10 smart city cases*. Business School, TEI of Thessaly, Greece, Larissa, ring road, GR41110 Larissa, Greece, http://dx.doi.org/10.1016/j.cities.2016.10.005.

Basili, V. R. (1993). *Applying the Goal/Question/Metric paradigm in the experience factory* (pp. 21–44). Software Quality Assurance and Measurement: A Worldwide Perspective.

Basili, V., Heidrich, J., Lindvall, M., Münch, J., Regardie, M., Rombach, D., & Trendowicz, A. (2014). GQM + Strategies: A comprehensive methodology for aligning business strategies with software measurement. *Proceedings of the DASMA Software Metric Congress (MetriKon 2007): Magdeburger Schriften zum Empirischen Software Engineering*, pages 253-266, Kaiserslautern, Germany, November 15-16 2007.

Behkamal, B., Kahani, M., Bagheri, E., & Jeremic, Z. (2014). A metrics-driven approach for quality assessment of linked open data. *Journal of Theoretical and Applied Electronic Commerce Research*, 9(2), 64–79.

Ben Letaifa, S. (2014). The uneasy transition from supply chains to ecosystems. *Management Decision*, 52(2), pp.278-295.

Ben Letaifa, S. (2015). How to strategize smart cities: Revealing the SMART model. *Journal of Business Research*, 68(7), pp.1414-1419.

Boström, E. and Celik, O., C. (2017). *Towards a Maturity Model for Digital Strategizing A qualitative study of how an organization can analyze and assess their digital business strategy*. Department of informatics IT Management Master thesis 2-year level, 30 credits SPM 2017.09.

Brunelli, M. (2015). *Introduction to the Analytic Hierarchy Process. SpringerBriefs in Operations Research*. P. 83. 978-3-319-12502-2. 10.1007/978-3-319-12502-2. Available at: https://core.ac.uk/download/pdf/80714029.pdf [Accessed 17 Jun. 2019].

Budde, P. (2019). *2015 Australia - E-Health, E-Education, E-Government*. [online] Budde.com.au. Available at: https://www.budde.com.au/Research/2015-Australia-E-Health-E-Education-E-Government [Accessed 1 Apr. 2019].

Business Tampere. (2016). *Tampere, Finland, is investing 6-10 Billion Euro in development of smarter city by 2030 - Smart Tampere possibilities on display at the Smart City Expo World Congress in Barcelona - Business Tampere Magazine*. [online] Available at: https://businesstampere.com/tampere-finland-is-investing-6-10-billion-euro-in-development-of-smarter-city-by-2030-smart-tampere-possibilities-on-display-at-the-smart-city-expo-world-congress-in-barcelona/ [Accessed 17 Jun. 2019].

Chourabi, H., Nam, T., Walker, S., Gil-Garcia, J., Mellouli, S., Nahon, K., Pardo, T. and Scholl, H. (2012). Understanding Smart Cities: An Integrative Framework. *2012 45th Hawaii International Conference on System Sciences*. doi:10.1109/hicss.2012.615.

Chudiniva, O. and Afonina, M. (2018). Formation of "Urban planning" indicators for "Smart City" concept (on the example of SKOLKOVO, Moscow). *MATEC Web of Conferences*, 170, p.02021.; https://doi.org/10.1051/matecconf/201817002021.

Dodson, K. (2019). *Top 10 Smart City Trends for 2018*. [online] blogs@Cisco - Cisco Blogs. Available at: https://blogs.cisco.com/government/top-10-smart-city-trends-for-2018 [Accessed 17 Jun. 2019].

Eder, M. (2017). *Common elements of a successful digital strategy*. Available at https://www.researchgate.net/publication/322078143_COMMON_ELEMENTS_OF_A_SUCCESSFUL_DIGITAL_STRATEGY.

Fritz, M., Rauter, R., Baumgartner, R. and Dentchev, N. (2018). A supply chain perspective of stakeholder identification as a tool for responsible policy and decision-making. *Environmental Science & Policy*, 81, pp.63-76. doi:10.1016/j.envsci.2017.12.011.

Giffinger, R.,Fertner, C.,Kramar, H., Kalasek, R., Pichler-Milanović, N., Meijers, E. (2007). *Smart cities - Ranking of European medium-sized cities*. [online] Centre of Regional Science (SRF), Vienna University of Technology in October 2007. Available at: http://www.smart-cities.eu/download/smart_cities_final_report.pdf [Accessed 17 Jun. 2019].

Gobble, M. (2018). Digital Strategy and Digital Transformation. *Research-Technology Management*, 61(5), pp.66-71.

Grünig, R. and Kühn, R. (2018). Strategic Planning. *The International Encyclopedia of Strategic Communication*, pp.1-11. Robert L. Heath and Winni Johansen (Editors-in-Chief), Jesper Falkheimer, Kirk Hallahan, Juliana J. C. Raupp, and Benita Steyn (Associate Editors). © 2018 John Wiley & Sons, Inc. Published 2018 by John Wiley & Sons, Inc. DOI: 10.1002/9781119010722.iesc0177.

Guanochanga, B., Cachipuendo, R., Fuertes, W., Benitez, D. S., Toulkeridis, T., Torres, J., ... Meneses, F. (2018). "Towards a RealTime Air Pollution Monitoring Systems Implemented using Wireless Sensor Networks: Preliminary Results". *2018 IEEE Colombian Conference on Communications and Computing (COLCOM)*. doi:10.1109/colcomcon.2018.8466721.

Harrison, J.S., John St, C.H., (1998). Strategic Management of Organizations and Stakeholders: Concepts and Cases, 2nd ed. Southwestern College Publishing, Cincinnati, OH.

ITU-T FG-SSC (2015a). *Master plan for smart sustainable cities*. [online] Focus Group Technical Report. Available at: https://www.itu.int/en/ITU-T/focusgroups/ssc/Documents/website/web-fg-ssc-0314-r5-ssc_framework.docx [Accessed 17 Jun. 2019].

ITU-T FG-SSC (2015b). *Key performance indicators definitions for smart sustainable cities*. [online] Focus Group Technical Report. Available at: https://www.itu.int/en/ITU-T/focusgroups/ssc/Documents/website/web-fg-ssc-0100-r9-definitions_technical_report.docx [Accessed 17 Jun. 2019]. (ITU-T Focus Group on Smart Sustainable Cities, 2015).

ITU-T FG-SSC (2015c). *Key performance indicators related to the use of information and communication technology in smart sustainable cities*. [online] Focus Group Technical Report. Available at: https://www.itu.int/en/ITU-T/focusgroups/ssc/Documents/website/web-fg-ssc-0268-r5-KPIs_ICT.docx [Accessed 17 Jun. 2019].

Kane, G., Palmer, D., Phillips, A., Kiron, D. and Buckley, N. (2015). *Strategy, not Technology, Drives Digital Transformation*. [online] MIT Sloan Management Review. Available at: https://sloanreview.mit.edu/projects/strategy-drives-digital-transformation/ [Accessed 17 Jun. 2019].

Kanter, R. and Litow, S. (2009). Informed and Interconnected: A Manifesto for Smarter Cities. In: *Harvard University Advanced Leadership Initiative Think Tank on Poverty, Justice, and Jobs*. [online] USA, p.https://hbswk.hbs.edu/item/informed-and-interconnected-a-manifesto-for-smarter-cities. Available at: https://www.hbs.edu/faculty/Publication%20Files/09-141.pdf [Accessed 17 Jun. 2019].

Kitchin, R., Lauriault, T. and McArdle, G. (2015). Knowing and governing cities through urban indicators, city benchmarking and real-time dashboards. *Regional Studies, Regional Science*, 2(1), pp.6-28.

Korachi, Z. and Bounabat, B. (2018). Data Driven Maturity Model for Assessing Smart Cities. *ICSDE'18, October 18–20, 2018, Rabat, Morocco; © 2018 Association for Computing Machinery; ACM ISBN 978-1-4503-6507-9/18/10; ENSIAS Rabat; Morocco.*

Lange, M. (2018). From real-time city to asynchronicity. *Time for mapping.* https://doi.org/10.7765/9781526122520.00021.

Lea, R. (2017). *Smart Cities: An Overview of the Technology Trends Driving Smart Cities*. IEEE, licensed under a Creative Commons Attribution-Non-Commercial 3.0 United States License.

Lombardi P. (2011). New challenges in the evaluation of Smart Cities. In: *NETWORK INDUSTRIES QUARTERLY*, vol. 13 n. 3, pp. 8-10. - ISSN 1662-6176.

Lombardi, P., Giordano, S., Farouh, H. and Yousef, W. (2012). *Modelling the smart city performance.* http://dx.doi.org/10.1080/13511610.2012.660325; Innovation – The European Journal of Social Science Research Vol. 25, No. 2, June 2012, 137-149.

London City Hall. (2019). *Smarter London Together.* [online] Available at: https://www.london.gov.uk/what-we-do/business-and-economy/supporting-londons-sectors/smart-london/smarter-london-together [Accessed 17 Jun. 2019].

Madakam, S. and Ramaswamy, R. (2016). Smart Cities [Meixi (China) × Kochi (India)] Notions (Sustainable Management Action Resource Tools for Cities). *Advanced Computing and Communication Technologies*, pp.269-277. DOI 10.1007/978-981-10-1023-1_27.

Mannaro, K., Baralla, G. and Garau, C. (2018). A Goal-Oriented Framework for Analyzing and Modeling City Dashboards in Smart Cities. *Smart and Sustainable Planning for Cities and Regions*, pp.179-195. doi:10.1007/978-3-319-75774-2_13.

Masdar.ae. (2019). *Home.* [online] Available at: https://masdar.ae/en [Accessed 17 Jun. 2019]. MASDAR CITY in Abu Dhabi.

Mattern, S. (2015). *Mission control: A history of the urban dashboard.Places Journal, March.* [Online] Available at: https://placesjournal.org/article/mission-control-a-history-of-the-urban-dashboard/ [Accessed 01 Jun. 2019].

Nabil, A. (2015). *Action plan for a smart city.* [online] Fr.slideshare.net. Available at: https://fr.slideshare.net/AhmedMohamedNabil/action-plan-for-a-smart-city-45796767 [Accessed 17 Jun. 2019].

Pellicer, S., Santa, G., Bleda, A., Maestre, R., Jara, A. and Skarmeta, A. (2013). A Global Perspective of Smart Cities: A Survey. *2013 Seventh International Conference on Innovative Mobile and Internet Services in Ubiquitous Computing.*

Picioroaga, I., Eremia, M. and Sanduleac, M. (2018). SMART CITY: Definition and Evaluation of Key Performance Indicators. *2018 International Conference and Exposition on Electrical And Power Engineering (EPE).*doi:10.1109/icepe.2018.8559763.

Songdo.com. (2019). [online] Available at: http://songdo.com/ [Accessed 17 Jun. 2019]. (Songdo.com, 2019)

Southekal, P. (2017). *Data for business performance: The goal-question-metric (GQM) model to transform business data into an enterprise asset.* Published February 15th 2017 by Technics Publications, LLC. ISBN 1634621840 (ISBN13: 9781634621847).

Suakanto, S., Supangkat, S., Suhardi and Saragih, R. (2013). Smart city dashboard for integrating various data of sensor networks. *International Conference on ICT for Smart Society*. doi:10.1109/ictss.2013.6588063.

Teknomo, K. (2006). *Analytic hierarchy process (AHP) tutorial.* Revoledu. com. Available at: https://www.researchgate.net/profile/Rafik_Karaman/post/there_is_any_details_about_AHP_method/attachment/59d63b9179197b80779989cd/AS:411365203300368@1475088515401/download/AHP_Tutorial.pdf [Accessed 17 Jun. 2019].

UN DESA. (2018). *2018 Revision of World Urbanization Prospects | Multimedia Library - United Nations Department of Economic and Social Affairs*. [online] Available at: https://www.un.org/development/desa/publications/2018-revision-of-world-urbanization-prospects.html [Accessed 5 Jun. 2019].

United Smart Cities, (2019). *The way to become a Smart Sustainable City - News - United Smart Cities.* [online] United Smart Cities. Available at: http://www.unitedsmartcities.org/news/the-way-to-become-a-smart-sustainable-city-34/ [Accessed 17 Jun. 2019].

United smart sustainable cities (2017). *Collection Methodology for Key Performance Indicators for Smart Sustainable Cities*. [online] Available at: https://www.itu.int/dms_pub/itu-t/opb/tut/T-TUT-SMARTCITY-2017-9-PDF-E.pdf [Accessed 17 Jun. 2019]. ISBN 978-92-61-25221-2 (Paper version); 978-92-61-25231-1 (Electronic version). Published in Switzerland Geneva, 2017.

Vogt, G., Dashja, E., Robinson, S. (2013). KPIs for S.M.A.R.T. Cities, DOI: 10.2759/42792, *Proceedings of the 1st Workshop organised by the EEB Data Models Community ICT for Sustainable Places*. Nice, France, 9 th -11 th September, 2013.

WHO (World Health Organization) and ITU (International Telecommunication Union), (2012). *National eHealth Strategy Toolkit.*

WHERE DOES TECHNOLOGY FIT IN THE GEOSPATIAL DESIGN AND PLANNING PROFESSIONS?

Carlos J. L. Balsas
Ph.D., AICP, Dep. of Geography and Planning
1400 Washington Ave., University at Albany, Albany, NY 12222, U.S.A

ABSTRACT

The societal transformations facilitated in part by geospatial design technological advances have brought new challenges to territorial planning. This paper analyzes the evolution of geospatial design and planning education in the United States by emphasizing the criticality of sustainable transportation planning in facilitating the partial resolution of some of the land use – transportation problems commonly found in environmental justice communities. The paper is in six parts. Part one is a review of geospatial design and planning education in the United States. Part two progresses from education to desired planning skills and a smart cities' framework. Part three is an overview of the dilemmas found in environmental justice communities. Part four explains why technology based on vehicles alone will not create more sustainable transportation. Part five is the case study of an environmental justice community in Albany, New York. Finally, part six makes some concluding remarks.

KEYWORDS

Geospatial Design, Urban and Regional Planning, Smart Cities, Environmental Justice, Sustainable Transportation

1. INTRODUCTION

Societal transformations facilitated in part by geospatial design technological advances have brought new challenges to territorial planning (Castells, 1996; Townsend, 2014). The relationship between place and information has been partially strengthened through placemaking and geographical notions of technological progress (Corey and Wilson, 2006). Geospatial design and planning professions such as geography, urban and regional planning, and urban design have had important theoretical and methodological affinities for a long time. The *foci* of these various disciplines have changed and evolved over the years. Also, new technologies have impacted the practice, scholarship and career paths of many professionals as well as the territory where we live.

The territory has been compressed and flattened, the world has gotten spikier, time and chronology have accelerated, spatiality and governance are ever more interrelated, and the number of professional challenges has increased exponentially. These challenges pose a series of important questions: What kind of scientific relationships should schools nurture? What changes should be made to the curricula? Is there a set path for academic careers? How should schools recruit, promote, deliver and offer education in the geospatial design and planning disciplines? (Balsas, 2000, 2017).

This paper analyzes the evolution of geospatial design and planning education in the United States by emphasizing the criticality of sustainable transportation planning in facilitating the partial resolution of some of the land use – transportation problems commonly found in environmental justice communities. It is argued that millennials (i.e., broadly defined as individuals born in the mid–1980s onwards) comprise a very different generational group than their predecessors; millennials tend to be more environmentally conscious, to drive slightly less, have more access to information, have earned more degrees, see value in their continuing education, and utilize information and communication technologies (ICT) like no previous generation did ever before in history. Such high degree of technological ubiquity has been facilitated by geospatial design and planning technological advancements and it tends to reinforce and perpetuate certain patterns of urban development and societal features (Dixon et al., 2005; Eubanks, 2018).

The paper is in six parts. Part one is a review of geospatial design and planning education in the United States. Part two progresses from education to desired planning skills and a smart cities' framework. Part three is an overview of the dilemmas found in environmental justice communities. Part four explains why technology based on vehicles alone will not create more sustainable transportation. Part five is the case study of an environmental justice community in Albany, New York. Finally, part six makes some concluding remarks.

2. GEOSPATIAL DESIGN AND PLANNING EDUCATION

Geospatial design and planning professions include mostly geography, urban and regional planning, and urban design. Although these disciplines are relatively autonomous, they have some overlaps in terms of theoretical and methodological affinities. New technologies have impacted the practice, scholarship and career paths of many professionals as well as territorial development. Geospatial design and planning require the ability to collect, manipulate, analyze, and present data in tabular, spatial and visual formats.

Of these three disciplines, the planning profession in the United States has evolved from its initial concerns with public health during the reformist period to a role centered more on issues of power, politics, and persuasion (Hoch, 1994; McClendon and Catanese, 1996; Dalton, 2007). Planning education was mostly formalized from the 1950s onwards. Formal training in urban planning was initially proposed in 1957 and the Massachusetts Institute of Technology (MIT) soon thereafter created a doctoral program in planning in 1958 (Rodwin and Sanyal, 2000). The profession's roots can be traced to its geospatial, architecture and landscape architecture traditions. However, the social sciences upbringings of the ecological movement of the Chicago School also provided an impetus to formalize education in planning, mostly from a sociological perspective (Caves and Wagner, 2018). The functionalist investments in planning during the 1930s, which created the planning machinery of maps, zoning codes, tax laws, and other regulations anchored in the Enabling Acts of the 1920s, would be materialized in subsequent decades.

Planning education has also benefited from the positivist revolution in the 1960s and 1970s when planning developed its emphasis on policy analysis (Friend and Hickling, 2005). Although planning had been represented by the American Institute of Planners (AIP) and the American Society of Planning Officials (ASPO), which were consolidated into the American Planning Association (APA) in 1978, planning education and scholarship only started to receive systematic attention with the creation of the Association of Collegiate Schools of Planning (ACSP) in 1969. ACSP started organizing a separate conference (from the AIP/APA's) in 1981 (Lauria, 2010). Both ACSP's publication outlet and its regular annual conferences aim at the presentation and dissemination of scholarly findings on planning, planning education, and research.

Seminal papers on the core planning competencies and skills in the planning curriculum at both the graduate and undergraduate levels have been published over the years (e.g., Friedmann, 1996; Edwards and Bates, 2011; Greenlee et al., 2015). For a long time, the traditional view of a generalist with a specialization has been challenged with the growth of planning specializations (Balsas, 2015). The core education of planning consists of theory and philosophy of planning, planning history, planning law, planning methods, and planning studios (Friedmann, 1996). The specializations range from land use and transportation to environmental planning, housing, community development, etc.

The debate between planning and urbanism has also continued and even accentuated in recent years mostly due to the rise of New Urbanism (Duany et al., 2001) and Landscape Urbanism (Waldheim, 2016). What and how to teach has changed slightly depending on regional nuances and national sensibilities. Social planning and advocacy planning emerged in the 1970s, partially in response to the civil rights movement and the national environmental programs. Nonetheless, the courses in the core curriculum have been offered consistently throughout most of the country (Frank, 2006). Specializations have grown in number and in depth and breadth of content and methods (Bayer et al, 2010).

3. PLANNING SKILLS AND SMART CITIES

Planning skills include writing, speaking, and analytical competencies in math, drawing, map making, geographical skills, leadership, and decision making, among others (Wilson, 2015). These skills are directly related to planning goals' orientation toward the future, diversity and social justice, equity and equality of opportunity, economic efficiency and environmental sustainability (Banai, 2013; Freestone, 2012; Greenlee et al., 2015). Sandercock (1999) has identified planning literacies fundamental in planning education that range from technical, analytical and multi- or cross-cultural, to ecological, and design.

The *ACSP Guide to Undergraduate and Graduate Education in Urban and Regional Planning* has been an important document to help individuals know more about program offerings in the United States, specialization requirements, faculty and tuition costs. The Planning Accreditation Board (PAB) was created in 1984, traditionally as a stamp of guarantee on the accredited planning programs, even though a gap between planning theory and practice has always persisted (Baum, 1997; Dalton, 2007). Although PAB is unique to planning programs in North America, the Association of European Schools of Planning (AESOP) has also recently implemented a quality control program along similar lines, although such task may prove much harder given the different European cultures and slightly distinct national planning traditions (Frank et al., 2014).

The interconnectedness of seamless interoperable technological systems is referred to as Smart Cities. Smart cities map and partially recreate the physical world into the virtual environment as a referencing framework for decision making (Eckardt, 2008; Townsend, 2014). The study of new technologies within a smart cities framework have included geographical information systems (GIS); new technopoles; E-government; public participation geographic information systems (PPGIS); intelligent transportation systems (ITS); E-commerce; the use of new technologies to help conserve energy; the deployment of Wi-Fi technology in public spaces via wireless networks; and the digital divide (Horan, 2000; Graham, 2004; Forsyth and Crewe, 2010).

Visualization techniques have also gained prominence due to technological advances and gains in affordability. The sketching and visioning of ideal community conditions has been put forward with before and after illustrations aimed at gaining community support for urban revitalization, site design, neighborhood planning, and streetscape improvements (Kotval, 1996; Kempenaar et al., 2016). For instance, SketchUp is an example of a software utilized for that purpose. Smart cities also reflect a new mentality in planning theory and practice, which to a certain extent, encapsulates a significant change from digital to intelligent development (Corey and Wilson, 2006).

Technological advances are also being appropriated by planning's cognate profession of urban design (Arefi and Al-Dourib, 2016). Ferrandino (2014) has written about how a GIS, as an interdisciplinary pedagogical tool, has also been incorporated in Masters of Public Administration (MPA) programs. Safety and homeland security agencies are also utilizing new technologies to improve safety conditions in cities. Finally, big data collected and utilized to identify trends as well as the Internet of Things (IoT), as the use of linked sensors in a myriad of devices and processes, are two of the latest tendencies in technological advancements (Meyer-Schoenberger and Cukier, 2014).

4. ENVIRONMENTAL JUSTICE COMMUNITIES

Environmental justice is the fair treatment and involvement of all people regardless of race, ethnicity, income, national origin, or educational level in decisions pertaining to our natural and built environment and the societal dynamics ensuing from those same governance processes (EPA, 2018). Unfortunately, many minorities and poor communities of color still face a disproportionately higher number of social and environmental issues than socio-economically balanced constituencies in relatively more privileged neighborhoods (Boone and Modarres, 1999; Pastor et al., 2001; Agyeman et al., 2003; Bullard, 2007).

Examples of those injustices resulting partially from inadequate land use – transportation decisions include daily exposure to air and noise pollution from heavy travelled highways, roadways, and industrial activity (Allen et al., 2009), higher likelihood of living in close proximity to contaminated soil and water sources, higher rates of preventable diseases, higher infant mortality rates, and lower life expectancy (Corburn, 2007; Bullard et al., 2014; Carrier et al., 2016). Figure 1. shows a map from the Environmental

Justice (EJ) Atlas displaying reported environmental conflicts in the United States. Figure 2. shows EPA's RMPs for high-risk industrial and commercial facilities. According to Coming Clean and the Environmental Justice Health Alliance for Chemical Policy Reform (2018: 3) "almost 124 million people (39% of the U.S. population) live within 3 miles of one of about 12,500 hazardous facilities included in the Environmental Protection Agency's Risk Management Plan (RMP) program."

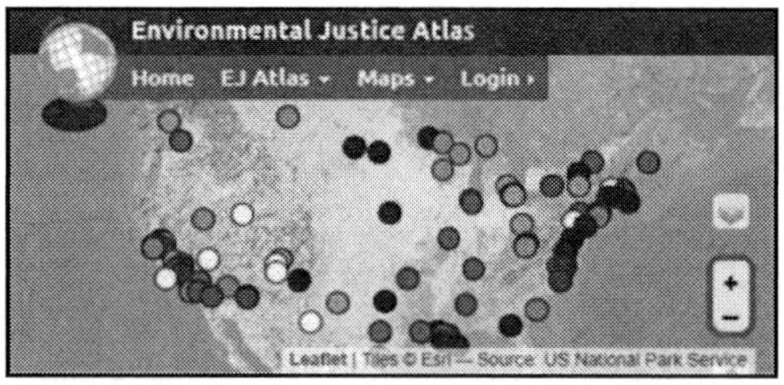

Figure 1. Environmental Justice (EJ) Atlas displaying reported environmental conflicts in the United States (<https:// ejatlas.rg/country/united-states-of-america> May 25, 2019)

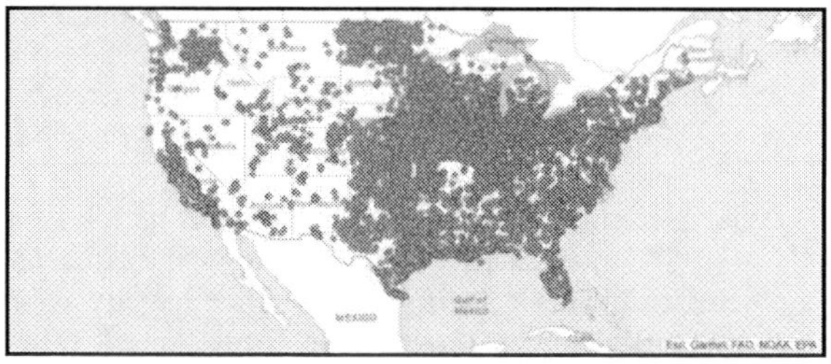

Figure 2. Environmental Protection Agency's Risk Management Plan (RMP) program for high-risk industrial and commercial facilities (<https://ej4all.org/life-at-the-fenceline> May 25, 2019)

In spite of some recent progress leading to the decontamination of polluted brownfield sites in former industrial areas in North American cities, certain regions of the Northeast and Midwest still possess a high number of such sites named by Hollander (2009) as HI–TOADS (i.e., High-Impact Temporarily Obsolete Abandoned Derelict Sites). In certain cases, present situations of environmental racism were created decades ago due to inexpensive land available in places near industrial sites and other LULUs (i.e., local unwanted land uses) (Bolin et al., 2005; Schively, 2007).

The individuals responsible for said land use – transportation decisions may no longer be in the same public office and therefore, it may be difficult to attribute responsibilities to individual decision makers or agencies (Pulido, 1996; Rohe and Freeman, 2001; Krizek and Levinson, 2005). Those who have inherited and are now responsible for managing those complex situations may not have the knowledge or the necessary resources to resolve those environmentally unjust situations (Kennedy, 2015). Therefore, incremental decisions may serve only to perpetuate unjust environmental problems without ever eradicating said state of affairs (Schweitzer and Stephenson Jr, 2007).

Effective environmental advocacy is still urgently needed in many communities throughout the United States, as the Hollywood film *"Erin Brockovich"* demonstrated in the early 2000s (Banks, 2002). That advocacy has to occur not only with the help of community leaders, elected officials and progressive media outlets, but also with effective and responsible decision making (Kurtz, 2005), which needs to provide resourceful solutions to those most affected by environmental nuisances. Urban and Regional Planning Departments in institutions of higher education ought to engage with those situations and train students in their resolution (Susskind and Amundsen, 1999; Corburn, 2005; Bullard et al., 2014).

5. SUSTAINABLE TRANSPORTATION PLANNING

Transportation is critical to the proper functioning of the economy (Goodwin, 1998). The U.S. has an extremely high dependence on automobiles for everyday transportation (Balsas, 2001). However, technology based on vehicles alone will not create more sustainable transportation (Hillman, 2012; Velazquez et al., 2015). More environmental advocacy within a smart cities framework ought to be taken into consideration by those with responsibility for public policy and territorial administration (Evans-Cowley and Manta Conroy, 2006).

With the current societal transformations, the emphasis on environmental problems in North America may have subsided slightly, but perhaps more than ever, there is a great need for pro-active strategies to minimize carbon emissions, to create participatory governance arenas, and to utilize new technologies in addressing the problems created not only by changing demographic patterns and lifestyles, but also by current urbanization trends. The skill sets brought forward by professionals in inter-related areas of study, which have city-region ecosystems and global approaches as their *foci*, will be increasingly required by those in future positions of power in city, regional and national governments as well as in the private and non-profit sectors, including academia (Schon, 1987; Caves and Wagner, 2018; Balsas, 2019).

The federal government, together with many states and non-profit organizations, has only partially attempted to reduce automobile dependence in the United States by incentivizing alternative modes of transportation, such as mass transit, light rail, walking and bicycling (Raco and Flint, 2011). Walking and bicycling in particular have received some attention in recent years in connection with the need to stimulate healthier lifestyles and to reduce the threat of chronicle diseases. Central to those developments was a combination of hard and soft responses to improving transportation infrastructure and the built environment, and to influence the transportation habits of the general population.

It is important to augment the results of previous research and policy programs by multiple stakeholders and to study how best practices can be understood and implemented within a framework of social justice, policy innovation, urban and metropolitan governance, sustainable transportation planning, and smart cities (Banister, 2008; Forsyth, 2012). At the core of such research lies the fundamental dilemma where more endowed communities and agglomerations, usually exclusively car-oriented, are able to provide better infrastructure and to support programs to improve transportation conditions than those with fewer means and resources (Eubanks, 2018) – therefore, perpetuating the resource/poverty gap.

The induced outcomes have led to less sustainable, perhaps contradictory results, which tend to increase automobile dependence instead of reducing car ownership, vehicle miles travelled, gasoline consumption, air and noise pollution, and accidents (Zavestoski and Agyeman, 2015). Guarantying better mobility conditions in communities with fewer means is a social responsibility matter and an opportunity to strengthen living conditions and sustainable livelihoods. Planning schools in the United States ought to pay more attention to these dilemmas in their curricular offerings, research commitments and public engagement responsibilities.

Our research and teaching experience on sustainable transportation planning has led us to believe in the need to strengthen and increase the impact of non-motorized modes of transportation in order to create safer and more livable cities, with lower levels of greenhouse gas emissions, and therefore less propensity to contribute to global climate change (Shay and Khattak, 2010; Balsas, 2019). Market economics aided by community advocacy and public involvement, responsible technological advances, and community-oriented development ought to help accomplish public policy goals that result in safer transportation infrastructure (e.g., road redesigns, bridges and tunnels, bicycle trails and lanes) also in poor communities in the United States and elsewhere. However, those economic measures ought to also emphasize social programs that de-market the automobile and instead attempt to popularize the general use of mass transit and non-motorized transportation for the daily transportation needs of everyone (Portney, 2005; Hajer et al., 2012; Buehler and Hamre, 2015). The next section discusses an alternative town-gown citizen science public engagement in an environmental justice community in upstate New York.

6. ALBANY'S SOUTH END TOWN-GOWN ENGAGEMENT

Town-gown applied learning activities constitute a useful methodology in many universities with undergraduate and masters programs in Urban and Regional Planning. Many of those programs involve capstone studios. Often (paying) clients approach the Planning Departments with requests for specific studies. The faculty and student labor is usually perceived as more affordable, more qualified, and under a clout of independence not easily found in professional consulting services provided by firms operating in the marketplace. However, the political economy of host cities tends to privilege certain places and neighborhoods at the expense of others (Soja, 2010; Sassen, 2014). Business districts, commercial corridors, certain residential suburbs, industrial parks, and open space areas tend to receive the most attention. On the other hand, complex planning situations such as environmental justice communities, abandoned ethnic neighborhoods, and areas surrounding landfills required strong epistemological motivation to defray the medium to long-term commitments necessary to turn those places around (Forsyth, 2012; Khan, Moulaert and Schreurs, 2013).

At the beginning of summer 2018, we were alerted to the possibility of helping to provide some planning suggestions to the resolution of a very complex environmental health situation involving the residents at a public housing complex in an environmental justice community in Albany, New York, called Ezra Prentice. Such housing complex is transversed by a busy state arterial road and is located adjacent to a railyard depot in the proximity of the Port of Albany (see Figure 3.). The residents, mostly low-income population of color, have been exposed to various types of air pollution generated by heavy roadway traffic and port-related operations such as crude oil transport by rail, among others (Houston, Li and Wu, 2014).

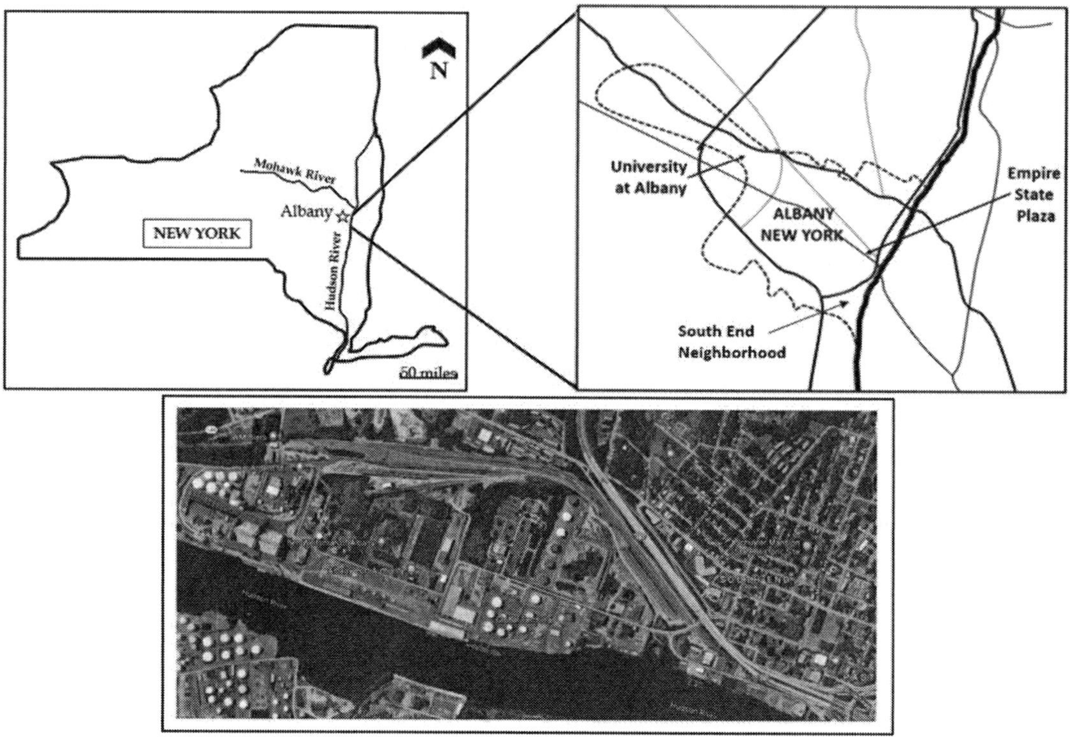

Figure 3. Location of the South End neighborhood in Albany, NY

Severe health problems such as high rates of asthma and other respiratory illnesses have been documented, most likely, in connection with the poor air quality and noise pollution in the area. Prior environmental advocacy by the residents themselves and the leaders of various non-profit organizations in Albany (e.g. AVillage and Radix), since at least 2014, served to alert various elected officials and decision makers to the severity of the problems in the area (Times Union, 2016). In response, in 2017-2018 the NYS Department of Environmental Conservation (DEC) invested about $500,000 in equipment and human resources to conduct an air quality study (NYSDEC Division of Air Resources, 2017) (see Figure 4.)

Figure 4. Air monitoring station in the South End neighborhood of Albany | Figure 5. Citizen science public engagement with high school students in June 2018

Furthermore, the Capital District Transportation Committee (CDTC) has just finalized a study in June 2018 aimed at finding solutions to the heavy truck traffic in the area. This study was conducted to help reduce the number of freight and heavy-traffic vehicles circulating on the main arterial road (Monios, Bergqvist and Woxenius, 2018). In collaboration with scientists from NYS DEC and a group of high-school students from the University at Albany's S.T.E.P. (i.e. Science and Technology Entry Program) we conducted visits to the study site to analyze the possibility of utilizing placemaking urban design strategies, including streetscape improvements and the installation of a greenwall to reduce the encroachment of air pollutants into the housing and playground areas located adjacent to the heavily travelled road through the housing complex. The high school students had meetings with air quality scientists and planners, a guided tour of the air monitoring station, conducted their own air quality measurements, tested the feasibility of installing a greenwall pilot project, and then presented their findings at the 2018 SUNY Albany S.T.E.P. Summer Institute/Smart Scholars Summer Bridge Closing Ceremony on Friday, July 20, 2018 (Figure 5.).

The main objective of this town-gown engagement was to study how the University at Albany could become more relevant to underserved communities in the Capital Region of upstate New York. Collaborations in urban planning and design professions are central to progressive educational models and professional practice. The political economy of recipient university-host communities tends to shape the conception and development of town-gown engagements. A certain dissatisfaction with traditional educational models has led us to explore the applicability of alternative educational paradigms based on citizen science, community engagement and creative arts and culture interventions to resolve structural problems in cities, and in our particular case, in the city of Albany.

We believe that the empathy that resulted from individual and collective social struggles and the affirmation of one's own cultural values on an even playing field, as well as the personal feelings of having been able to accomplish challenging tasks, has serve to motivate us in advancing to higher levels of research performance as well as personal and professional realization. During this town-gown engagement with the S.T.E.P. program we realized that there is power in accomplishing something with the knowledge we had acquired instead of being only the passive recipient (or deliverers) of transmitted knowledge. Although we were not able to reduce – nor to eliminate – the air pollution problem in the South End neighborhood during this short public engagement of various weeks, we are confident that the *in-loco* visits, the meetings with the scientists and planners, and the brief interactions with the residents revealed the potential of an applied citizen-science research approach. Such approach was mostly aimed at creating higher levels of awareness of the severity of the land use – transport planning problem for the local residents as well as to expose the high school students to geospatial design and planning educational skills. One of the most important lessons learned might well have been the need to better understand the proper siting and management of public housing developments and other sensitive infrastructure in contexts of environmental justice and the eradication of deeply imbedded decades old racist behaviors in urban development.

7. CONCLUSION

This paper has analyzed the evolution of geospatial design and planning education in the United States by emphasizing the criticality of sustainable transportation planning in facilitating the partial resolution of some of the land use – transportation problems commonly found in environmental justice communities. Over the past two decades, some of the most recent transformational changes in geosciences have included: Open source (suite of software packages) versus proprietary software (e.g., ESRI); smart communities (interoperability of systems); digital communities; data acquisition, manipulation, analysis and the extraction of useful findings; human, ecological, political, and technological transformations; tools (e.g., GIS, GPS, PPGIS, remote sensing, drones); self-reporting and volunteer programmers helping to produce maps for humanitarian reasons (e.g., *Openstreets,* and earthquake and tsunami recovery efforts in Haiti and Japan); smart phones and big data, in certain cases making GPS devices obsolete; cloud computing; and wayfinding technology (Rheingold, 2009).

On the other hand, some of the most recent changes in urban and regional planning have included: Renewed emphasis on decision making and technical recommendations; the facilitation and bridging of knowledge with interdisciplinary teams; conflict mediation and consensus building; more encompassing public participation processes; stronger articulation with urban design and architecture; brownfields and smart growth principles; climate change adaptability and resilience; disaster emergency preparedness; greater need for visualization technologies; the need to address socio-economic, age, gender and class diversity; E-government; incorporation of geospatial tools; multidisciplinarity in researching non-physical problems (e.g., role of emotions, mental health, environmental nuisances; sedentary lifestyles), and the emergence of 'hybrid' specializations (e.g., landscape urbanism, sustainability, LEED certifications) (Corey and Wilson, 2006).

Two of the most pervasive forces in geospatial design and planning have been the sustainability movement (Hakansson and Asplund, 2002) and the influence of technology (Townsend, 2014). New technologies have had a critical role in shaping digital communities and influencing patterns of urban development. Within a smart cities' framework, new technologies are definitely powerful tools capable of facilitating access to information and of enabling knowledge to be deployed in socially, environmentally, and economically responsive ways. However, it is dangerous to believe that new technologies alone will resolve our complex societal problems (Adams, 1996).

Finally, the South End case study demonstrates the dual potential of a town-gown citizen science public engagement to expose students to complex land use – transportation planning conflicts of siting affordable housing near industrial facilities on one hand, and of using geospatial design and planning skills such as placemaking, air pollution monitoring within a smart cities framework and green infrastructure to partially resolve those same issues, on the other. In closing and from an educational perspective, we demonstrate that geospatial design and planning skills can also be applied to the human utilization and governance decisions of the territory, the creation of more walkable public spaces, and the optimization of public policy decision making processes, especially in environmental justice communities.

REFERENCES

Adams, J. 1996. "Can technology save us?" *World Transport Policy and Practice*, Vol. 2, No. 3, pp. 4–17.

Agyeman, J., and Evans, T. 2003. "Toward just sustainability in urban communities: Building equity rights with sustainable solutions." *The Annals of the American Academy of Political and Social Science,* Vol. 590, pp. 35–53.

Allen, R.W., Davies, H., Cohen, M.A., Mallach, G., Kaufman, J.D., and Adar, S.D. 2009. "The spatial relationship between traffic-generated air pollution and noise in 2 US cities." *Environmental Research,* Vol. 109, No. 3, pp. 334–342.

Arefi, M., and Al-Dourib, F. 2016. "Exploring pedagogical opportunities between architecture and planning." *Planning Theory & Practice,* Vol. 17, No. 1, pp. 72–92.

Balsas, C. 2001. "Cities, automobiles and sustainability." *Urban Affairs Review,* Vol. 36, No. 3, pp. 429–432.

Balsas, C. 2015. "Sustainable transportation planning, the evolution and impact of a new academic specialization in the USA." *International Journal of Transportation Science and Technology,* Vol. 4, No. 1, pp. 1–16.

Balsas, C. 2017. "Blending individual tenacity with government's responsibility in the implementation of US non-motorized transportation planning (NMT)." *Planning Practice and Research,* Vol. 32, No. 2, pp. 197–211.

Balsas, C. 2019. "Progress and 'acts of god' in the age of climate change virility." *International Journal of Global Environmental Issues,* Vol. 18, No. 2, pp. 1–19.

Banai, R. 2013. "Cities and regions: The urban sustainability, planning, pedagogy, and technology nexus." *Journal of Sustainability Education,* No. 5. <http://www.jsedimensions.org/wordpress/wp-content/uploads/2013/06/Reza-Banai-finalproofMay2013–1.pdf> (March 17, 2018).

Banister, D. 2008. "The sustainable mobility paradigm." *Transport Policy,* Vol. 15, No. 2, pp. 73–80.

Banks, S. 2002. "The Erin Brockovich Effect." *Environmental Law and Policy Journal,* Vol. 26, pp. 219–251.

Baum, H. 1997. "Teaching practice." *Journal of Planning Education and Research,* Vol. 17, pp. 21–29.

Bayer, M., Frank, N., and Valerius, J. 2010. *Becoming an Urban Planner: A guide to careers in planning and urban design.* John Wiley & Sons, Hoboken.

Bolin, B., Grineski, S., and Collins, T. 2005. "The geography of despair: Environmental racism and the making of South Phoenix, Arizona, USA." *Human Ecology Review,* Vol. 12, No. 2, pp. 156–168.

Boone, C.G., and Modarres, A. 1999. "Creating a toxic neighborhood in Los Angeles County: A historical examination of environmental inequity." *Urban Affairs Review,* Vol. 35, No. 2, pp. 163–187.

Buehler, R., and Hamre, A. 2015. "The multimodal majority? Driving, walking, cycling, and public transportation use among American adults." *Transportation*, Vol. 42, No. 6, pp. 1081–1101.

Bullard, R. 2007. *Growing Smarter.* The MIT Press, Cambridge.

Bullard, R., Johnson, G.S., Smith, S.L., and King, D.W. 2014. "Living on the frontline of environmental assault: Lessons from the united states most vulnerable communities." *Revista de Educação, Ciências e Matemática,* Vol. 3, No. 3, pp. 33–61.

Carrier, M., Apparicio, P., and Séguin, A.M. 2016. "Road traffic noise in Montreal and environmental equity: What is the situation for the most vulnerable population groups?" *Journal of Transport Geography,* Vol. 51, pp. 1–8.

Castells, M. 1996. *The Rise of the Network Society*. Blackwell Publishers, Cambridge.

Caves, R., and Wagner, F. 2018. "Are planning programs delivering what planning students need? Perspectives on planning education from practitioners." In: Frank, A., and Silver, C. (Eds.) *Urban Planning Education: Beginnings, global movement and future prospects.* Springer, Cham, pp. 323–337.

Coming Clean and the Environmental Justice Health Alliance for Chemical Policy Reform. 2018. Life at the Fenceline: Understanding Cumulative Health Hazards. <https://ej4all.org/life-at-the-fenceline> (May 25, 2019).

Corburn, J. 2007. "Urban land use, air toxics and public health: Assessing hazardous exposures at the neighborhood scale." *Environmental Impact Assessment Review,* Vol. 27, No. 2, pp. 145–160.

Corey, K.E., and Wilson, M. 2006. *Urban and Regional Technology Planning*. Routledge, New York.

Dalton, L. 2007. "Preparing planners for the breadth of practice." *Journal of the American Planning Association,* Vol. 73, No. 1, pp. 35–48.

Dixon, T., Thompson, B., McAllister, P., Marston, A., and Snow, J. 2005. *Real Estate & the New Economy.* Blackwell Publishing, Oxford.

Duany, A., Plater-Zyberg, E., and Speck, J. 2001. *Suburban Nation: The rise of sprawl and the decline of the American Dream.* North Point Press, New York.

Eckardt, F. 2008. "E-City: From researching the virtual towards understanding the real urban life." In: Bucher, U., and Finka, M. (Eds.) *The Electronic City*. BWV Verlag, Berlin, pp. 9–24.

Edwards, M.M., and Bates, L.K. 2011. "Planning's core curriculum: Knowledge, practice, and implementation." *Journal of Planning Education and Research*, Vol. 31, No. 2, pp. 172–183.

EPA. 2018. "Environmental Justice." <https://www.epa.gov/environmentaljustice> (Accessed July 9, 2018).

Eubanks, V. 2018. *Automating Inequality: How high-tech tools profile, police, and punish the poor.* St. Martin's Press, New York, NY.

Evans-Cowley, J., and Manta Conroy, M. 2006. "The growth of e-government in municipal planning." *Journal of Urban Technology*, Vol. 13, No. 1, pp. 81–107.

Ferrandino, J. 2014. "Incorporating GIS as an interdisciplinary pedagogical tool throughout an MPA program." *Journal of Public Affairs Education*, Vol. 20, No. 4, pp. 529–544.

Forsyth, A. 2012. "Alternative cultures in planning research—From extending scientific frontiers to exploring enduring questions." *Journal of Planning Education and Research,* Vol. 32, No. 2, pp. 160–168.

Forsyth, A., and Crewe, K. 2010. "Suburban technopoles as places: The international campus-garden-suburb style." *Urban Design International,* Vol. 15, No. 3, pp. 165–182.

Frank, A.I. 2006. "Three decades of thought on planning education." *Journal of Planning Literature,* Vol. 21, pp. 15–67.

Frank, A.I., Mironowicz, I., Lourenço, J., Franchini, T., Ache, P., Finka, M., ..., and Grams, A. 2014. "Educating planners in Europe: A review of 21st century study programmes." *Progress in Planning*, Vol. 91, pp. 30–94.

Freestone, R. 2012. "Futures thinking in planning education and research." *Journal for Education in the Built Environment*, Vol. 7, No. 1, pp. 8–38.

Friedmann, J. 1996. "The core curriculum in planning revisited." *Journal of Planning Education and Research*, Vol. 15, No. 2, pp. 89–104.

Friend, J.K., and Hickling, A. 2005. *Planning Under Pressure*. Routledge, New York.

Goodwin, P. 1998. "Unintended effects of transport policies." In: Banister, D. (Ed.) *Transport Policy and the Environment.* E & FN Spon, London, pp. 114–130.

Graham, S. 2004. *The Cybercities Reader.* Routledge, London.

Greenlee, A.J., Edwards, M., and Anthony, J. 2015. "Planning skills: An examination of supply and local government demand." *Journal of Planning Education and Research*, Vol. 35, No. 2, pp. 161–173.

Hajer, M., Hoen, A., and Huitzing, H. 2012. "Shifting gear: Beyond classical mobility policies and urban planning." In: AISSR (Ed.) *Keep Moving, Towards Sustainable Mobility.* Eleven International Publishing, The Hague, pp.151–178.

Hakansson, M., and Asplund, E. 2002. "Planning for sustainability and the impact of professional cultures." In: Thornley, A., and Rydin, Y. (Eds.) *Planning in a Global Era.* Ashgate, Burlington, pp. 387–404.

Hillman, M. 2012. "The implications of climate change for the future of the car." *World Transport Policy and Practice,* Vol. 17, No. 4, pp. 18–29.

Hoch, C. 1994. *What Planners Do: Power, politics, and persuasion*. APA Planners Press, Chicago.

Hollander, J.B. 2009. *Polluted & dangerous: America's worst abandoned properties and what can be done about them.* UPNE, Burlington.

Horan, T.A. 2000. *Digital Places: Building our city of bits*. ULI-the Urban Land Institute, Washington, D.C.

Houston, D., Li, W., and Wu, J. 2014. "Disparities in exposure to automobile and truck traffic and vehicle emissions near the Los Angeles–Long Beach port complex." *American Journal of Public Health,* Vol. 104, No. 1, pp. 156–164.

Kempenaar, A., Westerink, J., van Lierop, M., Brinkhuijsen, M., and van den Brink, A. 2016. ""Design makes you understand"—Mapping the contributions of designing to regional planning and development." *Landscape and Urban Planning,* Vol. 149, No. May, pp. 20–30.

Kennedy, M. 2015. *Globalizing Knowledge – Intellectuals, universities, and publics in transformation.* Stanford University Press, Stanford.

Khan, A., Moulaert, F. and Schreurs, J. 2013. "Epistemology of Space: Exploring relational perspectives in Planning, Urbanism, and Architecture." *International Planning Studies,* Vol. 18, No. 3-4, pp. 287–303.

Kotval, Z. 1996. "Telecommunications" *Cities,* Vol. 16, No. 1, pp. 33–41.

Krizek, K., and Levinson, D. 2005. "Teaching integrated land use-transportation planning." *Journal of Planning Education and Research,* Vol. 24, pp. 304–316.

Kurtz, H. 2005. "Alternative visions for citizenship practice in an environmental justice dispute." *Space Polity,* Vol. 9, No. 1, pp. 77–91.

Lauria, M. 2010. "ACSP at 50: Introduction." *The Town Planning Review*, Vol. 81, No. 2, pp. i–ii.

McClendon, B.W., and Catanese, A.J. 1996. *Planners on Planning: Leading planners offer real-life lessons on what works, what doesn't, and why.* Jossey-Bass Inc., San Francisco.

Meyer-Schoenberger, V., and Cukier, K. 2014. *Big Data: A revolution that will transform how we live, work and think.* First Mariner Books, New York.

Mitchell, W.J. 1996. *City of Bits: Space, place, and the infobahn*. MIT Press, Cambridge.

Monios, J., Bergqvist, R., and Woxenius, J. 2018. "Port-centric cities: The role of freight distribution in defining the port-city relationship." *Journal of Transport Geography,* Vol. 66, pp. 53–64.

Murrain, P. 2013. "Landscape Urbanism: Supplement or substitute?" In: Duany, A., and Talen, E. (Eds.) *Landscape Urbanism and its Discontents.* New Society Publishers, Gabriola Island, pp. 141–158.

NYSDEC Division of Air Resources (2017). "South End Study Progress Update." <https://www.dec.ny.gov/docs/air_pdf/albsouthend011018.pdf> (Accessed July 13, 2018).

Pastor, M., Sadd, J., and Hipp, J. 2001. "Which came first? Toxic facilities, minority move-in, and environmental justice." *Journal of Urban Affairs,* Vol. 23, No. 1, pp. 1–21.

Phelps, N., and Tewdwr-Jones, M. 2008. "If geography is anything, maybe it's planning's alter ego? Reflections on policy relevance in two disciplines concerned with place and space." *Transactions of the Institute of British Geographers,* Vol. 33, pp. 366–384.

Portney, K. 2005. "Civic engagement and sustainable cities in the United States." *Public Administration Review,* Vol. 65, No. 5, pp. 579–591.

Pulido, L. 1996. "A critical review of the methodology of environmental racism research." *Antipode,* Vol. 28, No. 2, pp. 142–159.

Raco, M., and Flint, J. 2011. "Towards a new politics of urban mobility." In: Flint, J., and Raco, M. (Eds.) *The Future of Sustainable Cities: Critical reflections.* Policy Press, Bristol, pp. 243–251.

Rheingold, H. 2009. *Smart Mobs: The next social revolution.* Basic Books, Cambridge, MA.

Rodwin, L., and Sanyal, B. (Eds.) 2000. *The Profession of City Planning: Changes, images, and challenges: 1950–2000.* Routledge, New York.

Rohe, W.M., and Freeman, L. 2001. "Assisted housing and residential segregation." *Journal of the American Planning Association,* Vol. 67, No. 3, pp. 279–292.

Sandercock, L. 1999. "A portrait of postmodern planning" *Plan Canada*, Vol. 39, pp. 12–14.

Sassen, S. 2014. *Expulsions: Brutality and complexity in the global economy.* Harvard University Press, Cambridge.

Schively, C. 2007. "Understanding the NIMBY and LULU phenomena: Reassessing our knowledge base and informing future research." *Journal of Planning Literature,* Vol. 21, No. 3, pp. 255–266.

Schon, D. 1987. *Educating the Reflective Practitioner.* Jossey-Bass Publishers, San Francisco.

Schweitzer, L., and Stephenson Jr, M. 2007. "Right answers, wrong questions: Environmental justice as urban research." *Urban Studies,* Vol. 44, No. 2, pp. 319–337.

Shay, E., and Khattak, A. 2010. "Toward sustainable transport: Conventional and disruptive approaches in the U.S. context." *International Journal of Sustainable Transportation,* Vol. 4, pp. 14–40.

Soja, E. W. 2010. *Seeking Spatial Justice.* University of Minnesota Press, Minneapolis.

Susskind, L., and Amundsen, O. 1999. *Using assisted negotiation to settle land use disputes: A guidebook for public officials.* Lincoln Institute of Land Policy, Cambridge.

Times Union. 2016. "Editorial: Time to close Prentice." *Times Union,* August 21.

Townsend, A. 2014. *Smart Cities.* W.W. Norton & Company, New York.

Velazquez, L., Munguia, N., Will, M., Zavala, A., Verdugo, S., Delakowitz, B., and Giannetti, B. 2015. "Sustainable transportation strategies for decoupling road vehicle transport and carbon dioxide emissions." *Management of Environmental Quality: An International Journal,* Vol. 26, No. 3, pp. 373–388.

Wachs, M. 2000. "Education for transportation planning in a new century." In: Rodwin, L., and Sanyal, B. (Eds.) *The Profession of City Planning: Changes, Images and Challenges 1950–2000.* Rutgers, New Brunswick, pp. 128–139.

Waldheim, C. 2016. *Landscape as Urbanism: A general theory.* Princeton University Press, Princeton.

Wilson, M.W. 2015. "On the criticality of mapping practices: Geodesign as critical GIS?" *Landscape and Urban Planning*, Vol. 142, pp. 226–234.

Zavestoski, S., and Agyeman, J. (Eds.). 2015. *Incomplete Streets: Processes, Practices and Possibilities.* Routledge, New York.

HOW DO SMART BUILDING PROJECTS DEFINE AND DELIVER VALUE? A CLASSIFICATION OF BUSINESS MODELLING CHARACTERISTICS TO SUPPORT DESIGN AND DEVELOPMENT

Adriano Tanda and Alberto De Marco
Politecnico di Torino, Department of Management and Production Engineering
Corso Duca degli Abruzzi 24, 10129, Torino

ABSTRACT

Both public administrations and real estate developers have been investing in innovative Smart Building projects to reduce energy consumption while improving housing quality and occupant comfort. Despite a booming market and an ever-growing academic interest in Smart Building technologies, few studies are available to understand the value generated by Smart Building projects and how these initiatives are able to achieve business success and distribute value to their stakeholders.

To fill this gap, this study presents an empirical analysis of 300 Smart Building projects implemented internationally. The projects' characteristics have been analyzed on a business model framework in order to identify general concepts and discarding redundant information. The result of this effort has been a classification of business modelling characteristics able to illustrate the main value and business objectives pursued by Smart Buildings projects and the strategies through which these projects distribute and deliver value to their customers and stakeholders.

This study presents two main implications. First, it helps scholars in their study on the development and implementation of Smart Building projects. Second, it supports the decision-making processes of both public and private developers acting as a collection of best practices for the design and development of Smart Building initiatives.

KEYWORDS

Smart City, Intelligent Buildings, Smart Buildings, Business Models, Case Study

1. INTRODUCTION

In 2017 the world's population exceeded 7.5 billion people and will grow up to 9.77 billion by 2050 (United Nations, 2017). One of the direct consequences of this trend is the ever-growing need for greater housing capacity and new buildings. On average, between 20 and 40% of the world's energy consumption is due to buildings (Arditi et al., 2015) making them the source of 40% of the annual Green House Gas (GHG) emissions (Kleissl and Agarwal 2010), and accounting from 5 to 10% of an average firm operating cost (Ghayvat et al., 2015). Furthermore, occupant comfort and quality of life is of paramount importance as it is linked to higher satisfaction and productivity (Holopainen et al., 2014). Indeed, housing quality correlates to psychological well-being (Wilner et al., 1962), improved children school performances, and has a positive effect on occupant depression and anxiety (Elton and Packer,1986). The Smart City (SC) and in particular Smart Buildings (SB) have been emerging as paradigms whose goals are fostering urban economic and social growth, guaranteeing the city's global competitiveness, and improving its environmental sustainability and the quality of life of its citizens (Michelucci et al., 2016) (Caragliu et al., 2011). Given these considerations, it is not surprising that the market for SB technological solutions is booming (Tanda and De Marco, 2018a) with Garner Insight (2018) reporting that by 2023 the market for these technologies will reach $31.74 billion from the $7.42 of 2018.

Nevertheless, there is a scarcity of studies investigating how SB initiatives are able to create value. The majority of these seminal works address these topics from a business modelling perspective (Tanda and De Marco, 2018b) as it considered to be the best tool to describe how an organization creates, captures, and delivers value (Osterwalder and Pigneur, 2010). Even fewer studies focus on developing a prescriptive approach to the topic by presenting classifications and taxonomies of SC business models. It is the case, for example, of Perboli et al. (2014) who develop a taxonomy of SC projects' business model characteristics based on a case study analysis of 28 SC initiatives or Cledou et al. (2018) who synthesize the business model characteristics of 42 SC services on a taxonomic framework describing how these initiatives are designed and developed.

However, these approaches present several criticalities. First, the related literature is quite limited, and the approaches presented are heterogeneous. Furthermore, no one presents a comprehensive approach to the topic, which should address together both value creation and stakeholder relationships. Finally, these focus on single vertical SC domain, mostly ignoring the building domain and SB technologies. As a contribution to filling these literature gaps, this study aims to address the following question: how do SB initiatives define and deliver value?

To answer this question, the goal of this work is to study the value creation processes of SB projects and services and develop a classification of their business model characteristics able to describe:

- Which value SB projects aim to deliver;
- How the intended value is created and distributed in relationship with projects' stakeholders;

To this end, the author collected 300 world-wide distributed SB projects focusing on small scale self-contained initiatives in order to capture a finer level of detail. For each of these projects, the author has synthesized their characteristics into a classification framework. This study will provide a tool able to assist academics in their studies on SB projects and aid city managers and private organizations in their decision-making processes designing, developing, and implementing SB projects.

This study is structured as follows. First, an overview of the literature is given (Section 2). Second, the methodology is explained (Section 3). Then, results are presented and discussed (Section 4). Finally, the authors draw conclusions and underline implications and limitations (Section 5).

2. LITERATURE OVERVIEW

Buildings are increasingly integrating technological systems in order to become "smart" (Arditi et al, 2015). Modern information and communication technologies allow the integration of control platforms to monitor and control buildings' infrastructures (Minoli et al., 2017) providing for a more efficient and cost-effective building ownership (So et al. 1999) and a more comfortable living experience by achieving the optimal combination of comfort and resource consumption (Chen et al., 2013) (Kwon et al., 2014). Intelligent solutions can be implemented in order to remotely control monitoring and automating the operations, performances and consumptions of a building HVAC system (Kolokotsa et al.2011), with the goal of reducing energy, eliminate wastes and improve comfort (Weng and Agarwal 2012). Similar technologies can be deployed in order to automate the operation of a building's lighting system, monitor its status and consumption and remotely control it (Tao et al., 2016). Similarly, the building's plumbing and irrigation system can also be remotely controlled, monitored, and automated in order to reduce water consumption and wastes (Kleissl and Agarwal 2010) (Minoli et al., 2017) while monitoring and controlling lifts and elevators guarantee a higher level of operational efficiency and safety (Arditi et al., 2015). Sensing technologies can also be implemented to monitor and control the building environment with the overall goal of improving the living comfort and the residents' well-being (Kwon et al., 2014). Indeed, all the buildings' air and water quality parameters, such as air and water temperature, air pollutants, humidity and noise pollution can all be easily monitored (Doukas et al. 2007). Remote control systems can also guarantee a higher degree of resident safety thanks to modern security and automatic access control systems (Doukas et al. 2007) (Ghayvat et al., 2015). Finally, new technologies can provide faster and more effective systems for fire prevention, detection, and extinguishment (Doukas et al. 2007).

Considering the vast field of applications, the authors decided to implement the taxonomic definition in Neirotti et al. (2014) who define of the domain "buildings" by breaking it down into three main sub-domains:

- Facility Management (FM): technologies and services aimed at improving aspects related to cleaning, maintenance, and property management;
- Building Services (BS): technologies and services for improving buildings' existing infrastructures such as electric networks, elevators, fire safety, telecommunication, centralized HVAC, and water supply systems;
- Housing Quality (HQ): technological solutions related to house automatization and the quality of life in a residential housing such as comfort, lighting, and safety;

3. METHODOLOGY

The authors developed a qualitative inductive data analysis approach with the objective of using data in order to extract theory (Glaser and Strauss, 2017). In particular, this study is based on a multiple case-study methodology, as it is a collective "robust" and "reliable" method (Baxter and Jack, 2008) most appropriate when researching the "why" and "how" of a contemporary issue or set of events (Johnson, 2008), followed by the empirical analysis of gathered data.

3.1 Data Gathering

The data gathering process was based on the definitions given in the previous section. To avoid the classical weaknesses of a single-case (holistic) model (Yin. 2013) such as lack of statistical significance and, most importantly, selection biases, for each of the three listed sub-domains, the author collected and analyzed 100 projects, for a total of 300 internationally distributed projects. This number was found sufficient in saturating the sample (O'Reilley and Parker, 2012). The research process has been conducted on the Internet by searching, on the search engine Google, for a query composed as follows: "name of the sub domain" AND "case study". The result of this search process allowed the author to gather projects from multiple sources such as: project reports to funding bodies, company websites and press releases, case-study white papers, and minutes of city council meetings. The multitude of different sources allow to confirm the validity of the process (Yin, 2013) and enhance the credibility of the study (Baxter and Jack, 2008). To populate the sample, the authors selected only the projects having the following characteristics:

- Small-scale and contained;
- Were, currently are, or are planned to be implemented, and/or are or have been commercially available;
- With enough information available in order to evaluate their business model characteristics;

Figure 1 shows the geographical distribution of the sample by international region, while Figure 2 shows their year of implementation. From Figure 1 is it possible to notice that most projects can be found either in Europe or North America. Furthermore, despite the data gathering process not being limited to a specific timeframe to avoid potential recency biases, from Figure 2 it is possible to observe that the overwhelming majority of projects have been implemented in the last ten years, between 2008/2009 and 2019/2020, highlighting the dramatic impact that recent technological advancements had on the development of innovative SB solutions (Theodoridis et al., 2018).

3.2 Framework Design

The second step of the study has been the development of a framework of main business modelling elements onto which the projects' characteristics can be analyzed and confronted. Given its prominence in the literature on SC business modelling (Schiavone et al, 2019), the author decided to use the business model canvas by Osterwalder and Pigneur (2010) as the reference framework for this study. However, while it allows to understand the value proposed by an organization and how it can deliver that value to its intended targets, it does not map two important elements useful to describe how specific projects are developed, namely the project's ownership and the project initial financing source. To this end, the author integrated the business model canvas following the framework model presented by Perboli et al. (2014) where "project initiator" of a SC project is classified as either a public entity, a private organization or a mix of the two, and the "financial resources" of a SC can come from either public or private sources.

3.3 Analysis

For the last step, each project has been analyzed individually, and its business model characteristics classified on the framework. The author started by identifying the project's owner and its financing sources. After this preliminary step, the other business model characteristics of the projects have been synthesized on the remaining nine elements of the framework. Finally, the author started an iterative process of refinement to identify similarities between different projects business model characteristics. The result has been the emergence of general concepts and patterns (Baden-Fuller and Morgan, 2010) that captured the essence of the projects' value creation process while discarding redundant information.

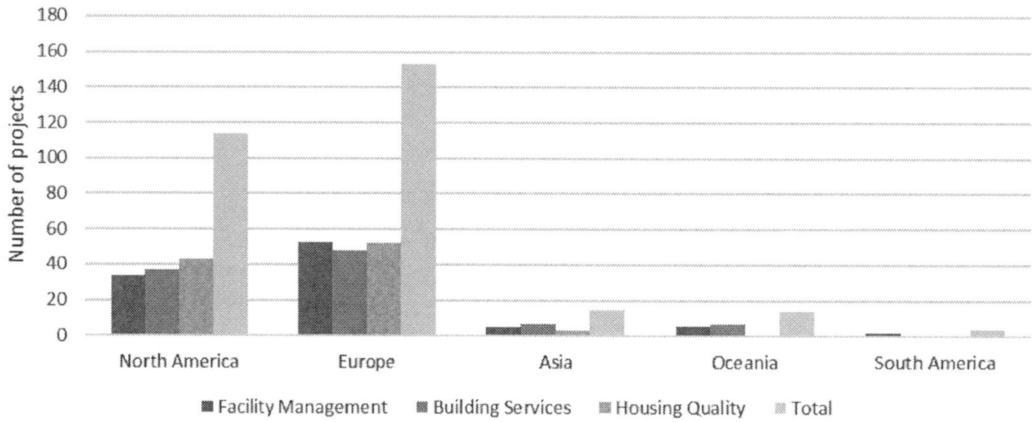

Figure 1. Geographical distribution of SB projects

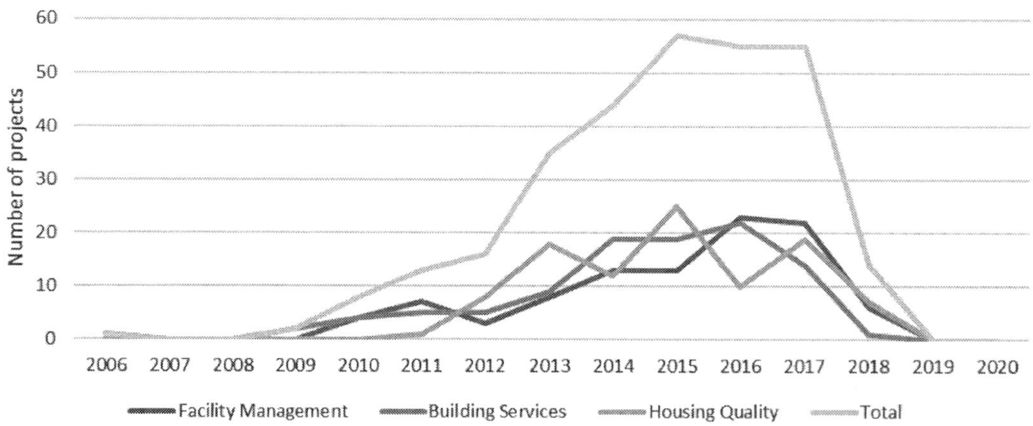

Figure 2. Implementation year of SB projects

4. DISCUSSION OF RESULTS

4.1 Facility Management

Chotipanich (2004) argues that the main role of FM is to support business operations and activities while managing human resources and the work environment through an efficient management of resources and services. Hence, the value propositions that can be observed in Table 1 are not surprising. The main objective of FM smart projects is to provide cost savings: 71% of FM projects aim to reduce operations costs by improving efficiency and productivity, consistently with FM acting as a key support for businesses' operations, while 49% of FM projects aim to increase energy efficiency. The FM domain involves a wide array of operations (Nutt, 2002) all using different environmental resources. Hence, the second most pursued objective of FM projects (70%) is to reduce pollution and the environmental impact of the buildings' FM operations.

Table 1. Classification of business modelling characteristics for FM projects

Key Partners	*Key Activities*	*Value Proposition*	*Customer Relationships*	*Customer Segments*
Commercial partners (100%); Technology providers (95%); Public entities (29%); University / research centers (2%);	Systems remote control and automatization (68%); Data gathering (49%); Energy management (45%); Lighting management (30%); Air and water quality management (14%); Plumbing system management (13%); Waste management (11%);	Operation cost savings (71%); Pollution reduction (70%); Energy saving (49%);	Dedicated custom solutions (100%);	Private organizations (64%); Public entities (36%);
	Key Resources		*Channels*	
	Research and intellectual property (100%) Hardware & Software (100%) Commercial relationship (43%)		Physical interaction (100%); Web / digital applications (98%);	

Cost Structure	*Revenue Streams*
SG&A (100%);	Sales (96%); Software licensing (76%);
Ownership	*Financing*
Private (65%); Public (35%);	Private (64%); Public (36%);

These objectives are achieved through multiple activities. Most FM projects reach their goals through the deployment of systems able to remotely control, program, and automate FM operations (68%) and able to sense and collect buildings' data (49%). Direct energy management activities are implemented in 45% of projects, while 30% implement solutions to directly manage the building lighting systems. The management of the building's environmental parameters (air and water quality) is pursued by 14% of projects, while 13% of FM initiatives are deployed to control and automate the building's water and plumbing infrastructures. Finally,

11% of the projects manage waste and recycling systems. The main targets of FM projects are private organizations (64%) while 36% of projects target public entities. There is virtually no overlap between targeted segments as FM projects are developed custom made for a specific customer. Partnerships are key for the implementation of FM projects, both with commercial entities (100%) such as retailers, distributors, and technicians, and with technical suppliers (95%). Public entities are a partner in 29% of projects. The almost complete lack of partnership with research institutions (2%) highlights the technological maturity of these projects. Finally, sources of revenue are quite traditional: the overwhelming majority of FM projects' revenue (96%) comes from direct sales of goods and services and 4% of projects generate revenue through software licensing. This suggest that the market of FM smart solutions tends to have more traditional monetization structures. Finally, while most FM projects are owned and financed by private organizations, a sizeable minority of them are owned and financed by public entities (35 and 36% respectively) suggesting a relatively high level of involvement of the public sector in the development of these projects.

4.2 Building Services

From data reported in Table 2, 66% of the sample projects have reducing the building environmental impact as one of the main goals, while 57% aim to improve their energy efficiency. Finally, 51% of the projects aim at reducing the building operations costs.

Table 2. Classification of business modelling characteristics for BS projects

<table>
<tr><td rowspan="2">Key Partners

Technology providers (100%);
Commercial partners (100%);
Public entities (36%);
University / research centers (2%);</td><td>Key Activities

Data gathering (95%);
System remote control and automatization (87%);
Energy management (51%);
Lighting management (41%);
Utilities consumption management (37%);
HVAC management (32%);
Safety system management (31%);
Air and water quality management (25%);
Plumbing system management (12%);</td><td rowspan="2">Value Proposition

Pollution reduction (66%);
Energy savings (57%);
Cost savings (51%);
Improve safety (50%);
Improve comfort (35%);</td><td>Customer Relationships

Dedicated custom solutions (100%);</td><td rowspan="2">Customer Segments

Private organizations (87%);
Public entities (13%);</td></tr>
<tr><td>Key Resources

Research and intellectual property (100%)
Hardware & Software (100%)
Commercial relationship (89%)</td><td>Channels

Physical interaction (100%);
Web / digital applications (89%);</td></tr>
<tr><td colspan="3">Cost Structure

SG&A (100%);</td><td colspan="2">Revenue Streams

Sales (100%);
Software licensing (71%);</td></tr>
<tr><td colspan="3">Ownership

Private (87%);
Public (13%);</td><td colspan="2">Financing

Private (83%);
Public (17%);</td></tr>
</table>

However, safety and security are the main reasons behind the design and development of SB technologies (Ghayvat et al., 2015) (Kleissl and Agarwal 2010). Hence, it is not surprising that improving building security results as the objective of 50% of the sample projects. Similarly, the main objective of a smart building is to provide a high level of living comfort and wellbeing to its occupants (Doukas et al., 2007) (Kwon et al., 2014). This is reflected in the sampled projects: in fact, improving comfort and resident wellbeing is the main objectives for 35% of the sample.

BS projects implement technologies able to sense the building environment and remotely and automatically act (95 and 87% respectively). Other key components of the building infrastructure directly managed by smart solutions are the energy system (51%), the lighting system (41%) and the HVAC system (32%). Finally, together with environmental sensing (the building's air and water quality), security management allows for a direct improvement of the occupant safety. Unsurprisingly, most customers are private organizations (87%), with public entities target of only 13% of the projects. Even more than for FM, BS projects are developed for specific customers. This is why the lack of overlapping in the targeted customer segment of these projects is observed. Technology providers and commercial partners are essential for the implementation of BS projects (100%), while public entities act as partners in 36% of the projects. Universities and research centers are almost absent (2%), which suggests a strong maturity of these technologies. Finally, it is possible to observe a traditional monetization approach in all the projects with direct sales of goods and services as the main revenue stream. This strengthens the idea that the market of SB solutions is relatively traditional regarding how they make money. Private organizations are the main owners and financiers of BS projects, with the public sector relegated to a minority position.

4.3 Housing Quality

As stated above, innovative technologies in the home environment have the objective of improving comfort, energy efficiency, safety and security (Ghayvat et al., 2015). It comes as no surprise then, from the data in Table 3, that improving comfort is by far the most pursued objective for HQ technologies (in 89% of projects), followed by safety improvements (42%). Interestingly, HQ projects are less concerned with providing cost saving measures (only 18% of HQ projects) and reducing the housing environmental impact (24%) suggesting that HQ projects are driven more by the potential positive impact that they can have on the occupants' quality of life than by cash or environmental considerations.

HQ projects implement a multitude of smart solutions. Systems able to sense and collect building information while automatically react upon these data or allowing for the possibility of remote intervention can be found in a majority of the project sampled (67 and 56% respectively). 73% of projects aim to directly manage home lighting, while 58% manage HVAC systems. Entertainment-oriented solutions are offered in 52% of projects, while 32% of the projects offer safety and security technologies. Finally, only a minority of projects deploy technology for energy, consumption and water management (29, 22, and 22% respectively). Projects in the HQ domains are related to housing safety and security, and home automation. Hence, these projects mostly target homeowners and private users (100%). Unsurprisingly then, while technology providers maintain their role as key partners in most HQ projects (98%), commercial partners lose their relevance (18%), as most of HQ solutions are distributed through retail and do not require specialist technical support for installation and maintenance. HQ projects present a high degree of maturity, highlighted by the irrelevance of universities or research centers as main partners. Finally, revenue sources for HQ projects come from traditional sales of goods and services (100%). The public sector appears to be completely absent as either owner or financer of HQ projects, which is reasonable as these projects are targeted at consumers and homeowners.

Table 3. Classification of business modelling characteristics for HQ projects

Key Partners	*Key Activities*	*Value Proposition*	*Customer Relationships*	*Customer Segments*
Technology providers (98%); *Commercial partners (18%);* *University / research centers (1%);*	*Lighting management (73%);* *Data gathering (67%);* *HVAC management (58%);* *System remote control and automation (56%);* *Entertainment systems (52%);* *Safety systems (32%);* *Energy management (29%);* *Utility consumption management (22%);* *Plumbing system management (22%);* *Air and water quality management (16%);*	*Improve comfort (89%);* *Improve safety (42%);* *Pollution reduction (26%);* *Cost savings (18%);* *Energy savings (17%);*	*Automated services (86%);* *Dedicated custom solutions (34%);*	*Private citizens (100%);*
	Key Resources *Research and intellectual property (100%)* *Hardware & Software (100%)*		*Channels* *Physical interaction (100%);* *Web / digital applications (98%);*	
Cost Structure SG&A (100%);			*Revenue Streams* Sales (100%); Software licensing (7%);	
Ownership Private (100%);			*Financing* Private (100%);	

4.4 Discussion

From the data discussed above, it is possible to notice that all three SB domains present similar objectives and value propositions, all aiming to reduce costs and pollution while improving energy efficiency, safety and comfort. Furthermore, projects in the SB domains are able to deliver both public and private value and have both business-oriented and socially-conscious objectives. Indeed, cost reduction, energy savings, and comfort are key objectives, highlighting the business-oriented nature of these projects, the main goal appears to be reducing pollution, while improving the safety and security of buildings and building services, highlighting their socially-conscious orientation.

This is consistent with the related literature that identify the buildings as the most critical urban dimension in terms of energy consumption and emissions and highlight the possibilities of smart technologies in terms of cost reduction and improved quality of life (Arditi et al., 2015). To summarize, SB projects are able to deliver both socially-conscious public value (Emerson, 2003) and business-oriented objectives. In particular, the main objectives of these projects are reducing pollution and improving occupant's safety and security, while reducing costs and energy consumptions and improving living comfort.

SB projects implements several innovative technologies. Nevertheless, gathering data and implementing systems able to monitor, program and automate building functions, from lighting to the HVAC system, is the main key enabler for SB projects. As most of the projects in the SB domains are at least partially custom made for a specific customer, there are no overlaps between the projects' targets. Private organizations are the major customer for these projects, followed by homeowners and public entities. Partnerships are relatively homogeneous, with technology providers and suppliers, and distributors and technicians being the main key partners.

SB projects present a traditional approach to monetization strategies with sales representing the main revenue source. The lack of research and development as a meaningful cost item highlights the market maturity of these projects, as underlined by the almost total lack of research institutions as partners.

Finally, the public sector plays a minor role as both owner and financing source. However, projects implemented in the SB domains still deliver socially-conscious public value. One explanation for this may be that these objectives are, in reality, a byproduct of a business-oriented pursuit of energy efficiency. However, one other explanation is that the public sector is able to drive this socially-oriented innovation mostly through regulations and guidelines. The role of the public sector becomes to design regulations driving innovative smart building projects with the objective of prompting the implementation of socially-conscious technologies and solutions.

5. CONCLUSION

This paper proposes a classification of business modelling characteristics for SB innovative projects that addresses the following research question: how do SB projects define and deliver value?

To this end, the authors have collected 100 projects for each of the three domains composing the SB taxonomy. The business modelling characteristics of each project has been analyzed and classified on the business model canvas by Osterwalder and Pigneur (2010), chosen as a reference framework for this study, to capture the essence of these characteristics.

As a theoretical contribution, this classification is able to address the shortcomings of the academic literature on the design and development of SB projects. This classification helps understand how SB projects create and distribute value and how these structure change depending on the different domain. Therefore, this work presents a reference canvas for the analysis of SB projects and allows scholars to better understand and predict the strategies and decisions required for their implementation.

As a practical implication, this classification helps public administrators effectively and efficiently develop their own SB projects depending on the goals and objectives they aim to achieve. On the other hand, private vendors will be able to use these classifications as a way to discern what benefits are expected by their clients and how to effectively create and deliver it.

This study suffers from two main limitations. First, the overwhelming majority of projects analyzed comes from either Europe or North America. However, this reflects the limitations of the data gathering process due to the author's geographical and language constraints.

Second, by design this study limits the projects' collection to the definitions presented in the literature section. Any SB projects, and their relative characteristics, outside the scope of those definition are not included in the analysis.

REFERENCES

D. Arditi et al. (2015) "Assessing the Smartness of Buildings," Facilities 33:9-10, 553-572.

C. Baden-Fuller, M.S. Morgan (2010) "Business Models as Models," Long range planning 43:2-3, 156-171.

P. Baxter, S. Jack, (2009) "Qualitative Case Study Methodology: Study Design and Implementation for Novice Researchers," The qualitative report 13:4, 544-559.

A. Caragliu et al. (2011) "Smart Cities in Europe," Journal of urban technology 18:02, 65-82.

C. Chen et al. (2913) "The User Side of Sustainability: Modeling Behavior and Energy Usage in the Home," Pervasive and Mobile Computing 9:01, 161-175.

G. Cledou et al. (2018) "A Taxonomy for Planning and Designing Smart Mobility Services," Government Information Quarterly 35:1, 61-76.

S. Chotipanich (2014) "Positioning Facility Management," Facilities 22:13-14, 364-372.

H. Doukas et al. (2007) "Intelligent Building Energy Management System Using Rule Sets," Building and Environment 42:10, 3562-3569.

P. Elton, J. Packer (1986) "A Prospective Randomized Trial of The Value of Rehousing on The Grounds of Mental Health," Journal of Chronic Disease 39, 221-227.

J. Emerson (2003) "The Blended Value Proposition: Integrating Social and Financial Returns," California Management Review 45:4, 35-51.

Garner Insights (2018) Global Smart Buildings Market 2018 by Manufacturers, Countries, Type and Application, Forecast to 2023 https://garnerinsights.com/Global-Smart-Buildings-Market-2018-by-Manufacturers-Countries-Type-and-Application-Forecast-to-2023 Accessed November 12, 2018.

H. Ghayvat et al. (2015) "WSN-and IOT-based Smart Homes and Their Extension to Smart Buildings," Sensors 15:5, 10350-10379.

B. G. Glaser, A. L. Strauss (2017) Discovery of Grounded Theory: Strategies for Qualitative Research (UK, London: Routledge).

R. Holopainen, et al. (2014) "Comfort Assessment in The Context of Sustainable Buildings: Comparison of Simplified and Detailed Human Thermal Sensation Methods," Building and Environment 71:1, 60-70.

W. H. Johnson (2008) "Roles, Resources and Benefits of Intermediate Organizations Supporting Triple Helix Collaborative R&D: The Case of Precarn", Technovation 28: 8, 495-505.

J. Kleissl, Y. Agarwal (2010) "Cyber-Physical Energy Systems: Focus on Smart Buildings," paper presented at the Design Automation Conference (DAC) (Anaheim, CA, U.S.A., June 13-18).

D. Kolokotsa et al. (2011) "A Roadmap Towards Intelligent Net Zero and Positive Energy Buildings," Solar Energy 85:2, 3067-3084.

O. Kwon et al. (2014) "Sensor-Aware Elevator Scheduling for Smart Building Environment," Building and Environment, 72:1, 312-326.

F. V. Michelucci et al. (2016) "Defining the Role of the Smart-City Manager: An Analysis of Responsibilities and Skills," Journal of Urban Technology 23:03, 23-42.

D. Minoli et al. (2017) "IoT Considerations, Requirements, and Architectures for Smart Buildings—Energy Optimization and Next-Generation Building Management Systems," IEEE Internet of Things Journal 4:1, 269-283.

P. Neirotti et al. (2014) "Current Trends in Smart City Initiatives: Some Stylised Facts," Cities 38, 25-36.

B. Nutt (2000), "Four Competing Futures for Facility Management," Facilities 18:3-4,124-132.

M. O'reilly, N. Parker (2012) "'Unsatisfactory Saturation': A Critical Exploration of the Notion of Saturated Sample Sizes in Qualitative Research," Qualitative Research, 13:2, 190-197.

A. Osterwalder, Y. Pigneur (2010) Business Model Generation, (Hoboken, NJ, USA: Willey).

G. Perboli et al. (2014) "A New Taxonomy of Smart City Projects," Transportation Research Procedia 3, 470-478.

F. Schiavone et al. (2019) "Business Model Innovation for Urban Smartization," Technological Forecasting and Social Change 142, 210-219.

A. T. P. So et al. (1999) "A New Definition of Intelligent Buildings for Asia," Facilities 17:12-13, 485-491.

A. Tanda, A. De Marco (2018a) "Drivers of Public Demand of IoT-Enabled Smart City Services: A Regional Analysis," Journal of Urban Technology 25:4, 77-94.

A. Tanda, A. De Marco (2018b) "Business Model Framework for Smart City Mobility Projects," paper presented at the World Multidisciplinary Civil Engineering-Architecture-Urban Planning Symposium - WMCAUS 2018 (Prague, Czech Republic, June 18-22).

F. Tao et al. (2016) "Internet of Things in Product Life-Cycle Energy Management," Journal of Industrial Information Integration 1, 26-39.

E. Theodoridis et al. (2013) "Developing an IoT Smart City Framework," paper presented at the 4th International Conference on Information, Intelligence, Systems and Applications (Piraeus, Greece, July 10-12).

United Nations, Department of Economic and Social Affairs, Population Division (2017) World Population Prospects: The 2017 Revision, Volume I: Comprehensive Tables https://esa.un.org/unpd/wpp/Publications/Files/WPP2017_Volume-I_Comprehensive-Tables.pdf Accessed March 13, 2018.

T. Weng, Y. Agarwal (2012) "From Buildings to Smart Buildings—Sensing and Actuation to Improve Energy Efficiency," IEEE Design & Test of Computers 29:4, 36-44.

D. Wilner et al. (1962) The Housing Environment and Family Life: A Longitudinal Study of the Effects of Housing on Morbidity and Mental Health (Baltimore, MD, U.S.A.: Johns Hopkins Press).

R. K. Yin (2013) Case Study Research and Applications: Design and Methods (Thousand Oaks, CA, U.S.A.: Sage publications, 2013).

FACT-CHECKING & SOCIAL MEDIA SHARING BEHAVIOR AMONG UAE YOUTH

Ashraf Khalil[a], Salam Abdallah[b] and Kundan Noor Sheikh[1]
[a]*Department of Computer Science and Information Technology, Abu Dhabi University*
Abu Dhabi, United Arab Emirates
[b]*College of Business, Abu Dhabi University*
Abu Dhabi, United Arab Emirates

ABSTRACT

With the advent of the internet and social media, the spread of online misinformation has become a matter of serious concern for scholars and decision makers all over the world. Given this platform's relative lack of censorship and extensive as well as swift reach, the likelihood of unverified information content spreading unchallenged in the digital world has grown exponentially. This study aims to understand the patterns of content-sharing behavior on major social media platforms by young adults living in United Arab Emirates, and how this is influenced by various demographic and social factors in an individual user's life, such as social conformity and religiosity. A qualitative analysis of 6 semi-structured interviews on young adult users ranging between 18 to 24 years of age in the United Arab Emirates (UAE) was conducted to ascertain their sharing patterns as well as tendencies to verify content being shared via social media. The study finds that the need for social conformity and religiosity influence what users share on social media and how likely they are to verify information before sharing it.

KEYWORDS

Social Media, Online Misinformation, Privacy, Young Adult, Religiosity, Social Conformity

1. INTRODUCTION

Limited censorship in social media has led to unprecedented sharing of unverified content such as rumors and fake news. Hence recent works in the field of Human-Computer Interaction (HCI) have extensively studied sharing practices on social media and how the veracity of information being shared is a growing concern. Starbird, et al. (2016) have identified and described types of 'expressed uncertainty' in social media posts on Twitter during different points in a rumor's lifecycle, across different rumors, and within multiple crisis events. Using Artificial Intelligence (AI) nudges for fact-checking to influence human and machine behavior in an effort to make it more pro-social while preserving individual liberty has also been explored. (Matias, 2017) The effect of reciprocity in sharing behavior and engagement practices is also seen to have significant importance. (Grinberg, et al., 2016) Therefore, disambiguating the "social" aspect of sharing behavior is considered to be of prime importance in order to ensure safe sharing practices whereby content and information being shared and re-shared by young adult users is true and authentic.

Given its unique background and demographic composition, the UAE plays a pivotal and interesting role in the region with regards to content-sharing via social media, its importance and its impact. Despite being one of the smallest Middle Eastern nations in terms of population, the UAE is an Internet adoption leader in the Arab world, with a fast-growing base of internet users. Overall, in the Arab world, the media environment has started opening up recently, especially with social media platforms providing increased opportunities for self-expression and information sharing. (Wiest & Eltantawy, 2015) However, due to the socio-cultural values of most users in this region, concerns for privacy and reliability of information-sharing have been paramount. An initial study on the use of social media in UAE pointed out that overall users can be said to have a "guarded trust" of the media, especially for media they feel operate correctly and protect their privacy.

[1]kundanrulz@gmail.com

(Al-jenaibi, 2015) Exploring the meaning of "privacy" from the perspective of Qatari nationals, Abokhodair, et al. (2016) have concluded that in the Arab Gulf, the need for privacy is often supported by Quranic text, and privacy is framed as a communal attribute, including not only the individual, but the behavior of those around them; it even extends beyond one's lifespan. Such previously unexplored interpretations of privacy play a role in how users' social, cultural and religious contexts play a major role in how they navigate social media.

Hence, set against this backdrop cultural uniqueness and demographic diversity in the region, young adults in UAE are definitely likely to take into account certain socio-cultural factors when deciding not only what content to share on social media, but also how to verify the authenticity of what is being shared as they feel a high sense of social responsibility towards those who will interact with this shared content.

The aim of this research is to help identify a new angle of sharing habits relevant to this region in particular, where religion and culture is such an integral part of social interaction.

1.1 Religiosity

The terms religiosity is often defined as an individual's conviction, devotion, and veneration towards a particular religion or theology. In its most comprehensive use, religiosity can encapsulate all dimensions of religion, gauged by an involvement in religious practices and how much influence one's religious beliefs have on one's day-to-day dealings in life. (Gallagher & Tierney, 2013)

Religiosity has been used as a dominant factor in social sciences to determine patterns of religious influences among American adolescents. (Smith, 2003) Several reliable studies show that youth and their families who regularly participate in religious activities and rituals display greater overall satisfaction with their lives and feel better equipped to solve health-related problems than those who don't engage in such activities as often. A number of studies also show that religion is associated with more effective "coping" with problems by youth, among teens and young adults. (Shortz & Worthington, 1994; Varon & Riley, 1999)

A 10-item intrinsic Religious Motivation Scale proposed by Hoge (1972) with slight modifications to adjust for cultural norms in the Arab world (Abdel - Khalek, 2017).

1.2 Social Conformity

In order to identify the level of social conformity in our participants, our online survey took them through a series of statements to agree or diagree with using a likert scale. This was done using a Concern for Appropriateness Scale (CAS) developed by Lennox and Wolfe in 1984, which was validated fully by Martin A Johnson in 1989. (Johnson, 1989)

Melman, et al. (2009) have verified the applicability of the Hebrew version of CAS internationally beyond the Western culture recommending its use in the fields of social psychology, employment, business and personality research. Thus it was appropriate for us to apply it to the UAE population with slight cultural adjustments as suggested by the authors of this study.

Bliss & Brown (1994) have used Lennox and Wolfe's CAS to investigate the direct and indirect relationship between social conformity (representative of peer pressure, self-representation, etc.) and the use of alcohol and marijuana among 143 American college students. Not only did this scale directly predict Marijuana use, but also interacted with religiosity in the prediction of marijuana use. As for alcohol use, CAS did not directly predict alcohol use but this scale interacted with religiosity and gender in in the prediction of alcohol use. Thus proving the validity of the CAS as an index of social anxiety among young adults leading to specific behavior patterns just to 'fit in'.

We have thus applied similar principles in our study to find the correlation between CAS and patterns of sharing and verifying shared content on social media, as well as the interaction of CAS with religiosity (represented by the HOGE scale explained above) and the demographics of gender among our sample of young adults living in the UAE.

1.3 Personality

A brief 10-item measure of the Big-Five personality dimensions was used to determine the personality traits of our participants in the quantitative study along the scales of extraversion vs. introversion, openness vs. closedness to experience, conscientiousness vs. lack of direction, agreeableness vs. antagonism and neuroticism vs. emotional stability. (Gosling, et al., 2003; John & Srivastava, 1999) This scale was used to determine how these personality traits affect sharing behavior among participants directly and indirectly through social conformity.

2. BODY OF PAPER

Our study focuses on three main research objectives:

1. Identifying social, cultural and religious factors that influence the type of content that young adults share on social media
2. Determining the influence of these factors on the type of content shared
3. Determining what role this influence plays in the likelihood of users verifying the content before sharing it – and if so, how do they verify it?

To answer the above questions, we conducted an in-depth qualitative analysis into the motivations behind social media sharing behavior among young adults in the UAE, and what measures they took to verify the veracity of this information. Data were derived from young adults of various nationalities aged between 18 to 24 years residing within the UAE. Six face-to-face, semi-structured, in-depth interviews were conducted for this qualitative analysis. Before starting the interview, each participant was made to fill out an online survey designed using the Big Five Personality Traits, HOGE Scale for Religiosity (Hoge, et al., 1982) and Concern for Appropriateness Scale (CAS) for social conformity in order to determine the linkages between their score on these scales and their interview answers. (Lennox & Wolfe, 1984; Johnson, 1989)

2.1 Social Media Sharing and Verification Behavior

Six in-depth interviews, each longer than 20 minutes, were conducted. All participants were young adult students residing in the UAE. Three of them identified as male and three as female. All of them identified as Muslim. Research conducted by Dworkin (2012) was taken into consideration when deciding this sample size, whereby "An extremely large number of articles, book chapters, and books recommend guidance and suggest anywhere from 5 to 50 participants as adequate" for qualitative analyses using in-depth interviews.

The design of the interviews was semi-structured, whereby the focus was to get a general overview of participants sharing habits, mainly what type of content they share, what motivates them to share it and how they feel about the importance of credibility of information being shared through social media, especially sensitive content like religious quotes, breaking news, etc. Based on these detailed open-ended discussions, the following themes were extracted regarding the participants' sharing behavior on social media which give insights into their need for social conformity when sharing content as well as their motivations and ideas behind making the online information-sharing space a safe one.

2.1.1 Empathy and Concern for the Collective Value System

Empathy and concern for how their post makes others feel, emerged as a recurring theme throughout this study, as one participant mentioned upon being questioned about her motivations behind sharing sayings and inspirational stories on social media, "It's essentially just to spread the goodness." followed by "why spread the hate" when the discussion flowed into whether or not she would be inclined to share controversial religious content through her profile on Facebook.

Furthermore, participants in our study showed a keen sense of respecting collective beliefs and values prevalent in the society around them, acknowledging the fact that the same value system extends into their interactions and sharing habits on social media as well, when one participant observes, "Values shape everything about us…so if there is something that might be against my values or the values of my friends or family, for example, I wouldn't be sending it around or having a look at it myself even. So for example, some hate videos come up on Facebook against some religions and ethnicities, I don't even bother looking at them, because then I'm just wasting my time over things that are not worth my time." Another user, when questioned about how he feels regarding his friends and acquaintances on his social network sharing unverified religious content, stated, "Well, I stop paying attention to their posts in the future. I just ignore their posts. Their credibility goes down. For example, there are religious views, like a hadith or any saying from the Prophet Mohammed, which you are quoting in your status, then you NEED to write where it is taken from. It is very clear that we need to prevent a lot of unnecessary and false information from entering into our value system and our social beliefs".

2.1.2 Importance of Social Conformity and Preserving Self-Image

Another trend that was observed was the participants' unwillingness to debunk information publically on social media as "everyone's watching". In this context, when asked about their inclination to openly negate false information shared by friends on social media by, for example, commenting on such a post, one participant observed, "I won't really say anything to them by commenting publicly on Facebook, for example…but if we ever have a discussion about it face-to-face later, I would give my opinion. But otherwise, I won't oppose them on social media platform. I try to steer clear of getting involved in controversial issues on social media. Better to play it safe than be rude and offend someone you are friends with."

Another comment that made the concern for self-image fairly evident was, "I am very careful about what I post, as I don't want unsolicited, possibly incorrect, information to spread through me. I also feel that if I am not an authority on the subject, then I am not the right person to be sharing it. Like, for example, there are lots of people nowadays who share things after reading, say, just 'one' news article about it without any background knowledge about the subject matter. So I feel that is very wrong and extremely unfair to those you are sharing it with. So, for me, if I am not an expert on a particular topic, then maybe I don't have the right to post about it, you know."

2.1.3 Moral Responsibility towards Correcting the Information Space

Examining how users correct online rumors on Twitter, Arif, et al. (2017) uncovered three different objectives for taking correcting actions: correcting oneself, correcting the information space, and correcting another person (or organization). A deeper analysis was undertaken to identify users' rationale for their corrective actions in relation to these three correction objectives. Consequently several perspectives on the "locus of responsibility" for sharing and correcting rumors were identified, whereby when a user take the responsibility of correcting a rumor upon herself, she is most likely to correct her own previous post upon finding out the truth, while if a user presumes the responsibility of rumor-correcting upon the crowd accessing the information or the social media platform itself, then the likelihood of her correcting her own post after it has been debunked goes down. (Arif, et al., 2017)

A recurring concern participants in our study expressed was regarding the veracity of information being shared via social media and how checks and balance need to be incorporated by users themselves. None of the interviewees were of the opinion that unverified information should ever be shared on social media and most of them agreed that the onus of checking for its authenticity before sharing lies upon the users themselves. They expressed displeasure upon seeing inauthentic content being shared by their friends and acquaintances on social media, and went on to suggest ways of verifying sensitive content before sharing it, so as to cleanse the online social media sharing space of plagues such as fake news and misinformation. Expressing her concern for such instances, one participant said, "When people usually send these kind of videos with stats in them, a lot of times stats are actually exaggerated because that person just wants to drive their point home…so like instead of saying only about 50 people were affected, they'll say something like two-thirds of the population was affected, which is kind of an exaggerated way of saying just 50 people were affected…maybe because 50 sounds like a small number in comparison to the billions that we have on this planet. So, things like these, because they're usually exaggerated, I don't tend to go for them because I don't know if they're true or not…or how much they have been twisted just to drive a point across…"

On further probing about how such misinformation can be corrected, a sense of moral obligation was expressed, "let's say there's a blogger saying things against a certain minority, like some kind of hate message, you can't really stop them directly. But what you can do is stop spreading it if it comes up to you…prevent it from reaching others and stop the hate from spreading further". So there was a general resolve to not re-share information that has not been proven to be correct, so as to prevent the wrong from spreading.

The participants also shared details about their own ways of checking the authenticity of content they come across on social media, with one of them commenting, "whether I believe what I read or not, depends on the source. So if its let's say CNN, I'm more inclined to believe it…if its Huffington post, I would believe it. But is it's just a normal random page, like a blog or something…then I wouldn't believe it right away." Another participant added a similar view saying, "For me, if it's coming from a reliable source like Khaleej times or Gulf news, so I would consider that authentic. And they update it. So if I go to the website of Khaleej times and I am following a story, so I can get all the updates from it. So if at any point in time, the information is proven to be wrong, I can update it, and tell other people about it as well. But usually people don't do that, which is something I dislike. I feel we should keep a constant check on what we are posting on social media, so we can keep a track of whether it is right or wrong. It is our responsibility to share the truth."

As mentioned before, most participants were inclined towards correcting the online information space tacitly rather publicly, so when commenting on the measures taken on their part when their friends post controversial or unverified content, one of them said, "Mainly, I STOP trusting people who share such unverified content…because you see I don't tend to blindly share stuff just because everyone is doing it, but when and if I do share something, then it means that I have done some background research and I have fair knowledge about the subject matter…but I know that other people do not follow the same principles. They share things without checking, without verifying and end up spreading wrong information left, right and center…" when further probed about how this makes him feel, he added, "it really upsets me… I think that on a personal level, people should be aware of the fact that whatever they share should be verified because, in general, I'm sure no one is in favor of our future generations being exposed to knowledge and information which is misleading."

Discussing measures that can be taken to prevent such misinformation from spreading, he added, "So we should take the responsibility to correct this on our own. But if people are still not abiding by such basic values and principles, then perhaps awareness campaigns should be a thing. I know that it sounds like a rather trivial issue to be campaigning for, but it is extremely important at the same time. I mean, its free space, right? Anyone and everyone can post pretty much whatever they like, and that alone, comes with a sense of responsibility…so what's the difference between someone people who deliberately WANT to spread rumors and those who are doing it simply out of ignorance because they fail to 'check' before they post something. In the cyberspace, they're both equally wrong…there's no excuse for it! So we have to teach our youth where to draw the line. And for that I feel that awareness campaigns are a good idea…one of the better solutions to the problem. It is also a good idea to start it from our younger generation, since they are at the forefront and tend to use these platforms most frequently… So I think we should start awareness sessions in schools, colleges and then universities to introduce the idea of ethical sharing."

Mentioning people who misquote religious content on social media in specific, he further added, "I think we should minimize this by quoting the credentials and…that's something at we are being taught regularly even at university, you know…the importance of citation…whatever you write in your assignments, reports and research papers should be verified. Same principle applies, you know. Why blindly copy-pasted things without fair background knowledge? It makes sense, basically, to research a little on something that you are so confidently sharing on social media with hundreds and thousands of people…verify it, and cite the source where possible…else, steer clear!"

3. CONCLUSION

The qualitative analysis of our participants' sharing behavior proved that a need for social conformity and religiosity play a major role in determining the content that is being shared by young adults in the UAE. It also influences their decision to verify content being shared, especially sensitive information concerning religious beliefs, breaking news, etc. A sense of moral responsibility towards cleansing the information space to benefit other users and to save them from harm was also seen.

Based on our qualitative study, we can conclude that young adults in the UAE experience a collective sense of empathy and concern for the value system prevalent in the region. This was partially pointed out by Wiest & Eltantawy (2015) and has been proven further in a more multi-faceted context through our current study. In order to preserve 'peace' within their relations and bonds developing via social media, these youngsters were opposed to the idea of sharing controversial content against any religion or ethnicity, so as to not offend anyone in the diverse socio-cultural context of their region, just as they do in real life. Their primary objective for sharing content on social media was to spread goodness rather than negativity and to be a source of helping others network rather than harming them.

Secondly, not only are the youth concerned about conforming to the social, moral and cultural values of their surroundings when engaging with content on social media, they are also significantly concerned about their self-image when sharing, re-sharing or engaging with such content. This inculcates a high level of conscientious sharing behavior, whereby these users are generally very careful about what they post/share and always try their best to verify the source of any sensitive content they may be sharing, be it religious text or breaking news. The downside to this need for preserving self-image is that they are less likely to openly publicly debunk false information (such as fake news) being shared by their own family, friends and acquaintances on social media, as a high percentage of users interviewed expressed hesitation in making an effort to publicly correct their friends for posting wrong/controversial material on social media. So, for example, instead of commenting on a post saying "this is fake news", they would rather tell the original poster in private if they are close enough or just ignore it if they don't the personal too closely. However, they all agreed that such posters do lose their future credibility, and that information shared through such people would always be received with a grain of salt, i.e. being on the receiving end of such content, our young adults would always think twice about believing it without verifying on their own through other reliable sources. So 'trust but verify'!

Lastly, our participants were of the opinion that the onus of responsibility for verifying information shared via social media falls upon the user herself. Hence they showed a strong conviction/commitment towards always verifying sensitive information against various credible sources before posting it on their social media. They also displayed a certain level of resistance towards blindly believing anything posted by their friends on social media without verifying it for themselves, as they felt it was their own responsibility to consume/receive authentic information – be morally responsible consumers and sharers/posters of knowledge/information.

Future research will develop measurement instruments based on the findings derived from this research. These measurement instruments will provide us a better means for validating our hypothesis and testing for control and mediating variables.

REFERENCES

Abdel - Khalek, A. M., 2017. The Construction and Validation of the Arabic Scale of Intrinsic Religiosity (ASIR). *Psychol Behavioral Science International Journal*, Vol. 44, No. 4.

Abokhodair, N. et al., 2016. Privacy and Twitter in Qatar: Traditional Values in the Digital World. *Proceedings of the 2016 ACM Web Science Conference.* New york, USA, pp. 66-77.

Al-jenaibi, B., 2015. Use of Social Media in the United Arab Emirates: An Initial Study. *Global Media Journal*, Vol. 1, No. 2, pp. 3-27.

Arif, A. et al., 2017. A Closer Look at the Self-Correcting Crowd: Examining Corrections in Online Rumors. *Proceedings of the 2017 ACM Conference on Computer Supported Cooperative Work.* Portland, USA, pp. 155-168.

Bliss, S. K., & Brown, C. L.,1994. Concern for Appropriateness, Religiosity, and gender as predictors of Alcohol and Marijuana use. *Social Behavior and Personality*, Vol. 22, No. 3, pp. 227-238.

Dworkin, S. L., 2012. Sample Size Policy for Qualitative Studies Using In-Depth Interviews. *Archives of Sexual Behavior*, Vol. 41, No. 6, pp. 1319-1320.

Gallagher, S., & Tierney, W., 2013. Religiosity/Religiousness. In: M. Gellman, & J. Turner, *Encyclopedia of Behavioral Medicine*. Springer, New York, USA, pp. 108.

Gosling, S. D. et al., 2003. A very brief measure of the Big-Five personality domains. *Journal of Research in Personality*, Vol. 37, pp. 504-528.

Grinberg, N., et al., 2016. Changes in Engagement Before and After Posting to Facebook. *Proceedings of the 2016 CHI Conference on Human Factors in Computing Systems*, San Jose, USA, pp. 564-574.

Hoge, D. R., 1972. A Validated Intrinsic Religious Motivation Scale. *Journal for the Scientific Study of Religion*, Vol. 11, No. 4, pp. 369-376.

Hoge, D. R., et al., 1982. Transmission of Religious and Social Values from Parents to Teenage Children. *Journal of Marriage and Family*, Vol. 44, No. 3, pp. 569-580.

John, P. O., & Srivastava, S., 1999. The Big-Five Trait Taxonomy: History, Measurement and Theoretical Perspectives. *Handbook of personality: Theory and research*, pp. 22-34.

Johnson, M. A., 1989. Concern for Appropriateness Scale and Behavioral Conformity. *Journal of Personality Assessment*, Vol. 53, No. 3, pp. 567-574.

Lennox, R., & Wolfe, R. N., 1984. Revision of the Self-Monitoring Scale. *Journal of personality and social psychology*, Vol. 46, No. 6, pp. 1349-64.

Matias, J. N., 2017. MIT Media Lab (*via medium.com*). Retrieved January 3, 2018, from https://medium.com/mit-media-lab/persuading-algorithms-with-an-ai-nudge-25c92293df1d#.y62422rs5

Melman, R. B., et al., 2009. The Psychometric Properties of the RSMS and CAS in Hebrew. *European Journal of Psychological Assessment,* Vol. 25, pp. 8-15.

Shortz, J., & Worthington, E., 1994. Young adults' recall of religiosity, attributions, and coping in parental divorce. *Journal for the Scientific Study of Religion*, Vol. 33, pp. 172-179.

Smith, C., 2003. Theorizing Religious Effects Among American Adolescents. *Journal for the Scientific Study of Religion*, Vol. 42, No. 1, pp. 17-30.

Starbird, K., et al., 2016. Could This Be True? I Think So! Expressed Uncertainty in Online Rumoring. *Proceedings of the 2016 Conference on Human Factors in Computing Systems,* San Jose, USA, pp. 360-371.

Varon, S., & Riley, A., 1999. Relationship between maternal church attendance and adolescent mental health and social functioning. *Psychiatric Services*, Vol. 50, pp. 799-805.

Wiest, J. B., & Eltantawy, N., 2015. Mediatization in the Arab World: A Cross-cultural comparison of New Media use. *Online Journal of Communication and Media Technology*, Vol. 5, pp. 120-142.

DISCOVERY OF CUSTOMER SATISFACTION DIMENSION FROM TWEETS USING LATENT DIRICHLET ALLOCATION

Iqbal Hadiyan, Achmad Nizar Hidayanto and Satrio Baskoro Yudhoatmojo
Faculty of Computer Science, Universitas Indonesia
Kampus UI, Depok, 16424, Jawa Barat, Indonesia

ABSTRACT

Customer satisfaction of a service or product is reflected in the customer's attitude towards the service or product once the customer perceived or used the service or product. Customer satisfaction has many dimensions, and previous studies have identified and used those many dimensions to measure the customer satisfaction of a certain service or product. In this study, we explore the use of text mining techniques of modeling topic as a way of discovering customer satisfaction dimensions, and we used tweets data from Twitter as our dataset. These are our contributions. We believed that this approach had not been used for discovering customer satisfaction dimensions. We used Latent Dirichlet Allocation for the topic modeling, and perplexity model and topic coherence are used for optimizing the number of topics. We would then choose representative words for each topic formed using Latent Dirichlet Allocation. The name of the topic is added by analyzing the logical relationships between the representative words and find the semantic meaning of the representative words in the context of the original tweets. These are done manually by the authors. Once the labels have been identified, we associate the labels to the original tweets. The identified topics in our study become customer satisfaction dimensions. The last task in our study is comparing the identified dimensions with dimensions in previous studies. In this task, we needed to broaden the definition of dimensions from previous studies. The result shows our identified dimensions are fitted with the dimensions from previous studies. The main differences are the naming of the dimensions and the granularity of the dimensions. Our identified dimensions have finer granularity than previous studies. Our study enables the decision maker to be informed with the current dimensions, which are mattered by the customer in using the organization's services or products. Once the tweets are labeled to the identified topic names, we can sort the topics having the most documents. This result shows important issues which are discussed by the customers.

KEYWORDS

Customer Satisfaction Dimensions, Latent Dirichlet Allocation, Twitter, Social Media, Text Mining

1. INTRODUCTION

Social media holds a plethora of people opinions about various things. Social media detaches physical boundaries and gaps, which means people from various places, backgrounds, and beliefs can meet and communicate. Companies use social media as a platform for marketing their products and services. This way is more effective in spreading their products and services updates and also allows the customer to interact with the company intensively. Companies can review and give feedback to customer's comments or questions on social media. Thus, social media is a great platform to obtain information about the quality of the product or the performance of the service.

Studies about dimensions of customer satisfaction have been done by many researchers. They identified several dimensions and used the dimensions to measure the customer satisfaction of a product or a service. We have not found a study that customer satisfaction from social media by organically (or clustered) the data to form common topics which represent the dimension of customer satisfaction. This study is important in a sense that customer satisfaction dimensions are not concepts which are set in stone while rather, it is a dynamic concept that may expand or condense depending time and context at hand.

This study aims to discovery dimensions of customer satisfaction from social media post. We used Twitter as the social media and PT Indosat Tbk. as the company for our case study. We gathered tweets about PT Indosat Tbk. with the aim to clustered discussion topics in which these clusters would resemble dimensions of customer satisfaction. Our rationale is that social media users tend to give an opinion about the product or service they use through the social media platform. Thus, we assume that PT Indosat Tbk. customers would also give their opinion about PT Indosat Tbk. services in social media. The research questions of this study are: (1) "What are the dimensions of customer satisfaction found by analyzing social media post?", and (2) "Do the dimensions found resembles the dimensions previously studied or used in other researches?".

This paper is organized as follows. Section 2 describes the related works of this study. Section 3 describes the research methodology of this study. Section 4 describes the process of discovering the dimensions and comparison between the dimensions found with previous studies. Section 5 concludes our study.

2. RELATED WORKS

Customer satisfaction is the customer's view or attitude that his/her expectation of the product or service has been fulfilled or surpassed [Gerson, R. F., 1993] [Mowen, J., C., and Minor, M., 1997] [Kotler, P., T., and Amstrong, G., 2017][Kotler, P., 2009][Buttle, F., 2009]. The view or attitude can be positive or negative. The telecommunication industry is one of the growing industries in the past decades. The competition amongst player in this industry has intensified. Companies must increase their customer satisfaction so that in return, the customer loyalty rate is also increased.

Several studies have focused on customer satisfaction in telecommunication services. The following describes the result of our reviews. A study done by [Olatokun, W. M., and Nwonne, S. A., 2012] shows that service quality is a significant factor for customer to choose a mobile service provider. Moreover, [Olatokun, W. M., and Ojo, F. O., 2014] identified and validate five dimensions of service quality: reliability, responsiveness, assurance, empathy, and tangibility. Reliability and tangibility do not significantly influence customer satisfaction, while others have a positive and significant influence on service quality.

An evaluation of the effect of service quality and customer satisfaction on cellular phone service in Greece was done by [Santouridis, I., and Trivellas, P., 2010]. According to their study, service quality is the main predictor for customer satisfaction and customer loyalty [Santouridis, I., and Trivellas, P., 2010]. They used six dimensions of service quality: customer support, price structure, billing system, network quality, value added, and mobile device. Customer support is the only dimension which significantly influences customer satisfaction and customer loyalty, while price structure, billing system, and network quality show a positive influence on them. The value added and mobile device dimensions show no significant influence on customer satisfaction and customer loyalty.

A study by [Wang, Y., and Lo, H.-P., 2002] is based on the service quality model of China's telecommunication service. The model is a modified version of SERVQUAL model. The modification is based on the result of group discussion and opinions from experts to represent specific characteristics of the telecommunication industry and a unique culture in China. There are six service qualities used: tangibles, reliability, responsiveness, assurance, empathy, and network quality.

[Aydin, S., and Ozer, G., 2005] did a study about the history of customer loyalty in the Turkish mobile telecommunication market. They studied the relationship between customer loyalty and service quality, the perception of cost change, trust, and company image. The dimensions used in the study are service quality, trust, company image, and cost change.

In 2003, [Athanassopoulos, A. D., and Iliakopoulos, A., 2003]. A formulated a function of customer satisfaction in telecommunication industry using transaction points between the telecommunication operators and their customers as the foundation of the analysis. The dimensions of customer satisfaction formulated in this study consist of billing, product quality, branch services, company image, the establishment of new services, and troubleshooting problems.

[Khatibi, A. A., Ismail, H., and Thyagarajan, V., 2002] looked into what drives the customer to become loyal in using telecommunication services. There are three stages in the study. The first stage identified contributing factors for the service quality factor. The second stage used the regression analysis to identify the relationship between service quality element and customer satisfaction. The third stage is the analysis of the relationship between customer loyalty and customer satisfaction. There are 16 factors of service quality, which are grouped into four groups. The first group is competency/capability, which consists of the relationship between sales personnel and marketing material. The relationship has a direct influence on the customer's decision to buy. The second group is assurance, which consists of skills, employee knowledge and courtesy, the employee ability to deliver trust to the customer, and the trust amongst customer. The third group is tangibility, which consists of physical (tangible) services. The fourth group is reliability, which consists of the ability to deliver reliable and accurate services as planned. Table 1 shows customer satisfaction dimensions of previous studies.

Table 1. Customer satisfaction dimensions of previous studies

References	Olatokun, W. M., and Nwonne, S. A., 2012	Santouridis, I., and Trivellas, P., 2010	Wang, Y., and Lo, H.-P., 2002	Aydin, S., and Ozer, G., 2005	Athanassopoulos, A. D., and Iliakopoulos, A., 2003	Khatibi, A. A., Ismail, H., and Thyagarajan, V., 2002
The mapping of customer satisfaction dimensions	Service Quality	Network Quality	Network Quality	Service Quality		
			Tangibles			Tangibility
			Reliability			Reliability
			Responsiveness	Customer Support	Branch Service	
			Assurance	Trust	Troubleshooting Problems	Assurance
			Empathy			
					Product Quality	
						Competency/ Capability
	Call Rate (Price)	Price Structure		Cost Change		
	Service/ Product Availability					
	Promotion	Value Added			Provision of New Service	
	Brand Image			Company Image	Company Image	
		Billing System			Billing System	
		Mobile Device				

3. RESEARCH METHODOLOGY

There are three major steps in our study. The first one is the data collection. We used the Twitter API to crawl through Twitter to collect the data. The keyword "Indosat" is used as a base for crawling the data.

The second step is the data pre-processing. There are three tasks in this step: (1) data pre-processing, (2) case transformation, and (3) pattern discovery. These three tasks used text mining techniques. The data pre-processing starts from removing data duplication that is walking through each tweet to find any duplicated tweets. If any, remove them from the data set. Next, we tokenized the tweets. Tokenization decomposed the tweet into token words. The decomposition is based on space between words and punctuation. After the tweets are tokenized, we performed the case folding process where we transform all letter cases into lower case letters. Lastly, we performed the part-of-speech (POS) tagging, where we labeled each part of a sentence. We used Hidden Markov Model (HMM) to label the words with a label such as noun, adjectives, etc.

The second task is case transformation, which consists of two sub-tasks: (1) stop word removal, and (2) stemming. Stop words are common words which largely occur in each tweet. The removal would enable us to obtain the semantic words of each tweet. Stemming is a process of transforming each word into its root form. The third task is pattern discovery, which gives the output a set of semantic words of each tweet known as bag-of-words.

The third major step is topic modeling or dimension modeling. The first task is to use Latent Dirichlet Allocation (LDA) to cluster words into a group of words which represent the topics. The second task is labeling the group of words into topics/dimensions. The third task is to associate the name of topic/dimension into the original tweet corpus. This is labeling the original tweet corpus with topic/dimension identified from the previous task.

4. ANALYSIS AND RESULT

In this section, we describe the analysis of our study and its result.

4.1 The Dataset

The collected tweets are tweets about services provided by PT Indosat Tbk. The initial data collected by crawling into Twitter is 101,532 tweets. Following the data pre-processing step, the data is cleaned up, and the result is decreased into only 44,586 tweets.

4.2 Corpus Representation

The tweets, or call them corpus, are transformed into bag-of-words. The bag-of-words model represents each corpus in an array where each array contains tokenized words. Each distinct word from the whole corpus is associated with an ID and added into a dictionary. A new corpus is introduced in the form of a set of tuples in an array for each document S [A1, …, An]. A0i is an ID of a word, and A1i is the frequency of that word.

4.3 Topic Modeling using LDA

It is assumed a priori that the corpus consists of a combination of topics/dimensions. It is because we collected data about the services of PT Indosat Tbk. using the keyword "Indosat" where we may have collected various kind of tweets containing that keyword. There are three tasks in modeling the topic/dimension: (1) optimizing the number of topics/dimensions, (2) identifying representative words using LDA, and (3) naming the topic/dimension based on representative words.

4.3.1 Optimizing the Number of Topics

We used the perplexity model and topic coherence to optimize the number of topics in our corpus. Gibbs sampling algorithm in the LDA model is used by iterating through the corpus until the likelihood model is optimal and does not change or known as the burn-in period. The process of optimizing the number of topics is done by building several LDA model with different values of topic k and choose the one with high coherence score. Choosing the k ends the growth of topic coherency, which provides important topics that are easy to interpret. If we chose a higher coherence score allows us to have detailed sub-topics, but the representative words are repeated/duplicated in every topic. Thus, choosing the optimal coherence score is the key to obtain representative words that are easy to interpret and less repetition/duplication of representative words in every topic. Table 2 shows the coherence score of the tested number of topics.

Table 2. The coherence score of the tested number of topics

Number of Topics	Coherence Score
2	0.3518
8	0.422
14	0.44
20	0.478
26	0.4778
32	0.4298
38	0.4309

As shown in Table 2, there is a decline of coherence score after 26. Thus, there is a possibility of the optimal number of topics between 26 and 32. We measured the perplexity and topic coherence between these two and found that 30 is the optimal number of topics by having 0.5238 as the coherence score.

4.3.2 Identifying Representative Words

We used LDA to identify representative words. For the 30 topics chosen from the previous task, there are five representative words. The list of representative words for each topic can be seen in Table 3.

Table 3. Representative words for each topic

Topic	Representative Words	Named Topic	Number of Corpus
Topic 1	package, *matrix*, number, card, quota	Subscription	1223
Topic 2	phone credit, bonus, 4g, upgrade, number	Bonus	282
Topic 3	community, check, number, community, id	Community	1071
Topic 4	*iflix*, number, pop, quota, collect	Content and Validity	55
Topic 5	*bts*, sweet, milk, business, professional	Corporate Communication	17
Topic 6	point, phone credit, content, number, package	Customer Loyalty	108
Topic 7	package, 4g, quota, internet, data	Data Services	**9064**
Topic 8	handphone, kiosk, bundling, package, max	Device Bundling	21
Topic 9	*iflix*, quota, *dompetku*, package, number	Digital Services	446
Topic 10	phone credit, legend, *patagihan*, mobile, 100k	Finance Function	1
Topic 11	service, active, data, center, local	*Indosat*	2
Topic 12	gives, receive, number, package, kiosk	Customer Interaction	5232
Topic 13	4g, signal, network, handphone, internet	Signal Strength	3750
Topic 14	retrieve, card, *mtronik*, email, check	Partnership	8
Topic 15	package, *matrix*, number, card, tariff	Configuration	158
Topic 16	*matrix*, *im3*, freedom, *mentari*, product	Quiz	3497
Topic 17	bills, email, *matrix*, name, month	Billing Sheets	163
Topic 18	profile, mention, stalking, admin, *indosat*	Mention	1
Topic 19	message, yesterday, *oot* (out of topic), reply, send	Message	1
Topic 20	*dompetku*, balance, PIN, promo, transaction	Mobile Commerce	314
Topic 21	package, phone credit, number, 4g, check	Multi Tweet	6635
Topic 22	*chelseaindo*, *ciscgoestolondon*, *chelsea*, *city*, *man*	Out of Topic	3587
Topic 23	*matrix*, package, card, number, date	Basic Plan	47
Topic 24	telephone, number, phone credit, calls, package	Calls	722
Topic 25	pay, bills, ATM, *matrix*, *cimb*	Payment	32
Topic 26	PUK, code, name, mother, PIN	Customer Profile	1776
Topic 27	*32000an*, coin, line, amount, refund	Refund	1
Topic 28	phone credit, date, content, hour, success	SIM card	4687
Topic 29	SMS, *indosat*, number, handphone, fraud	SMS	758
Topic 30	based, internet, super, volume, multi	Twitter	2

4.3.3 Naming the Topic/Dimension based on Representative Words

The resulting representative words from the LDA model show distribution of words of certain topics in which the names of the topics are unknown at this moment. This task has a purpose of naming these topics manually based on the logical relationship between the representative words in each topic and randomly sampled the original corpus to derive the semantic meaning of the words. Amongst the 30 topics/dimensions, there is one topic/dimension which the label cannot be determined. It cannot be determined because the representative words are too random. Thus, it is difficult to find the logical relationship between the words. This topic/dimension is labeled as "Out of Topic" (OOT), and further sampling to the original corpus showed that the corpus with this label contains advertisements which are not related to PT Indosat Tbk. but they mentioned or created a hashtag using the word "Indosat." The result of naming the topic/dimension is shown in Table 3 in the third column.

4.3.4 Associating the Topic/Dimension to Corpus

The process of associating the topic/dimension to the corpus is done by looking at the probability of the topic in each corpus. Each corpus may contain more than one topic; thus, we need a threshold value for the probability value of the topic. The threshold is measured by averaging the probability of the topic from the whole corpus.

We iterated the whole corpus against the representative words for each topic/dimension which would give us the result of the probability of that corpus belong to certain topics/dimensions. The number of corpora associated with the identified topics/dimension according to the representative words can be seen in Table 3 on the fourth column. Data Services topic has the largest number of the corpus.

From Table 3, there 18 topics/dimensions which have a number of corpora more than 100 corpora. We assumed 100 corpus and above are large enough to conclude these topics/dimensions to be hot topics/dimensions. Next, we compared our identified customer satisfaction dimensions with the ones identified by previous studies done by Olatokun and Nwonne (2012), Santouridis. I and Trivellas. P (2010), Wang. Y, and Lo. H (2002), Aydin. S and Ozer. G (2005), Athanassopoulos. A and Iliakopoulos. A (2003), and Khatibi. A, Ismail. H, and Thyagarajan. V (2002). We broaden the definition of previous studies' dimensions so that our identified dimensions can be classified into the previous studies' dimensions. The mapping result can be seen in Table 4.

Table 4. The number of corpus per-topic/dimension according to its representative words

Identified Topic/Dimension of Our Study	Dimension from Previous Studies
Customer Interaction	Responsiveness, Customer Support, Branch Service
Signal Strength	Network Quality
Partnership	Competency
Configuration	Reliability
Quiz	Promotion/ Value Added/ Provision of New Service, Empathy
Billing Sheets	Billing System
Mention	Responsiveness, Customer Support, Branch Service
Message	Responsiveness, Customer Support, Branch Service
Mobile Commerce	Product Quality, Product Service/ Product Availability
Multi tweet	Responsiveness, Customer Support, Branch Service
Indosat	Brand Image
Basic Plan	Product Quality, Product Service/ Product Availability
Calls	Network Quality
Payment	Billing System
Customer Profile	Trust / Assurance
Refund	Trust / Assurance
SIM card	Product Quality, Product Service/ Product Availability
SMS	Network Quality
Twitter	Responsiveness, Customer Support, Branch Service
OOT	-

In general, all dimensions from previous studies can be found in our identified dimensions using LDA method applied to the Twitter posts. Furthermore, by using data from social media such as Twitter, we can get a finer granularity of a dimension from previous studies. For example, a dimension from previous studies called "Product Quality" is mapped to several dimensions of our work, such as "Digital Services," "Mobile Commerce," "Basic Plan," etc. as seen in Table 4. This allows decision makers to narrow down the focus of improvements. By using data from social media, we would have a real-time data that we can analyze and provide to the decision maker, and the decision maker can create strategies based on the analysis result for the best interest of the organization.

5. CONCLUSION

Our study used tweets from Twitter to identify topics/dimensions, which becomes the factor for customer satisfaction. We used PT Indosat Tbk. telecommunication services as the case study. We used the perplexity model and topic coherence to find the optimized number of topics/dimensions. Once we have the optimized number of topics/dimensions, we identify the representative words for each of the topics/dimensions. The name of the topic/dimension would then be decided manually by looking at the logical relationships between the representative words and the semantics of the words used in the original corpus. The identified names of topics/dimension are associated to the original corpus (labeling the corpus). We counted the number of the corpus with each topic to have a statistic of popular topics. Furthermore, we rationalized our identified topics/dimensions by comparing them with dimensions identified/used by previous studies. We had to broaden the definition of the dimensions from previous studies and able to find matching pairs between our identified topics/dimensions with the previous ones. This shows that the result of our method for discovering topics/dimensions of customer satisfaction agrees with previous studies.

Furthermore, our study enables dynamic discovery of customer satisfaction dimensions because the data that we used are social media data (real-time data). The benefit of using social media data is that we can get analyze this real data so that we get the current situation of the issues regarding customer satisfaction. Thus, decision-makers can decide more accurate solutions or strategy to the solution.

The limitation of our study is limited by the data we obtained from Twitter. First, Twitter has a rate limit policy, which is 15 minutes per-token, and Twitter only serves a small portion of data to be streamed. This means we are only getting a sample of data in that 15 minutes window time. Second, since tweets are temporal data, this means analysis on different time may discover different topics/dimensions. Nevertheless, this allows us to adapt to the real issues handed at that time. Thus we may react to issues that matter at that time. If the data collection is done regularly, we may analyze the data for a bigger picture and long-term strategy of the company. We may discover recurrent topics/dimensions and the ones which appear randomly or isolated on a certain period in time. To conclude our study, we have managed to used text mining techniques to discover topics from tweets data and label the topics as dimensions of customer satisfaction dimensions for telecommunication services of PT Indosat Tbk.

ACKNOWLEDGEMENT

This publication is funded by a research grant called PITTA-B number NKB-0515/UN2.R3.1/HKP.05.00/2019 provided by Universitas Indonesia. We are grateful to be funded by Universitas Indonesia. We also thank the Faculty of Computer Science, Universitas Indonesia, for supporting us in researching and publishing our work.

REFERENCES

Athanassopoulos, A. D., and Iliakopoulos, A., 2003. Modeling Customer Satisfaction In Telecommunications: Assessing The Effects Of Multiple Transaction Points On The Perceived Overall Performance Of The Provider. *Production and Operations Management*, pp 224-245.

Aydin, S., and Ozer, G., 2005. The analysis of antecedents of customer loyalty in the Turkish mobile telecommunication market. *European Journal of Marketing*, Vol. 39, No. 7/8, pp 910-925.

Buttle, F., 2009. *Customer Relationship Management – Concepts and Technologies*. Butterworth-Heinemann.

Gerson, R., F., 1993. *Measuring Customer Satisfaction*. Crisp Publication.

Khatibi, A. A., Ismail, H., and Thyagarajan, V., 2002. What drives customer loyalty: An analysis from the telecommunications industry. *Journal of Targeting, Measurement and Analysis for Marketing*, Vol. 11, No. 1, pp. 34-44.

Kotler, P., 2009. *Marketing Management an Asian Perspective*. Pearson.

Kotler, P., T., and Amstrong, G., 2017. *Principles of Marketing 17th Edition*. Pearson.

Mowen, J., C., and Minor, M., 1997. *Consumer Behavior Fifth Edition*. Prentice Hall.

Olatokun, W. M., and Nwonne, S. A., 2012. Determinants of Users' Choice of Mobile Service Providers in the Nigerian Telecommunications Market. *African Journal of Computing & ICT*, Vol. 5, No. 4, pp19-32.

Olatokun, W. M., and Ojo, F. O., 2014. Influence of service quality on consumers' satisfaction with mobile telecommunication services in Nigeria. *Information Development*, Vol. 32, No. 3, pp 398-408.

Santouridis, I., and Trivellas, P., 2010. Investigating the impact of service quality and customer satisfaction on customer loyalty in mobile telephony in Greece. *The TQM Journal*, Vol. 22, No. 3, pp 330-343.

Wang, Y., and Lo, H.-P., 2002. Service quality, customer satisfaction and behavior intentions: Evidence from China's telecommunication industry. *Info*, Vol. 4, No. 6, pp 50-60.

THE EFFECTS OF COLLECTIVISM AND SOCIAL NETWORK SELF-CONGRUITY ON ENGAGEMENT

Sara Santos[1] and Pedro Espírito Santo[2]
[1]*Escola Superior de Educação de Coimbra, R. Dom João III, 3030-329 Coimbra, Portugal*
[2]*Instituto Politécnico de Coimbra, ESTGOH, Rua Gen. Santos Costa, 3400-124 Oliveira do Hospital, Portugal*

ABSTRACT

In recent years, social media and special social networks are being part of people's everyday lives and consumers use a variety of social media channels daily. For firms, it has become a key tool in the promotion of brands, products and services. Furthermore, people have different characteristics of individualism, collectivism and congruity with social networks. However, empirical research on consumer–brand engagement on social networks is still scarce.
The aim of this research is to understand the relation among collectivism, self-congruity with social network and social networks engagement.
Using an online questionnaire conducted across 484 participants in Portugal, the results show that collectivism has a positive influence on social network engagement (consumption and contribution).
Our finds also reveal that self-congruence of individuals has influence on their engagement with social networks.
In practical implications, marketers should see the values and lifestyle of their users to improve their social networks pages.

KEYWORDS

Collectivism, Individualism, Self-Congruity, Social Networks, Engagement

1. INTRODUCTION

In recent years the exponential growth of social media and special social networks sites leads to increase of interactions and continuous connection between users and brands, between users and even between brands and brands. It is important to distinguish between social media and social networks sites. Kaplan & Haenlein (2010) consider that social media facilitates interaction, collaboration and content sharing and there are six types of *social media plataforms*: blogs (Wordpress, Tumblr or Twitter - microblogging), collaborative sites (e.g. Wikipedia), content creation communities (e.g, YouTube), virtual worlds (World of Warcraft), virtual social worlds (e.g, Second Life) and social networking sites. Social network sites are "web-based services that allow individuals to construct a public or semi-public profile within a bounded system, articulate a list of other users with whom they share connection, and view and traverse their list of connections made by others within the system" (Boyd & Ellison, 2007, p. 211).

In this study we analyze the relation among collectivism, self-congruity with social network and social networks engagement (consumption and contribution).

2. LITERATURE REVIEW

2.1 Social Networks Engagement

In the last decade consumer engagement, namely consumer-brand-engagement (CBE) has been the target of several studies (Hollebeek, Glynn, & Brodie, 2014). However, there is no consensus regarding its definition (Dessart, Veloutsou, & Morgan-Thomas, 2015).

Social media engagement is a specific context of consumer engagement (Brodie, Ilic, Juric, & Hollebeek, 2013) and it could begin with "liking" a Facebook page (Beukeboom, Kerkhof, & de Vries, 2015). In order to analyze this engagement in social media, Muntinga, Moorman, & Smit (2011) proposed a Consumer Online Brand-Related Activity (COBRA) model which distinguishes consumer engagement in three types of behavior (from lower to higher engagement): consumption (when consumers view images and videos, read information, comments and reviews), contribution (when users like or comment photographs and videos and engage in conversations about the brand); creation - users produce and publish content related to the brand (Mutinga et al., 2011). These users proactively create brand content on their personal networks (Men & Tsai, 2014).

2.2 Individualism / Collectivism

Culture, defined as the patterns shared by individuals in a society, represents the dominant values of a set of people and are socially accepted (Frank, Enkawa, & Schvaneveldt, 2015). Culture represents the values of most people and influences the behavior of individuals in their personal behavior.

In this context, it is accepted in the literature that individualism as opposed to the collectivism of individuals depends on the culture of each individual (Hofstede, 1984) since as individuals internalize the norms, rules, and values in a society they share the perception of their social environment that modifies the way individuals behave, interact, and build relationships (Kim, Sohn, & Choi, 2011).

Based on the analysis by Kim et al. (2011) the role of culture in communication has been studied by comparing two distinct cultures - individualism and collectivism. Goncalo and Staw (2006) describe that the cultural values of individualism and collectivism differ in their relation to the group. These authors report the study of Markus and Kitayama (1994) to explain that in individualistic cultures, people are seen as independent and have a unique pattern of characteristics that distinguish them from others while in collectivist cultures people are linked to their social group (Kim et al., 2011).

Thus, the two types of individuals (individualists and collectivists) have distinct communication styles. Kim et al. (2011) recognizes that individuals with a higher level of collectivism tend to communicate and interact more with groups, so this study will test the following research hypothesis:

H1a: the level of collectivism of individuals has a positive influence on the consumption of content in social networks.

H1b: the level of collectivism of individuals has a positive influence on the contributions of individuals in social networks.

2.3 Social Network Self-Congruity

In brand relationships with individuals, brand proximity in terms of beliefs, values and personality is defined as the self-congruence of the brand with the individual (Su *et al.*, 2015). In this sense, congruence with a brand is a mental representation (Beerli, Meneses, & Gil, 2007) and refers to the relevance, adequacy or compatibility between a brand and the image each individual has of himself.

In the field of brands management, congruence has been analyzed and, in this context, Sirgy, Lee, Johar, and Tidwell (2008) describe that the results in the literature demonstrate the significant influence of this congruence with the brand, the brand image (Sirgy, 1982, 1986) social interactions and emotional attachment to the brand (Beerli *et al.*, 2007).

According to the theory, individuals tend to prefer brands that are congruent with their identities (Hollenbeck & Kaikati, 2012). As social networks improve collaboration between individuals, the relationship between the level of collectivism and the self-congruence of the individual with social networks is real. This relationship arises through the facilitation, acquisition and diffusion of knowledge (Bodin & Crona, 2009). In this sense, this study aims to test the following hypothesis of investigation:

H2: the level of collectivism has positive effects on self-congruence (individual-social networks).

Therefore, this study investigated how users use social networks as a consequence of their self-congruence that, based on the study of Koo, Cho, and Kim (2014), it is possible to affirm that the degree to which the images of a brand correspond to the self-image of the individuals exerts a significant influence on the behavior of the consumer in several contexts, namely when forming online attitudes. Thus, this study aims to test the following hypothesis of investigation:

H3: Self-congruence of individuals influences their engagement with social networks.
H3a: Self-congruence of individuals influences their consumption of social networks
H3a: Self-congruence of individuals influences their contribution with social networks
Schivinski et al. (2016) based on the COBRA model (Muntinga *et al.*, 2011), consider that there is a hierarchical relationship between the three dimensions of engagement: consumption, contribution and creation. This study analyzes whether the same hierarchical relationship (consumption-contribution) happens. Thus, the last hypothesis is:
H4: Consumption of content in social networks has influence on contribution.
This formulation of hypothesis resulted in the conceptual model shown in figure 1.

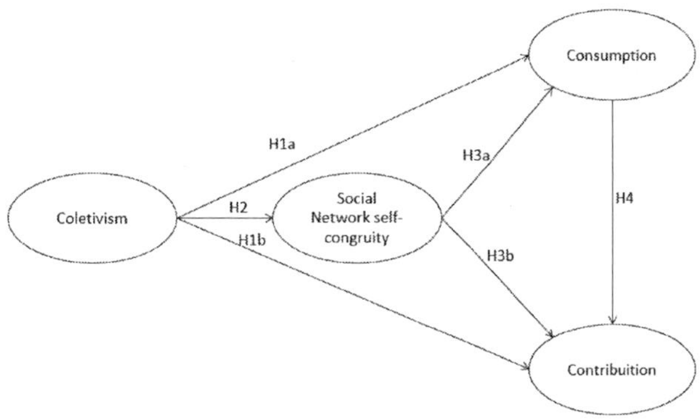

Figure 1. Conceptual Model

3. METHODOLOGY

The present study of a conclusive-causal nature had simple transversal characteristics whose unit of analysis were the individuals that use social networks in general. The request for the questionnaire response was sent by sharing the questionnaire link through different social networks guaranteeing the anonymity of the individual's response. Considering the concepts under study, the concepts were operationalized through 5-point Likert scales, already tested in the literature and whose original studies of which were adapted are described in table 1.

Table 1. Constructs, Items and References

Constructs	Items	Code	References
Social Network self-congruity	I use social networks, because it reflects who I am.	SNC01	
	I use the social networks, to make a better impression on other people.	SNC02	Park & John (2010)
	I use the social networks, to feel more positive about myself.	SNC03	
	I use the social networks, to communicate with other people.	SNC04	
Individualism / Colletivism	People should only pursue their goals after considering the welfare of the group.	COL01	
	Group success is more important than individual success.	COL02	Erdem, Swait, and Valenzuela (2006)
	Group loyalty should be encouraged even if individual goals suffer.	COL03	
Consumption	I read a lot of text information on social networks.	CONS01	
	I see many images on social networks.	CONS02	Schivinski, Christodoulides, and Dabrowski (2016)
	I see many videos posted on social networks.	CONS03	
	I read posts and comments on social networks.	CONS04	

Contribution	I click the like button in many publications.	CONT01	Schivinski et al. (2016)
	I often comment on publications, videos and images.	CONT02	
	I often share the publications with friends.	CONT03	
	I comment on publications, videos and images of unknown people.	CONT04	

From the data obtained, 484 responses were obtained from respondents whose characteristics are shown in table 2.

Table 2. Demographic Characteristics of Respondents

Variable	Category	Frequency	Valid %
Gender	Male	152	31,4
	Female	332	68,6
Age	Until 20 years	226	47,5
	20 to 29 years	178	37,4
	30 to 39 years	39	8,2
	40 to 49 years	27	5,7
	50 to 59 years	5	1,1
	60 to 69 years	1	0,2
	Missing values	8	

Following the previous analysis to the data, where the existence of outliers and the non-existence of multicollinearity (VIF<5) the model was estimated through the method of analysis of structural equations by partial least squares (PLS-SEM) (Hair, Hult, Ringle, & Sarstedt, 2016).

The first step is to analyze the measurement model whose objective is to evaluate the capacity of the items under study and measure their concepts in terms of reliability and validity. The evaluation to the measurement model provides confirmatory information about the reliability, factorial validity, convergent validity and discriminant validity of the constructs. This step was executed through the "PLS algorithm" function in the software SMART PLS version 3.2.7. The results obtained for the measurement model are shown in table 3.

Table 3. Results of the Measurement Model

Construct	Item	λ	Cronbach α (> 0,7)	Rho_A (> 0,7)	CR (> 0,7)	AVE (> 0,5)
Social Network self-congruity (SNC)	SNC01	0,801**	0,712	0,700	0,819	0,533
	SNC02	0,747**				
	SNC03	0,761**				
	SNC04	0,594**				
Individualism / Colletivism (COL)	COL01	0,820**	0,762	0,779	0,861	0,673
	COL02	0,819**				
	COL03	0,822**				
Consumption (CONS)	CONS01	0,826**	0,801	0,816	0,871	0,630
	CONS02	0,851**				
	CONS03	0,730**				
	CONS04	0,619**				
Contribution (CONT)	CONT01	0,665**	0,770	0,831	0,845	0,581
	CONT02	0,870**				
	CONT03	0,850**				
	CONT04	0,773**				

λ - Standardized Coefficients (*Standardized Loadings*); AVE – Average Extracted Variance; CR – Composite reliability; ** p<0,01

The analysis of the standardized coefficients (λ) verifies that these are greater than 0.5 and their significance is considered for p<0,01. It is considered the existence of factorial validity, convergent validity and composite reliability. The Cronbach α values are greater than 0.7 (α > 0,7).

In this study the analysis of the discriminant validity was evaluated through the following criteria: criterion of Fornell and Larcker (1981), cross-load analysis criterion and Heterotrait-Monotrait correlation coefficient analysis criterion (HTMT) (Henseler, Ringle, & Sarstedt, 2015). The results obtained for the analysis of the discriminant validity by the criterion of Fornell and Larcker (1981) are present in table 4.

Table 4. Discriminating Validity - criterion of Fornell and Larcker (1981)

	COL	SNC	CONS	CONT
Individualism / Colletivism(COL)	0,820			
Social Network self-congruity (SNC)	0,283	0,730		
Consumption (CONS)	0,207	0,453	0,794	
Contribution (CONT)	0,132	0,416	0,417	0,762

Table 4 confirms that the square root values of the extracted mean variance, whose values are presented in the main diagonal of the table, are superior to the square of the correlations between the respective constructs, and it is considered that the discriminant validity exists by the criterion of Fornell and Larcker (1981). Cross- loadings present in the items of the model were also analyzed. The results are shown in table 5.

Table 5. Discriminating Validity – Cross-loadings

	COL	SNC	CONS	CONT
CONT01	0,169	0,298	0,665	0,230
CONT02	0,178	0,404	0,870	0,282
CONT03	0,175	0,385	0,850	0,298
CONT04	0,141	0,343	0,773	0,471
CONS01	0,109	0,388	0,460	0,826
CONS02	0,138	0,336	0,331	0,851
CONS03	0,075	0,274	0,251	0,730
CONS04	0,062	0,223	0,080	0,619
COL01	0,820	0,287	0,188	0,110
COL02	0,819	0,184	0,116	0,078
COL03	0,822	0,205	0,188	0,128
SNC01	0,193	0,801	0,291	0,410
SNC02	0,228	0,747	0,142	0,297
SNC03	0,255	0,761	0,154	0,264
SNC04	0,163	0,594	0,577	0,220

The results of Table 5 show discriminant validity since the coefficients (*loadings*) are higher than cross loadings for each item. For the discriminant analysis were also analyzed the correlation ratio of Heterotrait-Monotrait. The values that were obtained are present in table 6 (Henseler et al., 2015).

Table 6. Discriminating Validity – ratio of Heterotrait-Monotrait

	COL	SNC	CONS	CONT
Individualism / Colletivism(COL)				
Social Network self-congruity (SNC)	0,376			
Consumption (CONS)	0,258	0,523		
Contribution (CONT)	0,157	0,543	0,452	

According to the Heterotrait-Monotrait criterion, there is a discriminant validity, since the values presented (table 6) are lower than 0.9 as indicated in the literature (Henseler *et al.*, 2015).

Thus, the three criteria analyzed for the discriminant validity items confirm what is recommended in the literature, which leads to consider that the items have distinction between them. Therefore, the data obtained suggest that there is a discriminant validity so that we can proceed with the analysis to the structural model.

The second step is the analysis to the structural model through the evaluation of the structural path coefficients and analysis to their significance.

The second step of the analysis is the test to the structural model. For this purpose, we used the bootstrap resampling technique with 5000 sub-samples in order to be able to have stability in the obtained results. The accomplishment of this analysis allowed to obtain the results that will be used to test the hypotheses under study.

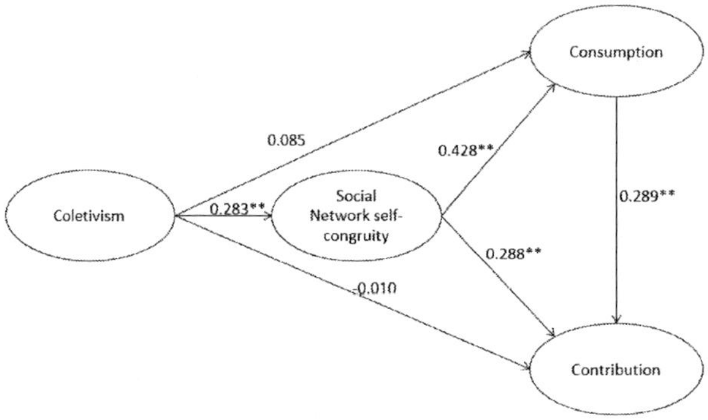

Figure 2. Structural Model

These results will be analyzed considering the values standardized β (table 7) and *t Student* values. This analysis will serve to validate the statistical significance of the parameters under analysis. Therefore, the results are summarized on the table 7.

Table 7. Hypothesis Testing - Direct, Indirect and Total Effects

		Direct Effects		Indirect Effects		Total Effects		
	Relationship to be tested	**β**	**t values**	**β**	**t values**	**β**	**t values**	
H1a	COL→CONS	0.085	1.880	0.121	4.832	0.207	3.986	Supported*
H1b	COL→CONT	-0.010	0.213	0.141	4.969	0.132	2.670	Supported*
H2	COL→SNC	0.283	5.741	--------	--------	0.283	5.741	Supported
H3a	SNC→CONS	0.428	8.604	--------	--------	0.428	8.604	Supported
H3b	SNC→CONT	0.288	5.235	0.124	4.189	0.412	9.531	Supported
H4	CONS→ CONT	0.289	5.593	--------	--------	0.289	5.593	Supported

* *Hypothesis corroborated by indirect effects*
Source: self elaboration

4. DISCUSSION

The results evidenced the explanation of the engagement in social networks by the variables included in the model. This analysis is done through two dimensions: the consumption of individuals (R^2_{CONS} =0,211) and the contribution (R^2_{CONT} =0,239) of individuals in social networks.

In the analysis of the hypothesis test carried out through the structural model, the individual or collectivistic characteristics of the individuals do not have significant direct effects on the engagement in social networks. This analysis is done by the values presented for the hypothesis H1a ($\beta_{COL \rightarrow CONS}$ = -0.010; t = 0,711; p > 0,05) and for the hypothesis H1b ($\beta_{COL \rightarrow CONT}$ = 0.085; t = 1.880; p > 0,05) from which it is verified that the direct effects of the collectivism of the individuals do not contribute to the explanation of the consumption nor the contribution of the individuals in the social networks. This analysis can make sense, since the respondents are individuals belonging to countries of the European Union very associated with low levels of collectivism and may not have corroborated the hypotheses H1a and H1b.

However, the engagement in the social networks of individuals has as a determining variable the congruence with the social network. This analysis is based on the results of the hypothesis H3a ($\beta_{SNC \rightarrow CONS}$= 0.428; t = 8.604; p < 0,001) and the hypothesis H3b ($\beta_{SNC \rightarrow CONT}$ = 0.288; t = 5.235; p <0.001). In addition to this analysis, the congruence with the social network with the individuals has a mediating capacity in the corroboration of the hypothesis H1a ($\beta_{COL \rightarrow SNC \rightarrow CONS}$= 0.121; t = 4.832; p < 0,001) and the hypothesis H1b ($\beta_{COL \rightarrow SNC \rightarrow CONT}$= 0.141; t = 4.969; p < 0,001) contributing for its indirect effects to be important so that the collectivism of the individuals is an important variable in the explanation of the engagement in the social networks thus supporting the hypothesis H1a and H1b, justifying the assertion of Kim et al. (2011) in the sense that individuals with a higher level of collectivism are more connected to the group, that through this study, it is verified that individuals connect to social networks if this social network has values appropriate to individuals.

5. CONCLUSION

Due to the centrality of social networks today, the empirical study presented here contributed to the advance of theoretical knowledge and has practical implications for management.

In the theoretical scope, this study presents as main contribution the importance of the self-congruence of the individuals with the social network so that it improves its engagement. Therefore, this work demonstrates that the engagement of individuals is directly due to the congruence of the values of individuals and the values of social networks, but also the collectivist culture promotes higher levels of engagement in social networks.

As practical contributions, this work has implications for companies, demonstrating that the management of social networks must consider the individual and his own values, without forgetting the culture in which they are inserted, by the importance that the collectivist culture must determine the consumption of content and the contribution of individuals in social networks.

In summary, this work has valid conclusions, however some limitations of investigation have arisen. From the limitations, the fact that the data were collected from a sample of young individuals up to the age of 30, in most cases. This evidence may have left out some conclusions that could be important to draw from the model under analysis. Another limitation is the analysis of a sample of individuals, not comparing different groups of people.

Thus, it is suggested that for future studies the data collection should be performed to a more balanced sample in the respondents' ages and that groups of individuals be compared in order to obtain more precise explanations about the engagement of individuals in social networks.

REFERENCES

Baldus, B. J. et al, 2015. Online brand community engagement: Scale development and validation. *Journal of Business Research*, Vol.68, No.5, pp. 978–985.

Beerli, A. et al, 2007. Self-congruity and destination choice. *Annals of Tourism Research,* Vol. 34, No.3, pp. 571-587.

Beukeboom, C. et al, 2015. Does a Virtual Like Cause Actual Liking? How Following a Brand's Facebook Updates Enhances Brand Evaluations and Purchase Intention. *Journal of Interactive Marketing*, Vol.32, pp. 26-36.

Bodin, Ö. et al, 2009. The role of social networks in natural resource governance: What relational patterns make a difference? *Global Environmental Change,* Vol. 19, No.3, pp. 366-374.

Boyd, D. et al, 2007. Social Network Sites: Definition, History, and Scholarship. *Journal of Computer-Mediated Communication,* Vol.13, No.1, pp. 210-230.

Brodie, R. J. et al, 2013. Consumer engagement in a virtual brand community: An exploratory analysis. *Journal of Business Research*, Vol.66, No.1, pp. 105–114.

Cheung, C. M. K. et al, 2011. Online social networks: Why do students use facebook? *Computers in Human Behavior*, Vol.27, No.4, pp. 1337–1343.

Dessart, L. et al, 2015. Consumer engagement in online brand communities: a social media perspective. *Journal of Product & Brand Management*, Vol.24, No.1, 28–42.

Erdem, T. et al, 2006. *Brands as Signals: A Cross-Country Validation Study*, 70, pp. 34-49.

Fornell, C. et al, 1981. Evaluating structural equation models with unobservable variables and measurement error. *Journal of Marketing Research,* Vol.18, No.1, pp. 39-50.

Frank, B. et al, 2015. The role of individualism vs. collectivism in the formation of repurchase intent: A cross-industry comparison of the effects of cultural and personal values. *Journal of Economic Psychology,* Vol.51, pp. 261-278.

Goncalo, J. A. et al, 2006. Individualism–collectivism and group creativity. *Organizational Behavior and Human Decision Processes,* Vol.100, No.1, pp. 96-109.

Hair, J. F. et al, 2016. *A Primer on Partial Least Squares Structural Equation Modeling (PLS-SEM)*: SAGE Publications.

Henseler, J. et al, 2015. A new criterion for assessing discriminant validity in variance-based structural equation modeling. *Journal of the Academy of Marketing Science,* Vol.43, No.1, pp. 115-135.

Hofstede, G. 1984. *Culture's Consequences: International Differences in Work-Related Values*: SAGE Publications.

Hollenbeck, C. R. et al, 2012. Consumers' use of brands to reflect their actual and ideal selves on Facebook. *International Journal of Research in Marketing,* Vol.29, No.4, pp. 395-405.

Hollebeek, L. D. et al, 2014. Consumer Brand Engagement in Social Media: Conceptualization, Scale Development and Validation. *Journal of Interactive Marketing*, Vol.28, No.2, pp. 149–165.

Kaplan, A. M. et al, 2010. Users of the world, unite! The challenges and opportunities of Social Media. *Business Horizons*, Vol.53, No.1, pp. 59–68.

Kim, Y. et al, 2011. Cultural difference in motivations for using social network sites: A comparative study of American and Korean college students. *Computers in Human Behavior,* Vol.27, No.1, pp. 365-372.

Koo, W. et al, 2014. Actual and ideal self-congruity affecting consumers' emotional and behavioral responses toward an online store. *Computers in Human Behavior,* Vol. 36, pp. 147-153.

Men, L. R. et al, 2014. Perceptual, Attitudinal, and Behavioral Outcomes of Organization–Public Engagement on Corporate Social Networking Sites. *Journal of Public Relations Research*, Vol.26, No.5, pp. 417–435.

Muntinga, D. et al, 2011. Introducing COBRAs. *International Journal of Advertising*, Vol.30, No.1, pp. 13–46.

Park, J. et al, 2010. Got to Get You into My Life: Do Brand Personalities Rub Off on Consumers? Journal of Consumer Research, Vol.37, pp. 655-669.

Schau, H. J. et al, 2003. We Are What We Post? Self-Presentation in Personal Web Space. *Journal of Consumer Research*, Vol.30, No.3, pp. 385–404.

Sirgy, J. 1982. Self-Concept in Consumer Behavior: A Critical Review. *Journal of Consumer Research,* Vol. 9, No.3, pp. 287-300.

Sirgy, J. 1986. *Self-congruity: Toward a Theory of Personality and Cybernetics*: Praeger.

Sirgy, J. et al, 2008. Effect of self-congruity with sponsorship on brand loyalty. *Journal of Business Research,* Vol.61, No.10, pp. 1091-1097.

Schivinski, B. et al, 2016. Measuring Consumers' Engagement With Brand-Related Social-Media Content. *Development and Validation of a Scale that Identifies Levels of Social-Media Engagement with Brands,* Vol. 56, No.1, pp. 64-80.

COMPLAINT HANDLING THROUGH SOCIAL MEDIA: PERCEIVED JUSTICE AND CUSTOMER SATISFACTION

Made Dwita Juliarta, Achmad Nizar Hidayanto, Ave Adriana Pinem and Putu Wuri Handayani
Faculty of Computer Science, Universitas Indonesia
Kampus UI, Depok, Indonesia

ABSTRACT

Nowadays, it is common for us to complaint about the service or product by using social media platform. Organizations are usually having their customer service or public relation to maintain their social media account such as Twitter, Instagram, Facebook or other platforms. This study aims to analyze perceived justice in complaint handling process through social media and its impact towards customer satisfaction. Customer satisfaction is evaluated together with trust and perceived product quality for their influence in e-WOM and continues usage. The sample of the study is customer of a telecommunication company who is the follower of its customer care account in Twitter. The questionnaires were distributed online, and 238 valid response were analyzed using CB-SEM. The results show that, customers would be satisfied if the complaint handling process is accurate and quick (procedural justice) and supported by compensation (distributive justice). The satisfaction would increase customer trust and perceived product quality and eventually increase their intention to continue using the service and spread positive e-WOM.

KEYWORDS

Perceived Justice, Satisfaction, Trust, Perceived Product Quality, e-WOM, Continues Usage

1. INTRODUCTION

In this era where the technology advancement is rapidly growing, and market transparency is increasingly high, and technology is growing rapidly, customer needs continue to increase, and their long-term loyalty is a difficult to achieve. Therefore, companies need a greater effort to improve their relationships with customer. Complaint handling management holds a key position, because it helps restore customer satisfaction and returns the customer's desire to repurchase (Johannsen & Zellner, 2015). Complaints submitted by customers are an indicator that one or more of the services provided does not work as they should. Effective complaint handling can change customers who feel disadvantaged to be more satisfied and become loyal customers. The main determinants of customer satisfaction in handling complaints perceived justice which are procedural, distributive, and interactional justice (Brock, et al., 2013). Perceived justice is identified as the main concept in the organization's response to handling service failures (Ding & Lii, 2016).

Nowadays, it is common for us to complaint about the service or product by using social media platform. Organizations are usually having their customer service or public relation to maintain their social media account such as Twitter, Instagram, Facebook or other platforms. Additionally, with the emergence of e-commerce, the sales of some services can be conducted easily using application without meeting directly with the customer. For example, the service provided by telecommunication company. Customer can top up their phone credit using mobile banking, or purchase internet data package through application. Thus, when having problem using the service, it is easier for customer to contact the provider using social networking sites.

In this study, we would like to assess the complaints handling process through social media and evaluate the perceived justice and satisfaction relationship. In handling conventional complaints where customers are handled directly through telephone lines and or face to face with complaints handling agents, perceived justice becomes an important thing to achieve customer satisfaction. There is a significant relationship between the four dimensions of perceived justice to customer satisfaction (Ding & Lii, 2016). While in this study, we would like to focus on the media for complaint handling which is social media that has a difference with the handling of conventional complaints. We also want to evaluate the impact of satisfaction towards trust, product quality, e-WOM and continuous usage. Previous researches had been conducted to study e-WOM and repurchase intention and both are influenced by customer satisfaction and trust. From the existing studies, the authors have not found any studies that discuss the effect of customer satisfaction and trust on perceived product quality. Therefore, we would like to evaluate the relationship between customer satisfaction and trust to perceived product quality as well as the relationship between perceived product quality and the concept of e-WOM and repurchase intention.

2. THEORITICAL BACKGROUND AND HYPOTHESIS DEVELOPMENT

2.1 Perceived Justice

Perceived Justice is the fairness that perceive by customers when they involved in the service recovery procedures in the communication and interpersonal activities, and it is the main antecedents in customer evaluation (Ding & Lii, 2016). And according to Adams (1965), perceived justice refers to the extent to which customers feel fairly treated during failures handling and service recovery (Ding & Lii, 2016). There are three dimensions of perceived justice, namely; distributive justice, procedural justice and interactional justice (Ding & Lii, 2016).

Distributive justice is an attribute that focuses on results and solutions of a problem. The solutions depict organization effort to compensate customer loss even if it occurs cost for the organization. This can be reflected by giving compensation to customers who experienced problem in using service or product. Distributive justice has a significant influence on the consumers' word of mouth. Procedural justice is an attribute that focuses on righteousness that should be accepted by consumers when filing complaints in accordance with the rules and policies set by the company. Procedural justice includes process control, decision control, accessibility, timing/speed, and flexibility when handling customer complaints. The third dimension is interactional justice that concerns to the matters relating to the response given by the organization to consumers in providing services on complaint handling. When the customer received good response from the organization, it will improve customer satisfaction with the services provided by the company. There are two types interactional justice namely: Interpersonal Justice and Informational Justice. Interpersonal Justice refers to the extent to which customers are treated with courtesy and respect by the organization or employees involved in implementing service recovery procedures. While Informational Justice focuses on whether consumers receive adequate and appropriate explanations in the recovery of services and/or handling complaints that they submitted (Ding & Lii, 2016).

2.2 Satisfaction, Trust, e-WOM, and Research Gap

Satisfaction is a pleasure or disappointment that initiates from a comparison between expectation and actual performance of a product or service (Kotler, 2009). Highly satisfied customers usually stay loyal for longer periods of time and make another purchase when the company introduces new products or launches the updated products. These customers will also share the positive information about the company and its products to others and do not pay much attention in competing brands, and more importantly they are not too sensitive about prices charged by the company. Satisfaction is especially crucial to be maintained when customer has bad experience or file a complaint regarding the product or service. The process in complaint handling can affect customer satisfaction and eventually determine their intention to repurchase and to spread the word-of-mouth. It depends on how the justice is perceived by the customer (Wirtz & Matilla, 2004).

Trust is defined as a phycological state to be open to vulnerability based on favorable expectation or behavior of other party (Fang, et al., 2016). In an online platform trust would be more difficult to gain since there are no direct interaction between to parties. e-WOM (electronic word of mouth) is a statement made by actual, potential consumers or previous consumers about a product or company that available in the internet (Hennig-Thurau, et al., 2004). e-WOM would increase transparency of a product or service, in other words consumers have a higher active role in the value chain cycle so consumers are able to influence products and prices based on individual preferences (Park & Kim, 2008).

Previous study had been conducted to evaluate the impact of perceived justice on customer satisfaction in the context of service failures in online games (Ding & Lii, 2016), in B2B context (Brock, et al., 2013), and hospitality industry (Karatepe, 2006). However, with the emergence of complaint handling through social media in telecommunication industry still difficult to find. On the other scope, other researches had been conducted to prove the impact of satisfaction towards trust, also the impact of trust toward Word-Of-Mouth (WOM) and repurchase intention in online shopping context (Fang, et al., 2016), in complaint handling process of an online games (Ding & Lii, 2016). Thus, perceived justice, satisfaction, trust, e-WOM and repurchase intention are captured in one picture on how complaint handling process, which supposed to be a disadvantage condition, if managed fairly will be profitable to the organization. Then research by (Bao, 2015) states that the desire of customers to continue to use services is significantly influenced by the level of customer satisfaction with service, product quality and product prices. The perception of good product quality will keep customers loyal using the products offered by the company. Hence, the perceived product quality will also be evaluated in this study on its relationship with satisfaction, trust, e-WOM and continuous usage.

2.3 Hypothesis Development

Based on previous studies and previous literatures, we develop conceptual model depicts thirteen hypotheses shown in Figure 1.

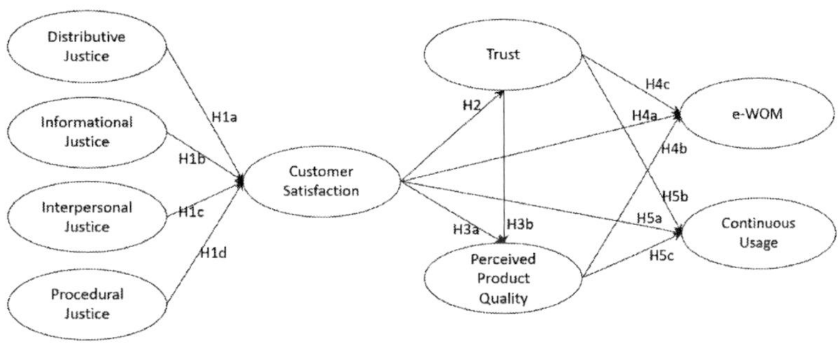

Figure 1. Conceptual Model

In complaint handling process, action and complement given to customers after they report the case will affects the level of customer satisfaction. Distributive Justice is an effort made by a company to allocate resources in fixing the service failures and focusing on compensation. If customer complaints are handled by providing appropriate compensation, the satisfaction will be achieved. In this study, we focused in complaint handling conducted through social media, thus the distributive justice given by company can be in a form of discounts or refunds to achieve higher level of satisfaction (Ding & Lii, 2016).

Informational Justice represented by an adequate explanation that in accordance with the reported complaints or company service improvement. In this context, customers want to understand what is happening, what the cause is, and what do the company is doing to deal with failure. An informative explanation is quite effective in helping customers and often used as complaints handling strategies. When a failure occurs, if the customers do not get enough information, they will assume that the process is unfair. We proposed that adequate information provided through social media influences customer satisfaction when they report a complaint. When customers get enough information, they will not wary to continuing next purchase and not chose other vendor and when a company offers adequate and specific explanations to customers, their satisfaction is increased during the service recovery process (Nikbin, et al., 2012).

Interpersonal justice is perceived when company focuses on treating the customer politely and respectfully when handling their complaints. In social media, although there is no face to face interaction with customers in handling complaints, interpersonal justice can still also be achieved with respectful comment or replies given to the customers. This interaction has a positive influence on customer satisfaction in handling complaints process (Tax, et al., 1998).

Procedural justice is the fairness perceived in specific policies, processes, and methods adopted by the company to deal with service issues and service failures restoration including timeliness, accessibility, control processes, and flexibility to adapt to customer needs. This procedural justice also includes accuracy, speed and procedures in matters of service handling and recovery. We proposed that the accuracy and speed in answering and/or resolving customer complaints through social media platforms is an important aspect to keep customer satisfied. In accordance with above explanations, the authors propose the research hypothesis as follows:

H1a: Distributive justice in complaints handling process through social media has positive impact on customer satisfaction

H1b: Informational justice in complaints handling process through social media has positive impact on customer satisfaction

H1c: Interpersonal justice in complaints handling process through social media has positive impact on customer satisfaction

H1d: Procedural justice in complaints handling process through social media has positive impact on customer satisfaction

In this study, customer satisfaction is particularly defined by the satisfaction perceived by customers when complaint handling process is ongoing and comes from the contentment of how the provider handles their complaints. When customers are satisfied with response given by customer service staff during the time, then the level of customer trust to the companies will increase. The staff response is the reflection of company's concern toward customer satisfaction. Thus, customer service and complaint handling agent are one of the frontlines that must be trained to communicate well with customers. If the level of customer satisfaction increases, then the level of customer trust also increases. Customer satisfaction with service providers can build customer trust. In the context of consumer behavior, trust is defined as an achievement of the level of satisfaction and loyalty that results from problem handling behavior (Johnson & Auh, 1998). Therefore, the authors propose the following hypothesis:

H2: The satisfaction level of complaint handling process through social media has positive impact on customer trust

In relation to product quality, we argue that when customers are satisfied with the complaints handling service provided by the company, they will be perceived that the product/service is also qualified. On other hand, customer trust would also be increased if customers are confident in the company's reliability and integrity. If it is associated with product quality, the authors argue that customer trust in the company will affect customer opinion about the quality of products/services offered by the company. Therefore, the we propose the following hypothesis:

H3a: Customer satisfaction in complaints handling process through social media has positive impact on customer opinion about the quality of the product/service provided

H3b: Customer trust in the company has positive impact on customer opinions about the quality of products/services offered by the company

e-WOM is used to find out how customers suggest, recommend, and engage in positive talk by word of mouth through internet related to product or service (Ding & Lii, 2016). When customers have satisfying experience with the provided services and is encouraged by the ease of access to social media, customers will spread e-WOM positively via their social media account. For mobile service providers it is very important to maintain or increase market share and profitability and retain customers. To achieve these goals, increasing customer satisfaction is one of the vital tasks. Satisfaction will retain current customer and increasing the chance that they will spread the positive review thus increasing others' interest in the product/service and higher purchase probability. On the other hand, customer satisfaction directs customers to loyalty and WOM.

Perceived product quality variable is used to find out how customers value the quality of products offered to them (Bao, 2015). In this case, product quality represents the extent of the product/service to meets customers' need and expectations. We suggest that if the quality could fulfill customer requirements, then customer will disseminate positive information to others regarding the product/service. Therefore, the authors propose the following hypothesis:

H4a: The level of customer satisfaction has positive impact on e-WOM

H4b: Product quality has positive impact e-WOM

H4c: The level of customer trust in the company has positive impact on e-WOM

Consumer satisfaction is the main motivation for consumers to continue using the product/service. Increasing customer satisfaction level can reduce the number of complaints and customers who terminate using services. Repurchase is important for the company's success because the costs incurred for gaining new customers are greater than retaining existing customers. When customer had bad experience when using the product/service, they could stop subscribing and switching to competitors' service/product (Johnson & Auh, 1998). Customer satisfaction with the services provided by complaints handling agents on social media has an influence on the customer's desire to reuse products services offered by the company.

Customer trust in corporation is a privilege owned by the company to maintain the continued use of the products/services offered. When customers trust in corporate services, customers will tend to be loyal and continue to use the product compared to the desire to purchase other competitors' product. Trust and commitment affect consumer intentions in repurchasing (Ding & Lii, 2016). In complaints handling process through social media, trust can have a positive effect on customers, so they want to reuse products/services provided. Additionally, when product quality perceived by customers meet their expectations, it is more likely that they will continue to use these products. This will maintain the continued use of the product. Perceived quality and willingness to buy have a positive correlation, so the perceived quality can be used in predicting the desire to repurchase or repeat use (Fang, et al., 2016). Therefore, we propose the following hypothesis:

H5a: Customer satisfaction in complaints handling process has a positive impact on the continuous of use
H5b: Customer trust has a positive impact on the continuous of use
H5c: Product quality has a positive impact on continuous of use

3. METHODOLOGY

Quantitative research approach was used to answer the purpose of the study. The population of this study is the followers of a customer care twitter account of a large telecommunication company in Indonesia. This organization provide individual customer GSM card that largely used in mobile phones. Customers can use the service to make phone call, send instant message and use the internet data package. To ensure that the respondents is customer of the service and has file complaint, we search the account who had a post or tweet related to a complain and mentioned the account and asked them as the respondent. Currently the number of followers is around 250 users. The data will be analyzed using structural equation modelling and the sample size suggested by (Hair, et al., 2011) is more than 100 data.

Nine variables were introduced based on the conceptual model with 29 indicators item. The exogenous variables are the dimensions of perceived justice, namely; distributive justice (3 items), procedural justice (4 items), interpersonal justice (3 items) and informational justice (3 items). We defined five endogen variables which are customer satisfaction (4 items), trust (3 items), product quality (3 items), e-WOM (3 items) and continuous usage (3 items). Then, indicators that represent all the variables were written in a questionnaire with five Likert scale 1 to 5 ranging from "strongly disagree" to "strongly agree". Prior to questionnaires dissemination, readability test was conducted by twenty respondents to assess the clarity of the statements in the survey. Data collecting was conducted online by asking the follower of the account who had sent complaint to the account. Then, CB-SEM was used to analyze the survey result using IBM SPSS AMOS 24 and IBM SPSS Statistics 20.

4. RESULT

4.1 Demographics of Respondents

The research data was collected in five weeks and we successfully obtained 250 respondents. However, there are several invalid questionnaires and omitted from the set, resulted 238 valid responses. The demographic of the respondents is shown in Table 1.

Table 1. Respondents' Demographic

Variable		Total	Percent.	Variable		Total	Percent.
Gender	Male	140	58.82%	Education	Primary Sch.	5	2.10%
	Female	98	41.18%		Junior High	112	47.06%
Age	<=20 years	46	19.33%		High School	9	3.78%
	21-30 years	132	55.46%		Diploma	22	9.24%
	31-40 years	52	21.85%		Bachelor	84	35.29%
	41-50 years	7	2.94%		Master	6	2.52%
	> 50 years	1	0.42%				

4.2 Reliability and Validity Testing

Convergent validity test is conducted by assessing the factor loading value of each indicator. The factor loading value that is more than 0.50 is an acceptable minimum value (Hair, et al., 2011). If the value is less than the threshold then the elimination of indicators is carried out as in the previous stage. After all the loading factors fulfill the threshold, we continued to the internal construct reliability test. Reliability testing is conducted by evaluating the Average Variance Extracted, Construct Reliability, and Cronbach's Alpha values (Table 2). Discriminant validity tests was conducted by comparing the AVE square root values with correlation values between variables. It can be fulfilled if the square root value is greater the correlation value with other variables. The goodness of fit (GFI) value is 0.846 and the model is statistically declared to be good fit.

Table 2. AVE, CR, CA Values

Variables	AVE	CR	CA	Variables	AVE	CR	CA
e-WOM	0.75	0.9	0.875	Interpersonal_Justice	0.653	0.849	0.959
Trust	0.826	0.905	0.882	Procedural_Justice	0.711	0.907	0.936
Continuous_Usage	0.626	0.77	0.849	Distributive_Justice	0.725	0.885	0.925
Customer_Satisfaction	0.734	0.917	0.906	Perceived_Product_Quality	0.685	0.867	0.818
Informational_Justice	0.716	0.883	0.894				

4.3 Hypothesis Testing

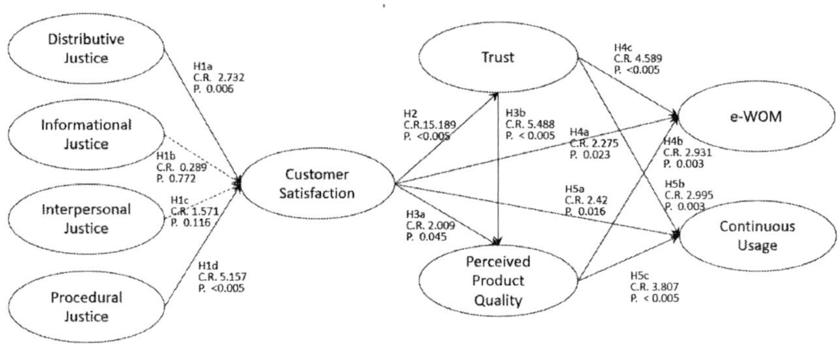

Figure 2. Hypothesis Testing Result

At this stage hypothesis testing will be carried out. Testing this hypothesis is done by measuring the level of significance of the relationship between variables in the structural model. For this significance test, the author uses the value of critical ratio (C.R) and p-value from the results of the regression weight bootstrapping as a reference. The p-value that must be fulfilled is less than (5%) or $| C.R | > 1.96$, which means that exogenous constructs have a significant effect on endogenous constructs at a 5% significance level with a 5% probability of error (Hair, 2014). Figure 2 shows the result of the hypothesis testing. Two hypotheses were rejected which was H1b and H1c with p value more than 0.005.

5. ANALYSIS AND DISCUSSION

Four hypotheses were proposed in evaluating perceived justice and customer satisfaction. The results show that distributive and procedural justice have positive influence towards customer satisfaction. However, it is not affected by procedural and interpersonal justice. In case of distributive justice, giving complementary would influence the level of customer satisfaction. When customer experienced service failure, the refund system will make customers feel satisfied with the complaints handling process. This is in accordance with the research conducted by (Ding & Lii, 2016), distributive justice such as discounts and refunds given by companies to customers after service recovery gives a higher level of satisfaction. Additionally, procedures that are fair to customers will affect the level of customer satisfaction. The procedure for handling complaints that includes the process, speed and timeliness in resolving complaints is very important. It is implied that customers want their complaints to be resolved more quickly and precisely. They will not want to wait long for the problem-solving process. In handling complaints through social media, this can be attributed to the speed and accuracy of responses from the customer service. This result is also consistent with the research by (Ding & Lii, 2016) and (Brock, et al., 2013), that procedural justice includes timeliness, accessibility, process control, and flexibility will increase consumer satisfaction. Informational and interpersonal justice in the other hand, are found to be not significantly affect customer satisfaction. In this case it can be explained that the customer does not need information that is really detailed about the service disruption that occurred. And the utilization of social media as the complaint handling communication tools do not required direct meetings with customer. Therefore, based on the results of this study, the fact that interpersonal justice is the attitude of the agent handling complaints is not too influential on the level of satisfaction felt by the customer.

From the results of hypothesis testing, it was found that the satisfaction in complaints handling process affected customer trust. When customers are satisfied with company's response regarding the complaint, the level of customer trust toward the company also increases. The factor of customer satisfaction with complaints handling process influences customer opinions about the quality of the service provided. They will assume that the quality is appropriate. Customer trust in the company also has a positive influence on customer opinions about the quality of services offered. This means that when the customer uses the service accompanied by trust towards to company they will perceived that the quality of the product is acceptable. The level of customer satisfaction with the services of a provider has a significant influence on e-WOM. Customer satisfaction will produce positive e-WOM about their experience. In addition, product quality influences e-WOM. This can be interpreted that acceptable service quality will affect the customers' desire to provide e-WOM positively. The level of customer trust in the company has a significant influence on e-WOM. This means that if the customer confidence level increases, the customer may spread positive information through e-WOM. When customers have trust in the corporation, then most likely customers will spread positive information about the corporation, especially in regard of the complaint handling case through social media.

Customer satisfaction with complaints handling services has a significant influence on continuous usage. When the customer is satisfied with the service of a complaint handling process, the customer's desire to use the service will increase or continuing the consumption of current service. Meanwhile, customer trust also affects the customer's intention to reuse. And, product quality has a positive impact on customer's intention to repurchase. This means that perceptions of good product quality will trigger customers to repurchase or continuing current service. Thus, in complaint handling process when it is typically a disadvantageous condition for the company, it could be managed so that the negative possible impact would turn into positive impacts where customer will repurchase or continuing current service and company could be advantaged by the positive e-WOM that would bring new customer in.

6. IMPLICATION

The theory of Perceived Justice defined four applicable justice which are distributive justice, informational justice, interpersonal justice, and procedural justice. The results of this study indicate that customer satisfaction is influenced by perceived justice which are distributive justice and procedural justice. We argue that in the context of handling complaints through social media, customers prioritize the time and accuracy in handling complaints (procedural justice) and are supported by compensation given to customers (distributive justice). In addition, the results of the study show that perceived product quality can be added to the e-WOM concept and continues usage. In previous research, the concept of e-WOM and continues usage (repurchase Intention) was only influenced by customer satisfaction and trust.

For practical implication, company will want to compensate and resolved the problem quickly when customers report their problem by using social media platform to increase customer satisfaction. So, in handling complaints, companies can prioritize distributive justice, which is providing appropriate compensation and procedural justice in the form of speed and accuracy in resolving customer complaints. This can be done by simplifying complaints handling. Customers who are satisfied with the services of tend to repurchase products and be loyal to the company. This loyal customer will help spread positive information through e-WOM through social media, which is a free and effective marketing tool.

7. CONCLUSION

The results of the study statistically prove that distributive justice and procedural justice are proven to affect customer satisfaction in complaint handling process. Meanwhile, informational justice and interpersonal justice are not proven to affect customer satisfaction. Of the two proven dimensions of justice, the most influential one is procedural justice. This means that in handling complaints process, customers prefer accuracy and promptness when they experience such condition. Results also show that the satisfaction of handling customer complaints affects customer trust and the perceived quality of the services offered by the company. Also, trust and perceived service quality affect the intention to spread e-WOM and reuse the service. When customers have trust in the corporation, it more likely that customers will spread positive information about the corporation, especially through social media. In addition, perceptions of good product quality will trigger customers to repurchase or continue use.

ACKNOWLEDGEMENT

This study is supported by the Universitas Indonesia Publication Grant (PIT9) entitled "Implementasi Sistem Enterprise di Indonesia" with contract number NKB-0012/UN2.R3.1/HKP.05.00/2019

REFERENCES

Bao, J., 2015. *The Impacts of E-service Quality on Customers' Repurchase Intention in Platform Online Retailing: An Empirical Investigation.* s.l., AIS Electronic Library.

Brock, C., Blut, M. & Evanschitzky, H., 2013. *Satisfaction with complaint handling: A replication study on its determinants in a business-to-business context.* Germany: Zeppelin University, Corporate Management and Economics.

Ding, M.-C. & Lii, Y.-S., 2016. Handling online service recovery: Effects of perceived justice on online games. *Telematics and Informatics,* 33(4), pp. 881-895.

Fang, J., Shao, Y. & Wen, C., 2016. Transactional quality, relational quality, and consumer e-loyalty: Evidence from SEM and fsQCA. *International Journal of Information Management,* Volume 36, p. 1205–1217.

Hair, 2014. A Primer on Partial Least Squares Structural Equation Modeling (PLS-SEM). *European Business Review,* Volume 26, pp. 106-121.

Hair, J. F., Sarstedt, M., Hopkins, L. & Kuppelwieser, V. G., 2011. PLS-SEM: Indeed a Silver Bullet. Volume 19, pp. 139-152.

Hennig-Thurau, T., Gwinner, K., Walsh, G. & Gremier, D., 2004. Electronic Word-Of-Mouth via Consumer-Opinion Platforms: What Motives Consumers to Articulate Themselves On The Intenet?. *Journal Of Interactive Marketing,* 18(1), pp. 28-52.

Johannsen, F. & Zellner, G., 2015. *Introducing a Professional Complaint Management: The Case of a Fleet Management Company.* Jerman: University of Regensburg.

Johnson, M. D. & Auh, S., 1998. Customer Satisfaction, Loyalty, and the Trust Environment. *Advances in Consumer Research ,* Volume 25, pp. 15-20.

Karatepe, O. M., 2006. Customer complaints and organizational responses: the effects of complainants' perceptions of justice on satisfaction and loyalty. *International Journal of Hospitality Management,* 25(1), pp. 69-90.

Kotler, P., 2009. *Manajemen Pemasaran.* 13 ed. Jakarta: Erlangga.

Nikbin, D., Marimuthu, M. & Armesh, H., 2012. Perceived justice in service recovery and switching intention: Evidence from Malaysian mobile telecommunication industry. *Management Research Review,* 35(3/4), pp. 309-325.

Park, D. & Kim, S., 2008. The Effects of Consumer Knowledge on Message Processing on Electronic Word-of-Mouth via Online Consumer Reviews. *Electronic Commerce Research and Applications,* Volume 7, p. 399–410.

Tax, S. S., Brown, S. W. & Chandrashekaran, M., 1998. Customer Evaluation of Service Complaint Experience: Implications for Relationship Marketing. *Journal of Marketing,* 62(2), pp. 60-76 .

Wirtz, J. & Matilla, A. S., 2004. Consumer Responses to Compensation, Speed of Recovery and Apology after a Aervice Failure. *International Journal of Service Industry Management,* 15(2), pp. 150-166.

SPONSORSHIP CONGRUITY AND ATTITUDE TOWARDS ADVERTISING IN MUSIC FESTIVALS: THE ROLE OF TRUST AND SOCIAL MEDIA ENGAGEMENT

Pedro Manuel do Espírito Santo[1] and Sara Santos[2]
[1]*Instituto Politécnico de Coimbra, ESTGOH, Rua Gen. Santos Costa, 3400-124 Oliveira do Hospital*
[2]*Escola Superior de Educação de Coimbra, R. Dom João III, 3030-329 Coimbra*

ABSTRACT

The number of festivals is increasing all over the world. Most people search for living moments and experiences that will retain in their mind and shared in social media. At the same time, social media change daily habits of people, special younger ones.
In this study, in the context of music festivals, it is analyzed the relation among trust, attitude toward "new" advertising, and congruence between the sponsoring brand and the event as influencing factors in social media engagement.
Results show that trust in the sponsoring brand of an event is explained by the congruence between the sponsoring brand and the event and by the attitude of individuals to creative brand advertising. On the other side, in social media engagement, consumption is influenced by congruence, by the attitude of individuals to advertising and by trust.
These results show that sponsorship congruity and attitude toward advertising have effects on consumption and trust. Thus, brands should look with special attention to the events before they sponsor them.

KEYWORDS

Sponsorship Congruity, Attitude Towards Advertising, Brand Trust, Social Media Engagement, Festivals

1. INTRODUCTION

Brands increasingly seek to build lasting relationships with their customers. Being present and sponsoring festivals has been a recurring strategy primarily to create closeness special to younger generations. Festivals are not only important to build relations and interactions with sponsors, brands, attendees and the community (Gursoy, Kim, & Uysal, 2004) but also to provide involvement with the cultural and social environment (Rowley & Williams, 2008). According to Crompton & McKay (1997, p. 429) “a festival implies that visitors are likely to be seeking cultural enrichment, education, novelty, and socialization”. For these authors there are four motives to attend a music festival: (1) cultural exploration, in other words, people want to experience different cultural activities; (2) novelty/regression, to live different experiences; (3) recover equilibrium, to escape from daily routine; (4) external interaction/socialization, to meet and to amuse with different people; (5) known-group socialization, spending quality and amazing time with friends; and (6) family togetherness, improving family relationships. For these reasons, brands used sponsorship strategies to get closer to its public and achieve marketing objectives.

On the other side, social media could help brands to build long-term relationships with attendees of festivals that share information with each other as well as non-attendees (Hudson, Roth, Madden, & Hudson, 2015). However, authors emphasize that this relation between social networks sites brands and festival attendees needs further investigation (Hudson et al., 2015).

In this study we search to deepener this investigation, analyzing trust, attitude toward "new" advertising, and congruence between the sponsoring brand and the event as influencing factors in social media engagement (namely in consumption and contribution). As little is known about how sponsorship of festivals drives engagement with brands on social media, we propose to contribute with theorical and practical results.

2. LITERATURE REVIEW

2.1 Sponsorship Congruity with the Event

Brands search to improve their image and perception through good memories in the consumer's mind through stimuli that strengthen brand associations. Therefore, there are several brands that seek a greater repeated exposure to potential consumers so that this stimulus increases the likelihood of relation with the brand and leads to an affective reaction to the brand (Woisetschläger & Michaelis, 2012).

Events are important assets for the growth of visitor flows to a region or city, improving the competitiveness of destinations and promoting the creation of local jobs and income. Nowadays, the financial viability of many regional festivals and events depends to a large extent on brand sponsorship (Shin, Lee, & Perdue, 2018).

Brand sponsorships allow to increase the exposure of these brands to an audience that might not otherwise have any contact with the brand. Sponsorship is summarized in the work of Chebli and Gharbi (2014) which describe the sponsorship of a brand to an event as an investment (financial or through the transfer of materials), about an activity, person or event and has access to a possible communication associated with that activity, person or event. However, event sponsorship literature has studied congruence theory as a theoretical tool for analysing whether the image of a sponsoring brand is consistent with the image of the event. This research focused mainly on the congruence between the visitor's self-image and the image of the event and the congruence between the sponsorship of the brand image and the image of the event (figure 1) (Shin et al., 2018).

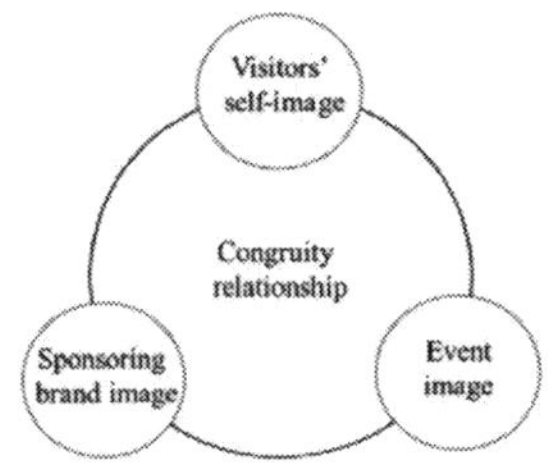

Figure 1. Congruity Relationship
Source: Shin et al. (2018)

Shin et al. (2018) refers that the exposure of individuals to a brand improves their involvement and the relationship that each individual has with the brand. Self-congruence with the sponsorship event helps to create a favourable attitude towards this event, and these positive feelings overflow to the company (Sirgy, Lee, Johar, & Tidwell, 2008). Engagement with brands improves when the congruence between the sponsored event and the brand is high, causing change in attitudes (Woisetschläger & Michaelis, 2012). It is no wonder that when individuals are involved with the event, they are more likely to spend more time and energy on the event and the positive feelings they have about the event are more likely to be transferred to the sponsored brands than when individuals are not highly involved (Sirgy et al., 2008).

Thus, this study intends to test the following hypotheses of investigation:

H1: The congruence between the event and the brand has positive effects on brand trust.

H2: The congruence between the event and the brand has influence in the engagement with the brand in the social networks.

2.2 Attitude towards Advertising (Novelty)

Creativity in advertising is essential to the effectiveness of advertising. Creativity has long been recognized as one of the most important concepts in designing and developing effective advertising (Baack, Wilson, van Dessel, & Patti, 2016).

Consumer responses may be affective, behavioural or cognitive (Pochun, Brennan, & Parker, 2018) and create systems of meanings and associations between the intended message and life experiences that trigger experiences and different emotions. As ad clutter exists, ad creativeness is even more important in generating attention and fostering trust. The attitude of each individual to innovative advertising promotes greater levels of brand's trust (Varki & Ashley, 2011). Thus, this study seeks to evaluate the following research hypothesis:

H3: The attitude to advertising (Novelty) has positive effects on brand trust.

Nowadays, the new communication formats are based on customized communication models that use social media/networks and events in an integrated way (de Waal Malefyt, 2015). Thus, the following hypothesis of investigation is formulated:

H4: The attitude to advertising (novelty) has positive effects on the consumption of content in social networks.

2.3 Brand Trust

Brand Trust is a concept widely study in marketing literature, mostly associated with brand loyalty. Lau & Lee (1999, p. 344) define brand trust as "a consumer's willingness to rely on the brand in the face of risk because of expectations that the brand will cause positive outcomes". In situations of information asymmetry, fear of opportunism or uncertainty, trust has the role of decrease this this doubts and make customers feel comfortable with the brand (Cheung, Chiu, & Lee, 2011). Therefore, brand trust is related with building strong relationship and brand loyalty. According with several authors (Cheung et al., 2011), trust is one of the main antecedents of loyalty. Burmann, Jost-Benz, & Riley (2009, p. 391) emphasize that brand trust represents "the basis for long-term customer relationship".

In online communities, brand trust has a mediating role in converting the effects of enhanced relationships in brand community to brand loyalty.

2.4 Social Media/Networks Engagement

Social media has changed the way people interact with brands as well as other people. Xiang & Gretzel (2010) define social media as internet-based applications that encompass media impressions created by consumers, resulted from experiences and archived or shared online and that could be accessed by other people. However, other authors evidence that not only for socialization but also entertainment, rewards, search information (Muntinga, Moorman, & Smit, 2011), among others.

Muntinga et al., (2011) proposed a Consumer Online Brand-Related Activity (COBRA) model which distinguishes consumer engagement on social media in three types of behavior: consumption (when consumers view images and videos, read information, comments and reviews), contribution (when users like or comment photographs and videos and engage in conversations about the brand); creation - users produce and publish content related to the brand (Muntinga et al., 2011). However, when applied to social network sites, Tsai & Men (2013) used the Muntinga et al. (2011) typology only with the variables "consumption" and "contribution". The study of Hudson, Huang, Roth, & Madden (2016) concluded that consumers who engage with their favorite brands using social media have stronger relationships with those brands compared with consumers who do not interact. Thus, the fifth hypothesis is:

H5: Brand trust has positive effects on the consumption of content in social networks.

Based on the COBRA model (Muntinga et al., 2011), Schivinski et al. (2016) consider that there is a hierarchical relationship between the three dimensions of engagement: consumption, contribution and creation. This study intends also to analyze whether the same hierarchical relationship (consumption-contribution) occurs in the engagement of the festivalgoers. Thus, the last hypothesis is:

H6: Consumption of content in social networks has influence on contribution.

This formulation of hypothesis resulted in the conceptual model formulated in figure 2.

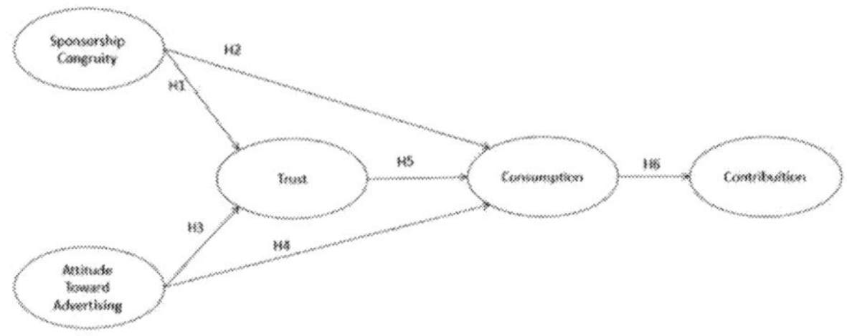

Figure 2. Conceptual Model

3. METHODOLOGY

The present study of a conclusive-causal nature had simple transversal characteristics whose unit of analysis were individuals who already had some experience in music festivals and who identified the sponsoring brands of the last festival in which they participated. The concepts under study were operationalized through 5-point Likert scales, tested in the literature, and whose original studies of which were adapted are described in table 1.

Table 1. Constructs, Items and References

Constructs	Items	Mean	Std Dev.	λ	Code
Attitude towards advertising (ATT) (Varki and Ashley, 2011)	Event sponsor ads are original.	3,54	0,91	0,835**	ATT01
	Ads from the event sponsor are memorable.	3,26	0,99	0,822**	ATT02
	I'm interested in the sponsorship ads of the event.	3,29	1,06	0,869**	ATT03
	Ads from the event sponsor are interesting.	3,43	0,96	0,919**	ATT04
	There is something different about sponsor advertising for the event.	3,17	0,99	0,874**	ATT05
Sponsorship Congruity (CONG) (Koo and Lee, 2018)	The advertising of brand sponsorship of the event is consistent with my way of being.	2,97	0,97	0,685**	CONG01
	The advertising of brand sponsorship of the event is consistent with how others see me.	2,81	1,01	0,653**	CONG02
	There is a logical connection between the music festival and its main sponsor.	3,56	1,06	0,806**	CONG03
	The image of the event and the brand image of the main sponsor are similar.	3,50	1,02	0,713**	CONG04
	The event and the main sponsor represent similar things.	3,23	1,04	0,822**	CONG05
	It makes perfect sense for this brand to sponsor the event.	3,63	1,00	0,796**	CONG06
Trust (TRUS) (Varki and Ashley, 2011)	The sponsor's brand of the event is sincere.	3,53	0,86	0,899**	TRUS01
	The sponsor's brand of the event is honest.	3,51	0,84	0,922**	TRUS02
	The sponsor's brand of the event is reliable.	3,71	0,83	0,878**	TRUS03
	Ads to this festival are compelling.	3,91	0,83	0,725**	TRUS04
Consumption (CONS) (Schivinski, Christodoulides, and Dabrowski, 2016)	I follow the social network pages of the sponsor of this event.	2,88	1,43	0,926**	CONS01
	I see the images in the social network pages of the sponsor of this event.	2,99	1,38	0,916**	CONS02
	I follow the comments on the social network pages of the sponsor of this event.	2,49	1,25	0,889**	CONS03
	I make "like" in the sponsor brand publications on Facebook / Instagram.	2,69	1,36	0,920**	CONS04
Contribution (CONT) (Schivinski, Christodoulides, and Dabrowski, 2016)	I create publications about the festival sponsor brand on Facebook / Instagram.	2,00	1,15	0,916**	CONT01
	Comment the publications made by sponsor brand or other users on the Facebook / Instagram page	1,98	1,03	0,896**	CONT02
	I share sponsor brand publications on Facebook / Instagram.	2,15	1,18	0,892**	CONT03

λ - Standardized Coefficients (*Standardized Loadings*); ** p<0,001

Individuals answered through a questionnaire available online between November and December 2018, which 272 responses were obtained from individuals younger than 30 years of age, 73.2% are female and 78.3% of the individuals attended to music events in recent months. For the sample procedure, preliminary analyses were carried out. It was concluded that the constructs don't have problems of multicollinearity (VIF<5) (Maroco, 2014). Data analysis was performed through the PLS-SEM estimation which the first step in the analysis through PLS is the analysis to the measurement model. The study of the reliability and validity of the measurement model will provide confirmatory information about the reliability of each construct, its convergent validity and its discriminant validity. In order to perform this step, the "PLS algorithm" function was executed in the software SMART PLS 3.2.7. From the obtained data we only considered the values that had standardized coefficients (λ) higher than 0.5 (table 1). From table 1, it is possible to verify the factorial and convergent validity of the constructs (Hair et al., 2016; Vinzi, Chin, Henseler, & Wang, 2010). Regarding the evaluation of the model of measures, the discriminant validity was confirmed through three criteria: criterion of Fornell and Larcker (1981) (table 3); cross-loadings evaluation criterion (table 4) and correlation ratio of Heterotrait-Monotrait (HTMT) of Henseler et al. (2015) (table 5).

Table 2. Results of the Measurement Model

Construct	Cronbach α (> 0,7)	Rho_A (> 0,7)	CR (> 0,7)	AVE (> 0,5)
ATT	0,915	0,920	0,937	0,747
CONG	0,841	0,846	0,884	0,561
TRUS	0,879	0,883	0,918	0,739
CONS	0,933	0,934	0,952	0,833
CONT	0,885	0,885	0,929	0,813

AVE – Average Extracted Variance; CR –Composite Reliability;

Table 3. Discriminating Validity - Criterion of Fornell and Larcker (1981)

	TRUS	ATT	CONG	CONS	CONT
Trust (TRUS)	0,860				
Attitude towards advertising (ATT)	0,429	0,864			
Sponsorship Congruity (CONG)	0,581	0,518	0,749		
Consumption (CONS)	0,452	0,509	0,496	0,913	
Contribution (CONT)	0,303	0,385	0,365	0,710	0,902

Table 4. Ratio of Heterotrait-Monotrait Correlations (HTMT)

	TRUS	ATT	CONG	CONS	CONT
Trust (TRUS)					
Attitude towards advertising (ATT)	0,476				
Sponsorship Congruity (CONG)	0,671	0,586			
Consumption (CONS)	0,501	0,548	0,559		
Contribution (CONT)	0,341	0,426	0,424	0,778	

Table 5. Discriminant Validity

	TRUS	ATT	CONG	CONS	CONT
ATT01	0,359	0,835	0,435	0,428	0,308
ATT02	0,309	0,822	0,338	0,373	0,296
ATT03	0,365	0,869	0,471	0,493	0,376
ATT04	0,401	0,919	0,487	0,447	0,341
ATT05	0,412	0,874	0,489	0,446	0,336
CONG01	0,390	0,472	0,685	0,407	0,396
CONG02	0,341	0,422	0,653	0,433	0,390
CONG03	0,440	0,368	0,806	0,325	0,163
CONG04	0,426	0,314	0,713	0,284	0,192
CONG05	0,443	0,353	0,822	0,391	0,264
CONG06	0,548	0,394	0,796	0,377	0,236
TRUS01	0,899	0,360	0,552	0,379	0,279
TRUS02	0,922	0,395	0,524	0,410	0,290
TRUS03	0,878	0,331	0,461	0,379	0,222
TRUS04	0,725	0,385	0,452	0,383	0,243
CONS01	0,444	0,466	0,453	0,926	0,605
CONS02	0,426	0,493	0,458	0,916	0,584
CONS03	0,369	0,433	0,450	0,889	0,694
CONS04	0,413	0,467	0,449	0,920	0,702
CONT01	0,250	0,353	0,333	0,627	0,916
CONT02	0,245	0,312	0,296	0,627	0,896
CONT03	0,321	0,375	0,355	0,665	0,892

The second step through the PLS-SEM methodology is the analysis to the structural model that aims to test the hypotheses under study through the analysis of path coefficients and the analysis of their significance (Avkiran & Ringle, 2018; Hair et al., 2016; Henseler et al., 2015; Vinzi et al., 2010). For this purpose, we used the bootstrap resampling technique with 5000 sub-samples to be able to have stability in the obtained results. The accomplishment of this analysis allowed to obtain the results that will serve to test the hypotheses under study through the analysis of the standardized path coefficients (Std β). In addition to this analysis, the significance of each relation was verified through Student's t-value, p-value from which the results presented in the figure 3 which are summarized in table 6.

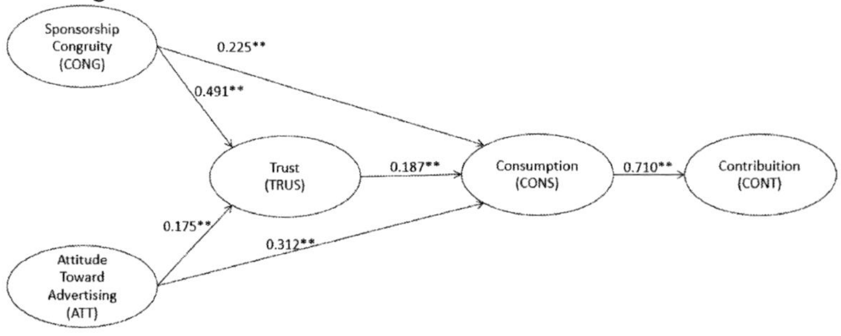

Figure 3. Structural Model

Table 6. Summary of Hypothesis Test Results

Hypothesis	Structural Relationship	Std β	*t-Value*	Results
H1	CONG→ TRUS	0.491***	9.118	Supported
H2	CONG→ CONS	0.225***	3.756	Supported
H3	ATT→ TRUS	0.175**	2.964	Supported
H4	ATT→ CONS	0.312***	5.485	Supported
H5	TRUS→ CONS	0.187***	3.466	Supported
H6	CONS→CONT	0.710***	24.483	Supported

* p<0.05; ** p<0.01; *** p<0.001

4. DISCUSSION

Brands have sought to increase exposure to their potential customers in several ways. Bringing audiences to the digital environments where brands communicate has been a present challenge. Therefore, this paper aims to explain the engagement of individuals with brands in the social media environment.

Engagement in social media is, according to Schivinski et al. (2016) based in Mutinga's COBRA framework (Muntinga, 2011), composed of three dimensions: consumption, contribution and creation. However, only consumption and contribution (base in authors such as Tsai & Men, 2013) were analysed in this study.

This study developed a research model that identified trust, attitude toward "new" advertising, and congruence between the sponsoring brand and the event as influencing factors in social media engagement. Thus, we tested the hypotheses of investigation, which were based on the analysis to individuals less than 30 years old. From the hypothesis test, the model explains that trust in the sponsoring brand of an event is explained (R^2=0.360) by the congruence between the sponsoring brand and the event ($\beta_{CONG \rightarrow TRUS}$ = 0.491; t = 9.118; p <0.001) and by the attitude of individuals to creative brand advertising ($\beta_{ATT \rightarrow TRUS}$ = 0.175 t = 2.964; p <0.01).

In the engagement in social networks, consumption is considered an initial level of engagement that, by the results obtained is influenced (R^2=0,355) by congruence ($\beta_{CONG \rightarrow CONS}$= 0.225; t = 3.756; p <0.001) by the attitude of individuals to advertising ($\beta_{ATT \rightarrow CONS}$= 0.312; t = 5.485; p <0.001) and by trust ($\beta_{TRUS \rightarrow CONS}$ = 0.187; t = 3.466; p <0.001).

It is thus explained that congruence and attitude towards advertising are important to create positive feelings and trust (Sirgy et al., 2008; Varki & Ashley, 2011) and the engagement with the brands is superior whenever the sensations are positive, leaving the brand reinforced (Woisetschläger & Michaelis, 2012).

At a higher level of engagement of individuals in social networks, the contribution is explained (R^2=0,504) by the individuals' own consumption of content ($B_{CONS \rightarrow CON}$ = 0.710; t = 24.483; p <0.001).

5. CONCLUSION

The results showed that the dimensions of engagement in social networks are explained by the variables included in the model tested. In this way, the work presents theoretical and practical contributions.

The theoretical advances focus mainly on the presented model that explains the involvement through the variables analysed. Thus, the congruence between the sponsored brand and the event is proving to be of utmost importance, as is the attitude towards advertising and also trust. Thus, at the practical level, this work has relevance for the management of brands since it reports that the brands should look with special attention to the events before they sponsor them. Greater engagement with brands increases the value of brands and, accordingly, congruence is a key factor in social networks. Thus, the sponsorship should follow a strategic analysis in order to enhance the engagement of the public with the brands.

Although the conclusions are relevant, this study had limitations because the analyzes are based on a sample of young individuals (under 30 years of age) and mostly female. These limitations suggest new studies with more diversified samples.

REFERENCES

Avkiran, N. K. et al, 2018. *Partial Least Squares Structural Equation Modeling: Recent Advances in Banking and Finance*: Springer International Publishing.

Baack, D. W. et al, 2016. Advertising to businesses: Does creativity matter? *Industrial Marketing Management,* Vol. 55, pp. 169-177

Burmann, C. et al, 2009. Towards an identity-based brand equity model. *Journal of Business Research*, Vol. 62, No. 3, pp. 390–397.

Chebli, L. et al, 2014. The Impact of the Effectiveness of Sponsorship on Image and Memorizing: Role of Congruence and Relational Proximity. *Procedia - Social and Behavioral Sciences,* Vol. 109, pp. 913-924.

Cheung, C. M. K. et al, 2011. Online social networks: Why do students use facebook? *Computers in Human Behavior*, Vol. 27, No. 4, pp. 1337–1343.

Crompton, J. L. et al, 1997. Motives of visitors attending festival events. *Annals of Tourism Research*, Vol. 24, No. 2, pp. 425–439.

de Waal Malefyt, T., 2015. Relationship advertising: How advertising can enhance social bonds. *Journal of Business Research,* Vol. *68*, No.12, pp. 2494-2502

Fornell, C. et al, 1981. Evaluating structural equation models with unobservable variables and measurement error. *Journal of Marketing Research,* Vol. 18, No. 1, pp. 39-50.

Gursoy, D. et al, 2004. Perceived impacts of festivals and special events by organizers: an extension and validation. *Tourism Management*, Vol. 25, No. 2, pp. 171–181.

Hair, J. F. et al, 2016. *A Primer on Partial Least Squares Structural Equation Modeling (PLS-SEM)*: SAGE Publications.

Henseler, J. et al, 2015. A new criterion for assessing discriminant validity in variance-based structural equation modeling. *Journal of the Academy of Marketing Science,* Vol. 43, No. 1, pp. 115-135.

Hudson, S. et al, 2016. The influence of social media interactions on consumer–brand relationships: A three-country study of brand perceptions and marketing behaviors. *International Journal of Research in Marketing*, Vol. 33, No.1, pp. 27–41.

Hudson, S. et al, 2015. The effects of social media on emotions, brand relationship quality, and word of mouth: An empirical study of music festival attendees. *Tourism Management*, Vol. 47, pp. 68-76.

Koo, J. et al, 2018. Sponsor-event congruence effects: The moderating role of sport involvement and mediating role of sponsor attitudes. *Sport Management Review.*

Lau, G. T. et al, 1999. Consumers' Trust in a Brand and the Link to Brand Loyalty. *Journal of Market-Focused Management*, Vol. 4, No. 4, pp. 341–370.

Maroco, J. (2014). *Análise Estatística com o SPSS. 6ª Edição*. Pêro Pinheiro: Report Number.

Muntinga, D. et al, 2011. Introducing COBRAs. *International Journal of Advertising*, Vol. 30, No.1, pp. 13–46.

Pochun, T. et al, 2018. Advertising effects? An elemental experiment. *Australasian Marketing Journal (AMJ),* Vol. 26, No. 4, pp. 338-349.

Rowley, J. et al, 2008. The impact of brand sponsorship of music festivals. *Marketing Intelligence & Planning*, Vol. 26, No. 7, pp. 781–792.

Shin, H. et al, 2018. The congruity effects of commercial brand sponsorship in a regional event. *Tourism Management,* Vol. 67, pp. 168-179.

Sirgy, J. et al, 2008. Effect of self-congruity with sponsorship on brand loyalty. *Journal of Business Research,* Vol. 61, No. 10, pp. 1091-1097.

Tsai, W.H. et al, 2013. Motivations and Antecedents of Consumer Engagement With Brand Pages on Social Networking Sites. *Journal of Interactive Advertising*, Vol. 13, No.2, pp. 76–87.

Xiang, Z. et al, 2010. Role of Social Media in Online Travel Information Search. *Tourism Management*, Vol. 31, No. 2, pp. 179-188.

Varki, S. et al, 2011. The Differential Effect of Ad Novelty and Message Usefulness on Brand Judgments AU - Sheinin, Daniel A. *Journal of Advertising,* Vol. 40, No. 3, pp. 5-18.

Woisetschläger, D. M. et al, 2012. Sponsorship congruence and brand image: A pre-post event analysis. *European Journal of Marketing,* Vol. 46, No.3/4, pp. 509-523.

VFX: A VISION-BASED APPROACH TO FORUM DATA EXTRACTION

Chen Hui Ng, Choon Jin Ng and Tong Ming Lim
Tunku Abdul Rahman University-College, Malaysia

ABSTRACT

Rapid development of the Internet has dramatically increased information available on the World Wide Web. Amongst these vast sources of information, discussion forums may be useful for businesses and organizations to get a glimpse of customer opinions or to extract product information. Little existing work reported in the literature has systemically investigated the problem of extracting user posts from forum sites. Extracting forum posts accurately raises a few challenges. First, forum comes in a variety of templates and this makes it hard to formalize general rules to extract forum posts. Second, each post record might appear relatively different from each other. This introduces inconsistency in the Document Object Model (DOM) for comparisons. Third, each post in the forum can consist of complicated subtrees rather than a single node in the DOM tree. To tackle these challenges, a vision-based approach was introduced to automatically extract posts from a web forum page based on its visual cues. In this paper, we propose a visual-based forum extraction (VFX) algorithm that can extract user posts in any types of forum without the need to inspect its template structure in advance.

KEYWORDS

Forum Data Extraction, Forum Visual Cues, Forum Layout Structure, Vision-Based Extraction

1. INTRODUCTION

The increasing accessibility of the Web has increased the proliferations of web based forums. This has enabled users to freely voice their views and promote discussions on a variety of topics ranging from politics, entertainment, to products and services reviews. As such, these silos of knowledge can conveniently become another important source of information. These extracted information can then be processed and used for monitoring and analysis. For instance, a company can monitor customer feedback on its products and services.

In this paper, we focus on the problem of automatically extracting posts in any forum site without the need to inspect its template structure in advance. In general, a web page contains not only useful data, but also other irrelevant data such as header, footer, navigational panels, advertisements, comments, and so on. These irrelevant data are known as noises. Reducing noises will reduce preprocessing complexities during the forum data analytics cycle. The goal of forum data extraction is to remove these noises from a web page and extract only the required data records from these pages. There are two main tasks in forum data extraction: (a) post record identification, and (b) post content extraction. Post record identification is to find out where the posts are located in a forum web page using visual cues. Once the position of post records is found, the next step is to extract individual post in the post records.

Obviously, it is impractical to manually inspect all forums' structures in order to extract their posts. Therefore, the goal of this project is to propose a general algorithm that can automatically extract user posts from any given forum page.

2. LITERATURE REVIEW

Liu et al. proposed an algorithm named Mining Data Records (MDR) (Bing, Grossman, & Zhai, 2004). MDR identifies data regions by searching for multiple generalized nodes using edit-distance similarity where generalized nodes are a fix combination of multiple child nodes and their corresponding subtrees. MDR does not identify the most relevant data records but rather reports each repetitive subregion contained in a Web page. Later, the author proposed an improvement of their system named DEPTA operating on a tag tree built according to visual rendering information (Liu & Zhai, 2005). Additionally, they mentioned that gap information is incorporated to eliminate false node combinations but nothing is said about the gap information. Finally, they proposed an approach for data record alignment by progressively growing a seed tag tree. The alignment is partial because only these nodes of a data record become aligned whose position for inserting into the seed tree can be uniquely determined. They tested their MDR system on a collection of handpicked sample pages with a precision of 100% and a recall of 99.8%.

Cai et al. proposed a vision-based page segmentation algorithm (VIPS) (Liu, Meng, & Meng, 2006). VIPS is proposed to extract the semantic structure for web page where semantic structure is a hierarchical structure where each node corresponds to a block. VIPS algorithm makes full use of a page layout feature. It first extracts all suitable blocks from the HTML DOM tree, then it tries to find the separators between these extracted blocks. Separators denote the horizontal or vertical lines in a web page that visually crosses those extracted blocks. These separators are also assigned weightage based on its visual cues. Finally, the separators with the lowest weight and the blocks beside these separators are merged to form new blocks. This merging process iterates until separators with maximum weights are met. VIPS algorithm takes advantage of visual cues to obtain the vision-based content structure of a web page and thus successfully bridges the gap between the DOM structure and the semantic structure. The page is partitioned based on visual separators and structured as a hierarchy. This semantic hierarchy is consistent with human perception to some extent.

Akpinar et al. then extended the VIPS algorithm (Akpinar, Elgin, & Yesilada, 2012). The original VIPS algorithm has a limited coverage on HTML tags. Any tags not covered are then referred to a single generic rule. This becomes an issue as most websites are now written in HTML5 tags. To tackle such problems, Akpinar et al. modified the heuristic rules of the algorithm by adding more visual features such as margin, float, and images. Besides, some rules required a threshold to be defined. It is also not possible to find a cue on how to calculate this threshold.

Song et al. proposed a VIPS-based algorithm to rank block importance for web pages through machine learning algorithms using spatial features (Song, Liu, Wen, & Ma, 2004). They extracted query-independent rankings for the fragments for the purpose of improving the performance of web search and also to facilitate web mining and accessibility. They partitioned a web page into semantic blocks with a hierarchical structure, constructed the spatial and content features, and used neural network and Support Vector Machine (SVM) to build the block importance model for ranking the importance of each block in the web page.

Simon et al. presented a fully automatic information extraction tools called ViPER (Simon & Lausen, 2005). ViPER provides a better sub-tree comparing method that allows consecutive data records with various lengths. The technique is based on the assumption that a web page contains at least two consecutive data records which exhibits some kind of structural and visible similarities. For example, a search engine's result page. ViPER is able to extract relevant data with respect to user's visual perception of the web page. It also introduces a multiple sequence alignment algorithm (MSA) that aligns maximal unique matches at different levels to extract the template of data records. With respect to the 676 correctly extracted data records by ViPER, only 11 data items could not be aligned correctly.

Shuyi et al. proposed a novel template independent news extraction approach to easily identify news articles based on visual consistency (Zheng, Song, & Wen, 2007). They first represent a page as a visual block tree. Then, by extracting a series of visual features, they can derive a composite visual feature set that is stable in the news domain. The visual features used included position, size, rich format features (font size, bold, and italic), and statistical features (number of images and hyperlinks, text length, number of paragraphs, number of paragraph with italic, number of table, number of paragraph with bold). Finally, they used a machine learning approach to generate a template-independent wrapper. Experimental results indicated that their approach is effective in extracting news across websites, even from unseen websites. The F1 performance was around 95%.

Zhao et al. presented the ViNTs algorithm for automatically producing wrappers that can be used to extract search result records from dynamically generated result pages returned by search engines (Zhao, Meng, Wu, Raghavan, & Yu, 2005). ViNTs automatically generates SRR (Search Result Record) extraction rules using visual context features and tag structure information. Therefore, it first utilizes the visual content without considering the tag structure to identify content regularities denoted as content lines and then combines them with the HTML tag structure regularities to generate wrappers. To weight the relevance of different extraction rules, visual and non-visual features have been used. ViNTs builds a wrapper for a search engine using several result pages and one no-result page. The resulting wrapper is represented by a regular expressions of alternative horizontal separators tags such as <HR> or

, which segment descendants into SRRs. Due to the fact that the ViNTs system only supplies horizontal separators, which is sufficient when considering document result pages, it could not separate horizontally arranged data records which will require vertical separators. Additionally, at least four data records must be present in a web page for building the wrapper. In case the data records are distributed over multiple sections, only the major section is reported.

3. SYSTEM OVERVIEW

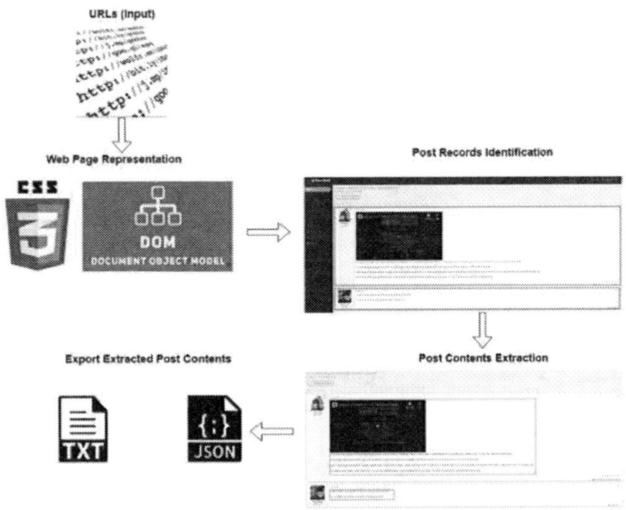

Figure 1. Overview of the Stages in the Visual-based Forum Extraction (VFX) Algorithm

Figure 1 shows the stages of the Visual-based Forum Extraction (VFX) algorithm. The first stage is to prepare DOM node information, render it in memory, and acquire its CSS properties. The second stage is to identify which block in a forum web page holds the post records. The third stage is to extract the post contents from the identified records. Finally, the last stage is to export those contents into a readable format such as the JavaScript Object Notation (JSON) or a comma separated value (CSV) file for further analysis.

3.1 Web Page Representation

The input to the VFX is the forum page's URL link. VFX will fetch the page and parse its HTML, simulate any JavaScript events, and render them into a DOM tree representation.

As HTML tags do not accurately reflect a semantic representation of a web page, visual information needs to be acquired from the post-rendered Cascading Style Sheets (CSS) in order to improve the extraction performance. Visual information in web page has proven to be a very useful feature for web data search and extraction, and several vision-based approaches have been proposed, such as those presented in Liu et al. (2006) and Akpinar et al. (2012). During the parsing process, useful visual information is obtained and attached to the nodes of the DOM tree. The visual information used in this paper is listed as the following:

- *Position*: The coordinate of the left-top corner of a node.
- *Size*: The width and height of the rectangle that a node occupies in the web page.
- *Font*: The text properties including its font size, font style, font colour and font weight.
- *Margin*: The margin applied to the rectangle area occupied by a node.
- *Colour*: The background colour of the node's rectangular area.

3.2 Post Records Identification

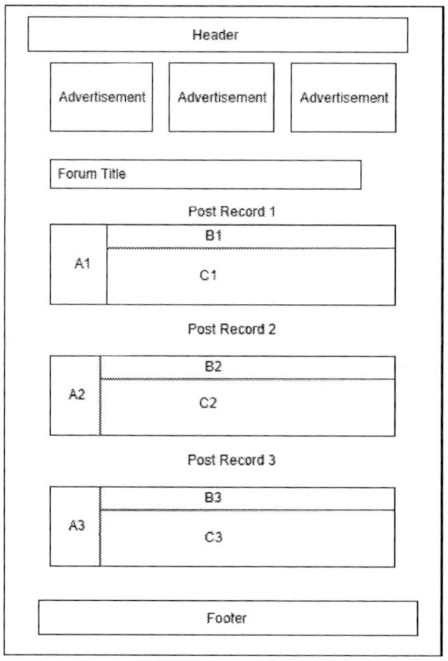

Figure 2. A Typical Web Forum Layout with the Post Title and the User Posts

To ease reader's convenience, forum pages are often designed to have regular layout of post records. Based on the observations of a large number of forum pages, a group of useful features and visual information is generalized to create a set of heuristic rules for post records identification. To help understand the features, Figure 2 shows a general layout of the post contents in a typical forum page. Based on Figure 2, the useful features are identified as below:

- *Feature 1*: Post records are arranged vertically with the same width and flushed left.
- *Feature 2*: The templates of the post records in one page are identical.
- *Feature 3*: The items with the same semantics in different post records are similar in appearance, including position and font, but the user-generated contents (post contents) can be different.
- *Feature 4*: Title is always located at top of the page and is bold.
- *Feature 5*: The title font size is larger than other text.

The components to be extracted are the forum thread title and the user generated posts, known as the post records. The first post record (post record 1) shown in Figure 2 is formed by blocks A1, B1 and C1. Amongst these blocks, C1 is the post content containing the user's post content.

On the other hand, blocks that are outside of the forum title and the post records are known as noises. In Figure 2, the noises are the header, advertisement and footer.

To be able to extract the title and user generated posts accurately, we need to identify which blocks are important. Every node in the DOM tree is checked to determine whether it forms a single block or not. If not, its children will be processed in the same way. Score will be assigned to each extracted block based on the block's visual cues. These scores are known as the TitleValue and the ContentValue. TitleValue is the score assigned to the block based on the heuristic rules in Table 1. The blocks with the highest TitleValue will be identified as the forum thread title. ContentValue is the score assigned based on heuristic rules to identify whether it is a post record. Blocks with equal ContentValue will be identified as the post records.

Then, the block with the highest TitleValue or equal ContentValue will be appended to a list for later extraction. A set of heuristic rules is produced to justify whether the node can form a single block and to assign the TitleValue and ContentValue. Tag cues and visual information acquired in the web page representation stage are utilized to produce the heuristic rules. Tags such as <H1>, <H2>, <B> and <STRONG> are often used to highlight a reader's attention such as the forum thread title. Thus, when a block has such tags, especially <H1> tag, higher TitleValue will be assigned to that particular block. The heuristic rules are listed in Table 1. The rules precedence are processed in the order of the rule set.

Table 1. Heuristic Rules for Post Records Identification

No.	Rules
1.	If the DOM node is a valid node (visible element) and has the following HTML tags: • If it has <h1> HTML tag, add 5 points to TitleValue • If it has <h2> HTML tag, add 3 points to TitleValue • If it has <b> or <strong> HTML tag, add 2 points to TitleValue
2.	If the top and bottom margin of the DOM node are nonzero: Add 2 points to TitleValue
3	If the font size of the DOM node is greater than the average font size: Add 3 points to TitleValue
4.	If the font weight of the DOM node is bold or the value is greater than 550: Add 3 points to TitleValue
5.	If the DOM node has a text node or a virtual text node as its child nodes, and their font colors are different: Add 2 points to TitleValue
6.	If the background color of the DOM node is different from its child nodes: Add 2 points to TitleValue
7.	If the text-align style of the DOM node is center: Add 1 points to TitleValue
8.	If the height of the DOM node occupied at least 70% of the page height and it is a visible element: Add 5 points to ContentValue
9.	If the DOM node's width is the same with all its sibling nodes: Add 5 points to ContentValue
10.	If the DOM node class name is same with all its sibling nodes' class name: Add 5 points to ContentValue

3.3 Post Contents Extraction

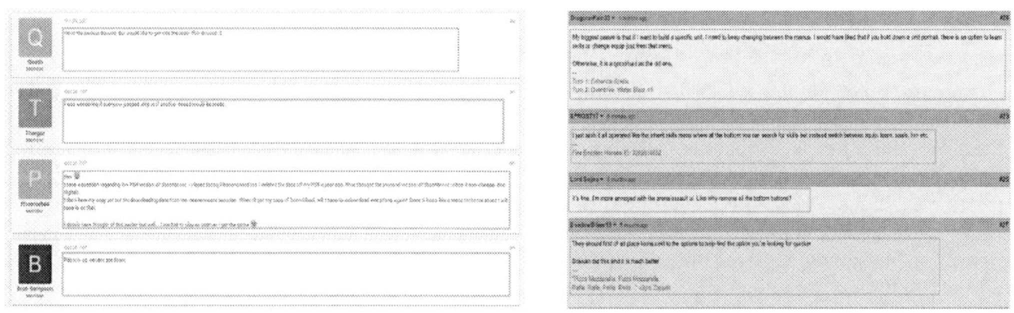

(a) NeoGAF forum sample

(b) GameFAQ forum sample

Figure 3. Sample Post Record from Different Source of Forums

Based on the observation on samples of forum pages, we found out that region containing post contents usually have greater width or greater height if compared to its sibling nodes. The blocks highlighted in Figure 3 show the regions containing the post contents. In Figure 3(a), the post contents have greater width when compared to their siblings (regions with the user profile details). In Figure 3(b), the post contents have greater height when compared to their siblings (regions with the user name and post number).

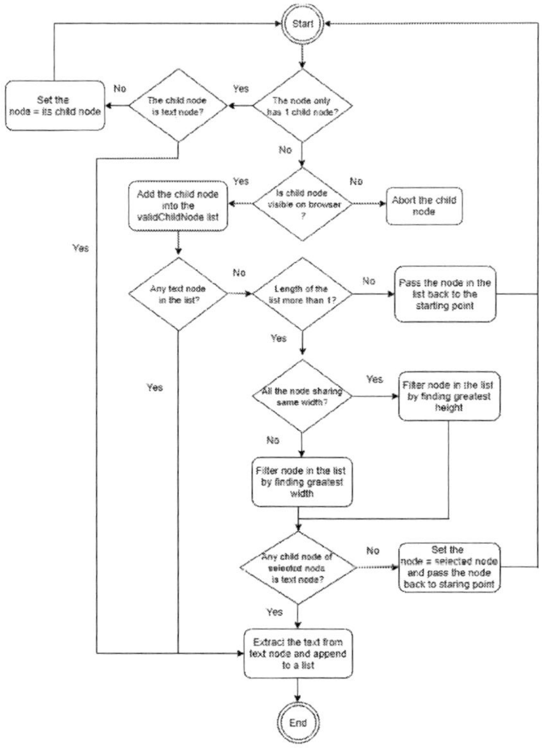

Figure 4. The Process Flow of the Visual-Based Forum Extraction (VFX) Algorithm

Hence, we conclude that a DOM node with greater width or greater height in a post records is the node that holds the post contents. Then, an algorithm is created based on these observations. Figure 4 illustrates the process of the VFX algorithm. Post records will be passed to this algorithm in order to extract post contents inside it. The post record is divided from the root of its DOM tree. This process is recursively repeated until all the post contents are extracted or all the DOM nodes in the post records are processed. However, not every forum page employs such layout. Some of the forum designed its post contents with lesser width and lesser height when compared to its sibling nodes. Thus, this algorithm only work on those forum pages where their layouts are consistent with the assumptions made in this paper.

In record extraction, all visual blocks with the same ContentValue are marked as the candidate blocks. These candidate blocks can potentially hold the forum posts and will be extracted. The visual blocks are always processed recursively starting from the root of the DOM tree. In this stage, the nodes in the post records with the highest width or highest height are marked as the post contents. However, the width measurement takes a higher priority over the height measurement. This process is illustrated in the example shown in Figure 5.

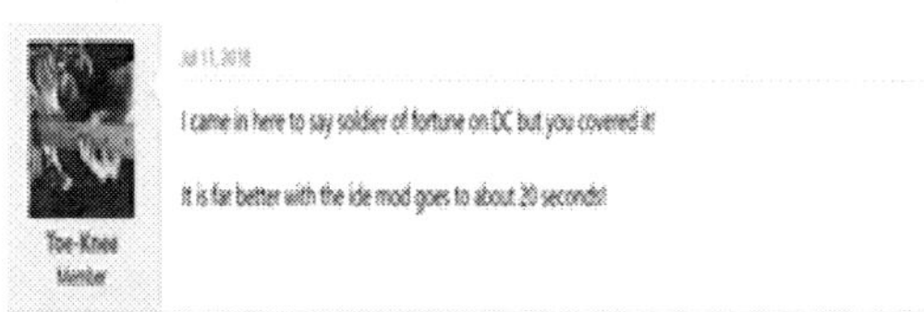

(a) Sample post record from the NeoGAF forum.

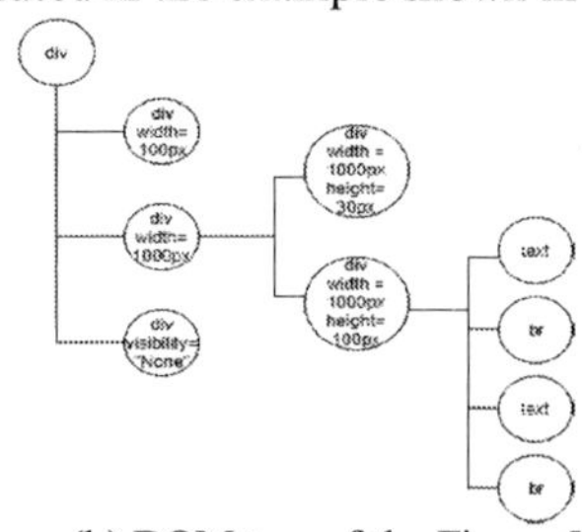

(b) DOM tree of the Figure 5(a)

Figure 5. An Illustration of the Rendered DOMs in the NeoGAF Forum

Figure 5(a) shows a sample post record from the NeoGAF forum while Figure 5(b) shows the DOM tree of that post record. In this example, the parent node is the first DIV node processed by the VFX algorithm. From there, there are three DIV child nodes. These nodes' visibility on the web browser is determined by inspecting some of their CSS properties such as the visibility property, size and coordinate. Out of these three child nodes, only two have been determined to be visible on the web browser while the third child node is not visible since its visibility property is "None". The two visible child nodes are then appended into a validChildNode list.

Among these two nodes in the validChildNode list, the node with the greatest width is selected. In Figure 5(b), the DIV node with the width of 1000px is selected. Its child nodes will be inspected to determine if there is a text node. If no text node is found, then the node will be passed to the start of the algorithm again. In this case, the selected node only has two DIV node and so it is passed to the start of the algorithm.

With this selected node (DIV node with 1000px width), as all its child nodes are not a text node, the visibility of the children are validated. Only visible child nodes are appended to the validChildNode list. In this case, all the children are visible so they are appended to the list. Then, two nodes in the list are compared in order to select the node with greater width. As both nodes in the validChildNode list share the same width, 1000px, the nodes are selected based on their height instead. Hence the DIV node with 100px height is selected.

For this selected node, two of its child nodes are text nodes, hence the texts are extracted from the text nodes and the process ends here. The extracted text is appended into a global list.

After all the visual blocks in the list are processed by VFX, a list that holds all the comments are generated. As extracted text may contain some special characters such as '\n', '\t' and '\a', these characters are cleaned from the final result before exporting.

4. RESULTS

In order to test the robustness of this algorithm, we have randomly chosen 50 forum pages for the implementation test. Throughout this test, the algorithm went through a few iterations of fixes to improve its accuracy.

After a few rounds of test-and-debug, 46 out of 50 forum web pages were successfully identified and extracted. However, to ensure this algorithm is template-independent we carried out a validation test with another 50 forum pages. The result of the implementation test and data validation test are shown in Table 2.

Table 2. Implementation Test and Validation Test Results

Implementation test	Validation test
No. of forum tested: 50 forum web pages	**No. of forum tested:** 50 forum web pages
No. of successful extraction: 46/50 (Approximate 92%) 1 forum failed in identification stage 3 forums failed in extraction stage	**No. of successful extraction:** 34/50 (Approximate 68%) 8 forums failed in identification stage 8 forums failed in extraction stage

(a) Number of success and failed cases in implementation test and validation test

Testing	Precision	Recall	F-measure
Implementation Test	92%	90%	91%
Validation Test	68%	89%	77%

(b) Overall performance between implementation test and data validation test

After going through data validation, the results were lower when compared to the implementation test. This situation occurs because improvements to the algorithm were made based on the failed cases in the implementation test. Hence, this might cause the algorithm to overfit the fifty forums in implementation test. By referring to Table 2, there is one failed case in implementation test and eight failed cases in validation test for the post record identification. These failures occurred because they did not comply with Rule 9 of Table 1. Our algorithm will only rate the nodes as potential post records if all the nodes under same parent are sharing the exact same width. Hence, our system will not classify the nodes as potential post records even their width differences with their siblings are drifted in a small decimal amount. Thus, this is the main reason that our algorithm failed to identify post records on some of the forum websites.

There are some limitations in the heuristic rules used in the post records identification stage. Rule 9 states that the node and all its siblings must share the same width. So, when there is the case that the node has different width with its siblings, the heuristic rules would fail to identify the content records. Besides that, as Rule 9 and Rule 10 need to compare sibling nodes in order to identify the content records, a forum page must have at least two post records. Hence, the algorithm would have failed to identify the post record if it has only one post record. Rule 10 states that if the node shares the same class name with its sibling nodes, then points are awarded to the node. However, not every post record can have the same class name. For some websites, the post records do not even have a class name. In order to solve these issues, more visual features should be added into the heuristic rules in order to identify the post records accurately.

5. CONCLUSION

In this paper, we introduced the VFX algorithm to automatically extract forum data without needing a user to explicitly identify the area of interest. This paper tackled the challenges posed by user-generated post contents where they can be highly variable. The solution mainly consists of two steps. First, to identify the post records in a forum page by comparing the similarities of post records. Then second, to find the post contents from the extracted post records. The experimental results on 100 forum pages indicated that there are still room to improve the accuracy of the algorithm.

REFERENCES

Akpinar, E., & Yesilada, Y. (2012). Vision based page segmentation: Extended and improved algorithm.

Liu, B., Grossman, R., & Zhai, Y. (2003, August). Mining data records for web pages. In *Proceedings of the ninth ACM SIGKDD international conference on Knowledge discovery and data mining* (pp. 601-606). ACM.

Liu, W., Meng, X., & Meng, W. (2006, June). Vision-based web data records extraction. In *Proc. 9th international workshop on the web and databases* (pp. 20-25).

Liu, W., Yan, H., & Xiao, J. (2011). Automatically extracting user reviews from forum sites. *Computers & Mathematics with Applications*, *62*(7), 2779-2792.

Simon, K., & Lausen, G. (2005, October). ViPER: augmenting automatic information extraction with visual perceptions. In *Proceedings of the 14th ACM international conference on Information and knowledge management* (pp. 381-388). ACM.

Song, R., Liu, H., Wen, J. R., & Ma, W. Y. (2004, May). Learning block importance models for web pages. In *Proceedings of the 13th international conference on World Wide Web* (pp. 203-211). ACM.

Zeleny, J., Burget, R., & Zendulka, J. (2017). Box clustering segmentation: A new method for vision-based web page preprocessing. *Information Processing & Management, 53*(3), 735-750.

Zhai, Y., & Liu, B. (2005, May). Web data extraction based on partial tree alignment. In *Proceedings of the 14th international conference on World Wide Web* (pp. 76-85). ACM.

Zhao, H., Meng, W., Wu, Z., Raghavan, V., & Yu, C. (2005, May). Fully automatic wrapper generation for search engines. In *Proceedings of the 14th international conference on World Wide Web* (pp. 66-75). ACM.

Zheng, S., Song, R., & Wen, J. R. (2007, July). Template-independent news extraction based on visual consistency. In *AAAI* (Vol. 7, pp. 1507-1513).

ASSESSING THE RELATIONSHIP BETWEEN INFORMATION TRANSPARENCY THROUGH SOCIAL MEDIA DISCLOSURE AND FIRM VALUE

Abdalmuttaleb M. A. Musleh Al-Sartawi
Ahlia University, Manama, Bahrain

ABSTRACT

The aim of this paper is to investigate the relationship between social media financial disclosure and firm value of the GCC listed firms. To answer to research questions, the researchers collected cross-sectional data from a sample of 241 firms listed in the financial stock markets of the GCC for the year 2017. An Index was used to calculate the total level of social media financial disclosure where the SMFD for each firm was calculated by dividing the total earned scores of the firm by the total maximum possible scours appropriate for the firm. The findings show that the 84% of firms in the GCC countries use social media, while 70% of these firms use SM for financial disclosure. The results also confirm the hypothesis that enhanced disclosure levels through various social media channels of GCC listed firms significantly influence the firm value of these firms. These results have implications for both social media disclosure literatures and value relevance literatures in the GCC countries.

KEYWORDS

Social Media Disclosure, Social Media Usage, Tobin's Q, GCC Countries

1. INTRODUCTION

Investors are constantly listening for financial information and tidbits, and these investors are usually made up of people who consume information differently. Offering a variation in the way financial information reach investors will ensure that firms are being heard. Technology is changing how stakeholders, and investors access a firm's data. Social Media (SM), in particular, has had a dramatic impact on how firms engage in dialogue with investors as it allows in producing immediate and large quantities of data in many forms including videos, images, and audios. SM is based on the technological and ideological foundations of Web 2.0 which allows the creation and exchange of user generated content (Kaplan and Haenlein, 2010), unlike the Web 1.0 which is a set of static websites that do not provide interactive content.

While many firms are still using paper-based means and static websites (Web 1.0) to disclose their financial information, others are jumping on the trending social media bandwagon (Web 2.0). In April 2013, the Securities and Exchange Commission issued a report stating that firms can use SM tools such as Facebook and Twitter to announce key financial information in compliance with Regulation Fair Disclosure (US. SEC, 2013). Based on the Canadian Investor Relations Institute (CIRI, 2012), the role of social media in financial reporting is increasing as firms that may have primarily used social media for marketing purposes are now expanding their scope to include investors. Similarly, Lodhia and Stone (2017) claim that the use of internet-based communications by firms, mainly social media, is growing rapidly. Whereas, firms ignoring SM will be disadvantaged within the investment community (Alexander and Gentry, 2014).

These developments have considerable implications for accounting practices due to the demand of stakeholders for instant access to wide-ranging information related to a firm's governance, performance, finances, operations, and practices (Lodhia and Stone, 2017). Therefore, amidst these significant developments the incentive for this paper is imminent, as it is important to examine how social media can be utilized to enhance the financial reporting process. Adams (2015) believes that the disclosure process should encompass the formal as well as the informal communications and interactions with the various stakeholders, and not simply sharing a single and static annual report on the firm's website. Alexander and Gentry (2014) found that institutional investors analyze firms and make recommendations based on information they find on social media searches.

Consequently, by improving the quality of communication and reducing information costs, firms may reduce the cost of their capital. According to William (2008), that firms which aim to increase their value might choose a disclosure position which will allow their higher position to be disclosed, as opposed to firms with lower performance, which will choose a disclosure position to legitimize their performance. It enhances transparency by disclosing symmetrical information and reducing the costs associated with the agency problem, thus adhering to the principles of corporate governance (Al-Sartawi and Sanad, 2019). This paper, henceforth, defines social media disclosure as the public reporting of financial and operating information by firms through social media.

Despite the importance of such a research paper, there are negligible studies that provide evidence on the relationship between social media disclosure and firm value, certainly none related to the GCC countries. Therefore, this explanatory paper attempts to develop a better understanding of the effects of social media financial disclosure on the firms listed in the GCC stock markets, whereby the main purpose is to determine whether information transparency has an impact on firm value, with a particular emphasis on Tobin's Q. This paper extends on previous research which focused on website-based disclosure through Web 1.0 and delves into social media disclosure through Web 2.0. The contribution of this paper is proposing a Social Media Disclosure Index (SMDI), which is based on the framework of prior studies relevant to web-based disclosure such as Al-Sartawi (2018). For this, this paper's research questions are: What is the level of SM disclosure in the GCC countries? And, what is the relationship between SM disclosure and firm value.

The GCC is selected as a context to study due to its unique environment in relation to the advancements in technology. They have recently introduced their own corporate governance codes to enhance the social and regulatory environments, hence attracting more investors by encouraging voluntary disclosure. According to its geographical location, the GCC is at the heart of the Middle East, providing quick and efficient access to every market in the region. It has, therefore, become an intended destination for many foreign investors. These investors ask for financial information and carry on with certain decisions whether to continue with a certain company or not, and this is provided through social media.

The GCC countries such as Saudi Arabia and UAE are among the world's leading nations in terms of social-media growth and use, driven by smartphone ownership, high levels of internet penetration and a large, digitally savvy youth population (Internet World Stats, 2018). Another study, the Arab Social Media Report (2015), states that in the GCC, consumers and investors believe that social media encourages consumer-centric and transparent approaches, and is an instant platform to get news and information. Moreover, they believe that it offers for a cheap means of communication despite that SM poses a threat to traditional media by taking a piece of their market shares. This willingness to accept SM in business provides an interesting perspective for investigating the level of SM usage by firms and its relation to firm value.

2. LITERATURE REVIEW AND HYPOTHESIS DEVELOPMENT

Disclosure is a fluctuating term that frequently changes among researchers. Joinson and Payne (2007) define that disclosure is the revelation of the previously unknown so that it becomes shared information. As a form of online disclosure, social media has boomed as a platform that people use to create content, share, network, and interact at a phenomenal rate. But, the question is: what are the implications of SM for firms with regards to information disclosure? Corporate social media facilitates firm-directed, one-to-many communications that bypass traditional media and allow a firm to broadcast its intended message to a large network of stakeholders which is instantly made visible to all (Lee et al., 2015). Miller and Skinner (2015) found out that Chief Financial Officers believe that their decisions which are related to disclosures have high implications. Therefore, Lardo et al. (2017), claim that the recent changes in technology, capital markets and the media affect and are affected by firms' disclosure policies, whereby regulators as well as companies are starting to embrace social media as a viable disclosure channel for important information.

Elliot et al. (2018) argue that social media provide investors, who have no direct channel of communication with the management, a voice to question decisions that give management incentives to take action. The use of SM for disclosure enables interaction between the stakeholders, and not merely between the stakeholders and the firms. This adds a new dimension to corporate disclosure, as what had been previously found regarding investors' reactions to corporate disclosures cannot be applied to their reactions in today's dynamic environment (Lardo et al., 2017). Cade (2018) argues that as investors and other stakeholders depend on SM for firm news and investment advice, firms that fail to take part in the conversation will be singled out for remaining silent. Hence, the previous researches which focused more on Web 1.0 need to be extended methodically to include more relevant issues such as SM disclosure.

SM channels are more widely available to investors and allow for interaction between users via postings and comments (Brad and Crossler, 2015). Firms usually choose SM as a part of their overall strategy to for online disclosure which aims to create a positive reputation and increase their value (Basouny et al., 2018). Firms also use SM as part of their strategy to reduce information asymmetry, increase transparency, and reduce agency-related costs (Blankespoor et al., 2014). Agency losses normally arise when there is a conflict between the desires or goals of the principal (shareholder) and the agent (manager), and it is difficult or expensive for the shareholder to determine what the manager is actually doing (Eisenhardt, 1989). The agency theory hence attempts to reduce agency losses by specifying mechanisms such as tying their compensation with shareholder returns.

Increased transparency is often achieved through voluntary disclosure. Therefore, to let the shareholders know what they are doing, managers need to reach stakeholders through different medium because they understand that the shareholders aim to control their behavior through monitoring activities. Consequently, managers have incentives to disclose more information to show shareholders that they are acting optimally. Managers might opt to disclose information through SM due to the wide-range of benefits it offers such as low cost, timely information, and a wide-reach two-way communication platform. More transparency and better disclosure are associated with equality among investors, less insider trading and lowers uncertainty in investment decisions (Mohamed and Basuony, 2016). For example, when the CEO of Netflix posted on Facebook that Netflix's monthly online viewing is more than one billion hours, the stock price increased in one day by 6.2 % (Zhou et al., 2015). This indicates that SM disclosure has a direct influence on stock price, and by extension firm value.

Blankespoor et al. (2014) argued that social media channels, mainly Twitter, reduces information asymmetry, as other researchers (Al-Sartawi, 2018) found that by increasing the dissemination of the same information leads to a reduction in information asymmetry. According to Al-Sartawi and Sanad (2019) enhancing voluntary disclosure can motivate top managers to improve firm value because of increased pressure from the intensive monitoring of outside shareholders. As market values depend on investor confidence presumably through increased and transparent disclosure, market evaluation could be measured using Tobin's Q. Tobin's Q is computed as the ratio of the market value of the firm's outstanding debt and equity divided by the book value of assets (Himmelberg et al., 1999). A prior study by Lishenga and Mbaka (2015) used Tobin's Q to examine the relationship between corporate disclosure and performance, and they reported a positive and significant association between the two variables.

Several researches have attempted to explore social media disclosure; however, as this is a new trend, these studies mainly focus on the literature, SM adoption, and the determinants of social media disclosure (Zhou et al., 2015; Mohamed and Basuony, 2016; Lardo et al., 2017; Cade, 2018). From these studies, we can assume that the topic of SM as a disclosure platform is gaining momentum, and this paper offers a contribution by taking part in the conversation. However, what differentiated this paper from previous studies is that this study empirically investigates the relationship between SM disclosure and firm value. This paper, therefore, hypothesizes that: There is a relationship between social media disclosure and firm value measured through Tobin's Q.

3. RESEARCH METHODOLOGY

3.1 Sample Selection

The empirical study of the current research depended on a sample which consisted of all the listed firms in the GCC stock exchange markets for the year 2017. The required data were gathered from 241 companies out of 289 companies listed under financial sector. The financial sector was chosen for the study due to the large size of the banking industry in the GCC countries. The GCC countries are gradually undergoing a shift in their economies, from oil-dependent economies to more diversified economies, focusing mainly on the financial sector as the largest non-oil contributor to their GDPs. Table (1) shows the sample distribution according to country and industry type (Banks, Insurance and Investment).

Table 1. Sample Distribution According to Country and Industry

Industry	**KSA**	**UAE**	**QAT**	**BAH**	**KUW**	**Per Industry**	
Banks	11	33	8	7	8	67	28%
Insurance	32	31	4	5	7	79	32%
Investment	7	19	4	10	55	95	40%
Per Country	**50**	**83**	**16**	**22**	**70**	**241**	**100%**

3.2 Measuring the Level of SMD

Consequently, the study applies a two-stage process to measure (1) the level of usage of Social Media (SM) in UAE firms as well as (2) the level of Social Media Financial Disclosure of those firms. Therefore, some firms might use social media, but not for reporting financial information. These were excluded from the study.

The first stage involved measuring the social media usage by GCC listed firms. In order to measure the percentage of usage of SM, the study use the binary data method, i.e., if a firm uses any type of social media platform (Facebook, Twitter, Instagram, Snapchat, YouTube, LinkedIn, others) it received a score of 1. However, if the firm did not use any form of SM platform it received a score of 0. Similarly, the second stage involved measuring the level of SMFD for firms using SM in stage 1. So, if a firm used SM to report financial information it received a score of 1, and if a firm did not use its SM to report financial information it received a score of 0. Accordingly, the Index for each firm was calculated by dividing the total earned scores of the firm by the total maximum possible scours appropriate for the firm. To secure the data on the social media applications and channels from any updates or changes during the time of the study, all information, hyperlinks and images were downloaded and saved as HTML files beforehand. Below formula shows the way of calculating the SMFD index.

$$SMFD = \sum_{i=1} \frac{di}{n}$$

Where:

di: ***disclosed item*** equals One if the bank meets the checklist item and zero otherwise.

n: equals maximum score each bank can obtain.

To test the hypothesis, the following regression model was developed using SMFD as an independent variable, and Tobin's Q as the criterion variable. Additionally, the study used firm age, firm size and financial leverage as control variables.

Model

$$TQ = \beta_0 + \beta_1 SMD_i + \beta_2 LFSZ_i + \beta_3 LVG_i + \beta_4 AGE_i + \varepsilon_i$$

Table 2. Study Variables

Code	Variable Name	Operationalization
Dependent variable		
TQ	Market value add	Total Market Value / Total Assets Value
Independent Variables –:		
SMFD	Social Media Financial Disclosure %	Total scored items by the company/Total maximum scores
Control Variables:		
LFSZ	Firm size	Natural logarithm of Total Assets
LVG	Leverage	Total liabilities/ Total Assets
AGE	Firm Age	The difference between the establishing date of the firm and the report date

4. DATA ANALYSIS

4.1 Descriptive Statistics

Table 3 reports the descriptive analysis of the independent, dependent and control variables. The overall mean of Tobin's Q was 1.07 by GCC firms with a minimum of 0.68 and maximum of 2.55 indicating that the majority of the firms are overvalued as their stocks are higher than the replacement costs of their assets. This proxy exposes the potential of added value of the firm as viewed by the market as a reflection of its performance. Therefore, if Tobin's Q is greater than 1, it indicates that the firm has a market value exceeding the price of the replacement of its assets. With regards social media usage, show the show that the overall level of firms in the GCC countries that use social media was 84%, which is considered as a moderate level of usage of SM. Additionally, the results show that of the 84% of firms that use SM, 70% use SM for financial disclosure, which again indicates a moderate level of disclosure through SM.

In addition to the dependent and independent variables, the descriptive statistics for control variables show that the mean of firm size was 84, 43,579, with a minimum of 4, 06,832 and a maximum 3,412,461.54, implying large firms. As according to table (5) firm size was not normally distributed due to the significance of the Kolmogorov- Smirnov test being less than 5% , so natural logarithm was used in the regression analysis to reduce skewness and bring the distribution of the variables nearer to normality. Moreover, the mean leverage of the firms was approximately 42%, with a minimum of 4% and a maximum of 87%, indicating that most GCC firms have a medium level of debts. Finally, firm age ranges from 2 to 64 with a mean of 33.45.

Table 3. Descriptive Statistics for continues variables

Variables	N	Minimum	Maximum	Mean	Std. Deviation
TQ	241	0.68	2.55	1.07	0.09025
Firm Size	241	406832.3	3412461.54	8443579	220268.40264
LVG	241	0.04	0.87	0.4254	0.26508
AGE	241	2	64	33.45	13.004

Descriptive Statistics for non-continuous variables

Variables	Achieved		Not achieved	
	Number	Percentage	Number	Percentage
SMFD	89	70%	38	30%
SML	96	84%	18	16%

4.2 Testing Regression Assumptions

A Variance Inflation Factor (VIF) test was used to check the data for multicollinearity. This test calculates the severity of multicollinearity and measures how much the variance of an estimated regression coefficient is affected by collinearity. The VIF should be lower than 10 and tolerance should not be below 0.2. The VIF scores for each variable, both independent and dependent, are reported in Table (4). The results indicate that since no VIF score exceeded 10 for any variable in the model, while no Tolerance score was below 0.2. So, it was concluded that there is no threat of multicollinearity.

Table 4. Collinearity Statistics Test

Model	Tolerance	VIF
SMD	.717	1.107
Firm Size	.805	1.206
LVG	.733	1.080
AGE	.826	1.098

In addition to test for homoscedasticity and linearity, an analysis of residuals, plots of the residuals against predicted values as well as the Q-Q and scatter plots were conducted. Therefore, wherever there was a problem of heteroskedasticity the data were transformed. Autocorrelation test was not conducted in this research as the data used are cross-sectional.

Table 5. Kolmogorov- Smirnov Test

	Statistics	Sig.
Tobin's Q	2.137	0.165
SMD	2.009	0.381
Firm Size	2.044	0.003
LVG	2.095	0.540
AGE	2.113	0.347

Finally, the Kolmogorov-Smirnov test used to assess the normality of the collected data for the variables. As table 5 illustrates, a significance level of more than 5% for all the variables except for firm size indicates that the data are normally distributed. With regards to firm size however, the variable was adjusted using natural logarithm.

4.3 Testing the Hypotheses

Table 6 reports the findings of the regression analysis. The findings indicate that the model was reflecting the relationship between the variables in a statistically appropriate way. According to the table, the model has an adjusted R^2 of 0.303 which shows that the model explains approximately 30% of the variation in the Tobin's Q amongst the GCC listed firms. Additionally, the probability of the F-statistic with a significance 0.026 means that the independent variables are significant in interpreting the dependent variable, Tobin's Q.

Table 6. Regression Analysis

Variables	Beta	T. test	Sig.
SMD	.432	8.678	.008***
Firm Size	.277	2.683	.187
LVG	-.056	-.938	.207
AGE	-.184	-1.546	.000***
R^2		.303	
F		16.283	
Prob. (F)		.026	

*Prob. <10%, **Prob. <5%, ***Prob. < 1%

The main hypothesis of the study states that there is a relationship between the level of social media financial disclosure and firm value (Tobin's Q) by firms listed in the GCC stock exchange markets. The result indicates that there is a significant and positive relationship between the level of SMD and firm value, that is, the higher the level of disclosure, the higher the Tobin's Q. This is in line with the studies conducted by Plumlee et al. (2015) who suggest that the level and quality of disclosure affect firm value. Another study conducted in the MENA region (Al-Akra and Ali, 2012) found a positive relationship between disclosure and firm value. However, an earlier study conducted by Hassan et al. (2009) in the Middle-East found no relationship between disclosure and firm value, which could be due to the lack of control for the endogeneity of the disclosure variable in relation to Tobin's Q. One reason for this could be the potential of SM as a two-way communication platform that allows timely dissemination of information to investors, shareholders and other stakeholders. This way all parties involved transmit information instantaneously, which helps them in making well-informed decisions. Furthermore, firms are able to receive instant feedback from their stakeholders which helps managers in making improvements accordingly, thus satisfying all parties involved and reducing costs related to agency.

With regards to the control variables, the study found a significant and positive relationship between firm value and age. Based on Susanti and Restiana (2018) who also found a positive association between age and firm value, investors have a higher level of confidence and trust in older firms due to their experience and maturity. On the other hand, this contradicts the study by Pástor and Veronesi (2003) who claim that firm value declines as investors learn about the firm's profitability or as their uncertainty resolves over time. Finally, the results show no relationship between firm value and the other control variables, firm size and leverage.

5. CONCLUSION AND RECOMMENDATIONS

The paper aimed to address several research questions: (1) the level of social media usage by GCC listed firms, (2) the level of social media financial disclosure (SMFD) by GCC listed firms and (3) the relationship between social media financial disclosure and firm value of the GCC listed firms. To answer to research questions, the researchers collected data from a sample of 241 firms listed in the financial stock markets of the GCC for the year 2017. Due to the nature of the data collected which is cross-sectional only one year was chosen to gauge the data at a specific point in time.

The findings show that the 84% of firms in the GCC countries use social media, while 70% of these firms use SM for financial disclosure. The results also confirm the hypothesis that enhanced disclosure levels through various social media channels of GCC listed firms significantly influence the firm value of these firms. The study was also checked for the possibility of non-linearity in the relation between social media disclosure and firm value by conducting various regression assumption tests such as Q-Q, scatter plots, collinearity statistics and the Kolmogorov- Smirnov tests.

From a theoretical standpoint, these results have implications for both social media disclosure literatures and value relevance literatures in the GCC countries. From a practical perspective, this study provides contributions to GCC's government, policy-makers and regulators with regards to a trending issue such as the modern disclosure tools that could be used by firms to increase transparency and reduce the agency problem. Policy makers and regulators in the GCC can make use of information from this research in setting new policies on social media financial disclosure in line with the Securities and Exchange Commission which recognized the potential of SM as a platform for disclosure.

This paper suggests having a study that further investigates the relationship between social media disclosure and other types of performance such as financial and operational performance. Future studies could also investigate the level of corporate social responsibility disclosure or intellectual capital of firms on social media.

REFERENCES

Adams, C. A. (2015). The international integrated reporting council: a call to action. Critical Perspectives on Accounting, 27, 23-28.

Al-Akra, M., & Ali, M. J. (2012). The value relevance of corporate voluntary disclosure in the Middle-East: The case of Jordan. *Journal of Accounting and Public Policy*, *31*(5), 533-549.

Alexander, R. M., & Gentry, J. K. (2014). Using social media to report financial results. Business Horizons, 57(2), 161-167.

Al-Sartawi, A. (2018), Does Institutional Ownership Affect the Level of Online Financial Disclosure? Academy of Accounting and Financial Studies Journal, 22 (2), 1–10.

Al-Sartawi, A., and Sanad, Z., (2019) Institutional ownership and corporate governance: evidence from Bahrain, Afro-Asian Journal of Finance and Accounting, 9 (1),101 – 115.

Arab Social Media Report (2015). Available at [http://sites.wpp.com/govtpractice//~/media/wppgov/files/arabsocialmediareport-2015.pdf.]

Blankespoor, E., Miller, G. S., & White, H. D. (2014). The role of dissemination in market liquidity: Evidence from firms' use of Twitter', The Accounfing Review 89 (1), 79–112.

Cade, N. L. (2018). Corporate social media: How two-way disclosure channels influence investors. Accounting, Organizations and Society.

CIRI (2012). The role of social media in performance reporting: A discussion brief. The Canadian Institute of Chartered Accountants, Available at [https://www.cpacanada.ca/-/media/site/business-and-accounting-resources/docs/role-of-social-media-in-performance-reporting-a-discussion-brief-2012.pdf?la=en&hash=394D1825712E8FC2F1ED7DBC68747B12F1E2225C]

Eisenhardt, K. M. (1989). Agency theory: An assessment and review. Academy of management review, 14(1), 57-74.

Hassan, O. A., Romilly, P., Giorgioni, G., & Power, D. (2009). The value relevance of disclosure: Evidence from the emerging capital market of Egypt. *The International Journal of Accounting*, *44*(1), 79-102.

Himmelberg, C. P., Hubbard, R. G., & Palia, D. (1999). Understanding the determinants of managerial ownership and the link between ownership and performance. Journal of financial economics, 53(3), 353-384.

Internet World Stats (2018). CIA World Factbook: Middle East Media.org. Available at [https://www.zdnet.com/article/whats-driving-middle-easts-rush-to-social-media/]

Joinson, A. N., & Paine, C. B. (2007). Self-disclosure, privacy and the internet. In A. N. Joinson, K. Y. A. McKenna, T. Postmes, & U. Reips (Eds.), The Oxford handbook of Internet psychology (pp. 237–252). Great Britain: Oxford University Press.

Kaplan, A. M., & Haenlein, M. (2010). Users of the world, unite! The challenges and opportunities of Social Media. *Business horizons*, *53*(1), 59-68.

Lardo, A., Dumay, J., Trequattrini, R., & Russo, G. (2017). Social media networks as drivers for intellectual capital disclosure: Evidence from professional football clubs. Journal of Intellectual Capital, 18(1), 63-80.

Lee, L. F., Hutton, A. P., & Shu, S. (2015). The role of social media in the capital market: Evidence from consumer product recalls. Journal of Accounting Research, 53(2), 367-404.

Lishenga, L., & Mbaka, A. (2015). The link between compliance with corporate governance disclosure code and performance for Kenyan firms. Net Journal of Business Management, 3(1), 13-26.

Lodhia, S., & Stone, G. (2017). Integrated reporting in an internet and social media communication environment: conceptual insights. Australian Accounting Review, 27(1), 17-33.

Miller, G. S., & Skinner, D. J. (2015). The evolving disclosure landscape: How changes in technology, the media, and capital markets are affecting disclosure. Journal of Accounting Research, 53(2), 221-239.

Mohamed, E., & Basuony, M. (2016). The use of social media for corporate disclosure by companies listed in the GCC. Information Technology Management Society ITMSOC–Transactions on Innovation & Business Engineering, 1(1), 14-20.

Pástor, Ľ., & Pietro, V. (2003). Stock valuation and learning about profitability. *The Journal of Finance*, *58*(5), 1749-1789.

Plumlee, M., Brown, D., Hayes, R. M., & Marshall, R. S. (2015). Voluntary environmental disclosure quality and firm value: Further evidence. *Journal of Accounting and Public Policy*, *34*(4), 336-361.

Susanti, N., & Restiana, N. G. (2018). What's the Best Factor to Determining Firm Value?. Jurnal Keuangan dan Perbankan, 22(2).

U.S. SEC. (2013). SEC Says Social Media OK for Company Announcements if Investors Are Alerted, Available at [https://www.sec.gov/news/press-release/2013-2013-51htm]

Williams, C.C. (2008). Toward a taxonomy of corporate reporting strategies. Journal of Business Communication 45: 232-264.

Zhou, M., Lei, L., Wang, J., Fan, W., & Wang, A. G. (2014). Social media adoption and corporate disclosure. Journal of information systems, 29(2), 23-50.

DIGITAL ME IN A VIRTUAL WORLD: IDENTITY CONSTRUCTION ON LINKEDIN BY AOTEAROA/NEW ZEALAND ENTREPRENEURIAL PROFESSIONALS

Sandra Jane Barnett[1]
Manukau Institute of Technology, New Zealand
[1]Dr

ABSTRACT

This study explores if, and how, the business social media site, LinkedIn, is providing for Aotearoa/New Zealand entrepreneurial professionals an alternative site for the construction of identity, and the tensions experienced in this process. The framework of exploration is based on identifying tensions in authentic online identity construction.

A two-dimensional model of these tensions is developed from the layers of sub-tensions, tensions and meta-tensions identified. In one dimension are identity tensions inherent in the specific context; in a different dimension are meta-identity tensions that have been identified in organisational contexts but are foregrounded in this virtual context.

The presence of these identity tensions confirms LinkedIn is becoming a site for professional identity construction. The study concludes with a discussion of how identifying and managing these tensions can be applied to tertiary education courses and to inform small business owners about LinkedIn use.

KEYWORDS

Linkedin, Social Media, Identity, Authenticity, Tensions

1. INTRODUCTION

Identity, both personal and social, is a major human preoccupation. Identity construction is an important process for situating individuals within the social landscape, and to answer the question, 'who am I'? Work or occupational identity has long been recognised as an important facet of an individual's identity (Albert & Whetten, 1985; Erickson, 1974; Watson, 2008), and the workplace has traditionally been the site where work identities, and to some extent personal identities, are constructed, performed, and validated (Goffman, 1959; Haslam, 2001; Oakes, 2004; Postmes, Baray, Haslam, Morton, & Swaab, 2006). In the late 20th and the 21st century, organisational structures have become more fluid than in 20th century industrialised economies; a new work order has emerged, characterised by differentiation and fragmentation (Gee, Lankshear, & Hull, 1996). The expansion of information communication technologies (ICTs) has accelerated and facilitated change, so that increasingly, the focus of work is moving outside co-located workplaces (Ancona & Caldwell, 1992; Kraut & Resnick, 2011; Nardi, Whittaker, & Schwartz, 2002). Additionally, restructuring and downsizing has led to the greater use of external consultants and contractors, often working virtually and independently. As a result, work has become more distributed and individual-centred; in addition, careers are more fragmented and dynamic, with identification individuals with organisations weakening (Kraut & Resnick, 2011; Reedy, King, & Coupland, 2016; Shirky, 2008). In addition the phenomenon of micro-entrepreneurship – a drive towards self-employment fuelled by the growth of the Internet and new digital technologies, has been identified as motivating a resurgence of entrepreneurialism in the current millennium, both globally and in Aotearoa/New Zealand (Clark & Douglas, 2014; Duffy & Pruchniewska, 2017; Fonseca, 2014; Wong, 2012).

All these trends in a world where traditional work structures of the 20th century are rapidly disappearing; the construction of work identity needs to be constantly re-examined to be relevant in the field of organisational studies and the discipline of communication. Social media as a communication technology is breaking boundaries between work and non-work life, as well as boundaries between professions and global boundaries is, as Linda Putnam (2017) explains:

> One big development in my discipline (communication) is the rise of social media in permeating and breaking boundaries – all kinds of questions are arising out of challenges to public-private and work-non-work as distinct boundaries. It's all about the new digital interface, convergence of media, and social media's influence in all walks of life – to the point that if you aren't situating your work in this space, you may not have a place in the discipline (communication). I think the work that people are doing on social media and its relationship to organization and organising is critical. It's about constructing a new understanding of what is going on in society and with social interactions (In Grant & Cox, 2017, p. 192).

Changes in the nature of work are evident in the daily work experience of the participants in this study, Aotearoa/New Zealand entrepreneurial engaged on LinkedIn. They have generally moved from employment as a professional in a larger organisation to self-employment, utilising the power of the Internet and social media, including LinkedIn to do so. This study aimed to explore the construction of identity on LinkedIn as an emerging and complex organisational environment. It is therefore is boundary spanning in that it spans the disciplines of: organisational communication and new forms of organisation; ICT and social media use; identity and identity construction (entrepreneurial, professional and digital); and globalisation, by juxtaposing the globalising effect of social media with local discourse.

2. BODY OF PAPER

2.1 Background and Research Approach

The approach of this study is that social 'realities' including identity are socially constructed (Berger & Luckman, 1966; Burr, 1995; Gergen, 1997). From this social constructionist perspective, identity is produced in the discourse of social relationships and encounters (Kuhn, 2006); it is not pre-formed in our subconscious and only reflected in, or transmitted through, communication channels (Kuhn, 2006; Mumby, 2011). Recent scholarship from a constructionist stance, conceptualises identities as fragmented, shifting, and conflicted (Ashcraft & Mumby, 2004; Knight & Weedon, 2014; Kuhn, 2006; Larson & Gill, 2017; Tracy & Trethewey, 2005). Identity then is a multiple construct, we have a number of social selves with each identity; we present a different self to different audiences, and they reflect back to us a version of ourselves as multiple selves. Through each of these identities, we present a different self, depending on the audience, for example people generally present different identities when they interact in a work context than in a social context (Ollier-Malaterre, Rothbard, & Berg, 2013). Consideration of context in identity construction is therefore fundamental to the interpretative approach of this study; the contexts of the social media context and LinkedIn, of Aotearoa New Zealand and of the personal context of the life and career of the participants.

On social media, though we may present different identities on different sites, the boundaries between these 'virtual worlds' are permeable, and identity is also multiply-interpreted by many different audiences. Multiple roles or identities can overlap and be more difficult to keep separate in the virtual world where individuals' different identities can be viewed and interacted with by multiple and overlapping audiences (Marder, Joinson, & Shankar, 2012; Marder, Joinson, Shankar, & Thirlaway, 2016). This unknown audience can be an issue for the construction of personal online self, but is possibly more be more problematic in the case of the online professional self, as misjudgement or lack of knowledge of audience can have a direct immediate impact on work and career (Ollier-Malaterre et al., 2013). The selves presented on online social networks are subject to simultaneous surveillance by multiple audiences that can occur 24 hours a day via many different search engines. This issue has been variously referred to and described in the literature as: the online multiple audience problem (OMAP) (Marder et al., 2016), context collapse (Marwick & Boyd, 2011), the problem of conflicting social spheres (Binder, Howes, & Smart, 2012), and the bridging of multiple heterogeneous social communities (DiMicco & Millen, 2007).

Another salient context is that of LinkedIn. As an online business networking site it has characteristics that are distinct from face to face networking: connections are made by explicit agreement, connections are publicly displayed, and they create a unique social world around each individual, regulated by the individual, and interaction only occur where there is an explicit digital connection (Papacharissi, 2011). In addition the context of LinkedIn is both local and global, in that it is worldwide, however, the participants are in a local context and this dual context can create tensions between global and local discourses (Gill & Larson, 2014a, 2014b).

As the general goal of this research was exploratory, that is to understand participants' experience of LinkedIn and how they constructed identity there, the subjective lens of interpretivism was the basis of this study. The interpretive approach, to understand the social world and human action by accessing the meanings participants assign to them, also underlies and informs the qualitative methodology. Accordingly, the research data was gathered through twenty-five in-depth semi-structured interviews conducted with those who responded to a request, on NZ SME groups on LinkedIn, to be participants and the interview transcripts were analysed through thematic analysis.

In the process of analysis, tensions, contradictions and paradoxes in identity construction emerged as a dominant concern. Tensions, such as identity tensions, have increasingly been identified a part of organisational experience (Putnam, Fairhurst, & Banghart, 2016; Trethewey & Ashcraft, 2004), and a growing body of literature posits that irrationality is a normal condition of organisational life, and is reflected in the tensions evident in the discourses around the construction of identity in organisations (Clarke, Brown, & Hailey, 2009; Larson & Gill, 2017; Tracy & Trethewey, 2005; Woo, Putnam, & Riforgiate, 2017).These tensions have increased as work increasingly moves to alternative or "less predictable settings of organizing"(Cheney & Ashcraft, 2007, p. 161) such as social media. Thus, whilst social media may have eased the process of relationship building (Jussila, Kärkkäinen, & Aramo-Immonen, 2014; Michaelidou, Siamagka, & Christodoulides, 2011), it has also added further layers of complexity and tensions (Quinton & Wilson, 2016; Rainie & Wellman, 2012). This tensional approach provided the framework for analysing and interpreting the data (Barnett, 2019).

2.2 Findings

Analysis of the participants' interview transcripts revealed 11 main tensional themes. These tensions were: two tensions around the virtual context of identity construction, four tensions around networking and making connections, and finally, five identity construction tensions around interacting and relationship-building on LinkedIn. These tensions are collated below in Table 1 and are discussed in more detail below.

Table 1. Tensional themes in discourses about engagement, networking, and interaction

Engagement	Networking	Interaction
Place vs space	Imperative to network vs reluctance to do so	Aligns with thought leaders but is also original
Risk of participating vs risk of not participating	Networks as living vs networks as fixed	Is an unassuming expert
	Openness vs closedness in networking	Sells without being a salesman
	Displayed network vs protected network	Separates and combines personal and professional identities
		Wants to surveil or watch others but doesn't want to surveil or watch others

When discussing their engagement with the virtual context and social media generally, a deep underlying tension was revealed in the analysis around the participants' use of contrasting discursive resources, which simultaneously described cyberspace in language that referenced images of both 'places' and 'spaces.' On one hand, the participants' discourse alluded to cyberspace as comprising boundaried, defined, separate 'places.' They referenced appropriate or expected behaviour and appropriate occupants to each 'place', seemingly ascribing a cultural context and imagined audience for interaction and identity presentation, based on a known or familiar context within the physical world (Boyd, 2007).

In contrast to images of 'places' within the discourses of the same individuals, a contrasting but simultaneously-held image of cyberspace was conveyed as a wide open, un-boundaried, flexible, unmappable, global, and disembodying 'space'. Participants' discourses conveyed the recurring theme that social and cultural mechanisms had not yet given clear meaning to this environment, and it was therefore chaotic, unregulated, and risky to enter, so much so that their sense of self became lost in this space, and they were unsure of where they were going in cyberspace, or why (cf.Massey, 1994).

When the analysis of the participants' discourses specifically focused on the specific context of LinkedIn, a second tension emerged, related to the first tension, but one that was considered separately to provide more insight into LinkedIn as an organisational setting. This tension was expressed in the paradox of LinkedIn being an important business tool that was necessary, risky *not* to use, but also risky *to* use, because of the many business, personal, and even social risks associated with its use, many of which echoed the concerns around context collapse.

When the analysis of the participants' discourses focused on networking through issuing and accepting invitations to connect, they indicated that online networking had opened up expansive and easy opportunities for connecting. They also felt a strong expectation, as a professional, to actively network on this site (more so now that they were a business owner or entrepreneur) and an imperative to create a digital network. However, in contradiction to this networking imperative, most participants said they preferred to, and did, limit accepting invitations to connect to people they knew, and to issue even fewer invitations themselves. They said they also did not like to be seen as networking incautiously, or even too actively or strategically.

The participants' discourse also revealed tensions around their displayed network. On one hand, they said that a large network of contacts reflected positively on their entrepreneurial professional identity. In contradiction though, they also indicated that a small, exclusive network aligned better with their sense of professional identity, and that displaying a large network may convey a message that they were not a genuine authentic professional; thus reflecting the traditional image of a professional as belonging to an exclusive network (Crane, 1972; Macdonald, 1995). Both views can be seen as consistent with the claim of Donath and Boyd (2004) that, "In this context, 'public displays of connection' present the center of identity performance and are typically viewed as a signal of the reliability of one's identity claims" (p.73). This tension around whether to display a large or limited network, illustrates the paradoxical nature of identity performance in this context. Many also expressed a trend to retreat from open active networking over time, rather than becoming habituated to it. They referred to their LinkedIn network as a database, rather than an active living framework of relationships, indicating they viewed their LinkedIn network as somewhat static. Also noted was a predominance of Aotearoa/New Zealand-born and educated participants expressing a stronger preference for passive networking (i.e. only accepting invitations and not issuing them), and a limited set of displayed connections.

When the analysis of the participants' discourses focused on interaction with others and relationship-building, their responses revealed other identity construction tensions. They expressed a need to appear to be experts and knowledgeable, but at the same time, modest and unassuming. Much of the professional identity construction work described in their discourse reflects the dominant global discourse around professionalism, for example, being polite and exclusive, and there were indications that these professional identity behaviours were being intensified online. However, there was also a cautiousness around volunteering expertise that made it difficult to present as an expert, a wariness of connecting with strangers, and a possible trend towards even greater insularity within a known group than in the physical world. There was little alignment with the dominant discourse around entrepreneurialism, of being assertive and taking risks, and this feature was more prominent in the Aotearoa /New Zealand-bred participants' discourses.

A prominent theme in the participants' discourse was that their own identity was very much aligned with the identity or brand of their business. On LinkedIn, which many referred to as a marketplace, they now felt personally responsible for getting their brand known, but there was tension in doing so, in that the process would reveal too much of their personal identity online. Additionally, they said that they needed to offer useful information to 'look the part', but not give away too much intellectual property to strangers. Furthermore, they were concerned that they may come across as 'selling' or being aggressive in marketing their business. There was also tension around the need for work or professional identity performances to be congruent with wider community identities and historical work identities, all of which are now publicly displayed on LinkedIn.

A further tension was evident in the participants' admission that they often viewed the LinkedIn profiles of others, even if they were not connected or did not want to connect with them. This surveillance feature of LinkedIn increased expectations that they were informed about others' background and careers as a part of their relationship-building process, but it also served to allow them to more easily reflexively evaluate their own and the careers of others, thus influencing their own identity construction. Their interest in watching others was offset by a concern that this was not polite and could be interpreted as 'stalking', creating tension around being observed as watching, or even simply knowing themselves that they were doing it. Participants stated that this behaviour was incongruent with their professional identity and even their own sense of self.

2.3 Discussion and Interpretation

In summary, the analysis of the participants' discourses overall revealed that LinkedIn was in fact being utilised as a site for the construction of entrepreneurial professional identity, and that this was becoming necessary and for many a normal, yet also complex and contradictory process, fraught with tensions. LinkedIn appeared to be simultaneously providing participants with a means to connect with others and construct a work/professional identity but also to be limiting their social work-world by connecting them only to those who they considered appropriate, that is, were like them. This self-boundaried world was having a regulating effect on their identity construction in this world. There were, however, divergent discourses. A few participants described actively expanding their network, curiosity about strangers, and an acceptance of and willingness to give praise and endorsements. These divergent discourses were almost exclusively from immigrants to Aotearoa/New Zealand, indicating a divergence between local contextual discourse and the wider global discourse related to professionalism and entrepreneurialism.

Further interpretation of these tensions revealed two dimensions of tensions. The first dimension related to the specific context, that is Aotearoa/New Zealand, LinkedIn, and the online entrepreneurial professional. This dimension of analysis accords with Cheney and Ashcraft (2007) advice to pay "particular sensitivity to institutional and contextual variation" (p.161) when researching identity construction in unpredictable organisational settings. The second dimension, described as meta-tensions, are more general tensional themes around identity work that surfaced in the analysis, and which align with those in prior studies in organisational communication, but which have taken on a different emphasis and character when experienced in the LinkedIn context.

The first tension in this dimension was a tension of 'space' versus 'place'. The participants in this study were negotiating with themselves and others, the meaning of the virtual world in which they interacted. This negotiation is important for identity construction if 'place' is regarded as an active character in the construction of identity (Gill & Larson, 2014b; Sampson & Goodrich, 2009). These different images were underscored by tension between whether this context, i.e. LinkedIn, was one of many defined 'places' for connecting and interacting online, or whether it was still an unorganised 'space'. This 'space' was an environment that had not yet been given clear meaning by social and cultural mechanisms (Massey, 1994); it lacked boundaries and regulated behaviour.

The second dialectical tension identified around the virtual context of LinkedIn as being both local and global, in that LinkedIn is worldwide, and global connection is as easy to establish as a local connection, purportedly making the world 'smaller'. However, in this study, there was global/local tension was evident in two specific aspects of the study. Firstly, when Aotearoa/New Zealand participants' discourses were contrasted with immigrants to Aotearoa/New Zealand, a tension was identified between the Aotearoa/New Zealand contextual discourse and the mainstream dominant discourse concerning entrepreneurialism and professionalism. For example, the need to be assertive and confident in communicating with others, set against the desire to be unassuming, and to not be viewed as a trying to be a 'tall poppy' (Fairburn, 1989; Sargent, 2001; Spoonley, 2014).

Secondly local/global tension was also evident in the implications of the design of LinkedIn. The technical digital context to some extent regulates identity construction work through the architecture and design of the site, a design that reflects dominant transcendent discourses around professional interaction, but these contrast with the discourses of Aotearoa/New Zealand participants around their professional interaction on LinkedIn. A prevailing assumption of the LinkedIn site's design is that, in this place, a professional or business person is one who grows and expands a network, and subsequently develops these relationships through assertive interaction. (e.g.Papacharissi, 2009). Despite espousing networking as an imperative, there was a reluctance to appear to need, or to be seen actively seeking out new business connections This reluctance to connect was consistently articulated more often and obviously by Aotearoa/New Zealand-born participants. This contradiction in their discourse aligns with Gill and Larson's (2014b) observations about mainstream and locale-specific discourse, i.e., "When they conflict, individuals are more likely to outwardly identify with the locale-specific discourse, yet still acknowledge the desirability of the transcendent discourse" (p.539). Such a tension between the networking imperative and reluctance to network to reflects an Aotearoa/New Zealand entrepreneurial type, where self-sufficiency and independence is valued, incongruent with the need to connect to others, implied by LinkedIn's design.

Another tension arose from the blending professionalism and entrepreneurial identity. The most prominent theme in the discourse of participants around professionalism online was the importance of being viewed as authentic. Yet being genuine and authentic as a professional, while promoting their business as an entrepreneur, was fraught with tensions.

The final tension was between bringing personal aspects to a LinkedIn identity, which then become both public and permanent (Young, 2013), and the desire to keep the personal private. This tension was increased by participants' awareness of "context collapse" (Marwick & Boyd, 2011, p. 114).

These tensions are illustrated in Figure 2 below. The 'push-pull' effect of contrasting tensions in the context represented by the double-ended arrows is illustrated as directly or indirectly influencing the construction of identity on LinkedIn.

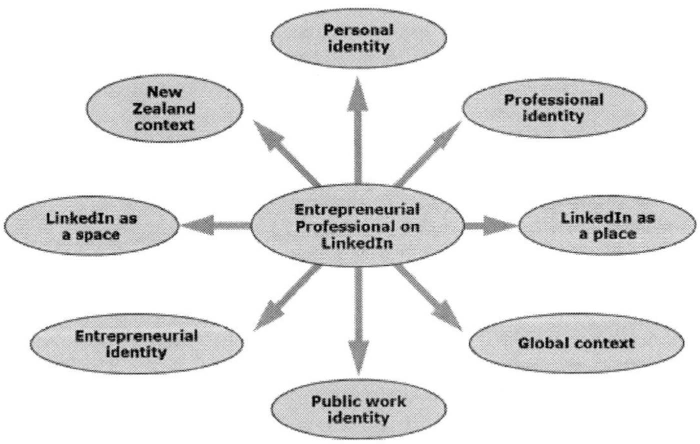

Figure 1. Dialectical tensions for an Aotearoa/New Zealand entrepreneurial/ professional on LinkedIn

In addition, these tensions are intersected in another dimension with three meta-tensions, which have already been identified in the literature on organisational identity construction (e.g.Cheney, Christensen, Ganesh, & Zorn, 2011), but which appear to be more prominent, significant, and with a different character in the setting of LinkedIn. These tensions are: openness vs closedness, autonomy vs connectedness, and equality vs superiority. Added to these three tensions is a further tension around peer-to-peer surveillance, that is, tension between the desire to surveil others versus a reluctance to do so.

The meta-tension of openness and closedness can be seen in the tension between the risks and benefits of sharing information (Cheney et al., 2011) and the willingness, or otherwise, to merge personal and professional digital identities. Social media may increase the flow of knowledge through passive information-seeking strategies (Ramirez, Walther, Burgoon, & Sunnafrank, 2002); however this knowledge flow on LinkedIn is limited by pressure to protect intellectual property and information that constitutes personal business brand and a reluctance to share with an audience that is somewhat unknown and therefore, untrusted. The second meta-tension, autonomy vs connectedness, is revealed in willingness, or otherwise, to accept the networking imperative. The tension of equality vs superiority is evidenced in the need to appear an expert, but to also be modest and unassuming, no better than anyone else, and even to not be 'too expert'.

The final meta-tension revealed in the study is in an interest and need to surveil, or watch, others for information and comparison, versus a hesitancy to do so out of politeness and respect for privacy, and the fear of being detected doing this. For the LinkedIn users in this study, the information gained by surveilling others was useful in relationship-building, and being surveilled was considered welcome attention, conferring professional recognition and increased social status (Marwick, 2012, p. 389). In contrast, being noticed watching others, they said carried the risk of being viewed as eavesdropping, voyeuristic (Marwick, 2012), and impolite or violating the privacy of others (Whitworth & Liu, 2013).These tensions are illustrated in Figure 2 below, by the double-ended arrows illustrating the push-pull effect of these identity meta-tensions in the organisational context of LinkedIn.

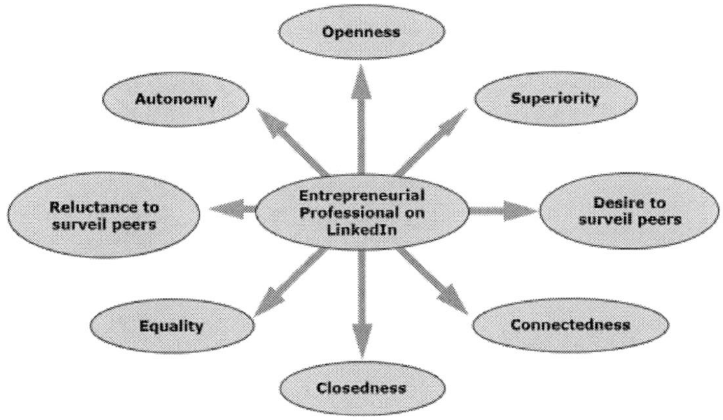

Figure 2. Meta-tensions on LinkedIn as an organisational context

A combination of these sets of dialectical tensions can be represented as intersecting tensions within these two dimensions (see Figure 3). The figure links the specific tensions experienced in constructing identity in the virtual context of LinkedIn (indicated by dotted lines) to the more general identity tensions present within organisations (indicated by a solid line).

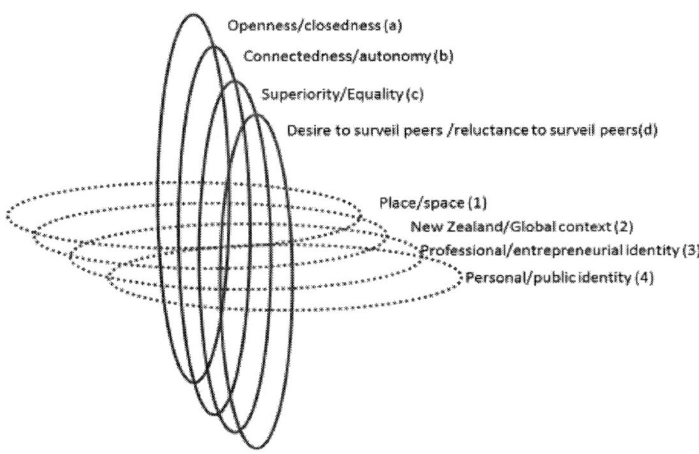

Figure 3. An integrated framework of identity construction tensions experienced by Aotearoa/New Zealand entrepreneurial/ professionals on LinkedIn

Vertical tensions interact with horizontal tensions at different levels and combine to create unique tensions for each individual. This conclusion echoes Gill's (2017) conclusion to a study of entrepreneurial identity, i.e. entrepreneurial identity resides not in the person themselves, but in the context (in the broadest sense) in which they engage. For the entrepreneurial professionals in this study, a similar conclusion can be made, although identity construction in digital contexts has become even more complex and multi-faceted, as social media is collapsing personal and professional, and global and local boundaries. Therefore, the tensions in constructing a digital identity are multi-faceted. Though likely to include those identified in the study, they are experienced in a unique combination for each individual and entrepreneurial/professional, depending on the situation or context. A visual conceptualisation of how these identity tensions crystallise in each individual is presented in Figure 4 below. The loops in Figure 4, signifying each identified tension (represented by numbers and letters) and in two dimensions (represented by dotted and solid lines), have been drawn out and rotated, so that that they intersect and crystallise at a central point. This point represents the unique identity tensions for an individual in a specific context.

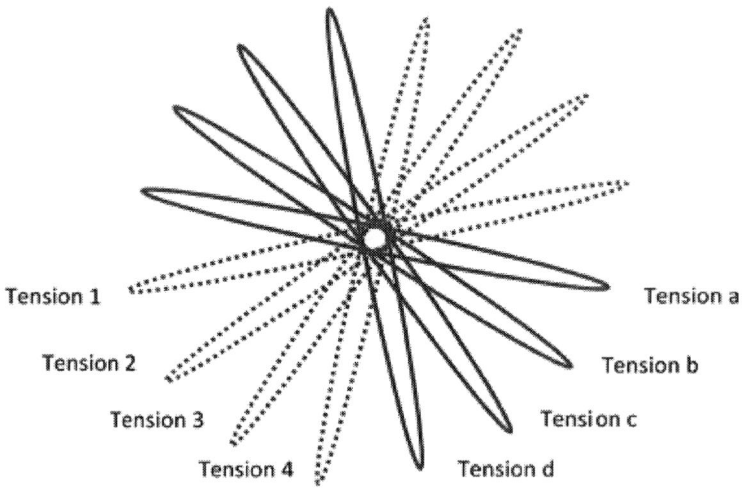

Figure 4. Conceptual image of identity construction tensions on LinkedIn for the individual

3. CONCLUSION

The study makes several contributions. Firstly, it identifies the tensions inherent in engaging in LinkedIn and constructing a digital identity there. Secondly, it provides evidence that LinkedIn has, in fact, become, or at least was in the process of becoming, an alternative organisational site, and thus a site for organisational identity construction. Thirdly, it presents in a multi-level and two-dimensional framework for analysis of identity construction in this context. In one dimension it suggests that identity construction on LinkedIn needs to be understood, in the context of personal work situation of the individual, of a local yet global site of communication, and in the context the unique features of a virtual social world. In another dimension, the identity construction needs to be understood as the tensions likely in an organisational setting. The research also provides some practical contributions.

The experience of these participants, and the findings around the likely tensions that arise and how they are managed, can be utilised to inform employment seminars and courses. Younger professionals are generally well-versed in using Facebook and other socially-orientated social media such as Instagram, but are generally less versed in using LinkedIn, the dominant social media site for work relationships (Florenthal & Dykhouse, 2012; Oslund, 2010). This study interviewed experienced professional LinkedIn users, and its findings can be used to broaden training courses beyond basic training, to create a curriculum vitae on LinkedIn (cf.Paliszkiewicz & Madra-Sawicka, 2016).

A limitation of this study is that, because of the paucity of literature on identity construction on LinkedIn, with none in the Aotearoa/New Zealand context, this research served as an exploratory study, and therefore, as the aim of the study is broad, the findings are broad in scope and somewhat tentative. A second limitation that may be raised about this study is that it was situated in Aotearoa/New Zealand, which limited its context, thereby raising the issue around whether these findings are generalisable elsewhere. However as this is an interpretive study the issue of generalisability is not appropriate. That said, the conclusions about tensions between Aotearoa/New Zealand entrepreneurial and professional identity and mainstream Western discourse are context-specific, however, they do suggest that similar differences may exist elsewhere, which can be explored.

The findings and limitations of this study suggest several avenues for future research. Firstly, future research can focus on the construction of the two different occupational identities, professional and entrepreneurial, within a virtual context, which will reveal deeper understandings about the construction of each. Such research can also include identifying how individuals reconcile the tensions, or find ways to "hold together necessary incompatibles" (Trethewey & Ashcraft, 2004, p. 84) in order to function effectively in this context.

Research into the local Aotearoa/New Zealand discourse around that is lacking and needed. entrepreneurship, particularly micro-entrepreneurship, is lacking and needed. This form of enterprise is an expanding phenomenon in Aotearoa/New Zealand (MBIE, 2017), with a drive towards self-employment (Clark & Douglas, 2014; Duffy & Pruchniewska, 2017). Such research, therefore, would provide a better understanding that is needed of the personal drivers of economic activity in this field. Finally, research that identifies how LinkedIn's architecture and design are utilised in different contexts, outside the home context of the US, and how design influences local engagement on the site, would be valuable

In conclusion, identifying LinkedIn as a new organisational context for work is possibly still a far-fetched notion for some; however, the experience of the participants in this study confirms it to be an important arena for their daily work lives. Furthermore, in the time that I conducted this research, LinkedIn membership worldwide expanded from 10 million users to 400 million users globally. This significant growth indicates the popularity of the site, and the ubiquity of social media in every aspect of life, including work life, and as such, should be a vital site of research for all aspects of social life.

REFERENCES

Albert, S. D., & Whetten, D. (1985). Organizational identity. In L. L. Cummings & B. M. Staw (Eds.), *Research in Organizational Behavior* (Vol. 7, pp. 263-295). Greenwich, CT: JAI Press.

Ancona, D., & Caldwell, D. (1992). Bridging the boundary: External activity and performance in organizational teams. *Administrative Science Quarterly, 37*(4), 634-665.

Ashcraft, K. L., & Mumby, D. K. (2004). *Reworking gender: A feminist communicology of organization*: Thousand Oaks, CA : Sage, c2004.

Barnett, S. J. . (2019). Identity construction by Aotearoa/New Zealand entrepreneurial professionals on LinkedIn: A tensional approach. (PhD.), Massey University, Albany, Auckland.

Berger, P., & Luckman, T. (1966). The social construction of reality: A treatise in the sociology of knowledge. New York: Doubleday.

Binder, J. F., Howes, A., & Smart, D. (2012). Harmony and tension on social network sites: Side effects of increasing online connectivity. *Information, Communication & Society, 15*(9), 1279-1297. doi:10.1080/1369118X.2011.648949

Boyd, D. (2007). Social network sites: Public, private, or what? *Knowledge Tree, 13.*

Burr, V. (1995). An introduction to social constructionism. London: Routledge.

Cheney, G., & Ashcraft, K. L. (2007). Considering 'The Professional' in Communication Studies: Implications for Theory and Research Within and Beyond the Boundaries of Organizational Communication. *Communication Theory, 2*, 146-175. Retrieved from http://ezproxy.massey.ac.nz/login?url=http://search.ebscohost.com/login.aspx?direct=true&db=edsggo&AN=edsgcl.172821364&site=eds-live&scope=site

Cheney, G., Christensen, L.T., Ganesh, S, & Zorn, T. E. (2011). *Organizational communication in an age of globalization: Issues, reflections, practices* (Vol. 2nd ed). Long Grove, Ill: Waveland Press.

Clark, Delwyn N., & Douglas, Heather. (2014). Micro-enterprise growth: Lessons from home-based business in New Zealand. *Small Enterprise Research: The Journal of SEAANZ*(1), 82. Retrieved from http://ezproxy.massey.ac.nz/login?url=http://search.ebscohost.com/login.aspx?direct=true&db=edsibc&AN=edsibc.776054436072976&site=eds-live&scope=site

Clarke, C. A. , Brown, A. D. , & Hailey, V. (2009). Working identities? Antagonistic discursive resources and managerial identity. *Human Relations, 62*(3), 323-352.

Crane, D. (1972). *Invisible colleges*. Chicago: University of Chicago Press.

DiMicco, J. M., & Millen, D. R. (2007, November). *Identity management: Multiple presentations of self in Facebook.* Paper presented at the 2007 International ACM conference on supporting group work . ACM.

Donath, J., & Boyd, D. (2004). Public displays of connection. *B.T. Technology Journal, 22*(4), 71-82.

Duffy, B. E., & Pruchniewska, U. (2017). Gender and self-enterprise in the social media age: A digital double bind. *Information, Communication & Society, 20*(6), 843-859. doi:10.1080/1369118X.2017.1291703

Erickson, E. (1974). *Dimensions of a new identity*. N.Y.: W. W. Norton & Company.

Fairburn, M. (1989). The ideal society and its enemies: The foundations of modern New Zealand society, 1850-1900. Auckland, N.Z.: Auckland University Press.

Florenthal, B., & Dykhouse, M. (2012). *How college students use LinkedIn, why some don't use it, and why it is important*. Paper presented at the DMEF Research Summit, Las Vegas.

Fonseca, M. (2014). Entreprenaissance: The renaissance of entrepreneurship. Retrieved from http://www.intelligenthq.com/startup/entreprenaissance-renaissance-entrepreneurship/

Gee, J. P., Lankshear, C., & Hull, G. (1996). *The new work order: Behind the language of the new capitalism*. St. Leonards, N.S.W.: Allen & Unwin.

Gergen, K. (1997). Social saturation and the populated self. In G. E. Hawisher & C. L. Selfe (Eds.), *Literacy, technology and society: Confronting the issues* Upper Saddle River, N.J.: Prentice Hall.

Gill, R. (2017). The entrepreneur in the age of discursive reproduction: Whence comes entrepreneurial identity? In T. N. Duening & M. L. Metzger (Eds.), *Entrepreneurial identity[electronic resource] The process of becoming an entrepreneur*. Cheltenham, U.K.: Edward Elgar Publishing Limited.

Gill, R., & Larson, G. (2014a). Making the ideal (local) entrepreneur: Enterprise discourse, place, and the construction of entrepreneurial identity. *Human Relations, 67*, 519-542.

Gill, R., & Larson, G. (2014b). Making the ideal (local) entrepreneur: Place and the regional development of high-tech entrepreneurial identity. *Human Relations, 67*(5), 519-542. doi:10.1177/0018726713496829

Goffman, E. (1959). *The presentation of self in everyday life*. Garden City, NY: Doubleday.

Grant, D., & Cox, J. W. (2017). Using a Discourse Lens to Explore Tensions and Contradictions in Organizational Theory and Change: A Conversation with Linda Putnam. *Journal of Change Management, 17*(3), 189-202. doi:10.1080/14697017.2017.1299289

Haslam, S. A. (2001). *Psychology in organizations*. London: SAGE.

Jussila, J.J., Kärkkäinen, H., & Aramo-Immonen, H. . (2014). Social media utilization in business-to-business relationships of technology industry firms. *Computers in Human Behavior, 30*, 606-613.

Knight, & Weedon, A. (2014). Identity and social media. *Convergence, 20*(3), 257-258. doi:10.1177/1354856514536365

Kraut, R. E., & Resnick, P. (2011). Building successful online communities: Evidence-based social design. Cambridge, MA: MIT Press.

Kuhn, T. (2006). A 'demented work ethic' and a 'lifestyle firm':discourse, identity, and workplace time commitments. *Organization Studies, 27*(9), 1339-1358.

Larson, G., & Gill, R. (2017). *Organizations and Identity*. Malden, MA., Cambridge, UK.: Polity Press.

Macdonald, K. M. (1995). *The sociology of the professions*. London: Sage.

Marder, B., Joinson, A., & Shankar, A. (2012). *Every post you make, every pic you take, I'll be watching you: Behind social spheres on Facebook*. Paper presented at the 45th Hawaii International Conference on System Sciences.

Marder, B., Joinson, A., Shankar, A., & Thirlaway, K. (2016). Strength matters: Self-presentation to the strongest audience rather than lowest common denominator when faced with multiple audiences in social network sites. *Computers in Human Behavior, 61*, 56-62. doi:http://dx.doi.org/10.1016/j.chb.2016.03.005

Marwick, A. (2012). The Public Domain: Social Surveillance in Everyday Life. *Surveillance & Society, 9*(4)), 378-393.

Marwick, A., & Boyd, D. (2011). I tweet honestly, I tweet passionately: Twitter users, context collapse, and the imagined audience. *New Media and Society, 13*(1), 114-133.

Massey, D. (1994). *Space, place, and gender*. Cambridge [England]: Polity Press.

MBIE. (2017). Small businesses in New Zealand: How do they compare with larger firms? Retrieved from http://www.mbie.govt.nz/info-services/business/business-growth-agenda/sectors-reports-series/pdf-image-library/the-small-business-sector-report-and-factsheet/small-business-factsheet-2017.pdf

Michaelidou, N., Siamagka, N.T., & Christodoulides, G. (2011). Usage, barriers and measurement of social mediamarketing: An exploratory investigation of small and medium B2B brands. *Industrial Marketing Management, 40*(7), 1153-1159.

Mumby, D. K. (2011). What's cooking in organizational discourse studies? A response to Alvesson and Kärreman. *Human Relations, 64*(9), 1147-1161. doi:10.1177/0018726711408367

Nardi, B., Whittaker, S., & Schwartz, H. (2002). Networkers and their activity in intensional networks. *The Journal of Computer Supported Cooperative Work 11*, 205-242.

Oakes, P. (2004). *Social cognition*. Oxford: Blackwell Publishing.

Ollier-Malaterre, A., Rothbard, N. P., & Berg, J. M. (2013). When worlds collide in cyberspace: How boundary work in online social networks impacts professional relationships. *Academy of Management Review, 38*(4), 645-669. doi:10.5465/amr.2011.0235

Oslund, C. (2010). Building a Professional Ethos on LinkedIn. In Tatyana Dumova & Richard Fiordo (Eds.), *Handbook of Research on Social Interaction Technologies and Collaboration Software: Concepts and Trends*. Hershey, PA, USA: ICI Global.

Paliszkiewicz, J., & Madra-Sawicka, M. (2016). Impression Management in Social Media: The Example of LinkedIn. *Management, 11*(3), 203-212. Retrieved from http://ezproxy.massey.ac.nz/login?url=http://search.ebscohost.com/login.aspx?direct=true&db=bth&AN=119349087&site=eds-live&scope=site

Papacharissi, Z. (2009). The virtual geographies of social networks: A comparative analysis of Facebook, LinkedIn and ASmallWorld. *New Media and Society, 11*(1-2), 199-220. doi:10.1177/1461444808099577

Papacharissi, Z. (2011). A networked self. In Z. Papacharissi (Ed.), *A networked self: Identity, community and culture on social network sites* (pp. 304-318). New York: Routledge.

Postmes, T., Baray, G., Haslam, S. A., Morton, T. A., & Swaab, R. I. (2006). The dynamics of personal and social identity formation. In T. Postmes & J. Jetten (Eds.), *Individuality and the group: Advances in social identity* (pp. 215-236). London: SAGE.

Putnam, L., Fairhurst, Gail T., & Banghart, Scott. (2016). Contradictions, Dialectics, and Paradoxes in Organizations: A Constitutive Approach. *The Academy of Management Annals, 10*(1), 65-171. doi:10.1080/19416520.2016.1162421

Quinton, Sarah, & Wilson, Damien. (2016). Tensions and ties in social media networks: Towards a model of understanding business relationship development and business performance enhancement through the use of LinkedIn. *Industrial Marketing Management, 54*, 15-24. doi:10.1016/j.indmarman.2015.12.001

Rainie, H., & Wellman, B. (2012). *Networked: The New Social Operating System*. Cambridge, Mass: The MIT Press.

Ramirez, A. Jr., Walther, J. B., Burgoon, J. K., & Sunnafrank, M. (2002). Information-seeking strategies, uncertainty, and computer-mediated communication: Toward a conceptual model. *Human Communication Research*(2), 213. Retrieved from http://ezproxy.massey.ac.nz/login?url=http://search.ebscohost.com/login.aspx?direct=true&db=edsgea&AN=edsgcl.85176496&site=eds-live&scope=site

Reedy, P., King, D., & Coupland, C. (2016). Organizing for individuation: Alternative organizing, politics and new identities. *Organization Studies, 37*(11), 1553-1573. doi:doi:10.1177/0170840616641983

Sampson, K. A., & Goodrich, C. G. (2009). Making Place: Identity Construction and Community Formation through "Sense of Place" in Westland, New Zealand. *Society & Natural Resources, 22*(10), 901-915.

Sargent, Lyman Tower. (2001). Utopianism and the creation of New Zealand national identity. *Utopian Studies*(1). Retrieved from http://ezproxy.massey.ac.nz/login?url=http://search.ebscohost.com/login.aspx?direct=true&db=edsglr&AN=edsgcl.771186827&site=eds-live&scope=site

Shirky, C. (2008). Here comes everybody: The power of organizing without organizations. NY: Penguin Press.

Spoonley, Paul. (2014). New diversity, old anxieties in New Zealand: the complex identity politics and engagement of a settler society. *Ethnic and Racial Studies, 38*(4), 650-661. doi:10.1080/01419870.2015.980292

Tracy, S. J., & Trethewey, A. (2005). Fracturing the real-self↔fake-self dichotomy: Moving toward "crystallized" organizational discourses and identities. *Communication Theory, 15*, 168-195.

Trethewey, A., & Ashcraft, K. L. (2004). Special issue introduction. Practicing disorganization: The development of applied perspectives on living with tension. *Journal of Applied Communication Research, 32*, 81-88.

Watson, T. J. (2008). Managing Identity: Identity Work, Personal Predicaments and Structural Circumstances. *Organization, 15*(1), 121-143.

Whitworth, B., & Liu, T. (2013). Politeness as a Social Computing Requirement *Examining the Concepts, Issues, and Implications of Internet Trolling* (pp. 88-104). Hershey, PA, USA: IGI Global.

Wong, J. (2012). The rise of the micro-entrepreneurship economy. Retrieved from https://www.fastcompany.com/2679903/the-rise-of-the-micro-entrepreneurship-economy

Woo, DaJung, Putnam, L., & Riforgiate, Sarah E. (2017). Identity Work and Tensions in Organizational Internships: A Comparative Analysis. *Western Journal of Communication, 81*(5), 560-581. doi:10.1080/10570314.2017.1312510

Young, K. (2013). Managing online identity and diverse social networks on Facebook. *Webology, 10*(2), 1-18. Retrieved from http://ezproxy.massey.ac.nz/login?url=http://search.ebscohost.com/login.aspx?direct=true&db=edsdoj&AN=edsdoj.54b68d0451914875ad20109a34f7628d&site=eds-live&scope=site

EXTREMIST TEXT DETECTION IN SOCIAL WEB

Dmitry Devyatkin[1], Ivan Smirnov[1], Fyodor Solovyev[2], Margarita Suvorova[1]
and Andrey Chepovskiy[3]
[1]*Federal Research Center "Computer Science and Control" of Russian Academy of Sciences, Moscow, Russia*
[2]*Institute of Computing for Physics and Technology, Moscow, Russia*
[3]*National Research University Higher School of Economics, Moscow, Russia*

ABSTRACT

Online or cyber extremism is one of the critical problem for the security of Russia and other countries as social web is widely used for radical activity and propaganda. This paper considers the problem of extremist text detection in Russian social media. We propose models and methods for identification of extremist text in Russian, which apply deep linguistic parsing and statistical processing of texts. We also present the dataset of terrorist, religious hate, racism and other radical texts in Russian and results of experiments on this dataset. It was shown, that low-dimensional psycholinguistic and semantic features of texts allow detecting extremist texts with quite good performance while lexical features allow recognizing topics of the detected extremist texts.

KEYWORDS

Cyber Extremism, Radical Texts Detection, Topic Identification, Psycholinguistic Features, Semantics, Extremist Lexis

1. INTRODUCTION

Due to their anonymity and quick diffusion of information social media are often misused for malicious intent. Extremist online recruitment and propaganda is one of them. Automatic detection of illegal activities on the Internet is a challenging problem for many reasons: great number of new messages per day, specificity of language for online communication and dynamic changes of content. In this paper we consider the problem of extremist text detection in the Russian-language segment of the Internet. By extremist texts we mean written materials that foment hatred toward a particular social or ethnic group, race, religion; vindicate terrorism, propagate superiority of a particular social or ethnic group, race, religion, etc. It stems from the language of Russian law "On Countering Extremist Activities".

Detection of extremist texts can be considered as a topic classification task where analyzed objects are texts form social networks and blogs. However, such an approach requires creating human annotated corpora [Cohen, K., et al, 2014] and pre-defined set of characteristics, e.g. keywords, results of complete linguistic analysis, and extracted named entities. Unfortunately, there are no such open corpora in Russian for a number of reasons.

This paper structured as follows: Section 1 contains a review of related works; Section 2 describes our methods for extremist text detection and classification; Section 3 describes a dataset of extremist text in Russian we created for the current research; and in Section 4 we provide results of experiments.

2. RELATED WORK

The problem of online extremism detection attracts attention of researchers since the early 21st century. By now there are vast amount of literature on this topic, including extensive reviews of existing solutions and methods with comprehensive analysis of their limitations, as well as trends and state-of-the-art in this field in general [Agarwal, S., & Sureka, A., 2015], [Correa, D. & Sureka, A., 2013]. Authors came to a conclusion that Link Based Bootstrapping and Text Classification are the most popular methods for extremist content detection. Text classification examines the linguistic features and makes decisions based on a machine learning classifier. Such an approach is akin to the one we use in our research. Moreover, Internet content is dynamic and trends to change patterns in time. This is the main limitation of Link Based Bootstrapping which Text Classification does not have. H. Chen presents several studies for open-source terrorism information collection, analysis, and visualization [Chen, H., 2007]. About 3,6 million web-pages were collected from sites of terrorist groups. This dataset is available for terrorist researchers on the Dark Web Portal. J.R.Scanlon and M.S.Gerber have set themselves a task to identify the recruitment activities of violent groups [Scanlon, J.R. & Gerber, M.S., 2014]. For this purpose they annotated manually 192 post of Chen's Dark Web Project dataset. Researchers achieved an 89% area under the curve (AUC) by SVM classifier and came to a conclusion that automatic detection of online terrorist recruitment is a feasible task.

Scientific studies rely heavily on open-source models and instruments, especially when it comes to PhD students or postdocs. In the field of social media analytics there are quite a number of them [Agarwal, S., et al, 2015]. Another challenge is that extremist users can create new accounts after being suspended. To deal with this problem one has to track extremists' accounts, analyze their behavior and connections to be able to identify multiple accounts of the same user [Klausen, J., et al, 2016]. Works on statistical analysis are relevant to our research as well. Statistical analysis implies such text characteristics as average length of words and sentences, frequency of special characters, syntax errors, frequency words of size n, structure of phrases and sentences, etc. Such methods of statistical analysis are usually applied for plagiarism detection and author identification [Zurini, M., 2015]. It is worth noting that in most of the observed approaches, simple lexical or statistical attributes are used as features for classification. This can make the approaches topic-dependent reduce their capabilities in real applications.

3. METHODS FOR EXTREMIST TEXT DETECTION AND DESIGN OF EXPERIMENTAL STUDY

3.1 Detection of Extremist Texts

Instead of widely used topic-dependent lexical features we studied more complex linguistic-based psycholinguistic and semantic features. The features [Vybornova, O., et al, 2011] were extracted from Russian text corpus. The values of psycholinguistic features are estimated on the basis of morphology of lexical units of the analyzed texts. Some examples of psycholinguistic features are:

1. Verbs-adjectives ratio in the text fragment.
2. Verbs-nouns ratio in the text fragment.
3. Infinitive-verb ratio.
4. Number of the pronouns in the first person plural form.
5. Number of the pronouns in the first person singular form.
6. Number of verbs in past tense, first person, singular.
7. Number of pronouns in the third person plural form.
8. Number of pronouns in the third person singular form.
9. Number of impersonal verbs.

Values of semantic features are calculated as frequencies of semantic roles in the corpus. We used SRL for the Russian language [Lyashevskaya O., 2010]. Some examples of semantic roles are present in the Table 1.

Table 1. Examples of semantic roles

Role	Definition
Causative	Reason for action or occurrence of a feature (e.g. reward for bravery).
Destructive	The object of destructive influence (e.g. blow up the house).
Situative	External situation, natural or social factors that determine the state of the subject (e.g. to carry out reforms under conditions of economic instability).
Comitative	Concomitant action, feature, an accompanying object, or accomplice (e.g. to discuss something with colleagues)

In addition to topic-independence, the proposed approach allows to significantly reduce the feature set dimensionality. That could leads to reducing of overfitting in small datasets. For representation of psycholinguistic and semantic feature of a text t we used the following approach. Let $\Phi = \{\varphi_1, \varphi_2, \ldots, \varphi_n\}$ be a set of all semantic and psycholinguistic features with cardinality n, $\varphi_i(t)$ be a value of a feature φ_i in a text t, where $i = 1,\ldots,n$. Then values of psycholinguistic and semantic features for each text t can be represented as a vector:

$$t_{psy} = (\varphi_1(t), \varphi_2(t), \ldots, \varphi_n(t)) \quad (1)$$

We created an experimental dataset, where each text is represented as a vector of values of these features (see expression 1) and tagged as extremist or neutral. Lexical features were excluded. During the experiment we evaluated the contribution of psycholinguistic and semantic features for text classification (into extremist and neutral). Classification quality was estimated by calculating F_1-score during 5-fold cross-validation. For classification we applied logistic regression, linear SVM, random forest, gradient boosting. For this experiment we used open source library of machine learning methods - Scikit-learn - where all above methods are realized [Pedregosa, F., et al., 2011].

3.2 Extremist Topic Identification

The meaning of concept of extremism is heterogeneous covering a variety of types of offences. We have developed a classification of the text collection being analyzed in our work. The classification comprises the following 7 topics: terrorism, ideological extremism, religious hatred, separatism, nationalism, aggression and calls for riots, fascism. The topics will be considered in detail in the experimental dataset description.

We propose the following framework for the problem of extremist text topic identification. Given a text corpus $C = \{C_1,\ldots,C_K\}$ with texts falling in K topics all the texts $C_i = \{t_1^i, \ldots, t_{C_i}^i\}$ within each topic C_i, $i = 1..K$ are concatenated into a single text T_i, $i = 1..K$. Given a text T_i a frequency dictionary $D_i = \{(x_1^i, f_1^i), \ldots, (x^i_{|D_i|}, f^i_{|D_i|})\}$ is built, where x^i_j is a j-th feature - a fragment of text obtained from the source text and f_j^i a frequency (number) of such fragments normalized by the total number of obtained text fragments. A set of features $\{x_1^i, \ldots, x^i_{|D_i|}\}$ of dictionary D_i is denoted as X_i. Feature may be represented as letter n-gramm, initial word forms or certain parts of speech, nominal groups, functional words. Each feature is related to single feature class F determined by the way the feature was obtained, e.g.: a class of initial word forms, a class of numerals, a class of 4-gramms, etc. A set $F_l = \{F_{l1},\ldots,F_{l|Fl|}\}$ of considered feature classes induces a set F_l of obtained features.

$$F\hat{}_l = F_{l1} \ldots \cup F_{|Fl|} \quad (2)$$

In our work we considered the following classes of features:

- Single alphabet symbols
- Sequences of symbols of lengths from 2 to 8
- Initial forms of nouns, adjectives, verbs, participles, adverbs, quantitative numerals, collective numerals, pronouns, last names, first names, middle names, vocabulary words
- Abbreviations
- Conjunctions
- Particles
- Prepositions
- Interjections
- Word stems
- Nominal and verbal groups

To filter the obtained features we used topical importance measure *Tic(w,τ),* calculated as follows [Mbaikodzhi, E., et al, 2012]:

$$idf(w,\tau) = log_2 \frac{|\tau|}{m(w,\tau)}, \quad (3)$$

$$\Delta I(w,c,\sigma) = idf(w, c \setminus \sigma) - idf(w,\sigma), \quad (4)$$

$$Tic(w,c,\sigma) = \Delta I(w,c,\sigma) H(\Delta I(w,c,\sigma)) \quad (5)$$

where *H(.)* - Heaviside function, *w* - some feature, *m(w,τ)* - count of texts in some set *τ* where *w* occurs, *c* - the experimental dataset *σ* - topical subset of the dataset. We filtered all features with zero topical importance. This way we significantly reduced the feature set dimension. In the experiment, we applied two models for features representation: a "bag of words" model and fastText word embeddings [Bojanowski, P., et al, 2016]. We used fastText because it allows creation of word embeddings for words missing in a training dataset. That is essential for social network analysis. As in the first experiment classification quality was estimated by calculating F_1-score during 5-fold cross-validation. For this experiment we also used Scikit-learn library.

4. DATASET OF EXTREMIST TEXTS

Unfortunately, there is no extremist dataset in Russian. Therefore, first of all we had to create a text corpus for the research. It includes not only extremist texts, but also topically similar texts that do not fall under the category of extremism (we call them neutral): political blogs, sites of opposition members, news, texts and posts from social networks about religion. When choosing texts for the corpus, we were guided by the law "On Countering Extremist Activities" and experts' opinion on what can be considered extremism and what cannot. The corpus includes 493 manually collected texts (650 000 words), 368 of them are extremist texts. The concept of extremism is broad and includes different types of offenses. Therefore, we classified all text on seven categories:

1. Terrorism (27 texts, 3,296 words) – materials from web-sites of outlawed in Russia organizations (the Islamic State, Hizb ut-Tahrir, etc.), where their ideology is propagated.
2. Ideological texts (26 texts, 21,131 words) affirms the superiority of some religion over others, or spreads false interpretations of sacred books.
3. Religious hatred (55 texts, 16,697 words) – texts that calls for cruelty against representatives of other religions, forming a negative image of other religions, attributing dangerous intentions to persons of another religion.
4. Separatism (7 texts, 852 words) - materials that disseminate the idea of separating some regions from the Russian Federation, and contain insults and threats against ethnic groups residing there.

5. Nationalism (208 texts, 19,399 words) - texts that affirm the initial hostility of a certain ethnic group, call for the physical destruction of its representatives, require restrictions of their rights and freedoms in Russia.
6. Aggression and calls for insurgency (43 texts, 6,757 words) - calls for unauthorized rallies and riots, deposing the government, threaten government officials and their families.
7. Fascism (13 texts, 2,059 words) - texts that justify neo-fascism and genocide, discuss forbidden fascist books, etc.

At the moment the corpus is not large enough and unbalanced: nationalism is larger than all other categories. In the future the above classification can be changed - similar categories can be combined and heterogeneous categories can be divided. Besides, we plan to expand corpus by new texts and apply the proposed method for Tatar text classification.

5. RESULTS OF EXPERIMENTS AND DISCUSSION

5.1 Results of Extremist Text Detection

We estimate F_1 binary score for the smallest class, because of the unbalanced dataset. On the basis of this experiment (Table 2) we make a conclusion that lincar classification methods (e.g. linear SVM and logistic regression) do not work well with psycholinguistic and semantic features (F_1-score stands at 55%). As for more complex methods - ensembles of decision trees – they give satisfactory quality without lexical features (F_1-score reaches 76%). Psycholinguistic and semantic features do not depend on the topic of the message as much as lexical features do. Therefore, their application for extremist text detection is more promising. However, this group of features needs additional research to improve the quality of classification.

Table 2. Comparative analysis of text classification methods (F_1-score, %)

Classifier	Psycholinguistic and semantic features	Psycholinguistic and semantic features + bag of words	Psycholinguistic and semantic features + fastText
Log-regression	55±6	60±4	91±5
Linear SVM	55±3	58±6	91±3
Random forest	76±3	85±4	92±4
Gradient boosting	76±3	85±5	93±3

5.2 Results of Extremist Topic Identification

Specialized topic dictionaries of keywords and all their morphological forms have been created based on the experimental dataset. Words from Russian dictionaries fall into three levels of their topic relevance:

1. The first level is represented with commonly used words, phrases usually in negative tone. Those words frequently occur in the texts on the topic at the same time not being directly related to the topic.
2. The words of the second level occur in the texts on the given and similar topics, describing the given topic without a direct relation to it.
3. Third level words most frequently occur in the texts on the topic having the strongest relevance to the topic.

Such a division is caused by the polysemy of the grammatical morphemes in the Russian language leading to a diversity of meanings for different phrases. The following dictionaries have been developed by the present day:

1. Extremism: first level – 1249 words, second level – 766 words, third level –310 words.
2. Terrorism: first level – 1060 words, second level – 254 words, third level –322 words.
3. Nationalism, social hatred: first level – 207 words, second level – 205 words, third level – 311 words.
4. Fascism: first level – 92 words, second level – 239 words, third level – 187 words.
5. Violence, cruelty: first level – 214 words, second level – 460 words, third level – 261 words.

Results of the second experiment are presented in Table 3.The separatism topic was excluded from the table because its texts were not detected by any classifier. The experiment shows that fastText embeddings model allow significantly improve the quality of topic classification in our unbalanced and small dataset, compared with the "bag of words" model. We believe that this is due to the smaller size of the feature set space produced by the embedding model. It can also be related to the property of embedding models to generate similar vectors for semantically similar words. Unlike the previous task in this experiment, linear classification methods reach better results than ensembles. This indicates that in this task we should rather continue to replenish and balance our experimental dataset than to complicate the models of machine learning that we used.

Table 3. Results of extremist topic identification using lexical features

	"Bag of words" model, F_1-score, %				fastText model, F_1-score, %			
	SVM	Log-regression	Random-forest	Gradient-boosting	SVM	Log-regression	Random-forest	Gradient-boosting
Aggression	–	–	–	–	56±2	57±4	35±2	47±7
Fascism	–	–	–	–	36±8	34±7	–	–
Ideological texts	33±5	35±2	32±4	25±2	34±5	33±3	30±3	27±5
Nationalism	86±9	86±1	86±1	85±1	85±6	86±1	83±1	83±1
Religious hatred	37±3	32±3	32±3	29±6	44±1	41±1	30±2	29±4
Terrorism	70±3	69±3	40±4	50±7	75±2	74±3	70±2	60±4

6. CONCLUSION AND FUTURE WORK

This research resulted in creation of experimental datasets in Russian that can be used for training and testing machine learning methods for extremist text detection. Specific lexis that characterizes different categories of illegal texts was extracted. The proposed psycholinguistic and semantic features were used in our previous research for sentiment analysis [Vybornova, O., et al, 2011]. It was shown that extremist text detection can be performed with satisfactory quality using machine-learning methods and set of psycholinguistic and semantic features. It was also shown that fastText embeddings allow significantly improve a quality of extremist topic identification for texts from social networks.

ACKNOWLEDGEMENT

The reported study was funded by RFBR according to the research projects № 16-29-09546, № 18-00-00606(18-00-00233), № 19-07-00806.

REFERENCES

Agarwal, S., Sureka, A., 2015. Applying social media intelligence for predicting and identifying on-line radicalization and civil unrest oriented threats. *arXiv preprint arXiv:1511.06858*

Agarwal, S., et al, 2015, Open source social media analytics for intelligence andsecurity informatics applications. *International Conference on Big Data Analytics.* Hyderabad, Telangana State, India, pp. 21–37.

Bojanowski, P., et al, 2016. Enriching word vectors with subword information. *arXiv preprint arXiv:1607.04606*

Chen, H., 2007, Exploring extremism and terrorism on the web: the dark web project. *Pacific Asia Workshop on Intelligence and Security Informatics*. Chengdu, China, pp. 1–20.

Cohen, K., et al, 2014. Detecting linguistic markers for radical violence in social media. *Terrorism and Political Violence*, Vol. 26, No.1, pp. 246–256.

Correa, D., Sureka, A., 2013. Solutions to detect and analyze online radicalization: a survey. *arXiv preprint arXiv:1301.4916*

Klausen, J., et al, 2016. Finding online extremists in social networks. *arXiv preprint arXiv:1610.06242*

Mbaikodzhi, E., et al, 2012. The method of automatic classification of short text messages. *Information Technologies and Computing Systems*, No.3, pp. 93–102.

Lyashevskaya O., 2010, Bank of Russian constructions and valencies. *LREC 2010*, Malta, Valletta, May, pp. 1802-1805.

Pedregosa, F., et al., 2011. Scikit-learn: Machine learning in python. *Journal of Machine Learning Research*, Vol. 12(Oct), pp. 2825–2830.

Scanlon, J.R., Gerber, M.S., 2014. Automatic detection of cyber-recruitment by violent extremists. *Security Informatics*, Vol. 3, No.1, pp. 1–10.

Vybornova, O., et al, 2011. Social tension detection and intention recognition using natural language semantic analysis. *Proceedings of European Intelligence and Security Informatics Conference.* Athens, Greece, pp. 277–281.

Zurini, M., 2015. Stylometry metrics selection for creating a model for evaluating the writing style of authors according to their cultural orientation. *Informatica Economica*, Vol. 19, No.3, pp. 107-119.

HUMAN INTERACTION IN THE DIGITAL AGE: SOCIOMATERIAL PRACTICE ON FACEBOOK GROUP IN INDONESIA

Wulan Widyasari[1] and Heidrun Allert[2]
[1]PhD Student at Institute of Education at Christian-Albrechts-Universität zu Kiel, Germany
Lecturer at Communication Department atUniversitas Muhammadiyah Yogyakarta
[2]Professor at Institute of Education at Christian-Albrechts-Universität zu Kiel, Germany

ABSTRACT

This paper analyzes the way of understanding and patterns of human interactions while using social media as constitutively entangled with the social practice and affordances of the technology that being carried out. Based on theoretical accounts we frame using media as socially and materially mediated. Using online ethnography, we see the different socio-material practice between the pro-LGBTQ and the anti-LGBTQ groups on Facebook regarding to the LGBTQ as a controversial issue in Indonesia. We analyse performative practices to see how the affordances of Facebook are enacted in co-producing the understanding of LGBTQ issues in both group. Although the issues discussed is the same issue in both Facebook groups, the socio-material practices that occur are different between the pro-LGBTQ and the anti-LGBTQ group. The data is collected from both groups using online observation in the period of March 2016 as the beginning of LGBTQ issues become a huge issue in Indonesia until July 2018 when LGBTQ was being criminalized by the Draft of the Criminal Code of Indonesia. As a result, we can see that the interaction pattern in both groups is different, depending on the issues that are being discussed and how the users perform the technology. The social practice is related to affordances and human interaction in a process that is constitutively entangled and performative.

KEYWORDS

Sociomaterial Practice, Affordances, Human Interaction, Facebook, LGBTQ

1. INTRODUCTION

Social media has changed the way people interact and communicate with others because of the digital technology being used as using media is socially and materially entangled. We can see it by looking at the sociomaterial practices occurring when groups create a collective understanding of a certain topic. According to Orlikowski (2009), the social and the material are considered to be inextricably related — there is no social that is not also material, and no material that is not also social. Furthermore, she also said that technology is here understood as material artifacts that are socially defined and socially produced, and thus as relevant only in relation to the people engaging with them. Thus, we can argue that the social practice and the material are constitutively entangled and that way we can understand knowledge process when people using technology. As Gherardi (2009) said, knowledge is therefore not only an activity situated in practices, but it is also an activity distributed between humans and non-humans. Objects, tools, and artifacts embody knowledge; they anchor practices in their materiality; they interrogate humans and are extensions of their memory.

It becomes interesting to see how human interaction using technology to produce knowledge when dealing with an controversial issue, such as LGBTQ. In Indonesia, the pros and cons of LGBTQ are widely discussed on social media. Until mid of 2018, the LGBTQ issues are heavily discussed regarding to the criminalization of LGBTQ in Indonesian Draft of the Criminal Code. It was started when the Indonesian Constitutional Court refused to try lawsuits about LGBTQ and adultery. Then, Indonesia's constitutional court rejects the petition for judicial review of some articles in Indonesian Draft of the Criminal Code, which regulate crime against decency, like adultery and LGBTQ. As a result of the rejection, the pros and cons of LGBTQ became a hot topic in the community. Namely *Perkumpulan Arus Pelangi* and *AILA Indonesia* are groups that are quite vocal in shouting LGBTQ issues. Both groups also have open Facebook groups dedicated to all Facebook users who are interested in gender and LGBTQ issues. The members of both groups were not recruited, every user who likes to join both groups and expressing their opinions are able to participate. Both group concern on LGBTQ issues, however they are on different position regarding to LGBTQ issues. Perkumpulan Arus Pelangi is a pro-LGBTQ group and AILA is an anti-LGBTQ group. Although both groups discuss the issue of LGBTQ, discussions are performed differently and affordances are enacted differently between them. They also perform different social practices taking account of the different affordances. We can see the example in Figure 1.

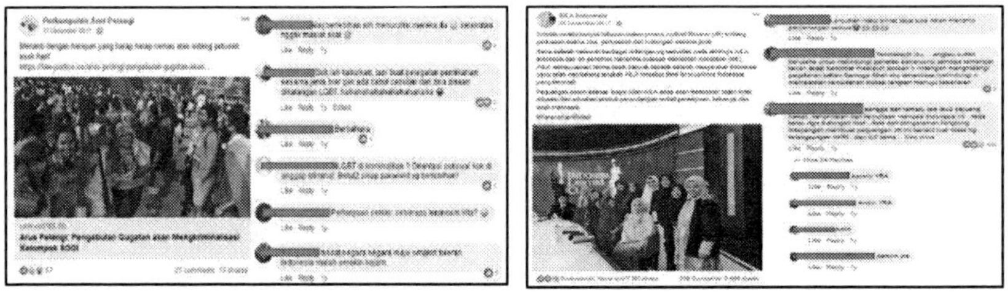

Figure 1. *Perkumpulan Arus Pelangi* and *AILA Indonesia* Facebook's post and discussions

The figure shows on how different is the interaction patterns of both group when dealing with LGBQ issues. In their Facebook's post, *Perkumpulan Arus Pelangi* waited for the result of judicial review from Indonesia's constitutional court regarding to Draft of the Criminal Code. The draft is important because if it was legalized, LGBTQ could be criminalized. In the comment, some users questioned why sexual orientation is criminalized and thought that it is a paranoid attitude. In contrast to *Perkumpulan Arus Pelangi* is a post from *AILA Indonesia*. The figure shows that *AILA Indonesia* accepts the constitutional court's decision and is grateful for the support of all parties. They also stated that their fight is not over yet. The comment shows a lot of support and prayer for AILA. Their support was more based on the argument of sake of the next generation. Taking account on how the affordances are enacted differently, *Perkumpulan Arus Pelangi* using a website link as an addition to their post while *AILA* Indonesia using a photo and *hashtag* to give illustration to their post.

As the basic assumption of our work is, there are different patterns in their interaction, we already see it in the comment section in figure 1. Furthermore, the use of *hashtag #KarenaKamiPeduli* (because we care) on *AILA Indonesia* post is also interesting because the *hashtag* is used as an expression and not to use it as an structuring *hashtag* function, which is to other users easily find a post with a specific content. This was only an example to introduce what we found in our analysis. Based on this case, our article researches how human interactions dealing with a controversial issue like LGBTQ is constitutively entangled with affordances of Facebook. We analyse the interaction on *Perkumpulan Arus Pelangi* and *AILA Indonesia* pages using online ethnography to answer this following question: How is the way of understanding of LGBTQ issues and the patterns of Facebook interactions on different groups constitutively entangled with the social practice and Facebook affordances? To answer the question, firstly, we need to describe the understanding of sociomaterial practices.

2. KEY CONCEPTS OF SOCIOMATERIAL PRACTICES

In social theory, practice-theroetical approaches promulgate a distinct social ontology: the social is a field of embodied, materially interwoven collective practices centrally organized around shared practical understanding (Schatzki, 2001). In this regard, the value of practice theory is to ask questions about what people are doing and how they categorize what they are doing, avoiding the disciplinary or other preconceptions that would automatically read their actions as, say, "consumption" or "being-an-audience", whether or not that is how the actors see their actions (Couldry, 2004). Based on practice theory, not only the practice is different but also the understanding that appears in individual minds. That is, individual understanding is mediated by the practice that is being carried out. Furthermore, differences in understanding as a co-result of these different practices becomes more complex when dealing with technology. According to Orlikowski (2007), technology is understood to be emergent within the practices evolving and the different ways in which people engage with it. Furthermore, materiality is integral to organizing, positing that the social and the material are *constitutively entangled* in everyday life. A position of constitutive entanglement does not privilege either humans or technology (in one-way interactions), nor does it link them through a form of mutual reciprocation (in two-way interactions). In her other work, she also argued that technology is here understood as material artifacts that are socially defined and socially produced, and thus as relevant only in relation to people engaging with them (Orlikowski, 2009). Corradi and Gherardi (2010) also said, central to the practice perspective is acknowledgement of the social, historical and structural contexts in which knowledge is manufactured. The concept of practice allows researchers to investigate empirically how constituents and practical knowledge is continuously (re-)produced and how competence is built around a contingent logic of action.

Thus, also the reason why we need to look at how social media users post on their feeds because one social practice enacts technological affordances differently to other social practices. As Bardone said (2011), the notion of affordance is fundamental because it defines the nature of the relationship between an agent and its environment. Then, according to Boyd (2011), networked technologies introduce new affordances for amplifying, recording, and spreading information and social acts. These affordances can shape the public and how people negotiate them. While such affordances do not determine social practice, they can stabilize and destabilize core assumptions people make when engaging in social life. Here, we can understand affordances as tools or materials of a technology and its specific applications. For example, Facebook and Instagram have their own affordances, Facebook cannot be used the way we use Instagram. While in Facebook we can upload a post that contains text only, in Instagram we need to upload a photo and use the text as a caption. Furthermore, taking account of affordances for human interaction on Facebook, sociomaterial practice helps to understand how social practice is constitutively entangled with the Facebook affordances. As Bjørn and Østerlund said (2014), sociomateriality emphasizes the *importance of material properties* of artefacts and the changes in social practices caused by enacting such technologies. Sociomateriality points to the *inseparability* of the social and the material.

3. RESEARCH METHOD

The data of this research are being analyzed using online ethnography because, from a practice-theoretical perspective, the ethnographic field is constructed by the actions and expressions of the people we study and by the ethnographer's decisions about the connections s/he follows and forms; the field constantly evolves as the fieldwork progresses (Cruz and Ardevol, 2013). According to Hammersley (2006), ethnography is the tension between trying to understand people's perspectives from the inside while also viewing them and their behavior more distantly, in ways that may be alien (and perhaps even objectionable) to them. In the context of internet, Geertz (in Beneito-Montagut, 2011) stated that ethnography analyses human practices in the context of culture and now the internet is part of our culture, with meanings, symbols, and a 'system of conceptions expressed in symbolic forms by means of which users communicate, perpetuate and develop their knowledge about attitudes towards life'. Here, to conduct online ethnography, the everyday life of the social media ethnographer involves living part of one's life on the internet, keeping up to date with and participating and collaborating in social media discussions. This is not simply a virtual experience but is connected to the material world in important ways (Postill and Pink, 2012). Thus, in this research, the data is collected by conducting online ethnography to observe both *Perkumpulan Arus Pelangi* (pro-LGBTQ group) and *AILA Indonesia* (anti-LGBTQ group) Facebook pages. The observation data is gathered in the period of March 2016 as the beginning of LGBTQ issues become a huge issue in Indonesia until July 2018 when LGBTQ was being criminalized by the Draft of the Criminal Code of Indonesia.

We use key concepts of sociomateriality from Barad and Orlikowski that are formulated by Harris and Abedin in their work to analyze the data. Their key concepts are *relationality practice, performativity practice, entanglement practice, sociomaterial assemblage practice* and *co-constitution practice* (Harris and Abedin, 2015). We also take account of the recent affordances of Facebook that being carried out because platforms, affordances and algorithms are continuously developed. The affordances enacted are always changing, so are its use. As Hutchby (2001) stated, the affordances can shape the conditions of possibility associated with an action: it may be possible to do it one way, but not another. Furthermore, the use of affordances is socially mediated within situated practices. To analyze the data, we started with capturing the Facebook posts related to LGBTQ issues on *Perkumpulan Arus Pelangi* and *AILA Indonesia,* and saved it in word format. We have 189 pages from *Perkumpulan Arus Pelangi* and 255 pages from *AILA Indonesia*. Then we went through the data to see the pattern of discussion using online ethnography. After that, we took some examples of the pattern and put it into our paper. Our findings in this paper is only example of the repetitive pattern of discussion that we find in our data. Finally, in order to do this research, both admin of both groups gave permission to use their data for this research. The captured data from social media was also censored and paraphrased to protect the identity of the users. Both are done under the consent of General Data Protection Regulation (GDPR) article 6 (a) and (b), that said processing shall be lawful only if and to the extent that at least one of the following applies: (a) the data subject has given consent to the processing of his or her personal data for one or more specific purposes; (b) processing is necessary for the performance of a contract to which the data subject is party or in order to take steps at the request of the data subject prior to entering into a contract (https://gdpr.algolia.com/gdpr-article-6).

4. FINDINGS: SOCIOMATERIAL PRACTICE IN UNDERSTANDING LGBTQ ISSUES

When discussing the LGBTQ issue, the different perspectives between *Perkumpulan Arus Pelangi* and *AILA Indonesia* as discussed on facebook pages can be explained as sociomaterial practices of both groups that are s constitutively entangled with the Facebook affordances. First, we can see it from the *relationality practice* that is being carried out. *Relationality practice* means online communities exist in relation to other assemblages. That is, within an online community, common interest unites agents, whereas across communities, differences in practices (such as participant needs) will create boundaries and potential conflict (Harris and Abedin, 2015). We can see the example in figures 2.

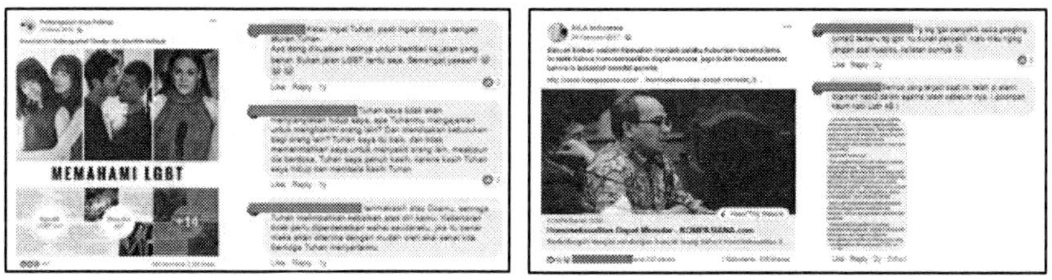

Figure 2. *Perkumpulan Arus Pelangi* and *AILA Indonesia* Facebook's post and comment section

In term of *relationality practice*, we found dominant interaction patterns from both groups. *Perkumpulan Arus Pelangi* has "LGBTQ is not a disease" as a pattern, which means LGBTQ is just ordinary human being. Figure 2 shows how *Perkumpulan Arus Pelangi* built narratives about LGBTQ when they used photos and info graphics to explain LGBTQ-related issues such as explaining LGBTQ notions, providing prove about LGBTQ are not diseases, giving examples of how animals also like same-sex relationship and so on. The post explained LGBTQ issues that are often discussed by the Indonesian community. In addition to this post, they also consistently builds narratives with facts that support LGBTQ, such as a post about the existence of gay priests in South Africa, how UK government vows to end practice of gay conversion therapy, an explanation of WHO views that state LGBTQ is not a disease and many others. These posts are consistent practices to create the pattern of discussion in the group so that they have common interest regarding to LGBTQ issues. Furthermore, in the comment section, we can see what happens when there are comments that are not in accordance with the common interest of the group. There was seen a user who stated that LGBTQ was not the right way because it was not following God's rules. The reaction that arose in response to this statement was a refusal, like when other users questioned why God judged others and wrote that God actually taught love and did not hurt others even though they sinned. In addition, the user also prayed that god will always be bestowed and suggested that the truth should not be debated because truth can always be accepted by common sense. From here, we can know the pattern of discussing LGBTQ issues on *Perkumpulan Arus Pelangi* group is using research and news about LGBTQ. The pattern of these rules is shown on many of their posts and discussion, mostly they refuse to accept opinions that are not based on facts. They also rarely use a religious perspective and when they do, they say it in universal language. Furthermore, we can see the affordances enacted on their post is infographic in the form of photo to explain about LGBTQ.

Meanwhile, the *relationality practice* carried out by *AILA Indonesia* is in stark contrast to *Perkumpulan Arus Pelangi* in understanding LBGTQ issues. Here, *AILA Indonesia* has "LGBTQ is a disease and threat" as a pattern, which means LGBTQ is dangerous for humanity. Figure 2 shows *AILA Indonesia*'s post about many victims of sodomy become homosexuals proving that homosexuality is contagious. They consistently builds anti LGBTQ narratives by selecting harsh words to mention LGBTQ such as perpetrator, threats, sexual deviations and other similar words in their posts. In addition, they have also consistently posted links that show the reason why they resistance to LGBTQ such as an explanation of LGBTQ as a Western secularism that is incompatible with Indonesia as religious country, news of the existence of gay prostitution that endangers the next generation, argumentation about natural disasters as a punishment from God because of LGBTQ and so on. The selection of these posts builds a narrative so that the members of *AILA Indonesia* have a common interest about how LGBTQ is a concern that needs to be addressed because it is contrary to their religion. Then, in the comment section, we can see the practice when a user disagrees with their understanding. There was seen a user suggest that people who said that LGBTQ was a disease need to find the latest journals about LGBTQ. Then, other users responded to that statement by including the Koran verses about the story of Prophet Lot and LGBTQ. These comments indicate that differences in views about LGBTQ lead to restrictions for discussion. They have discussion pattern that say LGBTQ is outsider perspective and undermines the morale of the Indonesian people. Their basic rule of argumentation is the Islamic perspective, so Islamic verses can be easily found in their discussions. This Islamic verses also shown on many of their posts, like when they explain about earthquake and blame the LGBTQ because of Prophet Lot story in Koran. Furthermore, we also can see the difference affordances that being enacted by *AILA Indonesia*. On their Facebook, *AILA Indonesia* is using a website link to explain the reason why LGBTQ is contagious and on their comment section, one of the user use a photo to explain their opinion about LGBTQ.

Second, we can see sociomaterial practice from the *performativity practice*. *Perfomativity practice* means relationships between community participants and social media technology are never fixed. Instead, the socio-material assemblage (online community) emerges from practice and defines how to practice. It is in the act of participating that the relation (between the participant and the social media technology) is defined, and each participatory act (re)produces (or performs) the socio-material practice (Harris and Abedin, 2015). Here, we found dominant interaction patterns from both groups. *Perkumpulan Arus Pelangi* has "diversity" as a pattern, which means LGBTQ as one of social diversity. In contrast, *AILA Indonesia* has "Islamic perspectives" as a pattern, which means LGBTQ must be seen in term of Islamic values. We can see examples of the differences in *performativity practice* conducted by *Perkumpulan Arus Pelangi* and *AILA Indonesia*. The religious template in *AILA Indonesia* remains the most dominant pattern, in contrast to *Perkumpulan Arus Pelangi* which uses universal value templates more often. The difference in *performativity practice* certainly forms different participation actions within the two groups where in *Perkumpulan Arus Pelangi* the argument about religion is a matter of mockery and sarcasm, but at AILA Indonesia is the main foundation that strengthens their perspective. Based on our observations, the member of *Perkumpulan Arus Pelangi* has discussion pattern when showing their support to LGBTQ, that is using the diversity and equality perspective, like the use of research data. In the other side, *AILA Indonesia* has different discussion pattern, that is using Islamic perspective when showing their rejection to the LGBTQ issues, like the use of many Arabic words in expressing their concern in the discussion. Furthermore, both groups also use different affordances. We can see on the use of rainbow sticker to show a support to LGBTQ in *Perkumpulan Arus Pelangi* and the use of writing text on *AILA Indonesia* comment's section.

Third, we can see the sociomaterial practice from the *entanglement practice* conducted by both groups. *Entanglement practice* means the material and the social emergently produce one another, as people, entangled with a variety of social media–based technologies, participate in online communities in the carrying out of their daily social practices (Harris and Abedin, 2015). *Perkumpulan Arus Pelangi* has "creativite features" as a pattern, which means they use creative and innovative way to spread their messages. In contrast, *AILA Indonesia* has "conservative features" as a pattern, which means they use traditional way to post their messages. For example, we can see how they uses info graphic images to explain the impact of negative media coverage on the LGBTQ community. Other than that, they also uses various Facebook's features in a creative way. In addition to using infographics, *Perkumpulan Arus Pelangi* also uses video feature to post songs about LGBTQ, films and profiles of inspiring LGBTQ people. Whereas *AILA Indonesia* prefers their posts in serious approach such as live video of the RKUHP trial in the Constitutional Court. *AILA Indonesia* never uses info graphics and mostly uses live video feature that contain dialogues and presentations from people who support *AILA Indonesia*. *Perkumpulan Arus Pelangi* used various Facebook *affordances* to update their posts on their page, meanwhile *AILA Indonesia* mostly use live video and writing text on their page. These enactments of *affordances* are seen throughout on both pages posts.

Fourth, we can see the sociomaterial practice from the *sociomaterial assemblage practice* conducted by bothe groups. *Sociomaterial assemblage practice* means an online community is a composite and shifting assemblage of the material and social, which change over time as those involved participate in online community activities to provide meaning, to exercise power, and to legitimate actions (Harris and Abedin, 2015). We found dominant interaction patterns in both groups when we see how users deal with legitimate action between humans and technology, such as "deleting comment". We can see the examples in figure 3.

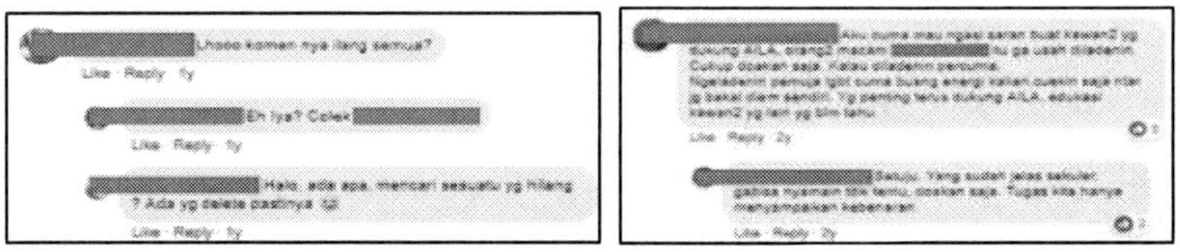

Figure 3. Facebook comments on *Perkumpulan Arus Pelangi* and *AILA Indonesia* post

Figure 3 shows the user interactions in the comment section of *Perkumpulan Arus Pelangi* and *AILA Indonesia* page. There are users in *Perkumpulan Arus Pelangi* who asks why many comments are missing. A user even feels confident to say that someone deleted those comments. This shows two things. First, when deleting a comment on Facebook, other comments under the deleted-comment will also be deleted. Second, a legitimate action to delete a comment in Facebook page is for both the administrator of the page and the user who posted the comment itself. In *AILA Indonesia*, we can see the interaction of users who discusses the need not to respond to comments from LGBTQ supporters because they have secular view. A user wrote a reason for ignoring the comments of the LGBTQ supporters because it only wastes their energy, while other users argue to pray for the LGBTQ supporters and keep telling the truth. This shows the legitimate action of the user can influence other users to comment on Facebook's discussions, even though this action does not have the absolute power to delete existing comments, the privilege is still in the hands of group's administrator. Figure 3 show how the ability to delete a comment on Facebook is a special characteristic of Facebook's affordances because of its ability to delete the following comment in sequence.

Finally, we can see the sociomaterial practice from the *co-constitution practice*. *Co-constitution practice* means the material (media technology) and the social are mutually constituted and inseparable. Structures and processes of an online community are enacted and emergent as participants draw upon communication features in their situated practices (Harris and Abedin, 2015). Here, we found dominant interaction patterns in both groups when we see how users use *hashtags* in their posts. *Perkumpulan Arus Pelangi* has "*hashtags* as campaign" pattern, which means they use *hashtags* for specific pupose. *AILA Indonesia* has "*hashtag* as emotion" pattern, which means they use *hashtags* to emphasize certain emotion. For example, we can see how *Perkumpulan Arus Pelangi* uses certain hashtags that are used to highlight certain issues such as the *#IDAHOT2016* to discuss LGBTQ issues related to International Day Against Homophobia Biphobia and Transphobia in 2016. Through the hashtag, *Perkumpulan Arus Pelangi* sought to call attention to LGBTQ issues that they are fighting for and point to further context, communities and informationspheres. Whereas in *AILA Indonesia,* there are users using the *hashtag* like *#elusdada* only to express their concern for LGBTQ issue. The use of *hashtag* is different from the use of hashtags conducted by *Perkumpulan Arus Pelangi* because the *hashtag* that being used is not intended for campaigns or easy access to look for certain information but as an expression of feelings. The use of *hashtags* also means structures and processes of affordances are enacted and emergent as Facebook users draw upon Facebook features in their situated practices. From the observation, *Perkumpulan Arus Pelangi* used a *hashtag* as tool of spreading information, and on the other hand, *AILA Indonesia* used a *hashtag* as affirmation of the statement that was being made.

From the data that has been described, we can say that all the practices are always related to *co-constitution practice.* Here, affordances can be seen as a force for *co-constituting practice.* Most relevant affordances in performing practices in these two groups are website link, photo, video, live video, sticker, *hashtag* and deleting comments. The very powerful one is the deleting comments because it is a legitimate action that can produce a different meaning and it cab even eliminate its meaning of the existing discussions.

5. DISCUSSION

Based on the data presented, it shows that interactions in social media related to the technologies co-produce the social practice. Producing an understanding of the issue of LGBTQ is socially and materially mediated. Facebook *affordances* that are shown, such as video feature or hashtags can provide different interaction meanings between two different groups. These affordances also helped shaping the different understanding of the LGBTQ issue between *Perkumpulan Arus Pelangi* and *AILA Indonesia* as they formed different narratives towards LGBTQ issues using different features on Facebook. *Perkumpulan Arus Pelangi* use the Facebook *affordances* to give meaning how LGBTQ is only sexual diversities that no difference with heterosexual and to give understanding about LGBTQ by using creative content like info graphics and music video. Meanwhile *AILA Indonesia* use the Facebook *affordances* in more affirmative way to create understanding that LGBTQ is a threat to Indonesian society. Of course, these differences in using Facebook *affordances* create a different practice in both groups. As Gherardi (2009) said, knowledge is therefore not only an activity situated in practices, but it is also an activity distributed between humans and non-humans. Objects, tools, and artifacts embody knowledge; they anchor practices in their materiality; they interrogate humans and are extensions of their memory. Practice is always related to the technology's affordances – but not in a deterministic manner. As we can see from the data, for example, when there is power relation take its roles by deleting a post or a comment, the context of the interaction change and we lost the understanding of the whole interaction. We can conclude that the most important Facebook *affordances* on both groups is the deleting tool because it can create different interaction and meaning of the discussion. This deleting-comment can produce different result of the discussion because it could stop the discussion.

Finally to answer the research question, we can say that the pattern of interaction between both groups are indeed different and it is related on how users deal with Facebook affordances as a social practice. The two groups co-produce different culture and pattern on understanding LGBTQ issues. We can also agree with van Dijk and Rietveld, although much in the behavior setting remains the same, in the newly unfolding socio-material context many affordances also change. In short, parts of the socio-material environment and the resulting behavior patterns are continuously re-arranged and reconfigured and other affordances enter the situation and dissipate as the departure time of the train approaches or the coffee is finished (van Dijk and Rietveld, 2017). It means, even though Facebook has affordances that can be used by any user throughout Facebook platform, however users can create different meaning and interaction based on the different socio-material practice that being carried out. As Costa (2017) said, practice theories can enable media scholars to move away from the limits imposed by the affordance and algorithm paradigm, and can enable them to grasp the varieties of possible uses of social media.

6. CONCLUSION

Dealing with technology in social life can create a different meaning of human interaction. It becomes indeed relevant when we deal with controversial issue, such as LGBTQ in Indonesia, where there is pros and cons as a political issue. The understanding of LGBTQ between the two different groups is different. Knowing is constitutively entangled with the socio-material practices and the technological *affordances*. As Kimmerle, Moskaliuk, Oeberst and Cress (2015) said, community as a whole develops and constructs new knowledge while the community members also individually advance and refine their own knowledge. So individual learning and collaborative knowledge construction are interdependent and occur simultaneously. Furthermore, when we analyze the socio-material practices we cannot exclude the power issues between humans and Facebook's technology that can shape human interactions on both groups. This power issue is related to how users can take control and action when using Facebook *affordances*. According to Boyd (2011), networked technologies introduce new affordances for amplifying, recording, and spreading information and social acts. These affordances can shape the public and how people negotiate them. Finally, the limitation of this research is that we only analyze the socio-material practice on Facebook pages and did not analyze on the individual Facebook accounts. Therefore, it needs future research to explain the difference of interaction pattern between Facebook page and individual Facebook account.

ACKNOWLEDGEMENT

This work was supported by Deutscher Akademischer Austauschdienst e.V. (DAAD) - Indonesian German Scholarship Program.

REFERENCES

Bardone, E. (2011). *Seeking Chances (From Biased Rationality to Distributed Cognition*. Berlin: Springer.

Beneito-Montagut, R. (2011). Ethnography goes online: towards a user-centred methodology to research interpersonal communication on the internet. *Qualitative Research* 11(6) 716–735.

Bjørn, P and Østerlund, C. (2014). *Sociomaterial-Design, Bounding Technologies in Practice*. Switzerland: Springer.

Boyd, D. (2011). Social Network Sites as Networked Publics (Affordances, Dynamics, and Implications). In Zizi Papacharissi (ed.). *A Networked Self (Identity, Community, and Culture on Social Network Sites)*. New York: Routledge.

Caliandro, A. (2017). Digital Methods for Ethnography: Analytical Concepts for Ethnographers Exploring Social Media Environments. *Journal of Contemporary Ethnography* 1–28.

Costa, E. (2017). Social Media as Practices: an Ethnographic Critique of 'Affordances' and 'Context Collapse, *Working papers for the EASA Media Anthropology Network's 60th*. Retrieved May 25, 2019, from: http://www.media-anthropology.net/file/costa_socialmedia_as_practice.pdf

Couldry, N. (2004). Theorising Media as Practice. *Social Semiotics* Volume 14 Number 2, August 2004.

Corradi, Gessica & Gherardi, Silvia. 2010. Through the practice lens: Where is the bandwagon of practice-based studies heading? *Management Learning* 41(3) 265–283.

General Data Protection Regulation. Retrieved May 20, 2019, from: https://gdpr.algolia.com/gdpr-article-6.

Gherardi, S. (2009). "Knowing and learning in practice-based studies: an introduction", *The Learning Organization* Vol. 16 Issue: 5, pp.352-359.

Hammersley, M. (2006). Ethnography: problems and prospects. *Ethnography and Education*, 1:1, 3-14.

Harris, G and Abedin, B. (2015). Participating or Not Participating? A Sociomaterial Perspective of the Embeddedness of Online Communities in Everyday Life. *Australasian Conference on Information Systems*, Adelaide.

Hutchby, I. (2001). Technologies, Texts and Affordances. *Sociology* Vol. 35, No. 2, pp. 441-456.

Kimmerle, J, Moskaliuk, J, Oeberst, A and Cress, U. (2015) Learning and Collective Knowledge Construction With Social Media: A Process-Oriented Perspective. *Educational Psychologist*, 50:2, 120-13.

Orlikowski, W. J. (2007). Sociomaterial Practices: Exploring Technology at Work. *Organization Studies* 28(09): 1435–1448.

Orlikowski, W. J. 2009. "The sociomateriality of organisational life: considering technology in management research." *Cambridge Journal of Economics* 34 (2009): 125-141.

Postill, J. and Pink, S. (2012). Social Media Ethnography: The Digital Researcher in A Messy Web. *Media International Australia incorporating Culture and Policy 145 (145): 123-134*. November 2012.

Schatzki, T. R. (2001). 'Introduction: Practice Theory', In: Schatzki, T. R., K. Knorr Cetina and E. von Savigny (eds) 2001. *The Practice Turn in Contemporary Theory*, London: Routledge, pp. 1-14.

van Dijk, Ludger & Rietveld, Erik. 2017. Foregrounding Sociomaterial Practice in Our Understanding of Affordances: The Skilled Intentionality Framework. *Front. Psychol. 7:1969.*

Short Papers

ICT4D & THE SUSTAINABLE DEVELOPMENT GOALS

Franz Ferdinand Rothe
Vrije Universiteit Brussel, imec-SMIT, Pleinlaan 9, 1050 Brussels, Belgium

ABSTRACT

The field of ICT4D (ICT for Development) entails using ICTs in support of the international development agenda, such as efforts against poverty or for better education in developing countries. The conceptualisation of ICT4D strongly depends on what is understood as international development itself. Hence, this paper argues that the introduction of the United Nations' Sustainable Development Goals (SDGs) in 2015 can be understood as a caesura not only for conceptualising development, but, in turn, for conceptualising ICT4D, as well. On the basis of literature review, this paper analyses the SDG framework and applies it to theories of ICT4D, outlining to which extent this new development agenda requires new approaches to ICT4D. In doing so, this article aims to sensitise the reader towards the challenges and potential dilemmas emerging from this transition and to spark debate on how to conceptualise ICT4D in response.

KEYWORDS

ICT4D, Sustainable Development Goals, Policy Coherence

1. INTRODUCTION

The field of ICT4D (Information and Communication Technologies for Development) is driven by the conviction that ICTs can support efforts of international development[1], such as the fight against poverty, for better education or reduced inequalities. Over the past decades, the notion of ICT4D has evolved alongside the shifting paradigms of development itself (Zheng *et al.*, 2017). Having advanced from a modernist focus on North-South ICT transfer for economic growth, ICT4D has been attributed increasingly multi-dimensional potential, as the international community has embraced concepts such as human or sustainable development (Heeks, 2009; Thapa and Sæbø, 2014). Coming from the early enthusiasm around, for example, colourful laptops that promised to automatically modernise not only the African classrooms but also the continent's economies and societies, scholars have reached the more nuanced conception that ICTs are only as valuable (or harmful) for development, as the interventions in which they are embedded.

Given that what we mean by ICT4D thus depends on what we mean by development, this paper argues that the introduction of the United Nations' Sustainable Development Goals (SDGs) in 2015, which mark a caesura for conceptualising development, should in turn be seen as a caesura for conceptualising ICT4D as well. However, research and guidance regarding the implications of this new development agenda for using ICTs for development is scarce. This paper responds to this gap, by translating the SDG framework onto the field of ICT4D. On the basis of a literature review, this paper analyses the SDG framework and applies it to theories of ICT4D, outlining the implications of transitioning to the post-2015 concept of *sustainable development*. In doing so, this paper aims to sensitise the reader towards the challenges and potential dilemmas emerging from this transition, and to spark debate on how to conceptualise ICT4D in response.

[1] As opposed to its definition in the field of IT, the term development will be used according to its definition in international development studies, describing socio-economic advances in so-called developing countries and beyond.

2. WHAT IS NEW ABOUT THE SDGs?

ICT4D can be defined as "technology [being] used to help deliver on the international development agenda" (Heeks, 2018, p. 18). Defining the *international development agenda* is thus integral to conceptualising ICT4D. When the SDGs were adopted with the 2030 Agenda for Sustainable Development in September 2015, the set of 17 goals encompassing 169 targets were the outcome of several years of consultations with governments, international organisations, the private sector, academia, and civil society. Therefore, the SDG agenda, while not being uncontested, arguably comes closest to representing a shared agenda for international development.

In order to assess what this new agenda means for ICT4D, we must consider the novel nature of the SDGs, in contrast to their predecessors such as the Millennium Development Goals (MDGs), the agenda that guided development efforts from 2000 until 2015. As LeBlanc (2015) synopsises, "[t]he novelty of the SDGs [...] is that they aim to cover the whole sustainable development universe, which includes basically all areas of the human enterprise on earth" (p. 11). In comparison to the earlier agenda, the UN (2015) resolution on the SDGs defines an agenda of goals and targets that are *universal*, *global* and *integrated*.

These notions represent three novel characteristics of the SDGs, which are (1) the holistic scope of targets, (2) their applicability for all countries alike, and (3) their essential interconnectedness and interdependence. While the former of these aspects has been subject to research from many sides, the latter two shall be central to the remainder of the paper. Focusing on the implications for ICT4D, section 3 will demonstrate the link between (1) the topical and (2) the geographical conceptual expansion before we discuss their implications for (3) policy coherence in Section 4.

3. ICT4D & UNIVERSALITY

First and foremost, as compared to the 8 MDGs, the SDGs cover a much larger scope of development objectives with 17 goals and 169 associated targets. This large amount of new goals, covering areas across the social, environmental and economic dimensions of sustainable development, can be understood as new opportunities for ICTs to play a role in international development. While ICTs are featured surprisingly little in the SDGs, being mentioned in merely 4 of the 196 targets, they are recognised as integral drivers for sustainable development and a significant amount of research has been produced to make the implicit potentials of ICT to support the SDGs explicit (NetHope 2015; Ericsson 2015; ITU 2016).

However, to conclude that the widening scope of goals merely suggests a widening *playing field* for post-2015 ICT4D would be a short-sighted assumption. In fact, the holistic architecture of the SDGs goes far beyond these new topical areas. As the following paragraphs will demonstrate, it also widens the horizon of development in a geographical sense.

3.1 ICT 4 Global Development

As opposed to the MDGs, the SDGs acknowledge sustainable development as a global challenge, being "universal goals and targets which involve the entire world, developed and developing countries alike" (United Nations 2015, para. 5). In fact, this is strongly linked to the broadened topical scope. The Global North might be more developed with regard to *traditional* development issues such as absolute poverty or health, which were at the core of the MDGs. Areas such as climate change, sustainable production, or reducing inequalities, however, are as much a challenge for the Global North as they are for so-called developing countries (Bertelsmann Stiftung and SDNS, 2016).

In the words of Jeffrey Sachs, "[t]he United States, just like Mali, needs to learn to live sustainably. The rich countries like the poor have to promote more social inclusion, gender equality, and of course energy systems that are low carbon and resilient" (2015, p. 484). In a post-2015 world, there is hence no longer such a thing as a *developed world*.

3.2 'Everything' is ICT4D?

This widened topical and geographic understanding of development leads to a number of potential dilemmas, when applied to ICT4D. Following the holistic and universal interpretation, ICT4D becomes a field going far beyond its traditional conception. To give an example, using big data to improve public transport in Brussels does, according to this definition, represent as much of an ICT4D intervention, as does a smart farming project in Burkina Faso.

On the one hand, this corresponds with the development challenges of our time. On the other hand, however, it might be understandable if ICT4D practitioners question the practicality of such a definition of their field. While the old and largely overcome understanding of ICT4D as merely fostering economic growth in the Global South is clearly misaligned and counterproductive to the global development efforts, taking the SDG narrative literally could arguably pose the risk of diluting the notion into a meaningless catch-all term. These two poles thus provide a spectrum, reaching from a clearly outdated development concept to an approach that might prove too idealistic to (yet) fully apply to ICT4D. This paper does not aim at providing an answer to this dilemma. Much rather it hopes to sensitise stakeholders towards this spectrum, along which ICT4D must consciously and rationally be situated.

4. ICT4 INTEGRATED DEVELOPMENT

As indicated in Section 3, a further defining novelty of the SDG architecture can be found in the "deep interconnections and many cross-cutting elements across the new Goals and targets" (United Nations, 2015, para. 17). The network character of the goals adds another crucial element of complexity. As the goals and targets are *integrated and indivisible* (United Nations, 2015), coherence must be ensured between all of the SDGs' 169 targets. The network architecture of the SDGs shall at this point briefly be outlined, before its implications for ICT4D are assessed.

4.1 A Network of Goals

In a Working Paper for the UN Department of Economic and Social Affairs, David Le Blanc (2015) analyses the manifold links between the 169 targets, which spin a complex network between the 17 goals, as most areas of sustainable development are featured not only in their specific goal, but are highlighted in the targets of other related goals as well. This network architecture responds to the fact that "[t]he interlinkages [...] of the Sustainable Development Goals are of crucial importance in ensuring that the purpose of the new Agenda is realized" (United Nations, 2015, p.4).

Acknowledging these interdependencies between the SDGs could "correct one of the drawbacks of the MDGs, in which 'silo' goals encouraged silo policies and did not make links and trade-offs across areas explicit" (Le Blanc, 2015, p. 11). Translating this post-silo architecture into development action that does take the whole of the SDG Agenda into account, will represent one of the biggest challenges for development practicioners, including and in particular for those working in ICT4D. As the following sections will demonstrate, this transition bears another potential dilemma for ICT4D, which should be debated within the community.

4.2 Coherence for Sustainable Development

On the one hand, the interconnectedness of goals indicates that an intervention in one of the areas of sustainable development can simultaneously support other goals as well. On the other hand, however, if the intervention is not coherent with the entirety of the SDG framework, its effects can undermine other objectives of the agenda. Policy coherence between the various actions taken within the development sector thus represents a multi-directional challenge. If actors in certain areas of sustainable development disregard their potential effect on other goals, their interventions risk doing more damage than good. Without internal coherence, it will thus be impossible to deliver on the SDGs as a whole.

The SDGs therefore bring forward the concept of PCSD, which urges development actors to strive for coherence within and between the various areas of development cooperation and take into account their potential (side-)effect on other goals, to avoid that their interventions do more damage than good. Finding synergies - or, at least, preventing negative side-effects – hence presents a central challenge for ICT4D in post-2015 development.

4.3 SDGs as a Deadlock for ICT4D?

The idea that measures to support one aspect of development should not undermine the rest of the international development goals may appear self-evident and rather straightforward. On a closer look, however, the multi-directionality of coherence required for sustainable development oftentimes makes this a highly complex challenge. Obviously, this challenge is not exclusive to the field of ICT4D but an issue for everybody working in international development. Yet, the multi-dimensional externalities associated with ICTs make the matter of coherence particularly relevant and challenging when utilizing them in a development context. ICT4D projects are likely to have (side-)effects on the three pillars of the SDGs, since the use of ICTs affects environmental, social and economic matters. The economic footprint of the ICTs, the labour conditions in their production and the inequalities that can arise from digitally including some and excluding others are merely a few of these inherent detriments. When using ICTs to support a particular development goal, their potential positive impact is thus bound to come at a certain developmental price.

For ICT4D, this holistic conception of development thus reveals another dilemma. Should projects be abandoned if they are incoherent with other goals? Clearly, if ICT4D projects contribute to environmental pollution or child labour, they can hardly be called 4D. In practice, however, it becomes obvious that a radical interpretation of these claims could put ICT4D, and arguably most other development sectors, into a deadlock. Considering the wide scope of externalities that are related to ICTs, it is nearly impossible to practice ICT4D without negative development effects. This begs the question, where a line should be drawn to avoid putting ICT4D in a deadlock? When is a project's positive impact in its target area outweighed by its negative side-effects on others? Surely, there will not be a one-size-fits-all answer to this dilemma. Yet, it must be discussed how ICT4D actors can guarantee that these side-effects are being thoroughly and transparently assessed.

5. CONCLUSION

The introduction of the SDGs marked a caesura for conceptualising development. In turn, it must be understood as caesura for conceptualising ICT4D as well. As this paper demonstrated, applying the new principles at the core of the SDGs onto the field of ICT4D requires us to fundamentally rethink certain aspects of ICT4D. If we are serious about using ICTs in support of this new agenda, we cannot stop at the comfortable task of embracing its new topical scope. Much rather, we must equally open the Pandora's Box of considering the complexity that results from this transition.

Should ICT4D open up to the Global North, as development is no longer an exclusive challenge for the Global South? How close can ICT4D come to meeting the holistic and integrated SDG approach without becoming an unworkable utopia? How far can it afford to stay behind without failing or even undermining the SDGs by doing more damage than good? And how can practitioners, to whom these questions might not seem pressing or even relevant, be incentivised to acknowledge that sometimes no ICT4D project is the better choice for sustainable development? By outlining this scope of challenges that a serious integration of SDG principles in the field of ICT4D would entail, this paper hopes to spark a meaningful debate around the future of ICT4D.

REFERENCES

Bertelsmann Stiftung and SDNS (2016) *SDG Index & Dashboards: A Global Report.* Bertelsmann Stiftung.

Ericsson (2015) 'ICT & SDG - How Information and Communications Technologies can Achieve the Sustainable Development Goals.' Ericsson in collaboration with Earth Institute at Columbia University.

Heeks, R. (2009) *The ICT4D 2.0 manifesto where next for ICTs and international development?* Manchester: University of Manchester. Institute for development policy and management (IDPM). Development informatics group.

Heeks, R. (2018) *Information and communication technology for development (ICT4D)*. New York: Routledge. Available at: http://search.ebscohost.com/login.aspx?direct=true&scope=site&db=nlebk&db=nlabk&AN=1554067 (Accessed: 18 January 2018).

ITU (2016) *Advancing Sustainable Development Through Information and Communication Technologies: WSIS Action Lines Enabling SDGs*. Geneva: ITU.

Le Blanc, D. (2015) 'Towards integration at last? The sustainable development goals as a network of targets', *Sustainable Development*, 23(3), pp. 176–187.

Mackie, J., Ronceray, M. and Spierings, E. (2017) *Policy coherence and the 2030 Agenda: Building on the PCD experience.* Maastricht: ECDPM.

Malone, D. and O'Dwyer, K. J. (2014) 'Bitcoin Mining and its Energy Footprint', in. Institution of Engineering and Technology, pp. 280–285. doi: 10.1049/cp.2014.0699.

NetHope (2015) *SDG ICT Playbook - From Innovation to Impact*. Fairfax (VA): NetHope.

Nilsson, M., Griggs, D. and Visbeck, M. (2016) 'Map the interactions between Sustainable Development Goals', *Nature*, 534, pp. 320–323.

Sachs, J. D. (2015) *The Age of Sustainable Development*. Columbia University Press.

Thapa, D. and Sæbø, Ø. (2014) 'Exploring the link between ICT and development in the context of developing countries: a literature review', *The Electronic Journal of Information Systems in Developing Countries*, 64.

United Nations, G. A. (2015) *Transforming our world: the 2030 agenda for sustainable development (A/RES/70/1)*. New York: United Nations.

Zheng, Y. *et al.* (2017) 'Conceptualizing development in information and communication technology for development (ICT4D)', *Information Technology for Development*, pp. 1–14. doi: 10.1080/02681102.2017.1396020.

WORKING IN THE DIGITAL AGE: MERGING A STATUS QUO BIAS PERSPECTIVE AND REFLECTIVE PRATICE

Frederike Marie Oschinsky[1], Hans Christian Klein[2] and Bjoern Niehaves[3]
University of Siegen, Germany

ABSTRACT

The pillars of digital change (new role models, new competences, changed attitudes) are most visible in the everyday practice of staff. In the digital age of continuous transformations, we need a theoretical basis that is capable of describing an individual's behavior in situations of uncertainty, instability, uniqueness and value conflicts. We approach this theoretical gap by joining the vision of "Reflective Practice" (Schön, 1983) and the status quo bias perspective (Kim and Kankanhalli, 2009; Lee and Joshi, 2017). By proposing a three-step mixed-method study, we try to answer the question of how work can be actually designed in the digital age. Based on our insight, we seek to develop a guideline to help organizations frame the working conditions in a future-oriented and comprehensible way.

KEYWORDS

Digitalization, Digital Work, Rational Choice, Reflective Practitioner, Cognitive Bias, Status Quo Bias Perspective

1. INTRODUCTION

Digitization is changing the way we work and organize. The use of information technologies (IT) makes it possible to fulfil tasks more effectively and to maintain or even increase the quality of service and data security. At the same time, IT use can save time, reduce errors and streamline internal processes. Nevertheless, digital change is accompanied by new roles and modified needs for (IT) competence (e.g., Hill, 2014; Malsbender et al., 2014; Ogonek et al., 2018, 2016), as well as a changing attitude towards digital solutions (e.g., Ogonek et al., 2018). This triad has been intensively studied and provides the basis for our investigation.

In order to explain decision-making of employees in the digital age, we consider the fundamental work in decision research. Nobel prize winner Herbert A. Simon (e.g., Simon, 1944, 1946, 1997; see also Sherwood, 1990) has stated that employees do not have access to all the necessary information and cannot process all facts correctly. Rationality is 'bounded'. His work is more prominent than ever in the digital age. Despite the high value of using technologies, many benefit from them only to a limited extent and encounter IT with skepticism or even fear. They insist on learned procedures and known solutions, although this perseverance objectively entails disadvantages (e.g., temporal, financial and emotional costs). This behavior is known as 'status quo bias' (Kim and Kankanhalli, 2009; Polites and Karahanna, 2012; Lee and Joshi, 2017; Li et al., 2016).

Current acceptance models and their underlying theories (e.g., Davis, 1989) often neglect the explanatory power of the status quo bias. We rely on the work of "Reflective Practice" (Bousbaci, 2008; Habib, 2017; Schön, 1983) as it pioneered to include cognitive biases and heuristics to explain how people interpret their working life and shape their behaviour accordingly. For this reason, we propose to expand research on competence building in the digital age and to include the aspect of this cognitive bias in order to shape the education and training of staff. Our research question is: How can work in the digital age be actually designed? Based on our insight, we seek to develop a guideline to help organizations frame the working conditions in a future-oriented and comprehensible way. For addressing our objective, we briefly present the theoretical background and research framework and then discuss the structure of our three-step methodological approach. Finally, we give an outlook.

---

[1] frederike.oschinsky@uni-siegen.de
[2] christian.klein@uni-siegen.de
[3] bjoern.niehaves@uni-siegen.de

2. RELATED WORK

In his seminal work "Reflective Practitioner – How Professionals Think in Action", Donald Schön (1983) develops the concept of practitioners, which goes far beyond *experts* using standard solutions (p.21). This concept is the basis for our further investigation. The concept consists of three parts (A) Knowing-in-Action (KiA), (B) Reflection-in-Action (RiA), and (C) Reflection-on-Action (RoA). The core of the concept is the phenomenon of RiA, which therefore builds the focal point of our framework.

KiA. Knowledge often is an unconscious and partly subconscious process. It forms the basis for action. Knowledge can be achieved through repetitions in a repertoire of expectations, representations and techniques in the practice of the expert (ibid., p.60). The repetitions make knowledge more and more specialized.

RiA. In everyday life, practitioners apply knowledge tacitly and implicitly (e.g., implicit perceptions, judgements, and skills). Schön describes the phenomena with the phrases "thinking on your feet", "keeping your wits about you" or "learning by doing" (ibid., p.49-50; p.54). RiA is not a matter of conscious thinking, but of feeling and intuition. The practitioner acts and works on a task and – sometimes ad hoc – situations arise in which he automatically calls up his existing knowledge (ibid, p.50). One can understand this as 'rules of thumb', illustrating the proximity to heuristics and cognitive distortions (ibid, p.63). The knowledge of the practitioner (KiA) in a rationally bounded manner. RiA can be divided in three subcategories:

(1) Framing – F: First, the problem framework is defined. When a satisfying solution is found, the process stops. Every practitioner understands the task of finding a satisfactory solution as unique and has to define and frame the problem in the first step (ibid., p.129).

(2) Reframing – RF: Second, the problem frame might need to be reset and reframed due to the complexity of a problem. The focus of the practitioner will be shifted away from the problem at hand to a different perspective of the situation. This can open up new design possibilities. A practitioner needs to solve the new problem with a kind of craftsmanship (ibid, p.130).

(3) Experiment – X: Third, the practitioner has to try whether the new solution is satisfactory. It is a kind of experiment. The new solutions will be examined with a new problem framework. The practitioner succeeds in spontaneously comparing, evaluation and finally favoring solutions (ibid., p.130).

RoA. The practitioner thoroughly thinks about the result of the situation or task. This reflection improves the practitioner's way of approaching the next task. This helps to improve the 'processing economics' (ibid., p.60) and possibly leads to 'overlearning' (ibid. p.60-61). Thus, it automatically influences KiA.

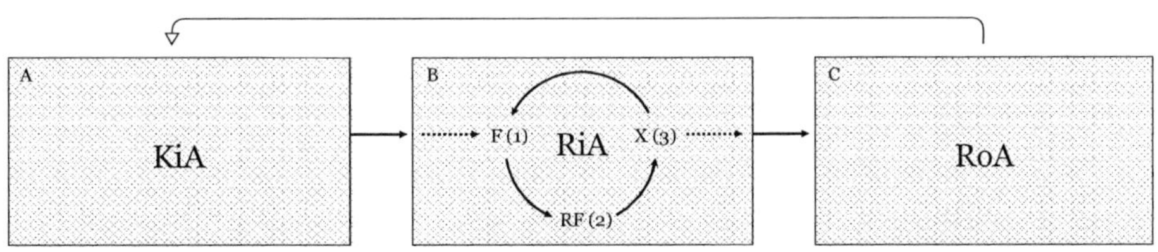

Figure 1. Reflection in Practice

Bounded rationality has its origins in the field of psychology (Tversky and Kahneman, 1974). Due to the explanatory power of the approach, it has been adopted in many other disciplines and serves to understand many previously puzzling phenomena. The approach follows the assumption that decisions are not always based on the weighing of costs and benefits. Instead, human judgment is influenced by heuristics and cognitive biases. Heuristics, or 'rules of thumb', help decision making in complex situations under uncertainty, and in situations that do not allow for long and reasoned reflection (Schön, 1983). However, cognitive biases, as systematic deviations from rationality, can lead to suboptimal and undesirable outcomes, for instance, because not all alternatives were considered or the effort of action wrongly estimated (Kahneman, 2003).

Undesirable outcomes are what we often observe when someone sticks only to a habitual decision making and behavior, even when better alternatives exist (e.g., the department head does not consider IT solutions, although digital workspaces require digital components (Fleischmann et al., 2014)). Samuelson & Zeckhauser (1988) were at the forefront to distinguish between three main constructs that influence the so called 'status quo bias': rational decision-making, cognitive misperception, and psychological commitment.

In IS research, Lee & Joshi (2017) supplement the perspective and offer the constructs. In particular, the authors adopted the categories and subdivided them even further. The dimensions are briefly summarized in the following.

Rational decision-making is not always possible under uncertainty. Uncertainty is the individuals' lack of information and/or expertise about the alternatives, which may impose search and analysis costs, and lead to decision paralysis (Samuelson and Zeckhauser, 1988). The concept was later on divided into anxiety costs as well as search and analysis costs (Lee and Joshi, 2017).

Cognitive misperception consists of loss aversion and anchoring effects addressing the perceived value. Loss aversion illustrates that individuals weigh losses heavier than gains in making decisions (e.g., Kahneman and Tversky, 1979; Kahneman, 2011). Anchoring effects refer to the individuals' propensity of setting a starting value and then assessing changes with reference to the initial state (Tversky & Kahneman, 1974).

Psychological commitment has three parts: sunk costs, regret avoidance and the effort to feel in control. Sunk costs in sequential decisions describe the continual selection of the same choice, where individuals' desire to justify previous commitments to a course of action by making subsequent commitments (Samuelson and Zeckhauser, 1988). Regret avoidance, which was later on divided into the categories regret avoidance and social norms (Lee and Joshi, 2017) shows that individuals are likely to avoid consequences in which they could make the wrong choice, even if in advance the decision appeared correct given the information available at the time (Samuelson and Zeckhauser, 1988). Finally, the effort to feel in control, which was later on added by the term 'self-efficacy' (Lee and Joshi, 2017), refers contexts where people have the freedom to make choices and thus perceive that they control the situation' (Samuelson and Zeckhauser, 1988).

3. FRAMEWORK

In merging the status quo bias perspective and reflection in action, we focus on two important points:

"Problem-ignoring". Type I-III occur when the application of existing knowledge (e.g., executing a standard solution) happens without reflection, and is thus based on a bias. A suboptimal solution thus appears to be the 'best' answer to a task.

"Not getting out of the wheel". Type IV-VI occur when the evaluation of the variants is not done rationally, but based on biases. Therefore, a rationally better solution is discarded.

After highlighting these two points, we identify two prominent cases where it is absolutely necessary to think rationally. Thus, the status quo bias has to be comprehensibly reduced. First, thorough RiA must be made possible. The practitioner has to recognize a situation as unique and new and thus frame a new problem in it, which involves reasoning and weighing of alternatives. Second, if the practitioner in the iterative process of RiA has to somehow recognize an outcome of his experiments as a satisfying solution. He has to formulate: "We stop experimenting. This is the solution and we start with the implementation!" The two cases where it is absolutely necessary to think rationally, will be acknowledged in our future studies.

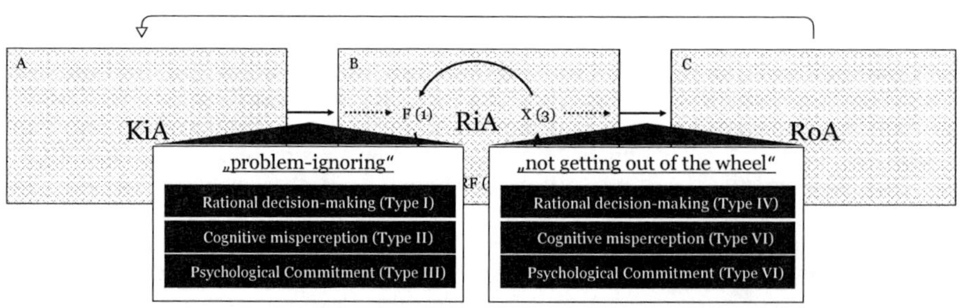

Figure 2. "Bounded" Reflection in Practice

4. RESEARCH AGENDA AND CONCLUDING REMARKS

Our aim is to develop an integrated model based on the status quo bias perspective and reflection in action. In order to obtain a holistic view of technology acceptance and the intended use of staff in the digital age among different organizations, we will conduct a preliminary mixed-method study in a municipality. The study will also be carried out in one small-sized and one medium-sized enterprise and a university of applied sciences. The three-stage mixed-methods study consists of a qualitative preliminary study, a pilot test and a quantitative survey. A subsequent workshop, which can be attended analogously and digitally, aims to mirror the results in practice, draw conclusions about new job profiles and shape and strengthen leadership. The findings of the study will be summarized and made available to the public free of charge. The study is structured as follows:

Qualitative preliminary study. Focus group with public administration managers to develop an activity scenario that includes innovative technologies (e.g., artificial intelligence). Moreover, we present the status quo bias perspective and the reflection in action approach. Thereupon, we identify missing variables.

Pilot test. The newly developed scenario is used as a priming tool for our questionnaire. The pilot test itself contains this scenario and the extended list of variables. In order to test the comprehensibility of our questions and the meaningfulness of the formulations, we perform a test with a small sample of employees ($N = 5$).

Survey. After revising the questionnaire, we carry out a large-scale online survey ($N = 300$). The aim is to develop our model in an explorative manner and to search for significant correlation and cause-effect relationships. After conscientious data cleansing and analysis, the results will be summarized. To present and discuss the project results, a workshop will be held, which can be attended in analogue and digital form. The aim is a future-oriented discourse on competence development and digital work.

To conclude, we seek to develop a guideline to help organizations frame the working conditions in a future-oriented and comprehensible way. By proposing a three-step mixed-method study, we try to answer the question of how work can be actually designed in the digital age. Because the pillars of digital change (new role models, new competences, changed attitudes) are most visible in the everyday practice of staff, we seek to test the newly developed theoretical basis (joining the status quo bias perspective and reflection in action). The findings of our study can be applied and refined in various settings of digital work.

REFERENCES

Bousbaci, R., 2008. "Models of Man" in Design Thinking: The "Bounded Rationality" Episode. Design Issues 24, 38–52.

Davis, F.D., 1989. Perceived Usefulness, Perceived Ease of Use, and User Acceptance of Information Technology. MIS Quarterly 13, 319–340.

Fleischmann, M., Amirpur, M., Benlian, A., Hess, T., 2014. Cognitive Biases in Information Systems Research: A Scientometric Analysis. ECIS 2014 Proceedings.

Habib, H., 2017. A Study of Reflective Practice and its Role For Teachers 5, 4.

Hill, H., 2014. Wandel von Verwaltungskultur und Kompetenzen im digitalen Zeitalter, in: Transparenz, Partizipation, Kollaboration. Nomos Verlagsgesellschaft mbH & Co. KG, pp. 123–148.

Kahneman, D., 2011. Thinking, Fast and Slow. Penguin, London.

Kahneman, D., 2003. Maps of Bounded Rationality: Psychology for Behavioral Economics. American Economic Review 93, 1449–1475.

Kahneman, D., Tversky, A., 1979. Prospect Theory: An Analysis of Decision under Risk. Econometrica 47, 263.

Kim, H.-W., Kankanhalli, A., 2009. Investigating User Resistance to Information Systems Implementation: A Status Quo Bias Perspective. MIS Quarterly 33, 567–582.

Lee, K., Joshi, K., 2017. Examining the use of status quo bias perspective in IS research: need for re-conceptualizing and incorporating biases. Inf. Syst. J. 27, 733–752.

Li, J., Liu, M., Liu, X., 2016. Why do employees resist knowledge management systems? An empirical study from the status quo bias and inertia perspectives. Computers in Human Behavior 65, 189–200.

Malsbender, A., Hoffmann, S., Becker, J., 2014. Aligning Capabilities and Social Media Affordances for Open Innovation in Governments. Australasian Journal of Information Systems 18, 317–330.

Ogonek, N., Distel, B., Rehouma, M.B., Hofmann, S., Räckers, M., 2018. Digitalisierungsverständnis von Führungskräften. Berichte des NEGZ, Nationalen E-Government Kompetenzzentrum e.V., Berlin, Münster 2.

Ogonek, N., Räckers, M., Becker, J., 2016. Rollen und Kompetenzen für eine erfolgreiche öffentliche Verwaltung im digitalen Zeitalter. Studie im Auftrag des IT-Planungsrats, Nationalen E-Government Kompetenzzentrum e.V., Berlin, Münster.

Polites, G.L., Karahanna, E., 2012. Shackled to the Status Quo: The Inhibiting Effects of Incumbent System Habit, Switching Costs, and Inertia on New System Acceptance. MIS Quarterly 36, 21–42.

Samuelson, W., Zeckhauser, R., 1988. Status quo bias in decision making. Journal of Risk and Uncertainty 1, 7–59.

Schön, D.A., 1983. The reflective practitioner: How professionals think in action. Routledge.

Sherwood, F.P., 1990. The Half-Century's "Great Books" in Public Administration. Public Administration Review 50.

Simon, H.A., 1997. Administrative Behavior, 4th ed. Free Press, New York.

Simon, H.A., 1946. The Proverbs of Administration. Public Administration Review 6, 53–67.

Simon, H.A., 1944. Decision-Making and Administrative Organization. Public Administration Review 4, 16.

Tversky, A., Kahneman, D., 1974. Judgment under uncertainty: Heuristics and biases. science 185, 1124–1131.

A METHODOLOGY FOR IMPROVING NEET YOUTH EMPLOYMENT IN THE ICT LABOUR MARKET

Luciana Oliveira, Anabela Mesquita and Adriana José de Oliveira
CEOS.PP ISCAP Polytechnic of Porto
Rua Jaime Lopes Amorim, s/n 4465-004 S. Mamede de Infesta, Matosinhos, Portugal

ABSTRACT

A global youth employment crisis and the transformation of the ICT labour market has been raising severe concerns and worldwide recommendations for the coordination of cross-field and cross-level agents, as well as the need for coherent strategies based on research and dialogue between workers, employers, organizations and youth groups to decrease the number of NEET. In this context, the Direction Employment project sets as a main objective to promote the integration of underprivileged minorities into the labour market, namely the NEET youth. To address the identified difficulties, an experimental educational and social intervention model was developed and will be implemented in different EU regional contexts, combining innovative pedagogical methodologies with social support structures for young people. This paper presents a methodology for the convergence of the main axis concerning NEET youth unemployment in the ICT labour market, namely educators and trainers, ICT employers and professionals, psychologists and young people, as well as the expected outcomes and key indicators for the assessment of the desired social/professional impact.

KEYWORDS

NEET Youth, Unemployment, ICT Labour Market, Methodology

1. INTRODUCTION

Despite the modest recent economic recovery, unemployment remains a major global concern. According to the International Labour Organization (ILO, 2017), unemployment affects especially young people who are entering the job market in record numbers and who are three times as much likely as adults to remain unemployed. A particularly concerning group are the young people who are not in employment, education or training (NEET) and, above all, young women. The youth employment crisis and reducing youth NEET rates is one of the primary targets of the 2030 United Nations Agenda for Sustainable Development Goals (UN, 2015).

The technological unemployment, which regained increased visibility in society and research, as a result of the 4th Industrial Revolution (Avis, 2018), has been causing high social and organizational distress, as it remains uncertain if there will be enough decent employment opportunities for the 25.6 million young persons entering the labour market between 2017 and 2030 (WEF, 2018). In the current combination of industrial revolution and gold rush, countless businesses have been jumping to trends by developing digital applications and platforms designed to monetise the new areas of potential that arise every day. *Platformization* is indeed one of the 4.0 Industry mega-trends (Baums, 2015), together with big data, and artificial intelligence. This represents both tremendous opportunities for business and organizations and challenges for the constant need to re-skill or up-skill the labour force with hard skills and soft skills, with special impact over the ICT market professionals. It also requires profound social changes to cope with the digitalization of personal and professional life (Gray and Rumpe, 2015, Rintala and Suolanen, 2005).

In the world of labour, however, it would be inappropriate to expect that it is a question simply of 'training' for the 'new digital economy' or of investment in skills and qualifications (Degryse, 2016, EC, 2015). In fact, and concerning youth employment, coordination and coherent strategies are needed based on research and dialogue with workers' and employers' organizations and youth groups (ILO).

In this paper, we introduce the Direction Employment (DE) project and the corresponding methodology proposal for addressing the youth unemployment crisis in the ICT labour market. The main expected outcomes and key indicators for professional and social impact are also presented and discussed in a call for participation among the researchers, social actors and companies.

2. THE DIRECTION EMPLOYMENT PROJET

The DE project sets as a main objective to craft and apply in different EU regional contexts, and within of timeline of 3 years, an experimental educational and social-professional intervention model, which prepares disadvantaged NEET young people for the structural labor market changes and digital transition. The consortium of the project is made up of partners from different sectors - NGOs, higher education, companies - from Bulgaria, Lithuania, Slovenia, Portugal, Ireland and Italy, who have a proven track-record of working for the social and labour market inclusion of young people from marginalized minorities.

The model and methodology are fully oriented towards the ICT labor market and fully aligned with the global tendencies for integral and democratic pedagogy, as well as with the top drivers of the digital transition, e.g. evolving preferences and behaviors of the business sector, globalization and new labor markets opportunities, coping with the increased pressure for learning and relevant knowledge and skills, increased demand for compliance with new and diverse standards and regulations.

The project is targeted to disadvantaged NEET youth aged 20-29 years at the European level, comprising the inclusion of specific groups at the local contexts of the participating countries, such as women, LGBT, immigrants and ROMA. The methodology for addressing the NEET youth unemployment crisis of this specific target is presented in the following section.

2.1 The 4.0 DE Methodology

The project's methodology is organized into seven main iterative stages, which combine research, intervention, evaluation and informing/reporting/refinement, as illustrated in Figure 1.

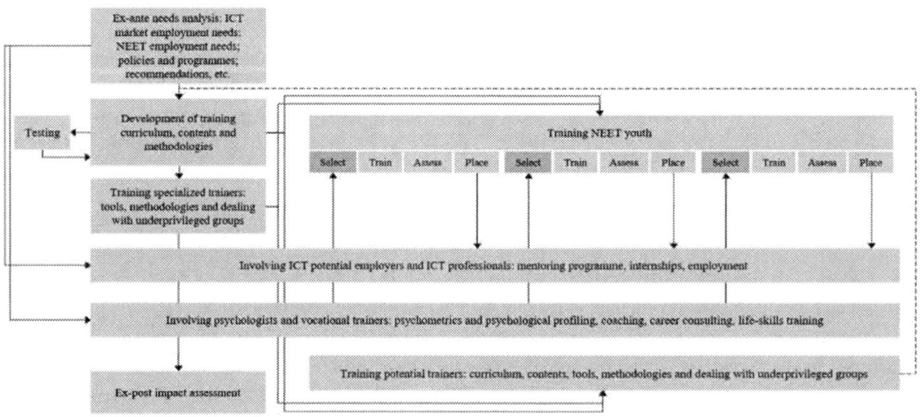

Figure 1. Overview of the 4.0 DE Methodology

The design stages are implemented at the national level, among the project's partners, and the informing/reporting among stages is also conducted transnationally, to benefit continuous improvement based on multicultural settings.

2.1.1 Ex-ante Needs Analysis

The first stage of the methodology consists of an ex-ante analysis of the ICT market and NEET youth employment needs, together with existing governmental and non-governmental employment and training policies and programs. This analysis is conducted not only on current needs, but also on future expectations and predictions for the ICT labour market and youth training. At this stage, desk research, questionnaires and interviews are conducted to gather quantitative and qualitative data and information that is used to provide recommendations as input for the development of a training curricula, contents and methodologies.

2.1.2 Development and Testing of Training Curriculum and Contents

An initial desk research on predictions and future trends for the ICT labour market is conducted during the methodology design, to establish provisional a set of domain areas, at the European level, to be included in the training curriculum. These areas include computer literacy, mathematics and logic, programming and web development. After that, the curriculum is tested with a group of 15 NEET young students and trainers using the short test-class sessions approach. Feedback and follow-ups are collected and reflected in the curriculum, which is, therefore, redesigned and adapted to local contexts. As the final step of the preparation of training, the consortium ensures the certification of the training by appropriate EU or international recognized standards (i.e. ECVET, certificate for vocational training (CP or FP) etc.).

2.1.3 Implementation of Training and Socio-Professional Support Structures for NETT Youth

Based on the ex-ante needs analysis and on the developed curriculum and contents, three series of seven months long training of up to thirty participants each are implemented in Europe. Each series is arranged in four main stages, as illustrated in Figure 1: one month for profiling and selection of participants, five months for core training and one final month for examination of competences and placement in the labour market. Psychologists and vocational trainers are involved in the selection phase to conduct psychometrics and psychological profiling, and also during the core training, to provide coaching, career consulting and life-skills training. The involvement of potential employers and professionals begins together with the core training in order to provide mentoring and internships to trainees, though their role is more prominent as labour market entry facilitators.

All through each of the three series of selection, training and placement the NEET youth will be accompanied by psychologists, vocational trainers, potential employers and ICT professionals. This is aimed at nurturing both personal and professional development of NEET youth, as well as building the necessary social settings for their market entry. Together with the vocational training and mentoring, in-family work with parents and siblings, personal development support, training visits, cultural development and meetings with ICT industries are included as continuous support initiatives.

In parallel, analysis of the group and individual experiences will be conducted, and feedback to the education methodologies and trainers will be provided on monthly basis. Reports of learning metrics, such as activity, learning flow, laziness etc., will be provided, and indexes for personal development will be introduced. The initial estimation of the trained NEET young students is 420, with at least 70% of the in-class training attended, and at least 90% of the course hours taken. The foreseen success rate of the trainees is 65%.

2.1.4 Development and Implementation of Training for Trainers (ToT)

Together with the development and implementation of training for NETT youth, a mobile smart classroom toolkit for training of potential trainers will also be prepared. The toolkit purpose is to train new trainers, and to transfer the 4.0 DE methodology into new regions of the participating countries. At least 2 new regions per country will be approached, and short-term trainings will be organized in parallel with the NEET youth main training. At least one train of new trainers per take-in (three overall) will be organized using the following structure: 3 months of MOOC combined with 3 days on-site training in preselected regions. The main criteria for selection of a new region will be to have at least 20 trainees enrolled in the course. The course content will be based on the following ToT curriculum modules: (a) how to use the curriculum; (b) how to prepare digital contents; (c) mobile smart classroom toolkit utilization; and (g) working with socially vulnerable groups. The ToT also envisions the creation of synergies among trainers to improve the curriculum, contents and pedagogical strategies for NEET youth training.

2.1.5 Ex-post and Impact Analysis

An ex-post and impact analysis and assessment will be conducted at the end of each of the training cycles, and six months after the NEET youth placement in the labour market. This is to ensure proper analysis and improvement of the methodology, the convenient personal and professional follow-up of trainees in the labour market and the measurement of employment rates and social impact. To do so, the World Bank Social Safeguards methodology and the Aspen Institute Social Impact methodology will be used together with other in-house developed social impact and assessment tools, which will be informed, among others, by peer reviews and empathic deep interviews with NEET trainees, trainers, employers and other stakeholders.

The WBS Safeguards propose, among others, guidelines for the Assessment and Management of Environmental and Social Risks and Impacts which set out responsibilities for assessing, managing and monitoring environmental and social risks and impacts associated with each stage of a project supported by the Bank, in order to achieve environmental and social outcomes consistent with the Environmental and Social Standards (ESSs).

2.2 Expected Outcomes

The methodology of the project envisions three main domains of expected outcomes: tangible outputs, research outputs and social impact. The tangible outputs include the development and provision of an education/training model, a curriculum and contexts for the upskilling/reskilling of NEET youth in the ICT labour market and a toolkit/course for training trainers. The research outputs are expected to emerge from the project's methodology, from the synergies established with trainers, stakeholders and researchers as well as from the project's annual international conferences. These consist of methodologies, current state analysis, models, forecasts, revisions, recommendations, assessments and results expressed in tools, reports and scientific publications.

The most relevant expected outcome resides on the potential of the social impact achieved with the methodology of the project, this is why the methodology is key and subject of revision. The evaluation of the social impact will be based on the following key indicators: (1) 52% of the trainees have received placements; (b) 75% of the trainees have reported changes in behaviour/self-assessment; and (c) *55% of the employers have reported changes in their perception of the employability of disadvantaged NEET youth, which leads to increased sustainability.

3. CONCLUSION

This paper presents a methodology for the convergence of the main axis concerning NEET youth unemployment in the ICT labour market, namely educators and trainers, ICT employers and professionals, psychologists and young people. At his stage, the main contribution relies on the conceptual and practical potential of the methodology to address the needs of the multiple key-players in the integration of NEET youth in the ICT labour market, providing guidelines and procedures for the convergence of synergies that are in line with core European and global recommendations.

Since the methodology design and procedures reunite cross-field and cross-level of domains of expertise, it can be applied to other specific targets for researchers and practitioners aiming at addressing local and global employability issues.

The main limitations of this work, at the stage, reside essentially on the absence of a detailed ex-ante needs assessment as an entry point, which is not yet fully conducted, but which will be presented to the scientific and social community in future research.

ACKNOWLEDGEMENT

This work is supported by the EEA and Norway Grants for Youth Employment within the project Direction Employment, project index no. 2017-1-294.

REFERENCES

Avis, J. 2018. Socio-technical imaginary of the fourth industrial revolution and its implications for vocational education and training: a literature review. *Journal of Vocational Education & Training,* 70, 337-363.

Baums, A. 2015. Industry 4.0: we don't need a new industrial policy but a better regulatory framework. *Social Europe,* 21.

Degryse, C. 2016. Digitalisation of the economy and its impact on labour markets. *ETUI Research Paper-Working Paper.*

EC 2015. A Digital Single Market Strategy for Europe. European Commission.

Gray, J. & RUMPE, B. 2015. Models for digitalization. *Software & Systems Modeling,* 14, 1319-1320.

Ilo 2017. Global Employment Trends for Youth 2017: Paths to a better working future. Geneva: International Labour Organization.

Rintala, N. & Suolanen, S. 2005. The implications of digitalization for job descriptions, competencies and the quality of working life. *Nordicom Review,* 26, 53-67.

UN 2015. Transforming our world: the 2030 Agenda for Sustainable Development. United Nations.

WEF 2018. The Future of Jobs Report 2018. Geneva: The World Economic Forum.

A MOBILE APP TO EXPLORE CULTURAL AND HISTORICAL ASSOCIATIONS BETWEEN EUROPE AND THE ARAB AND THE ISLAMIC WORLDS

Ahmed Dahroug, Mohamed Aborizka[1], Martín López-Nores[2] and José Juan Pazos-Arias[2]
[1]*Arab Academy for Science, Technology and Maritime Transport*
Marshal Ahmed Ismail Street square 1159, El-Sheraton buildings, Cairo, Egypt
[2]*Department of Telematics Engineering, University of Vigo*
EE Telecomunicación, Campus Universitario s/n, Vigo, Spain

ABSTRACT

Globalization and migration patterns have led to a significant intensification of the encounters between Europeans, on one hand, and Arabs and Muslims, on the other. Increasingly, politics, economics and culture transcend national boundaries, but the relations between Europe and the Arab and Islamic worlds are threatened by polarization and hostility. Grounded on theories of sociology, pedagogy and cognition, this paper presents a mobile app that seeks to promote mutual knowledge and understanding by highlighting the associations between the two sides, driven by the commonalities and disparities between the historical characters of Richard I of England and Salah ad-Din.

KEYWORDS

Mobile Applications, Historical and Cultural Symmetries, Storytelling, Multi-Perspective Education

1. INTRODUCTION

History and cultural heritage are often presented at schools, at museums and in the media in strongly-politicized ways that nurture attachment to the idea of homogeneous nations that transcend class divisions and erase local specificity (Phillips, 1996; Jaskulowski and Surmiak, 2017; Sung and Yang, 2009). The reinforcement of such siloed and one-sided structures of collective memory is seen as one of the most pressing contemporary challenges (Al Ashmawi et al., 2012). Accordingly, many scholars and institutions have advocated for cultural diversity and the promotion of transnational understandings of History, focusing on pedagogy to embed democratic principles of inclusion, inquiry, multiple interpretations and freedom of expression (Holden, 1996; Guyver, 2016; Bodenhamer, 2012).

Since textbooks have fixed structures, museum exhibitions are quasi-static, and most of the mass media have well-defined editorial policies (not to say ideological bias), the use of Internet-enabled devices and social networks could be one key to realizing a shift to these new models, helping people develop awareness of their own personal and national identities through an understanding of their own and others' histories and cultures (Bellino and Williams, 2017; Wong, 2015). In this line of thinking, we have developed one mobile application that delivers narratives and quiz games focused on the relationships between Europe, on the one hand, and the Arab and the Islamic worlds, on the other. The goal is to foster reflection and re-interpretation of history and heritage driven by the commonalities and disparities between two notable historical characters, namely Richard I of England and Salah ad-Din, who have been traditionally regarded as heroes by one side and villains by the other because of their roles in the Third Crusade. These two characters help to develop an interactive experience grounded on the three core principles highlighted in (Al Ashmawi et al., 2012):

1) Reflecting the diversity of Europe and the Arab and Islamic worlds.
2) Acknowledging the positive aspects of intercultural encounters.
3) Developing a multi-perspective approach to the study of the past.

Next section presents the main features of the app, along with a set of snapshots. Section 2 summarizes the results of preliminary evaluation, conducted by means of questionnaires on a small sample of volunteers from Spain and Egypt. Section 4 contains conclusions and a motivation for further development and testing.

2. APP DESIGN AND FEATURES

Figure 1 shows the starting screen of the app, which provides brief descriptions and visual contents about the different locations around the Mediterranean Sea that were relevant to the lives of Richard I and Salah ad-Din, as well as to the historical event of the Third Crusade. These locations were chosen to quickly highlight the diverse cultural landscape of the 12th century and the notable differences to the political maps of the 21st.

The app offers successive rounds of storytelling, gameplay and reflection, each one focused on a different reflective topic: "*Life in year 1180//575*", "*Political, military and religious leaders*", "*Alliances around the Mediterranean*", "*Fighting and co-existing*", "*811//835 years later*". These topics are weaved together by successive bits of a story (see Figure 2) that serve to confront the points of view of an English peasant and a shepherd from Jerusalem, about their societies, their political leaders, their culture, their faith, their involvement in the Battle of Jaffa, and the aftermath of the Crusade, when neither side was entirely satisfied with the results. The writing was supervised by Humanities experts in order to reinforce the increasingly-recognized capabilities of storytelling to integrate multiple viewpoints in cultural settings (Wong, 2015).

Figure 1. Initial screens

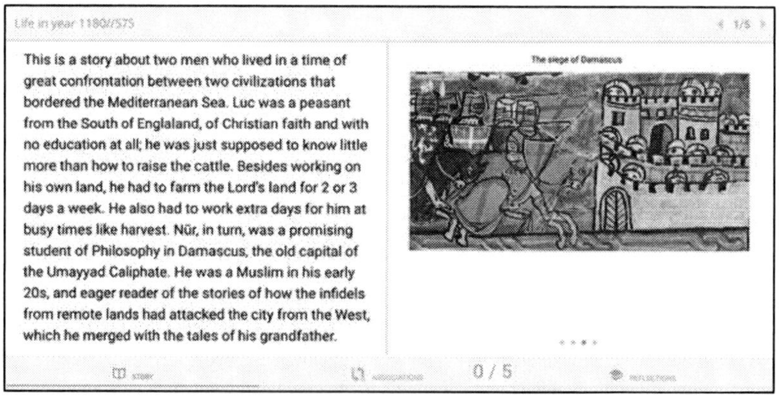

Figure 2. A bit of a story and related visual contents

The gameplay features lie within the exploration of the associations among the selected locations and the historical characters, filling in some questions left blank by the experts. Figure 3 shows a mesh of concepts and connecting properties related to the reflective topic of "*Political, military and religious leaders*". We have developed these associations, again with the aid of Humanities experts, in order to delve into the common and opposing features between Richard I and Salah ad-Din. Likewise, within the reflective topic of "*811 or 835 years later*", we have developed a symmetry between the history of Richard I of England and Salah ad-Din and the modern-day events of the Gulf Wars, trying to favor retention thanks to associations with the characters of Tony Blair (who, just like Richard I, had power in England and was educated in Oxford) and Saddam Hussein (a ruler from the Arab world, born in Tikrit, Iraq, just like Salah ad-Din).

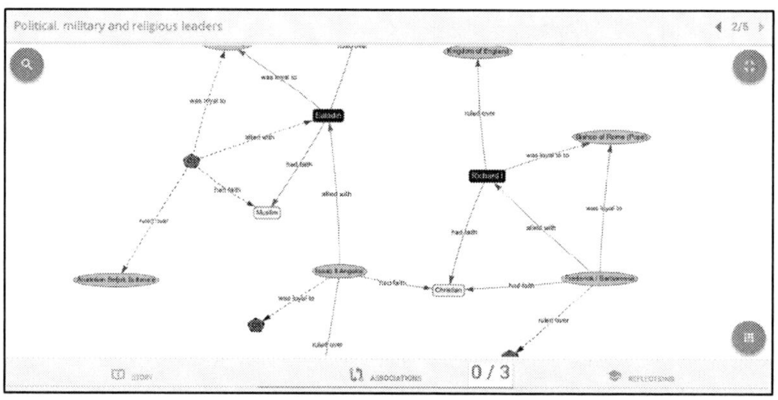

Figure 3. A mesh of associations and questions.

The user can drag the nodes around, zoom in/out and click on the pale blue nodes to display a gallery of visual contents related to the corresponding characters, locations or events. If he/she clicks on the question nodes (labeled Q1 to Q4 in Fig. 3), a pop-up appears including a question title and a set of choices (Figure 4). The user must reply correctly to all the questions before the next reflective topic is unlocked.

In relation to each reflective topic, the user can also display a handful of highlights, chosen by Humanities experts according to the messages that we aim to convey and the reflection we aim to instigate, with a particular focus on acknowledging the positive aspects of intercultural encounters before and after the 12th century. By clicking on each pieces of text, the user can again display a gallery of pictures and/or videos related to each fact. The user can give some quick feedback too, by clicking on one of the emojis of Fig. 5, to indicate different emotions: "*that's good to know*", "*that makes me think*", "*that's surprising*", "*I knew that already*" and "*who cares!*". This feedback is one of the sources of information for the experiments to conduct in the future for the full validation of our proposal. Prior to that, we have resorted to volunteers and questionnaires for the preliminary evaluation of the next section.

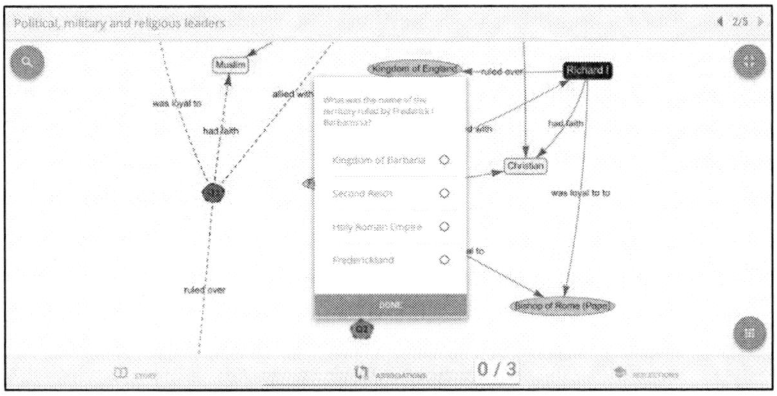

Figure 4. A multiple-choice question

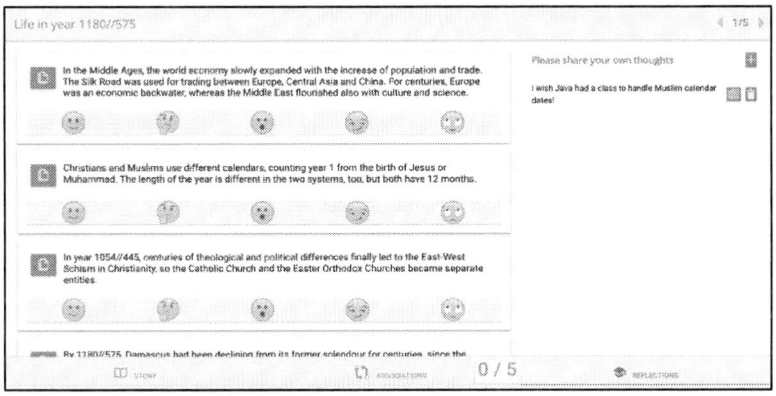

Figure 5. Seeking quick feedback about reflection points

3. PRELIMINARY EVALUATION

The first version of our app has been assessed in collaboration with 16 volunteers from Spain and Egypt (9+7) through experiments conducted in January and February 2019. The assessment looked at the feedback gathered through the emojis interface and the replies to a paper-based questionnaire.

The volunteers tried the app in one only session each, lasting for an average of 35 min. Then, they proceeded to fill in the questionnaire, which contained 31 statements to rate on a Likert scale, plus 8 questions requiring textual answers (about the user experience, the features they liked the most and the least, suggested improvements, etc.). The results yield the following observations:

- While the users were faced with an average of 13.2 highlights in the app, they rated only 4.7 with one of the emojis, either because they did not read the rest of the highlights or they did not find any of the emojis to be representative enough. From among the replies, 62% of the users would express interest, thinking or surprise; 32% would click on the smirking face, and only 6% would express indifference or lack of interest.
- Nearly 1/4 of the users had negative opinions about the app, and more than 1/3 did not perceive much added value in the graph visualizations of concepts and associations. This datum correlates with their suggestion that it would be better to use the app on a larger screen than offered by a smartphone, and that things would be much easier to understand with a teacher or guide browsing/explaining the contents. In contrast, the features related to the bits of the stories, the multiple-choice questions and the reflection points were appealing to nearly 88% of the users.

- 37% of the users indicated that they ended up with a richer understanding of the happenings of the 12th century, while 56% had a neutral opinion. It is likely that the statement in the questionnaire was too ambitious for the relatively short time spent with the app.

We are using the feedback gathered during these experiments to update the implementation of the app and to complete its contents. More extensive evaluation will be conducted once the new version has been finalized, with a broader spectrum of participants and an effort to use the app in primary/secondary education settings.

4. CONCLUSIONS AND FUTURE WORK

We have created and tested a mobile app that aims to contribute to bridging the gap between Europe and the Arab and Islamic worlds through a new pedagogical approach, rooted on the historical and cultural similarities and differences existing among locations, characters, events and any other elements of already-established identities and dominant narratives. Our design integrates different means to instigate curiosity, reflection and re-interpretation from a multi-perspective approach.

Our preliminary evaluation has yielded positive findings that encourage us to keep improving the app, dealing with usability issues and refining the contents. Subsequent studies will focus on investigating the use of the app in educational settings, contributing to a carefully-constructed history curriculum that enables pupils to challenge stereotypes, to avoid the superficial and to develop a deep understanding of controversial histories. On the technological side, we are interested in introducing means to personalize the contents of the app according to the age and the level of historical knowledge of each student, aiming to tailor the complexity of the writing and the difficulty of the quiz game accordingly.

ACKNOWLEDGEMENT

This research received funding from the European Union's Horizon 2020 research and innovation programme under grant agreement No 693150, as well as from the European Regional Development Fund (ERDF) and the Galician Regional Government under agreement for funding the AtlantTIC Research Center for Information and Communication Technologies, and from the Ministerio de Educación y Ciencia (Gobierno de España) research project TIN2017-87604-R.

REFERENCES

Al Ashmawi, F., Reiss, W., Dougi, N., Riley, M. et al., 2021. *On a common path: New approaches to writing history textbooks in Europe and the Arab and Islamic worlds: The case of the Mediterranean.* http://unesdoc.unesco.org/images/0022/002270/227041e.pdf, Rabat, Morocco.

Bellino, M.J. and Williams, J.H. (Eds.), 2017. *(Re)constructing memory: Education, identity, and conflict.* SensePublishers, Rotterdam, The Netherlands.

Bodenhamer, D., 2012. *History in the Digital Age.* Routledge, London, UK.

Guyver, R. (ed.), 2016. *Teaching History and the changing nation state – Transnational and intranational perspectives.* Bloomsbury Academic, London, UK.

Holden, C., 1996. Enhancing History teaching through a human rights perspective. *Evaluation & Research in Education*, Vol. 10, No. 2, pp. 113–127.

Jaskulowski, K. and Surmiak, A., 2017. Teaching history, teaching nationalism: A qualitative study of history teachers in a Polish post-industrial town. *Critical Studies in Education*, Vol. 58, No. 1, pp. 36–51.

Phillips, R., 1996. History teaching, cultural restorationism and national identity in England and Wales. *Curriculum Studies*, Vol. 4, No. 3, pp. 385–399, 1996.

Sung, P.-F. and Yang, M.-L., 2009. National identity and its relationship with teachers' historical knowledge and pedagogy: the case of Taiwan. *Asia Pacific Journal of Education*, Vol. 29, No. 2, pp. 179–194.

Wong, A., 2015. The whole story, and then some: Digital storytelling in evolving museum practice. *Proceedings of Museums and the Web*, Chicago (IL), USA.

EVOLUTION OF THE CONCEPT OF GOVERNABILITY IN THE CONTEXT OF DIGITALIZATION

Leonid V. Smorgunov, Kirill A. Neverov and Konstantin S. Kondratenko
Saint Petersburg State University
7-9 Universitetskaya Emb., St Petersburg 199034, Russia

ABSTRACT

New information technologies are used in public administration as part of the introduction of e-open government. Present paper focuses on the study of the centrality of governability for the digitization of public administration, affecting their architecture, processes and effects, including their social and political expression. Digital technologies generate not only hopes, but also challenges, and their distribution and use in public governance is associated with reasonable risks. Practical relevance to the project is given by the fact that at present digital technologies have become a common tool for the formation of a digital economy, society and government in Russia and in most countries of the world. The ontological basis of these findings is considered to be the phenomenon of socio-technical systems of power that are emerging in the process of the fourth technological (digital) revolution. The article traces the development of governance as base of governability, emphasizing nature of governability as a network effect of digitalization.

KEYWORDS

Digitalization, Governability, Network Effect

1. INTRODUCTION

New information technologies are used in public administration as part of the introduction of e-open government. Network technologies of distributed data (registers), which began to be used first in the financial sphere (2008), and then began to spread to the service sector, trade, public administration, art, etc., became a new and relevant step in advancing this issue. Meantime the social and political nature of this technology has not been studied. Moreover, the available studies reveal only certain aspects of the sociopolitical nature of digital technologies and are mainly descriptive and presumptive. The studies are dispersed between different branches of knowledge, which reduces their effectiveness given the humanitarian technical nature of the technology of distributed data. In this respect, the development of the fundamentals of the new synthesized scientific field of "digital social humanities" is significant. From this point of view, the formulated problem is relevant, since focuses the study of digital technology, taking into account its interdisciplinary nature, with a focus on the institutions of governing procedural processes. The subject of the paper and the formulated basic scientific problem are among the few that allow us to demonstrate the high potential of the integration synthesis of methodology and theory as a need for modern scientific knowledge focused on holism and complex thinking. The scientific relevance of the problem is also related to the fact that it focuses on the study of the centrality of governability for the digitization of public administration, affecting their architecture, processes and effects, including their social and political expression. Digital technologies generate not only hopes, but also challenges, and their distribution and use in public governance is associated with reasonable risks. In this regard, the relevance of the stated problem is expressed in combining scientific knowledge with critical thinking, which allows defining the limits of reasonable use of digital technologies in the interests of sustainable and dynamic development, as well as formulating the necessary algorithms to counter their irrelevant use in the public sphere. Practical relevance to the project is given by the fact that at present digital technologies have become a common tool for the formation of a digital economy, society and government in Russia and in most countries of the world. The Russian state program "Digital Economy", program documents of such international structures as the UN, the OECD, the World Economic Forum, the World Bank orient the modern sustainable development policy towards the prospects of the fourth technological revolution, which began with blockchain technologies. Consequently, the study of the political ontology of new digital formats of state governability is relevant from the standpoint of creating a scientific basis for evaluating and promoting the digitalization policy in public spheres and coordinating the world community in confronting grounded risks in this regard. So we stated following research question: could governability be a network effect of digitalization?

2. THE CONCEPT OF GOVERNABILITY AND DIGITALIZATION

The concepts of governability over the past three decades have evolved under the influence of new information and communication technologies. ICTs of the first, second and third generations defined state governability from functional (electronic public services), organizational (electronic participation) and communicative (monitoring democracy) positions. The network theory of public administration has formed a radical concept of "governance without government". The fourth generation of ICT has developed a distributed database technology (registers), a blockchain based on the ability to perform direct transactions between users of distributed networks based on cryptographic protocols and algorithms, almost without trust and bypassing third parties, including the state (Antonopulos 2014; Swan 2015). Blockchain was also examined for administrative purposes, its challenges, risks and limitations (Cusumano 2014; Shermin 2017; Danaher et al. 2017; Scott, Loonam, Kumar 2017). Primary studies of ontological issues of digitalization (philosophical, political, sociological) formed the idea of transition from institutional-rigid governance architecture with a stable representation and hierarchy (centralism) to institutional and procedural, based on a humanitarian-technical platform of network cooperation with free identification, organized anarchy and distributed knowledge. In this regard, the question is raised whether digital technologies are a complex system with non-linear connections that create difficulties for the algorithmic and institutionalization of governance and action in it, or can we talk about complex, algorithmic, but institutionalized digital governance. Along with the optimistic position regarding the political, social and technological performance of digital technologies, there is a reasonable judgment about the risks and challenges for society associated with the deinstitutionalization of interactions, instability and imbalance in the development of public life, the use of crime and terrorism. One of the central issues in the optimistic and critical areas is the lack of clarity regarding the new nature of the organization, and therefore governance and governability in distributed networks and digital platforms, including their use in the public sphere. Often this is described by the opposition of two political strategies related to the digitalization of public administration: "digitalization of politics" vs "politics of digitalization". The first direction relates to incremental, adaptive policy strategies for introducing digital technologies into politics and public administration. At the same time, digital technologies are not considered to invade the nature of the political, but are merely a technological means of increasing the level of efficiency in the execution of functions. The second direction is a more radical, proactive strategy for introducing digital technologies based on the identification and use of their institutional-procedural political properties and capabilities. In this case, there are many assessments of their properties - from the substantiation of the anarchist nature of digital technologies to allegations of their internal focus on new forms of political control, domination and subordination (neoliberal, republican and foucaudian criticism of digitalization). The ontological basis of these findings is considered to be the phenomenon of socio-technical systems of power that are emerging in the process of the fourth technological (digital) revolution.

3. NETWORK DEVELOPMENT OF GOVERNANCE AS BASE FOR GOVERNABILITY

The concepts The phenomenon of governability is closely related to the concept of governance, which, despite its popularity in the social sciences, is rather blurred in the subject field. To summarize, the following aspects can be distinguished as they follows.

Political governance, by which we mean not only public administration, but also, in a broader sense, governance of policy making and implementation processes - public policy, public affairs (Rhodes, 1996). Of particular importance are works that describe the signs of state governability arising on the basis of various models of public administration - scientific management, new public management, management of public values (Cass, Vigoda-Gadot E., 2009; Stoker G., 2010; Kooiman J., 2010; Kooiman J., 2010; Lynn L., Jr., Robichau R. W., 2013; Smorgunov L.V., 2012; Swanson D, Bizikova L., 2014).

The transformation of this category is traced in the works of J. Habermas, who, in fact, emphasized the governability of society through the development of communication, dialogue and cooperation in society. In modern Russian studies, the problem of governability is considered in this context. Among the works of domestic authors can distinguish research by Rubtsova M.V., engaged in identifying the relationship of governability with the self-organization of society, uncertainty and power (including the value aspect of governability), (Rubtsova M.V., 2010). In papers of Kupryashina G.L., Gritskevich T.I. manageability serves as a criterion for the success of the strategy of administrative reforms and public administration as a whole, since it generally reflects the realization of the management capacity of state structures (Kupryashin, 2011; Gritskevich, 2007).

The key role in the study of governability is played by the development of governance networks and policy networks that arise in connection with the allocation of resources, the growing influence of non-state actors on decision-making processes and, consequently, the decline in the role of the state as a key political actor. In this context, members of the research team developed the concept of a "coordinating state", the main idea of which is that the authorities in the new conditions, although they retain a central role in the processes of policy development and implementation, but increasingly perform the function of coordinating network interactions (Börzel, 1998; Koliba, Meek, Zia, 2011;Klijn, Edelenbos, 2012). In the context of the development of globalization based on network governance, a belief arises about the possibility of the existence of a "governance without government" (Rosenau, Czempel, 1992; Peters, 1998). M. Castells called modern society network, but today there are works that suggest that as a result of the fourth industrial revolution (Schwab, 2016). Of course, horizontal ties continue to dominate, but they are becoming less stable. Relationships become discrete in time, and the period of their existence is rapidly decreasing. Why capitalize on your social or institutional ties if modern technologies allow them to be established very quickly? In addition, there is a limit to the glut of bonds, since it is impossible for both individuals and institutions to maintain a large number of relationships equally effectively. Challenges of governability in this aspect are not of a subjective nature, as is the case with political governance, where challenges are facing the state, but rather relate to the governability of society as a self-organizing system.

The study of distributed networks contributed to the formation of a whole scientific field related to the study of the socio-political nature of digitalization (Berry, David, 2014; Floridi, 2015; Cormier, 2016; Carolan, 2018). In the center of this direction is the interaction of the three main critical waves - neoliberal, republican and foucaudian. There is still no integrated vision of the nature of digital technology as a socio-technical system. The concept of algorithmic public administration has been characterized by the technocratic basis of the description and contains a number of contradictions in the description of the possibility of governability, based algorithms in the public domain. In this regard, digital public administration requires its own social and political substantiation (Arkhipova, 2016; Digital Government - 2020: Prospect for Russia, World Bank, 2016; Ayad Al-Ani, 2017; IGI Global, 2015; O'Reilly, 2011; Margetts & Dunleavy, 2013).

In connection with the development of the network governance methodology, the study of the practice of introducing new information technologies based on Web 1.0, 2.0 and 3.0 is becoming increasingly important. The concept of e-government has been developing actively since the late 1990s. The idea of actively using new information and communication technologies (ICT) to increase the effectiveness of government activity emerged during the implementation of administrative reforms based on the ideology of New Public Management, which began to be carried out in Western countries (primarily Anglo-Saxon) in the early 1990s. The term itself is electronic government (e-government), however, it appears later in 1997 on the initiative of the National Science Foundation of the USA. The concepts of public governance over the past three decades have evolved under the influence of new information and communication technologies. ICTs of the first, second, and third generations have defined functional governability of government (Schedler, Summermatter, 2007), organizational (Evans, Yen, 2006; King, 2012; Bovaird, Loffler, 2012) and communicative (Chadwick, 2003). Of particular importance when studying e-government is the question of its openness and new technologies for using information and knowledge. Network electronic technologies are considered as the most appropriate structures for receiving, transmitting and diffusing knowledge, which significantly reduces management costs, transaction costs of interaction and increases the overall level of governability in organizations and in the public sphere (Milner, 2000; Barquin, 2001; Bellamy, 2002; Tsoukas, 2005).

4. CONCLUSION

The main contribution of this article was an examining of the concept of governability effected by vast and swift development of information and communication technologies in the past few years. It's showed changing attitude towards governability emphasizing the uncertainty of the political-institutional nature of digital technologies and the selection of relevant designs for their compatibility with government, ensuring the governability of the public sphere in the context of the contemporary technological revolution. The concepts of governability over the past three decades have evolved under the influence of new information and communication technologies. ICTs of the first, second and third generations defined state governability from functional (electronic public services), organizational (electronic participation) and communicative (monitoring democracy) positions. The network theory of public administration has formed a radical concept of "governance without government". The fourth generation of ICT has developed a distributed database technology (registers), a blockchain based on the ability to perform direct transactions between users of distributed networks based on cryptographic protocols and algorithms, almost without trust and bypassing third parties, including the state. However, digital technologies are not considered to invade the nature of the political, but are merely a technological means of increasing the level of efficiency in the execution of functions. We started from governance as a core concept for the following consideration of what governability in context of digitalization is. Then we studied the development of governance networks and institutions and policy networks that arise in connection with the allocation of resources, the growing influence of non-state actors on decision-making processes and, consequently, the decline in the role of the state as a key actor politicians. Challenges of governability in this aspect are not of a subjective nature, as is the case with political governance, where challenges are facing the state, but rather relate to the governability of society as a self-organizing system. In the fin of our paper we focused on the study of the practice of introducing new information technologies based on Web 1.0, 2.0 and 3.0 is becoming increasingly important, pushed forward by connection with the development of the network governance methodology.

ACKNOWLEDGMENT

The author disclosed receipt of the following financial support for the research, authorship, and/or publication of this article: This work was supported with a grant from the Russian Science Foundation (grant 19-18-00210 "Political ontology of digitalization: Study of institutional bases for digital forms of governability").

REFERENCES

Antonopulos, A., 2014. *Mastering Bitcoin: Unlocking Digital Crypto-Currencies.* Sebastopol, Ca.;

Arkhipova, Z. V., 2016. Transformation of "e-Government" into "Digital Government". *In Proceedings of Baikal State University,* Vol.26, No.5, pp. 818–824;

Ayad, Al-Ani, 2017. Government Platform: Services, Participation and Policies', *in Friedrichsen, M. and Kamalipour, Y. (eds.) Digital Transformation Journalism and News Media.* Cham: Springer, pp. 179-196;

Berry, D. M., 2014. *Critical Theory and the Digital.* New York: Bloomsbury;

Börzel, T.A., 1998. Organizing Babylon : On the Different Conceptions of Policy Networks. *In Public Administration*, Vol.76,No.2, pp.253-273;

Bovaird, T. and Loffler, E., 2012. From Engagement to Co-production, *in Pestoff, V. et al. New Public Governance, the Third Sector and Co-production.* New York and London: Routledge, pp. 35-60;

Carolan, M., 2018. 'Smart' Farming Techniques as Political Ontology: Acceleration of the Neoliberal and Not-So-Neoliberal Worlds'. *In Sociologia Ruralis*, Vol.58, No.4, pp. 745-764.

Cass, Vigoda-Gadot E., 2009. *Building Strong State. Improving Governance and Public Management.* Farnham: Ashgate Publishing Company;

Cormier, R., 2016. *Basic Cable: Notes: Toward Digital Ontology.* PhD dissertation;

Cusumano, M., 2014. Technology Strategy and Management: the Bitcoin Ecosystem. *In Communication of the ACM*, Vol.57, No.10, pp. 22-24.

Danaher J. et al, 2017. Algorithmic Governance: Developing a Research Agenda Through the Power of Collective Intelligence. *In Big Data & Society*, Vol.4, No.2, pp. 1-21;

World Bank, 2016. *Digital Government - 2020: Prospect for Russia*;

Floridi, L., 2015. *The Onlife Manifesto: Being Human in a Hyperconnected Era*. Springer;

Gritskevich, T. I., 2007. Modern Reforms: Manageability and Epistemological Uncertainty. *In Bulletin of Novosibirsk State University, Series: Philosophy,* Vol.5, No.1, pp. 60-64;

IGI Global, 2015;

King Ch., Cruickshank M., 2012. Building Capacity to Engage. *In Community Development Journal*, Vol.47, No.1, pp. 5-28;

Klijn E.H., Edelenbos J., 2012. The Influence of Democratic Legitimacy on Governance Networks. *In Administration & Society*, Vol.45, No.6, pp. 627-650;

Koliba, Ch. et al, 2011. *Governance Networks in Public Administration a nd Public Policy*. Roka Raton, London, New York: CRC Press;

Kooiman, J., 2010. *Governing as Governance*. London et all: Sage;

Kupryashin, G.L., 2011. Modernization and Governability. *In Moscow University Bulletin. Series 21: Governance (state and society)*, Vol. 2, pp. 67-86;

Lynn, L., Jr., Robichau, R. W., 2013. Governance and Organizational Effectiveness: Towards the Theory of Government Performance. *In Journal of Public Policy*, Vol.33, No.2, pp. 201-228;

Margetts, H. and Dunleavy, P., 2013. The Second Wave of Digital-Era Governance: a Quasi-Paradigm for Government on the Web. *In Philosophical Translations of the Royal Society A*, Vol.371, pp.1-17;

O'Reilly, T., 2011. Government as a Platform. *In Innovations,* Vol.6, No.1, pp. 13-40;

Peters, G., 1998. Governance without Governme: Rethinking Public Administration. *In Journal of Public Administration, Research and Theory*, Vol.8, No.2, pp. 227-243;

Rhodes, R.A.W. 1996. The New Governance: Governing without Government. *In Political Studies,* Vol.44, No.4, pp. 652-667;

Rosenau, J. and Czempel, E.-O., 1992. *Governance without Government: Politics.* Cambridge: Cambridge University Press;

Rubtsova, M.V., 2010. *Conceptual Foundations of the Study of the Phenomenon of Controllability in Sociology of Management.* SPb .: Book House;

Schedler, K., Summermatter, L.2007. Customer Orientation: Motives and Effects. *In Government Information Quarterly,* Vol.24, No.2, pp. 291-311;

Schwab, K., 2016. *The Fourth Industrial Revolution.* World Economic Forum.

Scott, B. et al, 2017. Exploring the Rise of Blockchain Technology: Towards Distributed Collaborative Organizations. *In Strategic Change*, Vol.26, No.5, pp.423-428. https://doi.org/10.1002/jsc.2142;

Shermin, V., 2017. Disrupting Governance with Blockchains and Smart Contracts. *In Strategic Change*, Vol.26, No.5, pp. 499-509;

Smorgunov, L.V., 2012. *In Search of* Governability*: Concepts and Transformations of Public Administration in the 21st Century.* SPb .: Ed. St. Petersburg University;

Stoker, G., 2010. *Governance Theory: A Cross-Disciplinary Approach.* Basingstoke: Palgrave;

Swan, M. 2015. *Blockchain.* Sebastopol, Ca.: O'Reilly Media.

Swanson, D., Bizikova, L., 2014. *Thrift Ch. and Governors of the Nexus of Sustainability, Accountability and Adaptability*. Manitoba: IIPG.

SMART CROSSWALKS: A SAFE ALERT SYSTEM THAT MINIMIZES THE CONFRONTATION BETWEEN VEHICLES AND PEDESTRIANS

João Branquinho[1], Carlos Senna[2] and André Zúquete[3]
[1]IT, University of Aveiro, Portugal
[2]Instituto de Telecomunicações, Portugal
[3]DETI / IEETA / IT, University of Aveiro, Portugal

ABSTRACT

A key characteristic of Smart Cities is the ability to reduce conflicts between different agents coexisting in a dynamic system, such as vehicles and pedestrians. This paper describes a system to augment the awareness of vehicle drivers regarding the presence of pedestrians in nearby crosswalks. To address this need, the system interconnects crosswalks to Road Side Units (RSUs), and RSUs to vehicles, in order to spread to vehicles the information about pedestrians in crosswalks. To prevent false information spreading, RSUs authenticate the alert messages they broadcast and all vehicles can validate them. This poses strong security requirements, such as non-repudiation of alert messages, as well as strong real-time requirements, such as minimum message propagation delays among vehicles approaching a crosswalk of interest. Because of this, the system minimizes the usage of asymmetric ciphers, which are fundamental to assure non-repudiation but increase performance penalties, and uses mostly symmetric ciphers for source authentication. To do so, we designed a new protocol, called Nimble Asymmetric Cryptography (NAC), which is useful to broadcast authenticated, implicit messages.

KEYWORDS

Smart Cities, Security, Smart Crosswalks

1. INTRODUCTION

Smart cities are a new reality, and an important branch of smart cities are Vehicular Ad-Hoc Networks (VANETs), where interconnected vehicles interact among themselves, with citizens and with the city itself. Currently, in Porto city, Portugal, buses interact among themselves and with the city itself in order to provide several services, such as Internet connectivity or information about the estimated time of arrival (Santos et al., 2018).

The goal of our work is to help car drivers to get alerts relatively to the presence of pedestrians in a crosswalk they are heading to. For reaching this goal, we assumed that crosswalks have a trustworthy pedestrian detection system, which they use to gather information to convey to a nearby Road Side Unit (RSU). This information is then spread along a variety of vehicles of interest in the neighborhood of the source crosswalk using the VANET formed by the vehicles themselves.

To prevent false information spreading, alert messages broadcast by RSUs must be authenticated, and all vehicles (or their On Board Units, OBUs) must validate them. This poses strong security requirements, such as non-repudiation of alert messages, as well as strong real-time requirements, such as minimum message propagation delays among vehicles approaching a crosswalk of interest. Thus, in this crosswalk-vehicle interaction scenario, maximizing efficiency while maintaining safety requirements is mandatory. Considering that RSUs and OBUs must perform several parallel tasks, such as (i) maintaining an Internet connection, (ii) control of car sensors and (iii) driver assistance mechanisms, the authentication procedure can't be a burden.

The Wireless Access in Vehicular Environments (WAVE) is a communication protocol widely used in VANETs. For routing services, WAVE makes use of asymmetric cryptography in order to guarantee both authenticity and non-repudiation ("IEEE Standard for Wireless Access in Vehicular Environments–Security Services for Applications and Management Messages," 2016). However, asymmetric cryptography, which is computationally more intensive than symmetric cryptography, impacts the validation process of messages (Cirne, Zúquete, Sargento, & Luís, 2019). This is particularly true when used in vehicles' OBUs, given they have limited processing power (Cirne, Zúquete, Sargento, & Luís, 2019). Consequently, it is associated to delays and to the degradation of applications related with emergency braking signaling (Studer, Bai, Bellur, & Perrig, 2009).

Considering the crosswalk scenario, we propose a solution mainly based on symmetric ciphers for origin authentication. Our proposal still uses asymmetric ciphers, which are fundamental to guarantee non-repudiation, but minimizes its usage to decrease performance penalties.

2. RELATED WORK

Several works, such as (Nambisan, Pulugurtha, Vasudevan, Dangeti, & Virupaksha, 2009), deal with the detect pedestrians in crosswalks as an improvement to smart cities; yet, often they do not include security measures related to information transmission. Anderson et al. (Anderson et al., 1998) proposed the Guy Fawkes protocol, a message chaining mechanism that includes the hash of the $i + 1$-th message in the i-th message. However, the loss of a single chain element forces the reestablishment of the full chain. Moreover, the non-repudiation criteria is only accomplished if the first message source can be proved to be the supposed sender (RSU). Perrig et al. (Perrig, Canetti, Tygar, & Song, n.d.) presented TESLA (Timed Efficient Stream Loss-tolerant Authentication), a protocol for broadcast authentication that relies on both keychains and time synchronization among the different nodes. TESLA uses a combination of easy-to-compute Message Authentication Codes (MACs) and hash functions as an authentication technique, which enables it to take low computation effort to authenticate broadcast streams. By using "time delays", packet buffering and a tight time synchronization, TESLA can tolerate packet losses as well. Perrig et al. also developed TESLA++ (Studer, Bai, Bellur, & Perrig, 2009) as an improvement of TESLA and a more efficient approach for ad-hoc networks. However, TESLA requires time delays in receivers to properly handle delays, which goes against our real-time requirements.

3. PROPOSAL

Taking into account the characteristics of VANETs (mobility, intermittent connectivity, long and variable delay in information delivery), it is important that message validations are performed even if a node loses one or more packages. Our proposal (explained in detail in Section 3.1) makes use of asymmetric ciphers, which are fundamental to guarantee non-repudiation, but minimizes its exploitation to decrease performance penalties.

Our proposal inherits some of the characteristics of the Guy Fawkes Protocol (Anderson et al., 1998)5, therefore we will overview it first. We will as well highlight its limitations regarding fault tolerance to packets losses and vulnerabilities to Man-in-the-Middle (MitM) attacks.

The Guy Fawkes protocol broadcasts two types of packages: Message packages P_i^m and Validation packages P_i^v (see Figure 1). The Message package P_{i+1}^m contains: (i) a random key K_{i+1} that, when hashed, conforms with Message package P_i^m ; (ii) the message contents M_{i+1}; and (iii) the hash of the random key K_{i+2} contained in the next Message package, P_{i+2}^m. The existence of K_{i+1} in P_{i+1}^m and its hash in P_i^m confirms that no message was lost.

A Validation package P_i^v consists of a hash over the Message package P_i^m that follows it; it is a commitment used to avoid MitM attacks. Once a message P_i^m gets accepted and P_{i+1}^v gets known by its recipients, only someone knowing both K_{i+1} and M_{i+1} can produce and send P_{i+1}^m, which creates an authentication chain. The protocol's bootstrap uses digital signatures in order to authenticate the message chain source.

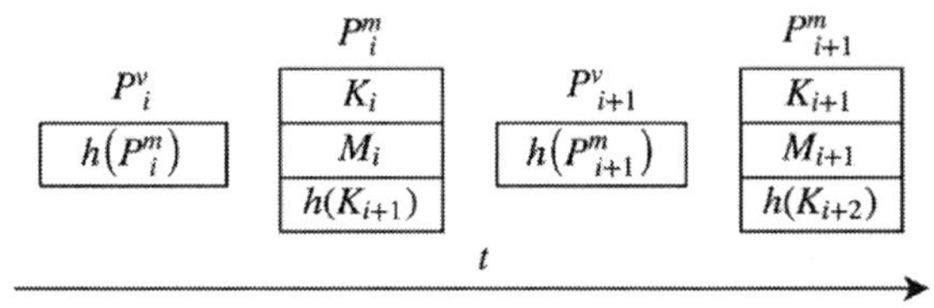

Figure 1. Sequence of packages in the Guy Fawkes protocol. P_i^v and P_{i+1}^v are Validation packages; P_i^m and P_{i+1}^m are Message packages

This protocol presents qualities that can lead to symmetric and efficient cryptography with authenticity and non-repudiation properties. Yet, it does not fit our scenario, since there are several problems with its integration to our use case. Firstly, the high probability of a message being lost in an ad-hoc network. If the recipient misses a packet, one cannot guarantee the authenticity nor the non-repudiation of the next Message packet, because (I) K_i and K_{i+1} are independent and (ii) Validation packages are critical to chain validations.

Under some circumstances, it is vulnerable to MitM attacks. In fact, if an attacker is able to deploy a physical barrier to packet broadcasting (e.g. by intercepting the wiring of the antenna of the broadcasting device), it can perform the following attack: (i) block the broadcast of genuine packets from P_i^m onward; (ii) wait until receiving both P_{i+1}^v and P_{i+1}^m; (iii) Change M_{i+1} in P_{i+1}^m to F_{i+1} (fake message) and recompute P_{i+1}^v accordingly; (iv) broadcast the tampered packets P_{i+1}^v and P_{i+1}^m and repeat the process in the following packets. Clock synchronization and fixed reception windows can avoid this problem, but they impose a fixed transmission rate that increases the medium occupancy.

3.1 Nimble Asymmetric Cryptography (NAC) Protocol

In general, the IoT sensors used in crosswalks emit a very reduced number of information values from finite sets. Crosswalk sensors, for instance, only transmit one binary message: either someone is using the crosswalk or no one is there. Our proposed solution, called Nimble Asymmetric Cryptography (NAC) and showed in Figure 2, was inspired by the Guy Fawkes protocol but designed in accordance with these characteristics.

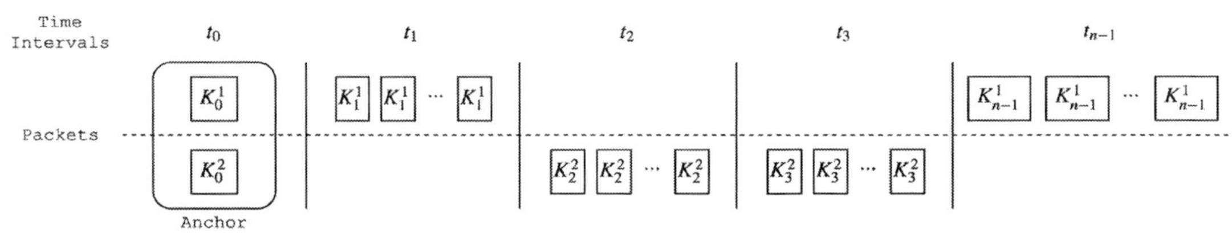

Figure 2. Sequence of messages broadcast with the Nimble Asymmetric Cryptography (NAC). This process is cyclic, at t_0 the RSU broadcasts an anchor message. At t_n, n time intervals after that, the RSU brodacasts a new anchor message, which will contain new K_0^1 and K_0^2 values

NAC uses hash chains of keys. Keys are computed and disclosed in the reverse order of a hashing chain: $K_i = h(K_{i+1})$. NAC also assumes global time synchronization and that the keys K_i are only valid during a particular time frame. The steps of the NAC protocol are:

1. At time interval t_0 the RSU broadcasts an anchor message (Section 3.2) containing two values, K_0^1 and K_0^2. Both these values are the end of two separate hash chains: $K_0^1 = h^n(K_n^1)$ and $K_0^2 = h^n(K_n^2)$. K_n^1 is a secret key that will be used to advertise the presence of people crossing the crosswalk; similarly, K_n^2 will be used to advertise the opposite.
2. At each time interval t_i a new key K_i is used in RSU alerts. K_i must belong to one of the two hash chains, i.e. it must be either K_i^1 or K_i^2. In order for each OBU to confirm the authenticity of a received K_i it must verify if $\mathrm{h}^i(K_i)$ equals K_0^1 or K_0^2. This way, each OBU can have implicit guarantees about the existence of people in the crosswalk. Note that, given a previously received (an authentic) message with $K_{i-\delta}$, if K_i belongs to the same hash chain it can be checked by computing only δ hash operations, instead of i, because $K_{i-\delta} = h^\delta(K_i)$. Observing Figure 2, we can validate K_3 by checking if $K_2 = h(K_3)$.

3. In order to guarantee that OBUs receive at least one message per time interval, the RSU broadcasts the same message more than once during its validity period. The repetition rate can vary according with the relevance of the implicit message for the safety of pedestrians: messages signaling an occupied crosswalk should be repeated more than for a free one.

Note that with NAC it is impossible for an attacker to tamper transmitted messages, contrarily to the Guy Fawkes protocol, because messages are implicitly given by each key hash chain. In other words, the key is the message, K_i is also M_i.

NAC requires clock synchronization between OBUs and RSUs. The OBUs need this synchronization to properly validate K_i keys and, therefore, to evaluate the correctness of the implicit message that they convey regarding the current occupancy of the crosswalk. The Global Positioning System (GPS) is not only a navigation system, but also a good option for time-transfer system (Lewandowski, Azoubib, & Klepczynski, 1999). In our testbed, OBUs and RSUs have GPS, and NAC will use this resource for clock synchronization.

The origin and duration of the time intervals used by NAC do not need to be established globally. In fact, they can be dynamically established by each anchor message.

3.2 Anchor Messages

The trust in messages is chained: a recipient trusts in a message because it trusts on some previously received messages. Therefore, there must be some trust anchor, in which a recipient relies, in order to trust the chain that follows it. Such anchor must be a self-protected message with non-repudiation properties and with the two keys, K_0^1 and K_0^2 at the end of the two hash chains. The widely used method to achieve these properties is with digital signatures and public key certificates.

The RSU is subject to two extra tasks: anchor re-sending and anchor updating. New vehicles entering the RSU radio range are not aware of the trust chain. Therefore, the anchor message must be re-sent by the RSU. The length of time interval between anchor disclosures will be subject to further investigation in future work. The RSU is also responsible for updating the anchor messages it sends. When a new vehicle enters the range of an RSU at time t_{n-1}, if n is a sizable number the OBU would take a significant amount of time to compute $h^{n-1}(K_{n-1})$ in order to validate K_{n-1}. This would create unnecessary overheads. Therefore, it is important that the RSU keeps the size n of key chains under maximum limits, and anchors are updated after n time intervals with new K_0^1 and K_0^2 values, belonging to two new hash chains.

The overhead added by asymmetric cryptography in anchor messages is redeemed by the validation of hash chains, since longer chains reduce the prevalence of overheads due to validations of anchor messages. However, longer hash chains may as well increase the cost of validating hash chains under heavy packet losses; the search for the right balance between chain size and asymmetric usage will be subject of further research.

3.3 Message Retransmission

In VANETs, vehicles moving through a city will be constantly switching their access points (RSUs). NAC was designed to address the mobility requirements of the VANET, as we discuss bellow.

1. *Anchor Messages:* when a recipient (OBU) is in the transmission range of an RSU responsible for a crosswalk, it may already be too late for getting an anchor message directly from the RSU. To minimize this characteristic, NAC uses the spreading of anchor messages between vehicles, maximizing the knowledge of "authenticators" of alert sequences encapsulated within hashing chains.
2. *Alert messages:* in some cases, due to excessive physical distances or to the presence of physical barriers, OBUs may not receive relevant alert messages direct from the RSU. Consequently, their drivers might not be warned of a possible risk situation. Alert messages can be relayed by OBUs.

NAC covers this possibility with two complementary measures: (i) an RSU broadcasts key K_i within time interval t_i more than once, for maximizing the nearby reception of alert messages; and (ii) vehicles may relay alert messages, namely the critical ones, up to a maximum range, as they do with anchor messages.

Relatively to alert relaying, vehicles should only relay alerts belonging to the current time frame. Otherwise, the network would be overloaded with bogus messages. Anchor relaying, on the other hand, must occur during the time validity of the anchor, an even a bit before, because new OBUs might be approaching the crosswalk and must be aware of the hash chains to be used.

3.4 Using NAC to deal with Other City Sensors

The NAC protocol conveys implicit messages, being these as many as the number of hashing chains allowed by anchors created by a given source. There are a variety of sensors in a smart city that follow a similar principle, and thus are suitable for being handled using NAC. Traffic lights, for instance, broadcast only three message types: the light is either red, yellow or green. Thus, one can explore NAC with three different hash chains and broadcasting at each time frame the correspondent key for the chain. Other sensors, such carbon dioxide, methane and even trash weight sensors, are often boolean: given a threshold value, they either emit "under the threshold" or "over the threshold" signals. Thus, they could also be handled with NAC.

Concluding, NAC takes advantage of time constraints and the distinctiveness of hash chains in order to achieve broadcast message authentication, while maintaining message loss tolerance and deciphering efficiency. This set of advantages can be of much use in smart cities, where most sensors broadcast a finite set of signals, and in scenarios where message interpretation times can make the difference between life or death.

ACKNOWLEDGMENT

This work is funded by FCT/MEC through national funds under the project S2MovingCity CMUP-ERI/TIC/0010/2014 and by the European Regional Development Fund (FEDER), through the Competitiveness and Internationalization Operational Programme (COMPETE 2020) of the Portugal 2020 framework, and Financial Support National Public (FCT)(OE); Project, MOBIWISE, POCI-01-0145-FEDER-016426.

REFERENCES

Anderson, R., Bergadano, F., Crispo, B., Lee, J.-H., Manifavas, C., & Needham, R. (1998). A New Family of Authentication Protocols. SIGOPS Oper. Syst. Rev., 32(4), 9–20. https://doi.org/10.1145/302350.302353

Cirne, P., Zúquete, A., Sargento, S., & Luís, M. (2019). The impact of ECDSA in a VANET routing service: Insights from real data traces. Ad Hoc Networks, 90, 101747. https://doi.org/10.1016/j.adhoc.2018.08.017

IEEE Standard for Wireless Access in Vehicular Environments–Security Services for Applications and Management Messages. (2016). IEEE Std 1609.2-2016 (Revision of IEEE Std 1609.2-2013), 1–240. https://doi.org/10.1109/IEEESTD.2016.7426684

Lewandowski, W., Azoubib, J., & Klepczynski, W. J. (1999). GPS: primary tool for time transfer. Proceedings of the IEEE, 87(1), 163–172. https://doi.org/10.1109/5.736348

Nambisan, S. S., Pulugurtha, S. S., Vasudevan, V., Dangeti, M. R., & Virupaksha, V. (2009). Effectiveness of Automatic Pedestrian Detection Device and Smart Lighting for Pedestrian Safety. Transportation Research Record, 2140(1), 27–34. https://doi.org/10.3141/2140-03

Perrig, A., Canetti, R., Tygar, J. D., & Song, D. (n.d.). The TESLA Broadcast Authentication Protocol. 12.

Santos, P. M., Rodrigues, J. G. P., Cruz, S. B., Lourenço, T., d'Orey, P. M., Luis, Y., … Barros, J. (2018). PortoLivingLab: An IoT-Based Sensing Platform for Smart Cities. IEEE Internet of Things Journal, 5(2), 523–532. https://doi.org/10.1109/JIOT.2018.2791522

Studer, A., Bai, F., Bellur, B., & Perrig, A. (2009). Flexible, extensible, and efficient VANET authentication. Journal of Communications and Networks, 11(6), 574–588. https://doi.org/10.1109/JCN.2009.6388411

A PROPOSED TECHNOLOGY SOLUTION FOR PREVENTING MARINE LITTERING BASED ON UAVS AND IOT CLOUD-BASED DATA ANALYTICS

George Stengos[1], Stavros T. Ponis[2], George Plakas[2] and Athanasios Yamas[3]
[1]*CycleFi IKE, Melissou 24, Athens 11635, Greece*
[2]*National Technical University Athens, Heroon Polytechniou 9, Zografos 15780, Athens, Greece*
[3]*Altus LSA, Renieri 9, Chania 73134, Greece*

ABSTRACT

Pollution in the marine environment is a global problem with severe consequences on marine and terrestrial ecosystems and to human health. It is estimated that every year, eight million tonnes of debris find their way into the world's oceans, mostly consisted of valuable materials which by following land-based routes are finally finding their way into the sea, instead of being recycled and reused, thus disrupting the Circular Economy value circle. Especially in the case of shorelines, which are in the spotlight of the research presented in this paper, fifty to eighty percent of the rejected debris is made of plastic. The research presented in this paper prescribes an innovative technology solution with the potential of mitigating the severity of the marine littering problem. The proposed solution utilizes the combined power of two emerging Industry 4.0 technologies, i.e. UAVs (Unmanned Aerial Vehicles) and Sensor technology. These two technologies are integrated in a proposed technology system capable of data collection, analysis and presentation through a cloud based platform of software services available to all system users and stakeholders. Furthermore, the proposed solution will provide tools for facilitating and triggering the pro-active role of responsible citizens, while creating a societal consensus through a user friendly and gamified citizens' awareness platform.

KEYWORDS

Circular Economy, Marine Littering, Blue Growth, Internet of Things, Unmanned Aerial Vehicles, Wireless Sensor Networks, Gamification

1. INTRODUCTION

Marine pollution is a severe global problem, which is getting worse as millions of tons of waste end up in the oceans every year causing multiple environmental, economic, health and aesthetic concerns with serious implications (Gallo et al., 2018). Apparently, the way products and goods are currently discarded fails to capture the economic benefits of a more 'circular' approach and harms the environment. In fact, marine litter is clearly a demonstration of a resource inefficient economy. Valuable materials are polluting beaches and damaging the environment instead of returning into the economy (Newman et al., 2015). In that sense, European and international directives and legislative pressures have been set forth to figure out ways to tackle the challenges of marine littering. Therefore, a Circular Economy approach, which puts the emphasis on preventing waste and on reuse of materials and products in the first place, seems the most efficient solution to the marine litter problem (Eriksen et al., 2017). Until today, estimations on marine littering seem to be in an assumption-based approach, making it nearly impossible to provide an exact measurement, due to the lack of a worldwide systematic monitoring mechanism. In fact, the lack of systematic monitoring of the origin, patterns and distribution of plastic waste ending up in the marine environment, results to the absence of a worldwide prevention mechanism (Borrelle et al., 2017).

Currently, there is very limited information from existing studies regarding the inland flow of the plastic marine litter. (ibid) So far, large land-based sources of marine litter include waste coming from landfills located near coastal zones or on the banks of rivers, ports, touristic and recreational activities taking place at the coasts and food packaging, which is the most common category of discarded materials directly associated with recreational activities (Mouat et al., 2010). Although the clean-up of the sea is imperative, the prevention of marine littering from debris entering the sea, remains the top priority. However, the lack of public awareness related to marine littering and best practices for waste disposal exacerbates the situation (Hasan, 2004). Unfortunately, up to today current efforts seem inadequate and inefficient since they are traditionally limited to high cost campaigns to raise awareness on marine littering and responsible citizenship. It is now clear to policymakers that they will not be able to tackle the marine littering challenge in an effective, impactful and cost-efficient manner, unless increased and ongoing citizens' participation is safe guarded (UNEP, 2018). In that direction, a cost-effective awareness program that creates a positive citizens' experience to maintain ongoing engagement for prevention of marine littering, seems an imperative.

As a solution, in this paper, the authors propose an integrated technology solution, which utilizes state of the art technologies such as drones, IoT wireless sensors, and mobile station centers in one cloud-based platform solution, launching and landing drones to prevent and/or divert debris from entering the marine environment while at the same time providing services to both public authorities (i.e. municipalities) and citizens inhabiting coastal areas. Furthermore, the proposed technology aims to promote the active role of responsible citizens, enhancing awareness and empowering the pro-active role of local policy to reduce marine pollution in general. In doing so the introduction of a 'Serious' Game is proposed, that plays a central role in the adoption, acceptance and sustainability of the system, by a) attracting beach management authorities to adopt the solution and creating a network of participants that gain visibility and recognition with the introduction of an eco-label similar to the well stablished 'Blue Flag' label and b) activating as many citizens as possible through raining awareness actions and making them part of the ecosystem by giving and receiving real-time information on the current environmental status of the beach (e.g. uploading a photograph of stacked plastics that need to be collected before they enter the sea) and participating in information / education programs on recycling / cyclical economy issues and conscious recycling behavior.

The proposed solution is in line with the European Strategy for Plastics (16/01/2018/EU) (European Commission, 2018) and the actions of the European Union, in the areas of Blue and Circular Economy for the design and successful implementation of innovative technological solutions that support the recording of quantities and the identification of sources of marine pollution from plastic waste.

2. THE PROPOSED SOLUTION

The proposed solution involves the development of network of wireless sensors operating on a LPWAN (Low Power Wide Area Network) such as LoRa (https://lora-alliance.org/), a set of integrated modules utilizing UAVs with imaging sensors supported by a mobile land-based station (van) and a specialized cloud platform for the reporting of results to system users. More specifically, The Monitor & Detect module is responsible for identifying and monitoring the various land sources of marine debris, while calculating the disposed quantities and recording their catchment areas in the marine environment. For these purposes, the configurable UAS (Atlas 8) drone model is proposed, equipped with powerful optical sensors, state of the art thermal sensors, dual optical payloads and environmental sensors (www.freeflysystems.com/alta-8). Next the Collect module will provide 24/7 autonomous drones by supplying a mobile land-based station van. The drones will carry out the assigned tasks, such as monitoring and detecting any kind of debris in the marine environment, before landing back on the mobile land-based station vans. Once landed, the drones are recharged and made ready for the next flight, whilst field data is transmitted wirelessly (through nG/GPRS) back to the cloud central server. This kind of all-encompassing solution appears to be the way forward in connecting drones to a wider Internet of Things array, while the ability to recharge and be maintained on the station pad could further lessen human involvement paving the way for a fully autonomous future operation. The Aggregation & Filtering module will provide users with an advanced data analysis tool and an integrated monitoring system. The abundance of data from thermal and optical cameras, video & audio sensors etc., received from the station will be analyzed with the use of an algorithm developed and run on the MongoDB, NoSQL database. The Report & Process Center will serve as an integrated content management system, customized for the efficient storage, management, archiving, processing and logging of multimedia/heterogeneous content through a modular architecture. The platform will be capable of providing data to all involved operators with authorized access, so they can manage data in tabular form. A dashboard (e.g. Jasper Reports) will be used for monitoring and reporting purposes. Finally, the Engagement Module will provide tools for facilitating and triggering the pro-active role of 'Responsible Citizens', while creating a societal consensus through a friendly responsible citizens awareness platform. The platform will constitute a user-friendly interface, implementing two core functionalities, namely a) inform all citizens (recreational users and residents) through a real time debris value calculator algorithm, on the marine debris status of a selected area, providing key metrics corresponding to the environmental impact on the specific area and b) promote the "Responsible Citizen" role to manage their waste by encouraging the proper procedure of sorting/throwing away garbage and stimulating behavioral change to prevent marine littering.

The platform will integrate data into a gamified environment to enable goals' attainment. The gamification mechanism will be centered around a set of competition scenarios among the municipalities adopting the proposed solution. Leaderboards and ranking will be displayed through self-sufficient solar powered screens, which will announce performance related information. The authors believe that influencing citizens to get more involved and educated on marine littering challenges, albeit important, is not a sufficient solution. As citizens undoubtedly play an integral part in the success of tacking marine littering challenge, a gamified, engaging, citizens-focused approach with an element of social pressure is the answer that can potentially boost citizen's responsibility, promote the desired behavior effectively, and maintain a serious, profound and long-term commitment to both coastal and marine environment. A schematic of the proposed solution is presented in Figure 1.

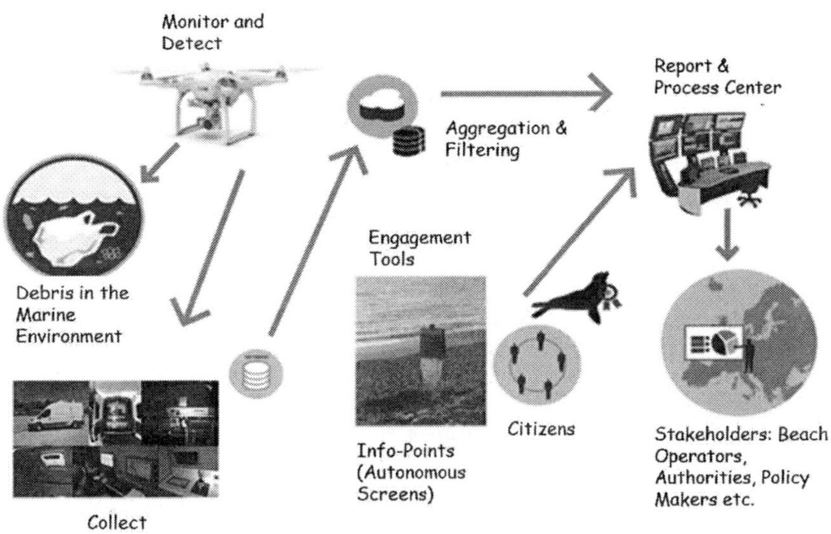

Figure 1. The proposed technology solution

The authors are currently in the phase of assessing the technical viability of the system and testing of its technological performance and underlying key components while at the same time identifying possible ways for conceptual design improvements. Their future objective is to produce a small-scale but fully customized and pilot tested Proof of Concept [POC] of a First of a Kind [FOAK] integrated infrastructure of product, service and business model including:

- A heavy-lift, multi-rotor Unmanned Aerial Vehicle [UAV] platform,
- A collection of State-of-the-art Sensors,
- A mobile land-based station (van)
- An advanced data analytics S/W for a holistic marine littering measurement & monitoring system
- A fully integrated Web Reporting tool for the users of the system, able to analyze streaming data from the UAVs and produce meaningful and customized results, e.g. Dashboard Designer
- A system integrated Serious Game that promotes environmental awareness of marine pollution and engages citizens into helping to reduce it.
- A novel debris value calculator able to determine, in real time, key metrics corresponding to the environmental impact of the most common marine debris.

3. CONCLUSION

The proposed solution aspires to promote the preservation of marine and coastal ecosystems and aims to be an ideal turnkey solution for coastlines and beaches that are willing to tackle the problem of marine littering. In doing so, it provides a reliable monitoring and gamified solution that drives competitive advantage and greater outcomes through enabling superior Citizen Engagement, while diverting debris away from marine environment. The proposed solution is improving the innovation capacity in the field of anti-marine littering technology systems, by leveraging the power and participation of citizens and enhancing their effectiveness and reliability. In terms of environmental long-term sustainability, the proposed solution accelerates the shift to a sustainable future and adds a people-driven dynamic, transforming the current efforts to raise awareness on marine littering and responsible citizenship, in which citizens passively receive information, to a two-way flow of information where citizens contribute on marine littering prevention, resulting in significant social and -above all- environmental positive impact.

ACKNOWLEDGEMENT

This research has been co-financed by the European Union and Greek national funds through the Operational Program Competitiveness, Entrepreneurship and Innovation, under the call RESEARCH – CREATE – INNOVATE (project code: T1EDK-05095).

REFERENCES

Borrelle, S., Rochman, C., Liboiron, M., Bond, A., Lusher, A., Bradshaw, H. and Provencher, J. (2017). Opinion: Why we need an international agreement on marine plastic pollution. *Proceedings of the National Academy of Sciences*, 114(38), pp.9994-9997.

Eriksen, M., Thiel, M., Prindiville, M. and Kiessling, T. (2017). Microplastic: What Are the Solutions?. *The Handbook of Environmental Chemistry*, Springer Open, pp.273-298.

European Commission - European Commission. (2019). EU Plastics Strategy. [online] Available at: https://ec.europa.eu/commission/news/eu-plastics-strategy-2018-nov-20_en [Accessed 1 Apr. 2019].

Freefly Systems. (2019). Freefly ALTA 8 - Multirotor Camera Drone for Cinematographers. [online] Available at: https://freeflysystems.com/alta-8 [Accessed 1 Apr. 2019].

Gallo, F., Fossi, C., Weber, R., Santillo, D., Sousa, J., Ingram, I., Nadal, A. and Romano, D. (2018). Marine litter plastics and microplastics and their toxic chemicals components: the need for urgent preventive measures. *Environmental Sciences Europe*, Volume 30, No. 1.

Hasan, S. (2004). Public Awareness Is Key to Successful Waste Management. *Journal of Environmental Science and Health, Part A*, Vol 39, No 2, pp.483-492.

Lora-alliance.org. (2019). Home page | LoRa Alliance. [online] Available at: https://lora-alliance.org/ [Accessed 1 Apr. 2019].

Marine plastic debris and microplastics: global lessons and research to inspire action and guide policy change. (2018). Nairobi: United Nations Environment Assembly of the United Nations Environment Programme. Available at: https://papersmart.unon.org/resolution/uploads/unep_aheg_2018_1_inf_4_unea2_edited.pdf [Accessed 1 Apr. 2019].

Mouat, J., Lopez Lozano, R. and Bateson, H. (2010). Economic Impacts of Marine Litter. [ebook] KIMO (Kommunenes Internasjonale Miljøorganisasjon). Available at: http://www.kimointernational.org/wp/wp-content/uploads/2017/09/KIMO_Economic-Impacts-of-Marine-Litter.pdf [Accessed 1 Apr. 2019].

Newman, S., Watkins, E., Farmer, A., Brink, P. and Schweitzer, J. (2015). The Economics of Marine Litter. *Marine Anthropogenic Litter*, Springer Open, pp.367-394.

HOW ORDINARY CITY SHIFT TO SMART CITY? A CASE STUDY "CITIZEN-CENTERED"

Hosni Seffih[1,2], Myriam Lamolle[1], Aurélie Pradelles[2], Ayoub Chouchou[3] and Christian Fluhr[2]
[1]LIASD-EA4383, IUT de Montreuil, Univ. Paris 8, 140 rue de la Nouvelle France 93100 Montreuil, France
[2]Geolsemantics, 12, avenue Raspail 94250 Gentilly, France
[3]Transfero, 39, cite Mayen Djeloul, 19000, Setif, Algeria.

ABSTRACT

The Smart City concept is a very recent one, which, nevertheless, has already implemented in several cities around the world (for example, Dubai, Moscow, Paris). The satisfactory results are encouraging more and more cities to experiment with this concept; given that the normal city of the future will be the smart city, regardless of its size and location. We have noticed during November 2018 Sétif start-ups fair, in Algeria, the strong desire of local authorities and investors to shift to a smart management of their city (Elmoudjahid, 2019). In this article we will study the transition of an ordinary city into a smart city, whatever its socio-economic environment. The concept of a smart city will be presented, in the first instance, then we will examine various examples of cities in view of transitioning to smart city, so as to propose an application at low-cost based essentially on the collaboration of the inhabitants (which we will call "smart Citizen-centred city"), this way we will pass over the lack of developed systems benefitting from open data, sensor networks, etc. Because of this, we have selected the theme "intelligent transport", presenting a simple transport application in the Wilaya of Sétif, which will depend on the connected people.

KEYWORDS

Smart city, Smart Transport, Smart Community, NLP, Data-Mining

1. INTRODUCTION

Since its conception, the idea of a "smart city" has evolved, going from the execution of specific projects to the implementation of global strategies with a view to facing the cities' greatest challenges. It is therefore necessary to obtain a view of all the available possibilities and to relate them to specific challenges. A smart city is representative of the innovation of the running of the city, its services and its infrastructure. A common definition of the term has not yet been decided (O'Grady and O'Hare, 2012).

We note that the smart city concept has emerged within the last 20 years, whether in scientific writing or in political discourse. The city has a big social, economic and environmental imprint (Mori and Christodoulu, 2012). According to (UN 2008), more than 50% of the world's population live in an urban environment. That is expected to reach 75% in 2050. According to the same report, cities consume between 60 and 80% of the world's resources.

According to (Turcu 2013; Berardi 2013a; 2013b), cities should respond to the needs of their inhabitants by finding durable solutions. The smart city concept is not just limited to the application of new technologies to the running of a city, but also is linked to the concept of the sustainable city.

As stated before there are many definitions of the concept of the smart city and even more if we topple the adjective "smart" in favour of "digital" or "intelligent". The term was used for the first time in the 1990s; at that time, studies focused on information and communication technology (ICT) and its impact on modern infrastructure in cities.

According to (Harrison et al. 2010), the term "smart city" applies to the cities that can capture and integrate data in real time using sensors, meters, domestic appliances, interconnected personal appliances, etc. The term "intelligent" refers to analysis, modelling, optimisation of resulting data to aid decision taking.

For (Ballas, 2013), the term "smart city" refers to governmental politics, which place upon "intelligent" strategies, to achieve sustainable development, an economic development and a better quality of life for citizens (Albino et al, 2015).

We can deduct from these definitions that the concept of a smart city implicates an approach for the management and development of the city that can be used globally. These definitions show a balance of technological, economic and social factors put in place within an urban ecosystem. These definitions reflect a global approach to urban problems taking part in new technologies to redefine the urban model and the relationships between the parties involved (Caragliu, Del Bo and Nijkamp 2009; Harrison et al, 2010; Correia et al, 2011; Nam and Pardo, 2011; Batty et al, 2012 and UN-HABITAT, 2015).

However, it can be pointed out that infrastructure is a central element of the smart city and technology is the catalyst which allows it, combining the two is fundamental to the transition of the ordinary city to smart city (Nam and Pardo, 2011).

2. RELATED WORKS

Many research projects have worked on the question of how to transform an ordinary city into a smart city or how to have a smart management in the city, which includes a smart economy, a smart environment, smart transport, etc, (Advancity et al, 2016) whether within cities which already have a smart infrastructure and management, which we will call the "northern cities", or whether they be the cities which have started to test certain concepts of smart management, which we will call the "southern cities".

For example, in Casablanca, (Safia et al, 2018), with the use of Geographical Information Systems sensors, present their approach to plan the distribution of food products from a single depot to multiple customers with variable demand rates, beginning by collecting data to model the problem of directing their heavy goods vehicles. Through this approach, they have presented the real-life case of a distribution firm in the food sector in a southern country using a multi-channel distribution circuit. The objective of this case study is to select the optimal configuration to satisfy clients, reduce business costs and avoid congestion in the city. In Algeria, an ontological solution has been developed to economise on energy thanks to a smart home in the city of Adrar (Boudaa et al, 2018). Using a Natural Language Processing (NLP) tool (Namiot et al, 2018), have tried to progress towards smart transport. The objective is to model the journeys of passengers and to create a pattern using the model of social and economic behaviour of residents in the Russian capital Moscow.

Studies on the concept of smart city itself have been carried out, as with ASCIMER (Monzon, 2015), a project developed by the Universidad Politecnica of Madrid (UPM) for the EIBURS call on "Smart City Development: Applying European and International Experience to the Mediterranean Region" The stated objectives were:

- To define the concept of the smart city and understand how it could contribute to the achievement of priorities for urban development.
- To develop a methodology to evaluate and prioritise Smart City projects.
- To elaborate guidelines for the implementation and direction of Smart City projects.
- To characterise the challenges of Mediterranean cities and develop a transitional strategy for Smart City projects.

The cities considered as belonging to the North Mediterranean Region are those located in countries of the European Union. The countries in the South and East Mediterranean region that have been considered in the study are: Morocco, Algeria, Tunisia, Libya, Egypt, Jordan, Israel, Lebanon, Syria and Turkey. It is imperative to study the applicability of the concept in all these regions, and to have a history of places where this has succeeded.

In all the preceding examples, a certain level of technology is necessary (for example, a network of GIS sensors, a well-defined terminology of the places in the case of Moscow), but this is not necessarily available. In the case of transport networks, many cities do not have the technology for sensors, or for machine validation of tickets, or standardised linguistic terminology for the referencing of locations.

3. CASE STUDY

At the centre of the Hautes Plaines region in the east of Algeria, the city of Sétif benefits from a strategic positioning in a traffic network, which has been reinforced, in recent years, by the doubling of all national routes and the implementation of the east-west route. With more than 300,000 inhabitants in the capital city and more than 400,000 inhabitants in the urban area, Sétif constitutes an important human concentration, a very attractive place for its activities, its production of services and its potential for development due mainly to its accessibility (Kebiche, 2017). The expansion of the city of Sétif is characterised by the phenomenon of the "urban transition" (WIEL M, 1999), the urban transition or the shift from the pedestrianised to the motorised city.

Knowing that we have at our disposal the database of all the stations in the city of Sétif, we will create a "smart citizen-centred transport" application, it's a small urban parc with 350 operators, 15 lines and 426 vehicles in 2015[1]. The principal objective is the participation of users to report the progression of buses from one station to the other and send alerts in the event of any bus failure. The collaborative area must take into consideration the fact that the stations referenced in the database for the city of Sétif do not necessarily correspond with the names given in "street vocabulary". Timetables are therefore calculated step by step by the signals from inhabitants while considering the adaptation to the vocabulary.

To do this, the calculation of times requires a data-mining module based on the users' reports. The adaptation of vocabulary is made by a module of natural language processing (NLP) to complete the dictionary of different names given to different places.

We hope that during the use of this application, the relevance of the developed timetables will be closer and closer to reality, bringing more and more residents to use public transport.

3.1 Datamining Module

Once the application is propagated, we will carry out a data-mining operation on the data sent by the users, by using an unsupervised learning algorithm coupled with a Bayesian inference. We will be able to identify the location of means of transport in real time and estimate the time in which it will reach the next station. The data sent by the user can be the GPS coordinates, but if there is only a declaration of place from the user, we will apply a comment section this is will allow users to declare events and places on what's holding the traffic, of course the GPS will not be always enabled. Therefore, we will have to extract the place from the comment, even if we will have to deal with many problems like fake notifications, a problem that has both manual and automatic solutions, we can start by allowing other users that are in the same area to confirm the event, and then we using those confirmation we can build a model and use machine learning to predict future fake notifications (Guibon et al, 2019), it will be necessary to identify the place and collect its coordinates. For this, we will have need of an NLP module.

3.2 Natural Language Processing (NLP)

The automatic treatment of the natural language will be a great help to us in this context. We are confronted with two challenges: the first being the identification of location, as the users tend to name places differently to their official name, whether by the old name of the street, abbreviated name or in slang (e.g. *Dallas* (common name) -> *Cité du 1 Nov*embre (official name)). It is therefore necessary to create a dictionary of the different names given to a place. The other challenge is that names can be written in different ways: phonetic spelling, reversing letters, etc. Because of this, we will install a spell checker to propose corrections (e.g. telefone -> telephone) or try different linguistic methods to suggest the appropriate spelling to the user.

It is necessary to use an NLP module for places recognition inside users' notifications, especially when it concerns names not containing proper nouns. It may then be interesting to mix the NLP module with GPS information when it is accessible, in order to be sure to link the official name of the stop with the one used by users.

[1] Source : ONTA organisation nationale des transporteurs algériens, 2015

4. CONCLUSION

A successful smart transport network can constitute a gateway to other domains that will appear in a smart city. Each region presents different challenges. In our case study, we will have to overcome the absence of databases and GPS tool based, by relying on a collaborative system, in the same manner as Waze. The NLP will help us to position the means of transport and above all to predict the time of passage at each station and the best itinerary for the user. We will also try to resolve the problem of places naming, and deal with the difference between official names and the names more commonly used by the public for the same place; a disambiguation which will surely aid those passing through Sétif. Later, the user will also be able to announce an incident, her/his text will immediately be analysed and serve to create an alert.

It remains to be seen if citizens will be receptive and will permit the development of this application. Up until now we have seen encouraging results with Yassir and Jumia which have respectively added a model akin to Uber and to Amazon on the Algerian market, solving in an elaborate way the problem of the lack of online payment methods in Algeria. Of course, we will have to deal with the problem of how to make our app viral, advertising around the stations and the buses will be our first stage, this should help us build a community we will then have to find ways to make this community active, this will be discussed in our next article.

REFERENCES

Elmoudjahid, 2019. *Le salon de l'emploi et des start-ups s'ouvre aujourd'hui à Sétif.* [online] Available at: http://www.elmoudjahid.com/fr/actualites/130889 [Accessed 27 Mar. 2019].

O'Grady, M. and O'Hare, G., 2012. How smart is your city? *Science,* 335(6076), pp. 1581-1582.

Mori, K. and Christodoulou, A., 2012. Review of sustainability indices and indicators: Towards a new City Sustainability Index (CSI). *Environmental impact assessment review,* 32(1), pp. 94-106.

UN, United Nations, 2008. *World Urbanization Prospects: The 2007 Revision Population Database.* United Nations

Turcu, C., 2013. Re-thinking sustainability indicators: local perspectives of urban sustainability. *Journal of Environmental Planning and Management,* 56(5), pp. 695-719.

Berardi, U., 2013a. Clarifying the new interpretations of the concept of sustainable building. *Sustainable Cities and Society*, 8, pp. 72-78.

Berardi, U., 2013b. Sustainability assessment of urban communities through rating systems. *Environment, development and sustainability,* 15(6), pp. 1573-1591.

Harrison, C., Eckman, B., Hamilton, R., Hartswick, P., Kalagnanam, J., Paraszczak, J. and Williams, P., 2010. Foundations for smarter cities. *IBM Journal of Research and Development,* 54(4), pp.1-16.

Ballas, D., 2013. What makes a 'happy city'? *Cities,* 32, pp. S39-S50.

Albino, V., Berardi, U. and Dangelico, R.M., 2015. Smart cities: Definitions, dimensions, performance, and initiatives. *Journal of Urban Technology*, 22(1), pp. 3-21.

Caragliu, A., Del Bo, C. and Nijkamp, P., 2009. Smart Cities in Europe. *3rd Central European Conference in Regional Science – CERS.* Slovakia.

Correia, L.M. and Wünstel, K., 2011. Smart cities applications and requirements. *White Paper. Net!Works European Technology Platform.*

Nam, T. and Pardo, T.A., 2011. Conceptualizing smart city with dimensions of technology, people, and institutions. *In Proceedings of the 12th annual international digital government research conference: digital government innovation in challenging times* pp. 282-291. ACM.

Batty, M., Axhausen, K.W., Giannotti, F., Pozdnoukhov, A., Bazzani, A., Wachowicz, M., Ouzounis, G. and Portugali, Y., 2012. Smart cities of the future. *The European Physical Journal Special Topics,* 214(1), pp.481-518.

UN-HABITAT, 2015. *The state of African cities 2014: Re-imagining sustainable urban transitions. United Nations Human Settlements Programme.* UN-Habitat.

Advancity, Cap-digital, and systematic, 2016. Livre Blanc "Le Numérique Et La Ville". [online] Available at: https://systematic-paris-region.org/wp-content/uploads/2017/05/LIVRE-BLANC-2016-Le-numérique-et-la-ville.pdf [Accessed 27 Mar. 2019].

Safia, L., Jamal, B., Mustapha, A., Salma, M. and Sabry, A.H., 2018. Optimization of Vehicle Routing for Smart City: Real Case Study in Casablanca. *Smart Application and Data Analysis for Smart Cities (SADASC'18).* Casablanca, Morocco.

Boudaa, B., Hammoudi, S. and Benslimane, S.M., 2018. Towards an extensible context model for mobile user in smart cities. *In Computational Intelligence and Its Applications: 6th IFIP TC 5 International Conference, CIIA 2018,* Oran, Algeria, May 8-10, 2018, Proceedings 6 (pp. 498-508). Springer International Publishing.

Namiot, D., Pokusaev, O. and Kupriyanovsky, V., *Data Mining on the Use of Railway Stations.* [online] Available at: http://ceur-ws.org/Vol-2268/paper7.pdf [Accessed 27 Mar. 2019].

Monzon, A., 2015. Smart cities concept and challenges: Bases for the assessment of smart city projects. *In Smart Cities and Green ICT Systems (SMARTGREENS), 2015 International Conference.* Lisboa, Portugal. pp. 1-11. IEEE.

KEBICHE A., 2017. Le tramway de SETIF: une opportunité d'articuler urbanisme et mobilité pour un «projet de ville». *Cahiers Géographiques de l'Ouest*, n°12-13, 2017.

Wiel M., 1999. *La Transition urbaine: ou le passage de la ville pédestre à la ville motorisée.* Editions Mardaga. Belgique.

Guibon G, Ermakova L, Seffih H, Firsov A and Le Noé-Bienvenu G., 2019. Multilingual Fake News Detection with Satire on Vaccination Topic. *Conference on Computational Linguistics and Intelligent Text Processing Cicling 2019.* La Rochelle, France

BLOCKCHAIN FOR IMPROVED SAFETY OF SMART BUILDINGS

Salam Abdallah, Nishara Nizamuddin and Ashraf Khalil
Abu Dhabi University
United Arab Emirates

ABSTRACT

In this paper, we propose a blockchain powered automated self-incited fire detection sensors connected to smart buildings. This solution is based on utilizing Ethereum smart contracts to coordinate and monitor the interaction between the service providers, smart connected devices, and the end users. The smart contracts monitor the status of the fire detecting sensors; interact with a service provider according to pre-negotiated contract terms and conditions, and carries out the maintenance task in an automated fashion. When a failure occurs within the device, an internal sensor which indicates the failure generates a request for service on the blockchain. This transaction informs the service provider about the nature of the failure, identifying the specific device. The service provider can respond to the service request in a timely manner. Upon completion, the sensor reading indicates the completion of the maintenance/repair work carried out and can release payment to the service provider on the blockchain. Moreover, the proposed solution automates the payment process between the client and the service provider.

KEYWORDS

Smart Buildings, Fire Detecting Sensors, Blockchain, Ethereum, Smart Contracts

1. INTRODUCTION

The rapidly evolving internet technology and interrelated computing devices and the Internet of Things (IoT) have led to the integration of millions of sensors and smart devices that can interact with one another without any human guidance or intervention (Alaba et al, 2017) (Atzori, Iera, and Morabito, 2010). The need for a large scale deployment of IoT devices and sensors is ever growing and has gained wide acknowledgement and prevalence. The innovation in the IoT technology and cloud computing has paved a way to the perpetual global connection of devices, people, services and sensors. The term "things" in the IoT comprises of physical devices such as sensors that monitor and collect a huge amount of data about machines and day to day activities of human life (Yan et al, 2014). In the era of information technology, smart homes once a myth has now become a reality where any device in one's home that uses electricity can be put on the home network and at the user's command. Whether that command is given by voice, remote control, tablet or smartphone, the home reacts and responds (Aldrich, 2003). Most smart home applications relate to lighting, home security, home theatre and entertainment, and thermostat regulation (Aldrich, 2003) (Ding et al, 2011).

One of the most crucial and lifesaving sensors that are employed in modern day buildings are fire detection sensors. However, these sensors fitted in the smart homes come with a life time of 10-15 years, which doesn't guarantee resistance to malfunction in due course of time (Home-security-systems, 2019). Many modern day smoke detectors will signal the "end-of-life" warning with a beep sound when their lifetime comes to an end. Despite the widespread use of fire detectors in both residential and industrial environments, the fire still claims many lives, causes grievous injuries and leads to huge financial loss. In the USA, over 362,000 residential fires were reported, leading to 2,500 deaths, 13,200 injuries and a loss valued at $6.65 billion in the year 2010. As shown in Figure 1, in Europe, some 20,000-25,000 deaths occur due to fire each year (Bogue, 2013). Figure 1 shows the pictorial representation of the analysis of the death dataset taken from (U.S. Fire Administration, 2017). Some of the most common causes of fire detection system failures are identified as high ceilings, dirty smoke detectors, and wrong detection type. Poor maintenance, negligence or unidentified malfunction leads to fatal outcomes and claims human lives. Figure 2 shows the overall non-residential building fire, injuries, fatalities, and losses due to fire during the year 2006-2015 based on National Fire Protection Association, National Fire Incident Reporting System, and consumer price index in the US.

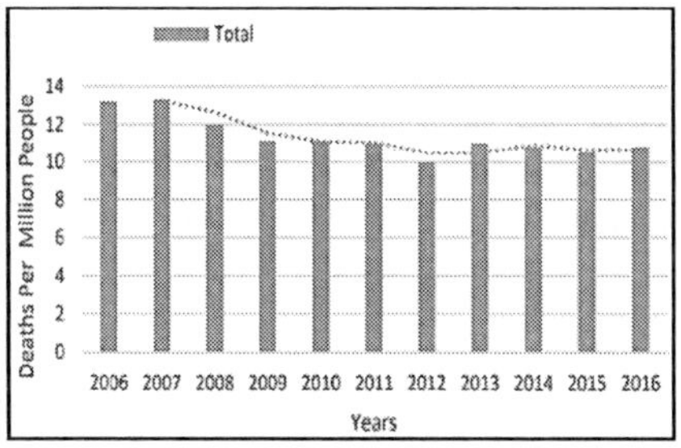

Figure 1. Fire deaths per million people

Overall Nonresidential Building Fires and Fire Losses (2006-2015)

Year	Fires (in thousands)	Fire Deaths	Fire Injuries	Fire Dollar Loss Adjusted to 2015 Dollars (in $ millions)
2006	98.9	75	1,350	$2,756.6
2007	103.0	90	1,275	$3,278.1
2008	97.1	100	1,250	$3,800.4
2009	89.2	90	1,500	$3,048.6
2010	84.9	80	1,375	$2,609.5
2011	85.4	80	1,100	$2,566.5
2012	92.8	65	1,450	$2,550.9
2013	93.7	65	1,425	$2,504.3
2014	99.5	60	1,200	$2,579.1
2015	104.6	70	1,325	$2,691.1

Figure 2. Non-residential building fire & losses
(U.S. Fire Administration, 2017)

1.1 Problem Statement

There is a considerable amount of time spent in identifying, reporting and maintaining faulty fire detection sensors. The conventional approach used is reliable but is tedious. Figure 3 shows the conventional approach of maintenance and repair of fire detection sensors in the smart buildings. The service provider sends its representative to address the reported issue by the sensors attached to the smart buildings.

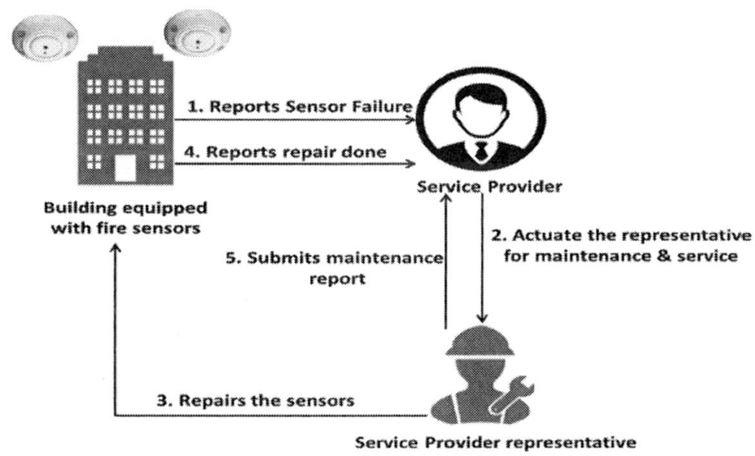

Figure 3. Classical model for security maintenance of buildings

In large scale deployments of thousands of smart devices, maintenance and repair is still predominantly a manual process. Service requests from clients and payments are handled by administrators (from the service provider) who manage their maintenance, monitoring, and repair. The process is slow and time-consuming. Both the parties heavily rely upon the maintenance reports withheld by the respective parties. There arises a need for a robust solution that manages the maintenances and repairs of smart sensors in a much faster and dependable manner.

Since its initiation in 2008, blockchain continues to be one of the augmenting technological concepts following the success of Bitcoin, a cryptocurrency system based on decentralized infrastructure (Nakamoto, 2008). Blockchain implements a distributed ledger which is shared among all the authenticated participants in the network based on consensus property. The presence for a third party authenticator is phased out, making the system secure and decentralized. The transactions are digitally verified by all the miner nodes, validated and is finally logged in the blockchain. This growing list of records is linked using cryptography is completely decentralized, time-stamped and tamper proof ledgers (Nakamoto, 2008). Blockchain technology has gained importance and has been utilized in several industries such as healthcare, energy sector, and supply chain. Ethereum is a public, blockchain-based, open source, a platform featuring smart contract functionality. It uses

Ether as currency to carry out payments on Ethereum blockchain. Smart contracts are self-executing shared ledgers that use blockchain as the underlying technology to verify the prosecution of predefined terms. A smart contract not only defines the rules and penalties related to an agreement in the same way that a traditional contract does, but it can also automatically enforce those obligations. This is carried out by taking information as input, assigning values to that input through a set of rules in the smart contract and executes the actions. For example, determining whether an asset should go to one entity in the network or should be returned to other entity from which the asset originated (Christidis and Devetsikiotis, 2016) (Luu et al, 2016). Smart City initiatives by both government and private sector businesses to invest in information and communication technologies to find sustainable solutions to the growing issues has been an important factor in the effective management of smart cities. The Internet of Things (IoT) couldn't exist without smart sensors, and the growing use of smart technology is already transforming how manufacturers implement the IoT. Smart sensors are also bringing more connectivity and analytics to the development of smart cities and are the indispensable enablers of the IoT and the industrial IoT (Zanella et al, 2014). Smart sensors are particularly in residential apartments and warehouses because they can keep track of heat, temperature, and humidity, log data for historical records and quality management or be used as triggers for alarms or process management (Hancke et al, 2013) (Su et al, 2011). As the sensor networks have been playing a crucial role in setting up the smart cities, smart sensors compound to be crucial elements in the information technology world.

2. PROPOSED BLOCKCHAIN BASED SOLUTION

Motivated by the importance of having a practical and robust maintenance service of smart sensors and the implementation of blockchain in various fields, we propose a blockchain powered solution combined with sensing–as-a-service model in the safety of smart buildings maintenance and management. Figure 4 shows the proposed blockchain based solution for improving the safety of smart cities. There are 2 smart contracts namely- fire sensor smart contract and service provider smart contract. As shown in figure 4, in case of sensor failure, the smart contract dedicated to fire sensor is logged with a fire sensor failure transaction, which in turn raises a service request on the service provider smart contract. The service provider opens/raises a ticket for the issue. The service providers' representative is contacted who then repairs and fixes the issue raised. The fire sensor contract then propagates the message to complete the payment for the service provider following which the payment settlement is completed in an automated fashion. The union of smart sensors technology and blockchain can manage the log data effectively, improve the service provided with the help of a shared distributed database. Smart contracts can be utilized to automate the tasks that benefit the smart building maintenance in terms of safety. The automation afforded by the blockchain and smart contracts can regulate and automate the communication between multiple stakeholders, eliminate the need for a trusted third party (i.e. administrators from service provider's side) and prevent the occurrence of delay to service a malfunctioned/ defective fire detecting sensor in a building. Upon raising the service request, the smart contract executed will guarantee the enforcement of predefined rules such that all the authorized stakeholders can check the outcome of a transaction.

Blockchains are built for transaction consistency in a data store, allowing for auditability, atomicity, linearizability, durability, and data integrity (Nakamoto, 2008). They serve a similar purpose to distributed databases using data models and transaction mechanisms, where different replicas can be hosted by mutually cynical organizations. The models continually check each other's integrity and use a consensus protocol to agree on the transactions that should be executed. Blockchains use cryptographic auditing that relies on Merkle trees. Though blockchain has gained importance across many industries, there are several research issues still to be addressed before implementing a completely decentralized application such as Security flaws, Transaction costs, network speed, scalability, sustainability setting regulations and standards and a full swing adoption of this technology is still under research.

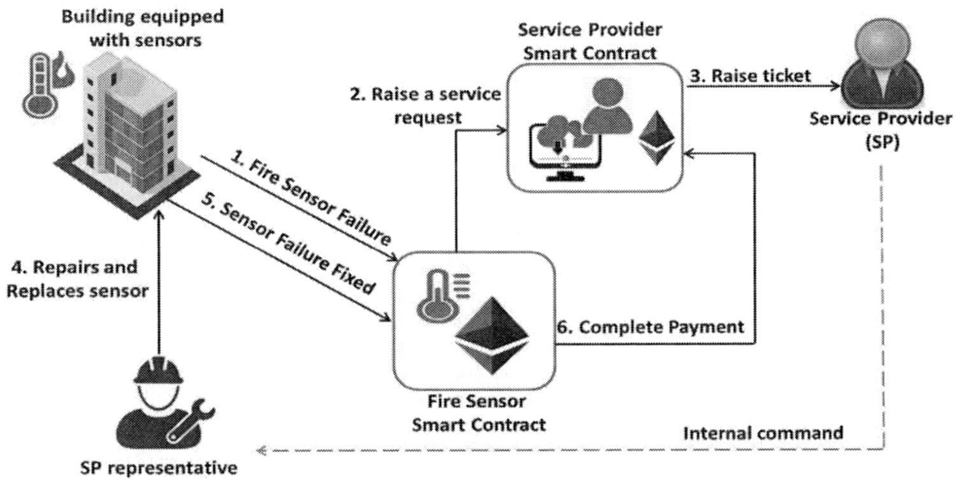

Figure 4. Blockchain-powered smart building security against fire sensor failures

3. FUTURE RESEARCH PLANNED

As a part of future research towards a blockchain-powered smart building security management, we are currently working on this project to contribute the following:

- To build the device self-service prototype using the Ethereum platform and smart contracts written in Solidity programming language on Remix IDE.
- To present a system that monitors safety by utilising the data and sensors' events in the smart buildings which help in detecting any sensor malfunction or repair and log events through smart contract.
- To offer a novel design that eliminates the need for a trusted third party (administrators in this case) between the service provider and the client.
- To carry out security vulnerability analysis of the smart contract code.

4. CONCLUSION

To date, the safety measures and maintenance of fire detecting sensors in smart buildings have been time consuming where the outcome of maintenance is manually administered or verified. In the near future, it is conceptualized that consumers and service providers will not settle for less than a tamper proof, secure and decentralized system especially when it comes to critical building services such as maintenance of fire detection sensors. Blockchain technology affirms and regulates safe and secure transactions. In this paper, we have proposed a model for improved safety of smart building maintenance by deploying smart contracts. Further, efforts and innovation are required by the research fraternity to design and build precise architecture, open source frameworks, and packages to execute critical sensor data-based services using blockchain platforms.

REFERENCES

Alaba, F. A., Othman, M., Hashem, I. A. T., & Alotaibi, F. (2017). Internet of Things security: A survey. *Journal of Network and Computer Applications*, *88*, 10-28.

Aldrich, F. K. (2003). Smart homes: past, present and future. In *Inside the smart home* (pp. 17-39). Springer, London.

Atzori, L., Iera, A., & Morabito, G. (2010). The internet of things: A survey. *Computer networks*, *54*(15), 2787-2805.

Bogue, R. (2013). Sensors for fire detection. *Sensor Review*, *33*(2), 99-103.

Christidis, K., & Devetsikiotis, M. (2016). Blockchains and smart contracts for the internet of things. *Ieee Access*, *4*, 2292-2303.

Ding, D., Cooper, R. A., Pasquina, P. F., & Fici-Pasquina, L. (2011). Sensor technology for smart homes. *Maturitas*, *69*(2), 131-136.

Hancke, G., Silva, B., & Hancke Jr, G. (2013). The role of advanced sensing in smart cities. *Sensors*, *13*(1), 393-425.

Home-security-systems. Smoke Detector Problems and How to Solve Them. [Online] Available: https://www.home-security-systems-answers.com/smoke-detector-problems.html, Accessed 01 April 2019.

Luu, L., Chu, D. H., Olickel, H., Saxena, P., & Hobor, A. (2016, October). Making smart contracts smarter. In *Proceedings of the 2016 ACM SIGSAC Conference on Computer and Communications Security* (pp. 254-269). ACM.

Nakamoto, S. (2008). Bitcoin: A peer-to-peer electronic cash system.

Su, K., Li, J., & Fu, H. (2011, September). Smart city and the applications. In *2011 international conference on electronics, communications and control (ICECC)* (pp. 1028-1031). IEEE.

U.S. Fire Administration. Available online: https://www.usfa.fema.gov/data/statistics/. Accessed on 01 April 2019.

Yan, Z., Zhang, P., & Vasilakos, A. V. (2014). A survey on trust management for Internet of Things. *Journal of network and computer applications*, *42*, 120-134.

Zanella, A., Bui, N., Castellani, A., Vangelista, L., & Zorzi, M. (2014). Internet of things for smart cities. *IEEE Internet of Things journal*, *1*(1), 22-32.

MULTI-LAYER AGGREGATION IN SMART GRIDS
A BUSINESS MODEL APPROACH

Lasse Berntzen, Thomas Brekke and Marius Rohde Johannessen
School of Business, University of South-Eastern Norway
P.O. Box 235, 3603 Kongsberg, Norway

ABSTRACT

This paper describes a business model innovation approach to multi-layer aggregation in smart power grids. Multi-layer aggregation makes it possible to sell and buy electrical power in the local market. To make this feasible, it is necessary to innovate an efficient business model and technology to handle the transactions between sellers and buyers. The proposed business model will use blockchain and smart contracts to handle transactions between the actors.

KEYWORDS

Smart Grid, Supply-Demand, Solar Energy, Smart Contracts, Blockchain, Disruptive Innovation, Business Model Innovation

1. INTRODUCTION

The smart grid describes a power distribution grid with intelligent components that seek to optimize power consumption based on dynamic pricing. Power consumption varies throughout the day, week and year, and the price of electricity is based on supply and demand. When the supply is limited, and the consumption is high the price increases, and in periods with ample supply and low consumption, the price decreases. During the winter, electricity is in demand for heating. During the summer, the demand is lower (and production higher, especially solar energy). Power consumption is higher during days than nights.

The smart grid optimizes energy use by shifting energy use to periods with lower prices. One typical example is the heating of water. A water heater is an insulated container that can keep water warm for several hours. A regular water heater has a thermostat that turns the heating element on when the temperature drops below a threshold. An alternative is to have a lower threshold and turn the heating element on during the night when electricity costs are lower.

The same solution is relevant to refrigerators. They also turn on when the temperature drops below a given threshold. Electric vehicles with batteries may also be charged at times when the price of electricity is lower.

The next section provides an overview of existing research on smart grid business. Section 3 introduces multi-layer aggregation, followed by a section describing blockchain and smart contracts. Section 5 discusses the business model, followed by a section providing conclusions and future work.

2. EXISTING RESEARCH ON SMART GRID BUSINESS

Smart grids have been on the research agenda for quite some time, and many researchers have proposed various business models. In this section, we present a brief overview of selected papers.

Shomali and Pinkse (2016) reviewed the disruptive consequences of smart grids (Table 1) for value creation, value delivery, and value capture. They found both enabling and constraining factors affecting existing business models. The authors conclude that for new business models to emerge, we need to see consumer engagement, new players on the supply side as well as strong government intervention.

Table 1. Impact on the Electricity Firms′ Business Model Innovation

	Enabling	Constraining
Value creation	• New value propositions based on renewable energy & energy services • Increased demand for high-quality electricity • Customers′ demand response helps balancing the network	• Empowered customers control and reduce electricity usage • Consumer generate their own electricity and become prosumers • Consumer engagement does not materialize
Value delivery	• Improved optimization of the electricity network • Improved marketing based on real-time data on electricity usage • Leverage assets of specialized ICT or energy service providers	• The value of conventional power plants erodes • The risk that new entrants become competitors • Increased complexity of the value network requires new capabilities
Value capture	• New revenue streams based on services and big data • Potential to become central actor on a multi-sided market • Reduced costs from less grid maintenance and load-shift	• Reduced revenues from selling electricity • Increased costs from investments in smart infrastructure • Uncertainty about the potential changes in revenues and costs

Electric vehicles have a disruptive potential for the power grid, as fast charging of vehicles requires large amounts of power delivered in a short time, putting stress on the grid's capacity. Several different business models have been developed to address this challenge. One example is presented by Budde Christensen, Wells, and Cicigan (2012), who propose a battery leasing scheme, where batteries are owned by a company and customers instead of charging can go to a station and change the battery when needed. This helps alleviate some of the added stress to the grid, as batteries can be charged at times of low demand. The company would be a major purchaser of electricity and could use this purchasing power to negotiate prices and overall lower the cost of running an electric vehicle. The multi-layer aggregation proposed in this paper could further help reduce the running costs.

Giordano and Fulli (2012) also present business models for electric vehicles, as well as for smart homes. They examine the actors involved and the relations between these actors, and their main conclusion is that for smart grid services to succeed, we need system system-level approaches to integrate the different components into a smart ecosystem.

Ubilla et al. (2014) present two different business models for so-called microgrids, which are local energy grids in rural areas with little or no access to the national grid. Using a variety of renewable energy sources, they show how their business model can help with the entire process from financing to implementing and running the local grid. Both models include a local management structure which is in charge of operation and maintenance. The first model has a cooperative structure, made for communities with no dependence on outside actors. The second model is a hybrid structure where the community is still strong, but where there also an added layer of administration hired to handle the operation and management.

Instead of focusing on a particular application area, Rodriguez-Molina et al. (2014) present a review of various prosumer (producer/consumer) business models for smart grids. They identify four different models and present the value-propositions for each. Their conclusion echoes that of Shomali and Pinkse in that they stress the need for active consumers (prosumers) in developing the smart grid: "*Prosumers are likely to become the major actor in the development of the smart grid and are no less than the part of the energy market value chain with the greatest potential of business creation based on the services in which they can take part.*"

3. MULTI-LAYER AGGREGATION

New technology makes it possible for households to produce their own energy. Solar power is the leading technology with solar panels installed on roofs, but also geothermal energy may be used. In most cases, the self-produced energy is a substitute for energy consumed from the power grid. The household may also produce surplus energy and sell it back to the grid.

The smart grid contains two key components: The smart meter (Meineche, 2017) that measures the amount of energy transferred between the power distribution grid and the household, and a contract with the distributor establishing payment for energy transferred from the grid to the household and from the household to the grid.

So far, the rates for exporting energy onto the grid has been set by the distribution network operator, operating in a monopoly setting. Even if the rates are based on market price, the price includes the administrative costs of the operator.

Smart multi-layer aggregation (Smart-MLA) is a concept to loosen up this monopoly and lower the transaction cost by selling energy to a local market. The concept is illustrated in Figure 1. The multi-layer aggregation makes it possible for a household with surplus power to sell its surplus to neighbors instead of putting it on the power grid. If the neighborhood produces surplus energy, the neighborhood can sell its surplus to the next neighborhood instead of putting the surplus onto the grid operated by the distribution network operator. This requires a new business model and technology that reduces administrative costs but also removes the risk of dealing with a network of sellers and buyers instead of one single operator. The technology includes components bridging the local distribution network with the power distribution network. The business model requires an effective and secure revenue stream, in addition to a distributed solution for handling billing between the actors. The bridging components are not discussed in this paper, but we propose to use blockchain and smart contracts to handle the billing process.

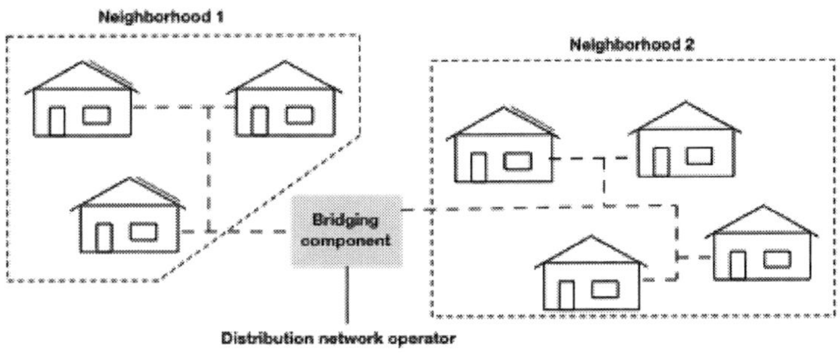

Figure 1. Smart-MLA concept

4. BLOCKCHAIN AND SMART CONTRACTS

Blockchain and smart contracts are intimately connected. Blockchain is the enabling technology for smart contracts.

4.1 Blockchain

Tapscot and Tapscot (2016) offer the following definition: "*Blockchain is an incorruptible digital ledger of economic transactions that can be programmed to record not just financial transactions but virtually everything of value*."

Blockchain is an immutable distributed ledger. Cryptographic techniques make sure that it is not possible to change the content of an entry when it is put on the blockchain. All entries are recorded in blocks that are distributed to many computers. If one or more computers fails, the data is still obtainable from the network. If there should be an inconstancy, the majority will win. Essentially, blockchain makes it possible to do transactions without an intermediary.

Themistocleous et al. (2019) discuss how blockchain can be used in the energy sector.

Blockchain may be a possible technology for supporting the business model outlined below. According to Hooper (2018), blockchain has the following features: Increased transparency, enhanced security, improved traceability, increased efficiency and speed, and reduced costs. To maintain the blockchain each transaction will incur a cost. Therefore, the transactions should be aggregated and written to the blockchain at regular intervals, e.g., once every day.

Other authors (e.g., Zheng et al., 2018) have argued that blockchain may not scale well, that it uses too much energy, and that in the future the technology may be replaced by some disruptive innovation discouraging support by platform operators. The risks are discussed below.

Ethereum is an open source blockchain platform with excellent support for writing smart contracts (Mukhopadhyay, 2018). The developer support offered by Ethereum makes the Ethereum platform a viable candidate for the Smart-MLA application. The main reason for using blockchain technology is that multi-layer aggregation involves multiple sellers and buyers without any centralized controlling entity.

4.2 Smart Contracts

A smart contract is a mechanism to store and verify data using self-executable code (Mohanta, Panda and Jena, 2018). The smart contracts run on a blockchain application platform, e.g., Ethereum. Smart contracts are autonomous and distributed. Mukhopadhyay (2018) shows how to write smart contracts that make it possible to store transaction information in the Ethereum blockchain. The smart contracts are written in a dedicated object-oriented programming language: Solidity.

4.3 Blockchain Risks

Being aware of the risks associated with blockchains is essential. Today, blockchain is distributed and free. However, there have been some warnings about the scalability and energy consumption to uphold the blockchain. Some future technology may make blockchain obsolete, and at some point, there may be an unwillingness to pay for the computer resources to run the blockchain. In our case the risks are considered low for two reasons:

- The transaction records are only needed for a limited period. The records are needed for fulfilment of payments, and maybe to generate reports for tax purposes.
- The blockchain will have limited size and may be transferred to a private blockchain infrastructure if the public blockchain structure breaks down.

5. BUSINESS MODEL

A business model defines how an enterprise creates and delivers value to customers, and then converts payments received to profits (Teece, 2010) in a specific marketplace. In this case, the marketplace is the electrical power market.

The business model handles transactions between sellers and buyers of electric energy in the market. The business model does not only consider customer needs more astutely, but also how to capture values from providing new products and services. According to Teece (2010), a good business model yields value proposition that is compelling to customers, achieves advantageous cost and risk structure, and enables significant value capture by the business that generates and delivers products and services. The value proposition of the smart grid should explain why the actors should prefer this solution compared to other competitive solutions in the marketplace.

5.1 Fair Price

The main goal of the new business model is to provide customers with a cost-effective solution for handling trade between themselves. For the consumer, the price should be lower than the market price. For the seller, the price should be above the price offered by the distribution network operator. Figure 2 shows the possible window of pricing. The selling price offered by the distribution network operator will in most cases be above the market price to cover the expenses of the operator. The buying price will normally be lower than the market price, also to cover expenses related to network operation and billing.

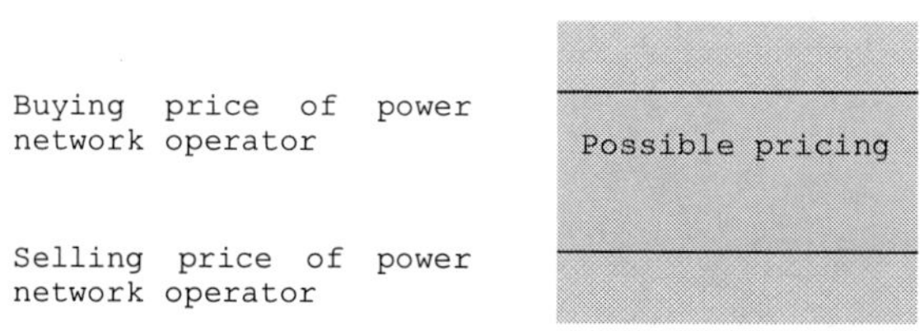

Figure 2. Market window

The costs will be related to smart meters and the bridging components to interconnect the local power grids with the distribution network operators grid.

5.2 Value Proposition

The value proposition of the Smart-MLA solution is to handle transactions between sellers and buyers in a cost-effective way. Electrical energy is dynamically priced, the price is decided on supply and demand. Normally, an intermediary handles the transactions between a seller and a buyer, and the intermediary is paid a commission to handle the transaction. Smart-MLA aims to reduce the transaction costs to a minimum. In practice, the transaction is conducted between the seller and buyer using the Smart-MLA solution for transaction fulfilment. By using blockchain technology, the transaction ledger is stored in the open, and since the blockchain is immutable, the transactions will be safely stored.

6. CONCLUSIONS AND FUTURE WORK

Multi-layer aggregation needs entrance of new disruptive smart grid business models that have the capacity to disrupt large energy distributors market monopoly of selling energy to household and propose new value proposition that is compelling to customers, achieves advantageous cost and reduce risk structure. This paper presents one possible business model based on the use of blockchain and smart contracts, and will be used for discussions with stakeholders in the energy business. Workshops for further refinement of the business model are planned and will be conducted during spring 2020.

ACKNOWLEDGEMENT

The research presented here was funded by The Research Council of Norway as part of the ERA-Net project: Multi-layer aggregator solutions to facilitate optimum demand response and grid flexibility, Project no. 295750.

REFERENCES

Budde Christensen, T., Wells, P. and Cipcigan, L., 2012. Can innovative business models overcome resistance to electric vehicles? Better Place and battery electric cars in Denmark. *In: Energy Policy*. 48, 498–505.

Giordano, V. and Fulli, G., 2012. A business case for Smart Grid technologies: A systemic perspective. *In: Energy Policy*. 40, 252–259.

Hooper, M., 2018. Top five blockchain benefits transforming your industry. Blockchain Pulse: IBM Blockchain Blog, February 22, 2018. [Retrieved May 2nd, 2019] https://www.ibm.com/blogs/blockchain/2018/02/top-five-blockchain-benefits-transforming-your-industry/

Meinecke, C., 2017. Potentiale und Grenzen von Smart Metering. Springer VS.

Mohanta, B. K., Panda, S. S. and Jena, D., 2018. An Overview of Smart Contract and Use cases in Blockchain Technology. *Proceedings 9th International Conference on Computing, Communication and Networking Technologies (ICCNT)*, IEEE, pp. 1-4.

Mukhopadhyay, M., 2018, Ethereum Smart Contract Development. Packt Publishing Ltd.

Rodríguez-Molina, J., Martínez-Núñez, M., Martínez, J.-F. and Pérez-Aguiar, W., 2014. Business Models in the Smart Grid: Challenges, Opportunities and Proposals for Prosumer Profitability.

Shomali, A. and Pinkse, J., 2016. The consequences of smart grids for the business model of electricity firms. *In J. Clean. Prod.* 112, 3830–3841.

Tapscott, D. and Tapscott, A., 2016. *Blockchain Revolution*, Portfolio Penguin.

Teece, D. J., 2010. Business Models, Business Strategy and Innovation. *In: Long Range Planning*, 43(2-3), 172-194

Themistocleous, M., Stefanou, K., Megapanos, C and Iosef, E., 2019. To Chain or Not to Chain? A Case from Energy Sector. The 15th European, Mediterranean, and Middle Eastern Conference on Information Systems (EMCIS 2018), Lecture Notes in Business Information Processing (LNBIP) 341, Springer, pp. 31-37, ISSN: 1685-1348, ISBN 978-3-030-11394-0.

Ubilla, K., Jiménez-Estévez, G.A., Hernádez, R., Reyes-Chamorro, L., Irigoyen, C.H., Severino, B. and Palma-Behnke, R., 2014. Smart Microgrids as a Solution for Rural Electrification: Ensuring Long-Term Sustainability Through Cadastre and Business Models. *In: IEEE Trans. Sustain. Energy*. 5, 1310–1318.

Zheng, Z., Xie, S., Dai, H-N, Chen, X. and Wang, H., 2017. Blockchain Challenges and Opportunities: A Survey. *International Journal of Web and Grid Services*. 14(4):352.

EXPLORING THE ROLE OF CUSTOMER REVIEWS IN DRIVING BUSINESS GROWTH

Rdouan Faizi and Sanaa El Fkihi
ENSIAS, Mohammed V University in Rabat, Morocco

ABSTRACT

Given the ubiquity of social media platforms and review sites, the popularity of online reviews has grown sharply over the past few years. These reviews have proven to help customers decide where to buy, where to eat and where to travel. Many studies have, actually, reported that up to 80% of customers trust these online reviews as much as personal recommendations. Therefore, our objective in this paper is to explore the business opportunities of using this valuable customer feedback. In this vein, it has been revealed that these reviews can boost business growth in a variety of ways. In fact, they help businesses gain invaluable insights on how customers perceive their products and services and enable them to identify areas for improvement. Using online customer reviews can also contribute in building branding, engagement, trust and connection between the business and its current and prospective customers. Moreover, since customer reviews rank high as important drivers of Search Engine Optimization, they can improve business online rankings. Taking into account all these benefits, we strongly believe that an effective use of customer reviews will not only enhance a business online reputation and credibility but will also boost its sales and revenue.

KEYWORDS

Social Media, Customer Review, Business, Opportunities

1. INTRODUCTION

Thanks to the rapid advances in information and communication technologies, the last two decades have witnessed the emergence and proliferation of a wide range of social media platforms. Today, these social online communities are widely used by millions of people around the world for a variety of purposes. Given the ubiquity of these digital networks, they seem to have affected nearly every aspect of our life. They have not only impacted how people communicate or interact with each other, but also influenced the way many regular operations are carried out in various domains.

As social media platforms have been growing in functionality and reach over the years, they have become a virtual space where people can voice their opinions on different issues and topics. Likewise, they have turned into an open service platform via which customers can express their views and feelings about different brands and businesses. With easy access to social media platforms such as Facebook, Yelp and Twitter at their fingertips, 21st century customers have the ability to post reviews on any product or service that they have purchased or used. This has enabled them to take a more active role as market players (Hennig-Thurau et al. 2010).

With the huge amounts of customer reviews that are posted online on a daily basis, this feedback is considered to be as important as word-of-mouth recommendation. This is, actually, why the great majority of customers tend to read these online reviews before making purchase decisions. Nonetheless, these reviews do not only impact the decisions of consumers but they also have the power to boost a company's online reputation and strengthen its credibility.

Given the importance of customer reviews, our objective in this work is to explore the impact of online customer feedback on business growth. The remainder of this paper is structured as follows. Section Two examines the reasons that motivate consumers to leave reviews. Section Three outlines the opportunities of using customer reviews to boost business. Finally, Section Four concludes this paper.

2. WHAT MOTIVATES CUSTOMERS TO LEAVE REVIEWS?

In a world of social presence, online reviews have become part and parcel of the buying experience of many customers. Before analyzing the positive impact of this customer data on businesses, our purpose in the present section is to examine the motives that drive people to post these reviews online (Yoo & Gretzel 2008).

A leading reason that motivates people to leave reviews, be they positive or negative, is that they want to help others make informed purchasing decisions. Many studies have reported that the great majority of people writing product reviews are mainly driven by altruism (Magno et al. 2018, Decker 2008, McQuarrie 2015). If a customer has a positive experience with a product or a service, he usually wants to let other people know about it so as to allow them to have the same enjoyable experience as he had. On the other hand, if his experience has turned out to be bad, his negative review serves as a warning to the online community to stay away from making a purchase they will later regret. Whether the purpose of the message is to incite to buy or not buy, the main objective of the reviewer is to help others save their time, efforts and money.

Another top reason that encourages consumers to write reviews is that they simply enjoy sharing their overall experience with others (Litvin et al. 2008). In today's ever-growing digital environment where groups of online individuals share interests and interact with one another, online reviews serve as an ideal means to voice one's opinions about different things. They are also a great opportunity for consumers to let other people know about their personal experiences with different businesses around the globe. Through reviews, consumers are given the chance to tell their side of the story and have it heard by peers. In such cases, the main motive behind writing a review is not to tell others about a positive or negative experience with a given brand. What really motivates the person to write the review is the enjoyment he feels when sharing information with the crowd (Wang & Fesenmaier 2002).

An additional reason that drives consumers to post reviews online is to reward a business for the excellent products or services it provided. These positive reviews are also an opportunity for shoppers to thank specific staff members for their efforts. Such reviews are, thus, a way of expressing gratitude to the business. Though the majority of online consumers do not write reviews, it has been reported that shoppers are more motivated to write positive reviews than negative ones. In fact, while about one third (33%) of the shoppers who write reviews are more likely to leave a review when they are especially satisfied with a product, only 2% of review writers are motivated by a negative experience (Delgado 2017).

Another motive that makes consumers leave online reviews is to help or compel businesses to improve their products, services or policy. Today, customer expectations are rising. As such, consumers expect all businesses to deliver a great customer experience. However, when the product or service of a given business does not quite live up to those expectations, the result is oftentimes a negative review on a social media platform or in a review site. Although very few of such reviews seem to have malicious intent, the main motive behind posting this set of hostile messages is simply to force the business to offer better products and services as well as establish better personal connections.

No matter what motive incites consumers to leave online reviews, this customer data is a valuable resource for both customers and businesses. In fact, these reviews not only help customers make informed buying decisions but they can also allow businesses enhance their performance in a variety of ways.

3. BUSINESS OPPORTUNITIES OF USING CUSTOMER REVIEWS

Over the last couple of years, the popularity of online customer reviews has grown considerably. These reviews have proven to help people decide which product or service that they should buy, which hotel they should stay in and even where they should eat. Over time, and with the abundance of reviews on social media platforms and review sites, this customer feedback has become a valuable resource for businesses thanks to the various opportunities that it presents (Faizi et al. 2017a, Faizi et al. 2018a, Faizi et al. 2018b, Ye et al. 2009, Zhu et al. 2010, Hu et al. 2008).

One of the major opportunities that online reviews offer is that they enable businesses to gain valuable insights on how customers perceive their products and services (Bassig 2017). Customer reviews are invaluable not only to prospective customers reading them but to businesses as well. In actual fact, they are a vital source of feedback about the way a given business is performing. In addition, they provide the business with information as to where it is meeting its customers' interests and where it is falling short.

Hence, by regularly gathering feedback that customers post on social media, businesses get a lot of opportunities to address customers' complaints and queries successfully in a timely manner before things spiral out of control. Handling the problems that customers have and responding to both negative (and even positive) reviews is likely to improve the perceptions that customers have towards the business. Responding to reviews shows that the business values both its customers together with the feedback they leave. This can help build a trusting relationship with customers who left the reviews as well as and with those who will read them, and will undoubtedly contribute in improving the overall customer experience (Faizi et al. 2017b).

Reviews can also help businesses identify areas for improvement. In addition to positive online reviews that boost a business online reputation, some other reviews may raise concerns about a specific product or service or even suggest improvements. As such, businesses can in real-time or near-real time spot difficulties that their clients are having and can identify prime issues of concern about the brand (Purcell 2011). If a given product is consistently getting mentioned in online negative reviews, a business can quickly react to solve the problem in question (El Fkihi & Faizi 2018). If an employee is frequently talked badly about, he may need to be coached. In the past, retrieving, analyzing and acting up on customer and brand data usually takes months. However, thanks to online reviews, a business can currently handle customer grievances and monitor its brand performance. Online reviews are also a good opportunity for the business to get valuable insights for enhancing business practices and for strategic analysis (Sarkar 2018). In fact, by being able to listen to what customers say about its products or services and taking into consideration the suggestions they make, businesses will not only be able to identify the potential opportunities for improving their current product line but will also be capable of designing or launching new products or services. Since products always need to be improved or upgraded to meet the evolving needs of customers, online reviews can be a great free source of great business ideas.

An additional benefit of using online reviews is that they have become one of the most trustworthy, engaging, and effective means to advertise a business products or services. Unlike traditional advertising, which can be highly expensive and oftentimes dishonest, online reviews are cost-effective, authentic, and largely unbiased. Today, every positive review that a customer posts on social media or on review sites serves as a free advertisement for the company. Through online reviews, people all over the world can get to know about different businesses and their products from real users. This is why 80 % of consumers trust online reviews as much as personal recommendations and more than advertisements and direct marketing messages (Sanyal 2016). This is simply because they serve as the digital era's word-of-mouth marketing. As such, these reviews provide mass advertising opportunities that no business might ever be able to afford through classical marketing channels. Henceforth, they are currently more vital than ever to any business seeking the most practical and profitable way to connect with customers online. Given these benefits, every business should cease every opportunity to invite happy customers to leave a review on a social media platform or on their own website after a successful customer transaction. Incorporating customer online reviews into marketing strategies will certainly help build branding, engagement, influence, trust and connection between the business and its existing and prospective customers.

In addition to the above-mentioned opportunities, customer reviews can also improve business online rankings. In fact, though search engines like Google, Bing and Yahoo have their unique ways of indexing and publishing webpages, they all value authentic and vivid content (Goldstein 2018). Yet, while there are a lot of factors that determine where a website should show up in search results, many studies have revealed that customer reviews rank high as important drivers of Search Engine Optimization (SEO) (Hodges 2018, Khan 2018). A steady pipeline of positive customer reviews is, thus, highly valued by search engines when deciding which results to return. Therefore, the more people talk about a business on the Web, the higher it is likely to appear in the top list of search results. In other words, the more online reviews a business has either on its own website or more importantly on third-party websites (such as Google, Facebook, Yelp, Amazon or Tweeter) the more chances the brand gets surfaced and clicked on. When a business website gets links (or backlinks) from other authoritative or quality sites, search engines see it as a vote of trust from users or consumers. And when the consumers' reviews are mostly positive, it is a signal for search engines that the business is trustworthy and is meeting the evolving needs of customers. Accordingly, it will certainly rank higher in search results. Therefore, in an era in which competition is increasingly getting tougher for both small and big businesses on the web, managing online reviews is an optimal way to improve search rankings and to build a solid online presence.

4. CONCLUSION

The objective of this paper was to explore the potential role of customer reviews in driving business performance and growth. The findings of the present study showed that this consumer feedback is a valuable resource of information for both customers and businesses. In fact, while these reviews can help customers make better buying decisions, they can also boost businesses in a variety of ways. In this respect, it was revealed that through this invaluable feedback, a business can know who its customers are and what their perceptions and attitudes are towards its products or services. Using these reviews will also enable businesses identify areas for improvement and will help them build branding, engagement, trust and connection with their existing and future customers. Furthermore, these customer reviews can enhance the business online rankings. All these opportunities will surely improve the online reputation and credibility of businesses and will, thus, boost their sales and revenues.

REFERENCES

Bassig M. (2017). Understanding Customer Experience Management. Retrieved from https://www.reviewtrackers.com/customer-experience-management/

Decker S. (2008). 94% of UK customers write reviews to help fellow shoppers. Retrieved from http://blog.bazaarvoice.com/2008/11/20/94-of-uk-customers-write-reviews-to-help-fellow-shoppers/

Delgado M. (2017). 5 Ways E-Commerce Websites Can Collect More Customer Reviews. Retrieved from https://clutch.co/website-builders/resources/how-to-collect-more-online-reviews-ecommerce

El Fkihi, S. & Faizi R. (2018). "How big data is reshaping the e-commerce industry," *Proceedings of the 31st International Business Information Management Association (IBIMA),* ISBN: 978-0-9998551-0-2, 25-26 April 2018, Milan, Italy, p. 2184-2189.

Faizi, R. El Fkihi, S., El Afia, A. & Chiheb, R. (2017a). "Extracting Business Value from Big Data," *Proceedings of the 29th International Business Information Management Association (IBIMA), ISBN: 978-0-9860419-7-6*, 3-4 May 2017, Vienna, Austria, p. 997-1002.

Faizi, R. El Fkihi, S. & El Afia, A. (2017b). "Leveraging Big Data to Improve Customer Experience," *Proceedings of the 30th International Business Information Management Association (IBIMA),* ISBN: 978-0-9860419-9-0, 8-9 November 2017, Madrid, Spain, p. 1405-1409.

Faizi, R. El Fkihi, S. & El Afia, A. (2018a). "Exploring the Potentials of Big Data Analytics in Marketing," *Proceedings of the 31st International Business Information Management Association (IBIMA),* ISBN: 978-0-9998551-0-2, 25-26 April 2018, Milan, Italy, p. 2109-2114.

Faizi, R., El Fkihi, S., Ezzahid, S.S., El Afia, A. (2018b). "Using sentiment analysis to derive business value," Proceedings of the 32nd International Business Information Management Association Conference, (IBIMA). ISBN: 978-0-9998551-1-9, 15-16 November 2018, Seville, Spain, p. 6781-6785.

Goldstein J. (2018). 5 Good Reasons Why Positive Online Reviews are Important to Your Business. Retrieved from https://www.sitepronews.com/2018/09/17/5-good-reasons-why-positive-online-reviews-are-important-to-your-business/

Hennig-Thurau, T., Gwinner, K. P., Walsh, G., & Gremler, D. D. (2004). Electronic word-of-mouth via consumer-opinion platforms: what motivates consumers to articulate themselves on the internet?. *Journal of interactive marketing*, *18*(1), 38-52.

Hodges M. (2018). Do Online Reviews Affect SEO? Retrieved from https://thrivehive.com/do-online-reviews-affect-seo/

Hu, N., Liu, L., & Zhang, J. J. (2008). Do online reviews affect product sales? The role of reviewer characteristics and temporal effects. *Information Technology and management*, *9*(3), 201-214.

Khan H. (2018). SEO and Why They Matter to Your Bottom Line. Retrieved from https://www.shopify.com/retail/119916611-how-online-reviews-impact-local-seo-and-why-they-matter-to-your-bottom-line

Litvin, S. W., Goldsmith, R. E., & Pan, B. (2008). Electronic word-of-mouth in hospitality and tourism management. Tourism management, 29(3), 458-468.

Magno, F., Cassia, F., Bonfanti, A., & Vigolo, V. (2018). The Effects of Altruistic and Egoistic Motivations on Online Reviews Writing Frequency. In Excellence in Services International Conference (pp. 447-455).

McQuarrie, E. F. (2015). The New Consumer Online: A Sociology of Taste, Audience, and Publics. Edward Elgar Publishing.

Purcell B. (2011). Bank of America Insights Make a Case For Social Media Data Analytics. Retrieved from http://beyondthearc.com/blog/2011/customer-experience/bank-of-america-insights-make-a-case-for-social-media-data-analytics#sthash.uYoy2PNL.dpbs.

Sanyal, P. (2016). Five Stars: Putting Online Reviews to Work for Your Business. *South Asian Journal of Management*, *23*(3), 221.

Sarkar S. (2018). Benefits of Sentiment Analysis for Businesses. Retrieved from https://www.analyticsinsight.net/benefits-of-sentiment-analysis-for-businesses/.

Ye, Q., Law, R., & Gu, B. (2009). The impact of online user reviews on hotel room sales. *International Journal of Hospitality Management*, *28*(1), 180-182.

Yoo, K. & Gretzel, U. (2008). What motivates consumers to write online travel reviews?. Information Technology &Tourism, 10 (4), 283-295

Wang, Y., Yu, Q., & Fesenmaier, D. R. (2002). Defining the virtual tourist community: implications for tourism marketing. Tourism management, 23(4), 407-417.

Zhu, F., & Zhang, X. (2010). Impact of online consumer reviews on sales: The moderating role of product and consumer characteristics. *Journal of marketing*, *74*(2), 133-148.

ANGER IN PROTEST NETWORKS ON TWITTER

Nazmiye Gizem Bacaksizlar[1], Samira Shaikh[2] and Mirsad Hadzikadic[2]
[1] *Santa Fe Institute, Santa Fe, New Mexico, USA*
[2] *University of North Carolina at Charlotte, Charlotte, North Carolina, USA*

ABSTRACT

We examine the influence relationships in online social networks and the distribution of anger during protests in Charlotte, North Carolina (2016) and Charlottesville, Virginia (2017). We extracted mention and retweet networks of users tweeting during these protests, and conducted emotion analysis on tweets to determine anger level of the users. We found that users with most followers receive most mentions and retweets. Anger levels peaked early on and then tapered off during both protests. The angriest users received few mentions and retweets. Our research has a potential to help understand influence dynamics in protest communication networks and provides insights for public policy implications.

KEYWORDS

Social Networks, Anger, Emotion, Twitter, Natural Language Processing, Protests

1. INTRODUCTION

Large political protests in the real-world are often reflected in numerous discussions on social media platforms. We investigate emotional contagion (specifically anger) in protest-related discussions on Twitter. The main research questions are: 1) What is the network structure of social media users who discuss protests on social media? 2) What is the level of anger among the users discussing the protests? 3) What is the relationship between the network position and anger level of the users?

Actual and potential protesters use Twitter and/or Facebook to connect with each other, communicate about the protests, and plan and organize their activities (Tufekci & Wilson, 2012, Valenzuela, et al., 2014). Social science theories on a threshold for political protest participation are helpful to define network structures for users (Granovetter, 1978 , Xie, et al., 2011). It has also been found that Twitter has an influence on spreading information and emotion in social networks (Anger & Kittl, 2011, Jansen, et al., 2009, Mitchell, et al., 2013, Taxidou & Fischer, 2014). However, there is a dearth of studies on how mention/retweet network structure influences spread of emotions related to protests (Tremayne, 2014). Here we focus on the spread of anger. Past studies have shown that anger is the triggering emotion for protests (Castells, 2015), but it has not yet been studied how anger spreads on social media after the protests have started.

We investigate contagion of anger in tweets after two recent protests: One occurred in 2016 in Charlotte, NC, where the police shooting of Keith Lamont Scott, who was African American, triggered the Black Lives Matter protests. These protests are known as the Charlotte uprisings or Charlotte riots (Lee, et al., 2016). The other is the Unite the Right rally that occurred in Charlottesville, VA in 2017. This protest, also known as the Charlottesville rally or Charlottesville riots, was a white supremacist rally (Astor, et al., 2017).

2. METHOD

To answer our research questions, we used a combination of empirical analysis of Twitter networks and natural language processing algorithms to detect anger levels of each user in the corresponding social network. In the first step, we gained access through Twitter' s proprietary firehose (Gnip Historical PowerTrack) to tweets that were sent in response to the two protests mentioned above, which used specific hashtags and keywords during the relevant protest periods. For Charlotte protests, between September 20 - 26, 2016, we extracted 1.36 million tweets. To identify the relevant tweets, only tweets with at least one of seven protest-related hashtags and keywords (e.g., #KeithLamontScott, #CharlotteProtest) were included in the data analysis. For Charlottesville protests, we extracted 390,915 tweets with relevant hashtags and keywords (e.g, #standwithcharlottesville, #HeatherHeyer) between August 11 - 18, 2017. These data sets have 430,260 (Charlotte) and 188,516 (Charlottesville) unique users. We conducted a comparative analysis for Charlotte and Charlottesville' s protests with these two datasets.

2.1 Network Analysis

We extracted user networks for both protests using mentions and retweets. Mentions in tweets appear as "@username". With retweeting, users simply copy the posted tweet from the target user. We call the user who mentions or retweets another user the *source user*, and the user who is mentioned or whose tweet is retweeted by the source user the *target user*. The resulting graph is a weighted directed network with links from the source to the target user weighted by the number of mentions or retweets of the target user by the source user.

We use this graph to investigate the influence level distribution between source and target users. We divided the users in two categories: *influential users* (those who have more than 10,000 followers) and *general public users* (with less than 10,000 followers). The most active influential users in our dataset were media channels, politicians, journalists, celebrities, singers, comedians, and actor/actresses. We select only active (not suspended) users and their non-duplicated tweets. We also remove all self-mentions. The network graph visualizations were created with the Gephi software (Bastian, et al., 2009). To have the datasets from the two protests more comparable, we sampled 5,000 tweets from each dataset (Hu & Lau, 2013), which were retweeted or mentioned by one or more source users.

2.2 Emotion Analysis

To detect anger, the Linguistic Inquiry and Word Count, or LIWC, analysis is applied on each tweet (Pennebaker, et al., 2015). LIWC is a text analysis application for language and disclosure studies, explorations with an expanded dictionary and a modern software designed in 2015. In the LIWC dictionary, words are categorized in different emotions and the frequency of words denoting each emotion are compared to overall number of words. We derived the level of anger for each tweet and calculated mean anger for each user over all of his or her tweets.

3. RESULTS

3.1 Weighted Graphs with Directed Links

For visualization purposes, the weighted graphs with directed links represent users as nodes, links between nodes as mentions or retweets of tweets, and node sizes as the number of mentions or retweets made for the node's tweets. A tweet can have more than one mentioned users. In the Charlotte's network, there were 6,259 nodes (all source and target users) and 5,656 edges. Figure 1(a) shows different communities in the network. The colors denote possible different communities in the network. The nodes with the highest in-degree tend to be influential users. For instance, users mentioned the Charlotte Mecklenburg Police Department, media channels (e.g., CNN), and one of the Black Lives Matter activists the most. The modularity score of this network structure is quite high: 97%. A high modularity score indicates possible presence of community structure, which means dense connections between the nodes within modules/groups but sparse connections between nodes in different modules (Newman, 2006).

In the Charlottesville network, there were 5,981 nodes (all source and target users) and 5,719 edges. Figure 1(b) shows different communities in the network. Again, the colors denote possible different communities in the network. In the same fashion as the Charlotte Twitter data set, most of the mentioned users in Charlottesville are also influential. This shows that influential users, such as Donald Trump and social media platforms (e.g., Facebook and Instagram), occur as the highest in-degree nodes. This might indicate that Twitter users aimed at taking the government attention and sharing tweets about the protest on social media. The modularity score of this network is a bit lower than for Charlotte protest: 90 %.

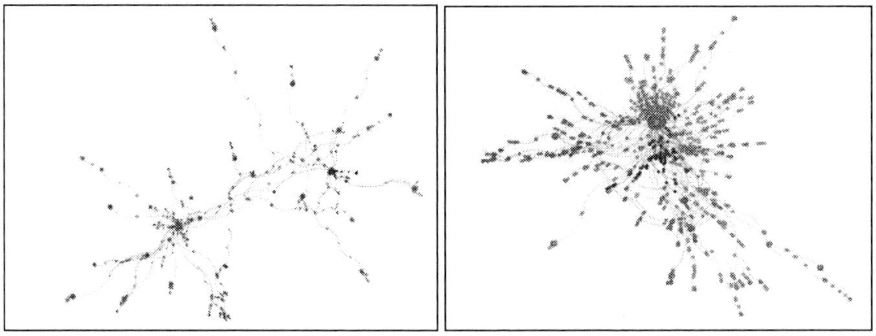

Figure 1. Network Sample for the (a) Charlotte Dataset Sample and (b) Charlottesville Dataset Sample

3.2 Anger Distributions across Protest Datasets

Figure 2(a) shows the mean anger per hour of the top ten angriest users (Max Anger), of the 32% of tweets that showed at least some anger (Mean Non-zero Anger), and of all users (Mean Anger), for the Charlotte protests. During the second day of the Charlotte protests, the anger level peaked which was likely due to the announcement that the Charlotte-Mecklenburg Police Department chose not to release the video of the shooting of Keith Lamont Scott. The percentage of users showing some anger in the Charlotte dataset is 47%. That means that angry users also tweet less than non-angry users.

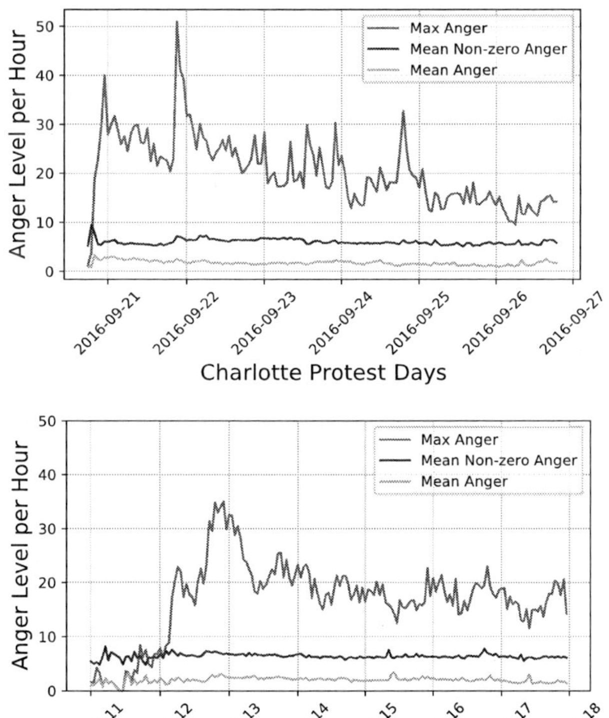

Figure 2. Anger Level Distributions of Tweets in (a) Charlotte Dataset (b) Charlottesville Dataset

Figure 2(b) illustrates the mean anger per hour of the top ten angriest users (Max Anger), of the 34% of tweets that showed at least some anger (Mean Non-zero Anger), and of all users (Mean Anger), for the Charlottesville protests. During the third day of protests, the angriest values peak, which likely stemmed from an appearance of the victim's mother in the media. The percentage of users showing some anger in the Charlottesville dataset is 45%. In sum, Charlotte protests tweets are with higher anger levels compared to tweets about Charlottesville protests. However, after early days of both protests, anger dies out. Although these two protests differ in their triggering points, they have similarities in their macro behaviors during the peak protest times.

3.3 Connection of Network and Anger

The percentages of influential users in Charlotte and Charlottesville datasets were 11% and 15%, respectively. The mean anger levels of general public users in Charlotte and Charlottesville datasets were 2.02 and 2.25, respectively. On the other hand, the mean anger levels of influential users in Charlotte and Charlottesville datasets were 1.90 and 2.08, respectively. Our results showed that the angriest users were general public users with the lower number of followers (see Figure 3). In other words, the angriest users had a relatively low impact level in the network: they were rarely retweeted or mentioned by other users. This suggests that directed links might be essential for the spread of influence and anger.

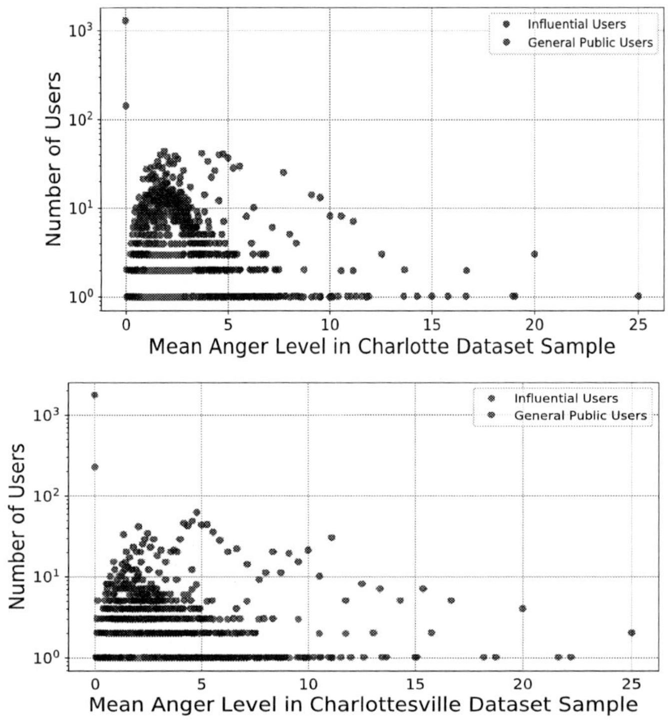

Figure 3. Mean Anger Level Distributions and Users in (a) Charlotte Dataset Sample (b) Charlottesville Dataset Sample

4. DISCUSSION

Our results show that despite being two distinct events, the Charlotte and Charlottesville protests follow similar patterns with distributions of anger and mentions/retweets based on their different network structures. Protest-related tweets of influential users (those with more than 10,000 followers) are more often mentioned and retweeted than the tweets of the general public users. Anger levels peak near the beginning of the protest and then tend to taper off. The anger levels in Charlotte protests are a bit higher. The angriest users had fewer followers, retweets, and mentions than less angry users. This could be the reason why anger does not persist in the two networks over time. If influential users were more angry, then the anger might have had a chance to persist for a longer time. Different network structures will have different effects on the dynamics of anger. In further work, comparing different network structures and applying these network structures within an agent-based model will help to investigate the effect of different influence algorithms on the spread of anger within online social networks. The law enforcement agencies, governors, and public policy makers can use our analysis to help make decisions about sharing relevant information with the public in a timely manner.

REFERENCES

Anger, I. & Kittl, C., 2011. Measuring influence on Twitter. *Proceedings of the 11th International Conference on Knowledge Management and Knowledge Technologies*. Graz, Austria, p. 31.

Astor, M., Caron, C. & Victor, D. 2017. A Guide to the Charlottesville Aftermath Video. [Online]. [Accessed 27 March 2019]. Available from: https://www.nytimes.com/2017/08/13/us/charlottesville-virginia-overview.html

Bastian, M., Heymann, S. & Jacomy, M., 2009. Gephi: an open source software for exploring and manipulating networks. *Third International AAAI Conference on Weblogs and Social Media*. San Jose, CA, USA, pp. 361-362.

Castells, M., 2015. *Networks of outrage and hope: Social movements in the Internet age*. John Wiley, Hoboken, NJ, US.

Granovetter, M., 1978. Threshold models of collective behavior. *American journal of sociology*, 83(6), pp. 1420-1443.

Hu, P. & Lau, W. C., 2013. A survey and taxonomy of graph sampling. *arXiv preprint arXiv*:1308.5865.

Jansen, B. J., Zhang, M., Sobel, K. & Chowdury, A., 2009. Twitter power: Tweets as electronic word of mouth. Journal of the *American society for information science and technology*, 60(11), pp. 2169 - 2188.

Lee, J. C., et al. 2016. Scenes and Voices from the Protests in Charlotte. [Online]. [Accessed 27 March 2019]. Available from: https://www.nytimes.com/interactive/2016/09/22/us/charlotte-police-shooting-protest.html

Mitchell, L., Frank, M.R., Harris, K.D., Dodds, P.S. and Danforth, C.M., 2013. The geography of happiness: Connecting twitter sentiment and expression, demographics, and objective characteristics of place. *PloS one*, *8*(5), p.e64417.

Newman, M. E., 2006. Modularity and community structure in networks. *Proceedings of the national academy of sciences*, 103(23), pp. 8577-8582.

Pennebaker, J. W., et al., 2015. *The development and psychometric properties of LIWC2015*.

Taxidou, I. and Fischer, P.M., 2014, April. Online analysis of information diffusion in twitter. In *Proceedings of the 23rd International Conference on World Wide Web* (pp. 1313-1318). ACM.

Tremayne, M., 2014. Anatomy of protest in the digital era: A network analysis of Twitter and Occupy Wall Street. *Social Movement Studies*, *13*(1), pp.110-126.

Tufekci, Z. & Wilson, C., 2012. Social media and the decision to participate in political protest: Observations from Tahrir Square. *Journal of communication*, 62(2), pp. 363-379.

Valenzuela, S. et al., 2014. Facebook, Twitter, and youth engagement: A quasi-experimental study of social media use and protest behavior using propensity score matching. *International Journal of Communication*, 8, p. 25.

Xie, J. et al., 2011. Social consensus through the influence of committed minorities. *Physical Review E*, 84(1), p. 011130.

THE IMPACT OF HOMOPHILY AND HERDING ON DECISION CONFIDENCE IN SOCIAL COMMERCE

Mariam Munawar, Khaled Hassanein and Milena Head
DeGroote School of Business
McMaster University
1280 Main St. West, Hamilton, ON, Canada

ABSTRACT

Social commerce is a new variant of e-commerce, fitted with social media technologies that allow users to interact with each other. These interactions may facilitate feelings of homophily, and may propagate herd behaviour within the online medium. This work-in-progress paper hones in on how homophily and herding arise within the social commerce context, and examines how it impacts a consumer's' decision-making process. A research model is proposed and an experimental methodology is outlined. Potential contributions to both theory and practice are discussed.

KEYWORDS

Homophily, Herd Behaviour, E-Commerce, Social Commerce

1. INTRODUCTION

Online shopping is experiencing exponential growth, with forecasts suggesting almost a 276.9% increase in the next couple years, culminating in a $4.9 trillion-dollar industry by 2021 (Orendorff 2019). This rapid uptake can be attributed to the emergence of social commerce (s-commerce) (Ramachandran 2018), a new variant of e-commerce fitted with social media tools that facilitate social interaction and sharing (Zhang and Benyoucef 2016). However, despite the growing popularity of this medium, shopping online is fraught with uncertainty, given the spatial and temporal separation between consumer and vendor (Pavlou et al. 2007). This is further complicated by the bells and whistles associated with the online space, resulting in information overload and complexity (Rodrigues 2018). These issues with online shopping can have a dire impact on a consumer's decision-making process (Gao et al. 2012), shaking his/her confidence in a purchase decision (Lee and Lee 2004). Although research in social commerce is gaining momentum (see Zhang and Benyoucef 2016), particularly in regards to consumers' buying intentions (eg: Hajli et al. 2017), one's confidence in his/her decisions through this medium has yet to be explored.

Decision confidence is a critical construct in understanding consumer behaviour and is important in understanding an individual's decision-making process (Oney and Oksuzoglu-Guven 2015). It is an important factor in influencing attitude formation and purchase intentions (Bennet and Harrel 1975), and has been suggested to reduce purchase uncertainty, anxiety, and post-purchase dissonance (Keng and Liao 2013). It is a predictor of future buyer behaviour (Chakrabarty et al. 1998), a predictor of household consumption (Dees and Brinca 2013), and an antecedent of brand commitment (Sung & Choi 2010). As can be seen through the literature, decision confidence is a critical construct that impacts an individual's behaviour, and investigating it within the social commerce context is both timely and needed.

Decision confidence is the belief about the goodness of one's judgments or choices, and has been described as the converse of subjective uncertainty in one's decisions (Sniezek 1992). One approach to reducing subjective uncertainty online, and thereby increasing confidence in one's decision, may be through identification with a group of similar others. This proposition is extrapolated from uncertainty-identity theory (Hogg 2000) which posits that individuals are able to overcome feelings of uncertainty by self-identifying with a group with whom they share similar attributes. Homophily is the extent to which individuals perceive themselves to be similar to others in either interests or demographics (McPherson et al. 2001). Research indicates that, in addition to reducing uncertainty, homophily also increases trust in others' recommendations or suggestions (Golbeck 2009). If individuals are able to perceive homophily within the online shopping space, it may be a valuable asset in aiding the decision-making process and building decision confidence.

The unique design of the s-commerce interface may facilitate perceptions of homophily. The s-commerce platform is integrated with specialized tools known as social media markers (SMM) which measure and track the activities and attributes of online consumers, providing convenient statistics on various measures, such as the total number of purchases or recommendations for a product (Munawar et al. 2017). Advances in data-mining technologies are making the design of SMMs more personalized, and these are now capable of providing information on the degree to which consumers are similar to one another in terms of interests and demographics (see Zafarani et al. 2014). There has been limited empirical research on the use of homophily within the social commerce context, and SMMs indicating measures of similarity are only just emerging.

SMM's are useful tools because they serve as heuristics, simplifying the complexity of online information overload. They are also partly responsible for the emergence of a phenomenon known as herd behaviour (Munawar et al. 2017), wherein individuals make decisions based on the observation of others' actions (Bikhchandani et al. 1992). Herd behaviour is quite prevalent in online shopping, due to the widespread use of SMMs that allow individuals to observe consumers' aggregated purchase-related information (such as the total number of recommendations or likes for a product). Its pervasiveness has led to a steady rise in empirical research on its occurrence in social commerce (Wang and Yu 2017); however, the research is sparse, and there remains a critical gap in understanding the interaction of herd behaviour with homophily, and its combined impact on the decision-making process.

Given the context outlined above, the purpose of this study is to build a more comprehensive understanding of a consumer's decision-making process by mapping the factors impacting decision confidence within the realm of social commerce. An attempt is made to uncover the elements of the s-commerce interface that serve as mechanisms for uncertainty reduction. In particular, this study focuses on the impact of homophily in reducing uncertainty, and in its interaction with herd behaviour to drive one's decision confidence.

2. RESEARCH MODEL

Our research model is rooted in the postulates of uncertainty-identity theory (UIT) (Hogg 2000; 2007) which suggests that uncertainty is an aversive state and that people are driven to reduce it. Identification with a group of others can serve as a means for uncertainty reduction because it allows for the development of a social comparative context that validates one's self concept, behaviours, and cognitions. In using UIT as a framework for our model, we are able to tease out perceived homophily (captured as interests homophily and demographic homophily) and herd size as factors impacting decision confidence as both these constructs aid in reducing subjective uncertainty within the online shopping context. UIT provides a theoretical underpinning for our research model, allowing us to integrate it with trust and sense of community as mediators that facilitate the reduction of uncertainty and the development of decision confidence. These mediators have been identified through their relationship to uncertainty reduction, as well as their relationship to homophily and herding.

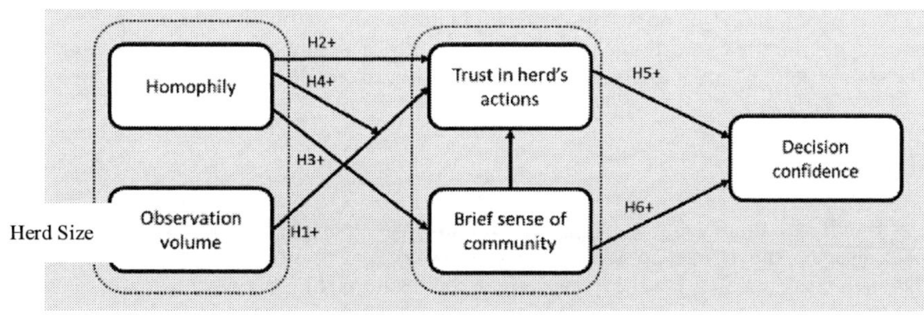

Figure 1. Research Model

3. RESEARCH METHOLOGY

The proposed program will be validated using an experimental study followed by administration of a survey. A factorial design will be employed to assess the main and interaction effects of homophily and herding on an individual's decision confidence within the social commerce context. Herding is captured through herd size, and will be operationalized as the total number of recommendations made for a product/service. Research indicates that herd size is an important factor in driving herd behaviour, and various studies report that the number of individuals in a herd will impact the likelihood of others joining and conforming to the actions of the collective. Homophily will be operationalized using a homophily index that will be presented as a percentage indicating similarity to consumers who are making these recommendations. Homophily is operationalized with four incremental levels (including a control zero level), based on the type of homophily being employed: (1) no homophily index; (2) demographic homophily; (3) interests-based homophily; or (4) both demographic and interest-based homophily. Interests-based homophily has been shown to be more potent in influencing behaviour than demographics-based homophily. Research also indicates that the combined impact of both may have stronger effects than either alone (Ensher et al. 2002).

Table 1. Research Design

Herd Size	**Homophily**			
	No homophily	*Homophily Demographics*	*Homophily Interests*	*Homophily D + I*
Small	40	40	40	40
Large	40	40	40	40

A fictitious website will be created where various treatments of these SSMs will be manipulated. Participants will view the homepage of the site, which will vary in these markers according to the experimental design. The website will be developed to simulate a social commerce platform, and subjects will be provided with a specific shopping related task. The research design will follow the approach utilized in other experimental studies on information seeking and decision-making behaviour (Tan, Teo and Benbasat, 2010), and will allow for the induction of mundane realism (Tan et al. 2010) to provide a realistic scenario. 40 participants will be randomly assigned to each treatment, for a total sample size of 320 subjects. After viewing the experimental site and completing the task, subjects will be administered a survey to answer questions about the various constructs utilized in the study.

4. PROPOSED ANALYSES

The research model will be analyzed using structural equation modeling (SEM) because of its ability to simultaneously assess both the measurement and structural model components, thereby resulting in a more rigorous methodological analysis (Gefen et al. 2011). The Partial Least Squares method will be applied because of its ability to allow modeling of latent constructs under conditions of non-normality and small-medium sample sizes. In an effort to triangulate results, a qualitative component will be included through use of open-ended questions to allow for more in-depth explanations and clarifications of the participants' experience. Content analysis techniques will be applied to identify emerging trends and patterns.

5. CONCLUSION

This research will aid in developing a clearer picture of a consumer's purchase behaviour through this medium. Because of the rising popularity of s-commerce, it is critical for vendors to understand how individuals make decisions in this setting, and the variables impacting their confidence, because of the central role confidence plays in driving satisfaction and channel adoption. In explicating the variables impacting decision confidence in social commerce, this research aids in bridging a gap in the academic literature; it also provides vendors with practical and relevant suggestions for improving the overall buying experience of its consumers.

REFERENCES

Bennett, P. D., & Harrell, G. D. (1975). The role of confidence in understanding and predicting buyers' attitudes and purchase intentions. Journal of Consumer Research, 2(2), 110-117.

Bikhchandani, S., Hirshleifer, D., & Welch, I. (1992). A theory of fads, fashion, custom, and cultural change as informational cascades. Journal of political Economy, 992-1026.

Chakrabarty, S., Chopin, M., & Darrat, A. (1998). Predicting future buyer behavior with consumers' confidence and sentiment indexes. Marketing Letters, 9(4), 349-360.

Dees, S., & Brinca, P. S. (2013). Consumer confidence as a predictor of consumption spending: Evidence for the United States and the Euro area. *International Economics*, *134*, 1-14.

Gao, J., Zhang, C., Wang, K., & Ba, S. (2012). Understanding online purchase decision making: The effects of unconscious thought, information quality, and information quantity. Decision Support Systems, 53(4), 772-781.

Gefen, D., Rigdon, E. E., & Straub, D. (2011). Editor's comments: an update and extension to SEM guidelines for administrative and social science research. Mis Quarterly, iii-xiv.

Golbeck, J. (2009). Trust and nuanced profile similarity in online social networks. ACM Transactions on the Web (TWEB), 3(4), 12.

Hajli, N., Sims, J., Zadeh, A. H., & Richard, M. O. (2017). A social commerce investigation of the role of trust in a social networking site on purchase intentions. Journal of Business Research, 71, 133-141.

Hogg, M. A. (2000). Subjective uncertainty reduction through self-categorization: A motivational theory of social identity processes. European review of social psychology, 11(1), 223-255.

Hogg, M. A. (2007). Uncertainty–identity theory. Advances in experimental social psychology, 39, 69-126.

Keng, C. J., & Liao, T. H. (2013). Self-confidence, anxiety, and post-purchase dissonance: a panel study. Journal of Applied Social Psychology, 43(8), 1636-1647.

Lee, B. K., & Lee, W. N. (2004). The effect of information overload on consumer choice quality in an on-line environment. Psychology & Marketing, 21(3), 159-183.

McPherson, M., Smith-Lovin, L., & Cook, J. M. (2001). Birds of a feather: Homophily in social networks. Annual review of sociology, 27(1), 415-444.

Munawar, M., Hassanein, K., & Head, M. (2017). Understanding the Role of Herd Behaviour and Homophily in Social Commerce. SIGHCI 2017 Proceedings. 11.

Oney, E., & Oksuzoglu-Guven, G. (2015). Confidence: A critical review of the literature and an alternative perspective for general and specific self-confidence. Psychological reports, 116(1), 149-163.

Orendorff, A. (2017). Global Ecommerce: Statistics and International Growth Trends. Shopify-Plus. Retrieved from: https://www.shopify.com/enterprise/global-ecommerce-statistics

Pavlou, P. A., Liang, H., & Xue, Y. (2007). Understanding and mitigating uncertainty in online exchange relationships: A principal-agent perspective. MIS quarterly, 105-136.

Ramachandran, M. (2018). The Evolution of Social Shopping in the Ecommerce Landscape. Retrieved from: https://www.adweek.com/digital/the-evolution-of-social-shopping-in-the-ecommerce-landscape/

Rodrigues, A. (2018). Our Brains Are Being Overloaded With Push Notifications About Nothing. Motherboard: Vice. Retrieved from: https://motherboard.vice.com/en_us/article/a3a848/facebook-notification-overload

Sniezek, J. A. (1992). Groups under uncertainty: An examination of confidence in group decision making. Organizational Behavior and Human Decision Processes, 52(1), 124-155.

Sung, Y., & Choi, S. M. (2010). "I won't leave you although you disappoint me": The interplay between satisfaction, investment, and alternatives in determining consumer–brand relationship commitment. Psychology & Marketing, 27(11), 1050-1073.

Tan, C. H., Teo, H. H., & Benbasat, I. (2010). Assessing screening and evaluation decision support systems: A resource-matching approach. Information Systems Research, 21(2), 305-326.

Wang, Q., & Shukla, P. (2013). Linking sources of consumer confusion to decision satisfaction: the role of choice goals. Psychology & Marketing, 30(4), 295-304.

Wang, Y., & Yu, C. (2017). Social interaction-based consumer decision-making model in social commerce: The role of word of mouth and observational learning. International Journal of Information Management, 37(3), 179-189.

Zafarani, R., Abbasi, M. A., & Liu, H. (2014). Social media mining: an introduction. Cambridge University Press.

Zhang, K. Z., & Benyoucef, M. (2016). Consumer behavior in social commerce: A literature review. Decision Support Systems, 86, 95-108.

Gap in pagination due to unavailable paper.

Pages 424-430

Reflection Papers

DIGITAL TRANSFORMATION IN ORGANIZATIONS: THE IMPACT ON WORKING LIFE QUALITY AND NEW RISK FACTORS

Emma Pietrafesa[1], Rosina Bentivenga[1], Sara Stabile[1] and Sergio Iavicoli[2]
Department of Occupational and Environmental Medicine, Epidemiology and Hygiene
INAL - Italian Workers' Compensation Authority
[1]Viale Stefano Gradi, 55 00143 - Rome, Italy
[2]Via Fontana Candida, 1 00078 - Monte Porzio Catone, Italy

ABSTRACT

The subject of the study is to analyse any critical factors related to the use and abuse of digital tools in the workplace, to assess their impact on work in terms of health and safety and to identify appropriate prevention and protection measures. This work aims to improve well-being and the performance of workers and organizations in relation to ongoing changes and challenges. For this purpose, a systematic international literature review was carried out with a special attention to the analysis of the validated questionnaires used in European and international contexts related to the evaluation of the impact of digital on working life quality and new risk factors. In this context, the digital transformation in the organizations, due also to the increasing use of information and communication technologies (ICT), determines changes in the workforce and management practices, with important effects, in terms of risks and benefits, on job characteristics and on the working life's quality too.

KEYWORDS

ICT, Well-Being, Workers, Occupational Health and Safety, Digital Transformation

1. INTRODUCTION

The World Health Organization defines health as 'a state of complete physical, mental and social well-being'. Health begins at home and in community where people live and work. According to the European Agency for Safety and Health at Work (EU-OSHA) strategy for 2013 – 2020, a more significant risk education is due to rapid development of the society, new technologies, globalization and changed demographic processes happened in the last decade. These changes have led to a redefinition of the world of work offering great opportunities for developing and increasing of the companies' competitiveness, but at the same time, they have had an impact on the characteristics and attitudes of the workforce, modifying the nature of the work itself, including the way in which the work is organized and managed. This digital transformation defines in the organizations the loss of traditional physical and temporal constraints, for companies and for employees both consider for example that everyone can be reached in any place (everywhere) and at any time of the day (always-on).

Starting from these assumptions, the EU-OSHA, in accordance with the basis of the strategies identified by the European Commission, has included among the research priorities in occupational health and safety at work (OSH) the impact of ICT on the job, emphasizing the need for an integrated and proactive approach for the identification of emerging risks related to changes in the world of work, which have to start from the design and development of new applications and the identification of appropriate prevention measures.

The current scenario of the labour market, in fact, is characterized by important technological innovations such as robotics, smart working, key enabling technologies (KETs), which will profoundly transform industrial processes, offering great prospects for development in terms of productivity and plant quality.

According to the latest World Economic Forum (WEF) study, within the next ten years, more than half of the current jobs are at risk of disappearing, while others will be created mostly related to technological innovation.

This landscape of the future of work will entail further complexities to manage and set in with a view to prevention, in order to increase the sustainability of work, including: new forms of work organization and new risks, the need to face important changes in the work management (e.g. flexible forms of work, new forms of work organization, psychosocial aspects). Technology innovation offers new opportunities to update and improve risk assessment and management using for example sensors and enabling technologies. This new setting, also known as the fourth industrial revolution, overcoming the Fordism and its conception of work, determines new paradigms in relation to roles, tasks and skills for workers and great opportunities for development and competitiveness growth for companies.

In this perspective, digital technology has significantly changed the way in which we communicate, interact and socialize by determining, also through the growing use of social and collaborative platforms, changes in the way we learn and share information, contents and "knowledge". Technology is also influencing the new organization of work, promoting coordination, capacity and shared knowledge with respect to centralization, but offering a new disruptive role face to a fragmented knowledge. In this situation, the technology, particularly the social and collaborative platforms are progressively interesting the workplace. In Italy, for example, the 2017 Survey of the National Statistics Institute finds that 72.1% of companies, with at least 10 employees, have their own website and/or web page (71.3% in 2016), and in 44.0% of cases they use one or more social networking platforms (39.2% in 2016). The spread of these solutions, is also affecting the new organization of work, primarily in terms of performance and well-being, but also in terms of development even because these tools can be used to satisfy customers and stakeholders.

2. METHODOLOGY

This study started from a systematic international literature review (from 2006 to 2016) through the following databases: Scopus, PubMed, Researchgate.net, ScienceDirect, with particular regards to scientific studies related to the evaluation of the impact of digital technology on the workers' well-being, followed by an examination of the validated questionnaires, more used in European and international contexts linked to the evaluation of the impact of digital in the workplace.

3. QUALITY OF LIFE AND NEW OCCUPATIONAL RISK FACTORS

The processes of innovation and digital transformation have an impact as well as on the increase of the company business, on the quality of the people working life and on the creation of new job opportunities. However, it can determine new risk factors for the workers due to the excessive workload, to the information overload and a pervasive use of digital tools, to a major exposure to continuous interruptions and intrusions and to the lack of separation between private life and professional life.

It is therefore important to observer and monitor changes in work organization, studying the effects on workers' health and safety because it is not always easy, in this regard, to distinguish between the use of digital tools at work and in private life. Working in a more flexible way, undoubtedly, represents an opportunity and a need for complex organizations, in terms of work-life balance and performance, without neglecting the effects on environmental sustainability of urban mobility given by the reduction of traffic and pollution. However, it is also necessary to evaluate carefully the aspects linked to the possible isolation of the worker - who carries out his activity outside the company context, such as in smart working, and who may not feel involved in company logics - and those related to performance evaluation, as there is still a strong correlation between career, progress and presence in the workplace. These aspects have repercussions especially in terms of gender question as they are often observed specifically in relation to the periods of women abstention from work for reasons of pregnancy and family care. Finally, the dynamics of the always-on, which should have negative consequences also in terms of dependence and abuse should not be underestimated, as some international studies have shown, a relationship between extreme use and high levels of anxiety, depression and stress (Booker 2014, Salanova 2013) and also anxiety when learning to use a new technology too, which eventually turns into psychological and emotional repulsion that prevents learning or use of the technology itself (Panova, 2016).

In the organizations, the stress linked to the use of ICT refers, above all, to data smog, multitasking madness, hassles computers, burnout, techno addiction and techno strain. Specifically, Salanova et all. (2013) have shown that this experience can be related to feelings of anxiety, mental fatigue, scepticism and inefficiency and have associated that with a negative psychological state related to use, or the prospect of having to use ICT. Technostress can therefore be traced back to a series of psychosocial factors such as work overload, interpersonal conflicts, ambiguity, conflict and role overload, conflict between work demands and family demands, insecurity. Booker (2014) has identified, in addition to five risk factors responsible for the onset of technostress: techno-overload, techno-invasion, techno-complexity, techno-insecurity and techno-uncertainty, three inhibitory factors that allow reducing the effect of stress linked to the use of technology and concerning literacy facilitation, technical support provision and involuntary facilitation.

Digital technologies have also renovated the way in which information is collected, used and remembered; for example in 2015, Kaspersky Lab has published a study in which it has described the attitudes of users to transfer the task of remembering information to their digital devices. This phenomenon called as digital amnesia affects the workplaces too.

Finally, the use of digital, by changing contextual references and work environments, expose workers also to new negative impacts such as violation of privacy, harassment and cyberbullying.

4. CONCLUSION

From the studies examined, it emerges that the most analysed areas are *use and familiarity* (Tarafdar 2011), *learning in the workplace* (Booker, 2014) and *relations with social media* (Lander, 2014). The main dimensions investigated trough the questionnaires related to the evaluation of the impact of digital on working life quality and new risk factors concern: Technostress, Offensive Content, Techno-overload, Techno-invasion, Techno complexity, Techno-insecurity, Techno-uncertainty.

As technostress inhibitors, Booker (2014) considers three factors, which represent mechanisms to decrease the effect of technology-related stress. The first one called literacy facilitation, which describes mechanisms that encourage and foster the sharing of ICT-related knowledge, reducing technostress because it helps users better understand ICTs and their uses. The second one identified as technical support provision that describes activities related to end-user support and reduces the effects of technostress by solving users' ICT problems relating. The last one is the involvement facilitation that could alleviate technostress by keeping users informed about the rationale for introducing new ICTs, by letting them know more about the effects of such introduction, and by encouraging them to use and experiment with new ICTs.

According to the Final report of Eu-OSHA (2018) some examples of OSH strategies which could help mitigate the challenges related to digitalisation in the workplace have to include:

- a strong 'prevention through design' approach that integrates a user/worker-centred design approach;
- a collaboration between academics, industry, social partners and governments on research and innovation in developments ICT-ETs/digital technologies to properly take account of the human aspects, in order to foster good quality work and good OSH;
- the involvement of workers in the implementation of any digitalisation strategies to identify the tasks best suited to automate and to structure work processes from the point of view of workers being assisted by digital technologies (rather than the other way around);
- a major challenge for the application of employment and social security laws, as well as for education and training approaches, relates to a more diverse and less well-defined workforce and to changes introducing more flexible working patterns (e.g. on-line platform working), which are expected to be brought about by an increase in the prevalence and spread of ICT-ETs.

This is because ICT-ETs allow work to be done virtually anywhere and at any time, and, for many workers, this is expected to fundamentally change the traditional employer-employee relationship. This also results in a blurring of the boundaries between work and private life. The impact of ICT-ETs on the location of work could also make defining work as the place where a problematical person is employed. These changes to the definition of work and workplace challenge the regulation and management of OSH.

In this perspective, our research activity is directed to the development of a questionnaire in order to better know and analyse the effects connected to the use and abuse of the digital technologies in the Italian workplaces through the assessment of workers' perception.

REFERENCES

Booker QE, Rebman Jr C M, Kitchens F L, 2014. A model for testing technostress in the online education environment: an exploratory study. *In Issues in Information Systems.* Vol. 15, Issue II, pp.214-222.

EU-OSHA, 2017. *Key trends and drivers of change in information and communication technologies and work location*. Luxembourg: Publications Office of the European Union.

EU-OSHA, 2018. *Foresight on new and emerging occupational safety and health risks associated digitalisation by 2025.* Luxembourg: Publications Office of the European Union.

Eurofound and the International Labour Office, 2017. *Working anytime, anywhere: The effects on the world of work.*

Landers R N, Callan R C, 2014.Validation of the Beneficial and Harmful Work-Related Social Media Behavioral Taxonomies Development of the Work-Related Social Media Questionnaire. *In Social Science Computer Review.* Vol. 32, Issue V, pp. 628-646.

Panova T, Lleras A, 2016. Avoidance or boredom: Negative mental health outcomes associated with use of Information and Communication Technologies depend on users' motivations. *In Computers in Human Behavior,* Vol. 58, pp.249-258.

Pietrafesa E., Bentivenga R., Stabile S., Persechino B., Iavicoli S., 2017. ICT e lavoro in ottica di genere: l'impatto sullo sviluppo professionale e sul work-life balance. *In Giornale italiano di medicina del lavoro ed ergonomia*, Vol. XXXIX, Issue III, p. 76.

Salanova S, Llorens Gumbau ML, Cifre Gallego SE, 2013. The dark side of technologies: Technostress among users of information and communication technologies. *In International Journal of Psychology*, Vol.48, pp. 422-436.

Stabile S, Bentivenga R, Ghelli M, Dentici MC, Pietrafesa E, Milana C, Iavicoli S. 2015 L'uso delle ICT negli ambienti di lavoro in un'ottica di salute e sicurezza. *In Giornale italiano di medicina del lavoro ed ergonomia*, Vol. 106, Issue II, p.106.

Stabile S., Bentivenga R., Pietrafesa E., (2017) *ICT e lavoro: nuove prospettive di analisi per la salute e la sicurezza sul lavoro*. Inail, Milan, Italy.

Tarafdar M, Qiang T, Ragu-Nathan T, 2011. Impact of technostress on end-user satisfaction and performance. *In Journal of Management Information Systems*. Vol. 27, Issue III, pp. 303-334.

World Economic Forum, 2018. *The future of the Jobs*.

WOMEN IN INFORMATION TECHNOLOGY EVENT: WHICH IS THE RESEARCH CONTEXT IN BRAZIL?

Pricila Castelini[1] and Marília Abrahão Amaral[2]
Postgraduate Program in Technology and Society (STS) - Federal University of Technology Paraná (UTFPR) – Curitiba, Brazil

ABSTRACT

Women participation in computer science and related areas in Brazil is fewer than men, considering quantitative researches on both labor market and academic space. Brazilian Society of Computing supports an initiative to discuss the disparities in this issue in Brazil: Women in Information Technology - WIT. We analyze 81 short papers published on 10th, 11th, and 12th editions of the event to highlight information on interests, practices, and origins of these papers. We base our analysis on Science, Technology, and Society (STS) and Feminist studies and we point out to plural and inclusive computing that open participation of all people in all spheres of society considering the social, cultural and historical aspects of society in the 21st century.

KEYWORDS

Women, Computing, STS Studies, Feminist Studies

1. THE CONTEXT

In a Brazilian context, practices on computing are culturally and socially naturalized as a male-dominant world. Monard and Fortes (2013) point out that women are not looking for undergraduate courses in computing. They indicate that computation undergraduate courses in Brazil do not follow the demand for gender equality. Open data from the National Institute for Educational Studies and Research Anísio Teixeira (INEP, 2018) show that women participation in computing in Brazil it is only 20,1%.

Meaning, it is assumed that men are those in charge of the production of technological artifacts for society. This trend has historical roots that can be traced to World War II. According to Abbate (2012) between 1940 and 1950 women worked in computing more than men did, but this initial success has historically declined. Hence, women "do not participate from design and development of the products" (WAJCMAN, 2006, p. 44). According to Gomes (2006), "our great challenge is to develop an ethical posture of not prioritizing differences and understand that no human and social group is better or worse than another. We're different" (GOMES, 2006, p. 22).

Women are the majority in university in Brazil, mostly enrolled in courses for teaching or personal caring, e.g., nursing and teacher (MONARD; FORTES, 2013). Traditional values, such as science purity and universality, are coincident with men's stereotypes. Hence, it constitutes another barrier to women entering the field. Women are not looking for these courses, with numbers showing that computing area does not follow the demand for gender equality (Abbate, 2012; Margolis, Fisher, 2002).

Women in Information Technology (WIT) is a venue to discuss and to improve the understanding of these issues. It aims to advance women participation in technology bringing together researchers and activists. Since 2016, WIT has included short papers in its call for work in progress. Is important to recognize that discussions, events, and programs in technology/computing area versing on women participation have begun with counterculture, feminism movements from 1960 and in academic research years later. Clearly, an event does not mean that the current barriers to women in tech are going to diminish, but it is an important space for the community concerned with more democracy on computation. Considering the feminism

[1] pricilacas@hotmail.com
[2] mariliaa@utfpr.edu.br

movements from the early 1960 and academic researches mentioned, we analyze the 81 published short papers from WIT 2016, 2017 and 2018. The second section presents the context of the event and 81 published short papers and the categories for analysis, the third section presents the categories analysis, and the fourth section presents final remarks.

2. *WOMEN IN INFORMATION TECHNOLOGY (WIT) – 2016-2018*

Women in Information Technology (WIT) is an initiative supported by the Brazilian Computing Society (SBC) to discuss gender in technology. Therefore, WIT focuses on women access to information technology, from the point of view of the labor market and Academia. Submissions are invited to discuss success histories; incentive policies; engagement of young people especially women associate with technological careers (CSBC, 2017). In 2016, 25 short papers were published, in 2017, 28 short papers, and in 2018, 28 short papers were published. Among the short papers submitted in the three editions of the event, some of them were written together by researchers from different regions of Brazil. In this case, we consider them separately.

As region distribution, WIT 2016 has: North of the country has published 2 short papers; Northeast, 6 short papers; Midwest, 5 short papers Southeast, 1 short paper; and South, 12 short papers have been published. WIT 2017 presents the following numbers: North, 4 short papers; Northeast, 7 short papers; Midwest, 6 short papers; Southeast, 3 short papers; and South, 8 short papers. In WIT 2018 we have found: North, 1 short paper Northeast, 11 short papers; Midwest, 7 short papers; Southeast, 7 short papers; and South, 3 short papers. Table 1 shows **recurring categories** lined up as similar categories and the second part presents the country **region** and the **quantities** of published short papers.

Table 1. Trends in topics of three event editions

WIT 2016		WIT 2017		WIT 2018	
Recurring categories	Region and quantities	Recurring categories	Region and quantities	Recurring categories	Region and quantities
Workshops, activities with high school students	9 South 3 Midwest 1 Northeast	Workshops or activities with elementary and high school students	4 South 1 Southeast 4 Midwest 3 North 2 Northeast	Workshops or activities with students	1 Southeast 2 Midwest 1 North
Presented incentive groups for women participation in the area	1 Northeast & Midwest 1 South 1 North	Analyze the participation of female students in educational institutions	1 Midwest & South 1 Northeast 2 Southeast	Incentive activity with students	7 Northeast 2 Southeast
Questionnaire with female audience	1 Northeast	Presented results of questionnaires applied with recent grads in computer science	1 South 1 North	Presented questionnaire applied with students	1 Southeast
Presented case study and examples of the reasons for women follow a computing career	1 South	Student profile analysis	2 Northeast 1 Midwest	Student profile analysis and case study	1 South 2 Northeast 2 Midwest
Teachers and students of higher education	1 Southeast 3 Northeast	Trajectories of black women teachers in computing	1 Northeast	Literature review that discusses black women in computing	1 Midwest

Table 2 shows unique **categories** and the second part presents the country **region** and the **quantities** of published short papers.

Table 2. Specific topics of three event edition

	Categories	Region and quantities
016	Games and apps	1 Midwest 1 South 1 North
2017	Examines gender violence in the computing area	1 South
	Analyses the speech in programs that encourage women participation in computing	1 South
	Presented research that discusses the regulatory and exclusionary constructions in computing	1 South
	Presented a mapping of harassment in public transport	1 Northeast
2018	Research on women barriers to access computing area	1 Northeast
	Women participation in game jams	1 Northeast
	Research with students about professional choice	1 South
	Research with students and undergraduate	1 Midwest & Southeast
	A platform that helps to evaluate work conditions for women	1 Southeast
	Presents a bibliographic analysis on women participation in game development process	1 South
	Research about women presence in electronic game development in Brazil	1 Midwest
	Qualitative study with men and women that work in a technology company	1 Southeast

3. WIT 2016, 2017 AND 2018 CATEGORIES OF ANALYSIS

We do our analysis on research categories: "quantitative data", "recurring topics", and "region". Based on STS and feminist studies, we identify disputes between ideas forged on technological determinism and neutrality of science, and views considering that the social aspects have a direct influence on the scientific-technological transformations. Also, we identify concerns about the environmental and social consequences on the people and the world.

In STS and feminist studies [WAJCMAN, 2006; HARAWAY, 1995], authors indicate disproportionality between men and women and points out the importance not only approximate women to the area, indeed to discuss the social and cultural values that move away from women to study and work in the computing area. This context is crucial in gender relations in Academia and the labor market because most of the short papers we analyze present misogynistic perceptions, repellent and aggressive to women presence in academic space and the labor market in computing.

In the category "recurring topics", authors showcase workshops and activities with elementary and high school students, composing 31 short papers in all three event editions. In the second place is the description of incentive groups for women participation in the area: 16 short papers. Reasons for women follow a computing career and students profile are present in 8 documents. Researches about student profile analysis and case study have 5 total. The last recurring category identified was about teachers of higher education and black women teachers in the area, has 6 short papers submitted.

In the category "quantitative data", we observe WIT receives researchers doing work with students in high and elementary school. The category "region and quantities" involves people participation from the whole country; in this category, we can identify that in Northeast and South had more submitted short papers the context in social, economic and cultural aspects may be an implication for future work. Most of the short papers analyzed reinforce the differences between men and women with exclusive groups. We point out the importance of closer participation of people with disabilities, race, and ethnicity, cultural and situated aspects [HARAWAY, 1995], it also has a reflective and activist on multiple identities and intersections in society that reflects on technology, on computing, on design, in everyday life and also in the labor market where there are several prejudices and gender discrimination.

4. CONCLUSION

In this short analysis of three event editions, we argue that woman participation in computing is very important for society, considering the cultural and historical conditions that invisibilized and silenced women to participate in decision-making and daily life in human history. We present this analysis based on plural and inclusive for computing. Based on STS and feminist studies, the authors indicate that it is not enough to approximate women to study and work in computing. It is also a reflection of daily actions, whereas society, culture, and history. Although there are many activities in the country to approach women in computing, there is still lack of reflections, activism, and discussion about an inclusive and not exclusive computing area, to bring all people and not to create exclusive groups.

Besides, as a future implication of this research is to discuss the social, cultural and economic aspects that are in the margins of society considering the multiple identities and intersections that need to follow this conception of society (and computing) free, unattended and without prejudices and judging. We observed that there is a plurality of approaches that are different for each person and each context and is even more visible by the support of cultural and historical discourse. We point out the importance to consider a wide, not restricted, and open participation of all people in all spheres of society, even in computing.

ACKNOWLEDGMENT

We thank the Postgraduate Program in Technology and Society (PPGTE) of the Federal University of Technology - Paraná (UTFPR) for the support in developing this research. This study was financed in part by the Coordenação de Aperfeiçoamento de Pessoal de Nível Superior (CAPES) – Finance Code 001.

REFERENCES

Abbate, J. *Recoding gender: women's changing participation in computing*. [S.l]: MIT Press, 2012.

Gomes, N. L. *Culture diversitym curriculum and race issue. Challenges for educational practise*. In: ABRAMOWICZ, Anete, BARBOSA, Maria de Assunção e SILVÉRIO, Valter Roberto (Orgs). Practical education difference. Campinas, Armazém do Ipê, pp. 21-40.

Haraway, D. 1998. *Situated knowledges: the science question in feminism and the privilege of partial perspective*. Vol. 14, No. 3. Feminist Studies, Inc. pp. 575-599.

INEP. Relatório Censo da Educação Superior 2018. Instituto Nacional de Estudos e Pesquisas Educacionais Anísio Teixeira. Available in: http://www.inep.gov.br/ Accessed in: 01 abr., 2019.

Margolis, J; Fisher, A. *Unlocking the clubhouse: Women in computing*. 2002. ed [S.l: s.n.], 2002

Monard, M. C; Fortes, R. *"A View of women participation in Computer Science courses in Brazil."* V Congresso de la Mujer Latinoamericana em La Computacion - LAWCC 2013, p. 6 - 12, 2013. Available in: <http://sites.labic.icmc.usp.br/pub/mcmonard/MonardLAWCC2013.pdf.pdf>. Accessed in: Apr 22, 2019.

Wajcman, J. 2006. *Technofeminism*. Ediciones Cátedra. Madrid.

ADOPTION OF MOBILE BANKING

Golan Carmi[1] and Nethanel Jay Drezner[2]
[1]*Information Systems Department*
[2]*Industrial Engineering & Management Department*
Jerusalem College of Technology, Havaad Haleumi 21 Jerusalem, 91160, Israel

ABSTRACT

The study examines which technical and psychological factors affect the willingness of the consumer to adopt a new financial application, as part of the transition to mobile banking. Six factors were examinee: relative advantage, complexity, compatibility, accessibility, trialability and perceived risk. To this end, a self-reported questionnaire was distributed via social media among 402 banking customers. Findings indicate that the four criteria with the significant impact on adoption of a financial application to smartphones are: relative advantage, compatibility, accessibility and trialability.

KEYWORDS

Financial Application, Smartphone Application, Application Adoption, Mobile Banking

1. INTRODUCTION

In recent decades the banking industry has undergone significant and revolutionary processes. The tools used by the customer for banking services have evolved and improved over time, due to technological changes: from services provided only by a traditional bank branch with clerks, through ATM operations and automated positions, telephone banking, online banking and financial applications. Nowadays, more and more transactions and acquisitions are controlled directly from mobile devices especially smartphones applications (Liu & Li, 2010). It is important to define the main technological and psychological factors that affect the choice of potential customers to adopt or prefer financial applications.

Previous studies have examined the adoption of financial applications based on a single theory as a theoretical basis (Al-Gahtani, 2003; Chen, Gillenson, & Sherrell, 2004; Koenig-Lewis, Palmer & Moll, 2010; McCloskey, 2006; Ndubisi & Sinti, 2006). In order to examine the phenomenon in a wider way, we used this study in two theories as a theoretical basis: DIT theory (Diffusion of Innovative Technology) suggested by Rogers (1983), and TAM model (Technology Acceptance Model) presented by Davis (1989). Finding the influence of the technological and psychological factors can help develop and implement future financial applications. Banks will be able to develop applications that truly meet the needs, desires and concerns of their target customers, thus able to save costs and improve their services to their customers.

2. BODY OF PAPER

The study involved 402 customers of the banks, when the questionnaire was distributed online by social media. An analysis of the questionnaires was found that 48% were men and 52% were women; most of the customers were married (68%), 40% were of age 18-25 and 43% between ages 26-35; most of them were academics (61% first degree and 20% second); about a third works in the high-tech and finance industries and the rest works in education, marketing, medicine, governmental and more; and 40% earn average wage in the economy and above.

Six independent variables were tested in this study: relative advantage, complexity, compatibility, accessibility, trialability and perceived risk. **(1) Relative advantage:** refers to the extent to which technological innovation is perceived as providing more advantages than its predecessor. A relative advantage results in increased efficiency, economic benefits, and improved status. The assumption is that when new technology is perceived to have a relative advantage or benefit there will be a tendency to adopt it. **(2) Complexity:** The extent to which we can relate to understanding and using technology. High complexity adversely affects the adoption of new technologies, and is the opposite of ease of use. Where ease of use refers to the extent to which a financial application is perceived as easy to understand and operate. The assumption is that the complexity of use is a major factor in the adoption of a financial application. **(3) Compatibility:** Refers to the extent to which the service is perceived as consistent with the values, beliefs, habits, and experiences of users. It is likely that there is a relationship between compatibility and adoption of a financial application. **(4) Accessibility:** The ability to access banking services at any time and in any place without waiting time or delay, without being dependent on the opening hours of banking branches and carrying out financial transactions immediately. It is assumed that advanced access to banking services over its advantages, especially availability, convenience and velocity will affect application adoption. **(5) Trialability:** Refers to the possibility of experimenting with new technology before adoption. It is assumed that users who are given the opportunity to try new technology will express less concern and feel more comfortable adopting the technology. **(6) Perceived risk:** This feature relates to the risk of using innovative technology. The risk perception is due to insufficient knowledge of the technology and the expected results from its use. In the context of banking services on the mobile phone, the risk perception is related to privacy and information security problems, such as: loss or theft of passwords or mobile devices, hacking into a mobile phone, leakage of financial information. The assumption is that there is a relationship between perceived risk and adoption of financial applications.

The main findings showed that four out of six variables: relative advantage, compatibility, accessibility and trialability - have significant positive effect on financial application adoption. The statistical analysis shows that, the higher the application's relative advantage, the adoption of financial application was more extensive; the higher the application compatibility, the adoption of a financial application was more widespread; as application accessibility was higher, there was widespread adoption of the mobile application; the more the customer has trialability the application, the more widespread adoption of the financial application. For variables, complexity and perceived risk, statistical significance was not found. In terms of demographic findings' it was found a significant negative correlation between age and relative advantage, so that as the age of the user increased the relative advantage decreased. A significant positive correlation was found also between age and accessibility, so that as the age of the user increased the accessibility decreased. No significant correlation was found between age and compatibility, complexity, trialability and perceived risk. In addition, it was found a significant negative correlation between age and the willingness to adopt a financial application, so that as the age of the subject increases the adoption willingness decreases. As for the other demographic variables: gender, family status, level of education, field of work and level of income - no significant correlation was found on adoption financial application.

3. CONCLUSION

The main conclusion of the study is that the four criteria with the significant effect on the adoption of financial application are relative advantage, compatibility, accessibility and trialability. Therefore, banks need to focus their development and marketing efforts on emphasizing the advantage and benefit of financial uses of the application over more familiar banking methods such as the Bank's website or face-to-face service at the bank's counter. Also, developers should ensure that the use of the financial application is as appropriate as possible for the use of the customers, that the interface is intuitive and fast-learning, especially for users who have been accustomed to performing operations on the banks' websites.

In addition, ensure that the services in the application are as accessible as possible and make sure that the application works 24/7 without any country or region restrictions. Periods of service unavailability or long waiting times when implementing an application will likely have a significant influence on customer usage. Moreover, enable customers experiment with the application to lessen concerns about using it, as well as offer a limited free option in addition to a unlimited paid option. Finally, the banks should take into account the age of the customers, as a parameter that particularly affects the adoption of a financial application on the smartphone, to conduct instruction in using the financial application as the customer age is higher.

We recommend programmers to focus on meeting the customers' needs that best match the criteria delineated above. By understanding the influencing factors, marketers should use these criteria to reduce the psychological concerns of customers that delay the adoption of a financial application. Since financial applications are becoming more useful as financial transfers, other behavioral aspects that influence the adoption of technology should be examined. We recommend conducting further research based on behavioral, economic and technological theories. A better understanding of the influencing factors will derive a better planning and development of financial applications, regarding the most significant factors: relative advantage, compatibility, accessibility and trialability. This process will result better and wider adoption of financial applications by customers, and will bring more customers to do banking operations and use financial transfers by smartphones.

Future studies can use other theoretical basis for research; to examine specific populations, for example, in terms of the third age or religious populations; and to examine cultural and social influences factors on the adoption of financial applications.

REFERENCES

Al-Gahtani, S. S. (2003). Computer technology adoption in Saudi Arabia: Correlates of perceived innovation attributes. *Information Technology for Development*, 10(1), 57–69.

Chen, L., Gillenson, M. and Sherrell, D. (2004). Consumer acceptance of virtual stores: A Theoretical Model and Critical Success Factors for Virtual Stores. *ACM SIGMIS Database*.

Davis, F. D. (1989). Perceived usefulness, perceived ease of use, and user acceptance of information technology. *MIS Quarterly*.

Liu, Y. and Li, H. (2010). Mobile internet diffusion in China: an empirical study. *Industrial Management & Data Systems* 110 (3), 309-324.

McCloskey, D. W. (2006). The importance of ease of use, usefulness, and trust to online consumers: An examination of the technology acceptance model with older consumers. *Journal of Organizational and End User Computing*.

Ndubisi, N. O. and Q. Sinti (2006). Consumer attitudes, system's characteristics and internet banking adoption in Malaysia, *Management Research News*.

Koenig-Lewis, N., Palmer, A. and Moll, A. (2010). Predicting young consumers' take up of mobile banking services. *International Journal of Bank Marketing*.

Rogers, E. M. (1983). *Diffusion of innovations* (3rd). New York: The Free Press.

THE PRACTICAL SIDE OF IOT IMPLEMENTATION IN SMART CITIES

Artyom Kravchenko
St. John's University, USA

ABSTRACT

Smart cities are an innovative concept of sustainable urban design that gains popularity across the globe. Its core premise is the provision of smart educational, utility, traffic, waste and resource management, and health services with an advanced level of connectivity. The Internet of Things (IoT) is employed as the technology powering that connectivity and ensuring that the smart services operate based on intelligent data collection, sharing, and analysis. However, while IoT is actively explored today and exhibits numerous tech achievements, there are still pressing challenges for its practical implementation in the smart city architectures. This article explores the unresolved challenges such as impaired device interoperability, vulnerability of IoT grids to hacks, data security and privacy issues, as well as the slow transition of governments to smart services. The study also offers insights into the future directions of IoT research and development to empower smart city creation.

KEYWORDS

Internet of Things, Smart Cities, Smart City Grids, Interoperability, Smart City Architectures

1. INTRODUCTION

Smart cities are taking shape day by day to respond to the citizens' needs for enhanced liveability, safety, revivification, and sustainability. They represent hubs of smart services in the areas of education, government, mobility, housing, an e-health; these services are strongly interconnected mainly due to the application of Internet of Things (IoT) (Hassanien, Elhoseny, Ahmed, & Singh, 2018). IoT is an innovative technological concept presupposing a high level of connectivity and enhanced information sharing possibilities within the smart grid, as well as the increasing degree of smart devices' autonomy to take specific actions on their owners' behalf (Adekumbi, 2018). Due to these features, IoT is highly relevant to the principles of smart cities' design, and IoT tech is now actively integrated into the urban strategies. Smart city designers envision IoT-enabled applications as empowering the street and traffic lights, enabling smart transportation, parking, maintenance, waste management, air quality, crime reduction, architecture, sustainable energy usage and distribution, traffic flow, and addressing the pedestrian and bicycle needs (Meyers, 2017). However, IoT, as any other technology, poses certain issues and challenges in the process of practical implementation. This article explores the practicalities of IoT integration in smart cities and proposes solutions to streamline that integration more smoothly and effectively in the upcoming Smart City projects.

2. IOT-BASED SOLUTIONS FOR SMART CITY GRIDS

IoT has become a critical component of the smart city architecture right from its inception, which is explained by the fact that smart cities are first of all oriented at providing highly customized services to users. For instance, smart homes are enabled by effective data collection by electronic home appliances shared and stored in a smart home environment. Similarly, smart cities aim at advanced energy and electricity use, provision of a convenient and economically sustainable infrastructure for the social well-being, which becomes possible with IoT application (Hammi, Khatoun, Zeadally, Fayad, & Khouhi, 2017). At present, such sectors as energy and electricity, architecture and construction, automation, transportation, security, and healthcare are the key aspects unified by IoT in smart cities. All of them can be empowered by IoT to deliver service quality and connectivity of a brand-new level, so the near future of smart city design deals specifically with the implementation of IoT in these spheres (Park et al., 2018).

In connection with such IoT objectives, the IoT platforms in smart cities have to be scalable due to the huge data storage requirements and, flexible to collect masses of miscellaneous data, and able to address the Big Data domain challenges. Thus, their key features include:

- Interoperability (enabling of communication and data transmission among heterogeneous IoT devices);
- Real-time data collection from a large number of sensors (fostering the provision of actual information about events or behaviors in the smart city);
- Near-real-time data transmission (implying the asynchronous communication enabled by the publish/subscribe communication paradigm);
- A microservice approach (presupposing the development of a single application as a suite of small services each running its own process and communicating with lightweight mechanisms);
- Awareness to end-users (IoT facilitates the interaction between users and things);
- Exposure of web services and API via open and standard data formats (fostering the design and development of novel services) (Patti & Acquaviva, 2016).

While IoT has already become a buzzword in the area of innovative urban design, there is still little understanding of the exact types of communication technologies expected to enable it. To date, the most suitable tech solutions for IoT in SCs include the power line communication (PLC) technology, ZigBee, WiMAX, third- to fifth-generation (3G-5G) cellular networks, the global system for mobile communication (GSM), general packet radio service (GPRS), and some more (Ejaz & Anpalagan, 2018). Since IoT is a modular approach, it is based on sensor integration (RFID, IR, GPS, laser scanners) into everyday objects to connect them over the Internet through specific protocols for information exchange, communication, and intelligent recognition, tracking, monitoring, and management (Saha, Auddy, Chatterjee, Pal, et al., 2017).

It is also noteworthy that for many, IoT is limited to connectivity of devices via the web, but the true implementation of IoT in smart cities is much broader. It suggests building a service based around the connectivity proposed to plug in with cloud integration and Big Data. IoT includes standards for connectivity, software, and even the clouds where the data is stored and processed. However, the implementation of IoT requires different control points and a variety of controlled parameters (Information Resources Management Association, 2018). Thus, the IoT technical architectures for smart cities require seamless integration of sensors in a mutual communication environment to create horizontal multiservice infrastructures and host all the city's systems. Such a task is challenging in many ways, and despite the technological advances of the recent years, the IoT sector still faces some pressing challenges as to the practical side of enabling smart cities.

3. CHALLENGES ON THE WAY TO AN IOT-ENABLED CITY

Since IoT is essentially about data retrieval, sharing, and storage, its critical weakness is vulnerability to hacks. Most connections in smart cities are enabled with RFID, which are highly vulnerable to all kind of hacking activities such as malware (a variety of harmful, dangerous computer programs such as worms, trojans, and viruses), ransomware (attacks on users with the purpose of money bribing), adware (attacks conducted to open ground for entering malware), etc. IoT grids also possess zero-day vulnerabilities (first-time system errors), side channels, phishing and spoofing, as well as RFID-related risks such as passive data monitoring, user identity scanning, and jamming of the RFID frequencies (Hassanien et al., 2018). Therefore, it is imperative to develop hack-proof IoT ecosystems to speed up the realization of smart city projects and to boost their development at a larger scale.

Another challenge inherent in the IoT architecture for smart cities is interoperability. While open standards have been in place for the past couple of decades, users still utilize interoperable systems rarely, which complicates scaling and a smart city's ecosystem creation. Various communication standards complicate the process of various processes' automation, as well as hinder the optimization, management, and reduction of accommodated energy. Even in the e-health sector of smart city services, the need to track medical team and facilities as well as healthcare-IT convergence services are imperative for the effective smart city functioning, which is hard due to the impaired interoperability (Park et al., 2018).

Security issues also play a role in the IoT implementation in smart cities because IoT systems are assumed to consist of very large heterogeneous networks of both constrained and unconstrained devices continuously operating without any power source. Because of these peculiarities, IoT architectures resist the implementation of strong security and privacy mechanisms. Major security challenges associated with IoT in smart cities include:

- Heterogeneity of communication technologies, software, hardware, and capabilities of multiple devices integrated into a single IoT grid;
- the constrained nature of numerous IoT devices possessing limited resources;
- the need to come up with scalable solutions to enable smooth IoT functioning at large-scale deployments;
- the need for energy-effective optimization in the use of IoT-empowering hardware and software (Angelakis, Tragos, Poehls, Kapovits, & Bassi, 2016).

Given these technical limitations inherent in the elements of an IoT grid, their creators face the challenge of balancing the system's agility and making it secure and privacy-preserving. According to the 2015 report of Hewlett Packard Enterprise, 90% of devices included in the IoT systems collect personal information, 70% of them use unencrypted traffic, and 60% of them have weak credentials (Rawlinson, 2015). Thus, no matter how secure the core IoT aspects are, the inherent weaknesses of peripheral devices may undermine the fundamental principles of user privacy and data protection.

Finally, it is noteworthy that while a transition from traditional cities to smart cities may be accelerated with the fast pace of technological development and disruptive technology's introduction in the global market, the path towards smart governments is much slower. Most often, governmental institutions and the public sector are the slowest to adopt new technologies, so the transition creates an unavoidable bottleneck on the way to establishing new smart city projects (Alenezi & Manuel, 2017). The modern-day imperative for the governments is to become more user-driven, responsive, flexible, and technology-oriented. Only after completing that evolutionary process, local and national governments may integrate into smart cities and complement them with innovative, technologically advanced governance.

infrastructures and host all the city's systems. Such a task is challenging in many ways, and despite the technological advances of the recent years, the IoT sector still faces some pressing challenges as to the practical side of enabling smart cities.

4. FUTURE DIRECTIONS OF IOT DEVELOPMENT IN SMART CITIES

IoT is already part and parcel of most smart city projects, powering the smart city technologies and infrastructure. Nevertheless, IoT also offers numerous additional business opportunities and possesses an enormous growth potential which may contribute to more efficient smart city development. To achieve greater progress with IoT in smart cities, recommendations for the future focus of developers include:

- prioritizing sensor-oriented technologies for wireless networking;
- developing technologies for network services;
- creating innovative energy-related technologies to power the energy load management technology, smart building energy management, and smart home cloud server technology.

Besides these recommendations for the industrial sector of IoT, technology needs for intelligent optimization, scheduling, and control of devices included in the IoT grids are pressing. Thus, the future of IoT development in smart cities is impossible without innovative solutions for intelligent collection, categorization, and analysis of Big data. Finally, IoT service provision may become more effective if employed via compatible integrated applications to ensure customization and end-user convenience (Park et al., 2018). Besides facilitating the development of smart city projects, numerous market players can embrace a promising business opportunity and increase their revenue by providing innovative solutions that the IoT requires.

5. CONCLUSION

As one can see, IoT is a highly promising aspect of smart city design without which the concept of connectivity and advanced end-user customization is simply unattainable. Thus, IoT is actively developed today, with new technologies emerging every day, to empower smart cities and make them sustainable socially, economically, and environmentally. Rapid technological advancement definitely contributes to the realization of smart city goals and visions, but the practical side of IoT implementation is still challenging in many ways. For instance, the implementation of most smart city projects is impossible without addressing such challenges as intelligent collection and analysis of big data, low interoperability, vulnerability of IoT grids to a wide range of attacks, and the lower speed of the public sector's technological advancement. Security still remains a pressing concern among smart city designers, so making IoT architecture work as it should presupposes the identification of IoT elements and assets requiring protection and development of system requirements for risk mitigation. The use of powerful encryption mechanisms and digital safety education for end users are also recommended steps to minimize the risks of hacking, data fraud, and data privacy breaches across the IoT grids in smart cities. Once these pressing issues are addressed and all aspects of smart city development are harmonized, smart city projects are projected to become more attainable and realistic.

REFERENCES

Adekunbi, A., 2018. Three ways IoT is shaping the smart cities of the future. *Entrepreneur*. Retrieved from https://www.entrepreneur.com/article/324345

Alenezi, A., & Manuel, P., 2017. Challenges of IoT based smart city development in Kuwait. *Thesis for Master of Information Technology*. DOI: 10.13140/RG.2.2.14375.04002

Angelakis, V., Tragos, E., Poehls, H. C., Kapovits, A., & Bassi, A., 2016. *Designing, developing, and facilitating smart cities: urban design to IoT solutions*. New York, NY: Springer.

Ejaz, W., & Anpalagan, A., 2018. *Internet of things for smart cities: technologies, big data and security*. New York, NY: Springer.

Hammi, B., Khatoun, R., Zeadally, S., Fayad, A., & Khoukhi, L., 2017. Internet of Things (IoT) technologies for smart cities. *IET Research Journals* (September 2017), 1-14.

Hassanien, A. E., Elhoseny, M., Ahmed, S. H., & Singh, A. K., 2018. *Security in smart cities: models, applications, and challenges*. New York, NY: Springer.

Park, E., del Pobil, A. P., & Kwon, S. J., 2018. The role of Internet of Things (IoT) in smart cities: technology roadmap-oriented approaches. *Sustainability, 10*, 1-13.

Patti, E., & Acquaviva, A., 2016. IoT platform for smart cities: requirements and implementation case studies. *2nd IEEE International Forum on Research and Technologies for Society and Industry Leveraging a better tomorrow (RTSI 2016), Bologna, Italy, 7-9 September 2016*, 1-6.

Rawlinson, K., 2015. HP study finds alarming vulnerabilities with Internet of Things (IoT) home security systems. *Hewlett Packard Enterprise*. Retrieved from https://www8.hp.com/us/en/hp-news/press-release.html?id=1909050

Information Resources Management Association, 2018. *Smart cities and smart spaces: concepts, methodologies, tools, and applications*. Hershey, PA: IGI Global.

Meyers, R., 2017. Smart cities using Internet of Things solutions. *IIoT World*. Retrieved from https://iiot-world.com/smart-cities/smart-cities-using-internet-of-things-practical-applications/

Saha, H. N., Auddy, S., Chatterjee, A., Pal, S., Sarkar, S., et al., 2017. IoT solutions for smart cities. *2017 8th Annual Industrial Automation and Electromechanical Engineering Conference (IEMECON)*. DOI: 10.1109/IEMECON.2017.8079565

REFLECTIONS ON EVOLVING URBAN CORRELATIONS FOR CONNECTED SMART CITIES

H. Patricia McKenna
AmbientEase
Victoria, BC, Canada

ABSTRACT

The purpose of this reflection paper is to explore emerging potentials for the use of correlation, in combination with a case study design, as a hybrid approach to identifying and understanding patterns and relationships in smart cities. A review of the research literature is provided for perspectives on correlation, the application of correlation in urban environments, and emerging approaches to the use of correlation in relation to smart cities. Focusing on people and their experience of urban spaces, elements, and digital interactions, the relationship of openness and connectedness is explored. Using multiple methods of data collection including survey and in-depth interviews, a combination of content analysis and explanatory correlational design is used in the analysis of data. Findings shed light on the relationship between openness and connectedness in smart cities. This paper is significant in that it contributes to the research literature on smart cities; advances the innovating of methodologies for the study of smart cities by combining case study and correlational design; sheds additional light on the connected dimension of smart cities; and highlights the importance of why correlation matters in smart cities.

KEYWORDS

Connectedness, Correlation, Mutual Information, Openness, Pearson Correlation, Relationships, Smart Cities, Urban Correlations

1. INTRODUCTION AND BACKGROUND

The purpose of this reflection paper is to explore emerging potentials for the use of correlation, in combination with a case study design, as a hybrid approach to identifying and understanding patterns and relationships, in smart cities. To this end, the research literature is reviewed for perspectives on correlation; the application of correlation in urban environments; and emerging approaches to the use of correlation in the context of smart cities. Focusing on people and their experience of urban spaces, elements, and digital interactions, the relationship of openness and connectedness is explored. Using multiple methods of data collection including survey and in-depth interviews, a combination of content analysis and explanatory correlational design is used in the analysis of data. This work is motivated by the need for approaches to "make visible what is normally not" (Quercia, Séaghdha, and Crowcroft, 2017) in smart cities while moving beyond the static to the dynamic in accommodating the "connected" and continuous nature of activities and interactions in technology-pervasive urban environments (Bermudez-Edo, Barnaghi, and Moessner, 2018). As such, this paper uses a combination of case study and correlational statistical research to explore patterns and relationships in smart cities. This paper is significant for at least four key reasons in that – it contributes to the research literature on smart cities; advances the innovating of methodologies for the study of smart cities by combining a case study design with an explanatory correlational design; sheds light on the connected dimension of smart cities; and highlights the importance of why correlation matters in smart cities.

2. CORRELATION: A REVIEW OF THE LITERATURE

Through a review of the research literature, perspectives are provided in this section on the use of correlation generally and on urban correlation in relation to smart cities.

2.1 Perspectives on Correlation

In the context of social research methods, Trochim (2006) describes correlation as "a single number that describes the degree of relationship between two variables" while from an information science perspective, Oakleaf (2014) highlights the need to "recognize the utility of correlational connections." Creswell (2018) describes correlational research in the context of education research as "designs to describe and measure the degree of association (or relationship) between two or more variables or sets of scores." Creswell (2018) indicates that correlation is also used to "predict an outcome" noting that types of correlational designs include explanatory design and prediction designs (2018). Correlation coefficients are described by Bermudez-Edo et al. (2018) as "tools to measure the dependency of two or more variables" such as the Pearson correlation coefficient and that of mutual information. Kaethler (Kaethler and Golchehr, 2017) problematizes "the correlation-based approach" to urban areas in the form of a lament, arguing that, "data mining will disorient the emergence and retention of urban narratives." For Kaethler (Kaethler and Golchehr, 2017), "the story telling that occurs, internally and externally" in urban spaces "is threatened by a data-centered approach." In response, in the form of a postscript in the same paper, Golchehr (Kaethler and Golchehr, 2017) articulates, "a defence of data mining as a new means through which socially innovative narratives can evolve." In the form of a "rebuttal", Golchehr (Kaethler and Golchehr, 2017) advances the importance of "an open mind" in support of the "use of correlation as the starting point for the narratives we create." Yin (2018) points to the "complementarity of case study and statistical research" where "case studies have been needed to examine the underlying processes that might explain a correlation."

2.2 Urban Correlation in Smart Cities

Lathia, Quercia, and Crowcroft (2012) use correlation to explore community well-being in urban areas in relation to mobility. Through leveraging the potentials of pervasive technology, Lathia et al., (2012) "test whether urban mobility – as measured by public transport fare collection sensors – is a viable proxy for the visibility of a city's communities." Quercia et al. (2012) "extract the subject matter of tweets using 'topic models'" from London census communities and use correlation to "study the relationship between topics and community socio-economic well-being." Hernando, Hernando, and Plastino (2013) demonstrate the use of space–time correlations in relation to urban sprawl. Dattakumar and Sharma (2016) explore the development of smart cities and knowledge societies in relation to correlation and causation or something altogether distinct from the two, advancing a "maturity model for smart cities and knowledge societies" while making a "conjecture that there may be a synergistic, rather than symbiotic, link" between the two. And it is worth noting that Gil-Garcia, Zhang, and Puron-Cid (2016) identify openness as one of several dimensions of smartness in government. Quercia et al. (2017) leverage the smartness of pervasive technologies to learn about people and well-being in making cities more livable based on the "creative use of network-generated data" in "capturing sensory and psychological perceptions at scale." Focusing on the human senses (e.g., sight, smell, hearing, and emotion), according to Quercia et al. (2017), it is "reasonable to assume that, from digital footprints" in social media and other spaces "one could derive good proxies for the different ways people perceive streets." Zhuhadar et al. (2017) describe systems capable of correlating events in smart cities and in the context of e-Government research, Joshi and When (2017) identified the variable of "citizen discussion via social media" highlighting people as "social sensors." Redi et al. (2018) "explored the possibility of using social media data to reliably map the ambiance of neighborhoods" throughout London while using correlation in "explaining neighborhood ambiance." Covatta (2018) highlights the importance of "play as an urban tool to reuse the infrastructure" using examples from the city of Copenhagen. Drawing on the research work of Gehl (1987) and his partner, Ingrid Mundt, Covatta (2018) notes that "data collection regarding citizens' movement and behavior become precious information for governments and municipalities" in support of "participatory design proposals" that are "based on the small scale intervention of people's behavior." Bermudez-Edo et al. (2018) provide an analysis of "real world data streams" using "spatio-temporal correlations" in smart cities as a "proposed method" to "analyze relations in IoT." Bermudez-Edo et al. (2018) argue that, "one of the main starting points to analyse these big amounts of data is correlation detection" claiming that their "analysis contributes to optimize the use of the available infrastructure" in order "to better plan the future urban deployments." Focusing on "road infrastructure" and traffic flow, the work of Bermudez-Edo et al. (2018) "demonstrated that for both, synthetic and real data, mutual information can discover dependencies in more general cases of distribution of data" while "Pearson correlation can discover linear distribution of data" concluding that "sample size is important" in that "it influences the correlation methods."

3. EXPLORING RELATIONSHIPS IN SMART CITIES

Using an exploratory case study approach in combination with an explanatory correlational design, this work seeks to provide insight into connectedness and openness in the context of smart cities. Data collection involved the use of survey and in-depth interviews focusing on the experience of smart cities. The study attracted a wide range of individuals from small to medium to large-sized cities, mostly in Canada and extending also to Europe, and Israel.

3.1 Connectedness and Openness in Smart Cities

Respondents were asked to assess the extent to which they associate smart cities with *openness* on a 7-point scale, with 1=Not at all, to 7=Absolutely. Responses were spread across the upper points on the scale with 25% at the neutral position of 4, 25% at 5, 25% at 6, and 25% at 7. When asked to assess connecting in smart cities on a 7-point scale, responses were slightly higher with 25% at position 5 on the scale, 25% at 6, and 50% at 7. Using the Real Statistics data analysis tool in Microsoft Excel, the correlation is calculated for openness and connecting in smart cities. A scatter plot diagram of the data shows the direction of the correlation to be positive, taking a linear form, with the strength of the relationship considered to be very good, falling as it does in the .66 to .85 range (Creswell, 2018), based on a Pearson Correlation coefficient of .67.

Through open-ended survey questions and in-depth interviews, people contributed additional insights with their comments about connecting and openness, where a city councilor observed that, "vibrancy is created by people and connections between people" describing technology "as a tool that will allow people to connect to each other and to their surroundings" as in, "creating activity." A technology consultant described "smart city thought processes" as "wonderful things that connects all the pieces." Referring to public data, city information technology (IT) staff indicated that, "fundamentally there is a desire to be very, very open with the available data." City IT added that "we are interested in putting physical infrastructure in place" and "how we interpret using it is still open." An educator identified the need for schools to open their "walls", when asked how "to get people more involved in the city and the community." Cities were described as affording "a sense of freedom and openness" when asked, "what do you like about being in the city?"

3.2 Limitations and Future Directions

Going forward, the use of correlation in smart environments provides an opportunity or, in the words of researchers such as Bermudez-Edo et al. (2018), a "starting point" for the analysis of relationships and for "the narratives we create" (Kaethler and Golchehr, 2017) in urban spaces. Indeed, considering the work of Quercia et al. (2017) where correlation is used to "make visible" what is not visible, this would seem to support the relevance of correlation for smart city-related research where the characteristic of invisibility is said to be a particular challenge (McKenna, 2019), offering possibly novel analytic methodologies and approaches with implications for urban theory. While this paper is limited by a small sample size and a focus on only two variables (e.g., openness and connectedness), opportunities exist to enlarge the exploration to include more participants and variables going forward and it is worth noting that Dattakumar and Sharma (2016) articulate a range of questions for future research such as, "can smart cities enhance creativity?"

4. CONCLUSION

This work probes the relationship of openness and connectedness in contemporary urban environments as a starting point for learning more about what contributes to the making of smart cities. A combined case study and correlational research design was used, informed by a review of the research literature for smart cities and correlation, as an approach to the exploration of connected smart cities that are characterized by more aware people interacting with increasingly aware and pervasive technologies. Findings show a positive and reasonably good relationship between openness and connectedness. Going forward, this work sets the stage for further work focusing on variables surfaced by researchers (Dattakumar and Sharma, 2016; Joshi and When, 2017; McKenna, 2019) in urban spaces. Enabled by more aware people interacting with aware technologies, this type of exploration provides novel opportunities for continuing to push at the edges of the use of correlation in smart cities, communities, and regions, in figuring out what contributes to the success of smart city projects and of smart cities more broadly. This paper is also significant in that it contributes to the research literature by highlighting the importance of correlation in the context of smart cities; demonstrates the use of correlation as an approach to exploring what is it that makes smart cities connected and why this matters; and extends urban theory and methodological approaches to include correlation.

REFERENCES

Bermudez-Edo, M., Barnaghi, P., and Moessner, K., 2018. Analysing Real World Data Streams with Spatio-Temporal Correlations: Entropy vs. Pearson Correlation. *In Automation in Construction*, Vol. 88, April, pp 87-100.

Covatta, A., 2018. From Infrastructure to Playground: The Playable Soul of Copenhagen. *UD/MN Journal of Urban Design and Mental Health*, Vol. 5, No. 3.

Creswell, J. W. (2018). *Educational Research: Planning, Conducting, and Evaluating Quantitative and Qualitative Research (6th Edition)*. Pearson.

Dattakumar, A. and Sharma, R. S., 2016. Smart Cities and Knowledge Societies: Correlation, Causation or Distinct? *Proceedings of the 2016 IEEE International Conference on Management of Innovation and Technology (ICMIT)*, volume and issue numbers, pp. 193-197.

Gehl, J., 1987. L*ife Between Buildings: Using Public Space.* First published in Danish in 1971. New York: Van Nostrand Reinhold.

Gil-Garcia, J. R., Zhang, J., and Puron-Cid, G., 2016. Conceptualizing smartness in government: An integrative and multi-dimensional view. *Government Information Quarterly* 33(3):524-534.

Hernando, A., Hernando, O., and Plastino, A., 2013. Space Time Correlations in Urban Sprawl. *Interface,* 11: 20130930.

Joshi, S., and When, U., 2017. From Assumptions to Artifacts: Unfolding e-Participation within Multi-level Governance. *The Electronic Journal of e-Government,* Vol. 15, No. 2, pp. 116-129.

Kaethler, M. and Golchehr, S., 2017. Correlation is Dismantling our Urban Narratives: A Lament and a Plea. In E. Bertoletti, H. Daam, F. Piredda, V. Tassinari (Eds.), *The Pearl Diver: The Designer as Story Teller.* Flanders, Belgium: Ku Leuven, Lirias pp. 120-127.

Lathia, N., Quercia, D., and Crowcroft, J., 2012. The Hidden Image of the City: Sensing Community Well-Being from Urban Mobility. In J. Kay, P. Lukowicz, H. Tokuda, P. Olivier, A. Krüger (eds), *Pervasive Computing*. Lecture Notes in Computer Science, Vol. 7319, pp. 91-98. Berlin, Heidelberg: Springer.

McKenna, H. P., 2019. Visibilities and Invisibilities: Methodologies and Theoretical Spaces for Ambient Urbanities. In *Ambient Urbanities as the Intersection Between the IoT and the IoP in Smart Cities*. Hershey, PA: IGI Global.

Oakleaf, M., 2014. Correlating Library Services, Expertise, and Resources with Student Learning. *Information Outlook*, Vol. 18, No. 2, pp 13-16.

Quercia, D., Aiello, L. M., and Schifanella, R., 2017. Mapping Towards a Good City Life. *UD/MN Journal of Urban Design and Mental Health*, Vol. 3, No. 3.

Quercia, D., Séaghdha, S. Ò., and Crowcroft, J., 2012. Talk of the City: Our Tweets, Our Community Happiness. *Proceedings of the Sixth International AAAI Conference on Weblogs and Social Media*, pp. 555-558.

Redi, M., Aiello, L. M., Schifanella, R., and Quercia, D., 2018. The Spirit of the City: Using Social Media to Capture Neighborhood Ambiance. *Proceedings of the ACM on Human-Computer Interaction,* Vol. 2, N. CSCW, Article 144, pp. 1-18.

Trochim, W. M. K., 20016. Correlation. *Research Methods Knowledge Base.* Retrieved 21 March 2019 from https://socialresearchmethods.net/kb/statcorr.php.

Yin, R. K. (2018). *Case Study Research and Applications: Design and Methods.* Thousand Oaks, CA: Sage.

Zhuhadar, L, Thrasher, E., Marklin, S., and Ordóñez de Pablos, P., 2017. The Next Wave of Innovation – Review of Smart Cities Intelligent Operation Systems. *Computers in Human Behavior,* 66: 271-281.

Poster

WELLNESS IN YOUR POCKET: UPDATE YOUR HEALTH

Susana Orrego, Karine Posada, Ana M. Ortiz and María M. Yepes
Seguros SURA Colombia
Carrera 64 B # 49 A 30 Medellín, Colombia

ABSTRACT

To build a system of sustainable healthcare, a private health insurance company in Latin America developed custom programs focused on achieving better solutions and delivering enhanced healthcare value to their members. The program developed is called "Update your health" (in Spanish "Tu Bienestar al Día") which means a way to keep members demographic and health status updated. The program, which use Information and Communication Technologies, enable members to manage their health risks by monitoring their health status and mitigating any risk. This is achieved through coordinated activities and help improve their health and quality of life. The insurance company take advantage of each contact with members to solve their health concerns and integrate their health information with their risk management. This paper describes the "Update your health" program five months after its implementation among members who required preventive services through screening tests, imaging, and medical consultation.

KEYWORDS

Patient Empowerment, e-Health, Risk Management, Healthcare Improvement

1. INTRODUCTION

"Update your Health" is a program that use the Information and Communication Technologies (ICTs) to promote healthy habits such as receiving necessary screening, and enable patients to know their health status and manage or mitigate their disease risks. The program allows the members to order screening tests, make appointments and other services through virtual access. The program uses members age, gender and comorbidities to define their needs for preventive or treatment services. This objective of this paper was to examine the effectiveness of the "Update your health" program five months after its implementation in a private insurance company in Colombia, South America.

2. BODY OF PAPER

This was a descriptive study which used members who seek screening tests, imaging, and medical consultation in a private insurer in Colombia between November 30, 2018 and March 12, 2019.

Members (n=211,327) who were deemed to need at least one the health service (lipid profile, glycemic blood levels, creatinine, prostate antigen, papanicolaou, mammography, total abdominal ultrasound, assessment by general practitioner, gynecologist or urologist) based on their risk profile as assessed using age, gender and comorbidities; were contacted using the programs "Marketing Cloud" platform to participate in the program. There were informed that preventive and medical services could be provided to them without the need to attend a face-to-face consultation. Once members agreed to participate in the program, health personnel contacted them through phone calls to schedule appointments to undertake the required service needed. Once the services were performed, the virtual health management team contacted those members and provided them with medical advice on test results, additional tests needed, the need to schedule additional appointments, and other recommendations as appropriate.

A total of 4,456 members agreed to participate in the program, of whom 843 were contacted by phone. Out of the 843 members contacted by phone, 107 completed the required medical services, 31 had completed some tests but were waiting to receive others, 3,981 were waiting to receive the services they required, and 337 decline to receive any service offered. Of the services provided, 1,342 members results came back normal, 418 had one or more abnormal results for lipid profile, glycemic blood levels, creatinine and prostate antigen.

3. CONCLUSION

The implementation of "Update your Health" program has had an impact on the health management of members through easy access to care, reduce wait times to receiving care, increased satisfaction, mobility, and savings in out-of-pocket expenses. "Update your Health" program is an innovative tool which focused on the insured and their life cycle, seeking to impact early detection of diseases in order to keep members healthier over time. Moreover, it has a direct impact on access to care, providing ICTs tools for health management virtually without the need for a face-to-face consultation.

ACKNOWLEDGEMENT

The program has achieved its three aims: improve health outcomes of members, reduce cost for the insurer and members, and increase members satisfaction. The program could be implemented in other countries. However, the challenge will be with being able to secure members information and providing the right information at the right time for each member.

REFERENCES

Hamine, S. et al, 2015. Impact of mHealth chronic disease management on treatment adherence and patient outcomes: a systematic review. *Journal of medical Internet research*, *17*(2), e52. doi:10.2196/jmir.3951.

Yara M. Asi. Et al, 2018. The role of digital health in making progress toward Sustainable Development Goal (SDG) 3 in conflict-affected populations. *International Journal of Medical Informatics,* Vol. 114, pages 114 – 120.

Meskó, B. et al, 2017. Digital health is a cultural transformation of traditional healthcare. *mHealth*, *3*, 38. doi:10.21037/mhealth.2017.08.07.

Sanjeev, B. et al, 2016. Mobile technology and the digitalization of healthcare. *European Heart Journal*, Vol. 37, issue 18, pages 1428 – 1438.

McConnell, M. et al, 2018 Mobile Health Advances in Physical Activity, Fitness, and Atrial Fibrillation: Moving Hearts. *Journal of the American College of Cardiology*, Vol. 71, Issue 23, pages 2691 – 270.

AUTHOR INDEX